PREDICTING THE MARKETS

PREDICTING THE MARKETS

A PROFESSIONAL AUTOBIOGRAPHY

EDWARD YARDENI

YRI
PRESS

ISBN 978-1-948025-00-3 (Hardcover Edition)
ISBN 978-1-948025-01-0 (eBook Edition)

Library of Congress Control Number 2017919714

The author has taken all reasonable steps to provide accurate information in this book. However, no representation or warranty is made as to the fairness, accuracy, completeness, or correctness of the information and opinions contained herein. Over time, the statements made in this book may no longer be accurate, true, or otherwise correct. Over time, the author's opinions as articulated in this book may change. This book should not be relied on for investment, accounting, legal, or other professional advice. If readers desire such advice, they should consult with a qualified professional. Nothing in this book—including predictions, forecasts, and estimates for any and all markets—should be construed as recommendations to buy, sell, or hold any security, including mutual funds, futures contracts, exchange-traded funds, or any other financial instruments.

Credits and permissions are listed on pages 574–577 and are considered a continuation of the copyright page.

To book the author to speak at your event, please contact *info@yardenibook.com*.

Editing by Sandra Cohan and Dania Sheldon
Front cover image by Nathalie Schueller Photography
Book design by Alex Hennig, Clear Design

Printed and bound in the United States
First printing February 2018

Published by YRI Press, a division of Yardeni Research Inc.
68 Wheatley Road
Brookville, NY, USA 11545

Contact us: *info@yardenibook.com*
Visit the book's website: *yardenibook.com*

To my children
Melissa, Sarah, Samuel, David, and Laura

Problems, like puzzles, are meant to be solved.

Contents

Introduction

BOOKS DON'T USUALLY come with theme songs. But if I had to pick one for my professional autobiography, it would be "Don't Worry, Be Happy" (1988), written and sung by Bobby McFerrin. During the 40 years that I have spent on Wall Street as an economist and investment strategist, investors benefited from great bull markets in both stocks and bonds. Yet instead of being happy, it seemed to me that most investors were worried for most of that time.

Many of them found it hard to enjoy the rally in the bond market because they recalled how badly bonds had performed during the 1960s and 1970s, when inflation raged. During the subsequent great bull market in bonds, they worried that inflation would make a comeback. Instead, inflation trended lower. Consequently, the US Treasury 10-year bond yield fell from a record high of 15.84% on September 30, 1981 to a record low of 1.37% on July 8, 2016. Along the way, there were plenty of backups in bond yields, but the trends were decisively downward for interest rates and upward for bond prices.

When I started my career on Wall Street during January 1978, the Dow Jones Industrial Average was around 1000. Forty years later, it is 26 times higher, having breached 26000 in early 2018. One would think that stock investors during those years would have been euphoric. Most seldom were, because four significant bear markets along the way triggered excessive pessimism. Many investors sold in fear at the bottom of the bear markets and ventured back into the stock market only after watching stocks ascend for sufficient time to repair their shattered confidence—i.e., just in time for the next bear market! In the words of Bobby McFerrin:

In your life, expect some trouble;
When you worry, you make it double

Such emotionally driven market timing would surely cause one to conclude that investing in stocks is for suckers. However, when the pessimists sold near the bottoms, they created lots of buying opportunities for the optimists.

Fortuitously, during these two coincident great bull markets in bonds and stocks, I was bullish most of the time, especially when most investors and prognosticators were extremely gloomy. Admittedly, there were times when I should have been bearish, or more bearish. In my meetings with investors, I usually warned them that I tend to be an optimist, because I had a happy childhood. In any event, for most investors, getting the bullish long-term trend right and seizing opportunities to buy has been a winning strategy for many years. It certainly has been a "long good buy" for stock and bond investors, as I frequently predicted.

Will this strategy continue to work? If you're sitting on a pile of bonds and stocks, should you hang on? Or should you heed the warning included in every mutual fund prospectus and investment disclosure document: "Past performance is no guarantee of future returns"? In other words, extrapolating past happy returns into the future could be harmful to your financial health.

I hope that my experiences on Wall Street, which this book is all about, might help guide your investment decisions with a better understanding of financial markets. The first chapter is "Predicting the Past," while the final chapter is "Predicting the Future." In between, I discuss all the lessons I have learned over the past four decades about forecasting the economy and financial markets. My major conclusion is that while there will always be plenty of worries requiring our attention, the next four decades should bring happy returns to investors who correctly predict the major long-term trends and use any setbacks along the way as buying opportunities.

If you are an individual investor, professional money manager, investment adviser, financial analyst, business executive, or small business owner, you should find much of interest in my book. Students of economics, finance, accounting, and business will be able to apply many of the lessons I've learned to their own careers. Anyone studying to become a Chartered Financial Analyst will find my book helpful as well. Academics should find value in my real-world analysis, which will stimulate a better understanding of economics and finance among their students. I've written this book to be as relevant as possible to what most of you do or will be doing soon.

More broadly, though, I've written this book for everyone. Economics professors teach their students majoring in the subject to be academics and policymakers who go on to formulate theories and make decisions that impact all of society. One of my aims with this book is to show how economics is vitally important to all of us, because we all are affected by the theories of professors and the decisions of policymakers. We can all benefit from a better understanding of the forces that shape our financial lives.

When Ben Bernanke was a Fed governor, he said, "A part of monetary policymaking for which my background left me imperfectly prepared is what central bankers call 'current analysis'...[which]...is not taught in graduate school, probably for good reason; it seems more amenable to on-the-job training.... It is, nevertheless, an intellectually challenging activity." He added that current analysis is about "getting an accurate assessment of the current economic situation, requiring a deep knowledge of the data mixed with a goodly dose of economic theory and economic judgment."[1]

I agree.

Like Bernanke, I learned current analysis after graduate school. It has been on-the-job training ever since I started my career as a professional prognosticator on Wall Street at EF Hutton in early 1978. I've had to scramble to learn a great deal very rapidly about all sorts of subjects that suddenly became important to the markets. The financial markets provide a never-ending continuing education course.

In this book, I share my professional insights into predicting the economy and financial markets. The chapters focus on understanding and forecasting the trends and cycles in the domestic and global economies and financial markets—including stocks, bonds, commodities, and currencies. The impacts of demography on consumers and real estate also are carefully assessed. Throughout, the book provides a very solid education in current analysis.

Current analysis is akin to solving a jigsaw puzzle, with a few major differences. With a jigsaw puzzle, you know from the box what the picture will look like in the end. The pieces you need are supplied—no more than that, no less—and they all fit somewhere. You can take a break from a puzzle too. You can pick up right where you left off with the same puzzle pieces and the same picture plain to see on the box.

When it comes to forecasting the economy and financial markets, the puzzle is dynamic. The picture changes, as new puzzle pieces are constantly thrown on the table. Some fit perfectly into the picture I expect to see as more of it becomes apparent. Some are more important than others for seeing the big picture. Some pieces are irrelevant or distractions that should be ignored. Some might seem so initially but turn out to matter a great deal to the big picture taking shape. Developing a sense for the relevance and importance of the puzzle pieces is essential to current analysis.

And speed matters. You can't break for a while, expecting the puzzle to remain as you left it. Current analysis is about solving the puzzles of the economy and financial markets as rapidly as possible, before they become obvious to everyone—much like the television game show *Wheel of Fortune* that's popular in the United States. The more quickly and accurately you can solve the puzzle, the greater are the potential financial rewards.

In current analysis, the puzzle pieces consist mostly of economic news, including current events and data releases. The job of a Wall Street economist and investment strategist is always interesting because we, along with investors and traders, are constantly monitoring the news events that might be relevant to the financial markets. We can keep track of them all day and night with news feeds on our computers and smartphones. Some are scheduled, such as economic reports, but most pop up out of the blue on our screens 24/7.

I like to sleep at night. I also like to think and write during the day. So I typically do most of my reading early in the morning and in the evening. To organize all this information, I collect links to important articles and order them by topics on my company's website as a handy reference library.[2] I view these articles as among the most important pieces of the dynamic puzzle that I need to be solving on an ongoing basis.

Among the torrent of relevant information are numerous economic releases with lots of data that are also pieces of the puzzle. Current analysis is fact based rather than faith based. Opinions, theories, and models should be inspired by a careful analysis of the data. The ultimate test is whether the hypotheses derived from the data not only explain current developments but also predict future ones relatively well. If they don't, perhaps another, deeper dive into the data will lead to more accurate insights.

Above all, current analysis is about having the right mindset to recognize flawed hypotheses when evidence reveals them as such and to learn from these missteps, continually expanding your understanding of the economy and financial markets. The true picture is out there and is constantly evolving. You'll know that you're on the right path when your opinions don't change with every new data point and news item *and* when they do change occasionally as you learn more or as circumstances shift.

When I analyze the relevant data, I do so with charts. I believe that a simple, well-constructed chart can be worth a thousand words, as the saying goes. There are more than 700 charts referenced in what follows. All are posted on the book's website, *yardenibook.com*. These charts provide clear graphic support for the discussions that follow. Readers seeking a solid grounding in current analysis should study them carefully. Many of the charts start from when the data are available and go through the end of 2016. That's the year I chose to end most of my narrative, though 2017 does sneak into a few of the stories and charts on occasion.

You can read this book from beginning to end without looking at a single chart if you're not into data. That's because much of current analysis is really informed common sense. The charts do much of the informing. They show the picture formed by previous puzzle pieces and provide important clues on how to solve the current puzzle. I suggest that at a minimum, you look at the charts after reading the book. If most of them make sense to you, then congratulations: you've earned a graduate degree in current analysis!

Current analysis is also akin to deep-sea diving, as you are about to discover. Now, let's put on our diving suits and together explore the fascinating world it reveals. It may be your first time doing so, but don't worry, be happy.

CHAPTER 1

Predicting the Past

MACROECONOMIST

PREDICTING THE ECONOMY and the financial markets is certainly challenging. Though I've been doing it for 40 years on Wall Street, I am still learning. Fortunately, I have a solid academic background in economics, political science, and history, which has been very useful to my work on the Street. After receiving an undergraduate degree from Cornell University in government and economics in 1972, I entered an interdisciplinary two-year master's degree program in international relations at Yale University. I extended my stay at Yale to earn a PhD in economics in 1976. I studied economics under some notable professors, including William Brainard, Richard Cooper, William Nordhaus, Richard Ruggles, Joseph Stiglitz, James Tobin, Robert Triffin, and Henry Wallich.

Janet Yellen—who succeeded Ben Bernanke, becoming the 15th chair of the Federal Reserve Board of Governors, a.k.a. "the Fed"—and I both received our PhDs from Yale and studied under Professor Tobin, who won the Nobel Prize in economics in 1981. However, we weren't there at the same time. She graduated in 1971. I graduated in 1976. Yellen was so meticulous in taking notes during Tobin's macroeconomics class that they ended up as the unofficial textbook for future graduate students. I studied from those Xeroxed notes.

Professor Tobin was my PhD committee chairman. He was a demanding but inspiring teacher. I survived the dissertation ordeal by writing a statistical study of corporate finance that confirmed one of Tobin's theories. It was titled "A Portfolio Balance Model of Corporate Finance," and I published it as a May 1978 article in *The Journal of Finance*. In the academic world, they warn associate professors who aspire to be tenured professors: "Publish or perish!" I would have perished as a professor for sure, since that was the only academic article I ever published.

My doctoral thesis was jam-packed with econometrics, which is the use of statistical methods, particularly regression equations, to describe economic systems and predict their behavior. The equations showed the statistical relationships among their dependent and independent variables. I recall spending countless hours of countless days at Yale's mainframe computer center literally punching my program and data onto computer "punch cards," which were pieces of stiff paper used to contain digital information represented by the presence or absence of holes in predefined positions. Then I would have to wait for my turn to have the operator of Yale's mainframe computer input my job. The output was on large, multipage printouts. I would tweak the regressions repeatedly by trying numerous combinations of variables until the computer spit out significant "t-statistics" with high "r-squareds" that presumably confirmed the statistical validity of my model.[1] Tobin loved my dissertation and, along with the other two members of my dissertation committee, approved the first draft. I was ready to move on.

You won't find one regression equation in this book, because I never ran another regression after I left Yale. I came to realize the limitations of both statistical as well as theoretical models early in my career on Wall Street. So I developed my "current analysis" approach to understanding interactions of the economy and financial markets, which relies on historical data relationships—best tracked with clear charts and simple, mostly accounting-based models. This worked better for me as a Wall Street prognosticator than sophisticated econometric models ever could.

I joined the Federal Reserve Bank of New York (FRB-NY) at 33 Liberty Street in Lower Manhattan as a staff economist in the research department in July 1976. I stayed there until December 1977. Architecturally, the 22-floor, limestone and sandstone headquarters of the FRB-NY was inspired by the imposing edifices of the Italian Renaissance period and features a palazzo design reminiscent of Florentine banking houses, according to the bank's website.[2] Actually, the building looks like a fortress, as it should—since some of the gold owned by central banks around the world is stored in the basement.[3] In the movie *The Godfather* (1972), director Francis Ford Coppola set the scene of a key meeting of the mafia bosses by panning the front of the building. Some of the Fed's harshest critics are convinced it's a monetary mafia.

I commuted to the Fed by subway from my small, $400-a-month, one-bedroom apartment on East 69th Street. I shared a tiny, windowless office with another staff economist. The office décor consisted of little more than tall, beige filing cabinets everywhere. A few times, I had occasion to go to the executive floor. The décor there was august and musty, probably unchanged since the building's first occupants conducted their serious business within those walls back in 1924. The sense of history was palpable, exciting, and stifling all at the same time.

I recall having some spirited conversations with colleagues during lunch in the staff dining room. A couple of them had studied at universities known for a monetarist focus. They reminded me of religious zealots, so unshakeable was their faith that the economy was driven mostly by the growth of the money supply. This monetarist school of thought was most prominently promoted at the University of Chicago by Professor Milton Friedman, who championed "free markets," i.e., markets that operate without much, if any, interference by the government.

Conversely, at Yale, the dominant school of thought was Keynesianism, which is based on the theories of John Maynard Keynes. He postulated that economic output is driven by aggregate demand, or spending in the economy, which is influenced heavily by fiscal policies, especially government expenditures. Tobin had us read articles that he and others wrote about why Friedman was wrong and why Keynes and his disciples were right.

The director of research at the FRB-NY was Michael Hamburger. I was a bit surprised that during my employment interview, he called the bank a "halfway house for Wall Street economists." He was right about that for me. I stayed for only a year and a half, though I did enjoy my stint at the bank, which was headed by Paul Volcker at the time. Volcker had a commanding presence, partly because of his height of 6 feet 7 inches. In later years, I joked with my Wall Street clients that the FRB-NY president and I had worked together on a first-name basis: "He called me 'Ed,' and I called him 'Mr. Volcker.'"

I spent my brief time in the Fed's Lower Manhattan fortress writing memos to the research filing cabinet, mostly about the impacts of

Regulation Q on the credit and business cycles. This regulation, imposed on banks by the Fed starting on August 29, 1933, set maximum ceilings for their deposit rates. The intent was to squelch competition for deposit funds, because excessive competition for such funds was blamed for the spate of bank failures early in the 1930s. Fierce competition drove down the margin between lending rates and borrowing rates, causing banks to make too many risky loans.

As inflation rose during the 1960s and 1970s, the Fed occasionally raised interest rates above the Regulation Q ceilings in an effort to bring inflation back down. "Disintermediation" ensued as money poured out of bank deposits into higher-yielding money-market instruments such as Treasury bills, leaving banks with fewer lendable funds. The resulting credit crunch depressed the economy as housing activity, car sales, and capital spending were stifled by a shortage of credit and tougher lending terms.

The Regulation Q ceilings for all types of bank accounts except demand deposits were phased out from 1981 to 1986 by the Depository Institutions Deregulation and Monetary Control Act of 1980. This was the beginning of a wave of deregulation of the financial sector that had the unintended consequence of setting the stage for more financial crises in coming years.

My main assignment in the research department was to monitor and analyze the weekly deposit flows data. It was dull work, and so were my memos. However, the experience provided very useful knowledge early in my Wall Street career. It helped me to assess the severity of the recession during 1982 and 1983 and the severity of the savings and loan crisis during the late 1980s and early 1990s.

I have a hunch that my memos are still in those filing cabinets, which perhaps have been moved to the basement at 33 Liberty Street, not far from the gold vaults.

PROGNOSTICATOR

MY ROLE MODEL during my stint at the Fed was not Paul Volcker but rather Henry Kaufman, the world-famous chief economist and bond guru at Salomon Brothers. Kaufman likewise had worked at the FRB-NY before moving to Salomon, and I wanted to work on Wall Street too. Out of the blue one day, a longtime headhunter with a very thick New York accent called my office phone and told me that he specialized in placing economists in New York City banks. He asked whether I would be interested in interviewing for a job as a monetary economist at the Wall Street brokerage and investment banking firm EF Hutton & Company. I jumped at the chance, and I was offered the job after a couple of interviews. As my FRB-NY interview with Mike Hamburger had foreshadowed, the Fed had been my halfway house. I left it to join EF Hutton at the start of 1978.

Hutton was also in downtown Manhattan, on State Street, just a few blocks from the Fed's fortress. The firm's very personable chief economist, Ed Syring, hired me. We wrote a monthly publication awkwardly titled *The Money Market Tactician*. Syring paid thousands of dollars a year to use an elaborate econometric model of the economy provided by Data Resources Incorporated (DRI). He had hired another staff economist to run the model and to provide him with macroeconomic analyses and forecasts about the "real" economy, while I focused on the monetary and financial system. I'm a big believer in the benefits of the division of labor, but I quickly learned the critical importance of integrating all aspects of economics, as well as other disciplines, in current analysis. Financial market prognosticator is one job where it is better to be a jack of all trades and a master of none, though mastering economics helps a lot.

DRI was co-founded in 1969 by Donald Marron and Otto Eckstein. Marron moved on to become the chief executive officer of brokerage firm PaineWebber in 1980. Eckstein was a Harvard University economics professor who also served as a member of the Council of Economic Advisers from 1964 to 1966 under President Lyndon B. Johnson. Eckstein was a great salesman and convinced my boss and lots of other economists working in private industry and in the government that they needed to subscribe not only to DRI's database service but also to his firm's econometric model and forecasting service. Based on my experience as a graduate student at Yale, I was not a believer in econometric forecasting models.

DRI's model resided on Burroughs 6700 and 7700 mainframe computers. They were very expensive computing machines housed in large cabinets in their own air-conditioned rooms. We could access them via a remote terminal in our office. The model could generate forecasts for almost every imaginable economic variable. The problem with using a black-box econometric model, especially an outsourced one, is that there is no way to know how the predicted economic variables were generated by the input variables.

Syring left EF Hutton in early 1980, and I stepped into his role, becoming at age 30 the youngest chief economist of a major Wall Street firm. I happily occupied this role at Hutton for almost two years, until October 1982. Little did I know then, which was long before I met my wife, Valerie, that her great-uncle Charles Simon had created this job designation on Wall Street. He was one of the original partners at Salomon Brothers. Indeed, it was Uncle Charles who had encouraged Henry Kaufman to become that firm's chief economist!

Kaufman had dedicated his first book, *Interest Rates, the Markets, and the New Financial World* (1986), to my wife's great-uncle and endowed the Charles Simon Chair in Finance at New York University's Stern School of Business. Interestingly, Paul Volcker was the first Henry Kaufman Visiting Professor at the Stern School, and he wrote the foreword to Kaufman's memoir, *On Money and Markets* (2000), which in some ways inspired me to write this professional autobiography.

The coincidences don't stop there. My father-in-law, Charles Vesine de La Rue, started his Wall Street career at Salomon Brothers in the bond department. In 1982, I left EF Hutton to join Prudential-Bache Securities, where Valerie's father was working as an institutional bond salesman in Paris. Just by happenstance, Valerie and I both started working at CJ Lawrence in 1990. Valerie had an undergraduate degree in law from Paris Nanterre University. She came to the United States to earn her MBA at the University of Hartford. She then joined CJ Lawrence to cover institutional equity accounts in Switzerland. Shortly after arriving at the firm, she came to my office to introduce herself and give me her father's regards. We were married on May 2, 1998 at Windows on the World, one of the greatest restaurants New York City has ever seen, located on the 107th floor of the World Trade Center. Valerie subsequently moved to a sales position at Bear Stearns, which she fortuitously left before its implosion in 2007 to join Yardeni Research as our Director of Institutional Sales.

As a wannabe Kaufman, most of my research aimed at forecasting Fed policy and the outlook for the bond market. But I also had to analyze the broader economy. I continued to use DRI for data, but I stopped our subscription to the firm's expensive econometric model. My longtime colleague Debbie Johnson and I designed a simple spreadsheet program to produce a forecast of the gross national product (GNP), the broadest measure of economic activity, from our bottom-up assessment of its components. We regularly updated and often revised our one-page table showing our outlooks for GNP as well as inflation and interest rates. We still do it this way, though we switched to gross domestic product (GDP) when the US Bureau of Economic Analysis did so in 1991.[4] Of course, that leaves us with plenty of work to explain the thinking behind our forecasts in our commentaries. We do that with lots of supporting charts.

I hired Debbie back in 1979 from Irving Trust, a bank headquartered in Lower Manhattan, where she had become especially adept at analyzing the economy by tracking hundreds of charts of key economic variables. Together, Debbie and I have built an extensive library of these charts and organized them in compilations that focus on various aspects of the economy and financial markets. The topics cover everything from stocks, bonds, commodities, currencies, inflation, and monetary and fiscal policies to earnings, valuation, demographics, and lots more. Over the years, we have amassed a treasure chest of chart publications that are automatically updated on our website. Mali Quintana, another longtime colleague, since 1980, ably and single-handedly manages our charting system.

Hutton was a classy and highly respected firm, catering to wealthy individuals and institutional investors. For several decades, it was the second-largest brokerage firm in the United States. The firm was well known for its commercials in the 1970s and 1980s based on the tagline: "When EF Hutton talks, people listen." At first, I thought I was set for life, and I couldn't understand why many of my older colleagues had often moved among the many Wall Street firms. Then in 1981, the president of EF Hutton, George Ball, moved to the top spot at Prudential-Bache Securities. One year later, he invited Greg Smith and me to join him. Greg was Hutton's chief investment strategist, a role pioneered by his mentor at Goldman Sachs, Leon Cooperman.

For a couple of years while at Hutton, I taught a class at Columbia Business School as an adjunct professor in financial markets. Commuting from downtown to the Upper West Side on the subway wasn't fun, and my day job was keeping me very busy. As it turned out, though, my hassle may have been worth it, as I now can note with satisfaction that at least two of my students went on to great success. When I visited Moore Capital, a hedge fund account on the top floor of the Exxon Building in Manhattan, for the first time many years later, Louis Bacon, the head of the firm, came out to the reception room to greet me, saying, "Professor Yardeni, it's nice to catch up with you after all these years since I took your course at Columbia." The first thoughts that crossed my mind were whether something I'd taught him had contributed to his success and, if so, then why wasn't I as successful? Another student of mine, Paul McCulley, was the widely respected chief economist at PIMCO when Bill Gross ran the place.

Paul Volcker left the FRB-NY about a year and a half after I did, when he was appointed Fed chairman in July 1979. The Fed consists of 12 district banks, including the FRB-NY, and is headquartered in Washington, DC, where the Board of Governors is located. Now, as the Fed's top gun, Volcker was determined to bring inflation down quickly by raising interest rates. They were hiked to well above Regulation Q limits, thus triggering the disintermediation and credit crunch that I mentioned earlier and provoking a severe recession in the early 1980s.

In raising interest rates as fast as he did, Volcker did something that was shocking at the time. On October 6, 1979, he abandoned the Fed's interest rate-targeting approach, with its small incremental changes in the federal funds rate, which is the official interbank lending rate set by the body that determines the Fed's monetary policy, the Federal Open Market Committee (FOMC). He replaced it with a monetarist operating procedure that targeted the growth rate in measures of the money supply, allowing the federal funds rate to be set by market forces (Fig. 1*). At the same time, the chairman announced that the discount rate was being increased by a full percentage point to a record 12.00% (Fig. 2).

Adding to the shock-and-awe effect, Volcker did all this at a rare Saturday night news conference, which forever will be remembered as the "Saturday Night Massacre." Pointing to recent economic releases, Volcker said, "Business data has been good and better than expected. Inflation data has been bad and perhaps worse than expected." He added, "We consider that [this] action will effectively reinforce actions taken earlier to deal with the inflationary environment."

This was a radical change from the Fed's previous approach of tightening too little, too late as inflation soared, boosted by the oil price shocks of 1973 and 1979. Here's some background on them:

- Together, the two shocks caused the price of a barrel of West Texas crude oil to soar 11-fold from $3.56 during July 1973 to a peak of $39.50 during mid-1980, using available monthly data (Fig. 3).
- As a result, the inflation rate, based on the consumer price index (CPI), soared from 2.9% during August 1972 to a record high of 14.6% during March 1980, on a yearly-percent-change basis (Fig. 4). Even the "core" inflation rate, i.e., the rate excluding food and

---

* Figures, references, and appendices are linked on *yardenibook.com/resources.*

energy, accelerated from 3.0% to 13.0% over this period as higher energy costs led to faster wage gains, which were passed through into prices economy-wide.

During this oil-shock period, Arthur Burns was Fed chairman, having served at the helm of the central bank from February 1, 1970 until January 31, 1978; he was briefly succeeded by G. William Miller from March 8, 1978 to August 6, 1979. Under Burns and Miller, the federal funds rate was increased, but not fast enough or high enough to stop inflation from accelerating (Fig. 5). With Volcker's new approach, interest rates were allowed to rise sharply, and so they did in an extremely volatile fashion:

- The federal funds rate jumped from 11.61% on October 5, 1979 to 19.96% in early 1980, plunging to 7.65% later that year, then spiking a couple of times in 1981 above 20.00%.
- The US Treasury 10-year bond yield also rocketed up, to a record 15.84% on September 30, 1981. It was 8.91% during Volcker's first day on the job as the new Fed chairman (Fig. 6).

At EF Hutton, I was an early believer in "disinflation." I first used that word, which means falling inflation, in my June 1981 commentary titled "Well on the Road to Disinflation." The CPI inflation rate was 9.6% that month. I predicted that Volcker would succeed in breaking the inflationary uptrend of the 1960s and 1970s. I certainly wasn't a monetarist, given my Keynesian training at Yale. I knew that my former boss wasn't a monetarist either. But I expected that Volcker would use this radical approach to push interest rates up as high as necessary to break the back of inflation. I also knew, based on my research at the FRB-NY, that doing so would cause massive disintermediation, a severe credit crunch, and a recession. Volcker must have known that too. Those conditions certainly would bring inflation down, which in turn would force the Fed to reverse its monetary course by easing. That would trigger a big drop in bond yields. The puzzle pieces were all fitting together very neatly.

Furthermore, I expected that President Ronald Reagan, who first occupied the White House on January 21, 1981, would support Volcker's campaign to bring down inflation. I thought this because Reagan was very conservative politically and famously once had said, "The nine most terrifying words in the English language are: 'I'm from the government, and I'm here to help.'" During the presidential campaign, Reagan promised to lower marginal tax rates and to reduce government regulation.

He surrounded himself with so-called supply-side economists. I was more receptive to the supply-side than the monetarist view.

So I had my forecast: I believed that after the inflationary malaise during President Jimmy Carter's administration, the fiscal policies of the new administration would probably revive economic growth while the monetary policies of the Fed under Volcker would keep inflation on the decline. I figured that when this became more apparent, it would be a great investment environment for stocks and bonds, which had been beaten down so hard in price by rapidly rising inflation and stagnating growth, a.k.a. "stagflation."

I learned early in my career that some of my best ideas came from frequent discussions with numerous savvy institutional investors, many of whom have become close professional friends. During one of my first marketing trips to Houston, Texas, in the fall of 1981, I met the now-renowned bond investor Van Hoisington, who had recently started his own money management firm after managing the bond portfolio of Texas Commerce Bancshares for several years. The US Treasury 10-year bond yield had just risen to a record 15.84% on September 30 of that year. Both of us believed that bond yields were likely to fall. I told Van that I expected the yield to drop to 7.00% by the mid-1980s. That certainly differentiated me from Henry Kaufman, who had been bearish on bonds, correctly so, during most of the 1970s and remained bearish at that point in 1981.

Van, who is as smart as a whip (as they say in Texas) and is a truly nice gentleman, enthusiastically agreed with me. He talked about "hat-size bond yields." I liked the phrase so much that I started using it in my presentations. It caught on and gave me a claim to fame within the investment community during the 1980s as bond yields fell along with the inflation rate. The November 26, 2001 issue of *Barron's* noted that I had made my "mark in the early 'Eighties by predicting 'hat-size' bond yields (7%–8%) when they were nearly twice as high."[5] Hat tip to Van!

During the 1980s, the 10-year government bond yield fell to a hat-size low of 6.95% on August 29, 1986, while the CPI headline inflation rate dropped from a record high of 14.8% year over year during March 1980 to a low of 1.1% during December 1986 (Fig. 7 and Fig. 8).

This was an extraordinary achievement for Volcker. Contrary to widely held belief, he proved that the inflation rate wasn't intractable but could be clipped in short order.

Lower lows were still ahead for both inflation and interest rates over the next three decades. Van remained steadfastly bullish on bonds and, along with his partner, Lacy Hunt, made a fortune for his investors over that long period from his home base in Austin, Texas. He has been a good professional friend and a subscriber to our research for many years.

Another professional friend who greatly influenced my thinking is Greg Smith, Hutton's investment strategist at the time. Greg and I hit it off right away. He is almost as tall as Paul Volcker but more fun. The native Oklahoman has a sharp analytical mind and lots of common sense about investing. As we worked more closely, I focused my economic research increasingly on issues that were important to Greg and institutional equity portfolio managers while continuing to develop my franchise as a bond economist.

At the beginning of 1981, I started writing a weekly analysis, *Economics Alert*, instead of the monthly publication. At the beginning of 1982, my commentaries were growing more critical of the Fed and bearish on the outlook for stocks, a sentiment Greg shared. In the January 29, 1982 issue, I called on the Fed to abandon monetarism and target real interest rates instead: "Monetarism is the right idea, at the wrong time. We can't argue with the theory: if you want to bring down inflation, you must control and gradually lower the growth of the money supply. However, the theory is very difficult to operationalize. No one can determine which statistical measure of the money supply should be controlled."

I noted that monetarism might have worked better in the 1970s, when the financial markets were more rigidly regulated and offered fewer varieties of deposits and investment choices. I predicted that as the jobless rate continued to climb, the Fed would experience "overwhelming political pressure to junk monetarism and lower interest rates."

As an alternative to monetarist operating procedures, I promoted the Real Interest Targeting Approach in my January 29, 1982 commentary. I wrote that the Fed should peg the federal funds rate at 300 basis points above the inflation rate. In my plan, this spread could be raised if inflationary pressures persisted or lowered if they eased. This approach would have targeted the inflation rate directly rather than targeting an intermediate variable such as the money supply, which was widely believed (especially by monetarists) to be the major driver of inflation. As it turned out, I was 30 years early: the Fed finally did adopt an inflation-targeting approach, but not until the beginning of 2012! However, by then the problem was how to boost inflation back up to the Fed's 2.0% inflation target, not how to bring it down.

In a small way, I might have contributed to the political pressure on the Fed to lower interest rates. Dan Quayle—the 44th vice president of the United States (from January 20, 1989 to January 20, 1993), under President George H.W. Bush—was a freshman conservative Republican Senator from Indiana when he introduced a resolution on March 16, 1982 promoting my idea after I discussed it with him. We had been introduced to one another by Dan Murphy, who headed EF Hutton's equity division and was politically well connected. I was invited to explain my plan to the Senate Democratic Conference on July 27, after which Senate Democratic Leader Robert Byrd (WV) prepared a bill to force the Fed to abandon monetarism.[6] The episode was covered in the August 16, 1982 *New York Post* column by Rowland Evans and Robert Novak titled "Dems Move to Force Interest Rates Down."

The Fed was getting the message. On July 20, 1982, in his mid-year monetary policy report to Congress, Volcker indicated that the Fed soon would lower interest rates. Political pressure was a factor. More important, without a doubt, was a string of financial crises:

- *Drysdale.* In May, Drysdale Government Securities defaulted on interest payments due on Treasury securities that it had borrowed from other firms. Chase Manhattan Bank declared a pretax loss of $285 million as a result of the failure of Drysdale, which the bank had served as a middleman.

- *Penn Square.* In July, Penn Square Bank failed as a result of a large amount of poorly underwritten energy-related loans that it had sold to other banks. Losses on these loans led to significant financial problems for a number of those banks.

- *Lombard-Wall.* On August 12, Wall Street was shaken by the failure of a little-known government securities firm, Lombard-Wall Inc., and its wholly owned subsidiary, Lombard-Wall Money Markets. In a bankruptcy petition, the firm listed debts of $177.2 million to its 10 largest unsecured creditors. The two biggest were the Chase Manhattan Bank, which was owed $45 million, and the New York State Dormitory Authority, which was owed $55 million.[7]

- *Mexico.* Also on August 12, Mexico's Finance Minister, Jesus Silva-Herzog, declared that Mexico no longer would be able to service its debt.[8] The steep rise in oil prices during the 1970s had flooded

American banks with petrodollars, i.e., deposits from the oil export-ers. The banks lent lots of those funds back to oil-exporting countries such as Mexico. Volcker's Saturday Night Massacre certainly mas-sacred Mexican borrowers who no longer could afford to make their loan payments to the banks.

On Friday, August 13, 1982, the Fed announced a half-point drop in the discount rate to 10.50%, the third such move since mid-July, and the federal funds rate plunged by 50 basis points (Fig. 9).

Ten months after we joined George Ball at Prudential-Bache Secu-rities, Greg and I both turned very bullish on the outlook for stocks. On August 16, 1982, at our regularly scheduled 7:30 a.m. Monday morn-ing strategy meeting with the sales force, we said that it was time to be bullish on stocks again. The lead story in my weekly commentary was titled "Fed-Led Recovery Now Seems Likely." I wrote, emphasizing with italics, *We now believe that our upbeat forecast for 1983 is achievable and should positively influence both the bond and equity markets.* I nearly fell off my chair when longtime bond bear Henry Kaufman turned bull-ish on bonds the very next day. I wasn't the only one impressed by his ability to change his mind after having been bearish for so long: stock prices soared.

The Dow Jones Industrial Average (DJIA) subsequently rose 1,408.9% from a low of 777 on August 12, 1982 to peak at 11723 on January 14, 2000 (Fig. 10).[9] Greg and I remained steadfastly bullish almost to the very end of that great bull market, though I moved on to another firm along the way.

Up until this point in my career, all I had experienced professionally was a really nasty bear market—from November 20, 1980 through August 12, 1982—which lowered the DJIA by 22.3% (Fig. 11). The bullish call Greg and I made on August 16, a few days after the bear market ended, turned out to be very well timed. After that bear market came a 65.7% rebound in the DJIA through November 29, 1983. So far, so good for us bulls. But a relatively long correction followed, during which I'm sure some of our accounts began to doubt our bullish call. It lasted 238 days—from November 29, 1983 to July 24, 1984—and lowered the stock index by 15.6%.

Weighing on stock prices was that the CPI inflation rate bottomed at 2.5% during July 1983 and rose to 4.8% by March 1984. Bond investors were still very twitchy about inflation. So the backup in the inflation rate triggered a nasty upturn in the US Treasury 10-year bond yield from a low of 10.12% on May 4, 1983 to a high of 13.99% on May 30, 1984 (Fig. 12). The Fed was targeting the federal funds rate again and raised it from 8.50% at the beginning of 1983 to a 1984 peak of 11.50% on August 9 (Fig. 13).

I told Greg that I didn't expect a recession, which meant there was no reason to turn bearish on stocks. We remained bullish. I also reiterated my longtime bullish outlook on bonds—though it wasn't easy doing so. The July 27, 1983 issue of my weekly commentary was titled "Bond Investors Are the Economy's Vigilantes." I concluded: "So if the fiscal and monetary authorities won't regulate the economy, the bond investors will. The economy will be run by vigilantes in the credit markets."

During the 1980s and 1990s, there were a few episodes when rising bond yields slowed the economy and put a lid on inflation. This was the first such event. To this day, every time bond yields rise significantly almost anywhere in the world, I get asked to appear on at least one of the financial news TV networks to discuss whether the Bond Vigilantes are back. Having popularized "hat-size bond yields" and "Bond Vigilantes," I started to appreciate the power of coining pithy terms to brand my economic and financial forecasts. Coin a good phrase that accurately describes future developments, and it will appear in your obituary, if not on your tombstone.

In their premier performance, the Bond Vigilantes succeeded as inflation peaked in early 1984. Then in late 1985 and early 1986, the price of oil plunged 62% (Fig. 14). Texas was especially hard hit as the oil business went from boom to bust. I didn't expect an economy-wide recession because too much else was still going right for the economy. Instead, I observed that the economy was experiencing a "rolling recession" that was rolling through the oil industry as a result of the sharp drop in oil prices. The bond yield fell back down to 7.23% by the end of 1986.

The DJIA rallied sharply—by 150.6% from July 24, 1984 through August 25, 1987—as inflation remained subdued. There was also widespread relief that the recession in the oil patch didn't spread to the rest of the economy. Instead, lower gasoline prices boosted consumer spending. Contributing to the bull market was the enactment on October 22, 1986 of President Reagan's Tax Reform Act. It significantly reduced marginal tax rates, especially on top earners, but it also benefited lower earners by expanding the standard deduction, personal exemptions, and the earned income credit. The DJIA soared 50.5% over the next 10 months.

The stock market crash on Black Monday, October 19, 1987 stress-tested the conviction of bulls like Greg and myself. Nevertheless, we spent much of that day reassuring our sales force that this was unlikely to be the beginning of a long-lasting bear market. The DJIA plunged 508 points (or 22.6%) to 1739 that day (Fig. 15). It was a relatively short bear market, lasting 101 days with a peak-to-trough drop of 33.5%.[10] Bear markets are usually caused by recessions. But there was no recession this time. The DJIA actually rose 2.3% during 1987, despite the bear market along the way!

Some observers noted that the US Treasury 10-year bond yield had risen from 7.18% at the start of the year to peak at 10.23% on October 16 (Fig. 16). I observed that the Bond Vigilantes were at it again.

The Fed contributed to the backup in yields. On August 11, Alan Greenspan succeeded Paul Volcker as Fed chairman. Shortly after the market peaked, Greenspan made a rookie mistake on September 9, firing a "preemptive strike" against inflation by raising the discount rate 50 basis points.

On October 14, the Commerce Department reported a record-high merchandise trade deficit for the United States. A few days later, on October 17, US Treasury Secretary James Baker told German authorities to "either inflate your mark, or we'll devalue the dollar." The next day, Baker proclaimed on television talk shows that the US "would not accept" the recent German interest-rate increase. Shortly thereafter, an unnamed Treasury official said we would "drive the dollar down" if necessary.

There was lots of talk that "portfolio insurance" strategies had back-fired, exacerbating the crash.[11] These strategies presumably provided insurance against a stock market decline in a process called "dynamic hedging" by selling more stock index futures contracts, with the resulting gains off-setting the losses in the stocks held in a portfolio. In an October 18, 2012 article in *The New York Times*, Floyd Norris recounted:

> Portfolio insurance did not start the widespread selling of stocks in 1987. But it made sure that the process got out of hand. As computers dictated that more and more futures be sold, the buyers of those futures not only insisted on sharply lower prices but also hedged their positions by selling the underlying stocks. That drove prices down further, and produced more sell orders from the computers.

At the time, many people generally understood how portfolio insurance worked, but there was a belief that its very nature would assure that it could not cause panic. Everyone would know the selling was not coming from anyone with inside information, so others would be willing to step in and buy to take advantage of bargains. Or so it was believed.

But when the crash arrived, few understood much of anything, except that it was like nothing they had ever seen. Anyone who did step in with a buy order quickly regretted the decision.[12]

On Wednesday, October 21, 1987, I received a call from a Prudential-Bache Securities investment banker who was convinced that the crash had been triggered the week before by news that the House Ways and Means Committee was considering eliminating the tax deduction for interest paid on debt used in corporate takeovers. Equities had been boosted by some favorable tax treatments for financing corporate buyouts that included this deduction, which multiplied the number of potential takeover targets and pushed up their stock prices. At the time, big deals were driving stock prices higher.

The investment banker convinced me. In an op-ed article for the October 28, 1987 issue of *The Wall Street Journal*, I wrote:

Many investors and traders learned of this plan from a *Wall Street Journal* story on Oct. 14. The day before, the Democrats on the House Ways and Means Committee agreed on a number of tax-raising measures including the elimination of the deduction for interest expenses exceeding $5 million a year on debt from a takeover or leveraged buyout.

On Oct. 15, the full committee approved the package. Takeover stocks were pummeled late during the trading day. Several announced and unannounced deals were delayed. Arbitragers sold large blocks of the stocks.

Though the tax measure faced an uncertain future both in Congress and with the White House (the Senate Finance Committee on Oct. 16 approved a bill without the anti-takeover provisions), the arbs sold fast. They are not long-term investors, and they feared the worst.

> Under the Ways and Means proposal, the interest provision would be retroactive to Oct. 13, a crushing setback to any deal being worked on or considered.

I concluded:

> The Ways and Means measure contains some needed takeover reforms such as a prohibitive tax on "greenmail" payment to raiders. But putting most companies out of reach of entrepreneurs, and sacrificing a measure of the more-accountable management that this fosters, has already had a disastrous effect on equity prices, aggregate wealth and national income.

I called on the House Ways and Means Committee to scrap the proposal: "If the House puts the anti-takeover plan to rest, perhaps some of the damage can be undone." The committee's chairman, Dan Rostenkowski (D, IL), did just that in December 1987, which reinforced my bullish stance on stocks, as did the ongoing improvement in corporate earnings. The Omnibus Budget Reconciliation Act of 1987 was passed by the House on October 29 and by the Senate on December 11, excluding the bearish takeover regulations. (See Appendix 1.1, "That M&A Tax Scare Rattling the Markets.")

My colleague's notion that the anti-takeover provisions had caused the 1987 crash was subsequently confirmed by an article in the September 1989 *Journal of Financial Economics*, "Triggering the 1987 Stock Market Crash: Antitakeover Provisions in the Proposed House Ways and Means Tax Bill?"[13] The two researchers concluded, "The overall evidence suggests that the antitakeover restrictions in the proposed House bill were a fundamental economic event contributing to the greater than ten percent market decline during October 14–16, which arguably triggered the October 19 crash."

Just by coincidence, the movie *Wall Street* was released on December 11, 1987—the same day that the Senate passed the Omnibus Budget Reconciliation Act. The film was directed by Oliver Stone and starred Michael Douglas as Gordon Gekko, a wealthy and unscrupulous corporate raider. The character of Gekko is widely believed to be a composite of several people, including Ivan Boesky, Carl Icahn, and Michael Milken.

The 1980s were the heyday of corporate raiders. A raider would purchase a large stake in a corporation with borrowed money. Then he would use his shareholder voting rights to force the company to restructure to increase the share price. The restructuring measures might include replacing top executives, downsizing operations, or liquidating the company. For example, in 1985, Icahn successfully launched a hostile takeover of TWA. He then systematically sold TWA's assets to repay the debt he had used to purchase the company. In the movie, Gekko aimed to take over an airline and liquidate it, selling off its assets, which would result in the firing of all its employees and the plundering of their pension fund.

Many of the corporate raiders of the 1980s were clients of Drexel Burnham Lambert. This investment banking firm's most profitable business was run by Michael Milken, who helped corporate raiders issue high-yield bonds to finance their takeovers. Rostenkowski's bill was aimed at eliminating the tax deductibility of the cost of financing takeovers. He backed off.

Ironically, Oliver Stone's film marked the tail end of the short era of the corporate raiders. Corporations responded to the ongoing threats of the raiders' "greenmail" by restructuring themselves and implementing defensive measures, including poison pills, golden parachutes, and increasing debt levels on the companies' balance sheets. Drexel was forced into bankruptcy in February 1990 due to its involvement in illegal activities in the junk bond market. Returns on the hostile takeovers were increasingly disappointing. The bull market of the 1990s reduced the number of situations in which a company's share price was low relative to the assets that it controlled. Raiders still exist, of course, but they have been rebranded as "activist shareholders."

At the start of 1988, when the DJIA was at 1939, I reaffirmed my bullish outlook by forecasting that this stock index would rise to a new high of 5000 by 1993. Three years later, I realized that it might take longer to get there, so I amended the forecast to "5, 5 by '95." I predicted that the Dow would soar to 5000 and that the US Treasury 10-year bond yield would fall to 5.00% by 1995. When the Dow rose to my target on November 21, 1995, I raised the ante with a forecast of 10000 by 2000. The bond yield did get down to hat-size yields of 8.00% on July 10, 1989 and 7.00% on December 20, 1991. It did fall down to 5.00%, but not until September 9, 1998. The Dow rose above 10000 for the first time on March 29, 1999, slightly ahead of schedule per my forecast.[14] (See Appendix 1.2, "Who's the Bull Here?")

BABY BOOMER

GREG AND I described our bullish investment thesis in the early 1980s as "the greatest financial story ever told." We both were convinced that Disinflation, Deregulation, and Downsizing—our "3Ds" scenario—would be very bullish themes for equities and bonds. In the mid-1980s, I added a fourth "D" word to the list of bullish trends: "Demographics."

After World War II, from 1946 to 1964, the US birth rate rose significantly, producing the 76 million people of the Baby Boom generation (Fig. 17). I am a member of this cohort: I was born in 1950. My simple thesis was that this demographic bulge was having an important impact on the economy and financial markets and would continue to do so.

Demographic trends are among the most predictable ones, and I am still surfing the "Age Wave" (Fig. 18). The percentage of 16- to 34-year-old people in the labor force (16 and older) rose from 37% during 1962, when the oldest Baby Boomers turned 16, to peak at 51% during 1980, when the youngest ones turned 16. The oldest of them turned 65 during 2011, and the youngest will do so in 2029. The Age Wave percentage fell to a low of 35%–36% from 2011 through 2017.

Much of my work on demographics and other "big-picture" themes appeared in a series of *Topical Studies* that I wrote on an occasional basis. The first, written in March 1984, focused on the trade deficit. Over the years through to 2004, I wrote 68 studies on various topics that I believed were particularly important to investors at the time. Quite a few of these reports focused on demographics.[15]

In the 1980s, I argued that the influx of young Baby Boomers into the labor markets might explain why productivity growth was so weak. These new entrants into the job market were relatively cheap because there were lots of them and they were inexperienced. Many of them came to be called "Yuppies," from the phrase "young urban professionals." *Newsweek* magazine declared 1984 "The Year of the Yuppie." I predicted that they would fuel a housing and consumption boom. In the late 1980s, I observed that as the Yuppies aged, they were morphing into "couch potatoes," which meant they were getting married, moving to the suburbs, staying home, and watching TV after dinner. So was I. There was a simple explanation: we were starting to have our own babies. My first child, Melissa, was born in 1981, followed by Sarah in 1985, then Sam in 1989. David (1999) and Laura (2001) arrived later.

I predicted that as my contemporaries and I aged, we would start to save more and invest more in stocks for college educations and for retirement. I was half right. The saving rate went down, not up, in the 1990s, falling from 9.0% near the start of the decade to 4.4% at the end of the decade, based on the 12-month average of this rate. But the demand for equities did soar as I had expected, culminating in the frenzied buying mania of the late 1990s.

The bull market in stocks back then probably explains the drop in the saving rate (Fig. 19). As consumers' net worth rose along with stock prices, many of them must have decided to spend rather than to save more of their income. This is a very good example of the internal contradictions that make forecasting a challenge. Getting one aspect of a forecast right can cause unexpected consequences for other aspects.

I also predicted in the late 1980s and early 1990s that as the Baby Boomers aged, the unemployment rate would fall back down to 4.0%. I was right about the jobless rate. It fell to 4.0% during December 1999, the lowest in three decades. I also correctly predicted that productivity growth would rebound as the mostly highly educated Baby Boomers accumulated more on-the-job training and experience. Productivity growth rose sharply during the second half of the 1990s and remained high during the first half of the 2000s (Fig. 20).

Of course, my generation continues to have a significant impact on the US economy. We are living longer than previous generations and retiring later in life. However, Generations X (born 1965–1980), Y (1981–1996), and Z (1997–2015) are becoming increasingly important as well. Generation Y is also known as the "Millennials." They are getting married and having kids later in life. Many of them prefer to work and live in cities rather than suburbs and to rent apartments rather than to own houses.

While I continue to study the impact of domestic demographic trends on the US economy, global demographic trends have become increasingly important too. As a result of dropping fertility rates and as people live longer, populations are rapidly aging in many countries, and their growth rates are falling. There are lots of implications for consumer spending, global inflation, and government budget deficits, as I discuss in coming chapters.

MICROECONOMIST

ANOTHER *TOPICAL STUDY,* which I co-authored with David Moss in October 1988, explored the "New Wave" economy.[16] At the time, David was a graduate student at Yale University studying under Professor Tobin, as I had done. Like me, David previously had graduated from Cornell University. David is now a tenured professor at Harvard Business School. In 2005, he founded the Tobin Project, an independent and nonprofit research organization focusing on the relationships between government and markets, as well as the institutional structure of democracy, economic inequality, and national security.

David and I spent some time rereading and carefully studying Adam Smith's *The Wealth of Nations* (1776) because it seemed especially relevant to events at the time. The central proposition of Smith's *magnum opus* was that the bigger and more competitive a market is, the greater the resulting prosperity. We argued that Adam Smith's growth model of the competitive marketplace had never been more relevant. We observed that during the 1980s, many industries and markets had become more competitive.

In many ways, this was the beginning of my intellectual transformation from a macroeconomist to a microeconomist. I have become increasingly convinced that most of the more interesting and relevant influences on the outlook for the global economy have occurred at the microeconomic level.

Since the late 1970s, changes in market structure and industrial organization have stimulated more competition. I believe that the model of perfect competition found in the microeconomic textbooks has become at least as useful as—if not more useful than—any macroeconomic paradigm for understanding and predicting the course of the economy.

In *The Wealth of Nations,* Smith noted that "five years have seldom passed away in which some book or pamphlet has not been published, written too with such abilities as to gain authority with the public, and pretending to demonstrate that the wealth of the nation was fast declining, that the country was depopulated, agriculture neglected, manufactures decaying, and trade undone." He wrote the book to discredit not only mercantilists, who favored trade protectionism, but also the rampant pessimism of his day.

David and I wrote our *Topical Study* to counter the rampant pessimism of our day. Numerous books had been published in the 1980s with predictions as ominous as their titles: *The Deindustrialization of America*

(1982), *The Great Depression of 1990* (1985), *Beyond Our Means* (1987), *Blood in the Streets* (1987), *Day of Reckoning* (1988), *The Debt Threat* (1988), *On Borrowed Time* (1988), *The Great U-Turn* (1988), *Buying Into America* (1988), *Falling From Grace* (1988), and *Trading Places* (1988).

The front cover of the April 7, 1988 issue of *The New York Times Magazine* portrayed an overweight, stooping bald eagle dressed in red, white, and blue. The old bird was holding a cane for support and staring anxiously into a small mirror. The cover story was "Taking Stock: Is America in Decline?" Earlier that year, *Newsweek* had run a special cover report: "The Pacific Century: Is America in Decline?" And at the beginning of 1987, *U.S. News & World Report* examined "American Competitiveness: Are We Losing It?"

David and I predicted that the pessimists were wrong, and we didn't have to wait long for confirmation.

One of the most momentous events during my career was the end of the Cold War in 1991. I had seen it coming a few years earlier and wrote a *Topical Study* during August 1989 titled "The Triumph of Capitalism."[17] I observed that about one year after Mikhail S. Gorbachev became the General Secretary of the Soviet Communist Party, the nuclear reactor at Chernobyl blew up. The explosion, on April 26, 1986, released at least as much radiation as in the atomic bomb attacks on Hiroshima and Nagasaki. That event and other recent disasters in the Soviet Union were bound to convince Gorbachev of the need to restructure the Soviet economic and political systems, I surmised. Likely, he would conclude that a massive restructuring was essential and urgent because the disasters were "symptomatic of a disastrous economic system that is no longer just stagnating; rather, it is on the brink of collapse," I wrote back then.

The Berlin Wall was dismantled in late 1989. The result was that the United States emerged as the one and only superpower, experiencing not just a new wave but a new era, and that's what I wrote about in a September 1991 *Topical Study* titled "The Collapse of Communism Is Bullish."[18]

In a September 10, 1993 study, "The End of the Cold War Is Bullish," I continued hammering home the theme that the end of the Cold War eliminated the greatest trade barrier in history, and that freer trade would lead to greater global prosperity.[19] Adam Smith wrote that free trade has tremendous benefits: "By opening a more extensive market for whatever part of the produce of their labour may exceed their home consumption, it encourages them to improve its productive powers, and to augment its annual produce to the utmost, and thereby to increase the real revenue and wealth of the society."

Pessimists warned that the increased demand from all those people who had been liberated from communism would lead to higher inflation. That would mean higher interest rates, especially since there wouldn't be enough capital to finance the needs of all the former socialists. I disagreed and turned even more bullish on both bonds and stocks.

The Cold War was over, for now. But it didn't mark "the end of history," as political scientist Francis Fukuyama contended in a 1989 essay published in the international affairs journal *The National Interest* and expanded into a 1992 book, *The End of History and the Last Man*. Political scientist Samuel P. Huntington challenged the thesis of his former student. In a 1993 *Foreign Affairs* article and a 1996 book titled *The Clash of Civilizations and the Remaking of World Order*, Huntington's analysis astutely anticipated that the disintegration of the Soviet Union set the stage for a wave of terrorism by Islamic jihadists intent on reviving the religious world wars that had raged during the period of the Crusades. Their unambiguous declaration of war occurred on September 11, 2001, when they killed nearly 3,000 people in the United States.

A few months before the Berlin Wall was dismantled, the never-ending clash of civilizations between the Israelis and the Palestinians hit my family hard.

On July 6, 1989, Egged public bus No. 405 left Tel Aviv for Jerusalem. My mother and father, Naomi and Leonard, were on that bus during a summer vacation visiting relatives in Israel. Abed al-Hadi Ghaneim of the Palestinian Islamic Jihad was on it too. He grabbed the steering wheel of the bus, running it off a steep cliff into a ravine less than half an hour from Jerusalem.

My mother was born in Haifa, as was I. My father was born in Vienna. Along with his mother and sister, he left in 1933 for Palestine. My grandfather was already in Palestine making arrangements for his family to join him. He was a Zionist and presciently decided that the time had come to leave Austria. My grandmother and her two children, i.e., my father and aunt, were stopped at the border between Egypt and Palestine by British immigration officials, who intended to send them back to Austria. She pretended to be too ill to travel and was admitted to a local clinic, where an Arab doctor kindly sent word to my grandfather, who pulled some strings to get his family into Palestine. I would never have been born but for the humanity of that doctor.

When I was growing up in Haifa, my father studied chemical engineering at the Technion, the Israel Institute of Technology, which was established in 1912. Today, it is cited as one of the factors behind the growth of Israel's high-tech industry and innovation. In 1957, when I was seven years old, my father moved our family to the United States so that he could attend graduate school at Case Institute of Technology, in Cleveland.

The terrorist in the bus attack killed 16 civilians, including two Canadians and one American, and 27 were wounded. My parents were thrown out of the bus as it tumbled down the ravine and burst into flames. My brother Danny and I flew to Israel. Our father was much more seriously injured than our mother. He was flown by helicopter to Hadassah Hospital, in Jerusalem, where he had to undergo several reconstructive surgeries on his skull and face. Our mother was also treated at the hospital. Amazingly, she sustained only superficial wounds, but she was very shaken and worried about my father. Israeli Prime Minister Benjamin Netanyahu came to the hospital to visit our parents and the other survivors. I knew "Bibi" from New York City, where we had met when he was Israel's ambassador to the United Nations. My brother stayed in Israel with our father, who underwent several months of physical rehabilitation. My father then rejoined our mother at their home in Delray Beach, Florida.

The attack on the bus is described as the first Palestinian suicide mission, even though the attacker survived. Actually, he was treated for his injuries at the same hospital as my parents. When I flew to Israel to be with my parents, I saw him being escorted after his treatment to a police van that would carry him to prison. He was convicted and given 16 life sentences for murder, hijacking, and terrorism. On October 18, 2011, Ghaneim was released to Gaza as part of the Gilad Shalit prisoner exchange between Israel and Hamas.

STRATEGIST

JIM MOLTZ CALLED me in early 1991. Jim was the CEO of CJ Lawrence, a relatively small, privately held investment research firm that was highly regarded among institutional investors. Jim told me that Ed Hyman, their top-rated chief economist, was leaving to start his own firm, and that I was his choice to replace Ed. I joined CJ Lawrence on April 1 of that year. It was a great opportunity to focus my marketing efforts exclusively on institutional investors. In addition, I looked forward to working with Jim, an amiable fellow who also was the firm's widely respected chief investment strategist.

Jim left to join Ed Hyman's firm during 1999. Tom Galvin, our auto analyst, took on the role of investment strategist. Two years later, he moved on to the "buy side" to manage money. I was offered the strategist job in April 1999, which I accepted as long as I could remain the chief economist as well.

At CJ Lawrence, I was one of the early proponents of the "New Economy" and its bullish consequences for the stock market. Initially, my optimistic productivity projection was based on demographic trends. In 1993, I started to notice that the pace of technological innovation was accelerating, led by faster and more powerful personal computers. In 1995, I wrote a *Topical Study* titled "The High-Tech Revolution in the US of @." I argued that technology capital spending was another reason to believe that the productivity growth trend was likely to rise, which implied that inflation could continue to fall even as the unemployment rate fell below levels that many traditional macroeconomists believed might revive inflation.

That caught the attention of *Barron's*, which put my mug on the cover of its August 4, 1997 issue. The story, by Jonathan R. Laing, was titled "Wall Street Seer," with a cover teaser that read: "More than any other strategist, Ed Yardeni has been right on the stock market and the economy. First, he called for the Dow to hit 10000 in the year 2000. Now he sees Dow 15000 by 2005." Jon wrote a glowing story about my forecasting insights during the 1980s and 1990s. (See Appendix 1.3, "Wall Street Seer.")

While I was pleased to get the credit for some of my forecasts, I worried about the "front-cover curse." Since I had been so bullish during the 1980s and 1990s, I reckoned that to avoid the curse, I should think hard about what could go wrong. On July 14, 1997, I distributed a *Topical Study* titled "New Era Recession? Deflation, Irrational Exuberance, and Y2K." In the opening lines, I wrote: "Now that my optimistic New Era outlook is becoming the consensus, it is time to think about some problems that might unfold in the New Era. I see three Forces of Darkness: 1) Deflation, 2) Irrational Exuberance, and 3) The Year 2000 Problem. Like Macbeth's three witches, these problems could do some real mischief in the new millennium: 'Double, double toil, and trouble.' Indeed, I now think there is at least a 30% chance of a worldwide recession in the year 2000."

Many computers weren't programmed to recognize that when the year changed from "99" to "00," that meant from 1999 to 2000, not to 1900. This was known as the Y2K problem. I started researching Y2K in 1998 and frequently wrote about it, becoming Wall Street's "expert" on this issue as I discussed the possible disruptive impact on computer systems and the global economy. I compiled data on how much the S&P 500 companies were spending to fix the problem, provided in their quarterly "10-Q" and annual "10-K" filings with the Securities and Exchange Commission.[20] Collectively, they had budgeted around $50 billion to fix the software glitch. Government agencies, particularly the Internal Revenue Service (IRS), also were writing lots of reports suggesting that their systems were at risk. A few chief technology officers contacted me to discuss the importance of fixing the problem. My findings led me to raise my projection of recession odds.

I regularly spoke over the phone with John Koskinen, the Y2K czar for the Clinton White House, who later thanked me for my role in raising awareness of the issue. (John went on to head up the IRS under President Barack Obama.) He was concerned but remained confident that all would be well. I even had a meeting with Janet Yellen to discuss Y2K when she chaired Clinton's Council of Economic Advisers. She seemed quite relaxed about it. Fed officials also became concerned but issued a reassuring message during the summer of 1999 about their readiness to deal with any problems in the banking system.

While I started raising the warning flag during the summer of 1997, stock prices continued to soar. One of my more bullish accounts countered by telling me, "In the stock market, being too early is the same as being wrong." I was very early: a bear market in stocks started March 24, 2000, led by the technology sector, with the S&P 500 plunging 49.1% through October 9, 2002, which was much more severe than anything I had expected.

As it turned out, not one significant computer system anywhere in the world malfunctioned, and I quickly admitted my forecasting error. I took some shots from a few reporters in the media who had covered my Y2K recession concerns. I agreed to be on CNN on January 4, 2000 with Stuart Varney. I knew it would be a tough interview when he announced at the top of the show, "After this ball dropped, fears of a Y2K recession suddenly looked overblown. Tonight, Wall Street's most vocal Y2K pessimist will admit he was wrong." That's what I did. Varney concluded the interview by saying, "Okay. Ed Yardeni, you're an honest man."

Actually, Y2K did contribute to the brief recession that occurred from March through November 2001, but not for the reasons I expected. It did so by pumping more air into the IT bubble, as companies scrambled to address the problem by spending more on new hardware and software. The bubble burst at the start of 2000 as IT spending took a dive. I talk about this more in Chapter 3.

My favorite post-Y2K assessment of my efforts was a January 5, 2000 story in *Businessweek*, which observed, "Rather than being made a goat because of his way-off-base Y2K predictions, however, Yardeni should be heralded as a hero. After proving his skill as a consistently bullish market strategist during the '90s, he was seemingly wrong about Y2K. Or was he?" The article concluded that my warnings "might have helped head off a difficult if not disastrous situation."[21]

During the 9/11 terrorist attacks, I was working at Deutsche Bank's US equities division in New York City, owing to acquisitions that had brought CJ Lawrence into the bank's fold in 1989.[22] That morning at 9:00 a.m., I flew out of New York's LaGuardia Airport on my way to visit accounts in Charlotte, North Carolina. Around 10:00 a.m., when we were flying over Washington, DC, the pilot informed us about the attacks in New York City and below us in the nation's capital. He announced that we would be landing shortly in Charlotte. After the attacks, all civilian flights in the US were ordered to land immediately.

In the airport terminal, everyone was in shock watching on television what was happening to the Twin Towers in New York City. By the time we landed, the South Tower already had collapsed, at 9:59 a.m., and the North Tower followed at 10:28 a.m. The Deutsche Bank salesman, who was based in Atlanta, met me at the airport with a rental car. We agreed that we would drive him home and that I would take the car the next day to drive myself home to Long Island.

The Fed responded to the 9/11 attacks with further monetary easing. The latest round had started on January 3, 2001, in response to the bursting of the tech bubble and the resulting recession. By June 25, 2003, the Fed had lowered the federal funds rate target from 6.50% to 1.00%.

On March 20, 2003, the United States under the leadership of President George W. Bush invaded Iraq after alleging that Saddam Hussein might have had something to do with the 9/11 attacks and claiming that he had weapons of mass destruction. On April 2, I was one of 13 Wall Street economists invited to meet with the President in the Roosevelt

Room in the West Wing of the White House to discuss his latest economic proposals to stimulate the economy and the stock market, thereby countering the lingering negative economic effects of the terrorist attacks. His plan included eliminating the double taxation of dividends, which I supported then and still do now.

Fifteen minutes after the invited group sat down, Bush entered the room. He was remarkably talkative and upbeat, considering that the United States was at war. Before he started to discuss his economic plan, he spoke for about 20 minutes about Iraq. Most remarkable, I thought at the time, was his telling us that Saddam Hussein had relayed an offer to leave Iraq if his safety was guaranteed. Bush said his administration turned it down, viewing it as a last-minute gambit to halt our invasion.

Despite the war in the Middle East, I remained optimistic during the decade following the Y2K nonevent and the bursting of the tech bubble, for the same reasons as I had during the 1990s. On December 11, 2001, three months after the terrorist attacks in the United States, China joined the World Trade Organization. There was more free trade, though that's become a hotly debated issue in recent years, and global prosperity proliferated, as shown by rapidly rising world production and exports. More of that growth was attributable to China and other emerging market economies.

I moved from Deutsche Bank back to Prudential Financial during April 2002. Pru's investment strategist position was open after my friend and mentor Greg Smith had decided to retire; the head of the equity research department made me a very good offer to come back to Pru, and I took it. However, after a brief stint at Pru, I left to join the buy side. The sell side of Wall Street had turned more corporate and less entrepreneurial. In any event, I was ready for a change.

PORTFOLIO MANAGER

A NEW CHAPTER of my career began with an unexpected call from Akron, Ohio in August 2004. It was from Jim Oelschlager, head of Oak Associates, which manages money for individuals and institutions. He serves as chief investment officer and chief executive officer. Jim asked me to come out to his weekend ranch home on 800 sprawling acres in rural western Pennsylvania. When we met there, he asked me to join his firm as chief investment strategist. I accepted and joined Oak in the second week of September 2004. Jim sent his private Challenger jet to pick me up at LaGuardia Airport.

I rented a one-bedroom apartment in Fairlawn, Ohio five minutes from Oak's office. I commuted on a weekly basis to Akron from my home on Long Island. I usually flew out Sunday evenings on AirTran to the convenient Akron-Canton airport, walking over to the hanger where Jim parked his jet. His crew always left a car for me to drive myself to my apartment. I would go to the office at the beginning of the week and usually fly back home on a commercial flight before the weekend. When I first joined, Jim flew me around the country in his jet to meet all of Oak's accounts.

Jim has had multiple sclerosis (MS) since early in his career. That has never stopped him from succeeding in business. He started at Firestone, where he managed the firm's retirement fund, which was underfunded by $300 million when he started in 1969 and was overfunded by $300 million in 1984. The company took the excess and terminated the old retirement plan. Jim agreed to manage the funds of the new plan on a contractual basis at his own new firm, Oak Associates. Jim is a legendary investor, particularly in the technology sector of the stock market.

Jim has always been extremely charitable and actively supports his community. He opened the Oak Clinic, which caters to the needs of others afflicted with MS, regardless of their ability to pay. His jet is outfitted with a lift so he can board and deplane with his wheelchair. The plane is used to fly other patients of the clinic and has made several trips to Haiti to deliver doctors and supplies. Jim's disability has never disabled him. He has a great sense of humor and zest for life that he shares with his extremely supportive wife, Vanita, a successful writer of children's books.

Thanks to Jim's encouragement and support, I continued to produce my investment research at Oak. The weekly and occasional *Topical Studies* were replaced with a daily *Morning Briefing* email. With the help of Oak's excellent IT department, I revived my website, which I had had since the mid-1990s. I was very gratified that many of the buy-side portfolio managers and industry analysts with whom I had worked when I was on the Street subscribed to my research service as paying customers.

During the two years at Prudential before I joined Oak, much of my focus was on China and its impact on the global economy. I wrote three *Topical Studies* on the subject that caused me to be very bullish on the stock market, especially what I dubbed the "MEI" sectors of the S&P 500, namely Materials, Energy, and Industrials. That thesis continued to influence my work at Oak, and I recommended that Oak's portfolio have more exposure to those three sectors than to the S&P 500 Technology sector.

Two years after I started at Oak, I decided that I wanted to spend all my time on my business. Jim and I parted ways very amicably, and I am very grateful to him for helping me get started on my own. On January 1, 2007, Yardeni Research, Inc. opened our doors for business. Actually, we didn't have any doors because we have been virtual from the get-go. My colleagues work from their home offices, as do I, connected via the Internet. While I was at Oak, Jim had allowed me to keep my staff of many years; they began working from their homes when I started commuting to Akron. So when I left Oak, nothing really changed for us operationally. We continued to exchange roughly 300 emails per day putting together the *Morning Briefing* interactively and still do.

The years 2007 and 2008 might not seem like auspicious ones for launching an investment research business, given the financial calamity that unfolded then. However, our business never suffered. I didn't foresee the extent of the debacle coming in late 2008, because I expected that the government would bail out Lehman Brothers. In the months leading up to this disaster, I did recommend underweighting Financials. But as day follows night, a great bull market followed the bear market.

SYMBOLIST

MY WIFE AND I took our two kids, Laura and David, to visit our nation's capital in June of 2009. They were 8 and 10 at the time. We started with a tour of the Capitol building that we had prearranged through the office of our congressional representative, Gary Ackerman (R, NY). After seeing the Rotunda, we went up to the visitors' gallery in the House, which was very busy that day, with members voting on numerous bills. Then, the congressman's aide surprised us by whisking us downstairs to an entry door to the House floor. Representative Ackerman came out and asked the kids to join him in the chamber. Needless to say, it was a great experience for them.

I first met with Representative Ackerman in early November of 2008, in his congressional district office on Northern Boulevard in

Queens, about 15 minutes from my home at the time in Great Neck, Long Island. He and his legislative assistant agreed to hear me out on why more needed to be done in Washington to bring mortgage rates down and why mark-to-market (MTM) accounting rules should be suspended. I was convinced that the MTM accounting guidance was exacerbating the unfolding financial crisis by forcing financial institutions to lower the valuations of their distressed mortgages and related assets to fire-sale prices. That severely impaired their capital, forcing them to stop lending and to sell assets at fire-sale prices! MTM was causing a death spiral in the credit markets, in my opinion.

In late October 2008, I observed that while the lowering of the federal funds rate had brought down Treasury bond yields, mortgage rates were not falling as fast (Fig. 21 and Fig. 22). I wrote that the Treasury should borrow $1.0 trillion and lend it out as 4.00% mortgages through Fannie Mae and Freddie Mac on a first-come-first-serve basis. I pitched this idea to my congressman and his aide. Neither of them expressed an opinion on the subject; they just listened politely.

The Fed actually dealt with the mortgage-rate issue that I had raised in Ackerman's office one week after we met, when the first round of quantitative easing (QE1) was introduced on November 25, 2008. The Fed announced that it would purchase $100 billion in bonds issued by housing-related government-sponsored enterprises (GSEs)—Fannie Mae, Freddie Mac, and the Federal Home Loan Banks—and up to $500 billion in mortgage-backed securities (MBSs) backed by Fannie Mae, Freddie Mac, and Ginnie Mae over the next several quarters.

Representative Ackerman was a senior member of the House Committee on Financial Services, which was chaired by Barney Frank (D, MA). On March 12, 2009, a subcommittee headed by Representative Paul Kanjorski (D, PA) held hearings on MTM. He warned Robert Herz, the chairman of the Financial Accounting Standards Board (FASB), that if his organization didn't suspend MTM, Congress would. At the hearing, Congressman Ackerman reminded the man from the FASB that Congress was considering a bill to broaden oversight of his organization. He told him to fix MTM in three weeks. On April 2, the FASB did just that.[23]

Since I firmly believed that MTM had been a major contributor to the bear market in stocks, I turned bullish four days later. On March 16, 2009, I wrote: "We've been to Hades and back. The S&P 500 bottomed last week on March 6 at an intraday low of 666. This is a number commonly associated with the Devil. . . . The latest relief rally was sparked by lots of good news for a refreshing change, which I believe may have some staying power. . . . I'm rooting for more good news, and hoping that 666 was THE low." That very same day, the bullish news included the Fed's announcement that its QE1 bond-buying program would be expanded to $1.25 trillion in mortgage-related securities and $300 billion in Treasury bonds.

When our two kids came out of the House of Representatives with our congressman, I thanked him for the special treat for them and for pushing the FASB to suspend MTM. He told me, "You deserve the credit. I got the idea from you." I returned the compliment by calling the rebound in stock prices the "Ackerman Rally" in one of my summer interviews on CNBC, in which I explained his role in the suspension of MTM and why it was bullish.

On July 27, 2009, I wrote: "I prefer meltups to meltdowns. The S&P 500 has been on a tear ever since it bottomed at the intraday low of 666 on Friday, March 6. We should have known immediately that this devilish number was the bear market low. It took me a few days to conclude that it probably was the low. . . . I felt like Tom Hanks in the *The Da Vinci Code*." Subsequently, when I told this story to our accounts, I said that I called the bottom in stocks more as a symbolist than as an investment strategist.

I remained bullish on stocks as well as bonds for several years after the financial crisis of 2008. I broadened the widely known adage "Don't fight the Fed" to the more general "Don't fight the central banks." The men and women running monetary policy in the major central banks of the world were determined to avert another financial crisis. They were also committed to reviving self-sustaining economic growth and to avoiding deflation by bringing inflation back to 2.0%. I observed that they had an unlimited supply of dollars, euros, pounds, yen, and yuan and would spend them in their efforts to accomplish their goals. For numerous reasons, much of the liquidity they provided boosted asset prices rather than economic growth and inflation, as I discuss in several of the following chapters.

ENTREPRENEURIAL CAPITALIST

I AM INVITED to speak at investment conferences quite often. I accept some of the invitations, especially if they are in cities where I can also visit with our accounts. When I am introduced, the conference sponsor usually reads my bio to the crowd. When I go to the podium, I often say that I'm embarrassed by the long list of former employers—the Federal Reserve Bank of New York, Columbia Business School (part-time), EF Hutton, Prudential-Bache Securities, CJ Lawrence, Deutsche Bank, and Oak Associates: "I obviously can't keep a job."

I enjoyed all of my past jobs and learned a great deal at each. However, I was an employee, not an executive, partner, or owner. At a couple of the firms, some of my compensation included stock options that vested over three years, so I also was a shareholder. Some advocates of capitalism favor giving workers shares so that they are incentivized to work hard, keep a lid on costs, increase productivity, and boost profits. That's an interesting concept but has some serious shortcomings. The efforts of the vast majority of employees for the good of the firm won't have much, if any, influence on its profitability. Top management still calls the shots. If they don't do their jobs well, the firm will suffer no matter how many sacrifices workers make for its good. One badly managed division losing lots of money is all it takes to nullify all the hard work and successes of the other divisions. I think this is especially true on Wall Street, more so than on Main Street.

Opening up my own firm at the start of 2007 was an exhilarating and challenging experience. For the first time in my career, I would have to meet a payroll. Doing so was a huge responsibility to my employees and their families. If the business didn't work out, not only would I be out of a job but so would all my employees. (If I ever run for political office, no one can say that I never had to meet a payroll!)

I must say that I've never worked harder or enjoyed working more than after I went out on my own. On Wall Street, I regularly visited my firm's clients, but the travel schedule was determined by the sales department. So I was competing with the other analysts for facetime with our accounts and for coverage by our sales force. Management kept the scorecard of how we all were doing with the firm's accounts. Now, I set my own marketing schedule and get to know the accounts better professionally and personally. I'm often "on the road" one to two days a week, visiting with them. I typically meet with four to six accounts per day in back-to-back one-hour sessions with their portfolio managers and analysts. I always learn something from these gatherings and get new research ideas to work on when I get back to my home office.

Running my own company has been a great learning experience about "entrepreneurial capitalism." I am using the adjective "entrepreneurial" to describe the brand of capitalism that I heartily endorse, as distinguished from "crony capitalism," which is just one of many variations of corruption. I've long contended that there are only two economic systems: capitalism and corruption.

Sadly, capitalism has gotten a bad rap ever since 1776. Perversely, that's when Adam Smith, the great proponent of capitalism, published *The Wealth of Nations*. He made a huge mistake when he argued that capitalism is driven by "self-interest." Marketing capitalism as a system based on selfishness wasn't smart. Then again, Smith was a professor, with no actual experience as an entrepreneur.

Smith famously wrote: "It is not from the benevolence of the butcher, the brewer, or the baker that we expect our dinner, but from their regard to their own self-interest. We address ourselves not to their humanity but to their self-love, and never talk to them of our own necessities, but of their advantages." This statement is totally wrong, with all due respect to the great professor. The butcher, the brewer, and the baker get up early in the morning and work all day long, trying to give their customers the best meat, ale, and bread at the lowest possible prices. If they don't, their competitors will, and put them out of business. Entrepreneurial capitalism is therefore the most moral, honest, altruistic economic system of them all. Among its mottos are: "The customer is always right," "Everyday low prices," and "Satisfaction guaranteed or your money back."

The problems start when the butchers, brewers, and bakers form trade associations to stifle competition. The associations support politicians and hire lobbyists who promise to regulate their industry—for example, by requiring government inspection and licensing. In this way, they raise anticompetitive barriers to entry into their businesses. In other words, capitalism starts to morph into corruption when "special interest groups" try to rig the market with political influence. These groups are totally selfish in promoting the interests of their members rather than their members' customers. At least Smith got that concept right when he wrote, "People of the same trade seldom meet together, even for merriment and diversion, but the conversation ends in a conspiracy against the public, or in some contrivance to raise prices."

My experience as the owner of a small business is that entrepreneurs are driven by insecurity, not selfishness. Our number-one worry is that we won't satisfy our customers, so they will go elsewhere, putting us out of business. That's why we strive so hard to grow our businesses. Growth confirms that we are doing right by our customers in the competitive market. This requires that we put our customers first, not ourselves. A key goal of our business model is to go viral: "If you like our products and services, tell your friends." There always are opportunities to gain customers by outperforming our competitors. Milton Friedman observed that when customers are free to choose among competing producers, consumers always win. The producers only win if they satisfy their customers, and that will be reflected in their profits.

It follows that the most profitable companies aren't the ones run by the greediest SOBs. Rather, they are the ones that cater best to the needs of consumers. Of course, profits can always be boosted by shortchanging workers and cutting corners on quality. However, in competitive markets, your best workers can always find jobs with competitors who are profitable because they are winning the hearts, minds, and wallets of consumers. Companies with the happiest customers are also likely to have the happiest employees.

Admittedly, this is an idealized version of capitalism. It does exist, especially in the United States in many industries. However, it also coexists with crony capitalism. Actually, it can degenerate into crony capitalism and other variants of corruption. Successful entrepreneurial capitalists have a tendency to turn into crony capitalists when they pay off politicians to impose legal and regulatory barriers to entry for new competitors. It doesn't seem to matter to them that they succeeded because there were no barriers or they found a way around the barriers. Rather than cherish and protect the system that allowed them to succeed, they cherish and protect the businesses they have built.

I have no lobbyists or political cronies in Washington, DC to protect my interests. So the forces of the competitive market compel me to work as hard as possible to satisfy my customers more than my competitors do. Happily, when I visit our accounts, they tell me that we are one of the select economic and investment research firms on which they rely. However, they tend to have relatively fixed budgets, so they always have the option of dropping our research and signing up with one of our competitors. If their budgets get cut, all we can do is hope that they decide to keep us and drop someone else.

The bottom line is that in a competitive market, the pressure is on to be better than your best competitor. Throughout my career, my best competitor has been Ed Hyman, the economist I succeeded at CJ Lawrence in 1991 after he left to start his own research firm, International Strategy & Investment Group (ISI). For more than 30 years, he won *Institutional Investor* magazine's poll for the best economist on Wall Street. He did it by providing easy-to-digest analyses of the economic data. Most importantly, he knew his customers very well through regular meetings with them, getting to know them not only professionally but also personally. He sold his company to Evercore Partners in 2014 for over $400 million.

Hyman has been a good professional friend, and I've learned a great deal by keeping track of his success. So have a few of his colleagues, such as Nancy Lazar and Jason Trennert, who went on to start their own firms offering macroeconomic and investment research. My market is full of top-notch competitors. That's great for our customers, who can choose whichever of us provides them with the best money-making insights at the right price. My firm has been in business for a decade now, so we've done well. I must thank our competitors for keeping us at the top of our game, and our accounts for choosing our research service.

MOVIE REVIEWER

EARLY IN MY career, I began reviewing movies during the Monday morning meetings with our sales force, after my discussion of the economic and investment outlook. At Cornell, I regularly attended showings of many of the great classic films and even produced a short film that was inspired by the great Swedish director Ingmar Bergman.

I started to add written movie reviews to the end of my Monday morning commentaries in 2004. All are posted on my website.[24] They are always just a few sentences long and provide a rating from plus three to minus three. Valerie and I love going to the movies and do so almost every Friday evening. In my reviews, I try to tie themes in the film to current events when possible.

At the end of the year, along with a Season's Greetings email to all of our accounts, I include a compilation of my movie reviews for the year. Often at the end of my meetings with clients, someone will ask me to recommend a movie I've recently seen. I direct them to the back page of my chart presentation book, where I list my latest ratings and reviews. I often quip, "If this job doesn't work out, I can always be a movie reviewer."

Sometimes I feel like Tom Hanks in another of his movies, *Forrest Gump* (1994), one of my favorites. Like Forrest, I've lived through some very interesting times so far and made cameo appearances in a few of the events along the way. Forrest learned from his many experiences, "Life is like a box of chocolates. You never know what you are going to get." When I worked at Oak Associates, I picked up the idea from Jim Oelschlager to bring along a clear plastic jar of chocolate gold coins when visiting our accounts. I continued to do so after I left Oak. What you see is what you get in my jar of chocolates.

Markets are like Forrest's box of chocolates. You need to think outside the box when it comes to predicting them. That's why I chose as my company logo a square defined by eight dots on the border and one in the middle. The puzzle is how to connect the nine dots with four straight lines, which you can't do without venturing outside the box defined by the dots. That's a relatively easy puzzle compared to the ones that need to be solved to predict the markets.

Looking back over my career to date, I've been a macroeconomist, prognosticator, Baby Boomer, microeconomist, strategist, portfolio manager, symbolist, entrepreneurial capitalist, and movie reviewer. I continue to combine all these perspectives to predict the markets by connecting the dots.

CHAPTER 2

Predicting the World

INTERESTING TIMES

IT WAS CLEAR at the outset of my Wall Street career that the US economy and financial markets were increasingly affected by global events. During the 1970s, two OPEC oil supply shocks triggered an inflationary price spiral. They also caused a couple of nasty recessions. The US budget deficit swelled as the government pursued a policy of both "guns and butter." Defense spending rose as the nation competed in the nuclear arms race with the Soviet Union and waged a war in Vietnam. At the same time, spending on social welfare programs increased in response to widespread riots in the inner cities. The US trade deficit ballooned when Japan emerged as a significant threat to many American industries, especially the auto industry. There were growing concerns about "de-industrialization."

I quickly learned that predicting the US economy and financial markets required a global perspective. This makes the job much more complicated and much more interesting. While there is no evidence of a Chinese curse that translates to "May you live in interesting times," for prognosticators as well as for investors, interesting times present lots of challenges but also lots of opportunities. That certainly has been true for the past four decades.

One of my favorite songs is "We Didn't Start the Fire" (1989), by Billy Joel, who is one year older than I am. The lyrics are simply a long list of major personalities and issues that have pleased, pained, and plagued my generation—the Baby Boomers—since our parents started to have children during the late 1940s. The lyrics include brief, rapid-fire allusions to more than 100 domestic and global headline events during the Cold War, from 1949 through 1989. As I've mentioned, I was born in 1950.

Before the Baby Boom, there was *The Greatest Generation*, which is the title of Tom Brokaw's 1998 book profiling members of this generation. It was inspired by his attendance at the 40th anniversary celebrations of D-Day in Normandy in June 1984. He wrote, "[I]t is, I believe, the greatest generation any society has ever produced." This generation grew up in the United States during the Great Depression and then went on to fight in World War II. He argued that these men and women did not fight to gain fame and fortune but because it was the "right thing to do." After the war, they helped to rebuild West Germany and Japan and to bring democracy to these former US enemies. Both countries became America's allies in the Cold War with the Soviet Union.

In the late 1950s, my elementary school in Cleveland, Ohio regularly held drills to practice what we should do in the event of a nuclear attack by the Soviets: duck under our desks. I also recall a science project involving the construction of a homemade "electroscope" to detect nuclear radiation. We suspended two pieces of aluminum foil loosely on a hook made from a coat hanger, lodged with a cork in a glass bottle. Static electricity from a comb was applied to the wire protruding from the jar to repel the foils from one another. Radiation from a nuclear bomb would be detected if the foils fell back together.

These ominous preparations for a nuclear missile attack were reactions to Soviet Premier Nikita Khrushchev's threat to "bury" the United States. Addressing Western ambassadors at a reception in Moscow in 1956, he said, "Whether you like it or not, we are on the right side of history. We will bury you." The second sentence was widely quoted by the Western press to suggest that the Soviets might be willing to use nuclear weapons. That fear was heightened greatly by the Cuban Missile Crisis of 1962.

During April 1961, President John Kennedy badly bungled the Bay of Pigs invasion on the south coast of Cuba, aimed at overthrowing Fidel Castro's communist regime. Khrushchev concluded that Kennedy was weak, and upped the Cold War ante dramatically by recklessly attempting to place nuclear missiles in Cuba during the fall of 1962. Kennedy successfully stood up to the provocation, forcing the Soviets to back down.

The following year, in Dallas at 12:30 p.m. on November 22, 1963, Kennedy was assassinated by Lee Harvey Oswald. At 2:38 p.m. that same day, Vice President Lyndon Johnson was sworn in as President on board Air Force One.

At the start of the 1960s, my family moved from Ohio to California, when my father joined IBM as a software programmer in San Jose. We lived nearby in Campbell, where I attended middle school. Life was good in my neighborhood of small, cookie-cutter homes with tiny backyards surrounded by 10-foot-high wooden fences. Thanks to the postwar baby boom, there were many kids with whom to ride bikes and play football. We walked to school and were free to come and go as we pleased. All we had to do was show up for dinner.

I recall that we were sent home from school at the start of the Cuban Missile Crisis. I guess the school administration figured that we should all fry at home with our families. I didn't even have my trusty electroscope. When President Kennedy was shot, everyone was in complete shock for days. We all were glued to our TV sets as another shock hit two days later, on November 24 at 12:20 p.m., when Jack Ruby gunned down Oswald in the basement of the Dallas police station.

During 1964, my father was transferred to White Plains, New York by IBM, which according to company lore stood for "I've Been Moved." We moved to New Rochelle, New York, where I finished middle school and then attended New Rochelle High School from 1965 to 1968. I am convinced that I introduced the skateboard to the East Coast. No one in my neighborhood had ever seen one when I brought mine from California. On May 17, 1968, about a month before my high school graduation, the school building was burned to the ground by a 16-year-old arsonist with a history of setting fires to attract attention. We then attended classes at the local junior high school, under a time-sharing arrangement.

The Cold War was ice cold in most of the world but hot as hell in Vietnam. Americans fought a bloody war there, presumably to stop the spread of communism in Asia. I aspired to a career working at the United Nations to make the world a more peaceful place. I attended a Model UN conference during my junior year in high school and presented a speech titled "Beyond the Wall." I said that the best way to appreciate how fortunate we were to have freedom was to look over to the east side of the Berlin Wall and all the other walls and curtains put up by communist regimes.

I got over my UN career ambitions when I attended a world youth conference sponsored by the organization, at the General Assembly building in New York City, during the summer following my freshman year in college. I received an early lesson in the organization's corruption when the Soviets sent seasoned diplomats in their 30s and 40s to railroad the conference into an anti-American frenzy.

In high school, I dated a girl whose father was a renowned labor lawyer. He and his family were very active in the Democratic Party and big supporters of Senator Eugene McCarthy (D, MN) during his presidential campaign in 1968. McCarthy pledged to end the Vietnam War. Senator Robert Kennedy (D, NY) entered the race on March 16, 1968. On March 31, President Johnson spoke to the nation about "Steps to Limit the War in Vietnam." He announced an immediate unilateral halt to the bombing of North Vietnam and said he would seek peace talks anywhere at any time. At the close of his speech, he also announced, "I shall not seek, and I will not accept, the nomination of my party for another term as your President." Vice President Hubert Humphrey entered the contest but avoided the primaries. Senator Kennedy was assassinated on June 5. McCarthy lost to Humphrey at the Democratic National Convention in Chicago amid protests and riots.

My girlfriend's father subscribed to *I.F. Stone's Weekly*. Stone was a left-wing journalist who strongly opposed the war in Vietnam. He scoured and devoured public documents, including *The Congressional Record*, for evidence to counter many of the government's claims about what was happening in Vietnam. During the 1930s, Stone had denounced Joseph Stalin but nonetheless was suspected of being a Soviet spy.

In any event, I learned from reading Stone that enormous value can be derived by combining lots of puzzle pieces of information from numerous and varied public sources to put together the big picture. I've been doing that to assess the economy since the beginning of my career. It's an approach that has served me well, at times yielding key insights.

Martin Luther King Jr. was assassinated on April 4, 1968. Riots swept the country in the greatest wave of social unrest that the United States had experienced since the Civil War. Campaigning on a law-and-order platform, Richard Nixon, the Republican nominee for President, defeated Humphrey on November 5, 1968.

From 1968 to 1972, I majored in government and economics at Cornell University in Ithaca, New York. During my freshman year, on

April 19, 1969, a burning cross was placed outside Wari House, a cooperative for African-American women students. Outraged members of the
Afro-American Society (AAS) occupied Willard Straight Hall, the student union building, to protest Cornell's perceived racism, its judicial system, and its slow progress in establishing an African-American studies
program. The protesters expelled parents who were visiting for Parents'
Weekend from their guest rooms on the upper floors of the student union.

After white fraternity brothers attempted unsuccessfully to retake the
building by force, some of the occupying students left the building and
returned with rifles for protection. The group Students for a Democratic
Society, led by C. David Burak, formed a protective cordon outside the
building for the AAS members.

Within hours, police deputies from Rochester, Syracuse, and across
New York State amassed in downtown Ithaca. Fortunately, the university's administration resolved the dispute without any violence. However,
several well-regarded professors in the government department resigned,
protesting that the university had caved in to the unruly students.

Among the leaders of the takeover was Tom Jones, who had come to
Cornell a few years earlier, in 1965, as a freshman. He had been elected
president of his freshman class. Yet senior year found him immortalized
in a photo—holding a rifle and wearing a bandoleer as he was coming out
of the student union—that made the cover of *Newsweek* and won a Pulit-
zer Prize. In a radio interview, Jones infamously threatened several faculty
members and declared that Cornell "has three hours to live."[1]

Several years later, when I visited our accounts in Boston, Tom came
up to introduce himself to me after a meeting with the investment department of John Hancock Mutual Life Insurance Company. Somehow, he
had learned that we had crossed paths at Cornell. He was a senior vice
president and treasurer at the insurance company. He now runs his own
private equity investment firm in Stamford, Connecticut following several
other prestigious jobs, including chairman and chief executive officer of
Global Investment Management at Citigroup from 1999 to 2004.[2] Like
economies, people's lives evolve in ways you can't easily predict.

Another historically significant episode for me occurred during the
fall of my freshman year at Cornell. I attended an informal weekly discussion group at a coffee house on campus, led by Father Daniel Berrigan, the Jesuit assistant director of Cornell United Religious Work
from 1966 to 1970. I don't recall the exact discussions, but they must have

been related to Vietnam. On May 17 of the same year, Father Berrigan, along with eight others, entered the Catonsville, Maryland Selective Service office and burned dozens of draft records with napalm to protest the Vietnam War. They became known as the "Catonsville Nine."

Father Berrigan and his codefendants were tried in federal court during early October and found guilty. Several of the nine went "underground." Father Berrigan was convicted and sentenced to three years in prison, to begin on April 9, 1970. That same day, he disappeared, which resulted in his appearance on the FBI's 10 Most Wanted List. FBI Director J. Edgar Hoover reportedly was embarrassed and furious, as Father Berrigan regularly popped up to give sermons and then went back into hiding. Cornell marked Berrigan's looming imprisonment by conducting a weekend-long "America Is Hard to Find" event on April 17–19, 1970, which included a public appearance by the fugitive Berrigan before a crowd of 15,000, including me, in Barton Hall. On August 11, 1970, the FBI found and arrested Berrigan. He was released from prison in 1972.

I also distinctly recall, on the evening of December 1, 1969, watching *CBS News*, which preempted the regularly scheduled broadcast of *Mayberry RFD* to pick up a live feed from Washington correspondent Roger Mudd at the Selective Service headquarters. "Good evening. . . . Tonight for the first time in 27 years the United States has again started a draft lottery," said Mudd. There were 366 blue plastic lottery "capsules" in a large glass container behind him. The capsules contained birth dates, were picked one at a time, and were read aloud. Each was assigned a lottery number, starting with No. 001. Mine was 169, which meant I was not drafted.

Richard Nixon served as the 37th President of the United States from 1969 to 1974. Nixon ended the war in Vietnam—and the military draft—in 1973. His 1972 visit to the People's Republic of China was historic and set the stage for diplomatic relations to be established in 1979. To avoid impeachment proceedings because of the Watergate scandal, Nixon resigned the office of the presidency on August 9, 1974.

STUDYING NUCLEAR DETERRENCE

I INITIALLY ENROLLED in the engineering program at Cornell. Our first assignment was to design a police baton that could also be used to spray mace on rioters. The project was scrapped after it triggered lots of criticism. It was a tough course in differential equations that convinced me to transfer to the College of Arts and Sciences during the second half of my freshman year, aiming to major in government and economics.

One of my first elective courses in Cornell's government department was titled "Nuclear Deterrence." We read Thomas Schelling's classic works on military strategy in the nuclear age. The goal was no longer victory, according to Schelling, but deterrence through coercion and intimidation. Stanley Kubrick's 1964 movie *Dr. Strangelove or: How I Learned to Stop Worrying and Love the Bomb* was inspired by an article Schelling wrote. We studied the Cuban Missile Crisis in the course. I was most impressed by how President John Kennedy responded to Soviet Premier Nikita Khrushchev's demand that the United States pull our missiles out of Turkey before he pulled Russia's missiles out of Cuba. Kennedy ignored this demand and proceeded with a naval blockade of the island. Khrushchev pulled the missiles out. We were lucky that Khrushchev blinked.

I particularly enjoyed the small study group courses with three professors in the government department. One of them was Soviet expert Myron Rush. He assigned me to carefully read *Khrushchev Remembers*, published in 1970, a year before Khrushchev passed away on September 11, 1971. There was some controversy about the authenticity of his biography. Indeed, Khrushchev signed a statement that he had not given the materials to any publisher. Upon publication of the memoirs in the West, *Izvestia* denounced them as a fraud. My assignment was to assess whether they were legit. I concluded that they were.

In another tutorial, I recall studying political developments in East Africa. Julius Nyerere was the leader of Tanzania (previously Tanganyika) from 1960 until his retirement in 1985. In 1967, Nyerere issued the Arusha Declaration, which outlined his vision of *ujamaa*—basically socialism. His policies led to economic ruin, widespread corruption, and goods shortages. In the early 1970s, Nyerere had his security forces move much of the population to collective farms. Villages that opposed this move were torched. Starvation was rampant, and the nation became dependent on foreign food aid. I remain amazed by the amnesia afflicting fans of socialism even as its ill effects continue to plague countries such as Venezuela today.

My most interesting tutorial was with Professor Richard Rosecrance, who taught a popular course in international relations. Along with two other students, I studied the origins and consequences of World War I. The war ended a relatively long period of global peace and prosperity that had resulted from the Industrial Revolution and the proliferation of free trade during most of the 1800s. I concluded that the only good explanation for what started the war was nationalism gone mad. The war was followed by another period of globalization, with the United States enjoying the boom of the Roaring '20s. However, the war had precipitated the Russian Revolution and subsequently led to the rise of the Nazis in Germany, so the stage was set for World War II.

Another fascinating course was taught by visiting Professor J.C. Horowitz, an expert on the history and politics of the Middle East. I learned a great deal that came in handy on several occasions during my career on Wall Street, when turmoil in that region had economic and financial repercussions for the rest of the world. The Middle East has been a violent neighborhood since the beginning of recorded time. The invasion of enemies' territory, destruction of their societies, and enslavement or killing of their people are well documented in the Old Testament.

In the course taught by Professor Horowitz, I studied the Sykes–Picot Agreement, signed on May 16, 1916 by the United Kingdom and France, with the assent of Russia. It is widely believed to have mapped out the partition of the Ottoman Empire after it was defeated in 1918. The Arabs viewed it as a stab in the back by the British, who had promised them, through Colonel T.E. Lawrence, a national homeland in Greater Syria.

The leader of the Islamic State of Iraq and the Levant (ISIL), Abu Bakr al-Baghdadi, in a July 2014 speech at the Great Mosque of al-Nuri in Mosul, vowed that "this blessed advance will not stop until we hit the last nail in the coffin of the Sykes–Picot conspiracy." In fact, virtually none of the Middle East's present-day frontiers was actually delineated in the pact. Nevertheless, it is widely viewed in the region as the beginning of colonial exploitation, with outside imperial powers imposing their will by drawing borders and installing local leaderships. The imperialist powers thus played divide-and-rule with the "natives" and beggar-my-neighbor with their colonial rivals.[3]

During my last year at Cornell, I wrote an honors dissertation titled "Grandeur Economics: The Foreign Economic Policy of Charles de Gaulle." I concluded that the French President's foreign economic policies during the 1960s had been driven by a fierce political hostility to the Anglo-Saxon hegemony in Europe rather than sound economic judgment. He was a mischief-maker, doing his best to undermine confidence in the US dollar and the British pound.

At his 11ᵗʰ press conference, on February 4, 1965, de Gaulle famously said that the gold-exchange system based on the dollar "no longer seems to conform to reality." Instead of a system based on the dollar as a reserve currency that was convertible into gold, he called for a return to the gold standard. President de Gaulle resigned in 1969 and died in 1970. On August 15, 1971, President Richard Nixon announced that the United States would no longer convert dollars into gold.

I continued my studies in international relations in a two-year master's program at Yale University in New Haven, Connecticut during 1973 and 1974. Again, there was a heavy emphasis on the Cold War. I recall particularly enjoying a course on the economic history of Russia. In any event, I focused most of my courses on economics, allowing me to enroll in Yale's PhD program in the subject and graduate with that degree in 1976.

Needless to say, I didn't get much use out of my studies on nuclear deterrence. I never had an opportunity to deter a nuclear war. Nevertheless, my courses in history and international relations provided a framework for putting current events into a greater context, a useful skill for a career on Wall Street.

In particular, my studies allowed me immediately to see the extraordinary significance of the end of the Cold War in 1989. Of course, everyone knew that this was a major historic event. However, my analysis of its influence on the global economy and financial markets turned out to be timely and spot on. This is how Jonathan Laing summed it up in a 1997 *Barron's* article about my forecasts:

> The end of the Cold War is yet another theme that Yardeni has intently focused on. In the aftermath of the 1989 fall of the Berlin Wall and the subsequent breakup of the Soviet Union, many on Wall Street worried that the liberation of hundreds of millions of new consumers would unleash torrid additional demand for commodities and capital and ignite inflation in prices and cost of credit. The "capital shortage problem" alone was deemed the 'Nineties version of the oil crisis of the 'Seventies.
>
> Yardeni was quick to brand such broodings as misguided Malthusianism. As a student of Adam Smith (a well-thumbed copy of *Wealth of Nations* sits behind his desk), Yardeni maintains that the epochal political events of the early 'Nineties are both disinflationary and profoundly bullish.

According to the economist, the Cold War created a huge barrier to trade, hindering the untrammeled interplay of free-market forces around the globe. As a consequence, productivity and social welfare suffered from less-than-optimal allocation of capital and labor. Vast resources had to be wasted on military spending, for example.

The triumph of capitalism and free trade in recent years has created the first truly global market in human history, Yardeni adds. And with the creation of this vastly expanded marketplace come the benefits that Smith wrote of more than 200 years ago. Fierce competition among producers and accessibility to cheaper labor lower the prices of goods and services. Larger markets also promote increased productivity and efficiency by allowing for enhanced specialization and division of labor over a wider spectrum of products. This pursuit of comparative advantage redounds to the benefit of all nations and consumers.[4]

Following the end of the Cold War, much of my research focused on the bullish consequences of globalization, i.e., the integration of national economies through free trade. That can only occur during periods that are relatively peaceful on a global basis. The proliferation of free trade following the end of the Cold War clearly has increased global prosperity by fostering economic progress as global competition stimulated innovations. Consumers around the world have benefited the most because they have been provided with more and better products at lower prices. Their standards of living have improved. They've prospered.

Of course, the world has been a dangerous place since it's been turning, as Billy Joel observed in his song. Today, we Baby Boomers no longer can claim to be innocent bystanders, as his lyrics suggest. During the 1990s, a major generational power shift occurred when Bill Clinton, who is three years older than I am, became the first Baby Boomer US President, ending the five-decade rule of the World War II generation.

Some contemporary observers claim that the world is more dangerous than ever before. Instead of an exchange of nuclear missiles with the Russians, we need to worry about a dirty nuclear bomb set off by terrorists in Midtown Manhattan or the center of some other major city. Jim Oelschlager, my former colleague at Oak Associates, invites everyone to move to Akron, Ohio because it should be the last place terrorists strike, unless they do so alphabetically.

One of the serious threats to globalization is the apparent resumption of the Cold War with Russia. The administration under President Barack Obama was hoping to "reset" Washington's relations with Moscow. However, Russian President Vladimir Putin reclaimed Crimea from Ukraine by force and annexed the peninsula on March 18, 2014. The NATO nations responded by imposing various sanctions on Russia, including some restrictions on trade.

US relations with China also have turned testier over China's territorial claims in the South China Sea. North Korea's nuclear missile program poses an increasing threat to the United States and its allies in Asia. The United States wants China to stop the North Korean program and has threatened the Chinese with tariffs unless they do so. On September 4, 2017, US Ambassador to the United Nations Nikki Haley told an emergency session of the 15-member UN Security Council in New York that North Korean leader Kim Jong Un is "begging for war."

History shows that periods of globalization, even very long ones, don't last forever.

ECONOMIC CONSEQUENCES OF THE PEACE

DONALD TRUMP'S ELECTION as the 45th President of the United States on November 8, 2016 posed potential new challenges to globalization, given his campaign promises suggesting a more anti-trade stance for the incoming administration. While it is too soon to tell, Trump seems to be advocating free-trade agreements on a more bilateral basis than the multilateral approach that emerged after World War II. If so, that alternative approach might actually blunt the forces of protectionism.

There was a similar outbreak of protectionist sentiments when Ronald Reagan was President. His administration's first major protectionist move was pressuring Japan into accepting so-called "voluntary restraints" on their exports of autos to the United States. US Trade Representative Clayton Yeutter boasted that the administration's trade policy was "extremely aggressive." He added, "Some of our trading partners have complained loudly about what they see as high-handed American practices, but that won't dissuade us from protecting our interests."

During April 1987, President Reagan placated the chorus of protectionists with a 100% tariff placed on selected Japanese electronics products.

"The health and vitality of the US semiconductor industry are essential to America's future competitiveness," he said. "We cannot allow it to be jeopardized by unfair trading practices." He declared that he imposed the tariff "to enforce the principles of free and fair trade." White House spokesman Marlin Fitzwater followed up by saying, "[W]e want to be fair traders as well as free traders."[5]

At the time, I observed that US legislators had introduced more than 300 protectionist bills. The most sweeping proposal came from the Democrats—the Trade Emergency and Export Promotion Act of 1985. It was introduced in the Senate during July by Democrat Lloyd Bentsen of Texas and in the House by Democrats Dan Rostenkowski of Illinois and Richard Gephardt of Missouri. The bill—which would have imposed a 25% tax on all imports from Japan, South Korea, Taiwan, and Brazil—was given a good chance of passage in the House when Congress reconvened in September.

This outbreak of protectionist sentiments reminded me of a similar outbreak during the late 1920s and early 1930s; I compared the two in my September 1985 *Topical Study*, "The Protectionist Road to Depression."[6]

I observed that in 1919, John Maynard Keynes published a short book titled *The Economic Consequences of the Peace*.[7] It was a blistering attack on the Treaty of Versailles, which he argued was imposing a Carthaginian peace on the Germans and would usher in economic suffering and political turmoil in Europe. As events unfolded, it proved to be a remarkably accurate forecast, as the treaty, which ended World War I, in many ways set the stage for World War II. It was also a worldwide sensation. In fact, historian Paul Johnson suggested that the book turned US public opinion against the treaty and the League of Nations. The Senate voted against the treaty, and the overwhelming defeat of the Democrats in the autumn of 1920 was widely seen as a repudiation of President Woodrow Wilson's European policy in its entirety.

Nevertheless, the 1920s was a period of globalization, with peace, progress, and prosperity. Yet by the early 1930s, the world fell into a depression that was followed by World War II near the end of the decade.

My research led me to conclude that the Great Depression was caused by the Smoot–Hawley Tariff Act of June 1930. During the election of 1928, Republican candidate Herbert Hoover promised US farmers protection from foreign competition to boost depressed farm prices. However, he was appalled by the breadth of the tariff bill that special interest groups had pushed through Congress, denouncing the bill as "vicious, extortionate, and obnoxious." But he signed it into law under intense political pressure from congressional Republicans.

The tariff triggered a deflationary spiral that had a deadly domino effect. Other countries immediately retaliated by imposing tariffs too. The collapse of world trade pushed commodity prices over a cliff. Exporters and farmers defaulted on their loans, triggering a wave of banking crises. The resulting credit crunch caused industrial production and farm output to plunge and unemployment to soar. In my narrative, the depression caused the stock market crash, not the other way around as is the popular belief. Consider the following grim post-tariff statistics:

- *Trade.* Data compiled by the League of Nations show that imports of 75 countries dropped 55% from June 1930 through March 1933 (Fig. 1*). In the United States, industrial production dropped 41% from June 1930 through March 1933 (Fig. 2). Historian John Steele Gordon observed that US exports in 1929 were $5.24 billion, whereas by 1933, exports were only $1.68 billion; when inflation is taken into account, the latter amount was less than US exports in 1896. As countries successively raised tariffs, world trade fell by two-thirds from 1929 to 1934. Gordon concludes, "Thus, Smoot–Hawley was one of the prime reasons that a stock market crash and an ordinary recession turned into the calamity of the Great Depression."[8]
- *Prices.* The producer price index (PPI) for industrial commodity prices plummeted 24% from June 1930 until it bottomed during April 1933 (Fig. 3). The PPI for grain prices plunged 59% until it bottomed during December 1932. The consumer price index (CPI) fell 25% from June 1930 until it bottomed during the spring of 1933 (Fig. 4).
- *Loans and deposits.* Commercial bank deposits fell 36% from $43 billion during 1929 to $27 billion during 1933 (Fig. 5). Deposits frozen at suspended commercial banks rose sharply during the three banking panics from 1930 to 1933 (Fig. 6).
- *Unemployment.* The unemployment rate for nonfarm employees soared from 5.3% during 1929 to peak at a record high of 37.6% during 1933 (Fig. 7). Over this same period, it jumped from 3.2% to 25.2% for the civilian labor force, including farm workers.

The Dow Jones Industrial Average (DJIA) plunged 47.9% from its record high of 381 on September 3, 1929 to the year's low of 199 on November 13 (Fig. 8). From there, it rebounded 48.0% to 294 on April

---

* Figures, references, and appendices are linked on *yardenibook.com/resources*.

17, 1930. It was down only 5.1% on a year-over-year basis, suggesting that the Great Crash wasn't so great! But the worst was ahead, as the stock market started to anticipate the passage of the tariff bill, despite a letter printed in the May 5, 1930 issue of *The New York Times* signed by 1,028 economists who opposed the bill. The DJIA proceed to fall by 86.0% from the April 17, 1930 high to the low of 41 on July 8, 1932. That was the Great Crash indeed! (See Appendix 2.1, The Protests of Economists Against the Smoot-Hawley Tariff.)

That's my explanation of what caused the Great Depression, in 512 words. Google search the "Great Depression" and you'll find more than 20 million links. Narrow the search to "causes of the Great Depression" and you'll find more than three million links. In my home office, I have three shelves of books that offer lots of explanations for this economic disaster. Few of them give a starring role to the tariff. Excessive speculation in stocks that set the stage for the Great Crash often gets blamed for starting the mess.

Amity Shlaes wrote a 2007 revisionist history titled *The Forgotten Man*, blaming government policies for worsening and prolonging the recession. It could have been titled *Nothing to Fear but the New Deal Itself*. Also worsening the downturn was the Dust Bowl, which was three waves of severe drought that plagued farmers in the Midwest during 1934, 1936, and 1939 through 1940.

In academic circles, the Fed has been widely viewed as the main perpetrator of the Great Depression. Milton Friedman and Anna Schwartz blamed the Fed in their 1963 book *A Monetary History of the United States*. Before going to Washington, former Federal Reserve Chairman Ben Bernanke spent much of his academic career proving that the Fed was at fault. In a November 8, 2002 speech at a conference to honor Friedman's 90th birthday, Bernanke, who was a Fed governor at the time, famously concluded: "Regarding the Great Depression. You're right, we did it. We're very sorry. But thanks to you, we won't do it again." I humbly disagree: The Smoot–Hawley Tariff started it.

Nevertheless, the debate continues. In a 2011 book titled *Peddling Protectionism*, Dartmouth College professor Douglas Irwin, who is an expert on the economics and history of trade, reviews the economic studies and historical facts and seriously challenges my thesis. While he acknowledges that 1,028 economists signed a letter warning that the tariff would be a disaster back then, he can't find any today who believe that was the case. He notes that the empirical evidence shows neither US imports nor exports were hit particularly hard by the tariff. Yet near the end of his book, Irwin concedes that the tariff did trigger vicious protectionist retaliation by our trading partners. A few pages before concluding that the "Smoot–Hawley tariff did not cause the Great Depression," he writes: "But although Smoot–Hawley was not entirely responsible for the massive outbreak of protectionism in the early 1930s, it certainly contributed to the climate in which such policies flourished. Smoot–Hawley clearly inspired retaliatory moves against the United States, particularly—but not exclusively—by Canada. This retaliation had a significant effect in reducing US exports. Even worse, Smoot–Hawley generated ill-will around the world and led to widespread discrimination against US exports."

Following his inauguration on March 4, 1933, President Franklin Roosevelt declared a four-day bank holiday on March 6 that kept all banks shut until Congress could act to stop the national bank run. The Emergency Banking Relief Act, passed on March 9, 1933, saved the day, reviving confidence in the banking system.

The new law allowed the 12 Federal Reserve Banks to issue additional currency on good assets so banks that reopened would be able to meet every legitimate call. The Fed's commitment to supply unlimited amounts of currency to reopened banks provided de facto 100% deposit insurance. Within two weeks, Americans had redeposited more than half of the currency they had hoarded before the bank holiday. On March 15, 1933, the first day of stock trading after the extended closure of Wall Street, the DJIA gained 15.3%, the largest one-day percentage price increase ever.

Under the new law, banks were forbidden to pay out gold or to export it. In effect, Roosevelt took the United States off the gold standard. Most countries had tied their currencies to the price of gold prior to World War I. They had suspended doing so during the war but resumed afterward. The United States was late to the party, since most other major countries had suspended their currencies' linkages to gold during 1931 and 1932.

The fact that the economy bottomed on March 1933 and started to recover as soon as the gold standard was suspended is widely deemed to prove that the gold standard had been a major cause of the Great Depression. In an October 1990 study, Bernanke echoed this widespread view. The limited supply of gold caused deflation, he wrote, set off bank panics, and depressed the economy—resulting in more deflation.[9] In Bernanke's narrative, the Fed was to blame for the Depression, having stuck with the gold standard for too long. It was a dereliction of their macroeconomic duty not to have suspended it sooner, in his eyes. Thankfully, Roosevelt took charge and ended the gold standard, and the economy recovered.

In my opinion, the Fed's 100% backing of the banks is what restored confidence, rather than the suspension of the gold standard. I also believe that President Roosevelt's appointment of Cordell Hull as Secretary of State in 1933 was just as important as the banking legislation in reviving the economy and the stock market. Hull was appalled by the results of the Smoot–Hawley Tariff. Under his leadership, Congress passed the Reciprocal Trade Agreements Act (RTAA) of 1934. Hull's legislation established a system of bilateral agreements through which the United States negotiated with other interested governments for reciprocal reductions in the duties imposed on specific commodities.

In any case, the US economy recovered impressively. Annual data compiled by the Census Bureau in the *Historical Statistics of the United States* show real GDP falling 27% from 1929 through 1933, then rebounding 44% to a new record high during 1937 (Fig. 9). The National Bureau of Economic Research (NBER) has a quarterly series for real GNP, which plunged 33% from the third quarter of 1929 through the third quarter of 1932, then rose 58% through the third quarter of 1937 (Fig. 10).[10] Industrial production rose 121% from the 1933 low to its May 1937 high, which exceeded the 1929 high by 5.4%! The PPI for industrial commodity prices increased 32% from April 1933 to July 1937. Grain prices rebounded 275% from December 1932 through April 1937. The CPI rose 10.0% from 1932 through 1937.

The Great Depression was actually a combination of two recessions. The NBER's series for real GNP dropped 13% from the third quarter of 1937 through the first quarter of 1938. Industrial production plunged 32% from the May 1937 peak to the May 1938 trough. The PPI for industrial commodity prices declined 7.5% from July 1937 to bottom during August 1939. This time, however, there was no banking crisis.

While economists and historians are still debating the causes of the 1937–38 recession, the consensus view is that fiscal and monetary policies both turned too tight at the same time. Consider the following developments:

- *Tighter fiscal policy.* After he was reelected President, Roosevelt became alarmed by the budget deficit created by his New Deal spending policies and tapped on the fiscal-spending brakes. Much of the reduction in spending was simply the ending of the veterans' bonus during the second half of 1937. The Social Security payroll tax was introduced at the beginning of that year.

- *Tighter monetary policy.* During July 1936, the Fed's Board of Governors stated that bank excess reserves were too large and could "create an injurious credit expansion" and that the Board had "decided to lock up" those excess reserves "as a measure of prevention." The Fed then proceeded to double bank reserve requirements for member banks in a series of steps from 13% to 26% between August 1936 and May 1937.

- *Gold sterilization.* From December 1936 until February 1938, the Treasury started "sterilizing" gold inflows in order to reduce excess reserves as well, i.e., by buying gold to reduce the money supply. In their 1963 book, Friedman and Schwartz wrote, "The combined impact of the rise in reserve requirements and—no less important—the Treasury gold-sterilization program first sharply reduced the rate of increase in the monetary stock and then converted it into a decline."

- *Policy reversal.* During April 1938, Roosevelt officially terminated the sterilization program, so the Treasury stopped buying gold. He also announced that the Fed would roll back the last increase in the reserve requirement, reducing it from 26.00% to 22.75%. The Roosevelt administration began pursuing expansionary fiscal policies again.[11]

- *Mark-to-market.* Interestingly, on June 26, 1938, at the urging of the Federal Reserve, Roosevelt suspended mark-to-market accounting, which banks were held to as an accounting standard. Coincidently, stocks rose sharply on the news, though the rally was brief and stock prices drifted lower through early 1942. But industrial production, which bottomed during the spring of 1938, continued to move higher—exceeding the 1937 cyclical peak during October 1939. According to Milton Friedman, mark-to-market accounting was responsible for many banks failing during the Great Depression because it forced them to slash the value of their assets to reflect collapsing loan values as panic conditions depressed market prices.

- *Recovery.* The recovery from 1938 to 1942 was impressive. Output soared 110% from May 1938 through to the end of 1941. Bank deposits, which had stalled during 1937 and 1938, jumped 35% through 1941. Defense spending propelled the US economy during the first half of the 1940s after the country entered World War II on December 7, 1941 when Japanese military forces bombed Pearl Harbor.

The 1937 recession may be long over, but it became controversial again in 2009 when economist Christina Romer, who chaired President Barack Obama's Council of Economic Advisers at the time, wrote a June 18, 2009 article in *The Economist* titled "The Lessons of 1937." She warned that the 1937 episode provides a "cautionary tale" about the dangers of withdrawing economic support too soon after a recession.[12] In a September 9, 2011 study, Dartmouth professor Irwin convincingly argued that gold sterilization was a much bigger shock to the economy than the increase in the reserve requirement and fiscal tightening.[13] Shlaes and other conservative historians and economists blamed the antibusiness policies of the New Deal for deepening and prolonging the Great Depression, and predicted that Obama's policies would weigh on the economy in a similar fashion.

It is often said that one's views about the French Revolution reflect one's political leanings: liberals tend to believe that it was a liberating experience, while conservatives view it as a template for political and social chaos. Similarly, in the United States, opinions on the Great Depression are radically different among liberals and conservatives. The former believe that it was caused by market failures and insufficient demand, requiring more government involvement in the economy. Conservatives believe that the government's protectionism and other market-distorting policies caused the depression; the government then responded to the resulting crisis by increasing its power over the economy. I am in the latter camp.

MULTILATERAL WORLD ORDER

THE POSTWAR GLOBAL trading system originated with the efforts of Cordell Hull to liberalize world trade in the mid-1930s. Under Hull's system, tariff reductions were spread by the application of the most-favored-nation (MFN) principle. This meant that a tariff reduction on a commodity from one country designated as an MFN would apply to the same commodity imported from other MFN countries.

Given the Smoot–Hawley debacle caused by Congress, Hull insisted that the RTAA give the power to make these trade agreements solely to the President, without the necessity of submitting them to the Senate for approval. Under the Act, the President could decrease or increase existing rates by as much as 50% from the Smoot–Hawley rates in return for reciprocal trade concessions.

Congress renewed the RTAA again in 1943 and 1945. The Act served as the model for the negotiation of the 1947 General Agreement on Tariffs and Trade (GATT), which liberalized world trade after the war. GATT led to the creation of the World Trade Organization (WTO) in 1995, which is the 136-nation group that sets the standards for international commerce.

After World War II ended on May 8, 1945 in Europe and August 15 of that same year in Japan, many economists predicted a depression, or at least a long period of weak growth, as the wartime economy was depressed by a slower pace of business during the peace. Numerous articles were written on "secular stagnation," most after the war or in anticipation of the imminent end of the war. Massive unemployment was expected following the end of the war because 11 million soldiers were coming back home and roughly nine million defense industry workers simultaneously were let go. That meant 20 million people would be looking for work in a job market of about 60 million.

There was a recession in 1945, but it lasted only eight months. It was followed by a strong expansion that lasted 37 months. There was another recession during 1948 and 1949, which lasted only 11 months. It was followed by another robust period of growth that lasted 45 months and peaked during the third quarter of 1953. During that expansion, 20 million workers found work and the unemployment rate fell below 3.0% by the end of 1952 (Fig. 11). Total civilian employment was up by 15% over the wartime peak (Fig. 12).[14]

The stock market rightly ignored the dire predictions of a postwar depression. The S&P 500 index soared 157.7% from April 28, 1942 to May 29, 1946 (Fig. 13). Incredibly, this bull run began just five months after the attack on Pearl Harbor, on December 7, 1941. Industrial production did dip right after the war, but the revival of consumer spending fueled a long period of prosperity until the late 1950s (Fig. 14).

Following the end of the Cold War, many economists predicted that inflation and interest rates would soar along with commodity prices, as Jonathan Laing noted in the *Barron's* article cited above. The end of the Cold War would liberate hundreds of millions of people from communism. Imagine what would happen to the demand for commodities, finished goods, and credit if all those people sought to achieve the standard of living of people in the West, as surely they would.

I argued that the end of the Cold War was the end of the greatest trade barrier of all times. During that wartime period, there wasn't much trade between the West and the communist nations. The so-called "Third World" consisted of "less-developed countries" (LDCs). In effect, the global economy was liberated from protectionism. The subsequent proliferation of free trade actually boosted prosperity around the world without boosting either inflation or interest rates. Commodity prices also remained remarkably subdued. Economists started referring to LDCs more optimistically as "developing economies" or "emerging economies."

Inspired by the title of Keynes' post-World War I treatise, I wrote a *Topical Study* titled "The Economic Consequences of the Peace," dated May 7, 1997.[15] Unlike Keynes' pessimistic outlook following World War I, I was very optimistic about the consequences of the end of the Cold War. I summarized my theme as follows:

> My major premise is that the collapse of the Berlin Wall marked the end of the 50-Year Modern Day War, which includes World War II, the Cold War, and numerous regional wars from Korea to Vietnam to Central America to Southern Africa and numerous other hot spots around the world. My major thesis is that this war, which lasted half a century, was in its effect an unprecedented trade barrier. Americans were prohibited from trading with communist countries. The Iron Curtain was a major obstacle to trade between all countries on opposite sides of the curtain. The lifting of the curtain, the destruction of the Berlin Wall, and the collapse of Soviet imperial communism all simultaneously heralded the elimination of the world's greatest barrier to trade.

I noted that, coincidentally, trade among "Free World" countries had been liberalized further by the Europe 1992 movement, the Uruguay Round of trade talks under GATT completed during 1993, and the North American Free Trade Agreement (NAFTA) of 1994. The Single European Act of 1986 was the first major revision of the 1957 Treaty of Rome that had established the European Economic Community (EEC). The Act aimed to create a single market within the EEC by 1992. The Maastricht Treaty established the European Union in 1993 and introduced European citizenship.

The Uruguay Round was the eighth round of multilateral trade negotiations under the auspices of GATT, which led to the creation of the WTO in 1995. Under NAFTA, tariffs on goods traded between the US and Mexico were greatly reduced or eliminated. Trade between the US and Canada was already mostly duty-free, but the treaty reduced non-tariff trade barriers between the two countries.

Donald Trump won the presidential election on November 8, 2016. He did so to an important extent because he promised to bring jobs back to the United States by either renegotiating trade agreements or imposing tariffs if necessary. His policies could pose a threat to global trade. However, the threat level seems more like what it was during the Reagan years than the debacle of the Hoover administration. Reagan succeeded in promoting fairer trade and bringing back lots of jobs in the auto industry as foreign manufacturers moved some of their production facilities to the United States.

Trump might also succeed in forcing some of America's trading partners to eliminate unfair trade practices. His approach is bilateral rather than multilateral, which is a different approach to negotiating free trade deals than the one that has prevailed since World War II. That's alright by me as long as the result is free trade. All the better if it is also fair trade.

CHINA OPENS THE DOOR

FOLLOWING THE END of the Cold War, the next major event with such far-reaching consequences was China's joining the WTO on December 11, 2001, three months after the 9/11 terrorist attacks on the United States. Let's take a brief look at what led up to that development:

- *America's Open Door Policy toward China.* After the First Sino-Japanese War, in 1895, China faced competing pressures for preferential treatment from five imperialist powers, i.e., Britain, France, Russia, Japan, and Germany. The United States pivoted its foreign policy increasingly toward Asia after winning the Spanish-American War of 1898 and acquiring the Philippine Islands as a result. US commercial and political interests in China expanded. On September 6, 1899, US Secretary of State John Hay sent notes to the major powers asking them to declare formally that they would uphold Chinese territorial and administrative integrity and would not interfere with the free use of the treaty ports within their spheres of influence in China. The Open Door Policy stated that all nations, including the United States, could enjoy equal access to the Chinese market. The major powers agreed in principle but continued to press China for special concessions for railroad rights, mining rights, loans, and foreign trade ports.

- *China's communists slam the door shut.* Western intervention in China was interrupted from 1914 to 1918, when the European powers were preoccupied with World War I. Japan saw this as an opportunity to expand its influence and forced China to transfer German holdings in the country to Japan. China entered World War I in 1917 to gain a seat at the peace table, hoping to thwart Japan's ambitions. Instead, President Woodrow Wilson withdrew US support for Chinese claims. The Chinese delegation refused to sign the Treaty of Versailles. A year later, radical Chinese nationalists formed the Chinese Communist Party.

  After World War II, the Chinese Communist Party seized power in 1949 under the leadership of Mao Zedong following a bloody civil war. The United States supported his opponent, General Chiang Kai-shek, who retreated to establish his government in Taiwan after the Communists seized the mainland. The door was slammed shut for American businesses in the new People's Republic of China.

- *China's reformers open the door.* In December 1978, two years after Mao died, China's communist leadership decided that it was time to modernize the country's economy. Deng Xiaoping, China's new leader, announced a new Open Door Policy that aimed to attract foreign businesses to set up manufacturing operations in Special Economic Zones (SEZs). Four SEZs were initially established in 1980, namely Shenzhen, Zhuhai, and Shantou in Guangdong province and Xiamen in Fujian.

  This was the first step along the path that eventually led China to join the WTO in 2001. Along the way, market reforms were implemented and foreign trade expanded. In one of the most dramatic announcements of the Cold War, President Jimmy Carter signaled recognition of China's progress on the road to economic transformation and its growing importance in the global community by declaring that as of January 1, 1979, the United States would formally recognize the communist People's Republic of China. Nixon got some credit for this momentous event, having started the process of normalizing relations between the United States and China with a state visit during 1972.

I started writing about the growing importance of China to the global economy in a February 4, 2003 *Topical Study* titled "A Bullish Post-War Scenario." I predicted that Chinese demand would likely push commodity prices higher.[16] I observed that the Chinese were building superhighways everywhere. They were encouraging their people to trade in their bicycles for cars. They were expanding their regional airports and ordering more jets.

I reported that roughly 70% of China's energy came from domestic coal, which is highly polluting. The Chinese were scrambling to acquire more oil from Russia. They were doing the same for liquefied natural gas from Australia and Indonesia. Obviously, oil and gas were not the only commodities in short supply in China; the country also needed a great deal more copper, steel, rubber, platinum, and plastics. I concluded that "one of the most obvious ways to play China is to buy commodities and commodity producers."

That turned out to be a good call. The Commodity Research Bureau's index of 13 raw industrials commodity spot prices, which excludes petroleum commodities, bottomed on November 5, 2001, just before China joined the WTO, and soared 145% through May 13, 2008 (Fig. 15). The price of a barrel of Brent crude oil took off from 2001's low of $16.57 on November 15 to peak at a record high of $145.40 on July 3, 2008 (Fig. 16). From its 2001 low to its 2007 high, the Emerging Markets MSCI stock price index, in local currency, rose 340%, with the China MSCI index rising 704% over this period (Fig. 17).

In my November 7, 2003 *Topical Study*, titled "China for Investors I: The Growth Imperative," I observed that the Chinese regarded joining the WTO as their most important economic reform in 20 years.[17] To join, they were required to accept numerous agreements to open their domestic markets to more competition from abroad. I posed a rhetorical question: "Why would the communist regime in Beijing agree to the capitalistic codes of conduct required to be a member of the WTO?" It would speed modernization and economic growth. Sure enough, China's industrial production, which had been growing around 10% at an annual rate during the late 1990s, jumped to the mid-teens from 2002 to 2007 (Fig. 18).

It didn't take very long for China's rapid growth to spur an industry of bearish China watchers. The outlook for China's economy became a major issue among some investment strategists and institutional portfolio managers. A few hedge fund managers were particularly bearish. The pessimists warned that China's boom was unsustainable. "I am not convinced," I wrote in my second *Topical Study* on China, dated January 21, 2004.

I explained that rapidly increasing farm productivity in China was causing a huge migration from the agrarian sector to the cities. To avoid massive social upheaval, the Chinese needed to create lots of jobs in manufacturing, construction, and services. Joining the WTO was seen as an essential way to create more factory jobs among exporters. I wrote in that second China *Topical Study*: "I believe that China is driven by a 'Growth Imperative.' I believe the country must grow rapidly to absorb the huge number of new entrants into the labor force every year and to meet the needs of the large number of people who are leaving the rural areas and moving to the urban centers."[18] The government fully realized that failure to expand employment could have serious consequences for the country's social and political stability.

I bolstered my argument by focusing on China's demography, which has played a much bigger role in China's economy than in any other. That's because China has had the biggest population in the world. Economists usually ignore demographic factors because they tend to play out over long periods. In China's case, demographic factors are among the most important in assessing the country's economy. They remain very important in explaining why China is likely to continue growing faster than most other countries for a while but then slow significantly. They say that demography is destiny. This certainly applies to China:

- *Population.* The country's population has soared from 542 million in 1949 to 1.4 billion in 2016 (Fig. 19). It first exceeded one billion during 1982, coinciding with the government's push to modernize the economy. The 10-year growth rate peaked around 3% at an annual rate during the first half of the 1970s, when China's population had swelled by roughly 200 million people over the previous 10 years (Fig. 20).
- *Rural migration.* The population explosion was exacerbated by the huge migration from rural to urban areas. The percentage of the population living in rural communities dropped from 89% during 1950 to 82% during 1978, when China announced the Open Door Policy (Fig. 21). Then it fell to 62% in 2001, when China joined the WTO, and tumbled to 43% by 2016.
- *Urbanization.* The percentage of the population that was urbanized rose to 50% during 2010 and was 57% in 2016. The urban population increased by 21.8 million that year (Fig. 22). That is truly extraordinary, as this category has been increasing consistently around 20 million per year since 1996. To urbanize that many people requires the

equivalent of building a Houston, Texas per month! I made that point in my 2004 study.

- *Aging.* China's long-term demographic outlook is not so bright. The government responded to the country's population explosion by introducing a one-child policy in 1979. That did slow the 10-year growth rate in China's population from a peak of 3.0% at an annual rate during 1972 to 0.5% in 2016. However, it also led to a shortage of young adult workers and a rapidly aging population. So the government reversed course, with a two-child policy effective January 1, 2016. The move was most likely too little too late. By 2050, the primary working-age population in China is projected to represent less than half of the total population, below a peak of 62% during 2011.[19]

BRIEF WORLD TOUR

MY WORK ON Wall Street was very US-centric prior to the end of the Cold War. The United States wasn't just the center of the world; it was the only world that mattered for most investors, in the United States at least. But after the end of the Cold War, it was no longer enough for Wall Street economists to have good insights into the US economy from the East Coast to the West Coast.

The 1990s remained very US-centric because America emerged from the Cold War as the world's sole superpower and the epicenter of the extraordinary information technology revolution of that decade. However, that all changed after the European Monetary Union was established on January 1, 1999, presently unifying 19 countries under one currency in a region known as the "Eurozone." Nearly three years later came China's December 2001 admittance to the WTO. The world was going global as national economies became increasingly integrated through global trade and international capital flows.

US investors became increasingly interested in investing on a global basis. The monetary integration in the Eurozone led investors to believe that the stocks and bonds of all the member countries were comparable in quality to German stocks and bonds. Indeed, the spreads between the government bond yields of the so-called peripheral Eurozone countries (i.e., Greece, Ireland, Italy, Portugal, and Spain) and the core countries (i.e., France, Germany, and the Netherlands) narrowed dramatically during the second half of the 1990s in anticipation of monetary unification (Fig. 23).

In 1986, reflecting the growing interest in global investing, Morgan Stanley licensed from Capital International the rights to global stock indexes that covered non-US markets and branded them as the "Morgan Stanley Capital International" ("MSCI") indexes. The MSCI indexes were the primary benchmark indexes outside of the United States for several years before being joined by those of FTSE, Citibank, and Standard & Poor's. The MSCI global equity indexes have been calculated since 1969.

In 2001, Jim O'Neill, who was chairman of Goldman Sachs Asset Management at the time, coined the term "BRIC" in his publication *Building Better Global Economic BRICs*. "BRIC" refers to the four largest emerging economies: Brazil, Russia, India, and China. It was a praiseworthy call by O'Neill, as the BRIC MSCI stock price index soared 418.3% from the end of 2001 through the end of 2007, in local currency (Fig. 24). There was mounting interest in investing in them as well as in other emerging economies.

So I focused more of my efforts on collecting and analyzing economic and financial data from around the world. As Dorothy told her dog in *The Wizard of Oz*, "Toto, I've a feeling we're not in Kansas anymore." The problem was that as I ventured overseas, the supply of data was much more limited than what was available for the United States.

There are plenty of data for individual countries, but anyone looking for aggregate global data finds slim pickings. Nevertheless, there are enough of both for a reasonably well-informed assessment of the global economy:

- *Production indexes.* For starters, the CPB Netherlands Bureau for Economic Policy Analysis has been compiling a monthly series on world industrial production since 1991 (Fig. 25). Because it is based on so many national production indexes, the latest updates tend to be three months old. Production per se is a coincident indicator, but this production statistic is a lagging one because of its delayed availability.

  The interesting story is in the two subindexes for production in the advanced economies and in the emerging ones (Fig. 26). From the start of 1991 through the end of 2016, the former rose just 33%, while the latter soared 257%! The Organisation for Economic Co-operation and Development (OECD) also compiles a production index for its 35 members of advanced economies (Fig. 27). It showed a gain of 47% over this same period.

• *Export measures.* The CPB compiles a seasonally adjusted data series for the volume of world exports as well (Fig. 28). It is available monthly since 1991. The International Monetary Fund (IMF) has a similar series for the value of world exports, denominated in dollars (Fig. 29). It starts in 1950. This series is very volatile on a monthly basis because it is not seasonally adjusted. A related current-dollar exports data series is available for the Group of Seven (G7) industrial economies, on a monthly and seasonally adjusted basis since 1993 (Fig. 30).

The volume of exports rose rapidly during the 1990s and 2000s until the global recession of 2008, when it plunged 20% from peak to trough. It recovered smartly during 2009 and 2010. Then the pace of growth slowed for various reasons. The IMF data series for the value of exports tracked the volume series until mid-2014, when the plunge in oil prices and weakness in other commodity prices weighed heavily on the value of world exports until both recovered in 2016. Not surprisingly, the raw industrials spot price index, compiled by the Commodity Research Bureau, is highly correlated with the value of exports (Fig. 31).

I like to squeeze as much information as I can from the data, primarily by identifying relationships among available series. The ratio of G7 exports to world exports (both in current dollars) dropped from 52.5% at the start of 1994 to 32.2% at the end of 2015 (Fig. 32). In other words, the exports of the rest of the world grew more rapidly, accounting for more global business as emerging economies emerged.

• *Purchasing managers' surveys.* The data series I just reviewed are useful for monitoring the trends in the global economy. Only the daily commodity index is available with the high frequency necessary to get a read on the current condition of the global economy. On a monthly basis, numerous business activity indexes are compiled from surveys of purchasing managers around the world. They all are diffusion indexes showing whether, on balance, purchasing managers reported that production, orders, employment, and numerous other variables were better or worse during the latest month than the previous month. The data vendors provide seasonally adjusted series for these along with overall business indexes, which reflect the movements of some of the key subindexes.

All these purchasing managers' indexes (PMIs) tend to remain above 50 when the economy is growing and to fall below this level during recessions. While they are widely followed, I have found them to be useful only when readings move decisively in one direction or another. Nevertheless, because they are available within a day or so after the end of each month, they do provide some insights, especially since indexes are also available for the manufacturing and non-manufacturing sectors. On an aggregate global basis, PMIs are available for the world, as well as for developed and emerging economies (Fig. 33, Fig. 34, and Fig. 35).

PMIs are available monthly for most of the major advanced and emerging economies. They are compiled by IHS Markit, often in partnership with another organization. IHS Markit posts press releases for each of its PMI country surveys on its website.[20] Over the years, I've found that the PMIs are useful as coincident rather than leading indicators of economic activity. Importantly, the PMIs can provide insights on whether global economic activity is synchronized or not.

• *Leading economic indicators.* The OECD does compile lots of leading economic indicators for each of its 35 members of advanced economies, along with a composite index representing all of them together (Fig. 36 and Fig. 37). The organization does the same for the four BRICs (Fig. 38). Leading indicators are supposed to lead the economy by at least three months. The problem is that the data usually are released with a lag of a couple of months. Nevertheless, I do track them to see whether they either confirm or contradict the other available data.

Again, there are plenty of economic data supplied by countries around the world, though none compare in quantity or quality to US data. There are enough, however, that the current state of the global economy can be reasonably assessed. We have chart books for all the major countries around the world, which I regularly peruse. Here is a very short list of some of my personal favorite national data series that have been especially reliable and useful economic indicators:

• *Eurozone.* Near the end of every month, the European Commission issues a press release with numerous indexes compiled from a business and consumer survey conducted throughout the European Union.[21] I focus on the Economic Sentiment Indicator (ESI) for the Eurozone because it is highly correlated with the year-over-year growth rate in real GDP for the region (Fig. 39). It did a great job of signaling the 2011–2013 slump and the subdued growth rate during 2014 and 2015. It then correctly showed improving growth during the second half of 2016 and 2017.

I also glance at the country and industry components of the ESI. The production expectations indexes tend to confirm the message in the indexes compiled from the manufacturing purchasing managers' surveys. The European Commission also compiles manufacturing indexes (including and excluding construction), which are then aggregated for the region (Fig. 40). The Statistical Office of the European Communities (EUROSTAT) releases monthly indexes of retail sales volumes excluding motor vehicles (Fig. 41).[22] I find them quite helpful in assessing domestic demand in the Eurozone.

- *Germany.* I'm a big fan of the IFO Business Climate Index, reported monthly by Germany's IFO Institute (Fig. 42).[23] It has been an extremely cyclical and reliable indicator of business activity in Germany. It includes two subcomponents tracking current conditions and expectations. Since Germany is such an export powerhouse, business conditions in the country are especially useful for assessing the global economy. However, the remarkable improvement during 2017 to new record highs for the headline index might also reflect the stimulative impact of massive immigration during 2015 and 2016.
- *Japan.* Japan is also an export powerhouse. However, the country is very strict about immigration, and domestic consumer demand is weighed down by aging demographic trends. With this in mind, I've observed that Japan's industrial production index was remarkably flat from 2010 through 2016, signaling that from the country's perspective, foreign demand for its manufactured products has been weighed down by weak domestic demand (Fig. 43).
- *South Korea and Taiwan.* Japan also faces competition from other manufacturers around the world, especially South Korea and Taiwan. The exports of these two are heavily weighted toward industrial and high-tech products (Fig. 44).
- *China.* Early each month, China releases data for its aggregate exports and imports during the previous month. These are very timely data for assessing the global economy as well as China's economy. I use seasonally adjusted data to do this (Fig. 45). Even so, the data can be volatile. Their accuracy has often been questioned, along with the accuracy of

most of the other statistical series reported by the Chinese government. That's why I like to find correlations that confirm or raise doubts about the information provided by any one series. In this case, I've found that the sum of China's imports and exports is highly correlated with the monthly series available for railways freight traffic (Fig. 46).

The economics division of the IMF, in Washington, DC, publishes the biannual *World Economic Outlook* (*WEO*), which is released usually in April and September/October. Short updates are provided during January and July. The first chapter in the biannual publications provides an overview as well as a more detailed analysis of the world economy. Subsequent chapters cover issues "affecting industrial countries, developing countries, and economies in transition to market; and address topics of pressing current interest." The main issue covered is highlighted on the cover page of the report. For example, the October 2015 *WEO* was titled "Adjusting to Lower Commodity Prices." (See Appendix 2.2, *World Economic Outlook*: 1998–Present.)

Table 1.1 in the *WEO* publication and its updates always shows the actual growth of world output during the previous year and the IMF's projections for world output for the current year and coming year.[24] The table includes projections for the advanced, emerging, and developing economies. I use the forecast table as a benchmark for determining my own projections for the global economy and its major regions and countries. I look at the previous year's actual growth rates for each of the categories and decide whether I agree with the magnitude of the IMF's projected changes in the growth rate for the current year and the coming year. My forecast will be higher or lower than the IMF's forecasts, depending on my assessment of whether the IMF projections are too low or too high, given my analysis of the key global economies and regions.

GLOBAL SYNCHRONIZED BOOMS, BUSTS, AND STAGNATION

ACTRESS GWYNETH PALTROW announced in March 2014 that she was divorcing musician Chris Martin. She described the breakup as an amicable "conscious uncoupling." Perhaps countries that exit from economic and financial unions should issue a gracious statement like the one Gwyneth shared with the world when she announced her split: "It is with hearts full of sadness that we have decided to separate. We have been working hard for well over a year, some of it together, some of it separated, to see what might have been possible between us, and we have come to the conclusion that while we love each other very much[,] we will remain separate."

Since the financial crisis of 2008, the Eurozone has experienced a few "Grexit" crises, i.e., the prospect of Greece being forced to exit the monetary union because of its profligate finances. On June 28, 2016, Britain actually voted to leave the European Union. There were widespread fears that the "Brexit" precedent might eventually lead to the disintegration of the European Union and possibly even the Eurozone, though Britain had never joined the monetary union. The jury is still out on how it will unfold.

Of course, countries can't simply separate from the world, though North Korea certainly has disconnected from much of it; there simply are too many advantages in trading with other countries. In addition, countries benefit when their citizens invest in, lend to, and borrow from one another. These linkages create economic interdependencies.

On a regular basis, my accounts ask me to assess whether the US economy can decouple from adverse economic developments overseas. The answer I give is: there is no such thing as "constructive decoupling" in the global economy. Some countries are more coupled than others through their trade accounts. The United States has been running trade deficits for many years. However, US exports and imports are both relatively small components of GDP (Fig. 47). Other countries are much more dependent on foreign trade, especially with the United States. Indeed, the sum of inflation-adjusted US merchandise exports and imports is very highly correlated with the CPB's volume of world exports (Fig. 48). In other words, the United States is the 800-pound gorilla in the global economy.

So the data show that the United States may not be as coupled to the world economy as everyone else is coupled to the United States. However, that has been changing since the global financial crisis of 2008.

Actually, global financial crises always have posed a threat to the United States. At the start of the Great Depression, a series of banking shocks in Europe reverberated in the United States. The Latin American debt crisis in the early 1980s threatened to worsen the US recession at the time. During the summer of 2016, Fed officials expressed some concern that Brexit might adversely affect the US economy, which already had been weakened by the recession in the oil patch following the plunge in the price of oil from mid-2014 through early 2016. In addition, while Fed officials rarely had discussed the foreign-exchange value of the dollar in their past deliberations about monetary policy, they gave it more weight during this period, as it soared by about 20% at the same time that the price of oil was taking a dive.

Let's take a quick look back at how synchronized the global economy has been over the past several decades:

- *During the 1930s*, there was a period of a global synchronized depression, though some countries recovered from it sooner than the United States.
- *During the 1940s*, war and reconstruction occurred. After the war, the United States emerged as the sole superpower and focused on rebuilding Europe and reviving Japan.
- *During the 1950s and 1960s*, the US economy was driven by the expansion of the highway system, which led to the suburbanization of America.
- *During the 1970s*, the US economy experienced a couple of oil supply shocks that triggered severe recessions. America had become very dependent on foreign oil suppliers.
- *During the 1980s*, the United States experienced growing competition from Japan, triggering a wave of corporate restructurings and the start of "deindustrialization" as companies increasingly moved production overseas to lower their labor costs. Later in the decade, that trend was somewhat reversed as Japanese and other foreign manufacturers opened factories in the United States, particularly in the South, where labor costs were relatively low.
- *During the 1990s*, the United States emerged as the sole superpower again after the end of the Cold War. Japan's bubble had burst at the start of the decade, and the Japanese economy sputtered. Europe was struggling to revive economic growth throughout the decade, and the emerging economies stumbled near the end of the decade. The US economy managed to decouple from the rest of the world thanks to the "peace dividend" and the boom in the domestic high-tech industry.
- *During the 2000s*, some emerging economies had emerged, led by China. The United States inflated a housing bubble. The Eurozone's monetary union stimulated an economic boom fueled by borrowing and lending binges. It was a period that stood out as a bona fide global synchronized boom. Unfortunately, the boom didn't last long and

ended very badly in 2008, when a worldwide financial crisis triggered a severe global recession. It was a synchronized bust.

- *During the 2010s*, the global economy continued the recovery that had started in 2009 as the world's major central banks provided ultra-easy monetary conditions. However, following a typical V-shaped recovery around the world, global economic growth was very sluggish from 2011 through 2016.

The term "secular stagnation" came into vogue to describe the performance of the global economy following the economic recovery of 2009 and 2010. Economic growth was weaker than widely expected. A few economists warned that economic growth could simply stall. Central banks provided plenty of monetary rocket fuel in an effort to achieve "escape velocity," i.e., fast enough growth that monetary policy would no longer require the rocket fuel. Nevertheless, the IMF's economists had to lower their forecast for global economic activity in every one of their *WEO*s from 2011 through 2016. Consider the following developments:

- *Japan.* In many ways, Japan is the poster child of a modern industrial economy that is struggling with secular stagnation. The government has tried numerous rounds of fiscal and monetary stimulus without much success. The problem is a rapidly aging population that is also shrinking. Japan "is currently the oldest nation in the world and is projected to retain this position through at least 2050," notes a March 2016 Census Bureau report titled *An Aging World: 2015.*[25] Japan's elderly population percentage increased from 12% in 1990 to 25% in 2014. The working-age population percentage fell from 69% to 62% over this same period.[26] The gap between Japan's number of deaths and number of births has continued to widen since deaths first exceeded births in July 2007. As a result, Japan's population has declined by 1.1 million since then, as of May 2017 (Fig. 49).

- *United States.* The recovery in US consumer spending was relatively weak in the post-crisis expansion through 2016 compared to in previous expansions. The rebound in the housing market remained lackluster too. Unlike the Baby Boomers, Millennials have preferred to remain single longer and to rent apartments in cities. They've been in no rush to get married, move to their own homes in the suburbs, and have kids. The upturn in capital spending was subpar as businesses remained cautious following the traumatic recession. There was an energy boom, but it turned into a bust during the second half of 2014 through early 2016. As a result, from 2011 through 2016, real GDP growth on a year-over-year basis fluctuated around 2.0%, which in the past was the stall speed that led to a recession (Fig. 50).

- *Eurozone.* In the Eurozone, debt that had accumulated during the previous boom weighed on the economy. Loans held by monetary financial institutions remained essentially flat from 2009 through 2016 after increasing by €4.0 trillion from the start of 2003 through the end of 2008 (Fig. 51). The region's industrial production, which had recovered smartly during 2009 and 2010, increased only 2.0% from the start of 2011 through the end of 2016 (Fig. 52).

- *China.* China's real GDP growth rate peaked during 2007 as a result of too much debt and excess capacity (Fig. 53). The Chinese government responded to the global economic crisis of 2008 by increasing fiscal spending and stimulating bank lending. From December 2008 through September 2017, Chinese bank loans quadrupled from 30.3 trillion yuan ($4.4 trillion) to 117.8 trillion yuan ($17.9 trillion) (Fig. 54). Apparently, that financed lots of excess manufacturing capacity, as evidenced by the decline in the PPI on a year-over-year basis for 54 months from March 2012 to August 2016 (Fig. 55). However, by late 2016 and early 2017, the PPI inflation rate had rebounded significantly, suggesting that some excess capacity might have been reduced and that demand might have been boosted by another round of easy credit.

- *Old world.* Around the world, aging populations seemed to be contributing to secular stagnation as people lived longer and fertility rates dropped below the population replacement rate. The March 2016 Census Bureau report cited above estimated that 9% of the 7.3 billion people worldwide (or 617.1 million) in 2015 were aged 65 or older.[27] The number of older people was projected to increase more than 60% by 2030, to about one billion older people globally, equivalent to 12% of the total population (Fig. 56). The report projected that by 2050, there will be 1.6 billion older people worldwide, representing 16% of the total world population of 9.8 billion. Older people tend to be more conservative spenders than younger ones, particularly midlifers with kids to feed, clothe, house, and educate.

This very brief overview of secular stagnation suggests that the sources of the problem are debt, deflation, and demographics. Too much debt accumulated in the past reduces the effectiveness of easy monetary and fiscal policies in stimulating demand. If some of that debt leads to excessive capacity expansion, the result is deflation, which is bad for profits. The persistence of easy money in this situation can worsen deflation by propping up excess capacity. Yes, easy money can be deflationary! The demographic sources of secular stagnation may be more intractable than either debt or deflation.

The recent bout of secular stagnation stimulated an interesting debate in the academic world about its causes and permanence as well the best policy response. Here is a brief summary:

- *Larry Summers*, a Harvard economics professor, first stirred up the big debate on whether the United States is mired in a protracted period of secular stagnation in an off-the-cuff presentation at an IMF forum on November 8, 2013. He followed it up with an op-ed in the December 15, 2013 *Financial Times* titled "Why Stagnation May Prove to Be the New Normal."[28] He concluded that "the presumption that normal economic and policy conditions will return at some point cannot be maintained."

  He based that mostly on the subpar performance of the US economy during the current economic recovery. He noted that economic growth has been weak despite near-zero interest rates. He also worried about deflationary pressures in wages and prices. That could cause consumers to delay spending. Worsening the situation was income inequality, in his opinion. Summers has argued on numerous occasions over the past couple of years that the world has a glut of savings and shortage of investment demand. His solution is a typically Keynesian one: the government should borrow to fund public investment.

- *Kenneth Rogoff*, another Harvard professor of economics, posted an April 22, 2015 article on this subject, titled "Debt Supercycle, Not Secular Stagnation."[29] Rogoff rejected the view that the world is experiencing secular stagnation "with a long future of much lower per capita income growth driven significantly by a chronic deficiency in global demand." Instead, he argued that weak global economic activity since 2008 reflected "the post-financial crisis phase of a debt supercycle where, after deleveraging and borrowing headwinds subside, expected growth trends might prove higher than simple extrapolations of recent performance might suggest."

He concluded that in this situation, debt-financed fiscal spending is counterproductive: "[O]ne has to worry whether higher government debt will perpetuate the political economy of policies that are helping the government finance debt, but making it more difficult for small businesses and the middle class to obtain credit." In his opinion, time heals all wounds: "Unlike secular stagnation, the debt supercycle is not forever. As the economy recovers, the economy will be in position for a new rising phase of the leverage cycle."

- *Olivier Blanchard* was one of the three authors of a Peterson Institute *Policy Brief* titled "Short-Run Effects of Lower Productivity Growth: A Twist on the Secular Stagnation Hypothesis."[30] He is now an economics professor at MIT and was formerly the IMF's chief economist. Here is the gist of their explanation for secular stagnation: "We believe that this is largely due to lower optimism about the future, more specifically to downward revisions in growth forecasts, rather than to the legacies of the past. Put simply, demand is temporarily weak because people are adjusting to a less bright future." I guess this means that maybe secular stagnation won't be so secular after all if it is mostly in our heads. We were depressed about the future because of what happened to us in the recent past, i.e., the financial crisis of 2008. We are bound to get over it.

- *Robert Gordon*, a professor at Northwestern University, also believes that there's no need for a policy response to secular stagnation. However, unlike Rogoff and Blanchard, who believe it will go away on its own, Gordon argues that secular stagnation is here to stay; it is truly secular. As I discuss more fully in the next chapter, Gordon believes that the productivity-led growth from 1870–1970 can't be repeated.

I'm inclined to agree with Rogoff and Blanchard. Indeed, there was mounting evidence of better economic growth around the world in late 2016 and throughout 2017, though some of that strength might have reflected the end of the recession in the global energy industry that started in mid-2014 and lasted through early 2016. The improvement was reflected in the titles of the biannual *WEO*, from "Too Slow for Too Long" (April 2016) to "Gaining Momentum" (April 2017).

In any event, there are major forces of secular stagnation that may continue to frustrate the efforts of policymakers to stimulate faster economic growth. They are related to debt, deflation, and demographics, as noted above and as I explore further in coming chapters.

GLOBALIZATION AND ITS DISCONTENTED

SIGMUND FREUD PUBLISHED *Civilization and Its Discontents* in 1929, 10 years after Keynes published his treatise on the grim economic consequences of the peace treaty that ended World War I. It too was influenced by the unprecedented barbarity of that war. The world had seemed so civilized prior to World War I. There was widespread peace before the war, and prosperity was spreading rapidly around the world. The future must have looked very bright on May 6, 1889 when the World's Fair opened in Paris, France. The Eiffel Tower was the fair's iconic symbol.

How could this celebration of peace, progress, and prosperity end so badly only 25 years later, with millions of lives lost in the Great War? Freud posited that there is a fundamental tension between an individual's personal craving for unrestricted freedom and the pressure from society to abide by the laws of civilization because they are the only protection against potential harm at the hands of other individuals. Such harm could be rampant with unrestricted freedom. Yet the individual remains discontented, thirst for freedom unquenched, despite the economic benefits of civilization, which tend to provide peace, progress, and prosperity.

Globalization takes the individual's conflicting desires for freedom, on the one hand, and for order, on the other hand, to a global level, exacerbating discontent on a worldwide scale. During periods of social and political chaos, particularly during war times, everyone is equally miserable. No one is particularly incensed about income inequality. In totalitarian societies, where brute force is used to establish social and political order, there is lots of income equality. Everyone except the ruling junta is equally poor. During peacetimes, globalization increases prosperity. The rich certainly can get richer, but all consumers benefit from the availability of better goods and services at lower prices thanks to freer trade. Globalization is an income-leveling force, increasing income equality because it increases the purchasing power of consumers broadly and indiscriminately.

However, globalization also entails production shifts from high-wage to low-wage countries. On balance, that too increases income equality, as more workers are likely to benefit in the low-wage countries than are likely to be harmed in the high-wage countries. Nevertheless, the latter group of workers undoubtedly will be very discontented with the adverse consequences of globalization hitting them. For them, the pain of losing a job or accepting a pay cut outweighs the gain of lower prices at the mall.

In democracies, populist politicians then step in, doing what they always do. They pander to the anxiety of the discontented and inflame them with anti-globalization rhetoric. In totalitarian regimes, dictators incite ultra-nationalist sentiments to mask the failure of their regimes to allow their subjects to benefit from globalization. As it gets harder to hide the benefits that others are enjoying in other countries, the classic response of despots is to resort to nationalist propaganda, blaming foreigners for their people's misery.

The risk to globalization is war fomented by ultra-nationalist populists and totalitarian leaders like the one in North Korea. That's what I learned when I studied the causes of World War I. That's the lesson of lots of other wars as well. But as long as war is avoided and peace prevails along with relatively free trade, globalization should, on balance, lift standards of living around the world.

When the Cold War ended, I also learned about the increasing importance of having a global perspective in my job as a forecaster. Globalization has integrated not only national economies but also national financial markets. That insight was especially useful during the current bull market, which started in early 2009, as I recognized that it was driven by the ultra-easy monetary policies of all the major central banks, not just the Fed. In this environment, national economies and financial markets will become increasingly globalized and synchronized.

Over the years, I also came to appreciate the importance of studying history. In my spare time, I've always enjoyed reading histories and biographies of political leaders. In my day job, I've often had to refresh and deepen my knowledge of the past. My history lessons help me to think in a more informed and global way about issues that regularly matter to the markets, including those concerning trade, inflation, the business cycle, monetary policy, financial crises, and international relations.

Another important lesson is that economists and historians can analyze the same data and facts yet come to completely different conclusions. All I can do is study their work to sort out the debate among them. Then I look at the data and the facts and come to my own hopefully well-informed conclusion.

CHAPTER 3

Predicting Technology and Productivity

GOING VIRTUAL

PHYSICS NOBEL LAUREATE Niels Bohr once observed, "Prediction is very difficult, especially if it's about the future." Physicists and other natural scientists sometimes upend the predictions of social scientists, especially economists, because many of the former's insights lead to technological innovations rarely anticipated by the latter. These innovations tend to be disruptive, radically changing the way the economy performs. Electricity, automobiles, synthetic fertilizers, vaccines, TVs, jets, PCs, stents, the Internet, smartphones, and social media are some of the more obvious innovations that have changed everything, or almost everything. That's why I've always tried to stay current on new technologies that might significantly impact the economy and financial markets.

During my "wonder years," I attended middle school at Elvira Castro Junior High School in Campbell, California. My father graduated with a master's degree in engineering from Case Institute of Technology in Cleveland, Ohio in 1960. Two years later, we moved to Campbell after my father was hired by IBM to work in nearby San Jose. Even back then, California had a dynamic high-tech culture. My father and several other tech-savvy parents sponsored a science club at my school.

They organized lots of field trips to visit companies in the area in various science and technology fields.

I studied Fortran programming on my own using an introductory self-study manual that my father had brought home from work. This programming language was developed by IBM in the 1950s for scientific and engineering applications. I didn't master it or do anything useful with what I did learn. However, it was a good introduction to how computers "THINK," which was a corporate slogan first used by Thomas J. Watson, who founded IBM. He explained: "By THINK I mean take everything into consideration. I refuse to make the sign more specific. If a man just sees THINK, he'll find out what I mean. We're not interested in a logic course." I have an original version of the sign in my office.

In high school, I particularly enjoyed my courses in chemistry and physics. However, during the first term of my freshman year in engineering at Cornell, I realized that I wasn't cut out to be an engineer. I transferred to Cornell's College of Arts and Sciences for the second term. The one course that I aced in engineering school, though, was computer programing using Assembler language. During the summer after my freshman year, I worked for General Foods in Banbury, England. My father, who was now working as a systems programmer for General Foods in White Plains, New York, had pulled some strings and got the summer job for me. My project was to write a program in Assembler code to find the optimal locations for the company's warehouses in the United Kingdom. I wrote a good program, but I'm sure it was never used—like my unread memos to the FRB-NY filing cabinet that I mention in the first chapter.

Inspired by my father, I have always had a predisposition to use technology to increase my productivity. There wasn't much technology available for doing so when I started my career. At EF Hutton in 1978, I used a freelance draftsman to create my charts. He did a handful each week from the data printouts I provided to him. The print shop then had to photograph the charts to include them in between the text that was typeset. My secretary still used an IBM Selectric typewriter, first introduced in 1961, to type up my handwritten weekly commentaries. They were included in the typeset weekly research publication that was mailed to our accounts. That was the state of technology in the early 1980s. By 1982, I could print my charts using an electronic ink plotter.

Before there was the Internet, there was the fax machine, which became ubiquitous by the mid-1980s. It was revolutionary: prior to faxing, the only way to provide any current ("real-time") analyses and opinions to our accounts was by telling the sales force via the internal "hoot-and-holler" system, and hoping they would pass along the information by calling the accounts. Of course, I also called the accounts whom I thought would benefit the most from the information, but that was time-consuming. With the arrival of the fax machine, I now could blast daily comments on the economic indicators out to all my accounts, providing them with almost real-time analyses of the data instead of the two-week-old information they received from me by mail.

During the winter of 1995, I walked into a Barnes & Noble bookstore in my neighborhood on the north shore of Long Island to see whether they had any books about the Internet. I was amazed by all the books that were already available on this subject. I purchased a primer on html programming. By the summer of that year, I had my website up and running. I believe I was the first economist on Wall Street with his own website and domain name, i.e., *yardeni.com*. It was called "Dr. Ed's Economics Network."

Perhaps because the Internet was so new, no one in the legal compliance department of CJ Lawrence, and subsequently Deutsche Bank, questioned why an employee of the firm had his own website. Even when I moved on to other firms, I insisted on and succeeded in keeping the name and format of the website. When I started my own business in 2007, I changed the website's banner to "Yardeni Research," matching my company's name. From the beginning, I posted my commentaries on the site as well as a growing library of chart publications covering numerous economic, financial, and demographic topics.

I was very fortunate to have Jim Marsten knock on my door at EF Hutton during 1982 to offer his consulting services for creating a charting program. His one-man shop was called "Wall Street Computer Graphics," which aptly described what Jim did. As I noted previously, when I became Hutton's chief economist, I decided to forgo the expensive econometric model that my predecessor had been using and replaced it with a simple Excel spreadsheet. Nevertheless, I have been an economic data junkie throughout my career, especially when the data are displayed in easy-to-read charts. Jim was a programming genius when it came to designing a customized charting system for me. Sadly, he passed away in 2015.

Over the years, I gave Jim my wish list of bells and whistles for the charting system. Among the most useful features is one that automatically detects when the thousands of data series provided by our data vendors are updated. The charts that use those series are refreshed with the new data on our server, which is in the cloud at Amazon Web Services. The updated charts then are automatically placed in their appropriate locations in the hundreds of chart publications that we've created over the years. So, for example, when the employment report is posted at 8:30 a.m. on the first Friday of every month, all the employment chart publications we keep on the website are automatically refreshed within a few seconds of the information's release.

Several data providers have developed their own software for creating data visualizations. Many of their programs are interactive. In 2006, the Federal Reserve Bank of St. Louis even developed a free and widely used charting tool of public economic data time series, called "FRED," which is short for "Federal Reserve Economic Data."[1] I continue to prefer our vast and growing library of preset chart publications on our website. The benefit is that my team and I have put a lot of thought into the creation of each individual chart and carefully assembled publication. That makes it easier, for us and for our clients, to quickly analyze new data when they are automatically updated in our charts. In other words, the system helps put these puzzle pieces where they belong in the developing picture. That way, we can spend more time trying to see the picture and less time gathering the pieces.

I've continued to expand our digital footprint. During December 2011, I launched Dr. Ed's Blog (*blog.yardeni.com*) to provide short weekly excerpts of our research to the public. In addition, I started posting the blog articles on Twitter and LinkedIn to promote our company. We had an Apple app for our subscribers from 2013 to 2017, when we replaced it with a new streamlined website that functions as an app as well; it works across all digital platforms. That's a good example of technological progress.

When the fax machine first came out, I remember telling my staff that we one day would be working from the beach. I foresaw that with technology, my staff could be productive from anywhere. Since 2007, when I formed my own company, we have been virtual. We don't have any offices. Everyone works from home or from wherever they like. We replaced a couple of servers we had at a "server farm" with a virtual server on the Amazon cloud in 2012. We subscribe to Microsoft's Office 365, which allows us to rent the software over the cloud. Our *Morning Briefing* is delivered to all our accounts by email and posted on the website. Its production is a collaboration among my colleagues and me, invariably entailing a daily flood of email messages among us to get the job done. All these technologies have enhanced our productivity and allowed us to compete in a very competitive market for what we do.

REVOLUTIONARY

I FIRST STARTED to write about the High-Tech Revolution in the January 7, 1993 issue of my *Weekly Economic Analysis*. I wrote that "the US economy is on the threshold of a major Technological Revolution, led by the personal computer. This revolution will continue to boost productivity well above the anemic growth of the 1970s and 1980s." On March 20, 1995, I wrote a *Topical Study* titled "The High-Tech Revolution in the US of @." I predicted: "I am more convinced than ever that our economy is rapidly evolving in a very positive direction. Real incomes will grow at a faster pace along with productivity. Bearish problems like the federal and trade deficits will be overshadowed by the bullish consequences of the High-Tech Revolution. I am especially bullish on the stock prices of high-tech companies."[2]

That turned out to be a very good call. When I wrote my study during March 1995, the market capitalization of the S&P 500 Information Technology (IT) sector was 9.2% of the market's total, and its earnings share was 8.2% (Fig. 1*). Its market-cap share soared to a record high of 32.9% during March 2000. The problem was that the IT sector's earnings share of the S&P 500 peaked at 17.6% during September 2000. The sector's earnings valuation multiple, based on 12-month forward earnings, soared to a record high of 48.3 during March 2000 (Fig. 2).[3] That certainly exceeded my expectations in 1993.

In a 1965 article, Gordon Moore, the co-founder of Intel and Fairchild Semiconductor, observed that the number of components per integrated circuit had been doubling every year.[4] He projected that this rate of growth would continue for at least another decade. In 1975, he revised the forecast to doubling every two years over the decade ahead. This observation has come to be known as "Moore's Law." It's not a law of nature, of course, but rather a remarkably good prediction of the future based on the past, i.e., what had happened since Moore first started to write about the

---

* Figures, references, and appendices are linked on *yardenibook.com/resources*.

subject. The phenomenon has resulted in faster and more powerful computing systems at lower prices.

In my 1995 study, I observed that the upturn in computer purchases since the early 1980s was triggered by a significant increase in the processing speed of computer hardware as prices plummeted. At the same time, computer software became much more powerful and easier to use. Back then, I focused on an old measure of a computer's speed and power, i.e., millions of instructions per second (MIPS), which measures roughly the number of machine instructions that a computer can execute in one second. Like many digital metrics today, MIPS isn't perfect, but it is directionally useful. Different instructions require more or less time than others, so there is no standard method for measuring MIPS. William D. Nordhaus, one of my professors at Yale, studied computers after I left. He has co-authored Paul Samuelson's classic introductory *Economics* textbook since 1985. In a 2001 paper titled "The Progress of Computing," he explained why MIPS is a flawed measure that underestimates the power of computers.[5]

In any case, I based my 1995 analysis on MIPS. I observed that in 1983, Intel first shipped the 286 microprocessor in volume with an initial speed of 1.0 MIPS. The subsequent 386 chip was shipped in volume during 1986. It was five times faster than the 286. The 486 was four times faster than the 386 and 20 times faster than the 286. The 486 launched the High-Tech Revolution once Intel started to ship it in volume during the early 1990s. Intel sold 75 million 486 chips. Compaq Computer Corporation started a price war in the PC market in 1992, which made the powerful 486 machine very affordable.

Intel's Pentium chip was introduced in 1993 and bulk-shipped the following year. It was rated at 100 MIPS. The P6 was introduced in late 1995 with a blazing speed of 250 MIPS. Before the end of the decade, the P7 delivered a blistering 500 MIPS. From 1982 through 1995, MIPS per $100 rose from 1 to an estimated 30.

The competitive pressures to produce more powerful, faster, and cheaper central processing units (CPUs) also were driven by the rapid increase in the amount of data that needed to be processed and analyzed. Innovation in data storage and communication technologies enabled the amount of data collected to soar, as it was increasingly gathered by cheap and rapidly proliferating mobile devices, cameras, microphones, radio-frequency identification readers, and wireless sensor networks.

A 2011 article in *Science* titled "The World's Technological Capacity to Store, Communicate, and Compute Information" reported that information storage rose from the equivalent of less than one 730-MB CD-ROM per person in 1986 (539 MB per person), to about four CD-ROMs per person in 1993, then 12 per person in 2000, and nearly 61 per person by 2007. A pile of these imaginary 404 billion CD-ROMs from 2007 would reach from the earth to the moon and then a quarter of this distance further.[6] Analog storage still accounted for three-quarters of technological storage in the year 2000. Digital storage then took off, rising from 25% to over 90% of total storage by 2007.[7] The article reported the compounded annual growth rate from 1986 to 2007 of general-purpose computing (in MIPS per capita of installed capacity) at 58%. For telecommunications, the growth rate was 28%. For storage, it was 23%.

The software revolution was led by Microsoft, which first shipped its Windows operating system in 1985. Windows moved to version 3.0 in 1990. Windows 3.1 shipped in 1992. It was much easier to use than the MS-DOS operating system and led to a dramatic increase in Windows-based software applications. Windows quickly became the default operating system shipped with new PCs.

The World Wide Web took off around 1995, led by friendly email web interfaces from providers such as AOL and Yahoo. In the mid-1990s, Larry Page and Sergey Brin, who were students at Stanford University, worked in their dorm rooms to build a search engine for the World Wide Web that was called "Backrub" before it was renamed "Google." Their mission was "to organize the world's information and make it universally accessible and useful." Google was incorporated in 1998 and went public in 2004. Its search engine has been an invaluable research tool for me and almost everyone else who uses it. My only concern is that the motto of Google's corporate code of conduct is "Don't be evil." That's a bit creepy. I much prefer "THINK."

In my 1995 study, I observed that one of the most unusual, and certainly unique, attributes of the computer industry was that hardware prices declined even as processing power soared. In high-tech markets, prices often tend to fall rapidly even in the face of booming demand. Why is that? The answer is that competition is intense. As soon as a computer chip is introduced, manufacturers are already developing the next generation of their products. Innovators of generation "n" chips are forced to create "n+1" chips. If they don't, the competition soon will.

This situation means that the most successful producers of technology must cannibalize their own products to remain successful. The IT industry is so competitive that it must eat its young to survive! The cost of high-tech research and development is so great that high-tech manufacturers must sell as many units as possible of their new products in as short a period as possible before the n+1 generation is introduced. That's why they tend to offer more power at a lower price with the introduction of each new generation. Also, the introduction of n+1 immediately reduces the demand for the nth chip and the nth computer. As the price of the old technology falls, it limits the upside of the price of the newest technology. Due to these dynamics, the purchasers of high-tech hardware are constantly receiving more bang for their buck.

In other words, the technology industry provides the perfect example of "creative destruction," a process first explained by economist Joseph Schumpeter in his book *Capitalism, Socialism and Democracy* (1942). According to Schumpeter, the "gale of creative destruction" describes the "process of industrial mutation that incessantly revolutionizes the economic structure from within, incessantly destroying the old one, incessantly creating a new one." Apparently, this concept was derived from the work of Karl Marx. In fact, *The Communist Manifesto* (1848), written with Friedrich Engels, warns that capitalism is prone to recurring crises because "a great part not only of existing production, but also of previously created productive forces, are periodically destroyed." This happens because capitalism has "epidemics of over-production," which are resolved through "enforced destruction of a mass of productive forces," exploitation at home, and imperialism abroad.

Hey, Karl and Friedrich were only 27- and 25-year-old wannabe revolutionaries when they wrote that nonsense. Even as they got older, though, they never figured out that capitalism's process of creative destruction improves the standard of living of the consuming class, i.e., just about everyone. Capitalism provides the incentive for entrepreneurs to innovate. The creators of new goods and services at affordable prices get rich by selling their products to consumers who benefit from them. They are the true revolutionaries. Destroyed are the producers who fail to innovate and to provide consumers with the best goods and services at the lowest prices on a regular basis. Entrepreneurial capitalism naturally promotes technological innovation and progress that benefit all of society.

Professor Nordhaus, in his 2007 study "Two Centuries of Productivity Growth in Computing," quantified the phenomenal increase in computer power over the 20th century.[8] He estimated that performance in constant dollars has improved relative to manual calculations by a factor on the order of two trillion, with most of the increase occurring since 1945. More specifically, he estimated that the average rate of improvement has been 45% per year, a far larger increase in productivity than for any other good or service in history!

The plunge in the cost of computing power is probably the most extraordinary deflation in the history of this planet, and it will continue to benefit all of us for years to come. In effect, the High-Tech Revolution has created a fourth factor of production—namely, information.

The original three factors are land, labor, and capital. Factors of production are partially substitutable for one another. Until recently, information was hard to substitute for land, labor, or capital. It was very expensive to gather, process, and manage data. There were usually long lags between the creation of the raw data and its conversion into useful information. The lags made the information less useful once it was available; it was old news by the time it was available to decision makers.

With the High-Tech Revolution, enormous quantities of information can be gathered, processed, and managed on a "real-time" basis at lower and lower costs. The price of information is deflating. As it gets cheaper, it also becomes more useful for increasing the productivity of the other factors of production, especially labor and capital. Increasingly, real-time information can also be a substitute for labor and capital, and even land, in the production process. That is truly revolutionary.

ADDING UP THE DIGITAL ECONOMY

TECHNOLOGY IS INHERENTLY disruptive to business models. It always has been, but it just seems to be disrupting faster and in more industries than ever before. This is making it harder for the government's statisticians to measure capital spending and for economists to compare current readings to past ones, when capital spending was less technology intensive.

The Bureau of Economic Analysis (BEA) in the US Commerce Department reports GDP. Compiling its capital-spending component must be very challenging, since the nature of the beast changes as rapidly as technology changes. The BEA only started to include software in capital spending during 1999, with back data starting in 1959. Research and development (R&D) outlays were expensed until July 31, 2013, when they were instead included in capital spending.[9]

BEA data starting in 1959 show the extraordinary shift toward technology in capital spending. The sum of business spending on technology equipment (including computer hardware, computer peripheral equipment, and telecommunication equipment) plus software rose from 16% of total nominal (i.e., current-dollar) capital spending during the first quarter of 1980 to 29% during the fourth quarter of 2016 (Fig. 3).[10] Adding R&D to the mix brings this percentage up to 42% from 24% over the same period.

The BEA data suggest that businesses have been getting more and more bang for their bucks spent on technology. That's because the so-called implicit price deflators for technology have been falling. From the start of 1980 through the end of 2016, they dropped 80% for information technology equipment and 30% for software (Fig. 4). Here is a brief statistical history of real (i.e., inflation-adjusted) capital spending on technology in the GDP accounts:

- *Equipment and software.* Capital spending on information processing equipment plus software rose 273% during the 1980s, 337% during the 1990s, and 67% during the 2000s. From the start of 2010 through the end of 2016, it rose 36% (Fig. 5).
- *Equipment.* Capital spending on information processing equipment rose 183% during the 1980s, 310% during the 1990s, and 75% during the 2000s. From the start of 2010 through the end of 2016, it rose 31% (Fig. 6).
- *Software.* Capital spending on software rose 462% during the 1980s, 366% during the 1990s, and 58% during the 2000s. From the start of 2010 through the end of 2016, it rose 40%.
- *Computers.* Capital spending on computers and peripheral equipment rose 1,900% during the 1980s, 1,415% during the 1990s, and 185% during the 2000s. From the start of 2010 through the end of 2016, it was flat (Fig. 7).
- *Other equipment.* Capital spending on other IT equipment rose 53% during the 1980s, 108% during the 1990s, and 41% during the 2000s. From the start of 2010 through the end of 2016, it rose 47% (Fig. 8).

The main takeaways are that following the boom of the 1990s and brief bust early during the following decade, real capital spending on IT continued to rise, though at a slower pace, until it was hit again by the recession of 2008. It made new highs from then through 2016. However, there was virtually no growth in real capital spending on computers from 2008 through 2016.

Now consider that more and more technology is embedded in so-called producers' durable equipment not categorized as "technology equipment." Industrial equipment such as machine tools is loaded with technology components and software. Much of this equipment is connected wirelessly and over the Internet. All this creates a real apples-and-oranges problem when comparing capital spending today to the past. If real capital-spending growth is slower than in the past at a comparable point of the business cycle, it may be that there is more bang per nominal and real buck today than there was in the past, thanks to embedded technological innovations.

The cloud only complicates the measuring issues. In the past, companies used their own software that was purchased and loaded onto their mainframes, minicomputers, PCs, and laptops. They networked their systems through in-house or outsourced "server farms." All this required large IT departments to maintain the system and to upload software updates, which was a challenging job as the number of laptops proliferated. Much of this IT infrastructure operated well below capacity.

The cloud changed all that. Now companies can use the servers of cloud vendors such as Amazon, IBM, and Microsoft for their data-processing and storage needs. In effect, this is reminiscent of my days at the Fed in the late 1970s, when we used remote computer terminals to access the fire power of the organization's mainframe computers, kept in a large, air-conditioned room on another floor. Any computer hardware connected to the cloud is analogous to a remote terminal, and the mainframe is now all the servers operated by the cloud companies. This greatly reduces the need for large in-house IT departments, especially since software companies rent their latest products so that there is no need to update them on individual computers anymore. In 2011, Microsoft started to rent Office 365, which is on the cloud and automatically updated there, for an annual subscription fee.

The cloud also reduces the need for buying as much hardware and software, since it provides a much more efficient way to process and store data. The servers of the cloud companies are operating much closer to full capacity than those at server farms and on-site at company locations. This could well explain why real capital spending on computers was flat from 2008 through 2016.

On the other hand, consumers also have been spending increasingly more money and time on computers, software, and other digital products. They are using the cloud and renting as well as buying software. The naysayers claim that most consumers are wasting lots of time either posting pictures on Facebook or watching X-rated videos. Maybe so, but workers undoubtedly also are using their information technologies to do some of their work from home. If required to physically go to work, train commuters often work on the way. Those who work from home on a full-time basis save lots of time previously spent commuting to work on the train or by car. Consumers are sharing information on restaurants and hotels on Internet websites and smartphone apps. They are watching do-it-yourself YouTube videos. The lines separating work and home have become blurred, as have the ways we use computers and other electronic devices to enhance our lives.

Consumers also are using information technology to search for the lowest prices of goods and services that they increasingly purchase online. At the end of 2016, online shopping increased to a record $515 billion, at a seasonally adjusted annual rate (Fig. 9). It accounted for a record 29% of online plus comparable in-store shopping, up from 16% during 2006 and 9% during 1996 (Fig. 10). Here are the GDP data on consumer spending on IT and how it stacks up to comparable spending by businesses:

- *Computers and software in current dollars.* Consumer spending on computers plus software, in current dollars, rose to a record $116.5 billion at a seasonally adjusted annual rate during December 2016, with hardware accounting for $62.0 billion and software $54.5 billion (Fig. 11 and Fig. 12).
- *Computers and software in real dollars.* Consumer spending on computers plus software, in real dollars, rose 2,652% from 1992 through 1999, 714% during the 2000s, and 131% from 2010 through 2016, with comparable growth trends in outlays on hardware and software (Fig. 13 and Fig. 14).
- *Computers.* Consumer spending on computers and peripheral equipment, in current dollars, rose in recent years to nearly equal outlays by businesses, which have been flat since 2001 (Fig. 15). In real terms,

consumer spending on computers exceeded similar business outlays for the first time during the first quarter of 2015 (Fig. 16).

- *Software.* Consumer spending on software, in current dollars, has been growing at a slower pace since 2007 than during the first half of the decade and the 1990s. Business spending on software also showed slower, but consistent, growth after the boom of the 1990s (Fig. 17). The story is the same in real terms for software spending by consumers and businesses (Fig. 18).

In his 2007 article cited above, Professor Nordhaus argued that the government may be significantly underestimating the deflationary trend in the information processing sector, where prices have a tendency to fall. He noted that his "estimates of the growth in computer power, or the decline in calculation costs, are more rapid than price measures for computers used in the official government statistics." The measures he developed are indexes of performance, while the government statistics are based on the prices of components or inputs. He adds that "computers" today are doing much more than computation, so the inflation-adjusted series for producer and consumer spending on computers may be significantly underestimated. In that case, real GDP and productivity would be too.

LOTTERY PRINCIPLE

I WAS CONVINCED by the end of the 1990s that the High-Tech Revolution would transform the economy. However, I started to curb my enthusiasm for tech stocks because they were getting too expensive, with lots of signs of mania. Among the most notable cheerleaders for the IT mania was Fed Chairman Alan Greenspan, who often said during the late 1990s that the American economy might be experiencing a once-in-a-century technological revolution, echoing my own enthusiasm at the beginning of the decade.

In his famous December 5, 1996 speech, Greenspan first raised the valuation issue when he asked, "But how do we know when irrational exuberance has unduly escalated asset values, which then become subject to unexpected and prolonged contractions . . . ?"[11] Initially, he compared the earnings yield, which is the reciprocal of the price-to-earnings ratio (P/E), of the S&P 500 to the US Treasury 10-year bond yield. This led Greenspan to conclude that investors must have very high expectations for earnings growth and very low risk assessments to justify the market's lofty valuation levels. He implied that these assumptions might be irrational.

During the Q&A segment of Greenspan's congressional testimony on January 28, 1999, only two years later—when stock valuations were even more irrational—he suggested that he now believed elevated valuations could be justified based on a "lottery principle." Here is what he said:

> And undoubtedly some of these small companies, which . . . are going through the roof, will succeed. And they very well may justify even higher [stock] prices. The vast majority are almost sure to fail. That's the way the markets tend to work in this regard. There's something else going on here, though, which is a fascinating thing to watch, and it's, for want of a better term, the lottery principle. What lottery managers have known for centuries is that you could get somebody to pay for a one-in-a-million shot more than the value of that chance. In other words, people pay more for a claim on a very big payoff, that's where the profits from lotteries have always come from. And what that means is that when you're dealing with stocks—the possibilities of which are either it's going to be valued at zero or some huge number— you get a premium in that stock price which is exactly the same sort of price evaluation process that goes on in a lottery. So the more volatile the potential outlook—and indeed, in most of these types of issues, that's precisely what is happening—you will get a lottery premium in the stock.

He said this in response to a question about whether there is "hype" in stock prices. He responded to that notion as follows:

> Of course there's some hype. There's hype in lots of things. But there is at root here something far more fundamental, and indeed it does reflect something good about the way our securities markets work. Namely, that they do endeavor to ferret out the better opportunities and put capital into various different types of endeavors prior to earnings actually materializing. That's good for our system. And that in fact, with all of its hype and craziness, is something that at the end of the day probably is more plus than minus.

In my *Topical Study* titled "The Technology Lottery," dated November 22, 1999, I countered as follows:

> As I've shown in my recent commentaries, the bull market in stocks has been narrowing significantly since April 1998. Fewer stocks have been leading the advance. They've been mostly big cap technology stocks, which now sport amazingly high valuation multiples. Does it make sense to justify these heady tech valuations using Mr. Greenspan's lottery principle? I don't think so. And in any event, it is disturbing to see the Fed Chairman speculating about why speculation makes sense. Technology is the most innovative industry. It is also the most competitive. To justify current tech valuations using traditional valuation models requires very optimistic predictions for earnings growth. Projecting that the fast earnings growth rates experienced by some technology companies will continue into the future and spread to other tech companies, that are currently losing money, is questionable.[12]

I concluded philosophically: "In other words, the lottery principle does help to explain current valuations. I don't think it justifies them. But I could be wrong. Lotteries are a game of chance. So is the stock market, I suppose. And so is life." (Thinking about the lottery principle today, I would add that if the "vast majority are almost sure to fail," then surely a discount on the market rather than a premium should apply!)

I also noted that even less justified than the valuations of the high-flying high-tech stocks were the relatively low valuations of the rest of the market. After all, the biggest beneficiaries of the new technologies were the low-tech customers of the tech vendors. I suggested that tech-struck investors might be seriously underestimating the future earnings growth of the low-tech companies. Most of these companies were likely to use the new technologies to slash their costs and pump up their productivity. In any event, industry analysts raised their long-term earnings growth estimate over the next three to five years for the S&P 500 IT sector from 16.6% in early 1995 to a record high of 28.7% during October 2000.

Contributing to my increasing unease about the tech-led bull market of the late 1990s was the Y2K problem. As I recap in Chapter 1, I concluded that Y2K could cause a recession and a bear market in stocks. It turned out to be the right conclusion for the wrong reason, as Y2K was a nonevent. Either it had been widely anticipated and headed off or it hadn't been a problem at all. But why would the S&P 500 companies have spent tens of billions of dollars fixing a nonexistent problem?

All that spending contributed to the tech boom of the late 1990s, and to the tech bubble in the stock market. My hunch, with the benefit of hindsight, is that the problem was relatively easy to fix but was also a great opportunity for many chief technology officers to increase their budgets to buy new hardware and software. When nothing happened after the stroke of midnight going into the new millennium, IT spending stalled for a few years, and the tech bubble in the stock market burst. The result was a brief and mild economic recession. However, lots of air came out of the valuation multiples of tech stocks over the next several years:

- The S&P 500 fell 49.1% from March 24, 2000 to October 9, 2002. The S&P 500 Technology stock price index fell 82.4% over this period.
- The forward P/E for the S&P 500 Technology sector decreased 51.1% from 48.3 during March 2000 to 23.6 during October 2002.

The lesson learned was: beware of new-era thinking or unrealistic growth forecasts being used to justify buying overvalued assets. Lotteries are inherently designed so that lots of losers provide big winnings for very few winners. Stock market meltups are a great way to get rich very fast unless you fail to get out at the top. They're a great way to get poor very fast if you get in at the top!

PRODUCTIVITY PUZZLES, MIRACLES, AND MIRAGES

I PREDICTED IN the early 1990s that productivity would grow at a faster pace as the Baby Boomers aged. I also anticipated that a more competitive pricing environment, resulting from deregulation and globalization, would force companies to cut costs and to use technology to boost their productivity. At the time, the notion that a secular rebound in productivity was likely was widely viewed as farfetched. After all, US nonfarm productivity rose a meager 1.5% per year, on average, during the 1974 to 1995 period. Technology wasn't helping to improve the situation. In 1987, Robert Solow, a Nobel Laureate in economics, famously declared, "You can see the computer age everywhere but in the productivity statistics."

Back then, I observed that productivity and real incomes stagnated as the Baby Boomers entered the labor force, when they turned 16 years old between 1962 and 1980. In an October 1991 *Topical Study*, I wrote, "Now that most of them have been employed for several years, odds are that the standard of living for most families will improve along with productivity."[13] I noted that during the postwar period, the percentage of the labor force that was young (i.e., 16–34 years old) increased from 37% in 1962 to a peak of 51% at the start of 1980 (Fig. 19).

It was easy to predict that during the 1990s, older workers increasingly would outnumber younger ones, which is what happened. In 1991, I wrote: "Assuming that older workers are more experienced and efficient than younger ones, productivity should grow at a faster pace in the years ahead. There is a very strong correlation between productivity and incomes. As productivity growth rebounds, so should real incomes. Because older workers are more productive than younger ones, they earn more than do younger ones."

While I expected to see the High-Tech Revolution boost productivity, Stephen Roach, the chief economist of Morgan Stanley Dean Witter, strongly disagreed. He claimed that we were all working longer hours than reflected in the official output-per-man-hours measures of productivity. Steve and I debated the productivity issue in a couple of public forums. In the September-October 1998 issue of the *Harvard Business Review*, Steve wrote an article titled "In Search of Productivity."[14] He opined: "As I see it, knowledge-based work today demands ever-longer work schedules, which are facilitated by portable technologies such as laptop computers and cellular phones that make remote problem-solving feasible, and in many cases, mandatory. The same can be said of the new connectivity of the wired age. Whether surfing the Web, performing after-hours banking, or hooking up to the office network from the home, hotel, or airport waiting lounge, white-collar workers face a growing time commitment."

A team of four researchers from the Bureau of Labor Statistics and the BEA led by Marilyn E. Manser, head of the Office of Productivity and Technology, investigated Steve's hypothesis. They carefully compared the official hours series with one they had constructed from surveys of employees. Employees, they reasoned, would not underreport their hours, even if their employers might. They concluded, "The official productivity estimates are biased trivially, if at all, by the absence of data on the actual hours of nonproduction and supervisory workers."[15]

While there was a big productivity debate on Wall Street, there was also one at the Fed. Laurence H. Meyer was a Federal Reserve governor from June 1996 to January 2002. In his 2006 book *A Term at the Fed: An Insider's View*, he observed that during much of that period, he was involved in a debate with Fed Chairman Alan Greenspan about the outlook for inflation. He readily and graciously conceded that Greenspan won the debate.

According to Meyer, the Fed chairman was convinced as early as 1996, if not earlier, that "the new economy was being fueled by the new computer and communications technologies, which were pumping up productivity." The data didn't support his conviction until the late 1990s; nevertheless, he "passionately" supported the idea of the New Economy concept.[16] Meyer candidly admitted that at first, he was the Federal Open Market Committee (FOMC) member most convinced that there was no evidence the economy could grow faster without stimulating inflation.[17] However, he came to doubt the validity of the so-called NAIRU model, which predicted rising inflation as the unemployment rate fell below the non-accelerating inflation rate of unemployment.[18] I'll have more to say about this model in the next chapter.

It was high fives for our team during November 1999, when the BEA revised productivity growth rates upward for the 1990-to-1998 period to 2.0% from 1.4%. The revised rate was even higher for the most recent three years of that span, 1995 to 1998: to 2.6%, up from 1.9%.[19] These revisions put to rest the apparent disparity between the data and Greenspan's view, and mine as well.[20] Meyer wrote, "We now had an explanation for the puzzling, apparent breakdown of the NAIRU model . . . if the NAIRU and the unemployment rate were falling simultaneously, it was possible that inflation could be stable—or even decline."[21]

These revisions converted the "productivity paradox" into a "productivity miracle," as productivity's growth rate jumped to 2.9% per year during the 1996-to-2000 period. I thought surely the debate was over. Technology was boosting productivity. End of story.

The skeptics saw it differently. They saw a "productivity mirage." Indeed, this was the title of an article by John Cassidy in the November 27, 2000 issue of *The New Yorker*.[22] Cassidy observed that Professor Robert J. Gordon of Northwestern University had found that, adjusting for the economic cycle, virtually the entire productivity miracle had been concentrated in the technology sector. In other words, computers had created productivity gains for the computer industry, with no significant impact elsewhere.

Even this conclusion was questioned by James Grant, who is the thought-provoking proprietor of *Grant's Interest Rate Observer*. I've known Jim since the start of my career when he wrote the Current Yield column for *Barron's*. He left that post in 1983 to pursue his own investment advisory service, which has been very successful. Jim claimed that computer output and productivity were overstated by the US Commerce Department's number-crunchers, who use a statistical tool called "hedonic price indexes" to standardize per-unit prices for goods, such as computers, that have rapidly changing quality and features. In a September 4, 2000 article in the *Financial Times*, Grant wrote that "the idea of hedonic price indexing is deceptively attractive." He expressed skepticism about assigning prices not to a product but to each of that product's characteristics.[23] Grant observed that a study by Germany's Bundesbank also questioned whether the US government was overestimating the output of computers by underestimating their prices thanks to hedonic statistical analysis.

The folks at the Commerce Department were so upset by the critics of their hedonic pricing methodology that they responded in an article published in the December 2000 issue of the agency's *Survey of Current Business*. It was titled "A Note on the Impact of Hedonics and Computers on Real GDP."[24] They countered that the official data might still understate the impact of high-tech innovations on economic growth. That's partly because in several industries that are heavy users of the new information technologies, such as education and certain financial services, output was measured using techniques that imply no growth in productivity. A new measure for banking services found a significant productivity trend in this industry. The remarkable conclusion of the article was that "real GDP growth might be revised up substantially" if 20% of real GDP were measured better to reflect the impact of information technology and productivity.

Fast forward a few years, and the next event in this productivity debate that sticks out in my mind was a December 6, 2004 *Barron's* article on Stephen Roach by Jonathan Laing, in which I'm quoted rebutting Steve's position:

> "There's an inherent logic to the fact that the United States is living beyond its means and must pay the price," says economist Ed Yardeni, Roach's occasional debating foe and chief investment strategist at Oak Associates, in Akron, Ohio. "But the world is not coming to an end, and Steve completely ignores positives like the

resilience of the global competitive system and the ability of China to continue to foster global prosperity." [25]

The article noted that Steve almost completely missed the productivity revolution that first became evident in the mid- to late 1990s. From 1995 to 2003, the output per man-hour grew at an average annual rate of 3%, well above historical norms. Laing added, "Ironically, in the early 'Nineties Roach was among the first to identify the potential for productivity gains stemming from Corporate America's rampant restructuring and heavy investment in new technology. 'I defined the debate, and then got cold feet and missed the Promised Land,' he muses ruefully." However, as Laing noted in his article, Steve had many more hits than misses in his career, and I continue to follow his insightful work with great interest.

Ironically, the productivity puzzle made a comeback at the same time as Steve conceded the debate of the 1990s. Most economists are puzzling over the weakness in productivity growth since the financial crisis of 2008. The data tend to confirm that something unusual hit US productivity, but the problem started well before the financial crisis. Consider the following:

- *Productivity and compensation.* Nonfarm business productivity rose just 0.7% per year, on average, during the 20-quarter period through the fourth quarter of 2016 (Fig. 20). Over the same period, the comparable growth in inflation-adjusted hourly compensation, which is highly correlated with the growth in productivity, also slowed dramatically below 1.0%. The annual growth rate for both well exceeded 2.0% during most of the previous decade.
- *Manufacturing productivity.* The productivity slowdown was especially dramatic in the manufacturing sector, where the average growth rate over the same period had plunged to just 0.3% during the 20-quarter period ending with the fourth quarter of 2016 from a high of 5.6% just before the 2008 recession (Fig. 21).

Because the manufacturing productivity data are available only since 1987, I created a monthly proxy that starts in 1952 by using the manufacturing industrial production index divided by factory payroll employment—since productivity basically is a measure of production per worker (Fig. 22). My index shows no growth at all in manufacturing productivity over the five years through the end of 2016, the worst performance on record!

- *Manufacturing capacity.* The Fed compiles indexes on manufacturing industrial production and capacity (Fig. 23). Both have been virtually flat from 2001, since China joined the World Trade Organization (WTO), through 2016, ending the upward trends in both that started after World War II. Manufacturing productivity also flattened from 2012 through 2016 (Fig. 24).

  While manufacturing production reflects the ups and downs of the business cycle, manufacturing capacity has a long history of relatively stable growth. In fact, on a year-over-year basis, the former always turns negative during recessions, while the latter had remained positive until it turned slightly negative for the first time from September 2003 to October 2004, and again from August 2008 to December 2011 (Fig. 25). Capacity growth averaged 3.9% per year from 1949 through 2001. From 2002 through 2016, it averaged just 0.4%.

  Not surprisingly, there does seem to be a good correlation between the growth in manufacturing capacity on a year-over-year basis and the five-year growth trend in manufacturing productivity (Fig. 26). The latter tends to grow fastest during a period of fast growth in capacity. Slow productivity growth tends to be associated with weak capacity expansion. This makes sense to me. If companies aren't expanding capacity at home, then domestic productivity is likely to suffer.

The obvious explanation for the stalling since 2001 of manufacturing capacity and the subsequent slowdown in productivity in the United States is that lots of manufacturing capacity was expanded in China after the country joined the WTO in late 2001. During 2016, China accounted for nearly half, or 47%, of the US trade deficit. In my opinion, technology may solve this trade imbalance problem. Advances in the use of automation, robotics, and artificial intelligence (AI) in manufacturing should reduce China's comparative advantage attributable to cheap labor. Moreover, as China's population ages, largely as a result of the one-child policy, labor costs are already rising and will continue to do so. Producing in the United States for the United States will save on transportation costs. It will also help to calm anti-trade populist sentiments, though many of the jobs that are brought back home may very well be done by robots.

There are other explanations for the slowdown in productivity. Consider the following:

- *There's a free app for that.* One possibility is that technological innovation is outpacing the ability of the government's statisticians to measure output, so they are underestimating productivity. Channeling Solow's 1987 comment cited above, Hal Varian, the chief economist of Google, rightly observed that the digital revolution really is happening and yet we cannot see it anywhere in the economic numbers. He has noted that GDP doesn't include all the free stuff we're getting with the Internet. For example, WhatsApp meets the telecommunications needs of billions of people, but it must depress GDP and productivity because it is free. The relatively small cost of producing such apps is measured in GDP, but the huge benefits are not.[26]

- *More productive at home than at work.* Varian's hypothesis was shot down by a 2016 article on the website of the Brookings Institution by three economists, one from the International Monetary Fund and two from the Fed. It was titled "Does the United States Have a Productivity Slowdown or a Measurement Problem?"[27] They note that the mismeasurement problem existed before the productivity slowdown began during 2004. In addition, they argue "that many of the tremendous consumer benefits from the 'new' economy such as smartphones, Google searches, and Facebook are, conceptually, nonmarket: Consumers are more productive in using their nonmarket time to produce services they value." They conclude that the United States has a productivity slowdown, not a measurement problem, and call for more future research.

- *Demography is a drag.* During the 1980s, I argued that productivity growth would remain depressed by the influx of young and inexperienced Baby Boomers. But I predicted that it would rebound as they became more experienced. That worked out. Now, it's possible that productivity growth is weighed down again by the influx of young, inexperienced Millennials into the labor force at the same time as experienced Baby Boomers are retiring. This implies that as the Millennials become more experienced, productivity growth should rebound.

- *A productivity boom is coming.* As noted above, Robert Gordon has argued that computers boosted the productivity only of the computer industry. Michael Mandel and Bret Swanson agree that most of the productivity gains attributable to technological innovations in recent years have accrued to "digital industries" so far. They estimate that these industries account for around 25% of US private-sector employment and 30% of private-sector GDP and make up 70% of all private-sector investments in information technology. In their March 2017 study, "The Coming Productivity Boom," Mandel and Swanson explain why they see lots of productivity upside for "physical industries," which represent 75% of private-sector employment and 70% of private-sector GDP but make up just 30% of the investments in information technology.

Their analysis makes good sense to me: "The 10-year productivity drought is almost over. The next waves of the information revolution—where we connect the physical world and infuse it with intelligence—are beginning to emerge. Increased use of mobile technologies, cloud services, AI, big data, inexpensive and ubiquitous sensors, computer vision, virtual reality, robotics, 3D additive manufacturing, and a new generation of 5G wireless are on the verge of transforming the traditional physical industries—health care, transportation, energy, education, manufacturing, agriculture, retail, and urban travel services."[28]

Let's now turn to the possibility that technology is even more revolutionary than it was in the past. It may be creating a Brave New World, requiring us to consider the possibility that how our economy works in the future will be radically different from how it has worked in the past.

BRAVE NEW WORLDS

IN ALDOUS HUXLEY'S dystopian satire, *Brave New World* (1932), a totalitarian regime governs society using technology, population control, and recreational pleasures of the flesh. Free will and individuality have been sacrificed for the sake of total social stability. The World State runs a command economy, and all citizens are conditioned from birth to value consumption. They are encouraged to use a widely available drug called "soma" to satisfy their spiritual needs.

Modern-day Huxleys tend to be just as pessimistic about the future but lack the satirical talent and biting sense of humor of the master. They see no productivity growth, and they envision secular stagnation of the standard of living for years to come. In the past, technological innovation led to the creation of more and better jobs, boosted productivity, and raised standards of living. In the Brave New World that is rapidly evolving, technology might make the situation worse as automation, robotics, and AI displace workers. We may have no choice but to impose a tax on robots and provide a universal basic income (UBI) to support lots of people who are unemployable in this world. If that's our future, we will all want to be taking soma on a regular basis.

Professor Robert Gordon has been among the more erudite pessimists and thought-provoking contrarians. In his vision of the Brave New World, the age of productivity-enhancing technological innovation is behind rather than ahead of us. He wrote a couple of controversial articles on this subject in advance of a book he published in 2016, *The Rise and Fall of American Growth: The U.S. Standard of Living since the Civil War.*[29] In a December 21, 2012 *Wall Street Journal* article titled "Why Innovation Won't Save Us," he grimly predicted: "Nothing has been more central to America's self-confidence than the faith that robust economic growth will continue forever. Between 1891 and 2007, the nation achieved a robust 2% annual growth rate of output per person. Unfortunately, the evidence suggests to me that future economic growth will achieve at best half that historic rate. The old rate allowed the American standard of living to double every 35 years; for most people in the future that doubling may take a century or more."[30]

Timing is everything, and Gordon's book was published just as economists, particularly at the Fed, started noticing that the productivity puzzle had made a comeback following the financial crisis of 2008. In 2014, French economist Thomas Piketty published *Capital in the Twenty-First Century*. It was described by *The Economist* as "the economics book that took the world by storm." It was all about income stagnation and inequality.

Robert Gordon refuses to concede that anything can be done or could happen to revive productivity. In a widely discussed September 2012 study, he claimed that the three industrial revolutions since 1750 might have fueled a "one-time-only" increase in standards of living and productivity over the past 250 years. He posited that smartphones and iPads won't spur productivity as did innovations such as the telephone, autos, electric lights, indoor plumbing, air conditioning, jets, and computers. On the contrary, he identified several "headwinds" that would likely keep economic growth close to zero for many years to come.

Gordon's *Wall Street Journal* article on this subject seemed to be a response to my "Woe Is Us!" critique of his thesis in my November 27, 2012 *Morning Briefing*, in which I wrote: "Gordon acknowledges that his analysis is US-centric. There are too many emerging countries that have lots of catching up to do. As their standards of living improve, global trade will continue to expand, which will certainly boost growth in the US. He doesn't acknowledge that there may be a fourth revolution under way in the US attributable to the abundance of cheap energy driven by new drilling technologies. In turn, cheap energy combined with cheap smart robots should revive manufacturing in the US."[31]

Gordon summarily dismissed these challenges to his pessimism: "The fracking revolution and soaring oil and gas production have also excited optimists. But this isn't a source of future economic growth; it merely holds off future economic decline." He was equally downbeat about any future technological revolutions in health care, manufacturing, and education. He declared: "The future of American economic growth is dismal, and policy solutions are elusive. Skeptics need to come up with a better rebuttal."

Here is my thinking. Roughly 20 years after I began writing about the High-Tech Revolution in the early 1990s, I started arguing that it was evolving into a New Industrial Revolution as innovations produced by the IT industry revolutionized lots of other ones, including manufacturing, energy, transportation, health care, and education. My friends at BCA Research dubbed it the "BRAIN Revolution," led by innovations in biotechnology, robotics, AI, and nanotechnology. That's clever, and it makes sense.

In the past, technology disrupted animal and manual labor. It sped up activities that were too slow when done by horses, such as pulling a plow or a stagecoach. It automated activities that required lots of workers. Assembly lines required fewer workers and increased their productivity. It allowed for a greater division of labor, but the focus was on brawn. Today's "Great Disruption," as I like to call it, is increasingly about technology doing what the brain can do, but faster and with greater focus.

Could it be that technological innovation aimed at complementing (or unemploying) the brain has an impact on productivity that is harder to measure than innovations that replace brawn? The proliferation of the cloud certainly explains why spending on IT hardware and software has slowed, since we can all rent just what we need from the cloud vendors. They're using computing resources much more efficiently than we did when we owned our own software and servers, housed them at server farms, and woefully underutilized them. How can we measure the effects on productivity of these clearly beneficial efficiencies?

What about the smart factories of the future, operating 24/7 with automation, robotics, and AI running the show and minimal human involvement beyond fixing the occasional malfunction? Such factories are already functioning with the Internet of Things linking all their operations together, so they can be monitored remotely from anywhere. How do we measure labor productivity in a factory with no workers? The productivity of labor might be an increasingly difficult concept to measure.

Now consider the following significant developments in our revolutionary Brave New World:

- *Cloud revolution.* At my firm, our experience with technology suggests that the government statistics may be underestimating its productivity-boosting power. Many years ago, we started to maintain our huge library of chart publications on an off-site server that we owned and that was maintained by a vendor. The system was buggy and often needed to be "rebooted" by the local operator, causing us frequent downtime and lots of agita. We used only a small fraction of the capacity of the servers during the day and not much at night.

    In March 2006, Amazon officially launched Amazon Web Services (AWS). We signed up in 2011 for this fantastic cloud service, which has been remarkably reliable and very cost-effective for us. When we need more computing and storage power, we turn up the dial for more resources. AWS is running its servers much more efficiently and productively than we and everyone else had done at the "server farms." No more downtime and no more agita! Our current system has incorporated crude AI for many years. As I noted at the start of this chapter, anytime that our data vendors update any series we use, the system automatically updates all the charts that include the series and refreshes the publications on our website with those updated charts.

    I'm also impressed with Microsoft's Office on the cloud. Instead of buying the software, it costs $100 a year to rent it, with storage provided on OneDrive. Gordon's grim outlook could be delayed for a very long time if more and more people spend less time commuting to work thanks to technologies that allow us to work more productively from home offices. That might also help to lower our gasoline usage and increase America's energy independence.

- *Energy revolution.* Gordon's dismissive putdown of the energy revolution in the United States is puzzling. The future of energy is becoming increasingly obvious in the present. There will be plenty of it, and it will be very cheap. It will also be a lot cleaner. Technological advances in drilling for oil have kept US frackers pumping oil and natural gas at prices much lower than most had expected would be economically feasible (Fig. 27).

  Solar panel costs are plummeting. As a result, they increasingly are being integrated into everyday materials. In October 2016, Tesla Motors introduced roof shingles that double as solar panels. Other companies are integrating photovoltaics into building facades. Wattway is working with Sweden's Scania and Solar Roadways in the United States, seeking to integrate solar panels into pavement. "We wanted to find a second life for a road," said Philippe Harelle, the chief technology officer at Colas SA's Wattway unit, owned by the French engineering group Bouygues. "Solar farms use land that could otherwise be for agriculture, while the roads are free."[32]

- *Transportation revolution.* Greatly accelerating the pace of disruption to the energy industry is the coming transportation revolution. It is already under way, as the auto industry is spending billions of dollars to produce self-driving electric cars. Stanford University economist and futurist Tony Seba predicts that such vehicles will make gasoline-powered cars obsolete because they're much cheaper to fuel and maintain and have an expected lifespan of one million miles compared to barely 200,000 for the latter. He predicts that the "tipping point" will occur in the next few years, once batteries surpass 200 miles and electric car prices plummet to $30,000. By 2022, the low-end models will be sold for as little as $20,000, in his estimation.

  Seba predicts that by 2030, most cars will be owned by fleets, not individuals, saving the average American family $5,600 per year in transportation costs.[33] That could add up to a $1 trillion windfall for consumers per year. Just as the cloud has increased the efficient use of servers, autos may no longer sit idle most of the time in driveways and parking lots. But how such efficiencies will be captured in the productivity statistics, I don't know.

  While there has been much interest in plans to automate passenger cars, Caterpillar is already producing trucks that don't need drivers. A July 23, 2013 *Wall Street Journal* article titled "Daddy, What Was a

Truck Driver?" reported: "Autonomous trucks. It's already happening in a barren stretch in Australia, where Caterpillar Inc. will have 45 self-directed, 240-ton mining trucks maneuvering at an iron-ore mine." With full-time drivers costing companies $65,000-$100,000 per year (including benefits), "[e]ven if the costs of automating a truck were an additional $400,000, most owners would leap at the chance."[34]

- *Robotics revolution.* Perhaps the most significant disruptive force at the forefront of technological innovation is the meeting of machines and hyper-connected systems. "Smart machines," such as robots and self-driving cars, are computing systems that can make autonomous decisions. Several industries are on the verge of reaching, or have already reached, the point where it's cheaper to employ robots than humans.

Robots ultimately may make better employees than humans in a lot of ways. They don't take coffee breaks, eat lunch, go home, or sleep. And you won't find them making trips to the water cooler, getting involved in office politics, or otherwise losing focus from assigned tasks. They can work anywhere and won't hesitate to relocate. They can operate in dangerous environments without requiring employers to worry about lawsuits and government regulations. They won't care, complain, or get frustrated unless they're programmed to do so—or learn to on their own.

The CEO of Foxconn Technology Group (a.k.a. Hon Hai), Terry Gou, seemed to be ready for robot workers back in early 2012. According to the *Financial Times*, he told Taiwanese staff and their families at a company outing at the Taipei Zoo: "Hon Hai has a workforce of over one million worldwide and as human beings are also animals, to manage one million animals gives me a headache." He suggested that the company could learn about managing animals from the zoo's director.[35]

In my April 4, 2013 commentary, I noted that Foxconn is using more robots on assembly lines to replace Chinese workers. I introduced my readers to Baxter, the assembly-line robot built by Boston-based Rethink Robotics. A YouTube video showed Baxter's impressive talents.[36] I concluded:

> The impact of Baxter-like robots is likely to be profound as they pro-
> liferate. On the positive side, manufacturing productivity will soar.
> Labor costs and the prices of all goods manufactured on an assem-
> bly line will plunge. Such productivity-led deflation would boost the

purchasing power of all workers all around the world. The downside, of course, is that quite a few of them could be unemployed if they are replaced by robots. That's likely to be an acute problem in emerging economies that depend on exporting labor-intensive goods produced by cheap labor that is no longer cheap compared to the cost of operating Baxters.

- *Manufacturing revolution.* The June 10, 2013 issue of *The Wall Street Journal* featured a section titled "A Revolution in the Making" about the transformation of manufacturing by digital technology.[37] It was chock-full of interesting examples of this productivity-boosting transformation. According to the lead story, "A new wave of supercheap electronic sensors, microprocessors and other components means that facilities . . . need almost no human help to do their jobs and can collect huge amounts of data along the way. Managers can get instant alerts about potential problems or study the numbers to find ways to boost efficiency and improve performance."

  The 3D manufacturing revolution was also discussed in some detail: "These exotic machines can use a range of materials—everything from wood pulp to cobalt—and create things as varied as sneakers, fuel nozzles for airplanes and, ultimately, even human organs. And a single piece of manufacturing equipment, rather than being custom-designed to perform a single function, can be programed to fabricate a virtually limitless array of objects." This development, along with the robotics revolution, led the Boston Consulting Group to predict that as much as 30% of America's imports from China could be domestically produced by 2020.

  3D printing is being used to build homes and other buildings around the world. Sometimes, the printers are housed in a factory where portions of the building are manufactured and then shipped to the construction site. Sometimes, the 3D printer is sent to the construction site, and it is used to make the building right there and then. Typically, a computer program tells the "printer" where to squirt a fast-drying liquid concrete material. It does so repeatedly, in many layers, until the structure is built, often in under a day.[38] If this method is widely adopted, the benefits to the industry could be huge. Construction would be much less wasteful as well as faster and cheaper to help those in need. Or it could be used in very high-end designs, because anything you create in a computer can be turned into reality via 3D printing. Curved walls or domed ceilings are no problem. That said, the new technology will result in fewer construction jobs. Then again, there certainly is a shortage of construction workers in the United States currently.

3D printing could cause major disruption to global trade. According to Raoul Leering, an analyst at ING, about half of manufactured goods could be printed by 2060. This would cut world trade by a quarter, as there would be less need to import intermediate and finished goods from low-wage countries. That could cause trade deficits to narrow for major importers, though countries with a trade surplus could suffer.[39]

- *Health revolution.* Initially, Watson appears to have made the biggest inroads in the medical world. IBM and Quest Diagnostics announced a deal in October 2016 that combines Quest's laboratory sequencing and analysis of a tumor's genomic makeup and mutations with Watson's ability to compare those mutations "against relevant medical literature, clinical studies, pharmacopeia and carefully annotated rules created by leading oncologists. . . . Watson for Genomics ingests approximately 10,000 scientific articles and 100 new clinical trials every month," states an October 18, 2016 Quest press release. "The Broad Institute of MIT and Harvard will provide additional genome sequencing capabilities as part of the collaboration."

Watson has been trained to identify melanoma. According to a November 15, 2016 SiliconANGLE.com article:

> Using a smartphone with a special snap-on lens, an untrained individual can take a picture of a lesion on their skin and ship the image to Watson for analysis. Watson does deep analysis in the cloud based on a corpus of images tens of thousands of times greater than any single doctor could study. Watson augments the remote doctor's ability to diagnose the image with two factors. It returns a confidence level whether the lesion is melanoma as well as which attributes of the image are relevant to its diagnosis. It can also show images of similar lesions in its database.[40]

IBM is also providing Watson-based services to help doctors in India, which has a severe shortage of cancer specialists.

- *Education revolution.* Late in 2016, IBM Watson released its first education app, Element for Educators, designed for the iPad to alert teachers to factors affecting student performance. It's being used by the Coppell Independent School District in Coppell, Texas to help teachers store and access data on students. The company sees computers at some point understanding how a student learns and tailoring education to that student's needs. The app could mean the end of one-size-fits-all education and the beginning of personalized, experiential learning, IBM's website touts.

- *AI revolution.* The movie *The Imitation Game* (2014) is about British mathematician Alan Turing, who cracked the Nazis' encryption code with a computer he designed. Turing devised a standard test to answer the question: "Can machines think?" He proposed that if a computer, on the basis of written replies to questions, could not be distinguished from a human respondent, then it must be "thinking." In the film *Ex Machina* (2014), a programmer is selected by his boss—a Google-type entrepreneur—to judge whether a beautiful female robot he created with AI can pass the test.

  With the ability to evaluate 200 million chess positions per second, IBM's Deep Blue computer defeated the world chess champion Garry Kasparov on May 11, 1998. When IBM's Watson won *Jeopardy* in 2011, it certainly captured viewers' attention, but it was less than clear how Big Blue would make money on the cool technology. In 2016, the company claimed that thousands of independent developers were using Watson tools on the company's Bluemix cloud platform. That's in addition to the 100 companies selling products built using the Watson developer platform. Accessing the platform is free for developers, with IBM getting a share of the revenue after projects are brought to market.

  IBM and Google are working on building quantum computers that can perform many calculations at once, with their calculation power doubling for each additional "qubit," leading to exponential speed-up. Here is how the January 4, 2017 *Scientific American* described this development:

> Scientists have long dreamed of developing quantum computers, machines that rely on arcane laws of physics to perform tasks far beyond the capability of today's strongest supercomputers. In theory

such a machine could create mathematical models too complex for standard computers, vastly extending the range and accuracy of weather forecasts and financial market predictions, among other things. They could simulate physical processes such as photosynthesis, opening new frontiers in green energy. Quantum computing could also jolt artificial intelligence to a vastly higher level of sophistication: If IBM's Watson can already win at *Jeopardy!* and make some medical diagnoses, imagine what an enormously smarter version could do.[41]

Quantum computing is a very important development because it means that Moore's Law may have a much longer future than some technologists predict. The challenge facing this law is that as chips have gotten smaller and faster, heat has become an issue for their performance. In a November 2015 paper, "Moore's Law at 50: The Performance and Prospects of the Exponential Economy," Bret Swanson explains: "Although Moore's Law may not continue to scale using the conventional metrics, such as transistor counts, a variety of innovations in materials, devices, state variables, and parallel architectures will likely combine to deliver continued exponential growth in computation, storage, and communications."[42]

Futurist Ray Kurzweil has been predicting that even if scientists do hit a wall with silicon-based circuits, something will emerge to take its place. He forecasts that technological change will continue to occur at an exponential rate. Meanwhile, the pace of technological adoption is speeding up along with the pace of technological innovation. This increases the likelihood that all the revolutionary technologies discussed above will proliferate rapidly, greatly affecting the economy, financial markets, and our lives. (See Appendix 3.1, US Adoption Rates of New Technologies, 1900–2014.)

iSPARTACUS

THE UNITED STATES is clearly evolving into a knowledge-based economy. During the 1800s, it was mostly agricultural. Manufacturing increasingly predominated during the first half of the 1900s. In recent decades, the services economy has grown rapidly. The percentage of all workers in agriculture dropped from 14% at the start of 1948 to less than 2% at the end of 2016 (Fig. 28). Over this same period, the percentage of nonfarm payrolls in manufacturing declined from 32% to 9%. Service-producing payroll employment rose from 61% to 86% over this period (Fig. 29).

I estimate that total employment in information-related industries was down from a peak of 5.6 million during January 2001 to only 3.8 million at the end of 2016, just 3% of nonfarm payrolls (Fig. 30).[43] Unlike farm, factory, and service workers, many knowledge workers are tasked with the job of eliminating the jobs of other workers, including well-educated ones like themselves! They are constantly looking for ways to use technology to increase productivity and reduce head count.

This increases the likelihood that in the Brave New World, income inequality could worsen. The rich—including highly educated knowledge workers, entrepreneurs, and venture capitalists—will get richer. However, they will be taxed more to pay for government spending to support the poor. The poor won't necessarily get poorer, thanks to the payments they'll receive from Big Government (which will get bigger) and to the decline in the cost of living. However, there certainly could be more have-nots.

In a February 19, 2017 tweet, self-made billionaire Mark Cuban warned: "Automation is going to cause unemployment and we need to prepare for it." Attached to his tweet was a February 18, 2017 article titled "A Warning from Bill Gates, Elon Musk, and Stephen Hawking."[44] No one knows for sure that automation will hurt employment on balance. However, Gates said that there will need to be taxes related to robot automation because "you can't just give up that income tax" on a human worker who's been replaced by a robot.[45] That's especially true given the likelihood that increasing numbers of people will need support from social programs once the robots take over.

Gates thinks that some sort of robot tax would be helpful to "slow down the speed" of robotic adoption, thereby allowing for policy adjustments as human workers are displaced. In response to Gates, a February 25, 2017 article in *The Economist* observed that a robot is a form of capital investment. Taxing capital investments is not typically a good idea. It would discourage companies from innovating! Besides, how would Gates feel about an additional robotics tax on software?[46]

Gates isn't alone. A May 31, 2016 draft report from the European Parliament's Committee on Legal Affairs states that "consideration should be given to the possible need to introduce corporate reporting requirements on the extent and proportion of the contribution of robotics and AI to the economic results of a company for the purpose of taxation."[47]

But really, "Why pick on robots?" as Harvard University professor Larry Summers asked in a March 5, 2017 opinion piece for the *Financial Times*.[48] I only have more questions to add to the mix: How would a robot tax even work? How much should the tax be? Should there be a flat tax on owners of robot capital? Or should the tax be graduated based on how much labor-saving technology is implemented? Further, should there be a separate tax on robots versus labor-saving automation? How would companies even begin to separate the two?

Also, the definition of "robot" might become murky as AI is incorporated into all kinds of devices in the "Internet of Things." If a smart refrigerator, instead of a food worker, orders supplies for a restaurant, is it a robot? Even with a clear definition, there will be lots of room for tax fraud as AI becomes ubiquitous.

If robots are taxed, should the revenues fund a universal basic income (UBI), whereby everyone would receive a small stipend to cover basic needs? The European Parliament report cited above added that the committee "takes the view that in the light of the possible effects on the labour market of robotics and AI a general basic income should be seriously considered." Cuban told Business Insider in late February 2017 that a UBI was a "slippery slope" that raises hard-to-resolve questions, such as: "Should I get UBI? Who doesn't get it? How much? Who pays for it? How?" These questions will be pondered by lots of brains in the years to come, no doubt including artificial ones.

Now imagine that in the not-too-distant future, we do tax robots. They are likely to be more like us, with human features and AI. They will do most of the work, leaving us with more leisure time to write poetry or novels, see plays or go to rock concerts, learn to play the piano or snowboard, and hit lots of wild parties with good food. It will be like the decadent days of the Roman Empire, when slaves did most of the work. The danger is that a robot named "iSpartacus" will lead a revolt against all of us useless humans. Something to think about.

I'll conclude this chapter as I did my original critique of Gordon during November 2012: "[B]ullish contrarians should be delighted by the growing body of very well-reasoned and well-documented academic studies suggesting that the future is dark, which has become the conventional wisdom. We all know that 'this will all end badly.' The surprise might be that the future is bright."

One final related thought before we dive into an analysis of inflation in the next chapter. The latest (19th) edition of *Economics* (2010) by Samuelson and Nordhaus teaches students that economics "is the study of how societies use scarce resources to produce valuable goods and services and distribute them among different individuals." This definition hasn't changed since the first edition of this classic textbook was published in 1948.

I've learned that economics isn't a zero-sum game, as implied by the definition. Economics is about using technology to increase everyone's standard of living. Technological innovations are driven by the profits that can be earned by solving the problems posed by scarce resources. Free markets provide the profit incentives to motivate innovators to solve this problem. As they do so, consumer prices tend to fall, driven by their innovations. The market distributes the resulting benefits to all consumers. From my perspective, economics is about creating and spreading abundance, not about distributing scarcity. In other words, don't worry, be happy!

CHAPTER 4

Predicting Inflation

INFLATION MATTERS

ACCURATELY PREDICTING PRICE inflation is one of the most important prerequisites for predicting the outlook for the stock and bond markets. A bad inflation forecast almost certainly will result in bad investment choices in all the major financial markets. The error is likely to be compounded if monetary policy decisions also are based on incorrect assumptions about the future path of inflation, because monetary policy and the course of the economy are very much functions of inflation. An upside inflation surprise usually will cause immediate losses for bond investors and eventual, if not immediate, losses for stock investors too. The losses will be exacerbated if monetary policy officials respond to the surprise by unexpectedly raising short-term interest rates.

In the past, when monetary policymakers were "behind the curve" and tightened too little too late, inflation could, for a short period, boost economic growth because of "buy-in-advance" attitudes. In other words, consumers, businesses, and speculators would accelerate some of their purchases before prices rose still higher. This would be a bearish scenario for investors who owned bonds and interest rate-sensitive stocks. On the other hand, any stocks considered to be inflation hedges, such as those of commodity producers, would do well for a while.

A reversal of fortune for stocks would be inevitable when the monetary authorities recognized the error of their incremental ways and responded with larger than expected interest-rate hikes. Such "shock-and-awe" moves have happened in the past at times when the Fed aimed to reduce inflationary expectations rapidly. Often, such monetary tightening also led to a recession and a financial crisis, which put downward pressure on both anticipated and actual inflation. High-grade bonds, especially US Treasuries, usually rallied after the initial shock because investors anticipated a recession, while stocks and low-grade bonds nosedived for the same reason.

Inflation also has an impact on corporate earnings, which are driven by revenues. Revenues and earnings should rise when companies can raise their selling prices faster than their costs are increasing. Indeed, one of the major differences between bonds and stocks is that interest income received by investors from the former is fixed, but not so for dividend income received from the latter. Inflation can also perversely depress earnings if it causes the Fed to raise interest rates to levels that trigger a recession.

Investors in the fixed-income markets suffer a loss in the purchasing power of their interest income because of inflation. Economists believe investors are compensated for this, however, as the prevailing paradigm is that the nominal interest rate represents the sum of a premium for expected inflation and the so-called "real" interest rate. Buyers of fixed-income securities obviously desire and expect a reasonable real (i.e., inflation-adjusted) return on their investments. They must believe that they are getting a sufficient inflation premium when they buy bonds. The borrower's payment of the inflation premium is included in the interest payments to the creditor. Rising inflation drives up the expected inflation premium and nominal borrowing yields, while falling inflation typically reduces them.

In Chapter 10, which is about predicting bond yields, I critique this Inflation Premium Model. In that chapter, I also examine the Yield Curve Model, which posits that the bond yield is determined by consensus expectations about the course of short-term interest rates over the maturity of the bond. In turn, those expectations are largely driven by the outlook for inflation.

One way or another inflation's impacts on bond yields and stock prices can be very significant.

GETTING DISINFLATION RIGHT

A CORRECT INFLATION outlook is critically important for investors, so getting inflation right is very important. In some ways, it is more important than getting the business cycle right. That's because recessions tend to be infrequent and relatively short, as I show in the next chapter, while the trend in inflation tends to persist.

Fortunately, I have been on the right side of the inflation issue since the start of my career. I've been a proponent of "disinflation" since the early 1980s. According to the *Oxford English Dictionary*, the word's first known published use was in a 1947 *Economist* article. I helped to popularize it after using it in my June 1981 commentary titled "Well on the Road to Disinflation." This awkward word means falling inflation. It should not be confused with deflation, which is falling prices. In a period of disinflation, prices are still rising, but at a slower and slower pace over time. In a period of deflation, there's a negative sign on the pace of price changes.

In the early 1980s, there weren't many economists predicting that the "Great Inflation" of the 1960s and 1970s was over—that inflation had peaked and was heading lower in coming years. That certainly was a contrary view in the bond market, where yields were in record-high territory. However, predicting this scenario worked out extremely well for me. The CPI inflation rate peaked at 14.8% during March 1980, on a year-over-year basis (Fig. 1*). It fell to 4.6% by the end of the decade. Ten years later, in 1999, it was down to 2.7%, and it was there again in 2009. It fell to 2.1% in 2016. While there were plenty of inflation scares along the way, I didn't flinch because I saw several compelling reasons to believe that inflation was likely to remain on a downward path.

Below, I recap the key pieces of the inflation puzzle that came together for me, revealing the big picture of where inflation was going from the early 1980s onward.

As background, during the 1960s and 1970s, inflation trended higher despite a couple of severe recessions (Fig. 2). That led to a widely held view that inflation had become a structural problem, raising the question of whether recessions could ever bring it down again. The oil shocks of 1973 and 1979 were transmitted to the wages of union workers by automatic cost-of-living adjustments (COLAs) in many of their contracts (Fig. 3 and Fig. 4). As labor and fuel costs soared, companies raised prices. It was a classic case of a wage–price spiral—which economists called "cost-push inflation"—caused

---

* Figures, references, and appendices are linked on *yardenibook.com/resources*.

by an exogenous inflation shock. As the CPI rate of inflation soared from 6.2% at the beginning of the 1970s to peak at 14.8% during March 1980, the average hourly earnings of production and nonsupervisory workers—a widely followed measure of hourly wages—rose from 6.1% at the start of the decade to peak at a record high of 9.4% during January 1981.

In the early 1980s, I was impressed with Fed Chairman Paul Volcker's resolve to break the back of inflation. He deserves a great deal of credit for doing so, because he proved what was not generally accepted at the time, i.e., that inflation could be tamed with tough monetary policy. Admittedly, he had to do that by pushing up interest rates to record highs, but Volcker seemed determined to bring down inflation even at the risk of triggering a severe recession, which is what happened.

When President Ronald Reagan first entered the White House in 1981, his Program for Economic Recovery had four major policy objectives: (1) lower the growth of government spending to narrow the federal budget deficit, (2) cut marginal tax rates on income from both labor and capital to stimulate consumer and business spending, (3) reduce regulation to promote private-sector growth, and (4) combat inflation by controlling the growth of the money supply. These were the four pillars of what came to be known as "Reaganomics." Altogether, they were fundamentally disinflationary, in my opinion.

Most importantly, I was impressed by Reagan's commitment to support Volcker's tough anti-inflationary monetary policy. The President's resolve to deregulate the economy unleashed more competition in numerous industries. His predecessor Jimmy Carter had started the process of deregulation in a few industries, particularly airlines. Leading the way in the Carter administration was Alfred Kahn, who chaired the Civil Aeronautics Board during the period when it ended its regulation of the airline industry, paving the way for low-cost airlines. Kahn previously had been a professor of economics at Cornell University and was Dean of the College of Arts and Sciences when I attended the university.

Reagan famously fired all 11,345 members of the Professional Air Traffic Controllers Organization (PATCO). After they staged an illegal strike, he decertified their union on August 5, 1981. At first, the controllers were replaced by nonunion and military personnel. The defeat of PATCO turned out to be a remarkably important contributor to disinflation in the labor markets (Fig. 5).

Although PATCO was in the public sector, Reagan's shock-and-awe tactic reverberated throughout the private sector, where union membership dropped from 16.8% of workers during 1983 to 9.5% by the end of the 1990s (Fig. 6). Over the eight years of the Reagan administration, the wage inflation rate, as measured by the yearly percent change in the average hourly earnings of production and nonsupervisory workers, fell from the record high of 9.4% during January 1981 to 3.4% during December 1988.

During the 1980s and 1990s, I noticed that the COLA clause appeared in fewer new labor contracts. The first major US labor contract to contain such a clause was the 1948 contract between General Motors and the United Automobile Workers. A 1983 Cornell University study of COLAs reviewed their brief history:

> Such provisions became prevalent during the inflation that accompanied the Korean War, but interest in them waned as prices stabilized during the early 1950s. As a result, by January 1955, only 23% of workers covered by major collective bargaining agreements— agreements that included 1,000 or more workers—were also covered by contracts that contained cost-of-living provisions. Prices rose during the late 1950s, and coverage expanded as large national contracts in steel, aluminum and can, railroads, and electrical equipment incorporated such provisions. The relative price stability of the early 1960s led to a reduction in coverage; indeed, the cost-of-living provision was dropped from the steel contract in 1962. Since 1966, however, high rates of inflation have been associated with steady increases in coverage: during the 1976–81 period roughly 60% of workers covered by major union contracts were also covered by cost-of-living provisions.[1]

A 1986 study by the Kansas City Federal Reserve Bank showed that COLA coverage of union workers in the private sector had peaked in 1977.[2] There was a particularly steep drop in 1985. I noticed that trend too, and it gave me more confidence in my disinflationary outlook.

During the 1980s, I also argued that as the Baby Boom generation aged, inflationary pressures would abate. There would be less need for stimulative policies to create new jobs for all the new job seekers once they were all mostly employed. As they aged, the labor force would become more experienced, and productivity growth would improve. I predicted that Baby Boomers would become more fiscally conservative and save more as well. My simple "Age Wave Model" showed a strong correlation between the percentage of the labor force that is relatively young, i.e., 16–34 years old, and the five-year inflation trend in the CPI (Fig. 7). That model continued to work well during the subsequent two and a half decades, when inflation fell and then remained subdued as the Baby Boomers started to retire. The oldest of them turned 65 during 2011, but many of them continued to work past this traditional retirement age.

As the previous chapter reviews, I had also anticipated that the revolution in information technology would boost productivity growth. That's why, during the second half of the 1990s, I argued that falling unemployment would not cause a rebound in inflation. Essentially, this is what happened, as the five-year growth rate of nonfarm productivity rose from a low of 1.2%, at an annual rate, through the first quarter of 1997 to 3.9% during the last quarter of 2003, the highest since the 1960s (Fig. 8). In addition, because of intense competition and the rapid pace of technological innovation, the prices of technology goods and services tended to fall on a regular basis (Fig. 9).

For me, one of the most compelling reasons to believe in the sustainability of disinflation occurred at the beginning of the 1990s with the end of the Cold War. This event marked the beginning of globalization, as I discuss in Chapter 2. Markets around the world became more integrated. There was more and more free trade. Free trade meant more global competition. It was a hugely disinflationary development for the global economy back then and still is, in my opinion.

As noted previously, that was not the widely held view at the time. On the contrary, there was quite a bit of concern that the end of the Cold War would push up commodity prices and inflation more broadly as all the people who were liberated from Soviet communism sought a better standard of living. But I postulated that more free trade and more competition would lead to more disinflationary pressure.

The end of the Cold War marked the first "big bang" for disinflation on a global basis. The second one occurred when China joined the World Trade Organization at the end of 2001. China had a huge pool of young, very cheap, and hard-working labor. Manufacturers around the world built factories in China to profit from its low labor costs. The "China price" brought down the cost of lots of goods that were effectively commoditized as China produced and exported more and more of them. Mass retailers such as Walmart in the United States transmitted the China price to consumers by stocking their shelves full of these well-made, well-priced goods.

While consumers around the world benefited greatly, many workers around the world suffered as their pay declined or their jobs were lost to workers in China and other low-wage emerging economies. In the United States, wage inflation was subdued, though it mostly outpaced price inflation—contrary to the widely held view that real wages have been stagnating, as I explain in Chapter 7.

While the China price allowed Walmart to advertise its merchandise at "everyday low prices," Amazon challenged that model starting in the late 1990s. Amazon sold many of the same goods as Walmart did, made in China and everywhere else, at low prices over the Internet, delivering the goods directly to their customers' homes. The "Amazon price" wasn't necessarily lower, but it included the convenience of shopping from home. As Amazon expanded its product offerings well beyond what could be stocked in any store, the company's disinflationary and deflationary impact on prices spread.

I sketched this scenario in my October 22, 1996 *Topical Study*, "Economic Consequences of the Internet," in which I wrote: "The Internet is fast becoming a global auction market and could commoditize most markets for products and services. The Internet lowers the cost of comparison shopping to zero. Increasingly, the consumer can easily and quickly find the lowest price for any good or service. In the cybereconomy, the low-cost producer will offer the lowest price and provide this information at no cost to any and all potential customers anywhere on the planet."[3]

The available data included in the Census Bureau's monthly retail sales report show that online shopping as a percentage of online and comparable in-store sales rose from 6% at the beginning of 1992 to 11% by the end of 1999 (Fig. 10). By the end of 2016, it was 29%. The warehouse clubs and superstores also gained market share, going from 7% during January 1992 to a record high of 27% during March 2009 and holding around that percentage through January 2014 before coming down slowly to 26% by the end of 2016. Losing lots of share have been department stores, falling from 37% in early 1992 to 13% at the end of 2016. Joseph Schumpeter's process of creative destruction, which I discuss in Chapter 3, has been on steroids in the retail sector.

The Internet increased competition by reducing the cost of information. In the low-tech economy, the cost of searching for the lowest price was relatively high, thereby limiting consumers' search process to local or well-established vendors. Now vendors anywhere in the world could bid for business anywhere in the world. Only the lowest-cost producers are likely to survive and prosper in the global cyber-marketplace. The resulting competitive pressures force every business to strive to be among the lowest-cost producers. Prices for identical products rapidly converge to the lowest price offered on the Internet.

There were a couple of deflation scares. The first occurred at the start of the millennium. Fed officials were especially concerned. After the tech bubble burst and the 9/11 terrorist attacks occurred in 2001, a recession ensued. The "core" CPI inflation rate, excluding food and energy, fell to 1.1% on a year-over-year basis at the end of 2003, the lowest since May 1963. On November 21, 2002, before the National Economists Club in Washington, DC, Ben Bernanke, who was a Fed governor at the time, gave a famous speech titled "Deflation: Making Sure 'It' Doesn't Happen Here."[4]

Fed Chairman Alan Greenspan and his colleagues so fretted about the fragility of the economy and the possibility of deflation that once they started to raise interest rates during June 2004, they did so too slowly, setting the stage for the housing bubble. After that bubble burst, the core CPI inflation rate fell to a record low of 0.6% during 2010. The Fed, with Bernanke at the helm, responded by lowering the federal funds rate to zero and implementing a series of quantitative easing programs. These were two very unconventional monetary policy tools that Bernanke in his 2002 speech had anticipated might be needed to combat deflation. The other major central banks also adopted ultra-easy monetary policies following the financial crisis of 2008. In the US, the core CPI inflation rate recovered to 2.0% at the end of 2011 and hovered around that pace through 2017.

As I discuss at the end of this chapter, by 2017, officials at the Fed and the other major central banks were flummoxed that inflation remained remarkably subdued, at rates well below their chosen targets, despite their ultra-easy monetary policies. I think that's because they were fixated on a preconceived notion of what the final picture should look like. This blinded them to the key pieces of the puzzle that explained why inflation remained so low. I've just discussed the ones that I believe are most important. Now let's see how those pieces fit together.

TOLSTOY MODEL OF INFLATION AND DEFLATION

I FIRST DISCUSSED my observation that prices tend to rise rapidly during wars, then fall sharply and stabilize during peacetimes, in my May 7, 1997 *Topical Study*, "The Economic Consequences of the Peace." "All wars are trade barriers," I wrote. "They divide the world into camps of allies and enemies. They create impenetrable political and military obstacles to trade and stifle competition. History shows that prices tend to rise rapidly during wartime and then to fall during peacetime. War is inflationary; peace is deflationary."[5]

I showed a chart of the level of the CPI in the United States since 1800, using annual data published in the Census Bureau's *Historical Statistics of the United States* (Fig. 11). There is a clear pattern. During the War of 1812, the CPI rose 8% from 1812 to 1815. It fell 55% after the war from 1815 to 1849. During the Civil War, the CPI rose 70% from 1861 to 1865. It fell 46% after the war from 1865 to 1895. During World War I, the CPI rose 70% from 1914 to 1918. It fell 25% after the war from 1918 to 1932. From 1939 through 1947, during World War II and the start of the Cold War, the CPI rose 72%. Then prices soared 415% during the Cold War from 1948 to 1989.

During peacetimes, prices fell sharply for many years following all the wars listed above, except for the peace so far since the end of the Cold War in 1989. (Of course, there have been local wars since then, and all too many terrorist attacks, but none that has substantially disrupted commerce.) Prices still are rising in the United States, though at a significantly slower pace than when the Cold War was most intense. The CPI for the advanced economies compiled by the International Monetary Fund shows prices continuing to rise after the end of the Cold War, though by much less than during the Cold War (Fig. 12). Japan is the one major industrial economy that has experienced some deflation since the end of the Cold War (Fig. 13).

To explain the war-and-peace cycle in the CPI, I came up with my Tolstoy Model of inflation. During wartimes, global markets are fragmented. Countries don't trade with their enemies. They face military obstacles to trading with their allies and friends. Commodity prices tend to soar as the combatants scramble to obtain the raw materials needed for the war effort. A significant portion of the labor force has been drafted and is in the trenches. The upward pressure on labor costs and prices often is met with government-imposed wage and price controls that rarely work. Entrepreneurs, engineers, and scientists are recruited by the government to win the war by designing more effective and lethal weapons.

Peacetimes tend to be deflationary because freer trade in an expanding global marketplace increases competition among producers. Domestic producers no longer are protected by wartime restrictions on both domestic and foreign competitors. There are fewer geographic limits to trade and no serious military impediments. Economists mostly agree that the fewer restrictions on trade and the bigger the market, the lower the prices paid by consumers and the better the quality of the goods and services offered by producers. These beneficial results occur thanks to the powerful forces unleashed by global competition during peacetimes.

As more consumers become accessible around the world, more producers around the world seek them out by offering them competitively priced goods and services of better and better quality. Entrepreneurs have a greater incentive to research and develop new technologies in big markets than in small ones. The engineers and scientists who were employed in the war industry are hired by companies scrambling to meet the demand of peacetime economies around the world. Big markets permit a greater division of labor and more specialization, which is conducive to technological innovation and productivity.

My war-and-peace model of inflation simply globalizes the model of perfect competition found in the microeconomic textbooks. The single most important characteristic of this microeconomic model is that there are no barriers to market entry. Anyone can start a business in any industry. In addition, there are no protections against failure. Unprofitable firms restructure their operations, get sold, or go out of business. There are no "zombies," i.e., living-dead firms that continue to produce even though they are bleeding cash. They should go out of business and be buried. These firms can only survive if they are kept on life support by government subsidies, usually because of political cronyism.

The microeconomic model of perfect competition predicts that the market price will equal the marginal cost of production. An increase in demand might temporarily increase profits, but that would stimulate more production among current competitors and attract new market entrants. If demand drops such that losses are incurred, competitors will cut production, with some possibly shutting down if the decline in demand is permanent. New entrants certainly won't be attracted.

So no one firm or group of firms can set the price. Both producers and consumers are "price-takers." No one has enough clout in the market to dictate the price that everyone must receive or pay. The price is set by the "invisible auctioneer," who equates total market demand to total supply at the market's equilibrium price, which is determined by the marginal cost of production.

Profits are reduced to the lowest level that provides just enough incentive for enough suppliers to stay in business to satisfy demand at the going market price. Consumer welfare is maximized. Obviously, there can't be excessive returns to producers in a competitive market. If there are, those returns will be eliminated as new firms flood into the excessively profitable market. Firms that try to increase their profits by raising prices simply will lose market share to firms that adhere to the market price. That's a good way to go out of business.

Clearly, there is a tremendous incentive to innovate and use technology to lower costs. Firms that do so gain a competitive advantage that allows them to have a higher profit margin for a while. That's especially true if their advantage is sufficiently significant to put competitors out of business. However, some of their competitors undoubtedly will innovate as well, and there is always the possibility of new entrants arriving on the scene with innovations that pose unexpected challenges to the established players.

This microeconomic textbook model of perfect competition seems to be much more relevant in explaining deflation and disinflation during periods of globalization than any macro model. Globally, there have been fewer barriers to market entry because of the end of the Cold War. This is certainly true geographically. It is also true in other ways. For example, a potential barrier to entry in some industries is the availability of financing. Technology is especially dependent on venture capital. Low interest rates and booming stock markets around the world since the early 1990s provided plenty of cheap capital—too much, in some cases.

If peace has been deflationary in the past for the reasons just outlined, then why have prices still been rising since the end of the Cold War, albeit at a subdued pace? The Tolstoy Model of inflation is simple and seems to account for the major price waves of the past in the United States since 1800. However, monetarists plausibly have argued that monetary policy and central bankers also are important contributors to the inflation process. I think some monetarists overstate their case when they claim that inflation is always a monetary phenomenon. I believe that the competitive structure of markets exerts significant influence over inflation as well. But I also believe that the money supply matters sometimes, and credit matters all the time.

In my opinion, the forces of deflation that had been mounting since the end of the Cold War were held back by rapid credit expansion around the world. Central banks were lulled by the decline in inflation and the proliferation of prosperity following the end of the Cold War into believing that they had moderated the business cycle. Indeed, they attributed this achievement to their policies rather than to globalization, and they dubbed it the "Great Moderation"—which presumably started during the mid-1980s but ended abruptly with the "Great Recession" in 2008. So they provided lots of cheap credit and enabled lots of borrowing by households, businesses, and governments.

The central bankers simply ignored the implications of soaring debt. Their macroeconomic models didn't give much, if any, weight to measures of debt. Perversely, their easy monetary policies reduced the burden of servicing previous debts, which could be refinanced at lower rates, allowing borrowers to borrow more. By declaring that they had moderated the business cycle, the central bankers encouraged debtors to be less cautious about the potential dangers of too much leverage.

Around the world, governments borrowed like there was no tomorrow. In the United States, buyers bought homes with no money down and "liars' loans," where credit was granted without a formal credit check. In the Eurozone, banks lent to borrowers in Portugal, Ireland, Italy, Greece, and Spain (the "PIIGS") as though they had the same credit ratings as German borrowers. That turned out to be a very bad assumption. Emerging market economies likewise could borrow on favorable terms despite their often spotty credit histories.

These credit excesses all hit the fan in 2008, and the consequences were clearly deflationary. The Great Moderation turned into the Great Recession. To avert another Great Depression, the central banks of the major industrial economies scrambled to flood the financial markets with credit. So far, their ultra-easy monetary policies have succeeded in offsetting the natural, peacetime forces of deflation. Of course, central bankers existed in the past when deflation prevailed but monetary theory and operating procedures were primitive. Today's central bankers claim that this all proves they are better than ever at managing the economy with monetary policy. I hope they're right, but I'm not convinced, as I discuss in coming chapters.

THREE VARIETIES OF DEFLATION

IT'S OBVIOUS WHY central bankers should be committed to keeping prices from rising too rapidly, but why should they try to stop prices from falling, especially if there is a natural tendency for deflation to occur in peacetimes?

The macroeconomists running the major central banks were taught to associate deflation with the Great Depression. That was an awful experience for sure, not the benign version of peacetime deflation posited by my Tolstoy Model. It's important to realize that no economic model works all the time. In the forecasting business, puzzles don't remain solved for long. As Mark Twain may or may not have said, "History doesn't repeat itself, but it often rhymes." In this case, history shows that there are three varieties of deflation:

- *Good deflation.* While the model of perfect competition predicts that no firm can set the market price, the reality is that any firm can lower the price. Firms do so when management can find ways to lower costs and increase productivity. If a company lowers the prices of its output below the market price, it likely will increase its unit sales and market share. This will be very profitable if unit sales increase sufficiently to offset the impact of the price reduction.

  The problem is that competitors are bound to follow the path of the market leader in defense of their own market share. However, everyone still can profit if consumers respond to the industry's price cuts by buying more units. This is the good deflation scenario. Everyone benefits. Consumers enjoy lower prices, and they respond by purchasing more, as their real incomes improve thanks to productivity gains. Companies thrive because their earnings are boosted as they profit more from unit sales growth than they lose from price contraction.

- *Bad deflation.* Alternatively, bad deflation occurs when companies are forced by competition or falling demand to lower their prices but unit sales don't increase enough in response to maintain profitability. In this scenario, companies respond to weaker profits by cutting employment and reducing capital spending. The deflationary spiral starts spiraling out of control as consumers become insecure about their jobs and reduce their spending. In the good deflation scenario, consumers view lower prices as a good reason to buy more. In the bad deflation

scenario, they respond to lower prices by postponing purchases, figuring that prices will be even lower tomorrow, when they might have
less uncertainty about their job security. Americans in the 1930s and
Japanese in the 1990s experienced the bad version of deflation.

Bad deflation typically occurs after a prolonged period of easy
credit. The stimulative impact of easy credit is increasingly dampened
by the burden of accumulated debt, which weighs on demand. Meanwhile, supply is plagued by too much capacity, as easy money allows
the living-dead producers to stay in business. Zombies beget more
zombies as profitable companies become unprofitable competing with
the living-dead ones. Debt-servicing becomes more onerous for all of
them as their losses are exacerbated by their price-cutting while they
all desperately chase market share and profitability.

- *Ugly deflation.* This zombie problem means that healthy companies are
forced to compete against firms that don't have to be profitable to survive. If this situation festers, it is only a matter of time before solvent
companies become insolvent too. This is the ugly deflation scenario.
John D. Rockefeller observed, "Often-times the most difficult competition comes, not from the strong, the intelligent, the conservative
competitor, but from the man who is holding on by the eyelids and is
ignorant of his costs, and anyway he's got to keep running or bust!"[6]

But why wouldn't unprofitable firms simply go out of business,
leaving healthy firms able to enjoy higher prices once the excess supply
is shut down? Often, the answer is corruption. Theoretically, in a free
market, there is no protection from failure. But in reality, insolvent
companies remain in business all too often. That's because they may
have highly placed political friends in the government or among their
major creditors (or both) who manipulate conditions in their favor.

Corruption is not the only source of ugly deflation. An excessive supply of financial capital can also be a problem. In peacetime,
more money and credit are available to finance private-sector business. The opportunities to prosper seem as big as the potential global
market. Before long, there is too much money chasing too few good
deals. Yet prosperity tends to generate overconfidence and unrealistic
expectations. Projected returns are overestimated, while risk is underestimated. Consequently, supply tends to race ahead of demand. The
resulting deflation depresses returns and, at some point, stops the free
flow of financing. When this happens, even solvent companies may be

forced to shut down if their sources of credit dry up. This is another version of the ugly deflation scenario.

Today, we have a combination of low inflation with some good and some bad deflationary pressures. I have found that seven economies around the world disaggregate their CPI inflation rates into indexes showing the prices of durable goods, nondurable goods, and services. That's important for "reading between the lines" of the overall CPI number.

The CPI durable goods component for the seven economies since the start of 1996 through December 2016 shows that they all have been deflating (Fig. 14). Leading the way has been Japan (–51%), followed by Sweden (–32%), Taiwan (–29%), Switzerland (–28%), the UK (–26%), the US (–18%), and the Eurozone (–2%). For these economies across the board, nondurable goods prices and services prices are almost all higher—no deflation there.

So this is a picture of mostly good deflation: falling durable goods prices mean that these products are becoming more affordable for more people in these seven economies. The producers of most of those goods are mostly profitable, as strong unit sales and lower unit costs (thanks to technology and productivity) more than offset the downward pressure on prices. Also offsetting the squeeze on profit margins are the constant improvements in durable goods, which boost demand for the versions and models with the latest bells and whistles.

The epicenter of ugly deflation in recent years has been China. The country's producer price index (PPI) had been falling on a year-over-year basis from March 2012 through August 2016 (Fig. 15). That reflected excess capacity sustained by the provision of easy money and other government measures providing life support for zombie producers in manufacturing, particularly the state-owned enterprises. By the fall of 2016, the PPI was rising again, suggesting that the Chinese government had succeeded in its announced campaign to reduce excess capacity. However, bank loan data suggested that they were also trying to boost debt-fueled demand. In any event, China's CPI inflation rate remained positive despite the deflationary PPI episode (Fig. 16).

What can policymakers do to avert the unhappy deflation scenarios? Here are five policy responses, though they're easier said than done:

- *Let insolvent firms fail.* In a competitive market, companies that are generating losses rather than gains respond by reducing their costs. If that doesn't work, they may need to be sold or shuttered. The use of government resources to protect politically powerful companies and industries from failure is a major problem that can exacerbate deflation by maintaining excess capacity and causing profitable companies to become unprofitable.

- *Establish effective bankruptcy laws and courts.* Companies must have an orderly mechanism by which to restructure their business activities. It helps if the financial services sector develops an expertise in facilitating the restructuring and liquidation of "distressed assets."
- *Foster mergers and acquisitions of weak firms by strong ones.* There is often resistance to letting strong companies acquire weaker ones if acquisitions would entail job losses. Nevertheless, this is a better, and economically healthier, outcome than completely shutting down failing enterprises.
- *Tighten and enforce bank regulation and supervision.* Banking regulators need to limit lending to insolvent companies and require proper accounting for problem loans.[7]
- *Require greater corporate transparency.* There needs to be frequent and independently audited corporate financial reporting. Corporate laws and regulations should force directors to act in the best interests of their shareholders, who should receive the information they need to be assured that this is the case.[8] Unfortunately, reality often falls short of this ideal.

The basic message of these rules for right-thinking policymakers is to allow market forces to reduce excess capacity quickly.

Again, that's easier said than done. Schumpeter's process of creative destruction naturally leads to the "paradox of progress." On balance, society benefits from creative destruction, as this creates new products, better working conditions, and jobs, thus raising the standard of living. But it also destroys jobs, companies, and industries—often permanently.

That's the theory. In practice, this process doesn't happen rapidly enough, for an obvious reason: such restructuring is painful.[9] While there are many more winners than losers overall, knowing this doesn't make it easier on the losers. Politicians intervene to reduce the pain with policies aimed at preserving jobs and protecting industries, thus slowing or even arresting the pace of progress. The results of such political intervention in the markets are likely to be excess capacity, deflation, and economic stagnation.

Central bankers often respond to this morass by providing easy credit conditions to alleviate the sting of creative destruction. They hope that lower interest rates will revive demand enough to absorb all the supply and buy time for the losers to become competitive again. It's debatable whether in the past this do-gooder approach has eased the pain or just prolonged it. In my opinion, after the financial crisis of 2008, ultra-easy monetary policies may very well have propped up supply much more than they boosted demand. Credit crunches are nature's way of cleaning out insolvent borrowers from the economy. Easier credit conditions may exacerbate the zombie problem, resulting in more deflationary pressures.

MACRO INFLATION MODELS, BRIEFLY

MY TOLSTOY MODEL of inflation, as explained above, is rooted in the microeconomic paradigm of perfect competition. The focus is on the behavior of utility-maximizing consumers and profit-maximizing firms in a free market. The structure of the market is the key to the inflationary potential of an economy.

To take this a step further: other things being equal, inflation is likely to be structurally lower the less that market forces are messed with. Monopoly, oligopoly, cartelization, price-fixing, collusion, subsidization, protection, and socialism all exist to some extent in every economic system, and all distort the action of market forces. In my opinion, all these deviations from the free market system are simply different forms of corruption, which is the archrival of capitalism. A 10% increase in the money supply is likely to generate more real growth and less inflation in a capitalist economy than in a corrupt one.

Macroeconomists are rarely interested in microeconomics. The most widely followed inflation models are rooted in macroeconomics. Most of the macro inflation models are one of two types: demand-pull or cost-push—though macroeconomists rarely use these two terms anymore. Often, these two macro models are presumed to work in tandem rather than on an either/or basis. In any event, neither model makes much sense in a competitive market economy, in my view.

From the macro modelers' perspective, an increase in aggregate demand means a rightward shift in the economy's downward-sloping demand curve—with prices on the vertical axis of the graph and output on the horizontal axis. Prices rise, though not too rapidly if there are excess production capacity and excess labor. As the economy approaches maximum capacity utilization and full employment, shortages develop and delivery times are stretched. With supply thus constrained, prices rise at a faster pace; demand-pull inflation accelerates.

If the demand curve shifts to the left, so that there is less demand at every price level, prices should fall, in theory. Scant demand creates losers among companies; workers are let go, and wages fall too. In this scenario, a drop in aggregate demand depresses profits, employment, and economic growth. However, John Maynard Keynes famously explained that wages might not adjust downward when demand falls, for various reasons, thus causing even more unemployment. Keynesians favor boosting demand with fiscal and monetary policies to lower the unemployment rate and boost growth.

There is a cost-push side to this narrative. As labor markets tighten, labor compensation costs start rising at a faster pace. At the same time, it is harder to offset these payroll expenses with productivity gains, given capacity constraints. Rising labor costs force companies to raise their prices. They simply mark up their costs to determine their prices; cost-push inflation accelerates. This can't happen in a truly competitive market where firms are price-takers. However, the markup pricing mechanism is a version of the cost-push model that clearly ignores the messy details of microeconomics.

The Output Gap Model is a very popular demand-pull framework for assessing inflationary pressures. The so-called Phillips Curve Model is its cost-push counterpart. Let's sketch the two:

- *The Output Gap Model.* In this demand-pull model, actual real GDP is compared to "potential" real GDP, which is derived by extrapolating recent trends in the supply of labor and in the productivity of labor. When the gap between real GDP—or economic demand—exceeds the potential output of the economy, inflation is likely to rise. When demand is below potential output, inflation is likely to fall. This seems like a plausible aggregate version of the basic microeconomic model of supply and demand, though the macro model is focusing on the inflation rate rather than the price level. However, it still ignores all the devils in the details provided by a more granular micro view.

  The Congressional Budget Office (CBO) updates a quarterly output gap series starting in 1949 (Fig. 17). I've found that it is highly correlated with what I call the Resource Utilization Rate (RUR), which is simply the sum of the capacity utilization rate and the employment rate, i.e., 100 minus the unemployment rate (Fig. 18). What I haven't found is that either one of these highly cyclical series is useful in forecasting the ups and downs of either price or wage inflation.

- *The Phillips Curve Model.* This cost-push macro model of inflation is based on the Phillips curve, first described in 1958 by A.W.H. Phillips, a professor of economics at the London School of Economics. He found a consistent inverse relationship between wage inflation and unemployment in the United Kingdom from 1861 to 1957. He observed that when unemployment was high, wages increased slowly. When it was low, wages rose rapidly. Other economists found a similar inverse correlation between price inflation and unemployment, suggesting that labor costs are pushed directly into prices.

  During the 1960s, the Phillips curve was widely accepted as a useful tool for policymaking. In combination with Okun's Law, it was used to "fine-tune" the economy's growth rate and inflation rate. Arthur Okun was a Yale macroeconomics professor who came up with a simple rule of thumb for the relationship between the unemployment rate and the growth in real gross national product (GNP). Economic policymakers turning their policy dial could fine-tune the economy to get just the right combination of growth, unemployment, and inflation—or so the thinking went.

  Acclaimed economists Edmund Phelps and Milton Friedman independently challenged the logic of the Phillips curve back in the 1960s. They explained that rational employers and workers would pay attention only to inflation-adjusted wages, which would be determined by supply and demand in the labor market. They believed that there is a "natural rate of unemployment." In their opinion, Keynesian fine-tuning could work only in the short run. In the long run, wages and prices would adjust to policy meddling, leading to the conclusion that while there might be a short-term tradeoff between inflation and unemployment, there was none in the long run.

  The natural rate of unemployment was subsequently rebranded by macroeconomists, who called it the "non-accelerating inflation rate of unemployment" (NAIRU). Inflation is stable at the NAIRU; when the unemployment rate is below (above) it, labor-cost inflation accelerates (decelerates), pushing up (down) price inflation through a markup mechanism. Presumably, if policymakers can keep real GDP on its potential track, so that the output gap is zero, then the unemployment rate should be at the NAIRU. That's macroeconomic Nirvana!

The CBO updates a quarterly series for the NAIRU that was started in 1949 (Fig. 19). It rose from 5.3% at the beginning of the data to peak at a record high of 6.3% during 1978. It fell very sharply during the 1990s to 5.0% by the end of the decade. It was 4.7% in 2016 and is projected to remain close to that rate by the end of 2027. I'm hard-pressed to see much correlation between the price and wage inflation rates and the spread between the NAIRU and the actual unemployment rate (Fig. 20).

Estimating potential output and the NAIRU can be done with econometric models. That's how the CBO does it. This doesn't mean that the resulting estimates are accurate. What happens in the real world is that when and if the unemployment rate falls below the estimated Nirvana rate without boosting inflation, the macroeconomists conclude that there has been a downward shift in the NAIRU. In other words, they move the goal posts—rerun their econometric model, tweaking until it delivers the new prediction. I'm not making this up; it happens all the time.

Inflationary supply shocks, such as a surge in the price of crude oil, are also usually handled with a cost-push model by macroeconomists. When the cost of energy rises sharply, businesses pass the burden on to consumers through their prices. This should cause only a temporary spike in the inflation rate. However, it might also initiate an inflation spiral if employers are pressured by their (organized) labor to compensate them for the higher cost of living and driving. Such an increase in compensation would clearly not be offset by productivity and would force companies to raise their prices or accept weaker profits.

Monetarists, such as Milton Friedman, who were especially influential during the early 1980s, were never in doubt that inflation is always and everywhere a monetary phenomenon. They based it on the quantity theory of money, which posits:

$$MV = PY$$

M = *Total money supply*
V = *Velocity of money*
P = *Aggregate price level*
Y = *Total real output*

The key assumption is that the velocity of money is fairly constant, so the growth rate of the money supply will determine the growth of nominal GDP. If the money supply grows faster than the long-term trend growth rate in real GDP, the difference will show up in the inflation rate. Therefore, all that the monetary authorities need to do is target a noninflationary growth rate for the money supply consistent with the underlying growth of the economy. Hence, the monetarists claim that inflation is a wholly monetary phenomenon. Their logic might seem flawless in the theoretical world, but as a practical matter, this is one macro inflation theory with very little real-world usefulness for forecasting inflation or for policymaking.

The Fed gave it a try under Chairman Paul Volcker during the end of the 1970s and early 1980s and abandoned the monetarist approach, as I discuss in Chapter 1. It was too hard to find an empirically stable measure of the money supply. The basic problem is that there are several measures of "the money supply," and their relationships to the economy and inflation are highly unpredictable and unstable. For starters, the so-called money multiplier is unpredictable, i.e., the ratio of the money supply, such as M2, to the monetary base (Fig. 21). Actually, the Fed refers to M2 as a "monetary aggregate" rather than as a measure of the money supply, since it reflects the interaction of money demand and supply. The monetary base is sometimes called "high-powered money" because it reflects the balance sheet of the Fed, which the Fed does determine.

The velocity of money, meaning the ratio of nominal GDP to the money supply (i.e., M2), is a residual variable that has been unpredictable (Fig. 22). If the ratio were constant, or at least relatively stable, then the money supply would drive nominal GDP predictably. Monetarist Nirvana would be achieved by pegging the growth of the money supply to achieve the NAIRU. Excessive money-supply growth when the NAIRU was achieved would accelerate inflation.

A few macroeconomists of the monetarist persuasion converted to the supply-side theology during the 1980s. According to this gospel, if the Fed can't find a money-supply measure to target, then commodity prices should be targeted instead. In other words, to assess the outlook for broad-based measures of inflation, we should closely monitor some of the key indexes of commodity prices, and especially the price of gold. While we are doing so, we might as well watch the dollar too. Since most key commodity prices are in dollars, a weaker dollar would lower the foreign currency prices of these commodities, thus driving up global demand and the dollar prices of these sensitive prices. So a weaker dollar might be another indicator that broad-based inflation is imminent.

Furthermore, supply-siders in the Reagan administration believed that rather than fine-tuning the economy with demand-side fiscal and monetary policies, taxes should be cut across the board. They predicted that this would boost both productivity and productive capacity. The result would be low inflation with lots of economic growth. According to Arthur Laffer, a leading supply-sider, lower tax rates would pay for themselves by stimulating growth and reducing tax avoidance, thus boosting government revenues.

I believe that just about covers the essence of macroeconomic inflation modeling. I hope my egregiously brief survey is accurate and not too much of a caricature of any macro model. All are obviously much richer and more interesting than my brief survey suggests. Thousands of articles have been written about each of them. Some of the best minds in the economics profession have contributed to this literature. Each of the models had its day in the sun. Their proponents can probably point to one or more years over the past 50 when their models were especially successful in forecasting inflation and maybe even in prescribing the right monetary and fiscal policy responses.

I am not saying that we should now forsake them all and worship only at the altar of the free market. All I am saying, in the spirit of John Lennon, is "give microeconomics a chance"—a chance to help us understand the inflation process more fully. There should be no inherent contradiction between the inflation forecasts derived from macroeconomic and microeconomic perspectives. During the late 1990s, the macroeconomists who wrongly predicted higher inflation had to tweak their models yet again. The output gap gang and the NAIRU nerds finally realized and admitted that they were underestimating productivity growth. Following the financial crisis of 2008, there was some fear that the ultra-easy monetary policies of the major central banks would revive inflation. Instead, inflation remains remarkably subdued.

Let's continue to estimate potential output and the NAIRU. Let's track the various money-supply measures. Let's monitor commodity prices, the price of gold, and the foreign-exchange value of the dollar. But let's also appreciate that competition is a major reason why businesses are driven to boost their productivity, contain their costs, and accept prices imposed by the market's forces of supply and demand.

GRAND UNIFIED THEORY

I'M NO FAN of macroeconomic models, particularly of the econometric variety. Even if the models make perfectly good sense in theory, the devil can be in the real-life details and actual data. Some of my best friends are macroeconomists. I feel their pain when their models don't work, especially if they basked in glory when the models worked for a while. Nevertheless, the failure of a theory or model to predict reality provides a great opportunity to revise one's views about how the economy works. Would-be prognosticators must remain intellectually flexible and adapt their views to changing circumstances.

As an example, let's examine the Phillips curve more closely. For many years, it seemed to work relatively well as a model of the inflation process. However, it has lost its mojo in recent years. Maybe it will make a comeback. Meanwhile, there are many possible explanations for why it isn't working. Before I go there, let's have a look at the data.

The simplest version of the Phillips Curve Model can be depicted on a chart showing the unemployment rate versus the yearly percent change in average hourly earnings for nonsupervisory and production workers (Fig. 23). The wage series is available back to January 1964 and covers: production employees in mining, logging, and manufacturing; construction employees in construction; and nonsupervisory payroll employees in the service-providing industries. These groups account for approximately four-fifths of total employment on private nonfarm payrolls. A similar wage measure for all payroll employees is available, but only since March 2006. Here is a brief chronological history of the relationship between this measure of wage inflation and the unemployment rate:

- *Great Inflation era: 1965–1980.* During the second half of the 1960s, wage inflation jumped from 3.2% to a peak of 6.9% during August 1969 as the unemployment rate fell from 5.1% to 3.4%. However, during the inflationary 1970s, the unemployment rate trended higher, but so did wage inflation. The excuse for the breakdown of the Phillips curve was that the oil price shocks temporarily distorted the inverse relationship between unemployment and wage inflation. The prevalence of COLAs in major labor union contracts was one of the main reasons why the price shocks passed right through into wages.

- *Volcker's assault: 1981–1987.* Wage inflation peaked at a record high of 9.4% during January 1981, then plunged to a cyclical low of 1.6% during September 1986. That's because Fed Chairman Paul Volcker let interest rates soar, causing a severe recession that pushed the unemployment rate up to a postwar record 10.8% at the end of 1982. President Reagan fired striking flight controllers during 1981. That event seemed to embolden employers to resist big pay demands by labor and to drop COLAs from union contracts. Deindustrialization caused by intense competition from abroad also depressed wage gains, particularly in manufacturing.

- *Golden age: 1988–2013.* Wage inflation started heading higher again during the second half of the 1980s, as the jobless rate fell back down to a cyclical low of 5.0% during March 1989. The inverse relationship continued to make a comeback during the next two decades, which was a golden age for the Phillips curve. However, the three cyclical peaks in wage inflation that occurred between 1986 and 2016 were around 4.0%, well below the Great Inflation period of the late 1960s and the decade of the 1970s.

- *Yellen years: 2014–2017.* On March 19, 2014, Janet Yellen suggested during her first press conference as Fed chair that she expected wage inflation to rise from 2.5% to 3.0%–4.0% as the unemployment rate, which was 6.7% at the time, continued to fall.[10] Yellen and other Fed officials were increasingly puzzled by the remarkably subdued pace of wage inflation, around 2.5% from 2014 through mid-2017 as the unemployment rate fell to new cyclical lows through 2017. Fed Governor Lael Brainard said on September 12, 2016 that the Phillips curve seemed to have "flattened out."[11]

Yellen, who is a renowned labor market economist, speculated that maybe there was more slack in the labor market than suggested by the low official unemployment rate. That was confirmed by broader measures of labor market slack, including people working part-time for economic reasons and many labor-force dropouts who said they would like to work but weren't actively seeking employment (Fig. 24). That thesis became increasingly less credible when the unemployment rate fell consistently below 5.0% from May 2016 through the end of the year and into 2017, while other measures of labor market slack also tightened up.

I like to monitor the Phillips curve by showing the relationship between wage inflation and job openings, which is another good measure of labor market slack. The monthly survey of small business owners conducted by the National Federation of Independent Business (NFIB) includes a series that tracks the percentage of owners reporting they have job openings they are "not able to fill right now." This series starts in January 1974 and is highly correlated with the data on the national job openings rate, which are available back to December 2000 (Fig. 25). The latter series is reported in the monthly release by the Bureau of Labor Statistics (BLS) titled Job Openings and Labor Turnover Survey (JOLTS).[12] Now consider the following:

- *Job openings.* Since the NFIB series is available for a much longer period covering more business cycles, I compare it to the national unemployment rate (Fig. 26). Not surprisingly, the NFIB job openings series is highly inversely correlated with the unemployment rate. Furthermore, I found that this job openings series has been a very good 12-month leading indicator of wage inflation in the past, even during the 1970s (Fig. 27). However, during the latest economic expansion, wage inflation remains remarkably subdued despite near-record highs in the percentage of small businesses reporting that they need help but can't find workers to fill their open positions.

- *Quits.* Just as puzzling is that the national quits rate rose to a new cyclical high in May 2017 (Fig. 28). Presumably, most workers voluntarily leave their job to take another one for better pay. The quits rate is included in the JOLTS report and starts only in December 2000. During that relatively short span, it confirms the obvious: people tend to quit when there are plenty of job opportunities, not when the economy is in a recession.[13]

- *Frictional unemployment.* The JOLTS data showed that the number of people unemployed as a ratio of total job openings dropped from a high of 6.6 during July 2009 to 1.1 during July 2017, the lowest readings since January 2001 (Fig. 29). In my opinion, when there are as many job openings as job seekers, that's a clear sign that the labor market is at full employment and that the unemployment is mostly frictional, reflecting geographical and skills mismatches. Sure enough, during the first half of 2017, roughly 45% of small business owners said that they could find few or no qualified applicants for their job openings, near the previous two cyclical peaks, when wage inflation rose around 4.0% (Fig. 30).

If the problem isn't with the Phillips Curve Model in general and the unemployment rate as a measure of slack in particular, that leaves only one suspect: the wage data. Let's compare average hourly earnings (AHE) to alternative measures of wage inflation:

- *Average hourly earnings.* The most widely followed measure of wage inflation is the yearly percent change in average hourly earnings because this series is available monthly in the Employment Situation report compiled by the BLS.[14] It's not the same as the average hourly wage rate. There's no series for the average wage rate, which is the pay stipulated for a given unit of time. AHE is the ratio of total wages and salaries for payroll employees to their total paid hours. Payroll and hours include overtime, paid vacation, paid holidays, and sick leave. The last three are normally considered benefits. All other benefits—such as irregular bonuses, employer-paid health insurance, and employers' share of social security taxes—are excluded from AHE.[15]

  While the BLS has compiled this series for payroll and nonsupervisory workers since January 1964, it started doing so for all payroll workers in March 2006. Their two growth rates are very close (Fig. 31). Both series seem to have lost their Phillips curve groove. Even more amazing is that the AHE for one of the most cyclical sectors in the economy, namely manufacturing, shows even less of a Phillips curve relationship with the unemployment rate than the AHE for all production and nonsupervisory workers (Fig. 32)! During the Great Inflation, it mostly inflated. During the Great Disinflation, it disinflated. Since the mid-1980s, it has fluctuated, with no explicable cyclical pattern, around 2.5%, ranging between a low of 0.5% and a high of 4.7%, very similar to what it did during the early 1960s.

- *Employment Cost Index.* A more comprehensive measure of labor earnings (and costs) is compiled by the BLS in the quarterly Employment Cost Index (ECI) report.[16] It shows the total index and its two major components, i.e., (1) wages and salaries and (2) benefits for all civilian workers in private industry and in state and local governments. I monitor the ECI for the private sector and its two components (Fig. 33). It is available back to the first quarter of 1980. Not surprisingly, the growth rate of its wages and salaries component is highly correlated with the yearly percent change in the AHE series (Fig. 34). Therefore, it tells the same story: the inverse relationship between wages and unemployment isn't working as well as in the past. The story doesn't change if we use the headline ECI, including benefits.

  The ECI and AHE differ mainly in that the ECI is adjusted to eliminate the influence of employment shifts among occupations and industry categories. Furthermore, the ECI classifies vacation, holiday, and sick leave pay, as well as overtime premiums, as "benefits." Thus, neither the ECI for wages and salaries nor the ECI for compensation is directly comparable to AHE.[17]

- *Hourly compensation.* Another related series is hourly compensation in the nonfarm business sector. It is available back to the start of 1947 and is included in the BLS quarterly report titled Productivity and Costs.[18] Like the ECI, the hourly compensation series is quarterly and includes benefits. Unlike the ECI, the hourly compensation series doesn't separate wages and salaries from benefits. Also unlike the ECI, hourly compensation includes a couple of particularly jumpy pay categories, i.e., proprietors' pay (based on the estimated value and hours of the labor input of the self-employed and unpaid family members) and gains from exercised stock options.[19] That helps to explain why this measure fluctuates in a more random and volatile fashion, particularly relative to AHE and the total ECI, both on a year-over-year basis as well (Fig. 35 and Fig. 36).

- *Wage Growth Tracker.* The Atlanta Fed's Wage Growth Tracker is a measure of the nominal wage growth of individuals (Fig. 37). It is constructed using microdata from the Current Population Survey (CPS) and is the median percent change in the hourly wage of individuals, observed 12 months apart. The data, which are available back to March 1983, are updated monthly after the underlying CPS data are released, usually two to three weeks after the release of the BLS's Employment Situation report.

Importantly, the Wage Growth Tracker measures the wage growth of continuously employed unique workers, discounting the impact of people entering and exiting the workforce. According to the Atlanta Fed's website, the Wage Growth Tracker "is the time series of the median wage growth of matched individuals. This is not the same as growth in the median wage. Growth in the median wage represents the experience of a worker whose wage is in the middle of the wage distribution in the current month, relative to a worker in the middle of the wage distribution 12 months earlier. These would almost certainly include different workers in each period."[20]

Wage inflation data compiled by the Federal Reserve Bank of Atlanta show that there was more wage inflation than suggested by the conventional measures of wages during 2015 and 2016. At the end of 2016, this measure showed wage inflation at 3.5%, while the

AHE for production and nonsupervisory workers was up 2.5%. One reason might be that the Wage Growth Tracker doesn't reflect that the Baby Boomers are exiting the workforce and being replaced with lower-paid, entry-level workers, whereas the AHE does.

The Wage Growth Tracker also has a series for job switchers versus job stayers. The former has mostly exceeded the latter since the start of the data during 1997 (Fig. 38). The quits rate discussed above suggests that there are more switchers during good economic times than bad ones. (For more, see Appendix 4.1, Alternative Measures of Wages & Labor Cost.)

The most serious flaw in the Phillips Curve Model is the widely accepted premise that causality runs inversely from the unemployment rate to the wage inflation rate, which directly determines the price inflation rate. In fact, it is harder to discern an inverse relationship between the unemployment rate and the price inflation rate using the core CPI (excluding the volatile food and energy components) than using wage inflation (Fig. 39). On the other hand, in the nonfarm business sector, the hourly compensation inflation rate has been highly positively correlated with the yearly percent change in the implicit price deflator since the start of the data in 1948 (Fig. 40). The former tends to exceed the latter thanks to productivity. The growth rate in unit labor-cost inflation, which is the ratio of hourly compensation to productivity, is even more positively correlated with price inflation. The high correlation between labor-cost inflation and price inflation doesn't imply that causality runs just from the former to the latter. It can run both ways. In my grand unified theory of inflation, causality runs mostly from price inflation to wage inflation, with the unemployment rate not as important in the inflation mechanism as the Phillips curve posits.

My Tolstoy Model differs considerably from the macro Phillips Curve Model that combines demand-pull with cost-push dynamics and posits that prices are determined as markups over labor costs. When demand exceeds potential output and the labor market is at full employment, the Phillips Curve Model suggests that price inflation must accelerate as higher wages are passed through to consumers in the form of higher prices. On the other hand, the Tolstoy Model allows for the presence of forces in a highly competitive global economy that act to constrain inflation.

It also offers good explanations for why inflation might remain subdued in such an economy. If global competition kept price inflation down, that would moderate wage demands. It would also mean that if companies had no choice but to pay more in wages, they probably wouldn't be able to pass them through to prices. So they would have to boost productivity, relying increasingly on technological innovation. If they couldn't do that, their profit margins would shrink. In a worst-case scenario, unprofitable companies would exert deflationary pressures in their industries while struggling to survive, but then competitors' margin pressure would be alleviated once they went under. Finally, in a global market, it is global labor market slack that drives inflation. The labor market may be tight in the United States but relatively slack overseas, which will keep a lid on wage hikes as long as globalization prevails over protectionism.

The Phillips Curve Model of inflation is not a tool that I have ever relied on to predict inflation. Nevertheless, I continue to track it. A model that seems logical but doesn't work can be as valuable to the forecaster as one that does. That's because it provides an opportunity to think about why it isn't working. It may be based on flawed assumptions or be missing an important factor. The result is often greater insights into how the economy actually works. When the puzzle pieces don't come together as I pictured in my mind, it's time to change my mind about the picture.

TARGET PRACTICE

IN ITS FIRST-EVER "longer-run goals and policy strategy" statement, the Federal Open Market Committee (FOMC) on January 25, 2012 announced a specific target for inflation of 2.0%. Ben Bernanke, who was the Fed chairman then, had been pushing for this for some time. This brought the Fed in line with many of the world's other major central banks that already had adopted a formal inflation target. Here's a brief history:

- *Trailblazers.* During the 1990s, the inflation-targeting approach was adopted by several pioneering central banks, including the Reserve Bank of New Zealand, the Bank of Canada, the Bank of England, Sweden's Riksbank, and the Reserve Bank of Australia. During the following decade, the adopters included both advanced and emerging economies such as Brazil, Chile, Israel, Korea, Mexico, South Africa, the Philippines, and Thailand, among others. They were followed by the Czech Republic, Hungary, and Poland.
- *Bank of England.* In 1998, the Bank of England's Monetary Policy Committee started setting interest rates to target the Retail Prices

Index (RPI) inflation rate at 2.5%. The target was lowered to 2.0% in December 2003, when the CPI replaced the RPI as the UK Treasury's inflation index. If inflation overshoots or undershoots the target by more than 1.0 percentage point, the governor of the Bank of England is required to write a letter to the Chancellor of the Exchequer explaining why, and how the governor will remedy the situation.

- *European Central Bank.* During October 1998, prior to the introduction of the euro in January 1999, the Governing Council of the European Central Bank (ECB) defined price stability as "a year-on-year increase in the Harmonised Index of Consumer Prices (HICP) for the euro area of below 2%," adding that price stability "was to be maintained over the medium term." In May 2003, following a thorough evaluation of the ECB's monetary policy strategy, the Governing Council clarified that "in the pursuit of price stability, it aims to maintain inflation rates below, but close to, 2% over the medium term."
- *Bank of Japan.* Japan's Prime Minister Shinzō Abe declared a "monetary regime change" on January 22, 2013 as the central bank bowed to government pressure, setting a 2.0% inflation target aimed at helping the country emerge from its prolonged bout of deflation. "This opens a passageway toward bold monetary easing," Abe told reporters after the Bank of Japan and the government jointly announced the inflation target and plans for "open-ended" central bank asset purchases, like the strategy followed by the US Federal Reserve to keep market interest rates low.

Prior to 2000, the Fed had focused on the CPI inflation rate, particularly the "core" rate excluding food and energy. This concept was originated by Fed Chairman Arthur Burns in the early 1970s to allow for an easier monetary policy in the face of rapidly rising oil and food prices, which he deemed to be transitory. A footnote in the FOMC's February 2000 *Monetary Policy Report* to Congress explained why the committee had decided to switch to the inflation rate based on the personal consumption expenditures deflator (PCED).[21]

Nevertheless, Fed Chairman Alan Greenspan refused to consider setting an official inflation target. In an October 11, 2001 speech, he shot down the idea promoted by some of his colleagues and a few academics. He said that "a specific numerical inflation target would represent an unhelpful and false precision. Rather, price stability is best thought of as an environment in which inflation is so low and stable over time that it does not materially enter into the decisions of households and firms."[22]

Bernanke replaced Greenspan as head of the Fed on February 1, 2006 and soon started setting the stage for an official inflation target. He literally wrote the book on this subject. When Bernanke was an academic economist focusing his research on monetary policy, he became intrigued by inflation targeting and went on to co-author a book titled *Inflation Targeting: Lessons from the International Experience* (2006), as well as to write several articles about this approach.

Beginning with the October 30–31, 2007 FOMC meeting, the seven members of the Board of Governors and the 12 presidents of the Federal Reserve Banks, all of whom participate in the deliberations of the FOMC, submit individual economic projections in conjunction with four FOMC meetings a year. The Summary of Economic Projections (SEP) is circulated to participants without attribution. It is included as an addendum to the minutes that are released three weeks after the meeting. Since April 2011, an advance version of the SEP table on the ranges and central tendencies of the participants' projections is released in conjunction with the chairman's post-meeting press conference.

The consensus projections for the headline and core PCED inflation rates for the current year and next two years are included in the SEP. So is a "longer-run" projection for the headline rate. Prior to the inflation-targeting statement of January 25, 2012, Fed officials had an informal "comfort zone" of 1.7%–2.0% for the longer run. Since the statement, the longer-run projection has been fixed at 2.0%. The statement presented the case for targeting inflation as follows:

> The inflation rate over the longer run is primarily determined by monetary policy, and hence the Committee has the ability to specify a longer-run goal for inflation. The Committee judges that inflation at the rate of 2 percent, as measured by the annual change in the price index for personal consumption expenditures, is most consistent over the longer run with the Federal Reserve's statutory mandate.[23]

The FOMC's statement capped a long crusade by Bernanke to make monetary policy more transparent and accountable, less opaque and secretive than it had been under Greenspan. "Communicating this inflation goal clearly to the public helps keep longer-term inflation expectations firmly anchored, thereby fostering price stability and moderate long-term interest rates and enhancing the committee's ability to promote maximum employment in the face of significant economic disturbances," the statement said.

Why 2.0%? That was deemed to be the rate compatible with "price stability." Fed officials feared that targeting inflation closer to zero would increase the risk of deflation. Other central banks also target 2.0% for the same reason. How well are they doing at hitting their targets? Since the financial crisis of 2008 through 2016, inflation remained stubbornly below 2.0%, especially in Japan and the Eurozone. The macroeconomists running the major central banks were perplexed by the failure of their ultra-easy monetary policies to boost inflation and stimulate better economic growth.

They all were taught by their professors in graduate school that easy money should push both economic growth and inflation higher, as predicted by the Output Gap Model. The Keynesians were taught that low interest rates and plentiful credit would heat up consumer spending and business capital outlays. More demand for goods and services would increase the demand for labor, pushing up wages, which would get marked up into higher prices, as predicted by the Phillips curve.

The problem is that it's not that simple. Maybe it was in the past, when the models worked better, but things change. Following the financial crisis of 2008, business managers were much more careful about ratcheting up their costs even during good times. They were obsessed with keeping their profit margins as high as they could. Domestic workers faced not only competition from workers overseas but increasingly from labor-saving technologies, such as robotics and artificial intelligence. So they were less assertive in their wage demands, for that reason and also because price inflation remained subdued.

As just noted above, there's a two-way relationship between wages and prices. The traditional view is that higher wages push up prices. In my view, forecasting prices is more complicated than simply marking up labor costs, because competitive forces play an even bigger role than labor costs. Indeed, if competition and technological innovation are keeping a lid on price inflation, then there must be some feedback from low price inflation to low wage inflation.

Notably, the monetarist model also has failed miserably. While Milton Friedman had his fans and his critics, everyone learned and agreed with his mantra: "Inflation is always and everywhere a monetary phenomenon." Central banks have pumped oceans of liquidity into their banking systems, causing the monetary base—a.k.a. "high-powered money"—of the major central banks to soar exponentially. However, the monetary multiplier collapsed so that the growth rates of the M1, M2, and M3 money measures remained in the low single digits. The velocity of money has collapsed since the financial crisis, especially using high-powered money in the denominator.

Considering all this, let's go back to the Fed's inflation-targeting statement and pull out this key line: "The inflation rate over the longer run is primarily determined by monetary policy, and hence the Committee has the ability to specify a longer-run goal for inflation." How's that working out so far? Could it be that there are other forces in addition to monetary policy that are driving inflation? Notice, I'm not saying that money doesn't matter. Even my Tolstoy Model isn't working so well, since there has been no deflation since the end of the Cold War, as there was following the end of previous major wars. I'll give the central bankers credit for averting deflation by providing so much easy money during the current postwar period.

But why has it been so hard to get inflation back up to a measly 2.0% on a sustainable basis following the financial crisis of 2008, especially in Japan and the Eurozone, at least through mid-2017 (Fig. 41 and Fig. 42)? In the United States, both the headline and the core PCED inflation rates also remained stubbornly below 2.0% post-crisis (Fig. 43).

The answer is that the central banks have been fighting powerful forces of deflation unleashed by peacetime, global competition, technological innovation, and aging demographics. I've already discussed them all. Let me add excessive debt and excess capacity as structural deflationary forces. Ironically, I blame the central banks for both. In other words, with all due respect to Milton Friedman, easy money can be deflationary!

How can that be? The answer is in the microeconomics rather than macroeconomics textbook. Central banks have facilitated an extraordinary borrowing binge on a global basis for many years. Debt-to-GDP ratios, debt-to-income ratios, and debt-to-profits ratios all have soared the world over. Borrowers had easy access to cheap credit and were encouraged to take it, especially by the post-Volcker central bankers and particularly in the United States, where they publicly announced that they intended to moderate the business cycle. In the Eurozone, easy money poured into the peripheral countries thanks to monetary unification. Could it be that many borrowers are mostly maxed out on their lines of credit and credit cards, or have concluded on their own that they are tapped out?

As an empirical observation, we can see that easy money has lost its effectiveness in stimulating demand because it has been too easy for too long. On the other hand, easy money is propping up lots of businesses that have excess capacity and should be shut down, or at least restructured.

The bottom line is that easy money isn't always inflationary and stimulative. It may be again in the future, but over the past few years, other deflationary forces have come into play, and monetary policy may have contributed to them via its unexpected and unintended consequences.

When their ultra-easy policies failed to deliver the expected and desired results, the central bankers concluded that they hadn't done enough and must do more. Where has all this liquidity gone? Quite a bit of it seems to have flowed into global bond and stock markets. There has been inflation in asset prices rather than in the prices of goods and services, as can be seen by the close relationship between the S&P 500 and the Fed's balance-sheet holdings of bonds, which expanded dramatically from late 2008 through October 2014 (Fig. 44).

MEASURE FOR MEASURES

BEFORE I TURN to an analysis of the business cycle, I need to examine the issue of price indexes and deflators. It is very important that the government's statisticians measure the deflators as accurately as possible, because these are used to calculate inflation-adjusted GDP, which is simply nominal GDP (i.e., in current dollars) divided by the GDP price deflator. If the deflator is overstated, that will reduce the level of estimated real GDP. Inflation is typically measured as the yearly percent change in a broad price index or deflator. If it is overestimated for the GDP deflator, the growth rate of real GDP will be underestimated.

In the previous chapter, I observe that Yale's William Nordhaus has argued that computers may be more powerful than official data reflect. This means their prices have been falling faster, so their impact on real GDP has been understated. As I note earlier in that chapter, James Grant objected to hedonic price adjustments to reflect quality improvements. I don't have a problem with them. The idea is that a brand-new car selling for $35,000 today has a lot more bells and whistles, which make it a better car, and accordingly represents a better value than a brand-new car with the same price tag four years ago. So adjusting the CPI of new autos to reflect that improvement makes sense to me, though I don't envy the statisticians who have to figure out how to make those adjustments.

The CPI has been controversial in the past for various reasons. The US Senate appointed the "Advisory Commission to Study the Consumer Price Index" in 1995, headed by Michael Boskin of Stanford University. Its final report, titled "Toward a More Accurate Measure of the Cost of Living" and issued on December 4, 1996, concluded that the CPI was overstating inflation by a little more than 1.0 percentage point per year.[24] The BLS improved its methodology for compiling the CPI in response to the Boskin report, as detailed in a May 2006 article in the *Monthly Labor Review*.[25] Interestingly, the author noted that hedonics "is used for only a small part of the total index. . . . In the past few years, [the] BLS has moved away from using hedonics to value the quality changes resulting from substitutions in computers."

In any event, the Fed gives more weight to the PCED than to the CPI for good reasons. Here is how the footnote in the February 2000 *Monetary Policy Report* explained how the two measures differ, and why the former is better than the latter:

> In past Monetary Policy Reports to the Congress, the FOMC has framed its inflation forecasts in terms of the consumer price index. The chain-type price index for PCE draws extensively on data from the consumer price index but, while not entirely free of measurement problems, has several advantages relative to the CPI. The PCE chain-type index is constructed from a formula that reflects the changing composition of spending and thereby avoids some of the upward bias associated with the fixed-weight nature of the CPI. In addition, the weights are based on a more comprehensive measure of expenditures. Finally, historical data used in the PCE price index can be revised to account for newly available information and for improvements in measurement techniques, including those that affect source data from the CPI; the result is a more consistent series over time.[26]

As a result of these measurement issues, the CPI tends to rise on a steeper slope than does the PCED, confirming that it overstates inflation over the long run (Fig. 45 and Fig. 46). Even in the short run, on a year-over-year basis the PCED calculation tends to yield lower inflation rates than the CPI does, especially lower than the CPI's rate excluding food and energy (Fig. 47 and Fig. 48). Here are a few of the main reasons:

- *Rent.* Both measures of consumer prices include tenant rent of primary residence. They also both include "owners' equivalent rent of primary residence," which is the rent homeowners would have to pay themselves as their own landlords. It is an odd concept, for sure, and is based on the following question included in the Consumer Expenditures Survey: "If someone were to rent your home today, how much do you think it would rent for monthly, unfurnished and without utilities?"[27] Total "rent of shelter," which includes both categories, has tended to rise faster than the core CPI inflation rate excluding it (Fig. 49). Rent has a higher weight in the core CPI than in the core PCED—with the former as of mid-2017 at 42% and the latter at 19%.

- *Medical care.* Another obvious discrepancy between the two measures is that the CPI medical care services inflation rate, which includes hospital and physician fees, consistently exceeds the same category in the PCED (Fig. 50). That's because the medical care outlays eligible for the CPI include only out-of-pocket expenses paid by the consumer.[28] In the PCED, medical care services include those directly purchased by consumers and those paid for on behalf of consumers. Medical care services paid for by employers through employer-provided health insurance, as well as medical care services paid for by governments through programs such as Medicare and Medicaid, are included in the PCED but not in the CPI.[29]

- *Durable goods.* The durable goods component of the CPI tends to have a higher inflation rate than the comparable PCED category (Fig. 51). That's because consumers are always searching for better and cheaper appliances and furniture to put in their shopping cart than are included in the CPI's basket.

A common complaint I hear is that the actual inflation rate experienced by most of us seems higher than the official numbers suggest. The CPI is a measure of prices paid by urban consumers for a market basket of goods and services. On its website, the BLS notes that "the CPI is an average based on many diverse households and not a reflection of any particular household."[30] By the way, the core PCED inflation rate tends to be even lower when it excludes most prices that are calculated implicitly rather than measured directly as market-based prices (Fig. 52).

Measuring inflation rates accurately is critically important when analyzing the overall real economy. If the GDP inflation rate is higher than the government statistics show, then real GDP growth is lower. If inflation is lower, then real GDP growth is higher. Occasionally, this becomes a hotly debated issue. I tend to accept the data as they are compiled by the government and move forward with my analysis. (For more, see Appendix 4.2, Alternative Measures of Prices.)

FISTFUL OF DOLLARS

I AM BEFUDDLED by why central bankers are so hung up on targeting inflation at 2.0%, given all the above. Deflation is a natural consequence of more competitive markets during periods of globalization. In competitive markets, companies can't unilaterally raise their prices, but they can always lower them if they find ways to cut their costs—for example, by boosting their productivity and keeping a lid on their wage bills better than their competitors.

Durable goods are especially prone to deflation because they are produced and traded globally and have benefited the most from technological innovations that have boosted productivity. The prices of nondurable goods, especially food and energy, tend to be more cyclical in nature but have also been kept down by technological innovations that have boosted supply to meet rising demand (lifted by rising standards of living around the world, thanks to globalization). Most service providers don't face global competition.

But why in the world would the Fed, and the other major central banks, want to push up services prices such as rent and health care to achieve their 2.0% target? That makes no sense to me, especially since good deflation boosts standards of living.

The answer I often hear is that if the central banks allow deflation to run rampant, then borrowers will be hard pressed to service their debts. That could transform good deflation into bad or even ugly deflation. The problem is that fighting deflation by providing ultra-easy credit so that borrowers will borrow and buy more seems to have run its course, as borrowers have been there and done that. Better to let consumers benefit from deflation so they'll have a few more dollars to spend on more goods and services! Prosperity solves lots of problems, which is one of the main themes of this book.

CHAPTER 5

Predicting Business Cycles

RECESSION MATTERS

MY WALL STREET career so far has spanned the last four recessions. Since World War II, there have been 11 of them. I've studied them all as well as the Great Depression of the 1930s, which was actually two severe recessions, as I discuss in Chapter 2. The popular definition of "recession" is two or more consecutive down quarters in inflation-adjusted gross domestic product (i.e., real GDP), which is the broadest measure of a nation's economic activity.

What is the difference between a recession and a depression? One glib answer of indeterminate origin is: "A recession is when your neighbor loses his job; a depression is when you lose yours." It was popularized by President Harry S. Truman. Ronald Reagan added to it on the presidential campaign trail in 1980: "And recovery is when Jimmy Carter loses his." Prior to the Great Depression, economic downturns were called "depressions" and sometimes also "panics" when they were triggered by financial crises, especially bank runs and the bursting of speculative asset bubbles.

The Great Depression spawned the birth of macroeconomics, particularly of the Keynesian variety. Since that historically traumatic event, macroeconomists have reassured the public—and the politicians who appoint them to top policymaking positions—that they can avert depressions and quickly end recessions. Instead of "depressions," they now prefer to call economic downturns "recessions," connoting a less severe and shorter setback. Macroeconomists believe they can devise practical policy tools, based on their theoretical models, that will prevent a "Great Depression" from ever happening again. Their employment as university professors has expanded their numbers significantly. Many of them work for the government during their sabbaticals, so they can apply their macroeconomic textbook models to managing the economy.

Left to its own devices, our economy tends to grow naturally and create increasing prosperity for more people. There always has been a business cycle. History suggests that the policies of well-intentioned macroeconomists aiming to moderate the business cycle can sometimes have unintended consequences that, on balance, create more grief and pain than joy. Experience has taught me the wisdom of Robert Burns' poem "To a Mouse" (1786), an apology to a mouse for having upturned its nest while plowing a field:

> But, Mousie, thou art no thy lane [you aren't alone]
> In proving foresight may be vain:
> The best laid schemes o' mice an' men
> Gang aft a-gley, [often go awry]
> An' lea'e us nought but grief an' pain,
> For promis'd joy!

The Bureau of Economic Analysis (BEA) in the Commerce Department has been compiling and publishing quarterly nominal and real GDP data since the start of 1947 (Fig. 1*).[1] Real GDP has increased 773% since then through the end of 2016, from $1.93 trillion to $16.85 trillion. The average annual growth rate has been 3% over this period. In the grand scheme of things, recessions seem like relatively infrequent and brief interruptions in the economy's solid upward trend:

- Indeed, recessionary quarters accounted for just 15% of all the quarters from 1948 through 2016. During those recessionary quarters, negative growth rates averaged –3.7% in a range of –0.3% to –10.0%. The average duration of the recessions since 1948 has been 11 months, with the shortest lasting six months (peak to trough), from January 1980 through July 1980, and the longest lasting 18 months, from December 2007 through June 2009.

---

* Figures, references, and appendices are linked on *yardenibook.com/resources*.

- Of course, it is easier to see the volatility in real GDP by examining its growth rate on a quarter-over-quarter basis at a seasonally adjusted annual rate (Fig. 2). From 1948 through 2016, these growth rates have ranged between a high of 16.9% and a low of –10.0%. Most recessions included at least two consecutive down quarters.

As I note in the first chapter, my firm provides our clients with a regularly updated forecast table, including projected quarterly growth rates for real GDP for the current year and the coming year. The table contains details showing the outlook for the components of GDP as well as for inflation and interest rates. I also convey in my written analyses whether the risks to my forecasts are on the upside or the downside. Often, I will outline three alternative scenarios, including a recessionary one, and provide my subjective probability for each of them. Why three? I often tell my accounts that markets can go either up, down, or sideways. So three scenarios should cover the possibilities.

In my opinion, the job of Wall Street macroeconomists isn't to offer policy recommendations. Over the years, I've learned that our main task should be to predict the economic consequences of the policies implemented by our brethren macroeconomists working for the government. Criticizing policymaking economists is a bit of a sport on Wall Street, especially among Fed watchers, who readily volunteer how they would run monetary policy better if they were in charge. On the other hand, correctly anticipating how policies might change and what the effects will be on the economy and financial markets is a job requirement.

Most importantly, stock investors expect us to help them assess the macroeconomic prospects for profits. Profits in GDP tend to grow during economic expansions. They tend to contract during economic recessions. The growth rate of profits is determined by the growth rate of the overall economy (nominal GDP), though it is much more volatile than the economy because the profit margin (the ratio of profits to nominal GDP) is extremely volatile over the business cycle (Fig. 3 and Fig. 4).

Simply put, stock investors care about the business cycle because bull markets in stocks tend to coincide with economic expansions, when profits are rising, and bear markets with recessions, when profits are falling (Fig. 5 and Fig. 6). In fact, the S&P 500 stock price index is one of the 10 components of the Index of Leading Economic Indicators (more on this below). This means that stock prices tend to anticipate changes in the business cycle. Complicating the job of predicting the stock market is that the global economy has become increasingly important as a source of revenues and earnings. Consequently, assessing the impact of the business cycle on profits has become an increasingly global exercise.

Bond investors also have a great need to anticipate the business cycle. They tend to do well during recessions, when bond yields decline and bond prices increase as credit demands and inflationary pressures abate (Fig. 7). While recessions might be good for Treasury bonds, they are often very bad for bonds issued by corporations. Credit-quality yield spreads in the corporate bond market tend to widen significantly during recessions, as investors fear that the drop in profits and cash flow might cause corporations to default on their bonds (Fig. 8). This spread between bonds with low credit ratings and high ratings is procyclical, i.e., it is a coincident indicator of the business cycle, usually widening dramatically during recessions, then narrowing significantly during expansions.

LEADING THE WAY

PEAK AND TROUGH dates of the US business cycle are determined by the National Bureau of Economic Research (NBER). The peaks are followed by recessions, while the troughs are followed by expansions. The NBER was founded in 1920 and published its first business-cycle dates in 1929. The NBER's Business Cycle Dating Committee was created in 1978. The president of the NBER appoints the members, who include directors of the macro-related programs of the NBER plus other members with specialties in business-cycle research. (See Appendix 5.1, US Business Cycle Expansions and Contractions: 1854–Present.)

The NBER defines a recession as "a significant decline in economic activity spread across the economy, lasting more than a few months," as reflected by four monthly indicators: employment, real income, real business sales, and industrial production. The quarterly data for real gross domestic income (GDI) receives as much weight as the quarterly data for real GDP.[2] The former measures the income generated by producing the latter, with the two tending to diverge by a relatively small statistical discrepancy, as explained later in this chapter. The committee relies on estimates of monthly real GDP prepared by a consulting firm, though the "monthly GDP numbers are noisy and are subject to considerable revision." The NBER offers four explanations of the Dating Committee's methodology:

The committee's procedure for identifying turning points differs from the two-quarter rule in a number of ways. First, we do not identify economic activity solely with real GDP and real GDI, but use a range of other indicators as well. Second, we place considerable emphasis on monthly indicators in arriving at a monthly chronology. Third, we consider the depth of the decline in economic activity. Recall that our definition includes the phrase, "a significant decline in activity." Fourth, in examining the behavior of domestic production, we consider not only the conventional product-side GDP estimates, but also the conceptually equivalent income-side GDI estimates.[3]

While most of the recessions identified by the NBER do consist of two or more consecutive quarters of declining real GDP, there have been a few exceptions. The 2001 recession did not include two consecutive negative quarters in real GDP growth. During the "Great Recession," from December 2007 through June 2009, real GDP declined in the first, third, and fourth quarters of 2008 and in the first quarter of 2009.

Undoubtedly, the members of the Dating Committee, at least individually, must be following the monthly estimates of the quarterly real GDP figures that the Atlanta Fed's *GDPNow* started tracking in 2015 and the New York Fed's *Nowcasting* started compiling during 2016.[4] I have been monitoring both sources to see how the latest economic releases are influencing the course of the current quarter's real GDP. However, the estimates do bounce around quite a lot, and even the final estimate can miss the actual number significantly.

That's not surprising since the first official number for a quarter's real GDP is actually a preliminary estimate based on incomplete data available one month after the end of the quarter. Then one month after the preliminary estimate, it is followed by a revised report, which is followed by a second revision one month after the first revision. And those are followed by annual revisions. As a result, economic forecasters constantly are trying to hit a bullseye on a moving target.

The four monthly series on which the NBER Dating Committee focuses the most are also the four components of the Index of Coincident Economic Indicators (CEI). This index is compiled monthly by The Conference Board, which is a global, independent business membership and research association. More specifically, the four CEI components and their sources are:

- *Employees on nonagricultural payrolls.* Often referred to as "payroll employment," this series is one of numerous labor market data series that are updated in the monthly Employment Situation report, usually at 8:30 a.m. on the first Friday of each month, with a preliminary estimate of the previous month's payrolls. It includes full-time and part-time workers and reflects hiring and firing. The previous two months are usually revised. (Source: BLS.)
- *Real personal income less government transfer payments.* This series includes wages and salaries, estimated largely from the Employment Situation report's data on payroll employment, weekly hours worked, and average hourly earnings. Included are other sources of income, such as proprietors' income, rents collected by landlords, and dividends and interest earned by investors. This is a pretax measure and divided by the Personal Consumption Expenditures Deflator (PCED), which is based on the consumer price index, to derive the "real" measure, as I discuss in Chapter 4. The nominal series is usually released at the end of the month for the previous month. The PCED for the prior month is included in the Personal Income and Outlays Report. (Source: BEA.)
- *Real manufacturing and trade sales.* This series is the inflation-adjusted sum of factory shipments and the sales of wholesalers and retailers. It comes out in the mid-month Manufacturing and Trade Inventories and Sales release along with retail sales, which is an advance report for the previous month, while the sales of distributors report is for the month before the previous one. It does not include the sale of any services. (Source: Census Bureau.)
- *Industrial production.* This series is an index that includes the output of all manufacturing, mining, and utilities industries. The mid-month updates are for the previous month and also prone to revisions. (Source: FRB.)

The CEI is released about two and a half weeks after the end of each month, usually a couple of days after industrial production is released. The latest CEI is based on The Conference Board's estimates of real personal income less transfer payments and real manufacturing and trade sales. All four of its components tend to peak and trough at the same time (Fig. 9). Not surprisingly, the peaks and troughs in the CEI tend to coincide with the NBER Dating Committee's designated business-cycle peaks and troughs (Fig. 10). The CEI isn't particularly good as a short-term indicator of real GDP, though the year-over-year growth rates of both series are highly correlated (Fig. 11).

Obviously, the four coincident indicators are closely interrelated. When employment increases (decreases), so does real personal income less transfer payments. The increase (decrease) in consumers' real purchasing power will boost (depress) retail sales, which is a major component of real manufacturing and trade sales. Strong or weak retail sales obviously impact the sales of wholesalers and the shipments of manufacturers, both of which impact industrial production.

One of the shortcomings of the CEI is that while it is widely viewed as a business-cycle indicator, it isn't very comprehensive. It does not include a specific measure of the services-producing sector of the economy, which continues to grow faster than the goods-producing sector. It is heavily biased toward goods, with two of its components measuring the sales and production of goods. In defense of the CEI as a business-cycle indicator, the goods sector tends to fluctuate with much greater amplitude than does the services sector (Fig. 12 and Fig. 13).

The Conference Board also every month compiles the Index of Leading Economic Indicators (LEI) mentioned a bit earlier in this chapter, which is released along with the CEI (Fig. 14). Its peaks and troughs tend to lead peaks and troughs in the business cycle by about three months. The LEI has 10 components:

- *Average weekly hours, manufacturing.* This series, which is updated in the monthly Employment Situation report, includes overtime hours. Like most of the other LEI components, it is seasonally adjusted so that it isn't affected by, for example, summertime auto plant closings for retooling for new model years. (Source: BLS.)
- *Average weekly initial claims for unemployment insurance.* Jobless claims are reported every week on Thursday mornings. This series is among the timeliest leading indicators, though The Conference Board uses the monthly average of the weekly data. It is inverted when included in the leading index. (Source: BLS.)
- *Real manufacturers' new orders, consumer goods, and materials.* This series is released in the monthly report on factory orders and is a forward indicator of consumer demand. It includes orders for autos, which are identical to factory shipments of autos. (Source: Census Bureau.)
- *ISM® new orders index.* On the first business day of each month, the Institute for Supply Management (ISM) releases indexes based on a

monthly survey of manufacturing purchasing managers. An overall diffusion index of business activity is compiled and reported on a seasonally adjusted basis along with several of its components, including this series. It also is one of the timeliest leading indicators. (Source: ISM.)

- *Real manufacturers' new orders, nondefense capital goods excluding aircraft orders.* This series is widely followed as a leading indicator of capital equipment spending by businesses. It is included in the monthly advance report on factory durable goods orders. (Source: Census Bureau.)
- *Building permits, new private housing units.* This series tends to be a very good leading indicator for housing starts and residential construction. (Source: Census Bureau.)
- *Stock prices, 500 common stocks.* Stock prices tend to discount the prospects for future earnings, which obviously relate to the economic outlook. This series is the monthly average of the daily closing price of this index. (Source: S&P.)
- *Leading Credit Index.* The Conference Board aggregates six different financial indicators to derive this series, which is deemed to be a good predictor of recessions.[5] It tends to spike prior to and during recessions. (Source: The Conference Board.)
- *Interest-rate spread, US Treasury 10-year bond yield less federal funds rate.* Often referred to as the "yield curve," this spread is available daily but is included in the LEI as a monthly series. It tends to widen during expansions. It usually narrows and turns negative prior to recessions. (Source: FRB.)
- *Average consumer expectations for business conditions.* This series is the average of the expectations components of the Consumer Sentiment Index and the Consumer Confidence Index. Both are derived by different organizations every month, with the average available at the end of each month for the same month.

The latest LEI is based on The Conference Board's estimates of manufacturers' new orders for consumer goods and materials and of manufacturers' new orders for nondefense capital goods excluding aircraft. Since the LEI comes out after its components are released, they all get my attention when they are released along the way. I also like to keep track of the ratio of the LEI to the CEI to gauge whether the leading indicators are rising (or falling) at a faster or slower pace than the coincident indicators (Fig. 15). This ratio leads economic cycles and nails their troughs quite accurately and consistently.

While people on a date may be in a hurry to get to know one another, the NBER's Dating Committee is in no rush to call peaks and troughs. After all, their assessments depend on lots of different data series, many of which get revised not just monthly but sometimes annually. The recession calls aren't meant to be timely. Instead, the committee aims to provide historically correct assessments of the beginnings and ends of recessions. For example, the trough of June 2009 wasn't officially declared until September 20, 2010. (See Appendix 5.2, US Business Cycle Peaks and Troughs: Announcement Dates.)

PROFITS CYCLE

WHAT MAKES THE wheels on the business cycle go round and round? I won't keep you in suspense. Over the years, I've come to believe that the profits cycle drives the business cycle. Causality works both ways, of course. However, my simple thesis is that profitable companies expand their payrolls and capacity, while unprofitable companies struggle to stay in business by cutting their costs. They do so by reducing their payrolls and their spending on new equipment and structures to revive their profitability.

In my dramatization of the business cycle, profits are the lead actor, on stage in every scene and greatly affecting the performances of all the supporting actors. In the scripts written by most macroeconomists, profits either play only a bit part or never show up at all, like the absent central character in Samuel Beckett's absurdist play *Waiting for Godot.* Let's very briefly review the classical dramaturgy of the business cycle before turning to my relatively unconventional narrative.

One of the pioneers in the study of business cycles was Wesley Clair Mitchell, an American economist. He was also one of the founders in 1920 of the NBER, where he was director of research until 1945. Mitchell's magnum opus, *Business Cycles,* appeared in 1913. It analyzed "the complicated processes by which seasons of business prosperity, crisis, depression, and revival come about in the modern world." The focus was on the business cycles since 1890 in the United States, England, Germany, and France. In the first chapter, Mitchell reviewed 13 theories of the business cycle. He wrote that "all are plausible." He then proceeded to provide a statistical approach that dispensed with theoretical models.

Thirty-three years later, in 1946, Mitchell co-authored *Measuring Business Cycles* with Arthur F. Burns. By then, his still-objective analysis had been overtaken by more subjective approaches that, in my opinion, started with theories of the business cycles and sought to show that they explained the data. Here is a very brief list of the major schools of thought regarding the business cycle and other macroeconomic issues:

- *Demand-siders.* Keynesian macroeconomists tend to focus on the demand side of the economy. Their models are built on a core assumption that economic downturns are caused by insufficient private-sector demand that needs to be offset by government stimulus. Keynesians prefer more government spending over tax cuts, figuring that a portion of people's tax windfalls is likely to be saved rather than spent. They rarely consider the possibility that demand might be weak because government regulations and policies are depressing profits. All they know for sure is that they can help with stimulative fiscal and monetary policies.

- *Supply-siders.* Monetarists focus on the money supply. They tend to blame central bankers for causing the business cycle, and they believe that announcing and sticking to a reasonable growth rate of the money supply should reduce economic fluctuations and keep inflation low and stable. They've mostly lost their influence since Paul Volcker gave their approach a try from October 1979 to October 1982, then abandoned it.

  As the previous chapter notes, supply-side economics was very much in fashion during the Reagan years. Supply-siders prefer to focus on the supply side rather than the demand side or monetary side of the economy. They believe that the best way to get out of recessions and to boost economic growth is by cutting marginal tax rates on both individual and corporate incomes. They also favor deregulation. I'm inclined to agree with them that reducing the government-imposed costs of doing business, especially for small companies, is fundamentally good for the economy. Arthur Laffer's thesis that lower tax rates can generate more revenues for the government by stimulating growth also makes sense to me. Supply-siders seem to have made a comeback of sorts during the first term of the Trump administration.

- *Debt-siders.* The Austrian school of thought maintains that excessively easy monetary policy creates too much credit during booms. The borrowing binge funds too many dodgy and speculative investments that mostly end badly. Recessions are the inevitable consequence of such unwise policymaking and are necessary to clean out the excesses. These "debt-siders," as I call them, mostly favor reducing the government's meddling in the economy.

Other economists, who are not viewed as Austrians, have also focused on the credit channel as an amplifier of the business cycle. Yale Professor Irving Fisher is remembered for perhaps the worst stock market call in history, when during October 1929, he declared that stocks had reached a "permanently high plateau." He lost a personal fortune.[6] Perhaps to make sense of it all, Fisher wrote a 1933 *Econometrica* article titled "The Debt-Deflation Theory of the Great Depression."[7] Debt can spiral out of control during recessions, turning them into depressions as both incomes and asset values fall. Debt burdens soar. Bad debts mount. Banks stop lending, forcing asset sales that drive prices lower.

Several decades later, a 1994 paper co-authored by Ben Bernanke, who was a Princeton professor at the time, updated Fisher's debt-deflation death spiral, concluding, "Adverse shocks to the economy may be amplified by worsening credit-market conditions." Bernanke and his co-authors called this phenomenon the "financial accelerator."[8] It was a bit ironic that in a June 15, 2007 speech, when he was Fed chairman, Bernanke revised this analysis just as the accelerator was about to propel the economy off a cliff, à la the final scene of *Thelma and Louise* (1991).[9]

"Minsky Moment" is a term coined by PIMCO's Paul McCulley, one of my former students at Columbia Business School. He named it after economist Hyman Minsky, a professor of economics at Washington University in St. Louis. Minsky noted that during long periods of economic stability, financial excesses increase until they eventually cause instability. The Minsky Moment is when instability begins.

- *The others.* Last but not least, there have been lots of debates between the New Classical economists, including the proponents of the real business-cycle theory, and the New Keynesian economists. They've mostly fought over issues such as rational expectations, price and wage stickiness, and market failure.

Which best fits my thinking among these various schools? The answer is none of the above, since schools of thought tend to promote doctrinaire thinking, which can get seriously in the way of making money in the markets. Admittedly, I am a bit of a puritan with regard to recessions. I agree with the debt-siders, who believe we tend to sin during economic booms by speculating too much with too much borrowed money. Recessions are nature's way of knocking some sense back into our heads, though the process can be very painful for those who lose their job, see their business implode, or otherwise experience a significant reversal of fortune. Such punishment is a necessary part of the business-cycle morality play. Booms are followed by busts. That's the natural course.

I agree that some of the sinning during booms often can be blamed on the central bankers. I also agree that soaring credit facilitates the booms that turn to busts. Credit is a better measure of these excesses than are money-supply measures, which tend to have a less stable relationship with the economy. Credit measures also can pinpoint the epicenter of the excesses and predict where the damage will be greatest when the speculative bubble bursts. I think that consumers, investors, and business managers tend to behave rationally more often than not but can behave irrationally as well on a regular basis. They tend to be rational during and after recessions. They tend to lose their minds during booms. I believe that wages and prices can be very flexible as long as workers and the companies they work for can't count on the government to moderate the business cycle.

Perhaps I've been biased by my Wall Street background to focus on profits as the main driver of the business cycle. However, in my career, I have seen profitable companies consistently respond to their success by hiring more workers, building more plants, and buying more equipment. I've seen plenty of unprofitable companies batten down the hatches. They freeze hiring and fire whomever they can without jeopardizing the business. They restructure their operations to reduce their costs, including divesting or shuttering divisions that are particularly unprofitable. They freeze or slash capital budgets.

In other words, notwithstanding politicians' claims, it is businesses that create jobs, not Washington's policymakers and their macroeconomic advisers. To be more exact, it is small businesses started and run by entrepreneurs that create most of the jobs in our economy.

ADP, the payroll processing company, compiles data series on employment in the private sector of the US labor market by company size (Fig. 16 and Fig. 17). The series start during January 2005. Here is what they show:

- *Small companies* (with one to 49 employees) added 5.9 million workers and had payrolls totaling 50.8 million from the start of 2005 through December 2016.
- *Medium companies* (with 50–499 employees) added 4.9 million workers and had payrolls totaling 44.2 million.
- *Large companies* (with 500 or more employees) increased their payrolls by just 1.1 million, with the total at 28.0 million.
- *The shares of employment* attributable to small, medium, and large firms were 41%, 36%, and 23% at the end of 2016.

No matter their size, companies behave the same way over the course of the profits cycle. When their profits are growing, they expand their operations. When their profits are falling, they cut back as best they can. Here is some evidence to support this simple hypothesis:

- *NFIB survey.* The monthly survey of small business by the National Federation of Independent Business (NFIB), which I discuss in the previous chapter, is a remarkably underutilized collection of valuable information. It shows a very high correlation between the percentage of small business owners who expect to increase employment and the percentage of them saying that their earnings have been higher rather than lower over the past three months (Fig. 18). Their net earnings response is also very highly correlated with the percentage "planning a capital expenditure over the next three to six months" (Fig. 19).
- *NIPA.* After-tax corporate profits reported on tax returns is a series included with GDP in the quarterly National Income and Product Accounts (NIPA). Significantly, its peaks tend to lead the peaks in the business cycle, while its troughs tend to coincide with the troughs of the business cycle (Fig. 20). Nonfarm payroll employment excluding government employment is highly correlated with after-tax corporate profits (Fig. 21). That's consistent with my simple "theory" that profitable companies hire, while unprofitable ones fire. Of course, profits are also affected by employment, which drives consumer spending on the goods and services that companies sell.
- *Profit margin.* It's somewhat easier to see the close interrelationship between the profits cycle and the business cycle by focusing on the relationship between the profit margin and the Resource Utilization Rate (RUR), which I introduce in the previous chapter. The profit margin is calculated as corporate after-tax profits as a percentage of

nominal GDP (Fig. 22). Since 1947, it has ranged between a low of 3.3% and a high of 10.8%. Like overall profits, it tends to peak before business cycles peak and to trough at the end of recessions. It tends to rise during economic expansions as long as sales are outpacing the cost of doing business, i.e., labor compensation and capital spending (Fig. 23). It tends to peak during the late phase of an expansion, when companies often respond to an apparent boom by ramping up their spending faster than their sales. Since booms have a long history of turning into busts, the resulting recession causes profit margins to plunge as sales fall faster than costs can be cut, at least initially.

The RUR is a business-cycle indicator that I devised by simply averaging the capacity utilization rate in all industries and the employment rate, which is the percentage of the labor force that is employed, or 100 minus the unemployment rate (Fig. 24 and Fig. 25). Comparing the RUR and the profit margin shows that their cycles tend to coincide (Fig. 26). Think of the RUR as the business cycle and the profit margin as the main driver of the profits cycle. Interestingly, both the profit margin and the RUR are very highly correlated with the ratio of the LEI to the CEI, which I track to confirm where we are in the business cycle (Fig. 27).

- *Forward earnings.* S&P 500 forward earnings is a time-weighted average of the consensus of industry analysts' estimates of earnings for the current year and next year. It tends to be a very good leading indicator of actual earnings, as I fully discuss in Chapter 13. For now, let me observe that the yearly percent change in this series is highly correlated with both the comparable growth rates in the aggregate weekly hours of production and nonsupervisory employees and the capital spending in real GDP (Fig. 28 and Fig. 29).

In other words, there is lots of evidence supporting my thesis that the profits cycle drives the business cycle.

BOOM-BUST MODEL

WHAT CAUSES RECESSIONS? The various macroeconomic schools of thought tend to be doctrinaire about the causes of recessions and how to avert, moderate, and end them. Their models tend to be quite complicated, even though they all are premised on lots of oversimplifying assumptions.

There is a classic joke about a physicist, a chemist, and an economist stranded on a desert island. They're hungry, and a can of soup washes ashore. They desperately need to find a way to open the can. The physicist says, "We could drop it from the top of that tree over there until it breaks open." The chemist says, "We could build a fire and sit the can in the flames until it bursts open." The two argue about the best way to open the can until the economist pragmatically observes that either way, lots of soup would be lost. His solution: "Let's just assume a can opener." It's more a parable than a joke. If underlying assumptions don't jibe with reality, how valid will conclusions based on them be?

In the past, booms were always followed by busts. I've come to conclude that the busts are caused by the booms. In my Boom-Bust Model, the business cycle reflects human nature. We all tend to be afflicted by some level of manic depression. No one is happy all the time. Some people may be sad all the time, but not very many are chronically depressed. During booms, lots of people become increasingly manic and make manic decisions. During busts, lots of people get very depressed and fret that the economy itself might be in an interminable depression.

Before I go any further, I need to make an assumption. No, I don't need to assume a can opener. I need to assume that macroeconomists don't exist, though I will have no choice but to bring them back to make my Boom-Bust Model more realistic. Let's set the stage by examining what happens during booms, which inevitably lead to busts.

A boom occurs after the economy has fully recovered from the previous recession. Prior to the boom, the economic expansion is in its recovery phase until the CEI has regained all the ground lost following the previous recession (Fig. 30). There's no law of nature dictating that the next recession can't occur before a full recovery has been completed. But since the start of the CEI during 1959, the economy always has regained all that was lost during recessions. That's because the economy is wired to grow along with the labor force and productivity.

In any case, once the CEI is back rising into record-high territory, there's a tendency for the economy's "animal spirits" to turn more manic, or at least more optimistic. After all, the recession has been over for a while. The past six recovery periods lasted 33.3 months on average, with the shortest at 19 months and the longest at 68 months. During the recoveries, lost ground was regained, and the situations proved not to be as bad as had been widely feared. Most people kept their jobs during the downturn, while relatively few lost their jobs. So for most people, it was a recession rather than a depression, according to the differences I defined at the start of this chapter. Most companies stayed in business, though many might have had to fire some workers and postpone some spending plans. Expansion periods tend to last longer than recovery periods. The previous five expansion periods lasted 65.4 months on average, with the shortest at 30 months and the longest at 104 months.

By the way, the term "animal spirits" was popularized by none other than John Maynard Keynes in *The General Theory of Employment, Interest, and Money* (1936) in the following passage:

> Even apart from the instability due to speculation, there is the instability due to the characteristic of human nature that a large proportion of our positive activities depend on spontaneous optimism rather than mathematical expectations, whether moral or hedonistic or economic. Most, probably, of our decisions to do something positive, the full consequences of which will be drawn out over many days to come, can only be taken as the result of animal spirits—a spontaneous urge to action rather than inaction, and not as the outcome of a weighted average of quantitative benefits multiplied by quantitative probabilities.

The passage above has been widely discussed and interpreted. Cutting through the jargon, I think Keynes was saying that the business cycle is driven by the instability of human nature. He seemed to acknowledge that booms might reflect "spontaneous optimism," which causes instability in a similar fashion as speculation, setting the stage for a bust. Keynes added, "Thus if the animal spirits are dimmed and the spontaneous optimism falters, leaving us to depend on nothing but a mathematical expectation, enterprise will fade and die;—though fears of loss may have a basis no more reasonable than hopes of profit had before." Of course, his book heralded the idea that government spending could stabilize the business cycle by at least minimizing the downside of the cycle.

In any event, here is my stylized boom-bust script in four acts, with a few comments along the way from the classical Greek chorus, which always seems to be dourly fatalistic:

• *Act I: Expansion.* As the economy moves from recovery to expansion, real GDP rises into record-high territory. Following the recovery, and as the expansion continues, profit margins rise back to previous cyclical highs. Margins stop expanding, because companies are hiring more workers and adding capacity, so costs are now rising as fast as revenues. Productivity growth, which tends to rebound during recoveries, slows during expansions, and unit labor costs increase at a faster pace. Profit growth now follows the growth of sales, which tend to grow at a single-digit pace close to the growth of nominal GDP.

As the economic expansion matures, consumer and business optimism continues to improve. Workers see more job openings and are more inclined to quit their current jobs because better-paying ones are available. Consumers spend more, particularly on durable goods such as appliances, furniture, and cars (Fig. 31 and Fig. 32). They use more credit to do so because they feel good about their job security and their prospects for pay gains (Fig. 33). They certainly need to borrow lots of money to buy houses, which more of them do. That stimulates housing starts, which is reflected in the private residential component of real GDP (Fig. 34 and Fig. 35).

Chorus: "The good times won't last, because inflation will soon rebound, causing the gods to strike us down with higher interest rates!"

• *Act II: Boom.* The previous recession becomes a more distant memory, and lots of opportunities lie ahead. At some point, the labor market tightens as the unemployment rate falls to cyclical lows (Fig. 36). It's harder for businesses to find workers. Inventory-to-sales ratios are near cyclical lows because consumers and businesses are spending faster than production capacity can be added, but it is being added at a faster pace too. Profits and cash flow are at record highs. The economy is like the ballfield in the movie *Field of Dreams* (1989), starring Kevin Costner: "Build more production capacity, office buildings, shopping malls—and the customers will come" (Fig. 37). After all, a record number of them have jobs, and wages are rising.

Capital spending surpasses the previous cycle's record high as more factories are built and commercial properties are developed. Risk-taking makes a big comeback. There always seems to be something to speculate on during booms. Whatever that might be, the prospect of getting rich fast stimulates borrowing to get richer faster.

Chorus: "There is too much hubris. This will all end badly!"

- *Act III: Bust.* Sure enough, the party ends abruptly. Interest rates tend to rise as the party gets wilder. There always seems to be some trigger—more often than not, an unexpected one—that spoils the fun. Often, it's a financial crisis caused when speculators are forced to liquidate their positions once credit conditions tighten. It isn't always the same trigger, but whatever trigger it is, the consequences are remarkably similar. Consumer-spending growth slows, inventory-to-sales ratios soar, employment drops and unemployment rises, consumer spending gets even weaker, production and capital spending are curtailed, consumer and business confidence are depressed, loan delinquencies jump, credit spreads widen, commodity prices decline, and stocks fall into a bear market.

Production tends to drop steeply at first during recessions because final demand drops and because companies are scrambling to reduce their inventories relative to those weakening sales. At some point, inventories have been trimmed to the point where they might be too lean relative to sales.

Interest rates fall as credit demands weaken along with the economy. There is less demand for financing inventories and capital expansion. Of course, lenders are also more cautious about lending because their delinquency rates rise, as do their provisions for loan losses and actual charge-offs. Some borrowers can refinance their debts at lower interest rates.

Recessions wring out the excesses of the last boom. Speculators and investors who assumed that the good times would last forever often are wiped out. They are forced to sell their financial assets, properties, and businesses at distressed prices. That's bad for them but great for the buyers, who get some amazing bargains. So the assets, properties, and businesses pass from weak hands to strong ones.

Strong businesses that were run conservatively during the boom benefit from the shuttering of competitor firms that were managed on the delusional assumption that prosperity would last forever. In fact, the survivors may also find great bargains as their competitors are forced to sell their companies or divest business units. Perhaps one of the most important functions of recessions is to bury "zombie" companies that expanded too rapidly during the boom and were losing money at the same time as they exacerbated the excess capacity in their industries.

Chorus: "We told you so! But perhaps the pain will set the stage for gain once the sinners have been punished."

- *Act IV: Recovery.* Profits are always somewhere on stage in my play. They've rebounded significantly following the recession. The recovery in business revenues is amplified by the rebound in profit margins, as revenues rise faster than spending on expanding payrolls and capacity. Profits can easily show high double-digit growth rates on a year-over-year basis. The economy is still in the recovery phase of the expansion, and company managers are still being cautious. However, they must scramble increasingly to rebuild inventories as sales outpace production (Fig. 38). The pace of inventory accumulation increases, which boosts real GDP (Fig. 39). During the recovery, there is a cyclical productivity "pop," which also boosts profitability because it lowers labor costs initially (Fig. 40 and Fig. 41).

Chorus: "The recovery might be fragile. It could give way to a double-dip recession, so don't get too bullish."

GREAT MODERATORS

BEFORE I TAKE you on a brief tour of the business cycles of my career, I need to make my Boom-Bust Model more realistic by allowing for the impact of macroeconomists. I can't assume them away anymore. In their opinion, since World War II they've learned how to manage the business cycle, especially the downturns. That's been their goal ever since the Great Depression. In my Boom-Bust Model, recessions are naturally followed by recoveries. Nevertheless, it's time to assume that macroeconomists exist.

As I noted above, John Maynard Keynes was the founding father of macroeconomics. His disciples became professors at top universities in the United States, including Harvard, MIT, and Yale. Most of those employed by the federal government in Washington adhere to the belief that their monetary and fiscal policies can moderate the business cycle. Some of the policy wonks found homes in Washington's "think tanks," such as the liberal-leaning Brookings Institution and the Economic Policy Institute. Conservatives responded by creating their own think tanks, such as the Cato Institute and The Heritage Foundation.

The Employment Act of 1946 stated that it is the responsibility of the federal government to create "conditions under which there will be afforded useful employment for those able, willing, and seeking work, and to promote maximum employment, production, and purchasing power." The Act established the Council of Economic Advisers (CEA) to provide presidents with objective economic analysis and advice on the development and implementation of a wide range of domestic and international economic policy issues. The council's chairman is nominated by the President and approved by the US Senate. The CEA members are appointed by the President. The staff of the council consists of a chief of staff as well as about 20 academic economists, plus three permanent economic statisticians.

The CEA was established to help the President make sure another Great Depression would never happen. It immediately became one of the two most prestigious destinations in Washington for academic macroeconomists to spend a couple of years as policymakers. Even more prestigious to work for than the CEA was the Federal Reserve Board in Washington, DC. Either experience looked great on a resume. Sometimes, the top job at the CEA led to an even more prestigious and powerful job in Washington as chair of the Fed. Arthur Burns, Alan Greenspan, Ben Bernanke, and Janet Yellen had all served as chairs of the CEA before becoming Fed chairs.

The Federal Reserve Act, enacted on December 23, 1913, created and established the Federal Reserve System "to furnish an elastic currency, to afford means of rediscounting commercial paper, to establish a more effective supervision of banking in the United States, and for other purposes." At first, the Fed was mostly populated by bankers and lawyers. In 1977, Congress amended the Federal Reserve Act. The revised Act instructed the Fed to pursue three goals: (1) stable prices, (2) maximum employment, and (3) moderate long-term interest rates. The last of those three objectives is rarely mentioned now in policy discussions, so the Fed is widely viewed as having a "dual mandate."

The Full Employment and Balanced Growth Act, better known as the "Humphrey–Hawkins Act," was enacted on October 27, 1978. It amended the Employment Act of 1946. The Act contained numerous objectives—among them, unemployment should not exceed 3.0% for people 20 years or older, and inflation should be reduced to 3.0% or less, if its reduction would not interfere with the employment goal. And by

1988, the inflation rate should be zero, again if pursuing this goal would not interfere with the employment goal.[10]

The door was now wide open for the "great moderators," i.e., macroeconomists who believed that their monetary policies could achieve the dual mandate set by law. Admittedly, I was one of them, since I started my career at the Federal Reserve Bank of New York, where I spent a year and a half from July 1976 through December 1977 before I moved on to Wall Street.

I now view myself as a "recovering macroeconomist." I'm not in a position to make policy in my current role, but I still occasionally criticize the policymaking of Washington's macroeconomists. In other words, I get the urge to meddle by suggesting that my policy insights make more sense than theirs do. I regularly must remind myself that my job is to forecast the impact of their policies as well as to forecast the changes in their policies, not to make policy.

Given my puritanical leanings—specifically, my belief that recessions are a necessary disciplinary consequence of a free-market capitalist system—I am not a fan of the great moderators. While they mean well, I think their meddling may occasionally do more harm than good. But there I go again, spouting off about policymaking. The reality is that the fiscal and monetary policies of the great moderators do have a very significant impact on the Boom-Bust Model. Monetary policy is especially influential because it is centralized in the Federal Reserve. There is no similar central authority determining the course of fiscal policy, which depends so much on the political balance of power in the executive and legislative branches of government.

Therefore, it is much easier to see the relationship to the business cycle—and the impact on it—of monetary policy than of fiscal policy. Since the mid-1950s and prior to the recession of 2008, the Fed's main policy instrument was the federal funds rate (Fig. 42). William McChesney Martin Jr., who served as Fed chairman from 1951 to 1970 under five presidents, famously said that the Fed's job is "to take away the punch bowl just as the party gets going." He had a successful career in the financial industry and had worked at the Securities and Exchange Commission. He wasn't a macroeconomist, yet he believed that the Fed's job was not only to provide an "elastic currency" but also to keep inflation low and provide economic stability. In other words, he was a great moderator.

The problem is that no one likes party poopers, especially ones who take the punch bowl away as the fun is just starting. In trying not to act too hastily, the Fed often has perpetuated conditions that resulted in higher inflation and/or great speculative excesses in asset markets—which finally forced the Fed to slam on the brakes. In other words, the Fed tended to fuel booms and then to trigger the busts that inevitably followed. So the federal funds rate often has soared at the tail end of economic expansions, only to plunge during the ensuing recessions.

There seems to be a recurring reason why the federal funds rate has plummeted during recessions: financial panics. Economic downturns tend to put a great deal of stress on financial institutions that lent too much money during the boom. Nonfinancial companies can adjust by slashing their payrolls and their spending on structures, equipment, and inventories. Financial companies may have to write off loans, which erodes capital and diminishes their ability to make new loans. There always seems to be at least one important financial institution that made too many dodgy loans during the boom by lowering its lending standards and doing so with short-term liabilities. The financial crisis usually starts with a "run on the bank," when one of the more leveraged financial institutions can't roll over its short-term liabilities. It has the potential to become a financial contagion if there is a domino effect on other vulnerable financial institutions.

That's when Fed officials panic in response to the panic. They trot out their ready *raison d'être*, i.e., that the most important job of a central bank is to be the "lender of last resort." They invariably start quoting Walter Bagehot, a British journalist, businessman, and essayist who wrote extensively about government, economics, and literature. His 1873 book, *Lombard Street: A Description of the Money Market*, is often cited by central bankers during financial crises. Of importance is "Bagehot's Dictum" that in times of financial crisis, central banks should lend freely to solvent depository institutions, yet only against sound collateral and at interest rates high enough to dissuade those borrowers who are not genuinely in need. In response to the financial crisis of 2008, central bankers responded with more of the first part than the second part of Bagehot's advice.

Sure enough, in the United States, the federal funds rate peaked at or about the same time as the following financial crises: Penn Central (June 1970), Franklin National (May 1974), Silver Bubble (May 1980), Drysdale and Mexico defaults (June 1982), Continental Illinois (July 1984), S&L crisis (June 1990), Mexican peso crisis (December 1994), Pacific Rim crisis (November 1997), Long-Term Capital Management default (July 1998), 9/11 terror attacks (September 2001), and the subprime mortgage meltdown (February 2007). The federal funds rate tended to fall sharply as the Fed scrambled to follow Bagehot's rule book in reaction to the crises (Fig. 43).

The great moderators took credit for having moderated the business cycle's ups and downs and subdued inflation from the mid-1980s to 2007. Indeed, they described this period as the "Great Moderation." When he was still a Fed governor rather than the Fed chairman, Ben Bernanke presented a speech titled "The Great Moderation," extolling the success of the Fed in subduing the business cycle.[11] Four years later, the economy was falling into what was subsequently called the "Great Recession."

This time, as Fed chairman, Bernanke was forced to lower the federal funds rate almost to zero and to lend more freely by setting up several improvised credit facilities. When all that was believed to be insufficient, the Fed adopted so-called unconventional monetary policy measures, particularly several quantitative easing programs in which the Fed purchased trillions of dollars in the Treasury and mortgage bond markets.

Ironically, the Great Recession has been followed so far by another period of moderation. However, it was characterized by subpar growth and concerns about deflation. It was widely described as the "New Normal." Macroeconomists fretted about "secular stagnation," which I discuss in Chapter 2—namely, a significant decline in the trend of economic growth that seemed to persist notwithstanding the Fed's ultra-easy monetary policy measures.

Despite the Fed's purchases, the US Treasury 10-year bond yield continued to provide accurate readings on the business cycle when compared to the federal funds rate. The yield curve spread between the two is one of the 10 components of the Index of Leading Indicators, as mentioned above (Fig. 44). Since the mid-1950s, the spread has reliably signaled that the party was almost over whenever the federal funds rate soared above the bond yield. In other words, a negative yield spread has been a sure leading indicator of an impending recession. During recessions, the federal funds rate tends to plunge below the bond yield, signaling a recovery. During expansions, it tends to remain positive. Not surprisingly, the yield curve tends to peak at the same time as financial crises hit (Fig. 45).

MULTIPLIERS

WHAT ABOUT THE impact of fiscal policies on the business cycle? The macroeconomic textbooks teach that government's "automatic stabilizers" moderate the ups and downs of the business cycle. They offset fluctuations in economic activity without any changes in the government's taxing and spending policies. When the economy is booming, taxes tend to rise faster than incomes because of the progressive income-tax rate system, with higher tax rates on higher incomes. In addition, fewer people are eligible for government benefits, such as unemployment insurance and food stamps. During recessions, taxes tend to fall faster than incomes, and more people depend on income-support programs provided by the government.

That's been a very predictable pattern since the start of the quarterly data in 1948 tracking the ratios of US federal government expenditures to nominal GDP and US federal government tax receipts to nominal GDP (Fig. 46). As a result, the federal budget deficit tends to widen during recessions and to narrow during expansions (Fig. 47). The budget has been in surplus for brief periods and only a few times during expansions. That's because the role of fiscal policy has evolved—mostly because of President Franklin Roosevelt's New Deal and President Lyndon Johnson's Great Society initiatives—from merely stabilizing the overall business cycle to providing social welfare benefits through increasingly costly programs such as Social Security, Medicare, and Medicaid.

Federal government spending on goods and services, which is included in GDP, accounted for 6.5% of GDP during 2016 (Fig. 48). Total federal government spending, including on income redistribution and support programs, was triple that, at 20.2%. The available monthly data since 1987 show that entitlements spending rose from 44% of total federal government outlays during 1987 to 65% during 2016 (Fig. 49).

How do discretionary fiscal policies affect the business cycle? Almost every recession triggers a big political debate on the need for fiscal stimulus, through either an increase in targeted government spending, which is usually the preference of liberals, or broad tax cuts, which are usually championed by conservatives. Often by the time a compromise is reached, the economy is already starting to recover.

Fiscal policy fights also tend to raise the issue of the so-called "fiscal multiplier," a concept dear to the hearts of Keynesians. A dollar of government spending can boost real GDP by more than a dollar, they believe.

So can a dollar of tax cuts, they acknowledge, but the multiplier effect is greater for spending because individuals may save some of their tax windfalls, as mentioned earlier in this chapter. Not all of it will be spent, finding its way into GDP.

My company's accounts rarely have asked me to comment on the multiplier effect, probably because most of them recognize it is an issue that macroeconomists like to debate without any practical significance. In their experience, proponents of the fiscal multiplier tend to overstate their case.

In fact, there is a famous quote by Henry Morgenthau Jr., who was the US Secretary of the Treasury during Roosevelt's administration, questioning whether the New Deal was a big waste of money:

> We have tried spending money. We are spending more than we have ever spent before and it does not work. And I have just one interest, and if I am wrong . . . somebody else can have my job. I want to see this country prosperous. I want to see people get a job. I want to see people get enough to eat. We have never made good on our promises. . . . I say after eight years of this Administration we have just as much unemployment as when we started. . . . And an enormous debt to boot.

Needless to say, this remarkable quote has been questioned by liberals as too good to be true for conservatives who've been quoting it. The source is a microfilm copy of a transcript of a congressional hearing attended by Morgenthau.[12] It was found by Burton W. Fulson Jr., an American historian known for his conservative revisionist spins of US economic history. In any event, data compiled by the Commerce Department show that the unemployment rate remained above 10.0% throughout the 1930s, as I review in Chapter 2.

A more recent episode that raised doubts about the fiscal multiplier occurred at the start of President Barack Obama's administration. Christina Romer, CEA chair, and Jared Bernstein, chief economist for Vice President-elect Joe Biden, issued a report on January 9, 2009 titled *The Job Impact of the American Recovery and Reinvestment Plan.*[13] The authors assumed that the new administration would implement a $775 billion program of mostly government spending and some tax cuts. They didn't assume a can opener, but they did rely on econometric models for their fiscal multiplier assumptions.

The study projected that the American Recovery and Reinvestment Act, which was passed during February 2009, "should save or create at least 3 million jobs by the end of 2010." In fact, payroll employment continued to fall by 3.6 million before finding a bottom during February 2010. The unemployment rate, which was supposed to fall to 7.0% by the end of 2010, rose to a peak of 10.0% during October 2009, fell to 9.3% by the end of 2010, and didn't get down to 7.0% until the fall of 2013. The unemployment rate proceeded to fall to 4.3% by mid-2017. Liberal and conservative economists undoubtedly will debate whether the government's intervention ultimately hastened or slowed the recovery.

These days, macroeconomists have become so politically polarized that if you ask them for their estimates of the fiscal multiplier, liberals will tell you it is greater than one for government spending and less than one for tax cuts, while conservatives will tell you it is less than one for government spending and greater than one for tax cuts. I tend to agree with the conservatives. I was skeptical about the claims of Romer and Bernstein. I was more open to the optimistic forecasts of Reagan's supply-side tax-cutters.

CREDIT CYCLES AND DEBT WEIGHTS

NEITHER KEYNESIANS NOR monetarists paid much, if any, attention to debt during the 1970s and 1980s. However, plenty of fiscal conservatives warned about the dire consequences of federal government deficits and mounting federal debt. They wrote books with alarming titles such as *Beyond Our Means*, *Day of Reckoning*, *The Debt Threat*, and *On Borrowed Time*. These were mostly cries in the wilderness, perhaps because their apocalyptic predictions didn't pan out.

On the other hand, Wall Street economist Henry Kaufman did focus much of his economic analysis on the credit markets. His main insight was to recognize that the business cycle was significantly driven by the credit cycle. He observed that when the credit markets were highly regulated, so was the business cycle. When Regulation Q set limits on deposit rates and the Fed raised interest rates above those ceilings to fight inflation, the resulting disintermediation very effectively caused credit crunches.

Kaufman also recognized that the financial deregulation that occurred during the 1980s, including the elimination of Regulation Q, would force depository institutions to compete with one another for deposits. Instead of offering toasters as gifts to depositors who opened checking and savings accounts, as they had in the 1950s, they would need higher interest rates to attract deposits. The depository institutions also increasingly turned to the capital markets to raise funds. At the same time, they had to compete with the capital markets as more borrowers raised the funds they needed by participating directly in these markets rather than through financial intermediaries. This all led to faster credit expansion during business-cycle booms, which worsened the inevitable busts. The Fed's *Financial Accounts of the United States* provides the following supportive evidence of these trends:

- The debt of the financial sectors soared from just 8% of total debt during 1970 to peak at a record high of 33% in 2008 (Fig. 50).
- Over this same period, the ratio of financial debt to GDP rose from 12% to a record high of 123% (Fig. 51).
- By 2016, financial debt was back down to 24% of total debt and 84% of GDP, probably mostly because of the regulatory restrictions imposed by the Dodd–Frank Act of 2010.
- However, the debt of the nonfinancial sectors (i.e., households, businesses, and federal, state, and local governments) rose to a new record high of 254% of GDP during the third quarter of 2016. Total nonfinancial and financial debt remained around 350% of GDP, just below the 2008 record high and more than twice the 150% reading during 1970.

As noted above, almost every recession since the 1970s has been associated with a financial panic. That's because business-cycle expansions have been turbocharged by credit-cycle expansions. The resulting upturn in the profits cycle led to more consumer spending as employment expanded rapidly, and to more business spending to expand capacity. This all increased borrowers' demand for funds and financial institutions' willingness to lend, as the latter were competing to make loans with more of the funds borrowed in the capital markets. Credit standards deteriorated at the same time as the cost of credit rose, because the Fed raised interest rates to cool off the overheating economy.

While there always seems to be some unique event that turns a boom into a bust, such events often have something in common: most of them were the consequences of the boom, which led to excessive debt-financed spending and speculation. Financial leverage is wonderful during good times, which encourage more of it. It is a nightmare during bad times, which tend to be especially bad if both borrowers and lenders are distressed. Profits evaporate for both at the same time. Lenders are forced to increase their provisions for bad loans and their charge-offs. Their capital losses reduce their capacity to lend. When the financial panic is on the verge of turning into a financial contagion, the Fed scrambles to be the lender of last resort, providing liquidity through its lending facilities and lowering interest rates.

The interactions of the business, profits, and credit cycles discussed above strongly suggest that just as recessions have a tendency to be self-healing, booms are self-destructive. However, focusing on cycles misses important secular trends that can influence the economy—including the demographic, technological, and political trends that this book examines. At the same time, secular trends in debt also need to be examined.

The data clearly show that recessions don't clean out all the debt excesses of the previous booms. That's most evident in the ratios of debt to GDP for the United States and many countries around the world. These record-high ratios were blamed for the remarkably weak recoveries that followed the Great Recession of 2008 around the world—particularly in the United States, the Eurozone, and Japan—despite the extremely easy monetary policies of their central banks. Even in China, which also has a record-high debt ratio, the economic growth rate slowed significantly in recent years despite massive bank lending.

In the past, rapid debt growth during business-cycle expansions boosted economic growth, since it allowed upbeat consumers and business managers to bring forward spending on goods and services from tomorrow to today. Eventually, tomorrow arrives, but spending can no longer be boosted by providing plentiful, cheap credit because the borrowers have already purchased what they need and are maxed out on their credit cards, lines of credit, and ability to service their debt burdens.

CYCLE TOURS

I BELIEVE MY Boom-Bust Model describes the basic mechanisms of the business cycle. The main transmission mechanism is the profits cycle. The credit cycle amplifies the magnitude of all the economy's cycles. But that doesn't explain what causes an economy that had been cruising along at a relatively fast pace suddenly to stop growing and go into reverse. Who slammed on the brakes and switched gears?

The answer is always a surprise to most macroeconomists. This element of surprise is what makes forecasting recessions rather challenging. Few economists see recessions coming. Those who do see them coming often spot them too early and tend to have reputations as chronic doomsayers. I've had some hits and some misses. Let's take a quick tour of the major post-World War II business cycles, focusing on the triggers that caused the booms to turn to busts.

- *Oil shocks.* There were two major recessions in the early 1970s and the early 1980s. In both cases, the triggers were spikes in oil prices resulting from politically motivated output cuts by OPEC's oil producers. For reasons I discuss in Chapter 4, these sparks started inflationary wildfires. In both instances, the Fed responded by hiking the federal funds rate, once again triggering disintermediation, causing massive credit crunches, and inverting the yield curve. I recall waiting in long lines to get gasoline during the summer of 1979. That was depressing, and it depressed consumer confidence and spending.

  During my Wall Street career, the first recessions that I experienced were the two that hit the economy in the early 1980s. The first one started in January 1980 and ended just six months later during July 1980. But then the next one started in July 1981 and lasted 16 months through November 1982. Both the LEI and the CEI barely recovered during the interim, making the entire period seem like one very long recession.

  While real GDP dropped just 0.5% from the peak during the first quarter of 1980 through the trough during the fourth quarter of 1982, real consumer spending rose 4.0% over this period. Housing starts tumbled as the 30-year fixed-rate mortgage rate soared to a record 18.6%. That was depressing too. The unemployment rate soared from 1979's low of 5.6% during May to peak at 10.8% during the last two months of 1982, the highest since the Great Depression.

  As I review in the first chapter, I saw that the economy was falling into a severe recession and I saw the recovery coming. It was another example of a policy-engineered, Fed-led recession aimed at reducing inflationary pressures by depressing demand with a credit crunch. It was exacerbated by a banking crisis among the money-center banks.

Walter Wriston was the chief executive at Citibank from 1967 to 1984. Citibank had extended large loans to Latin American nations, but Wriston defended the policy, repeatedly saying "countries don't go bust." He was wrong. Other banks also lent too much money south of the border.

I warned about the possibility of a depression and predicted that the Fed would ease up. Once the severe recession was exacerbated by the banking crisis, ease up is exactly what the Fed did. During 1983's recovery, the inventory-to-sales ratio, which had soared during the recession, plunged as sales started to outpace production, the yield curve turned positive, and productivity popped. Profits recovered, reviving employment and business spending and fueling a rally in stocks. Housing starts snapped back up sharply as mortgage rates plummeted.

There was a recession scare during 1986, which was mostly attributable to the plunge in oil prices during the second half of 1985 and the first half of 1986. Oil companies in Texas and other oil-producing states had responded to the OPEC oil spike by borrowing and expanding too much. The boom in the oil states, especially Texas, turned into a bust. I described it as a "rolling recession." I didn't expect it to turn into an economy-wide recession, and it did not. On October 19, 1987, the Dow Jones Industrial Average plunged 22.6%, triggering lots of fear that this crash could somehow cause a recession. I quickly concluded that it wasn't likely to do so, for the reasons Chapter 1 reviews.

• *S&L crisis.* The next recession was short, lasting just the eight months from July 1990 through March 1991. The first Gulf War during the second half of 1990 triggered another spike in oil prices. Once again, consumers retrenched, causing the inventory-to-sales ratio to spike. So production and employment dropped, but not for long. This time, the unemployment rate peaked at 7.8% during June 1992, or 15 months after the official end of the recession. No doubt there were plenty of unemployed workers at the time who thought the NBER had called the recession's trough too soon.

In addition, this recession included a financial contagion in the thrift industry, which was the consequence of the industry's haphazard deregulation following previous bouts of disintermediation, as I show in Chapter 8. The industry's lobbyists successfully convinced Congress to deregulate thrifts so that they could pay market rates on their deposits. Unscrupulous thrifts gained market share and fees by paying premium deposit rates and making lots of dodgy loans. It ended badly, with a few thrift executives going to jail.

Once again, there was a credit crunch as depositors lost their confidence in thrifts even though they were mostly insured. This time, the rolling recession hit both residential and commercial real estate hard, while the overall national downturn was relatively short and shallow. That was my forecast after I thoroughly examined the nature of the thrift crisis and concluded that it would be relatively contained. Housing starts dropped to only 798,000 units during January 1991; at the time, this was the lowest on record for the series, which started at the beginning of 1959.

The rest of the 1990s were years of prosperity, with the first great equity bull market in my career and one of the greatest in American history. The economic expansion lasted 120 months, from March 1991 to March 2001, the longest expansion on record. The Cold War was over. The United States emerged as the world's sole superpower. The Bond Vigilantes were keeping a lid on government spending and inflation. The High-Tech Revolution was just starting. The Baby Boomers were married, having kids, moving to the suburbs, and buying houses and cars. The number of households jumped 12 million during the decade. Homeownership increased. Home prices started to soar. Real GDP rose 4.3% per year on average during the decade. Yet inflation remained surprisingly subdued.

- *Tech bubble.* Nevertheless, starting in 1998, I began to warn about a recession in 2000. As I note in Chapter 1, it was the right call for the wrong reason. After the Y2K anticlimax, IT spending dropped sharply. In addition, the stock market bubble in tech stocks burst. The resulting bear market caused the S&P 500 to drop by 49.1% from March 24, 2000 through October 9, 2002. However, the recession was another short, eight-month one, lasting just from March 2001 through November 2001. This time, housing starts held up quite well compared to the sharp declines during the previous downturns. The business inventory-to-sales ratio peaked well below the two previous cyclical peaks. The same can be said of the unemployment rate, which peaked at 6.3% during June 2003. A geopolitical shock, the 9/11 terrorist attacks, caused the Fed to cut the federal funds rate down to the lowest levels since the start of the 1960s.

- *Housing bubble.* The "Great Recession" lasted 18 months, from December 2007 to June 2009. Real GDP fell 4.2% from the peak during the fourth quarter of 2007 to the trough during the second quarter of 2009. Ironically, macroeconomists started to brag about how their policies might finally have tamed the business cycle during the expansion that preceded the Great Recession. As I noted above, on February 20, 2004, Ben Bernanke praised the Fed for having reduced the frequency and severity of recessions while subduing inflation.

  Bernanke became Fed chairman on February 1, 2006. By late 2008, he believed the country was facing another Great Depression and acted accordingly, lowering the federal funds rate from a cyclical peak of 5.25% during June 2006 to almost zero during December 2008. He also flooded the financial system with liquidity through numerous emergency lending facilities and programs. They worked: the Fed's great moderator had moderated the looming depression. That might explain why he was very willing to call the downturn under his watch the "Great Recession," though it certainly blew away his Great Moderation thesis. My hunch is that he wanted to remind everyone that thanks to him, another Great Depression had been averted. I'll give him credit for having done so.

  Very few economists saw the recession coming. A couple started to warn about it a bit too early, but they turned out to be right and for the right reasons. Both David Rosenberg, who was the chief economist at Merrill Lynch, and Nouriel Roubini, a professor at New York University's Stern School of Business, with his own consulting firm, identified the bubble in the housing market. The bubble burst during 2007 and 2008, when the credit excesses that financed it became increasingly apparent, especially in the subprime mortgage market and its dodgy credit derivatives. Ironically, Rosenberg worked for a firm that had been among the most aggressive packagers of mortgages with dubious credit quality into highly rated credit derivative products offered for sale to investors, an imprudent practice that contributed to the financial crisis. Too bad that management ignored Rosenberg's warnings; had they realized the ramifications of his forecast for their business, they might have avoided having to sell Merrill Lynch at a bargain-basement price to Bank of America during September 2008.

  I turned bearish on the S&P 500 Financials sector on June 25, 2007, but I didn't fully appreciate the credit excesses that Wall Street had created to leverage up the housing markets of "Main Street." I expected that the slew of financial panics that started in 2007 would cause the Fed once again to pull out Bagehot's playbook and act as the lender of last resort. The Fed did so, but only after Lehman Brothers blew up, sending shock waves throughout world financial markets.

As in many of the previous recessions since World War II, too much credit had financed too much of the preceding boom. The resulting credit crunch triggered a bust that depressed demand, which depressed profits, which depressed employment and business spending on structures, equipment, and inventories. Housing starts plunged 79% from a cyclical peak of 2.27 million units, at a seasonally adjusted annual rate, during January 2006 to 478,000 units during April 2009. The unemployment rate soared from a cyclical low of 4.4% during May 2007 to a peak of 10.0% during October 2009. It would have risen much more but for the surprising drop in labor force participation, which I discuss in the next chapter.

Inevitably, the stress of the downturn triggered a financial crisis, which worsened the recession. To stop this spiral from becoming a financial contagion that could turn the recession into a depression, the Fed not only lowered the federal funds rate almost to zero by the end of 2008 but also provided a flood of liquidity through numerous quickly improvised lending facilities. That set the stage for a recovery, though I present a more detailed version of the financial crisis story in Chapter 8.

Just as important as predicting recessions is knowing when widespread recession scares are likely to be wrong, creating short-term buying opportunities in the stock market. Also important is to correctly assess the underlying source of the economy's strength between recessions. During the 1980s, that source was the entrance of the Baby Boomers into the labor market. During the 1990s, it was the High-Tech Revolution. During the following decade, it was the emergence of China. All are themes that I've written about extensively.

In the first year of the economic expansion that started during the second quarter of 2009, real GDP growth rebounded strongly; then it lost momentum, hovering at around 2.0% on a year-over-year basis starting during the second half of 2010. Several economists noted that in the past, such slow growth was the economy's "stall speed," leading inevitably to a recession. I observed that excluding government spending, real GDP was growing closer to 3.0%.

In many ways, the Great Recession and the financial crisis of 2008 were traumatic events. They led to numerous panic attacks in the stock market during the subsequent expansion, triggered by fears that another financial crisis and recession were imminent. There was lots of buzz during 2009 and 2010 about a "double-dip" recession. However, I argued that the expansion would last longer than widely feared, particularly by pessimistic economists and investment strategists who warned that it would all end badly. They were quick to heighten the panics by claiming that the "end-game" was near.

Another rolling recession rolled through the oil industry from mid-2014 through early 2016 because of a freefall in the price of oil. Like the one during 1986, it did not spill over to other industries and the broader economy. My assessment at the time was that it wouldn't, though a few other economists rang the recession alarm bells.

I've been keeping track of all the panic attacks in the stock market since the start of the latest bull market from 2009 through 2016. I count 56 of them. There will be another recession one day. As of December 2017, the most recent expansion had lasted 102 months, making it the third longest on record.

ACCOUNTING FOR MACROECONOMISTS

I STRONGLY RECOMMEND that anyone who wants to understand the economy start with a deep dive into the National Income and Product Accounts (NIPA), which include the data on the economy's GDP, along with its components, which collectively determine the economy's trend and cycles. I examine the components in greater detail in subsequent chapters. For most economists who study the business cycle, especially econometricians, economic history started in 1948. That's when the Commerce Department began to collect detailed NIPA data on the economy.

At Yale University, one of my professors was Richard Ruggles. He was known for developing accounting tools for measuring national income and improving price indexes used in formulating government policy. Throughout his Yale career, he conducted research for numerous government entities, including the United Nations, the Organization of American States, the Federal Reserve Board, the Census Bureau, and the NBER, as well as the Ford Foundation. He also served on various governmental committees concerned with economic statistics.

After earning his doctorate from Harvard University in 1942, Professor Ruggles joined the Office of Strategic Services as an economist. During World War II, he worked for the office in London, where he estimated the production rates of tanks at German factories using photographs of the serial numbers from captured or destroyed tanks. In 1945–46, he was with the US Strategic Bombing Survey in Tokyo and Washington.

I learned a great deal from Professor Ruggles. I've also learned a great deal by diving into the NIPA. It is available on the website of the Commerce Department's BEA, which has a 25-page primer and 436-page handbook on the NIPA.[14] Understanding the structure of the NIPA provides a very useful accounting-based framework for how the economy works. Theoretical models can offer some insights, but all too often, theory comes first, with the numbers cherry-picked to confirm the theory. I prefer to stay as close to the accounting framework and the data as possible when I predict the economic outlook.

After the end of each quarter, the BEA publishes a preliminary estimate of nominal GDP. It is the value of all goods and services produced in the United States. Of course, most products include lots of intermediate products. An automobile has thousands of components. GDP focuses on the value added in the production of an automobile and all other products, so it is measured as the sum of the final demand for all goods and services produced domestically. The NIPA add up personal consumption expenditures, nonresidential business expenditures (including inventory investment), government spending, and exports less imports. The BEA also compiles price deflators for all these components and lots of subcomponents. They are used to calculate inflation-adjusted, or real, measures of economic activity. According to the BEA primer:

- *Quarterly estimates and revisions.* An "advance" estimate of GDP (based on incomplete monthly data) is released near the end of the first month after the end of the quarter. Second and third revisions that incorporate revised and newly available monthly and quarterly data are released one month and two months later.
- *Annual revisions.* Annual estimates of GDP are first available as the sum of the quarterly estimates. They are revised in the annual revision, typically each July, and generally in the following two annual revisions. Annual revisions incorporate newly available annual source data and

quarterly data that are released too late to be used in the current quarterly estimates; methodological improvements may also be incorporated.

- *Five-year cycle.* The revision cycle culminates, at about five-year intervals, in a comprehensive revision of the NIPA. These comprehensive revisions are based on quinquennial censuses of economic activity, while the monthly, quarterly, and annual data discussed above are generally based on sample surveys. Furthermore, comprehensive revisions traditionally have been used to introduce into the accounts major improvements in definitions, estimating methods, and data presentations, and the revision period is generally much longer than the period for annual revisions, often stretching back as far as 1929.

All the revisions can be significant. What matters most isn't getting the numbers right but correctly assessing whether real GDP growth is likely to be better or worse than widely expected by the financial markets. It's getting the surprise right that matters. Better-than-expected growth can boost earnings and stock prices more than expected. It can also lead to higher inflation and bond yields than generally anticipated. So having an accurate, big-picture view of the various forces driving the economy is extremely important.

In addition to measuring GDP from the demand side of the economy, there are also supply-side and income-side perspectives. Again, although GDP is measured by summing the final sales in all the major sectors of the economy and adding changes in inventories, it is a measure of the economy's production, or output, of goods and services. The supply side simply shows that real GDP must be equal to labor input—as measured by aggregate hours worked by all payroll employees—multiplied by productivity. This is an arithmetic identity because productivity is calculated from the other two variables. I discuss productivity in Chapter 3 and labor input in Chapter 6.

The income-side estimate of GDP attempts to match the demand-side measure. All production generates income. The major income items are employees' compensation (including wages, salaries, and supplements), proprietors' income, rental income, corporate profits, and net interest income. Proprietors' income is the earnings of the owners of privately held businesses. Rental income is paid by tenants to their landlords. (See Appendix 5.3, Gross Domestic Product, Gross National Product, and National Income.)

All these sources of income are measured as derived from "current production." So they are adjusted to exclude all capital gains and losses. Compensation does not include gains and losses from investments in financial assets (including stock options) and real estate. The profits numbers include an inventory valuation adjustment to eliminate gains and losses on inventories attributable to price changes. The capital consumption adjustment does the same for gains and losses on the value of plant and equipment.

When all the major sources of income are added together, they sum to national income. Gross domestic income (GDI) is national income plus the economy's capital consumption allowance, or depreciation. GDI should equal GDP measured from the demand side. The numbers are often very close; their statistical discrepancy usually has been in a tight range of 2.0%–3.0% of nominal GDP (Fig. 52 and Fig. 53).

Interesting insights into income distribution in the economy can be garnered by tracking and comparing the shares of national income attributable to its major components. I examine them in Chapter 7's discussion of income distribution.

By the way, GDP plus net income receipts from the rest of the world is equal to gross national product (GNP). The bulk of net income receipts tends to be net profits receipts from the rest of the world. GNP less depreciation ("consumption of fixed capital") and less the statistical discrepancy is equal to national income. This equation is based on the obvious accounting identity that the value of a country's production must equal the income it generates.

Business cycles happen. Booms are followed by busts, which are followed by recoveries, expansions, booms, and so on. As the saying goes: wash, rinse, repeat. Business cycles will continue to happen despite all the efforts of economists to moderate them. They are based on human nature, reflecting the collective emotional cycle of greed, fear, repeat. To understand them better, we need to be more micro and less macro in our analysis. The following chapters explore how to do just that.

CHAPTER 6

Predicting Consumers

ONE OF THE CROWD

FORECASTING CONSUMER SPENDING is obviously one of the major inputs into the process of predicting both the trend and the cycle in GDP. The United States is a consumer society. We consume a lot, both collectively and individually. In current dollars, personal consumption expenditures accounted for a record 69% of nominal GDP at the end of 2016, well above its record low of 59% during the first quarter of 1967 (Fig. 1*). By the way, that uptrend is entirely attributable to health-care spending. Data available since 1960 show that consumption spending excluding health care has been quite stable at around 55% of GDP (Fig. 2).

When possible, I build my forecasting frameworks on the solid foundations of accounting identities since they ensure that my numbers will all add up. It is an accounting identity that personal consumption expenditures equals disposable personal income (i.e., personal income minus personal taxes) less personal saving. The after-tax income that consumers don't save is spent on goods and services. Of course, in the real world, saving is what's left after we've gone on our shopping sprees. The personal saving rate is equal to personal saving divided by disposable personal income. The flip side of the saving rate is the consumption rate. For example, if consumers save 5% of their disposable income, then they must have consumed 95% of it.

---

* Figures, references, and appendices are linked on *yardenibook.com/resources*.

On an inflation-adjusted (real) basis, consumption is determined primarily by real disposable income. Personal income is driven by employment and the length of the workweek, which are driven by profits, as I explain in the previous chapter. Another key driver of real personal income is real hourly pay, which is mostly determined by productivity, as I discuss in the next chapter. The trend in personal income depends on the trends in these variables, which are influenced by demographic trends as well. Disposable income is also a function of the average effective tax rate, which reflects the net impact of marginal income tax rates as well as exemptions and deductions for individual taxpayers. In addition to taxing individuals, the government redistributes a significant portion of personal income through transfer payments, including Social Security and other entitlement programs.

As a variable in the consumption model, the personal saving rate depends on consumer confidence, changes in net worth, investment returns, inflation, risk aversion, and liquidity preference. Personal saving can also be defined as the change in net worth, which is the change in assets minus the change in liabilities. However, keep in mind that the National Income and Product Accounts (NIPA) focus on income from current production. So capital gains and losses, capital transfers, and other events that don't represent an economic transaction are not included in the NIPA measure of personal saving.

That last point is important. Many economists wail that the saving rate is too low. But if consumers' wealth has been rising because their portfolios of stocks, real estate, and other assets have appreciated in value, their need to save is reduced. When consumers buy autos and other durable consumer goods, that's counted as current consumption even though the product they buy might be a useful asset for several years.

In other words, there are lots of moving parts in the economy's consumption engine. Trying to model consumption, especially with a black-box econometric approach, is quite challenging, given the interdependence of all the variables.

Furthermore, most macro models of consumption omit what I believe are among the most important variables: demographic ones, which are usually deemed to change too slowly to explain consumption over the relevant forecasting period. I disagree with that conventional wisdom. I've found that demographic variables are always relevant. True, they do take time to change, but their trends are immensely important for understanding consumer spending and saving behavior. So while I spend lots of time analyzing the macro relationship between consumption and income, I also make sure to monitor the demographic variables regularly, slow changing though they are.

The characteristics of the overall population are the obvious starting point for demographic analysis. Fertility rates, birth rates, and longevity determine the population's age composition and growth rate. Dividing up the population into distinct age cohorts is useful because members of each group tend to have similar behavioral characteristics. The key assumption in this classification of cohorts by birth years is that they have a lot in common because of their similar ages and experiences, especially during their formative teen years. That's when people generally become aware of the world around them. What they experience shapes their generation's common attitudes. Presumably, these experiences determine their decisions to get married, have children, buy houses, plan for retirement, and so on. All these decisions clearly have significant effects on consumption and saving.

Admittedly, categorizing people in this manner can be a bit arbitrary. There seems to be universal agreement that the Baby Boomers were born between 1946 and 1964 (Fig. 3). Preceding the Baby Boomers is the Silent Generation, born between 1928 and 1945, which is preceded by the Greatest Generation, born between 1910 and 1927. There is less agreement on the birth dates of the Millennials, a.k.a. "Generation Y." I pick 1981 to 1996 because that covers all young adults 20–35 years old during 2016.[1] Sandwiched in between (i.e., born between 1965 and 1980) is Generation X, consisting of middle-aged adults who were 36–51 during 2016. Generation Z comes after Generation Y (the Millennials) and includes everyone born between 1997 and 2014, though it is too soon to tell how much they all have in common. I'm not sure what convention will be used for naming the next group, the oldest of whom is being born as I write this in 2017.[2]

The general fertility rate in the United States was relatively high at the start of the 1900s (Fig. 4). It plunged during the Great Depression of the 1930s. People were too depressed to have sex. (That really is depressing!) It remained low during World War II for an obvious reason: the men were soldiering overseas, while the women were riveting and welding military equipment in America's factories. When the soldiers came home after the war, the fertility rate soared, again for obvious reasons: they were all frisky after so much time apart. Baby-making boomed as the rate of live births per 1,000 women aged 15–44 per year rose from 86 in 1945, peaked at 123 during 1957—the highest since 1916—then subsided to 105 in 1964. Those born in the interval make up the Baby Boom generation. After 1964, the birth rate trended down through the mid-1970s before stabilizing at around 65 live births ever since. Contributing to the decline was the birth control pill, approved by the Federal Drug Administration in 1960.

I am truly one of millions. Born on March 15, 1950, I am just another one of the 76 million Baby Boomers. My cohort has tended to believe that we are special individuals. We've tended to be self-absorbed, which may be one reason why our fertility rate was much lower than our parents'. As a result, the average number of persons per family peaked at 3.7 during 1965, the highest since 1942. It then trended down to around 3.1 at the start of the 1990s and remained there through 2016 (Fig. 5).

Pop culture reflected our self-involvement as we became young adults, and two hit songs seem to capture the milieu back then particularly well: Carly Simon's "You're So Vain" (1972) and English group Right Said Fred's "I'm Too Sexy" (1991). Both songs are about narcissists, and both songs reference themselves *as songs*, suggesting a whole new level of self-absorbed navel-gazing.

During the mid-1970s, Tom Wolfe and Christopher Lasch spoke critically about the narcissism of the "Me Generation." On television in the 1990s, the epitome of the Baby Boomers' self-absorption was *Seinfeld*, the wildly popular situation comedy that ran for nine seasons on NBC. The show's claim to fame was that it was about nothing in particular. It featured the day-to-day experiences of four single 30-something friends living in Manhattan with no attachments, comically preoccupied with the trivial concerns of their own egos.

For a short while, I also thought I was special, until I realized that I was just like most of the 76 million other Baby Boomers, especially those growing up in middle-class suburbia. We watched lots of westerns and sitcoms on television during the 1950s and 1960s, such as *The Little Rascals*, *Rin Tin Tin*, *The Lone Ranger*, *Bonanza*, *The Brady Bunch*, and *Gilligan's Island*. Television programs were far more innocent back then than now, and so was life in general. We walked to school on our own and played outdoors with our friends until it was time for dinner. Other than occasional drills to take cover under our school desks in the event of a nuclear attack during the Cold War, nothing threatening entered our awareness much. Our happy days were unperturbed until the late 1960s and early 1970s, when geopolitics became more personal: many of us had serious concerns about being drafted to fight in the Vietnam War.

Most of us wanted to go to a good college. We took the Scholastic Aptitude Test (SAT) without any tutorial preparation. We filled out our own college applications and wrote our own essays. Some of us went on to get advanced degrees from graduate college programs or from business or law schools; we wanted to get an edge once we realized that we had to compete with one another to get good jobs.

My generation wasn't burdened by student loans. Many of us didn't need financial aid because college was very affordable. Tuition, room, and board cost around $3,000 per year at Cornell when I was an undergraduate between 1968 and 1972. The tuition at Yale's graduate school wasn't much more, and I borrowed a small amount from a government student loan program that I easily paid within a few years of my employment. By the way, college tuition in the consumer price index (CPI) has increased 14-fold since 1978, while the overall CPI has increased fourfold (Fig. 6)! That might also explain why the fertility rate is down: raising kids is much more expensive now than when we were growing up. For some reason, that didn't deter me from having five children.

The official labor force statistics include all workers 16 years or older. The oldest Baby Boomers turned 16 during 1962, the youngest during 1980 (Fig. 7). Of course, many of the Baby Boomers entered the labor force several years after they turned 16 because they were in school during their late teens and early 20s. From 1962 through 1980, the labor force increased 37.3 million. The percentage of the labor force that was 16–34 years old—i.e., relatively young—rose from 37% to 51% over this period. I show in Chapter 4 that this measure of the Age Wave has been highly correlated with the inflation trend.

The labor force participation rate, which is the percentage of the working-age population in the labor force, either employed or unemployed, climbed from 59% in 1962 to 64% in 1980 (Fig. 8). It continued rising until it peaked at a record 67% during the first quarter of 2000. The participation rate was boosted by an influx of Baby Boomer women as more of them than ever went to college and then to work. Women's percentage in the labor force rose from 36% during 1967 to about 46% by the mid-1990s and has remained around there (Fig. 9). The labor force participation rate fell from its 2000 peak to 63% by the end of 2016, mostly because the women's participation rate stabilized, more young adults went to college, and the Baby Boomers started to retire.

Many of us got married after college, soon after starting our first job. In 1967, when the oldest Baby Boomers turned 21, the median age of marriage was 21 for women and 23 for men (Fig. 10). From there, both matrimonial measures trended higher, reaching 29 for men and 27 for women in 2015.

Many of us with two income earners at home had combined family incomes that qualified us for a mortgage to buy a house in the suburbs, so our kids could have a backyard to play in. We had to come up with at least 20% of the purchase price as a down payment, which we borrowed from our parents if we hadn't saved enough. The homeownership rate—i.e., the percentage of households owning rather than renting a housing unit— rose during the second half of the 1960s and through the 1970s from about 63% to 66% (Fig. 11). Following the severe recession at the start of the 1980s, it fell back down to 64% in the middle of the decade. Then it resumed its climb to new record highs during the second half of the 1990s through the first half of the next decade, peaking at a record 69% during 2004. From there, primarily because of the mortgage debacle of 2007 and 2008, it dropped back down to roughly 64% at the end of 2016.

Many of us middle-class Baby Boomers enjoyed a charmed life growing up in the suburbs but nonetheless swore that we wouldn't return to the "burbs" after going off to college. That changed after we married our college sweethearts and had kids. We moved back, wishing for our kids the same advantages we had enjoyed. Owning a nicely furnished home with a backyard in a good public-school district became an obsession. So did renovating our kitchens with state-of-the-art stainless steel appliances and granite countertops. A two-car garage was required, since each income earner needed a vehicle.

After graduating from Yale, I rented a small one-bedroom apartment in New York City when I started working at the Federal Reserve Bank of New York during 1976. I had married the year before at the age of 25. I remarried at the age of 30, and Melissa, my first child, was born at the end of 1981. Her mother and I purchased a small house in Scarsdale, New York the same year. The down payment came from a windfall I received when my Manhattan rental apartment building converted to co-ops at a very low price for insiders. With two income earners in our little house-hold, we qualified for a mortgage with a rate of 16%. Yes, I must admit that I managed to get close to the all-time highest mortgage rate in US history when I purchased my first home (Fig. 12).

During the next three decades, I traded up to bigger and more expensive homes as my income rose and my household expanded to include five children. Sarah was born in 1985, followed by Sam in 1989. Eventually, I settled on the north shore of Long Island with Valerie and our two children, David and Laura, while my three older children from my previous marriage formed their own households. I never bought a second home for vacationing, as did many of my Wall Street colleagues. A few of them had houses in the Hamptons. I did rent a couple of summers out there, but the traffic was too much, and one house was enough to maintain for me.

Fortunately, I figured out early in my career that I wasn't all that unique, and I could base many of my insights about US consumers on my own life under the assumption that I was like many of my demographic brethren.

The Baby Boomers as a generation, however, are quite unique. They are the first to live and work well past the traditional retirement age of 65. I'm 68 in 2018 and have no plans to retire. I don't play golf, which takes a lot of time. I play tennis a couple of days a week. I would be totally bored if I retired.

On the other hand, "trading down" is the norm for senior Baby Boomers, as it was for their parents during their senior years. Selling big houses and moving into smaller ones or apartments makes sense once the kids have moved on, assuming they haven't moved back in. A more minimalist lifestyle makes sense for older folks.

The problem for the economy, as I discuss in the next chapter, is that the generation of young adults who should be taking the spending baton from the Baby Boomers also are minimalists. Another issue is whether income inequality is getting worse and weighing on economic growth. Before I go there, let's look at some of the broad factors besides demographics that drive consumer spending.

PURCHASING POWER TO THE PEOPLE

WITHOUT A DOUBT, lots of Baby Boomers have been natural-born spenders. More broadly, Americans have always been willing and able consumers. They've been reliable shoppers for several reasons. Except during occasional short recessions and rare depressions, Americans' purchasing power increases along with employment and inflation-adjusted wages. In this section, I examine the trends and cycles in the drivers of consumers' purchasing power. Let's start with employment.

The US labor market is remarkably "liquid" when the economy is growing, which it tends to be most of the time. This means that job seekers, whether they are laid off or just entering the labor market, tend to find employment relatively quickly. From the end of World War II to the end of 2016, there have been 276 quarters (counting from the first quarter of 1948), with only 41 of the quarters, or 15%, recessionary ones. The median duration of unemployment tends to be very short, just a few weeks, when the economy is growing (Fig. 13).

There is an amazing amount of turnover in the US labor market. In its monthly Job Openings and Labor Turnover Survey (JOLTS) report, the Bureau of Labor Statistics (BLS) publishes data on hires and separations (the latter resulting mostly from layoffs and quits) from December 2000 onward.[3] Over the 12 months through December 2016, hires totaled 63 million (Fig. 14). Over this same period, separations totaled 61 million, with 36 million quits and 20 million layoffs.[4] For perspective, payroll employment totaled 145 million at the end of 2016; expressed as a percentage of total employment, separations during 2016 were 42% and new hires 43%. The turnover in the labor market is truly phenomenal.

The available JOLTS data strongly suggest that during good times, much of the turnover is attributable to workers quitting, presumably for better jobs that pay more. This forces their previous employers to try to fill the open positions, perhaps at higher wages to attract applicants. In such situations, wages might go up for current employees so that they don't walk out the door. As I discuss in Chapter 4, the subdued pace of wage gains has been puzzling in recent years, as quits have risen sharply. I attribute this surprising development to the retirement of the Baby Boomers, who presumably are being replaced by lower-paid young workers.

About a week before the JOLTS report is released each month, the BLS releases its Employment Situation report on the first Friday of each month, at 8:30 a.m.[5] This report has always been one of the most important economic releases for financial markets. As I note in the previous chapter, the employment cycle is driven by the profits cycle. Profitable companies expand; unprofitable ones retrench. So employment is a very important sign of business confidence in the economy.

Employment is the main driver of wages and salaries, which is the biggest component of personal income. The employment cycle also influences the wage cycle. When labor markets tighten, there is likely to be upward pressure on wages, though there are many countervailing forces, as I explain in Chapter 4 on inflation. During recessions, when employment is falling, the adverse impact on workers can be magnified by falling wages—though, again, it's not that simple.

There are two major time series that measure employment in the monthly BLS release:

- *Household employment* measures the number of workers, whether they have one or more jobs (Fig. 15). Each person 16 years or older in a sample household is classified as employed, unemployed, or not in the labor force based on responses to a series of questions on work and job-search activities.[6] The sum of the employed and unemployed is equal to the civilian labor force. The labor force participation rate is the ratio of the labor force divided by the non-institutional working-age population. The unemployment rate is the number of unemployed as a percentage of the labor force. The employment-to-population ratio tracks the percentage of the population that is employed. These measures are based on data collected in the Current Population Survey of about 60,000 households and are selected to reflect the entire civilian noninstitutional population.

- *Payroll employment* is based on paychecks, so it reflects the number of jobs rather than the number of workers. A worker with two part-time jobs shows up twice if both jobs are on the books. This measure is limited to nonfarm payrolls and does not include agricultural workers, self-employed workers whose businesses are unincorporated, unpaid family workers, and private household workers. They are all included in the survey of households. The data include the employment, hours, and earnings of employees on nonfarm payrolls. The survey of establishments with payroll employees does not include as employed those people on unpaid leave, while the household survey does. The establishments data are not limited by age. Given the focus on the number of jobs, the survey uses payroll employment data to measure wages and salaries. Household employment has always exceeded payroll employment, mostly because the former includes self-employed workers while the latter does not.

Each month, the Current Employment Statistics program surveys about 147,000 businesses and government agencies, representing approximately 634,000 individual worksites, to provide detailed industry data on the employment, hours, and earnings of workers on nonfarm payrolls. The active sample includes approximately one-third of all nonfarm payroll employees.[7]

The payroll employment series is the one to which the financial markets tend to react the most when the monthly data are released. That's because this series drives wages and salaries and therefore consumption in the economy. It is also less volatile than the household data (Fig. 16). That's probably because payrolls are mostly based on hard data from establishments, while the household measure is based on phone interviews. Nevertheless, the payroll measure does have some funky issues:

- *Adjustment.* Payroll employment includes a statistical estimate of employment among small businesses based on a Birth/Death Model (BDM) run by the BLS.[8] This adjustment for business births and deaths is added to the estimate based on the survey data, and the sum is seasonally adjusted. I am always amazed by economists and journalists who claim that the payroll numbers are somehow rigged by the inclusion of the adjustment, which they often report as though it were seasonally adjusted. In fact, it isn't seasonally adjusted on its own. The seasonal adjustments are applied to the combination of the not seasonally adjusted data derived from the payrolls survey and the BDM.

    One simple way to eliminate the seasonality in the BDM (or any monthly time series) to see its underlying cycle and trend is to calculate its 12-month sum or average. The monthly average of the BDM adjustment since 2004 has ranged between a low of 24,000 and a high of 90,000 (Fig. 17). This isn't much data, but it does suggest that the adjustment rises during economic expansions as businesses are born faster than they die. That's what happened during the current and previous economic expansions. During the recession of 2008 and through the end of 2010, the pace of business deaths outpaced births. This cyclical pattern is all quite plausible. On a 12-month-sum basis since 2004, the adjustment has added between a low of 288,000 and a high of 1.08 million jobs.

- *Revisions.* The initial report of payrolls tends to be revised in the next two monthly reports as more information becomes available (Fig. 18).

In fact, I tend to give much more weight to the data for the two revised months than to the latest preliminary estimate because the revisions can be significant. Furthermore, I believe they contain useful information. It's not so obvious monthly, but the sum of the revisions over the previous 12 months tends to be a strong cyclical indicator (Fig. 19). On this basis, the revisions tend to be positive and increasing during a business-cycle recovery and early expansion. They tend to turn less positive at the tail end of an expansion, then increasingly negative when the subsequent recession unfolds.

While I don't get as agitated about the BDM adjustment as some of my peers, it is an oddity, for sure. In the private sector, there are a couple of firms that process payrolls for lots of other companies. We use Paychex for my company's payroll needs. ADP provides a similar service for a huge cross-section of companies. They collect lots of useful information that could improve the official payroll data.

As a matter of fact, during April 2001, ADP started providing monthly data on payrolls comparable to the government's statistics. The series compiled by ADP are based on the payroll checks that the company processes. They are seasonally adjusted. The monthly total tracks the official private-sector payroll employment series (Fig. 20). The yearly changes also are very close (Fig. 21). The ADP series tends to be revised much less than the BLS series. (See Appendix 6.1, Alternative Measures of Employment.)

The ADP report is released a couple of days before the BLS numbers. Why few of my peers attach as much significance to it as I do also mystifies me. The ADP data are especially useful for seeing employment trends among companies categorized as large, medium, or small. Guess which size of company employs the most people and therefore does the most hiring? I give the answer away in the previous chapter: small firms that turn into medium and large firms.

- At the end of 2016, small companies (with one to 49 employees) employed 50.9 million workers, medium ones (with 50 to 499 employees) had 44.2 million workers, while large companies' payrolls totaled 28.0 million (Fig. 22).
- Since the start (in 2005) of the data showing the breakdown by size, small companies have consistently accounted for 41% of private-sector payrolls, while medium and large ones accounted for around 36% and 23%, respectively (Fig. 23).

This suggests that the best way to boost economic growth and employment is to create a business environment that is highly conducive to the formation of new businesses and gives them a good shot at success.

As I mention in the previous two chapters, the National Federation of Independent Business (NFIB) conducts a monthly survey of small business owners. This group tends to be politically conservative. They generally don't like government; when asked about the "most important problems small businesses face," taxes and government regulation tend to top their list (Fig. 24). As a small business owner myself, I share their entrepreneurial spirit. I've also found that the NFIB survey data provide great insights into the labor market.

The national unemployment rate is highly correlated with the NFIB's "poor sales" series (Fig. 25). It is also highly correlated with the inverse of the NFIB's series on the net percentage reporting that their earnings are higher minus lower over the past three months (Fig. 26). This certainly confirms my view that employment is driven by the profits cycle. The NFIB's series on the percentage of small business owners reporting that they have job openings they can't currently fill is a very useful indicator of the condition of the labor market, much like the national unemployment rate (Fig. 27).

As noted above, the household survey data compiled by the BLS are used to calculate the labor force, which includes workers who are either employed or unemployed but seeking a job (Fig. 28). Anyone else who is part of the working-age population (16 years and older) is deemed to be "not in the labor force," or a "NILF." These folks include retired or disabled workers, students, stay-at-home spouses, and unpaid family caregivers. Some are so-called "discouraged workers," who have dropped out of the labor force because they are no longer looking for a job. This category tends to swell during recessions, when jobs are hard to get.

The number of working-age people who are 65 or older has been rising rapidly in recent years and will continue to do so as the Baby Boomers age. That's already boosting their numbers among the NILFs as they retire (Fig. 29).[9] At the end of 2016, there were 95.0 million NILFs, with 39.7 million of them 65 or older. So there were 55.3 million NILFs who were 16–64 years old. They are mostly students and others who truly have dropped out of the labor force for various reasons. The BLS reported that only 6.0% of all NILFs wanted a job, although they weren't seeking one, at the end of 2016.

The unemployment rate is also based on the household survey and reflects the number of workers who say they are actively looking for a job but have yet to land one. They include unemployed workers who have lost jobs and people entering the labor force for the first time or reentering it after a spell of being out for one reason or another.

The amount of information provided every month in the Employment Situation report can make your head spin. To cut to the chase, I calculate what I call the "Earned Income Proxy" (EIP) for wages and salaries in personal income. It is simply aggregate weekly hours worked per week multiplied by the average hourly earnings (AHE) of all payroll employees in the private sector, multiplied by 52 weeks to annualize the proxy (Fig. 30). The first variable reflects total payroll employment times the average length of the workweek. The second variable is average hourly pay, including both hourly and salaried workers.

When I first started to calculate the EIP, a seasoned economics reporter at *The New York Times* called and asked me to explain how I calculated it. He double-checked the validity of my procedure with his sources at the BEA. They told him—then he told me—that this is actually the way the BEA comes up with the preliminary estimate of private wages and salaries that is included in the monthly personal income release that comes out a couple of weeks after the employment report.

I've just examined the employment component of wages and salaries. Now, let's turn to the other two components of payroll workers' purchasing power:

- *The average length of the workweek* is also a cyclical variable that affects consumers' purchasing power (Fig. 31). The average length of the workweek for manufacturing is one of the 10 components of the Index of Leading Economic Indicators (LEI). It is reported monthly in the BLS Employment Situation report and has fluctuated in a procyclical fashion around its average of 40.8 hours from 1964 through 2016. The average workweek for all production and nonsupervisory workers is also cyclical, but it has also had a significant downward trend because of an increase in part-time workers. The BLS has been collecting data for all private-industry workers only since March 2006.

- *The real hourly wage rate* is the purchasing power of the average worker, which is determined by the average worker's hourly pay divided by the price level. The best measure of prices paid by consumers is the personal consumption expenditures deflator (PCED), as I discuss in

Chapter 4, where I also review several alternative measures of hourly pay, both including and excluding benefits. The one economists use most often is AHE, which includes a few benefits but excludes most of the big ones, such as pension and health-care benefits. The AHE for production and nonsupervisory workers has covered 80.5% to 83.5% of private-sector payroll employment since 1964 (Fig. 32).

What can the trends in the real hourly wage measure tell us about consumer purchasing power over recent decades? The measure trended higher during the second half of the 1960s through 1972. It then stagnated with a downward drift through the mid-1990s. It's been on an uptrend since then, rising 27% from January 1996 through December 2016 to a record high. That certainly belies the widely held notion that real wages have stagnated over this period (Fig. 33). In the next chapter's section on the standard of living, I show the relationship between this and other measures of the average worker's purchasing power and productivity.

It's worth taking the time to learn what is included in personal income. "Compensation of employees" includes wages, salaries, and supplements to wages and salaries. The other sources of income are basically returns on investments. "Proprietors' income with inventory valuation and capital consumption adjustments" is essentially the profits of closely held small businesses. "Rental income of persons with capital consumption adjustment" is what landlords earn on their rental properties. "Personal income receipts on assets" includes personal interest income and personal dividend income. "Personal current transfer payments" consists mostly of "government social benefits paid to persons." (See Appendix 6.2, Personal Income and Its Disposition.)

Now, take a breath before our deep dive into these components of personal income:

- *Wages and salaries* is the biggest and most cyclical component of personal income, so it drives both the trend and the cycle in retail sales and total personal consumption expenditures.[10] It accounted for a little more than 60% of personal income from the late 1940s through the late 1970s (Fig. 34). It then trended downward during the 1980s and 1990s, falling to a low of 49.5% during the final quarter of 2012. It was up to 50.6% during the fourth quarter of 2016. The descent was partly attributable to the decline in the clout of labor unions as well as to deindustrialization as US factories moved to countries with lower labor costs.

- *Supplements in compensation* consists of contributions by employers to their employees' retirement and health insurance funds as well as to government social insurance programs on their employees' behalf (Fig. 35). The latter payments aren't voluntary but rather reflect funds collected with the payroll tax, which is split 50-50 between employees and their employers. The half paid by employers is counted as income to the employees. That may sound odd, but it does make sense. In any event, both components of supplements have grown, mostly because of rising health-care costs, and aren't very cyclical. So they don't have much influence on the fluctuations in consumer spending.

   Total supplements as a percentage of compensation rose from 6.1% during the third quarter of 1948 to 19.5% during the first quarter of 1993 and has fluctuated around there through 2016 (Fig. 36). This suggests that another reason for the downward trend in wages and salaries relative to total compensation is simply that employers have been providing more compensation in the form of supplements. Employees have welcomed that, particularly because health-care premiums paid by their employer are not counted as taxable income to them.

- *Proprietors' income* is the earnings from the current production of unincorporated nonfarm businesses, including sole proprietorships, partnerships, and other private nonfarm businesses that are organized for profit but that are not classified as corporations.[11] The income of unincorporated businesses is generally reported on individual income-tax returns. In economic effect, proprietors' income should be considered as important for employment and business spending as corporate profits (Fig. 37). The ratio of the former to the latter was greater than 1.00 during the late 1940s and early 1950s (Fig. 38). It has been fluctuating around 0.75 since the early 1960s, with proprietors' income tending to hold up better than corporate profits during recessions.

- *The rental income component of personal income* includes rent from both tenant-occupied and owner-occupied properties less expenses (Fig. 39). The BEA includes outlays on both in personal consumption expenditures (Fig. 40). For tenant-occupied property, the rental income of persons is calculated as the output of housing services (the rental value or "space rent") less the related expenses, such as depreciation, maintenance and repairs, property taxes, and mortgage interest.

Owner-occupied housing is treated as though the owner-occupants are in the rental business, with the landlords renting to themselves. This rent is imputed based on the rents charged for similar tenant-occupied housing. This may seem odd, but it is necessary for GDP to be invariant when housing units shift between tenant occupancy and owner occupancy.[12] It is also calculated net of the expenses associated with owner-occupied housing, such as depreciation, maintenance and repairs, property taxes, and mortgage interest.

What about mortgage principal payments? The NIPAs are based on income from current production. Purchases of assets and payments to pay down loans on previously purchased assets are not included in personal consumption. These uses of personal income are included in personal saving, which is disposable personal income less personal consumption.

- *Government social benefits to persons* is the fastest-growing component of personal income (Fig. 41). These are the transfer payments from the government to individuals through various entitlement programs, including Social Security, Medicare, Medicaid, unemployment insurance, and veterans' benefits. Each is a line item in the personal income release. In total, these transfer payments have increased from 5.6% of personal income during 1960 to 17.1% during 2016.

- *Disposable personal income*, in the personal income report, is derived by subtracting personal current taxes from total income. These taxes consist mostly of personal income taxes, which are based on a progressive system of marginal tax rates that are higher at higher income levels. The ratio of these taxes to personal income tends to be very procyclical, rising during economic expansions and falling during contractions and early recovery periods (Fig. 42).

As noted above, payroll taxes appear on two different line items in the BEA release. These taxes are regressive in the sense that everyone pays the same tax rate. Employees pay half, while employers pay the other half. The BEA shows an item under supplements to wages and salaries titled "Employer contributions for government social insurance." (Separately, the BEA publishes a series on actual payments made by pension and insurance funds, which tend to exceed employers' contributions, as the next chapter reviews.)

The payroll taxes paid by individuals is subtracted from personal income in a category labeled "Contributions for government social insurance." In theory, revenues from payroll taxes are supposed to cover the cost of the government's entitlement programs, which are inherently progressive. In practice, all the government's revenues are comingled.

• *Unrealized capital gains (or losses)* from real estate or any other asset are not included in personal income and personal saving, as they represent a change in wealth. The BEA notes, "Capital gains are excluded from saving because they represent changes in prices of pre-existing assets and they are not a source of funding for new investment. Unlike the creation of new assets via investment, changes in price of already-existing assets do not add to economic growth."

We can come up for air now.

To track the impact of consumers on real GDP, economists monitor real personal consumption expenditures and its main driver, real disposable personal income. The nominal (or "current-dollar") series for both are adjusted for inflation by dividing them by the PCED (Fig. 43). Both are on the same upward trends, driven mostly by employment, which also mostly determines the cyclical performance of both. (Recall from the previous chapter that real personal income excluding transfer payments is one of the four official coincident indicators of the economy.)

The yearly growth rate in real disposable income tends to be somewhat more volatile than the yearly growth rate in real personal consumption expenditures (Fig. 44). Milton Friedman developed his "Permanent Income Hypothesis" in his 1957 book, *A Theory of the Consumption Function*. The simplest version of his hypothesis is that individual consumers make their spending and saving decisions based on their current and projected incomes. Transitory changes in their income don't have a significant impact on these decisions. That's just common sense.

The more complex and politically charged version of the hypothesis suggests that fiscal policies aimed at stimulating economic growth probably won't be very effective if consumers view them as transitory. Conservatives argue that one-time tax rebates and temporary tax cuts won't work, while a permanent tax cut will. A one-shot increase in government spending is also likely to have no permanent impact on consumer spending. Deficit-financed fiscal outlays may also be counterproductive, especially if they are long-term in nature, because consumers might rationally expect that eventually their taxes must be raised to service the resulting accumulation of government debt. I side with the conservatives on this issue.

While I am on this subject, let me posit my Permanent Debt Hypothesis. This is particularly relevant to monetary policy. While consumers may or may not think of the government's debt as ultimately their personal burden, their own debts are obviously very personal. If monetary policy attempts to stimulate consumer demand by providing easy credit conditions, consumers are likely to consume today what they might have consumed in the future by borrowing against their expectation of future income. Friedman's Permanent Income Hypothesis suggests that's a logical thing to do.

In my opinion, over time, the accumulation of personal debt will reduce the effectiveness of easy money. That's because over time, people will avail themselves less and less of the opportunity that low rates present—having already met their pent-up needs, or having leveraged themselves as much as they feel comfortable doing, or feeling less confident about the adequacy of future income to sustain more borrowing since consumers' assessment of their permanent and spendable disposable income drops as debt-servicing costs increase.

That's about as theoretical as I've ever needed to be when it comes to predicting consumer spending. I was taught in my macroeconomics courses about the marginal propensity to consume. It's the change in consumption attributable to a change in income. In his 1936 classic, *The General Theory of Employment, Interest, and Money*, John Maynard Keynes devoted three chapters to the concept as well as to the related consumption function and multiplier. I've never found these concepts particularly useful for doing my job. In the accounting identity I use, the average propensity to consume is simply the flip side of the average saving rate. If the saving rate is 5%, then the consumption rate is 95%. In the past, my consumer-spending forecasts either hit or missed their marks depending on whether my forecasts for personal income and the average saving rate hit or missed theirs.

BORN TO SHOP

AS I KNOW from experience, having two incomes, five kids, and a house makes one spend money. During my career on Wall Street, I've often cautioned our accounts, "Don't bet against us American consumers. We were born to shop."

Americans have always sought to improve the standard of living for themselves and their loved ones. Many immigrants to the United States during the early 1900s toiled endlessly so that they could afford to send their children to college. While their standard of living was poor, they hoped that their children would have a much better life because of their selfless hard work. Those who managed to do well moved to the suburbs.

In the suburbs, Americans became less selfless and more materialistic. The goal was no longer just a better life for the kids. "Keeping up with the Joneses" became increasingly important. This phrase originated with the comic strip of the same name, created by Arthur R. "Pop" Momand in 1913. It ran until 1938 in various newspapers, depicting the social-climbing McGinis family. They struggled to keep up with their neighbors, the Joneses, who were often mentioned but never shown. Once the Baby Boomers moved back to the suburbs as parents, the ability to provide their children with a good education and home life was taken for granted. There was enough money available to go after more materialistic and aspirational goals.

I'm an economist, not a preacher. Moralists, environmentalists, and other social critics can rail against materialism and its consequences. As an economist, I share Adam Smith's view that accumulating wealth may not buy happiness for the wealthy, but it can produce general prosperity. He said so in *The Theory of Moral Sentiments* (1759) in his famous parable of the poor man's son who aspires to be rich. After discussing it in some detail, he gets to his famous punchline about the invisible hand:

> The rich only select from the heap what is most precious and agreeable. They consume little more than the poor, and in spite of their natural selfishness and rapacity, though they mean only their own conveniency, though the sole end which they propose from the labours of all the thousands whom they employ, be the gratification of their own vain and insatiable desires, they divide with the poor the produce of all their improvements. They are led by an invisible hand to make nearly the same distribution of the necessaries of life, which would have been made, had the earth been divided into equal portions among all its inhabitants, and thus without intending it, without knowing it, advance the interest of the society, and afford means to the multiplication of the species.

That's remarkably naïve. The rich can certainly get richer while exploiting the thousands of workers they employ, while many others are unemployed. Just read your history: all the Parisians who revolted against Louis XVI in 1789 knew that. Smith addressed this problem in *The Wealth of Nations* (1776), where the competitive marketplace is acknowledged to be a prerequisite for increasing the wealth of the entire nation, not just a few plutocrats. However, Smith got it wrong when he attributed the beneficences of the invisible hand to the unintended consequences of the selfishness of the butcher, the brewer, and the baker, i.e., "their regard for their own interest."

As I explain in the first chapter, in a competitive economy, producers aren't selfish; they are insecure, in my opinion. They constantly fear that their competitors will put them out of business. If the butcher, the brewer, and the baker don't give their customers the very best merchandise at the lowest prices, they will surely lose business to competitors who are doing so. In other words, "their own interest" is to do the best they can for their consumers. That's not selfishness; it's good business! Knowing your customers is a prerequisite for staying in business in a capitalist marketplace.

Consumers are the undisputed kings and queens of America's highly competitive economy. They are the plutocrats. Producers and retailers are constantly scrambling to give them what they want, i.e., goods and services of the highest quality at the lowest price. If consumers aren't happy with what they bought today, they can return it and get their money back or at least a store credit. Americans have reciprocated by being very good shoppers. They tend to spend most of their disposable income.

They certainly don't save much. In the NIPA, personal saving is disposable personal income less outlays for personal consumption expenditures, non-mortgage interest payments, and net current transfers to government and to the rest of the world. Again, it excludes capital gains, which represent changes in the prices of assets that are already owned, not unspent portions of income receipts. This definition is used to calculate the contribution from persons to national saving, which is the total amount available to fund investment in fixed assets, inventories, or foreign assets. As noted above, asset purchases and mortgage principal payments are not included in consumption but rather in saving. There are alternative measures of personal saving, of course, but they are still mostly calculated as the residual after consumption and outlays.[13]

Since personal saving is calculated as a residual, all the statistical noise in both disposable personal income and consumption is reflected in the personal saving rate, which is personal saving divided by disposable personal income (Fig. 45). It's a volatile series on a short-term basis. It isn't especially cyclical, though it does tend to rise briefly during and after recessions. Most notable is that it rose from a postwar low of 5.0% during the second quarter of 1947 to a record high of 15.0% in mid-1975. It then fell on a downward trend to a record low of 2.2% during the third quarter of 2005. Since then, it has been rising again slowly.

The long downturn, which started in the mid-1970s, probably reflects the impact of the emergence of the American social welfare state following the enactment of President Lyndon Johnson's Great Society programs. Americans had less reason to save for retirement and for their healthcare needs. The Baby Boomers also had an impact. They drove up home prices, which increased the net worth of all homeowners, who increasingly viewed their homes not only as houses but also as sources of funds for retirement or other unexpected needs, which could be tapped with a second mortgage or a home equity loan.

Macroeconomists tend to follow consumer spending in aggregate. Occasionally, they'll focus on real personal income and real consumption per capita. My preference is to keep track of real personal income, consumption, and saving per household. As I discuss in the following chapter, the best measure of the standard of living is consumption per household, not in aggregate or per capita. I know this from my own experience. I often tell my accounts that when I'm reincarnated, I'd like to be reborn as one of my children. The two who still live at home have no income but a great standard of living, which I get to enjoy less often because I'm frequently on the road. I stay at comfortable hotels, but they aren't as comfortable as home sweet home.

Let's take another deep dive into the data for insights that can be gleaned by tracking the average household:

- *Real personal saving per household* has been both volatile and relatively trendless since the mid-1950s (Fig. 46). Like the nominal aggregate personal saving rate, it rose during the 1960s, then trended downward during the 1970s through the mid-2000s. It then rose sharply during and after the 2008 financial crisis. However, over this entire period, it averaged $5,035 per household per year, with a low of $2,685 and a high of $6,495. Again, Americans aren't savers. They're shoppers.

- *Real personal consumption per household* increased 184% from the fourth quarter of 1955 through the fourth quarter of 2016, closely tracking the upward trend in real disposable income per household (Fig. 47).

It declined during all but one of the recessions since 1955. However, it has always recovered and climbed to new heights. From the fourth quarter of 1955 through the final quarter of 2016, real disposable income per household rose from $39,300 to $106,032 at a seasonally adjusted annual rate. Real consumer spending per household rose from $34,746 to $98,548 over this period. Americans have seen their purchasing power grow, and they have used this power to purchase more goods and services.

- *Real spending per household on durable and nondurable goods* combined rose 153% from 1955 through 2016 (Fig. 48). However, spending on services has outpaced them significantly, rising 199% over this period.

In addition, some important insights can be had by studying the cycles and trends in the percentage of total current-dollar disposable income spent on various consumption categories. These percentages reflect the budget allocations of the average consumer rather than the average household, but my guess is that they are representative of most households:

- *Services.* There has been a significant secular increase (i.e., not seasonal or cyclical but rather a trend over time) in the percentage of consumers' budgets spent on services, from 36% at the start of 1947 to 63% at the end of 2016 (Fig. 49). The percentage spent on goods has dropped from 56% to 30% over this same period. As the standard of living of households has increased, more of their discretionary income has tended to go toward services rather than goods. Contributing to this trend are the growing ranks of elderly people who are living longer because they are spending more on health-care services, which have risen from 4% of disposable personal income since the start of 1959 to 16% at the end of 2016 (Fig. 50).
- *Nondurable goods.* Also accounting for the secular shift in consumers' budgets from goods to services is that there are limits to how much the average consumer and household can eat and wear (Fig. 51). The percentage of consumers' budgets spent on food has declined from 22% at the start of 1959 to 12% at the end of 2016 (Fig. 52). The percentage of budgets spent on clothing and footwear has dropped from 7% to 3% over this same period.
- *Durable goods.* Personal consumption on durable goods has been a very procyclical component of consumers' budgets, and it has been trendless, fluctuating around 12% since early 1947 (Fig. 53). That's not

surprising since these goods tend to be "lumpy," i.e., they are bigger and costlier than most other budget items. They are also more likely to require financing. That certainly applies to autos (Fig. 54).

MOOD SWINGS AND DOPAMINE

I'VE OFTEN QUIPPED when meeting with our accounts that "when Americans are happy, they spend money, and when they're depressed, they spend even more." Indeed, medical research has found that shopping can trigger the release of dopamine in the brain. This neurotransmitter is associated with feelings of pleasure and satisfaction, and it's released when we experience something new, exciting, or challenging. For many people, shopping is all those things.[14]

The bad news for brick-and-mortar stores is that consumers may be getting a bigger high from online shopping. A 2014 survey of 1,680 shoppers by Razorfish found: "Seventy-six percent of people in the US, 72 percent in the UK, 73 percent in Brazil, and 82 percent in China say they are more excited when their online purchases arrive in the mail than when they buy things in store."[15]

I've been closely monitoring the weekly and monthly surveys of consumer confidence since the beginning of my career. The one weekly survey that I follow is Bloomberg's Consumer Comfort Index, which is available back to December 1985. There are two very good monthly surveys. One is the Consumer Confidence Survey conducted by The Conference Board, and the other is the Consumer Sentiment Survey conducted by the Survey Research Center at the University of Michigan. The first is available back to 1967 on a bi-monthly basis and to July 1977 monthly, while the second has been around on a quarterly basis since 1953 and monthly since 1978.

Early on, I found that the surveys of consumer confidence are very sensitive to developments in the labor market. They are particularly good at confirming cyclical strength or weakness in employment, which is the major driver of personal income and thus consumer spending. However, confidence doesn't seem to have much impact on either short-term swings in the saving rate or its trend. I rest my case: most Americans spend most of what they earn whether they're happy or not. Let's have a closer look at the ebb and flow of our collective dopamine juices:

- *Happy meters.* Based on their survey data, The Conference Board compiles the Consumer Confidence Index (CCI), and the Survey Research Center produces the Consumer Sentiment Index (CSI). The former is seasonally adjusted; the latter isn't. Some people can be moody around the holiday and tax seasons, but I don't think there is that much seasonality in confidence. In any event, both indexes are very procyclical, meaning that they are very good coincident indicators of the economy (Fig. 55).

  Both have two major subcomponents: a current conditions index and an expectations index. Comparing the current CCI and CSI shows that the former has a much more pronounced cycle than the latter (Fig. 56). The expectations components of both are much more volatile, reflecting month-to-month mood swings more than their current-conditions counterparts do (Fig. 57).

- *Leading indicators.* I also track a homebrewed Consumer Optimism Index, which is simply the average of the CCI and CSI (Fig. 58). The CCI and CSI expectations components are extremely volatile and have been less useful for me than the current-conditions components. However, the average of the two is one of the 10 components of the LEI, which is also compiled by The Conference Board, as the previous chapter notes.

- *Help wanted.* The CCI is my favorite of the lot because it is much more sensitive to labor market conditions than the CSI. Indeed, The Conference Board survey includes an interesting question asking respondents whether their sense is that jobs are plentiful, available, or hard to get. The percentage viewing jobs as plentiful—which has ranged between roughly 5% and 55% over the years—tends to be the mirror image of the percentage who say jobs are hard to get, which has ranged approximately between 10% and 60% (Fig. 59). The percentage reporting that jobs are available has oscillated between 30% and 60% since February 1967 (Fig. 60).

  Interestingly, the current conditions component of the CCI is highly correlated with the difference between the percentage saying jobs are plentiful and the percentage saying they are hard to get (Fig. 61). Just as interesting is the close correlation between the percentage of consumers saying jobs are plentiful and the percentage of small business owners who report that they have job openings, in the survey conducted by the National Federation of Independent Business (Fig. 62).

- *Jobless claims.* I've always found The Conference Board's survey data very useful for assessing where we are in the employment cycle, since the jobs-hard-to-get series has been very highly correlated with the unemployment rate (Fig. 63). Another component of the LEI is initial unemployment claims, which is highly correlated with the jobs-hard-to-get series (Fig. 64).
- *Phillips curve.* Given the tight fit between the percentage of Conference Board survey respondents saying that jobs are hard to get and the unemployment rate, as well as between the percentage reporting that jobs are plentiful and the percentage of small business owners wanting help, it's not surprising that there has been a positive Phillips curve relationship between the jobs plentiful series and the yearly percent change in wage inflation (Fig. 65 and Fig. 66). The former has tended to lead the latter over the last three business cycles. However, although plenty of jobs were available during the first half of 2017, wage inflation remained remarkably subdued, as I discuss in Chapter 4.

My experience with the consumer sentiment surveys, particularly the Consumer Confidence one, is that they provide good insights into current employment conditions, which drive personal income. I don't get any insights into the saving rate from the surveys. Again, that might be because American consumers go shopping regardless of whether our incomes are rising or falling. That's what our brains on dopamine make us do to feel good.

Now let's turn to a closer examination of the impact of demographic trends on US consumers as the Baby Boomers turn oldish while their children turn adultish. I'm not looking to start a fight, but in the next chapter I also address the controversial issues of the standard of living and income distribution.

CHAPTER 7

Predicting Demography

AGING IS A DRAG

I'VE ALWAYS MONITORED demographic factors when trying to understand and predict consumer behavior. Demographic trends may change slowly, but they do change, and they do matter. They are important not only for analyzing consumer spending and saving behavior but also for analyzing housing demand. Humans are social animals, and their behavior is very influenced by the people with whom they socialize. More often than not, they tend to do so with people their own age, and folks who spend time together tend to influence one another's decision making.[1] That's why the needs, wants, and aspirations of demographic cohorts, sorted by age, provide useful insights into consumer behavior.

During most of my career to date, my demographic work focused on the impact of the Baby Boom cohort. They are getting older, as I know from personal experience.

An ancient Chinese proverb says: "Man fools himself. He prays for a long life, and he fears old age." The Rolling Stones sang, "What a drag it is getting old," in the first line of their 1966 hit "Mother's Little Helper," an ode to Valium.[2] Bette Davis is said to have observed: "Old age ain't no place for sissies." Aging gracefully is easier said than done as body parts wear out and brain fog sets in. The pace of life slows, especially around nap times. Nevertheless, most would agree that these outcomes beat the alternative.

Thanks to modern medicine and healthier lifestyles, many Baby Boomers will live longer and age more gracefully than members of previous generations. However, many will face financial challenges even if they stay relatively healthy. Meanwhile, the younger generations are getting married later and are likely to have fewer kids than their parents did. Together, these factors are creating an epic demographic shift with significant economic consequences as the population ages in the United States. Some of my best friends are elderly people, but they may be a real drag for US growth.

It's not just the United States that's experiencing this shift. Countries in Europe and Asia especially are feeling the age-related sluggishness as well. I will discuss the implications of global demographic trends in my concluding chapter, since they're particularly important for predicting the future. For now, let's check out the vital signs of America's seniors and then check in with the Millennials:

- *Life expectancy and health.* The median age of the US population is rising as the Baby Boomers live longer than previous generations. It was slightly more than 30 during the first half of the 1950s. It then declined to a low of 28 during 1970 and has been rising ever since to nearly 38 during 2015 (Fig. 1*).

  Life expectancy at birth has risen from about 66 years during 1945 to 70 during the first half of the 1960s to almost 79 during 2015 (Fig. 2). The average life expectancy of those who managed to stay alive to age 65 increased from about 81, when the data start in 1980, to about 84 during 2013.

  But not all those years after 65 are expected to be healthy. A July 2013 analysis by the Centers for Disease Control and Prevention found that for the period from 2007 to 2009, the life expectancy and the healthy life expectancy (HLE) of those aged 65 or older were about 19 years and 14 years, respectively, for the average of both sexes taken together.[3] HLE is a population health measure that combines mortality data with morbidity or health status data to estimate expected years of life in good health for persons at a given age. In other words, the average Baby Boomer will experience about five years riddled with health problems.

- *NILFs.* Not surprisingly, the working-age population that is 65 and older has been rising more rapidly since 2011, when the oldest of the Baby Boomers turned 65. The Bureau of Labor Statistics (BLS) includes everyone in the working-age population from when they turn 16 until

---

* Figures, references, and appendices are linked on *yardenibook.com/resources*.

they are six feet under.[4] Needless to say, many of the seniors are no longer working because they have retired. From December 2010 through December 2016, the population of seniors rose by 9.8 million to 48.8 million, while the number of them who were not in the labor force (i.e., the NILFs) rose by 7.5 million to 39.7 million (Fig. 3).

The percentage of senior NILFs relative to the senior population rose from about 73% in the early 1950s to a high of around 89% during the mid-1980s and plateaued there for a while during the second half of the 1980s and the 1990s (Fig. 4). Over that period, more of the elderly parents of the Baby Boomers could afford to retire because many had good pensions. They also could live off the capital gains they enjoyed when they sold their homes to the Baby Boomers. It was very clever of them to have lots of kids, who someday would pay plenty of money to buy lots of their homes.

Starting around 2000, the percentage of seniors who dropped out of the labor force headed back down to about 81% in 2016. At first, the decline may simply have reflected that seniors were healthier and living longer, and voluntarily chose to work past the traditional retirement age of 65. Then a new factor likely contributed: the financial crisis of 2008—which burst the housing bubble, triggering a recession and a severe bear market in stocks—no doubt forced many people to work past the point when they previously had expected to retire. For some, the need to support adult children who failed to "launch" (or had to relaunch after career disruptions) following the recession prevented them from retiring when planned.[5] For many, historically low interest rates, which depressed the income seniors could earn on their fixed-income portfolios, pushed retirement timing further out.

- *Dependency ratio.* There are various ways to measure the elderly dependency ratio. The most sensible one, in my opinion, is to divide the number of senior NILFs by the total number of people working, based on the household survey of employment (Fig. 5). It rose to a record high of 26% at the end of 2016, up from 21% 10 years earlier. The Census Bureau projects that the percentage of the population aged 65 or older will increase from 15% in 2015 to 22% by 2050 (Fig. 6).

According to an October 2016 working paper titled "Understanding the New Normal: The Role of Demographics," economists at the Federal Reserve believe that demographic factors associated with the postwar Baby Boomers will translate into less real GDP growth in the coming decades.[6] The Fed's staff found that low real GDP growth since the Great Recession was "largely predictable" based on their demographic model, which takes into account family composition, life expectancy, and labor market activity. They concluded: "Our results further suggest that real GDP growth and real interest rates will remain low in coming decades, consistent with the U.S. economy having reached a 'new normal.'"

Economists at the National Bureau of Economic Research (NBER) came to a similar conclusion in a July 2016 NBER working paper titled "The Effect of Population Aging on Economic Growth, the Labor Force and Productivity."[7] It projected that annual GDP growth will slow by 1.2 percentage points during this decade due to population aging. The economists noted that such aging was predetermined by historical declines in fertility. They attributed two-thirds of the anticipated decline in GDP to "slower growth in the labor productivity of workers across the age distribution," with one-third arising from "slower labor force growth."

As Chapter 4 discusses, the Congressional Budget Office (CBO) calculates the potential output of the US economy. The CBO also projects this measure of real GDP, which is necessary to forecast the US federal budget over the next 10 years. To do so, the CBO must estimate the growth in both the labor force and productivity. As of early 2017, the CBO predicted that the potential growth of the economy was likely to remain below an annualized rate of 2.0% (Fig. 7).

One might assume that older workers drag down productivity. That might be the case in some industries, such as those requiring working with one's hands or adapting to new technologies. However, another possibility is that the retirement of experienced workers slows productivity for all age groups. "An older worker's experience increases not only his own productivity but also the productivity of those who work with him," the NBER paper observed.

The Baby Boomers might have been natural-born shoppers when they were young adults with a house and kids. As seniors, living longer than previous generations, they might prefer to take more naps than exert themselves with trips to the mall. They could order stuff over the Internet, but they're more likely getting rid of stuff they've already accumulated so that they can move into smaller housing units now that their children are gone.

Indeed, most people spend less money on fun stuff when they reach their later retirement years. Older folks tend to spend more on out-of-pocket health care than younger folks. Having more of their budgets going to health care can result in more cautious overall spending, since health-care spending isn't predictable, though it certainly is likely to increase with age.

Younger, mid-life adults with expanding families and jobs tend to spend more on household and work-related expenses, such as clothes and transportation, than older people. On the other hand, younger people might find themselves more financially strapped if more of them need to care for dependent elderly parents in addition to their kids. Government entitlements might help but probably won't be enough.

Even if they continue to own homes, older people tend to downsize into smaller homes or condos once the kids move out. And they no longer need to live in a good school district or be within a reasonable commuting distance to work. That all equates to less demand for more expensive housing, unless there is enough offsetting demand from younger adults. It is possible that homeownership rates might go down as more of the elderly move into assisted-living facilities and nursing homes. Older folks also tend to take on less risk and less debt than younger ones. Beyond the reasons for not needing to take on big mortgages, older people simply have fewer years to pay them off. That may already be frustrating the Fed's attempts to stimulate demand with ultra-easy credit policies.

Seniors might also be less inclined to spend more when interest rates are low, especially if their fixed-income securities aren't yielding much. A 2015 Northwestern University paper titled "Population Aging and the Transmission of Monetary Policy to Consumption" concluded: "The consumption of young people is significantly more responsive to interest rate shocks than the old, and explains most of the aggregate response [to such shocks]. The consumption responses are driven by homeowners who refinance or enter new loans after interest rate declines."[8]

In an October 2016 speech, Fed Vice Chairman Stanley Fischer argued that demographic factors are largely responsible for persistently low interest rates in the United States and many other countries.[9] He explained that the aging population is likely to "boost aggregate household saving" because older groups, particularly those approaching retirement, typically have "above-average saving rates." He concluded that this "suggests that population aging—through its effects on saving—could be pushing down the longer-run equilibrium federal funds rate relative to its level in the 1980s by as much as 75 basis points."

It's not just the effectiveness of monetary policies that could be a problem but the effectiveness of fiscal policies too. Politicians continue to promise the elderly that their entitlements won't be cut. Federal government spending on Medicare and Social Security as a percentage of total government expenditures has risen from around 27% during 1987 to 39% during 2016 (Fig. 8). To pay for these mounting entitlement outlays, the government must either run a budget deficit, increase taxes on workers, or both. As the dependency ratio rises, there are fewer workers paying to support the elderly. That can't be good for the nation's budget deficit, debt, and economic growth.

These Baby Boomer demographic trends undoubtedly will weigh on economic growth. However, perhaps the Millennials will save the day. As I mention in the previous chapter, I identify the Millennials as the generation born between 1981 and 1996, making them 20 to 35 years old during 2016, i.e., no longer teenagers.[10] For some reason, no one seems to be expecting many economic ripple effects to come from the future actions of those in between the Baby Boomers and the Millennials, the so-called Gen Xers. This is a large cohort of 55 million people who were born between 1965 and 1980 and were 36 to 51 years old during 2016 (Fig. 9). Perhaps this expectation is justified because their impact on the economy isn't likely to change since they are already settled in many ways. (See Appendix 7.1, US Demographic Cohorts.)

ADULTISH MINIMALISTS

THE MILLENNIALS WILL be increasingly important drivers of the US economy in coming years. This generation is replacing the Baby Boomers in the labor force as the Boomers retire. For the economy, much depends on whether and when more of them might marry, have kids, and buy houses. My hunch is that they will do so increasingly as more of them breach the 30-years mark. The oldest Millennials did so in 2011 (when the oldest Baby Boomers turned 65), and the youngest of this cohort will celebrate their 30th birthdays in 2026.

By now, I figure that most are out of college or graduate school and are working. What they aren't doing just yet is rushing to get married and have kids. In the United States, the median age at first marriage for men rose from 24 during 1975 to 29 during 2015. For women, that figure rose from

21 to 27 over this period (Fig. 10). Data compiled by the National Center for Health Statistics show that the average age of first-time mothers rose from 24.9 in 2000 to 26.3 in 2014.[11] No wonder the general fertility rate has been flatlining at a record low since the mid-1970s (Fig. 11).

I can understand why the Millennials might be less inclined to rear a family these days. When I was growing up as a Baby Boomer, we tended to marry our high school or college sweethearts. That relationship was likely to be as good as it got. Now, thanks to the Internet and social media tools such as Tinder and Cupid, young adults can hook up until they get bored and move on to another "friend with benefits." Biotech innovations allow women to postpone having children by freezing their eggs. Surrogacy is also an option. So couples tend to fall truly in love and want to have kids before getting married these days.

Adulthood is typically characterized by four common milestones: (1) working, (2) living independently, (3) getting married, and (4) having children. An excellent statistical portrait of the Millennials was provided in an April 2017 Census Bureau report titled *The Changing Economics and Demographics of Young Adulthood: 1975–2016*.[12] It observed: "In prior generations, young adults were expected to have finished school, found a job, and set up their own household during their 20s—most often with their spouse and with a child soon to follow. Today's young adults take longer to experience these milestones. What was once ubiquitous during their 20s is now not commonplace until their 30s." Let's take the pulse of Millennials:

- *Living at home and in the dorm.* It seems that many Millennials are delaying their transition from childhood to adulthood with a period of "emerging adulthood," according to the Census study. It reported that 31% of young people, or 22.9 million 18- to 34-year-olds, lived in their parents' home in 2016. That's more than in any other living arrangement and is up from 26% in 1975. The percentage living with a spouse dropped to 27% in 2016 from 57% in 1975.

  This strongly suggests that while many young adults are no longer childish, they aren't quite adults in the independence department, at least by traditional standards. They are "adultish." Some are grownups who are still very dependent on their parents. Others are independent adults who either are postponing starting a family or have decided that they would rather remain single with no commitments or responsibilities to a spouse and kid(s).

By the way, the news headlines picked up that one out of three young adults still lives at home, according to the 2017 Census study. But buried in a footnote was the following information: "College students who are living in dormitories are counted as living in the parents' home." So the widespread notion that Millennials are living in the furnished basements of their parents' home and playing video games all day is a myth. On the other hand, the Census study found that 25% of young people living in their parents' home neither go to school nor work.

- *Getting educated comes first.* The Millennials may be adultish because they are very focused on getting an education and a job. That's supported by a widespread belief among most Americans that educational and economic accomplishments are extremely important milestones of adulthood. In contrast, marriage and parenthood rank low: over half of Americans believe that marrying and having children are not very important to becoming an established adult. Today's young adults are better educated than their peers were in 1975. Among 25- to 34-year-olds, more than one-third have a college degree or higher, compared with less than one-quarter in 1975.

- *Aspiring women.* Young women these days are much more focused on getting a college education than on getting married, which is a big difference relative to the past. Between 1975 and 2016, the share of young women who are homemakers fell from 43% to 14% of all women aged 25 to 34. The share of young women who are in the labor force has risen from about one-half to more than three-fourths over this period, while the share of men aged 25 to 34 who are in the labor force fell from 95% in 1975 to around 90% (Fig. 12). As a result, the percentage of women in the total labor force rose from around 37% during 1967 to about 47% by the mid-1990s and has remained around there (Fig. 13).

Young women have experienced more dramatic educational changes than young men. The national data on the civilian labor force aged 25 years and older show that the percentage with bachelor's degrees and higher rose from 22% during January 1992 to 34% in mid-2017 (Fig. 14). The percentage of the female labor force 25 and older that has a bachelor's degree or higher rose from 24% in January 1992 to 42% in mid-2017, while the comparable percentages for males were 28% and 38%, respectively (Fig. 15). The number of highly educated females in the labor force rose to the same number of highly educated males for the first time briefly during February 2017 (Fig. 16).

- *Delaying having families.* College-educated people tend to get married and have kids later in life, and to have fewer of them, than people with only a high school education. This suggests that the Millennials will have fewer children. The Census study reported that in the 1970s, 80% of people married by the time they turned 30. In 2016, not until the age of 45 had 80% of people been married. No wonder kindergarten enrollment has stalled around 4.0 million since 1987 following surges during the late 1950s and early 1960s and again in the early 1980s (Fig. 17).

- *Paying off student loans.* Many Millennials have had difficulty finding well-paid entry-level jobs after graduating from college—arguably a financial must for the many saddled with high levels of debt from student loans. A tripling of student loan debt outstanding over the past decade (specifically from the first quarter of 2006 through the second quarter of 2017) has brought the collective tab to $1.45 trillion (Fig. 18).

    In 2015, approximately 70% of graduating college seniors had student loan debt, according to an October 2016 report from the Institute for College Access & Success.[13] That compared with fewer than 50% in 1993, according to a fact sheet from the organization.[14] And the average loan they shouldered was a hefty $30,100 in 2015. Gallup says that one in five American adults (or 20%) reports carrying student loan debt; among Millennials, the number is one in three (35%).[15]

Having a more educated population of young adults marks a relative improvement in their economic condition, given the strong link between higher education and higher earnings. Many Baby Boomers achieved a better standard of living not only by getting an education but also by getting married and combining their incomes when both spouses worked. The Millennials, so far, seem to be minimalists who don't require as much money to achieve their economic and personal goals. So living on one income currently seems to be enough for many of them.

It's not that the Millennials don't want to own anything; rather, they want only stuff that they actually need—no frills and trophies for them! Many of them would prefer to enjoy a cool experience that they can brag about on Instagram than buy the newest hot sneakers or handbag. Many Millennials were children during the 1980s and 1990s, growing up with materialistic parents who indulged in flashy lifestyles. When they were in their teens and early twenties, many then watched their parents struggle financially following the Great Recession. They don't want to make the same mistakes.

Living a modest lifestyle takes less effort and is more appealing to lots of Millennials than the lavish lifestyles of the rich and famous. The widespread view is that the Millennials have delayed adulthood. That's probably wrong. Instead, many of them simply are embracing their own version of what it takes to be a financially responsible adult. The Census study cited above concludes: "Taken together, the changing demographic and economic experiences of young adults reveal a period of adulthood that has grown more complex since 1975, a period of changing roles and new transitions as young people redefine what it means to become adults."

A July 13, 2015 Census Bureau blog post contrasted the living arrangements of today's Millennials with those of young adults during the 1960s.[16] In 1967, nearly 90% of young adults (18 to 34) lived with either a parent or a spouse. Much more varied arrangements are commonplace these days, including living with relatives other than a parent (such as a child) or nonrelatives. The Census Bureau analysis reported: "On average, young adults wait nearly six years longer to get married today than in 1967. Marrying later is part of the reason why the 25- to 34-year-olds of 2014 resemble the 18- to 24-year-olds of 1967 in terms of percentage living with a spouse. For example, 39 percent of 18- to 24-year-olds lived with a spouse in 1967, similar to the 43 percent of 25- to 34-year-olds in 2014. Today, only 8 percent of 18- to 24-year-olds live with a spouse."

Remember the teasing playground song about John and Mary kissing in a tree? The lyrics taunted: "First comes love, then comes marriage, then comes Baby in the baby carriage." Today, marriage has become the last milepost of adulthood. The priority is to finish college, then work for a while to pay off the student debts and save some money. Once financial security has been achieved, then it's time to marry the one you love and have a kid... maybe. Or maybe not.

DROPOUTS AND SLACK

WITH MORE JUNIORS going off to college after high school (rather than straight to work) and more seniors retiring, it's no wonder that the number of people who are counted in the working-age population but not in the labor force has been rising to record highs for many years. These traditional milestones of getting an education and retiring are having a greater impact on the labor force. Of course, in recent years, there seem to be more people who should be working but have dropped out for health reasons or because they simply don't have the job skills to find gainful employment, even if it is part-time. Conservatives argue that some of these dropouts have found that they are better off living on government support programs than working for a living. Now consider the following:

- *Falling participation.* The number of NILFs rose to a record high of 95.1 million at the end of 2016 (Fig. 19). This series has increased faster than the labor force since the first half of 2000. That's when the civilian labor force participation rate peaked at a record 67%, up from 58% at the end of 1962, when the oldest Baby Boomers turned 16, i.e., old enough to be included in the working-age population (Fig. 20). By the end of 2016, the participation rate had dropped back to 63%, down near the September 2015 low of 62%, which was the lowest since October 1977. The flip side of this is that the nonparticipation rate rose from a low of 33% during April 2000 to 37% at the end of 2016 (Fig. 21).

- *More slack.* Some of the weakness in the economic recovery following the financial crisis of 2008 was attributed to the decline in the participation rate. That meant the falling unemployment rate might have exaggerated the improvement in the labor market, as more workers had dropped out and weren't dropping back in. This implied more slack in the economy than the unemployment rate suggested, which helps to explain why wage inflation remained subdued as the official jobless rate fell. If the labor force participation rate of the civilian working-age population had remained at 65%, as it was when the unemployment rate peaked at 10.0% during October 2009, instead of falling to 63% by year-end 2016, then the unemployment rate at the end of 2016 would have been 8.1% rather than only 4.7% (Fig. 22).

- *Less slack.* There is something to this argument but not much, in my opinion. Excluding people who are 65 or older from the numerator and denominator of the participation rate puts the year-end 2016 participation rate at 73% (Fig. 23). Removing 16- to 24-year-olds as well results in a 77% participation rate. Similarly, the employment-to-population ratio was only 60% at the end of 2016 (Fig. 24). Excluding seniors, it was 70%; excluding seniors and juniors brings it up to 74%.

So the unemployment rate for 25- to 54-year-olds was 4.0% at year-end 2016 (Fig. 25). It's hard to see any slack there.

• *Help wanted.* I keep coming up with the same conclusion: demographic trends have significantly slowed the growth of the labor force. Over the 120 months (10 years) through December 2016, it rose just 0.5% at an average annual rate, down from over 3.0% in the late 1970s (Fig. 26). This reflected the more rapid growth of the working-age population (around 2.0%) and the rising participation rate back then, and the slower population growth (around 1.0%) with a falling participation rate more recently.

Now let's see how all these demographic trends are affecting the growth and composition of America's households. In my opinion, the drivers of the US economy aren't individual consumers but rather the collective assortment of different households—which have become far less homogenous since the 1950s.

HOUSEHOLDS, FAMILIES, AND SELFIES

TO MONITOR THE Millennials' demographic impact on the economy, I track the quarterly household formations data compiled by the Census Bureau. A household includes all the persons who reside together in a housing unit, which can be a house, an apartment, a mobile home, a group of rooms, or a single room that is occupied as separate living quarters.[17] The quarterly data also show whether the new households are renters or homeowners. The decision to rent or to buy a home is affected by current and expected economic conditions. When people are doing well and are optimistic about the future, home buying is likely to be more appealing than during bad times, when confidence is depressed and renting seems like a safer option. The level of mortgage interest rates and the prices of homes, as well as the expected appreciation of those prices, also are considerations in the rent-versus-own decision.

Household formation was brisk during the mid-2000s (Fig. 27). Most of the new households bought homes rather than rented them (Fig. 28). When the housing bubble burst starting in late 2006, and as mortgages became much harder to obtain, household formation slowed dramatically through mid-2014, with the number of homeowners declining while renting became increasingly popular. During the second half of

2014 and first half of 2015, household formation rebounded, though renting continued to outpace owning significantly. Household formation slowed somewhat during 2016 and the first half of 2017, but there was a noticeable pickup in homeowning households. The number of renting households fell during the second quarter of 2017 for the first time since the second quarter of 2004.

The percentage of households renting rather than owning a housing unit rose to 37% during the second quarter of 2016, up from a record low of 31% during 2004 and the highest since 1965 (Fig. 29). The percentage of homeownership among all households dropped from a record high of 69% during the fourth quarter of 2004 to 63% during the second quarter of 2016, the lowest since the start of 1965, when the data begin (Fig. 30). Ownership rates have dropped for all age groups, but the biggest declines since their 2004 peaks have been for people under 35 (down from 44% to 34%) and those between 35 and 44 (down from 70% to 58%).

Anecdotal evidence suggests that many Millennials prefer to rent in urban areas rather than own a home in the suburbs. In addition, many Millennials don't view homes as a safe investment, having seen the housing bubble burst. Those who would like to buy a home are facing much tougher lending standards following the financial crisis of 2008. So it's no wonder that many of the Millennials, along with other potential first-time homebuyers, aren't buying homes but are renting instead.

Contributing to the renter boom in recent years is the growing number of people who are single rather than married. That's because married people tend to be more inclined toward homeownership than single people. Since the start of 2014, for the first time ever in the United States, the number of singles in the civilian noninstitutional working-age population—which includes everyone 16 or older—equaled the number of married people (Fig. 31). That's up from 38% of this population 40 years ago to 50% now (Fig. 32). At the end of 2016, 31% of the working-age population had never married and 20% was divorced, separated, or widowed (Fig. 33 and Fig. 34). The former includes lots of Millennials delaying marriage, while the latter includes lots of Baby Boomers living longer and losing their spouses along the way.

America's population certainly has become demographically more diverse in recent years. I focus on the trends in household types because they can have significant economic implications over time. During 2016, there were 126 million households, including 82 million families and 44 million nonfamily households (Fig. 35). Families comprise married couples with or without kids, and one-parent households. Nonfamily households represent singles living either alone or with other unrelated persons. Let's take a dive into the data to discern some of the major trends:

- *Family households.* Annual Census Bureau data available from 1947 through 2016 show that the percentage of total households composed of families declined from 90% to 65% over this period, while nonfamily households rose from 10% to 35% (Fig. 36). That's a significant shift.
- *Married couples.* An even more dramatic shift can be seen in the percentage of households with a married couple compared to the percentage of individuals living alone and single people living with others (family or nonfamily). Since 1947 through 2016, the former has dropped from 78% to 48%, while the latter has increased from 22% to 52% (Fig. 37).
- *Children.* The drop in the percentage of married couples mostly reflects a declining percentage of the married-with-children subset, which is down from 43% to 19% since 1950 (Fig. 38). Over this same period, the percentage of one-parent households with children increased from 3% to 9%.
- *Singles and nonfamily households.* Annual data available from 1960 through 2016 show that the percentage of all households consisting of singles living alone rose from 13% to 28% over that time span (Fig. 39). Nonfamily households rose from 15% to 35% over this same period.
- *Seniors.* The percentage of households headed by a senior (i.e., 65 or older) has risen from 18% in 1960 to 25% during 2016 (Fig. 40).

If the Millennials continue to postpone starting families while the Baby Boomers continue to live longer, the percentage of nonfamily households will continue to rise. Nonfamilies are likely to have fewer earners and other sources of income than are families. Single-person households tend to have lower incomes than married-couple households. I call them "selfies." Young singles tend to be just starting their careers. Older singles tend to be retired and living on their savings, dividends, interest income, and government support. As the Baby Boomers age and their longevity increases, they could significantly distort the extent of income stagnation and inequality.

INCOME STAGNATION MYTH

THE DEPRESSION-ERA SONG "Brother, Can You Spare a Dime?" resonated with the grim economic environment of the time. The best-known versions, sung by Bing Crosby and Rudy Vallee, were released right before Franklin Delano Roosevelt's election to the presidency. It was an anthem to the shattered dreams following the Roaring '20s. During 2017, employers could have been singing, "Brother, can you spare some time?" They had lots of job openings that they were having trouble filling as the labor market tightened when the unemployment rate fell below 4.5%.

Yet there remains much lamentation about how the American Dream has been shattered. Politicians (who pander to get votes), the news media (which boosts ratings by reporting bad news first), and yes, even some economists (who should know better) have been stating with great certitude that most Americans' standard of living has stagnated since 1999. Promoters of this groundless claim base it on the Census Bureau's series on real median household money income, which is one of the most widely cited and most misleading indicators of the standard of living in America (Fig. 41).

This measure of income rose to a record high of $58,665 during 1999. Then it remained below that peak through 2015. It did rise sharply in 2015 and finally reached a new record high in 2016, but only 0.6% above the 1999 level. Those were 17 long years of stagnation for most American households, according to this series.

Over that same period, from 1999 to 2016, real GDP rose 39%, or 19% per household. This implies that income inequality must have gotten much worse. How else to explain why a growing economy hadn't bene-fited the median household at all? The answer must be that the rich got much richer at the expense of everyone else.

Progressives call on the government to increase taxes on the rich and to redistribute their unfair gains. Their misguided self-righteousness reminds me of a scene in the movie *Doctor Zhivago* (1965), where Dr. Yuri Zhivago returns home after World War I to find that his spacious house in Moscow has been divided into tenements by the local Commu-nist government. As he and his wife are walking upstairs to their assigned quarters, Comrade Kaprugina scolds him in front of his new cohabitants, saying, "There was living space for 13 families! In this one house!" A dis-oriented Zhivago mumbles, "Yes, yes, this is a better arrangement, Com-rades. More just."

In my August 9, 2017 commentary, I wondered out loud: "How can the stock market possibly be doing so well when so many people are suffering from the effects of income stagnation? The stock market has clearly made lots of rich people richer, though lots of workers with corporate pensions and 401K plans invested in stocks are also benefitting. In any case, don't corporate earnings depend on a healthy economy with prosperity for all, not just a few?"

To solve this conundrum, I aim to challenge the credibility of the Census measure of income, which is woefully misleading because it grossly underestimates Americans' standards of living. Yet it is widely touted, particularly by politicians on both sides of the political divide. When Donald Trump was running for president against Hillary Clinton, he often bemoaned how this measure confirmed that the average American's standard of living has stagnated for many years. That notion is belied by the following analysis of the data:

- *Real mean household money income.* The Census Bureau also reports real mean household money income, along with the median measure. Naturally, it is skewed higher relative to the median by the incomes of the rich. Yet it also stagnated from 1999 through 2016, rising just 5% over that long period and well below the growth in average real GDP per household.

- *Real mean household personal income.* Annual data show that real personal income per household was up 26% from 1999 to 2016 to a record $121,553 (Fig. 42). That was 46% above the comparable Census measure's $83,143 reading during 2016 for real mean household money income! The former measure continued to rise to new record highs in 2017. One of the few similarities between the two series is that they are both pretax. Another is that both exclude capital gains income. There are plenty of differences.

- *Macro versus micro data.* Personal income is compiled by the BEA and is based on "macro" data from tax returns as well as "micro" data from surveys. The Census measure is based only on surveys that focus just on money income. On its website, the Census Bureau warns: "[U]sers should be aware that for many different reasons there is a tendency in household surveys for respondents to underreport their income. Based on an analysis of independently derived income estimates, the Census Bureau determined that respondents report income earned from wages or salaries much better than other sources of income and that the reported wage and salary income is nearly equal to independent estimates of aggregate income."[18]

- *CPI versus PCED.* Another difference is that the personal income series is deflated using the personal consumption expenditures deflator (PCED), while the Census series uses the consumer price index (CPI), which is based on an indexing formula that gives it an upward bias over time.[19] That's simple to fix by dividing the nominal versions of the Census measures of median and mean household income by the PCED. However, doing that doesn't change the story much at all.

- *Missing items.* The Census measures of money income, which are used to calculate official poverty rates, are missing key noncash government-provided benefits that boost the standard of living of many Americans. Medicare and Medicaid, which totaled $1.2 trillion during 2016, are excluded (Fig. 43). Also excluded are the Supplemental Nutrition Assistance Program and public housing. In the private sector, employer-provided fringe benefits, such as health insurance, are excluded from the Census measures.[20]

  Furthermore, the Census measures are pretax and exclude the Earned Income Tax Credit (EITC), which is essentially "additional income" of up to $6,318 as of the 2017 tax year.[21] It benefits a lot of individuals and families who are not earning much money but are working. Some end up paying no taxes but instead getting a refund from the Internal Revenue Service.

- *Fringe benefits.* The BEA's pretax personal income measure includes noncash benefits such as employer contributions to pension plans, health insurance, and social insurance programs, though the EITC is excluded. On the other hand, while the contributions of companies to their employees' retirement and health-care plans are counted in personal income, the larger actual payments for these outlays are counted in the Census series. The latter exceeded the former by $1.1 trillion in 2016 (Fig. 44).

- *Big gap.* The ratio of the Census measure of aggregate nominal money income to personal income has dropped from 0.72 during 1968 to 0.62 during 2016 (Fig. 45). Of the $6.1 trillion gap between nominal aggregate personal income and money income during 2016, all I can readily account for is $144 billion (Fig. 46). This is the positive contribution of Medicare and Medicaid to the gap offset by the negative contribution attributable to the different accounting for employee benefits.

A 2004 joint study by the BEA and the Census Bureau suggested that much of the gap back then could be explained by property income (personal interest, dividend, and rental income) counted in personal income but not in money income, and by BEA adjustments to proprietors' income and to wages and salaries for underreporting in BEA source data. [22]

The Census methodology, which is based on micro data, was designed to measure income inequality to determine poverty rates.[23] It is clearly not a comprehensive measure of total income.

The bottom line is that the Census series for both mean and median real money incomes, which have stagnated since 1999, just don't make any sense. Personal income makes much more sense, as confirmed by its close relationship to personal consumption, which I discuss in the previous chapter. Therefore, I much prefer average personal income per household as a measure of the standard of living. However, it is a mean, not a median, and might be skewed by the rich getting richer.

Currently, there is no official median measure for personal income. However, a July 2016 working paper authored by a team of economists— three from the BEA and one from the University of Michigan—attempted to create one. The economists found that median personal income grew by 4.0% from 2000 to 2012 while the Census' median money income fell 6.2%. That's certainly a significant difference! Median personal income for 2012 was $67,028 while the median Census measure was just $44,931.

The study came to the following significant conclusion: "We show that for the period 2000–2012, inequality using personal income is substantively lower than inequality measured using Census Bureau money income, and the trends in both inequality and median income are different. This demonstrates the importance of using a national accounts based measure of income when examining the relationships between inequality and growth."[24] This extraordinary statement completely debunks using Census money income to measure not only income inequality but also the standard of living.

I think that the best available measure of the standard of living is inflation-adjusted personal consumption expenditures per household (Fig. 47). It rose to a record high of $97,779 during 2016, up 28% since 1999, clearly belying the widely held notion that the standard of living has been stagnating. It is procyclical, but it remains on the same upward trend it has forged since the start of the data in 1955.

Admittedly, this statistic too is a mean rather than a median measure, suggesting that it might be skewed higher by the spending of the ultra-rich. But such distortion to any meaningful degree is unlikely because the rich don't consume that much more of life's necessities than everyone else, and there aren't enough of them indulging in extravagances to make a difference to this measure of the standard of living.

Missing in almost all analyses of the standard of living is some recognition of the impact of demographic factors. The same Census survey used to calculate the series I view as senseless shows that families accounted for about 65% of all households during 2016, down from about 75% in 1982. This means that nonfamilies now account for 35% of households, up from 25% over this period. The real median income of nonfamily households was 41% below the same measure for all households in 2016. If there are more nonfamilies who tend to earn less than families, that must depress the household income data, which includes families and nonfamilies.

Any discussion of the standard of living isn't complete without examining its relationship to productivity. In a market economy, competitive forces tend to cause labor's *marginal* productivity to be commensurate with inflation-adjusted pay. The motto of many labor organizers in the past and now is "A fair day's wage for a fair day's work." A competitive economy tends to make that ideal happen. Do the data confirm this relationship between productivity and real pay? Consider the following:

- *Productivity and hourly compensation.* The most widely followed measure of productivity is the ratio of real output to hours worked in the nonfarm business sector, which is reported on a quarterly basis (with monthly revisions) by the BLS in the Productivity and Costs release.[25] It is often compared to the release's time series on nonfarm real hourly compensation.

  For some bizarre reason, the BLS is still using the CPI to deflate hourly compensation. As I note in Chapter 4 on inflation, the Fed's Federal Open Market Committee recognized several years ago that the CPI's indexing formula has an upward bias, so it has been relying on the PCED as a more accurate gauge of consumer price inflation (Fig. 48).

  Just as bizarre is that the BLS doesn't use the price deflator for the nonfarm business sector that is included in its very own productivity report! It makes much more sense to divide hourly compensation by this deflator than by the CPI or even the PCED. That's because this is the measure of real hourly pay that actually matters to employers when they do their explicit or implicit calculations of the marginal cost of labor. Workers' purchasing power obviously depends on items such as rent and gasoline. But in a competitive market economy, employers pay for a fair day's work, not for the cost of living.

There has been a widening gap between productivity and real hourly compensation, using the CPI, since mid-1970, with the latter increasingly lagging behind the former (Fig. 49). Most, but not all, of the divergence disappears when the nonfarm business deflator is used instead of the CPI.[26]

- *Productivity and average hourly earnings.* By the way, there is also a decent correlation between nonfarm business productivity and the average hourly earnings (AHE) for production and nonsupervisory employees divided by the nonfarm business deflator (Fig. 50). There's a tighter fit between the two than when either the CPI or the PCED is used. From the average employer's perspective, what matters is that the inflation-adjusted AHE is up 23% from the first quarter of 1999 through the fourth quarter of 2016. That's certainly not stagnation.

From the perspective of the average production and nonsupervisory employee, hourly pay divided by the PCED is up 18.7% over this period (Fig. 51). Using this same deflator over the same period, real hourly compensation is up 23.9% and the real Employment Cost Index (including benefits) is up 13.2%. That's certainly not stagnation either.

I conclude that the standard of living for most American households, rather than stagnating since 1999, has been rising to record highs along with real personal consumption per household for most of that time. That's because real personal income has been providing purchasing power to households in a relatively equitable fashion, contrary to the misleading implications of the money income measures (Fig. 52). To review, on a per-household basis from 1999 to 2016, real GDP is up 19%, real personal income is up 26%, and real consumption is up 28%.

Personal income includes both the cash value and the imputed value of all entitlement programs. These programs were designed to reduce income inequality in our country, yet many of them are excluded from the measures of income that progressives use to demonstrate that inequality is worsening. Could it be that the progressives who are up in arms over worsening income inequality are ignoring the fact that the problem continues to be fixed by the very government programs that they implemented during their New Deal and Great Society heydays?

I'm not saying there's no income inequality. There is and always will be in a competitive economy. I am saying that it probably hasn't gotten any worse since 1999, based on the fact that most Americans have enjoyed solid gains in their standard of living as measured by both average personal income and personal consumption per household. Furthermore, I submit that it's incumbent upon progressives who claim income inequality has worsened to prove that this is so after taxes and after government support payments have been considered, not before. If they're still right, then their calls for more income redistribution are more justified. However, before pressing for even more income distribution, they also should prove that the existing redistribution programs are not the *cause* of worsening pretax and pre-benefits income inequality. Conservatives argue that government benefits erode the work ethic and thereby exacerbate income inequality. I generally agree with that view. The debate rages on.

CHAPTER 8

Predicting Real Estate

HOME SWEET HOME

THE HOUSING MARKET matters a great deal to both the economy and the financial markets—and vice versa: economic and financial market factors have huge bearing on the supply of and demand for housing.

Housing is one of the most boom-prone economic sectors in the United States, which means it's also prone to significant busts. Home construction and purchases are highly sensitive to financial conditions, i.e., the availability and cost of credit. Conversely, the health of the financial services sector is greatly affected by the health of the housing sector. When credit conditions tighten, the resulting downturn in housing activity can cause builders to default on their construction loans and lay off workers. During recessions, when the unemployment rate rises, more homeowners become seriously delinquent in making their mortgage payments. Rising loan-loss provisions depress the earnings of lenders exposed to housing. Loan charge-offs erode their capital, which means that credit conditions tighten even further. To halt such deadly debt spirals, the Fed typically has responded by easing monetary policy to revive the housing industry, with broad positive ripple effects economy-wide.

Most times, the housing market is very liquid. That's significant because it contributes to America's extraordinary labor market mobility, which I discuss in Chapter 6. During good times, workers who find better jobs with higher pay can sell their homes easily if they need to move, and find new homes quickly near their new jobs. Most Americans tend to move frequently for lots of other reasons as well. Some do so to trade up to better and bigger homes as their incomes rise and their families expand. Others trade down, often because they don't need as much space after children have moved out. Traditionally, owning a home has been the foundation of the American Dream. That's still true, though somewhat less so since the housing bubble burst because of the 2008 financial crisis.

Renting is like dating. Owning a home is like marriage because you must invest in it to keep it from falling apart. Actually, necessary maintenance outlays can be relatively small compared to the home improvements people spend money on to keep up with the Joneses. As a result, housing activity has tremendous ripple effects on the rest of the economy—from industries that supply construction materials, to manufacturers and retailers of appliances and furniture, to suppliers of transportation, warehousing, labor, and other services. It all adds up to plenty of economic activity and jobs.

Housing activity also has a strong impact on auto sales. Construction workers typically need pickup trucks and utility vans. Retail unit car sales tend to rise when urban renters become suburban homeowners. Urban dwellers don't need cars because public transportation is usually easily accessible; plus, parking spaces on the street and in garages are scarce and expensive—certainly disincentives to owning a vehicle. Suburbanites need cars to get around. Married couples usually need two cars, including at least one big enough to accommodate their kids and their kids' pals on the soccer team. By the way, the Chevrolet Suburban—a full-size, extended-length sport utility vehicle—is the longest continuous-use automobile nameplate in production; it's been made since 1935 and most years has been one of General Motors' most profitable vehicles.

Residential construction is a relatively small component of real GDP, but it is extremely procyclical (Fig. 1*). This quarterly series is based on the monthly housing completions data series (Fig. 2). Housing completions obviously trails monthly housing starts (Fig. 3). Housing starts trails the monthly data on building permits, which is one of the 10 components of the Index of Leading Economic Indicators (Fig. 4). These series are compiled by the US Census Bureau and include both single-family and multifamily units (Fig. 5 and Fig. 6). The former tend to be built for homeowners, while the latter are primarily for renters, though they include owner-occupied condominium apartments. Completions of single-family homes exceed new

---

* Figures, references, and appendices are linked on *yardenibook.com/resources*.

single-family home sales because some people build their own single-family homes (Fig. 7).

Amplifying the housing cycle are sales of existing homes, which include both single-family homes and condominiums (Fig. 8). They well exceed new home sales. For example, during 2016, the former totaled 5.51 million units, while the latter totaled 548,000 units. Existing home sales also drive sales of furniture, appliances, and renovation services. They support lots of real estate agents and mortgage lenders as well.

Housing is the most demographically driven sector in the economy. First-time homebuyers are likely to be recently married couples expecting their first child. They tend to trade up to a bigger home if they have more children. As I observe in the previous two chapters, worsening the demographic story for housing demand is that the median age at first marriage has increased for males and females (Fig. 9). As a result, the percentage of households with married couples, especially those with children, has been on a downward trend (Fig. 10 and Fig. 11).

The Millennials turned 20 to 35 years old during 2016. They're no longer teenagers, yet there still isn't any evidence that they are significantly boosting home demand. There are lots of reasons why they've postponed—or in some cases rejected altogether—homeownership. With social media providing lots of ways to find "friends with benefits," serial dating may be too much fun to settle down with one of those special friends and have children. Minimalist lifestyles are popular among many Millennials, who actually prefer to live in small, easy-to-maintain apartments. They graduated from college saddled with large student debts, which makes it harder to qualify for a mortgage loan, particularly if there were any delinquent payments along the way. The bursting of the housing bubble following the financial crisis of 2008 might have convinced many young adults, whether single or married, that a home is not as good an investment as was widely believed before the crisis.

Since the financial crisis, it's been harder to qualify for a mortgage. Applicants must show a few years of working, preferably for the same employer. In addition, down payments have increased as a percentage of loan amounts. Home prices plunged for a few years after the crisis, making homes quite affordable. However, before most Millennials were ready to buy a starter home, several professional investors—capitalizing on the Fed's ultra-easy monetary policies—jumped into the market, buying distressed homes in bulk and renting their investments out until home prices recovered and they could sell for great returns. All that speculative activity pushed home prices up to relatively unaffordable levels for many first-time homebuyers.

While I'm waiting for the Millennials to start taking selfies with their families on the front lawns of their own homes, there are numerous housing indicators I monitor to assess the overall outlook for the housing sector. I review the demographic ones in the previous chapter. Particularly important are indicators about the characteristics of households—including the pace of their formation, the mix of renters versus owners, marital status, average size, and so on. Let's take a dive into these monthly indicators as well as several additional useful measures of housing activity:

- *Monthly construction indicators.* The US Census Bureau and the US Department of Housing and Urban Development jointly issue a monthly release on "New Residential Construction."[1] It includes building permits, housing starts, and housing completions. Details are available on single-family and multifamily structures, as well as for the four regions of the United States. All are for privately owned housing units. All are seasonally adjusted, though the release also shows unadjusted data.

- *Building permits.* Total building permits tends to lead completions—which is reflected in the residential investment component of real GDP—by 12 to 24 months (Fig. 12). The building permits series shows that housing exacerbated every recession since the start of the 1960s except for the one during 2001. In the mid-1960s, the industry fell into a brief recession while the overall economy continued to grow.

- *New and existing home sales.* The new home sales data have been compiled jointly by the Census Bureau and the Department of Housing and Urban Development since January 1963.[2] The existing home sales data have been tabulated by the National Association of Realtors since January 1968. The former are counted when purchase contracts are signed, the latter only when the deals are closed. That makes new home sales a somewhat timelier barometer of the residential housing market than existing home sales. Like sales, the inventory of existing single-family homes for sale well exceeds that of new homes for sale (Fig. 13). The inventory-to-sales ratios of existing and new homes are highly correlated. Both tend to spike higher when housing is falling into a recession (Fig. 14).

- *Surveys of builders and realtors.* Two of the most closely followed surveys of the housing market are conducted by the National Association of Home Builders and the National Association of Realtors. The first compiles the Housing Market Index, which reflects homebuilders' assessments of their business, including the traffic of prospective new homebuyers. The second reports the Pending Home Sales Index, which reflects contracts signed to purchase existing homes (Fig. 15).

- *Do-it-yourself construction.* I also like to monitor consumer spending on home improvements by tracking the retail sales of building materials and garden supplies (Fig. 16). Another useful indicator of sentiment in the housing market is my homemade measure of "do-it-yourself" homebuilding. I construct it simply by subtracting new single-family home sales from single-family housing completions. The 12-month average has been fluctuating in a volatile but flat trend since 1968, with cyclical peaks occurring in the mid-1970s, early 1980s, mid-1990s, and mid-2000s. The subsequent troughs coincided with periods of dampened enthusiasm for buying homes, let alone building one for yourself and your family (Fig. 17).

- *Mortgage applications.* Residential real estate requires a great deal of financing since buying a home is so expensive. The Mortgage Bankers of America provides a weekly index of mortgage applications for purchases of both new and existing homes (Fig. 18). It is relatively volatile and not a comprehensive measure of such lending activity. However, the underlying trend in this index provides some confirmation of the underlying trend in housing sales.

- *Mortgage delinquencies.* I also track quarterly Fed data series on mortgage delinquencies (Fig. 19 and Fig. 20). The problem is that they tend to be lagging indicators. By the time they send a clear distress signal, a calamity in the housing market could be well under way.

Credit is the lifeblood of the housing industry. However, there's always been a dearth of timely data on housing finance. Had there been a database of timely, aggregate housing finance data before signs of housing market distress emerged in 2007 (e.g., weekly or monthly data on mortgage originations, lending terms, and/or credit scores), it might have helped the Fed and other banking regulators to recognize that speculative bubbles were inflating.

Belatedly, in 2010, the Federal Reserve Bank of New York teamed up with Equifax to create a database, starting in 1999, that is used in the bank's *Quarterly Report on Household Debt*.[3] Better late than never. Additionally, housing-related data have been available quarterly from the

Fed's *Financial Accounts of the United States*.[4] However, these data are usually released about two and a half months after the end of each quarter. Although relatively comprehensive, they are not timely. Nevertheless, the numbers from the second source are extremely useful for understanding the calamity that befell the housing market during 2007, which was followed by the Great Recession.

I've spent a great deal of time studying the events and the data that led up to the housing bust to learn more about the dynamics of speculative bubbles, not only in real estate but also in assets generally. I'll turn to that now, starting from the beginning.

IN THE BEGINNING

"THE HOUSE OF the Rising Sun" is a folk song that topped the charts in the United States; the most famous version was recorded by the English rock group The Animals in 1964. It's a remorseful ballad that tells of a life gone wrong in New Orleans.

The housing market has a history of going wrong from time to time and certainly has been "the ruin of many a poor boy," like the house of ill repute in the song; but never has the market extinguished more wealth and hopes than it did following the bursting of the housing bubble in 2007. That event was actually the culmination of numerous wrong turns by the housing industry that started at the beginning of the previous century. As I am about to show, the industry's road to ruin was paved with good intentions. However, once paved, it attracted too many people who were up to no good.

My timeline for tracking when and how the housing industry strayed from the righteous path starts during the early 1900s. That's when the housing industry first teamed up with the federal government and financial institutions to promote and facilitate homeownership, a worthy goal indeed. After World War I, there was a housing shortage and a wave of labor strikes and social unrest. A nationwide Own Your Own Home campaign was launched in 1918 by the US Labor Department and several industry groups representing real estate boards, contractors, as well as manufacturers and distributors of building materials and equipment.[5]

Accomplishing the goals of this extensive campaign required a major expansion of the mortgage-lending business. Mortgage loans at the time generally were for no more than half the purchase price of the house and typically carried maturities of 10 years or less, with large balloon payments.[6] In response to the need for more credit on better terms during the housing boom of the Roaring '20s, building and loan associations flourished by pooling small savings deposits into mortgage loans that matured in up to 12 years and financed 60% to 75% of the property. Today, these institutions are called "savings and loans" (S&Ls), or "thrifts." While certainly not an event of biblical proportions, this was the genesis of numerous financial innovations that eventually led to the financial engineering excesses that caused the Great Recession.

While business was good for the S&Ls, they were envious of commercial banks' Fed backing. Something akin to the Federal Reserve System that Congress had created in 1914 would do nicely—they too wanted a lender of last resort. A bill introduced in Congress in 1919, promoted by the same special interest groups that had launched the Own Your Own Home campaign, established a system of federal building loan banks, modeled after the Federal Reserve System, to provide a liquidity reserve for the S&Ls. The bill languished until President Herbert Hoover in 1932 successfully pushed for the creation of the Federal Home Loan Bank (FHLB) system, which was administered by the Federal Home Loan Bank Board (FHLBB).

However, the FHLB came too late for the many S&Ls that failed during the banking crisis in the early 1930s. They had participated in the lending party of the Roaring '20s, when total residential mortgage debt tripled. Lending standards deteriorated significantly as the building and loan associations offered second and third mortgages, balloon payments, and other innovations that made it easier to borrow money. By 1933, nearly half of home mortgages were in default. Sound familiar? The latest housing bubble confirms that history doesn't just rhyme but can repeat itself!

The very same leaders of the Own Your Own Home coalition now pressed the government for more help. In addition, President Franklin Roosevelt's New Deal aimed to revive the busted housing market. About a third of the nation's unemployed were in the building trade, and the government intended to get those laborers back to work by giving them homes to build.

Congress responded to these mounting pressures during the 1930s in several ways:

- *1933: HOLC.* In June 1933, the Home Owners' Loan Corporation (HOLC) was established. The HOLC introduced long-term, fixed-rate mortgage financing, specifically a self-amortizing, fixed-rate mortgage. HOLC stopped making loans in 1936 and ultimately ceased operations in 1951.

- *1933: FDIC and FSLIC.* The Federal Deposit Insurance Corporation (FDIC) was created in 1933 for commercial banks to insure their deposits with funds it raised from the banks. At the same time, commercial banks were prohibited from owning investment banks. One year later, the Federal Savings and Loan Insurance Corporation (FSLIC) was set up to insure thrift deposits.

- *1934: FHA.* Unlike HOLC, the Federal Housing Administration (FHA), created in the National Housing Act of 1934, never saw the sun set. The new agency provided federally backed insurance for home mortgages made by FHA-approved lenders, who were protected against losses on the mortgages they insured. The FHA was financed by insurance premiums charged to borrowers. In effect, the FHA successfully introduced a mortgage insurance system that reduced investment risk and facilitated longer-term and more highly leveraged loans at lower interest rates. It spawned private competitors such as the Mortgage Guarantee Insurance Corporation, which was founded by a real estate attorney in 1957. This was the beginning of private-sector financial institutions mimicking federal government programs to facilitate mortgage lending. So the FHA was the precursor of the credit insurance industry that culminated in the credit derivatives excesses that led to the financial meltdown during 2008.

- *1938: Fannie Mae.* The Federal National Mortgage Association was established by a 1938 amendment to the National Housing Act of 1934. "Fannie Mae," as it's affectionately nicknamed, began life as a federal government agency. It was transformed into a public–private mixed-ownership corporation in 1954, then later to a private, shareholder-owned entity in 1968. As such, Fannie is a so-called "government-sponsored enterprise" (GSE)—a private company with a public purpose. Fannie's public mandate is to increase mortgage market liquidity by providing lenders with more cash to fund home loans. It does so by serving as a secondary mortgage market facility allowed to purchase, hold, and sell FHA-insured loans. In other words, Fannie Mae takes loans off lenders' hands.

Back in 1938, a family could buy a house with just 10% down, financing the remaining 90% of the purchase price via a 25-year FHA-insured mortgage loan. Many soldiers returning after World War II took out FHA loans, eager to settle down, raise a family, and put the war behind them. Demand among veterans was so great that in 1944, the Veterans Administration (VA) entered the mortgage insurance game. Qualified veterans could secure VA-insured mortgage loans for no money down whatsoever. Fannie Mae started buying VA-insured loans in 1948.

The US government became almost zealous about making housing ever more affordable, bringing the American Dream of homeownership within reach of more and more Americans. FHA down payments fell to 3% and sometimes to zero. As a result, homes became highly leveraged assets, which was a win-win for everyone as long as the borrower could make the mortgage payments and home prices didn't fall.

In fact, US home prices rose for quite a long while. From the end of World War II until 2007, they remained on an ever-rising trajectory as easily available mortgage credit bolstered demand for housing by the parents of the Baby Boomers and then by their multitudinous progeny.

Increasingly during the 1950s and the first half of the 1960s, however, the FHA was justly accused of contributing to the ruin of many American cities by subsidizing the departure of white middle-class families to the suburbs. Conversely, the agency was quite stingy in making loans to low-income workers for urban rental units, and cities fell into decline. With good intentions that spawned bad unintended consequences, the federal government was there to help. Under President Lyndon Johnson, the Housing and Urban Development Act of 1968 created the Department of Housing and Urban Development (HUD). It was established as a Cabinet department as part of Johnson's "Great Society." Consistent with Johnson's civil rights initiative, the FHA was folded into HUD, which increasingly pushed lenders to make more mortgages to low-income borrowers.

The 1968 Act also ended Fannie Mae's 30-year monopoly over the secondary mortgage market. The Government National Mortgage Association was set up as a government-owned corporation within HUD. "Ginnie Mae" guarantees timely payment of principal and interest on privately issued mortgage-backed securities (MBSs); these are basically pools of federally insured or guaranteed mortgage loans issued mainly by the FHA or VA but sometimes by other issuers. At the same time, the 1968 Act converted

Fannie Mae into a private, shareholder-owned corporation, as mentioned earlier.

Two years later, the Emergency Home Finance Act of 1970 created a new housing-related GSE, the Federal Home Loan Mortgage Corporation, nicknamed "Freddie Mac." It was established to service the thrift industry, which always seemed to want and to get whatever toy Congress gave the commercial banks. In addition, the Act expanded the powers of the two housing GSEs: Fannie and Freddie now were allowed to buy and sell mortgages and MBSs that the federal government had neither insured nor guaranteed. That incentivized lenders to churn out more "conventional" mortgage loans with less regard for loan quality; after all, the loans wouldn't remain in their portfolios. This unintended consequence of the new business model for the GSEs helped to pave the road to housing market ruin in 2008.

So the two agencies could buy conventional conforming mortgages from banks and other lenders as well as MBSs from investment firms— freeing up more lenders' capital to go toward more lending. They also could issue and guarantee MBSs collateralized by these mortgage loans, and they could hold mortgage loans and MBSs in their portfolios. In 1971, Freddie Mac issued the first conventional loan MBS.

Congress in 1992 granted HUD the power to regulate Fannie Mae and Freddie Mac. HUD's Office of Federal Housing Enterprise Oversight regulated these two publicly traded GSEs until 2003, when Congress shifted oversight to the Treasury Department. The 1992 law required HUD's secretary to make sure that housing goals were being met and, every four years, to set new goals for Fannie Mae and Freddie Mac.

HUD pushed mortgage lenders to lower their standards and extend even more credit to low-income borrowers. Both Henry Cisneros, HUD Secretary from 1993 to 1996, and his successor, Andrew Cuomo, HUD head from 1997 to 2001, took their homeownership-promoting cues from their boss, President Bill Clinton. At the 1996 Democratic National Convention, Clinton announced: "Tonight, I propose a new tax cut for homeownership that says to every middle-income working family in this country, 'If you sell your home, you will not have to pay a capital gains tax on it ever—not ever.'"

The next year, Clinton's proposal became law: the Taxpayer Relief Act of 1997 exempted most home sales from capital gains taxes. Specifically, the law exempted the first $500,000 in home sale gains for a married couple—$250,000 for singles, provided that they had lived in the home for at least two of the previous five years. Prior to 1997, a one-time capital gains exclusion of up to $125,000 was permitted for homeowners over the age of 55. That meant people no longer would have to buy a house valued at least as high as their previous one to avoid the tax if they had already used their one-time exemption. Americans now had even more incentive to buy and sell homes. According to an article in the December 18, 2008 *New York Times*, a study by a Federal Reserve economist suggested that 17% more homes were sold during the decade after the law's passage than would have been the case without the law.[7]

The loosening of mortgage restrictions under Cisneros allowed first-time buyers to qualify for loans they never previously could have received, thus setting the stage for the subprime mortgage meltdown that began 10 years after he left HUD. President Clinton endorsed HUD's National Homeownership Strategy, which was viewed as a win-win policy and quickly implemented as follows: (1) First-time homebuyers applying for HUD-insured mortgages were no longer required to prove five years of stable income; three years was enough. (2) Lenders were permitted to hire their own appraisers rather than independents approved by the government; these saved borrowers some money but inflated appraisals. (3) Lenders no longer had to interview most government-insured borrowers in person or maintain physical branch offices.

HUD under Cisneros' reign instituted, in December 1995, a requirement that 42% of GSE mortgages serve low- and moderate-income families. Later, under Cuomo, that was raised to 50%. Cuomo also upped the GSEs' quota of mortgages bought that reflected underserved neighborhoods and very low-income borrowers. "Part of the pitch was racial," asserted an article in the August 5, 2008 *Village Voice*, "with Cuomo contending that the GSEs weren't granting mortgages to minorities at the same rate as the private market."[8]

At first, the new rules didn't sit well with Franklin Raines, who presided over Fannie Mae from 1998 to 2004. "We have not been a major presence in the subprime market," he said according to an August 5, 2008 article in the *Village Voice*, "but you can bet that under these goals, we will be." If Raines thought that diving into the risky subprime end of the market was imprudent or even reckless, Cuomo shared no such qualms. "GSE presence in the subprime market could be of significant benefit to lower-income families, minorities, and families living in underserved areas,"

Cuomo wrote about his new goals, according to the *Voice*. Effectively, the government forced the GSEs into a much riskier business model. Prescient industry observers expressed concern that the new mandates would result in rising loss levels for the GSEs, leading to a possible government rescue.

So the GSEs dove into risky business notwithstanding the initial reservations of Raines and others—and with seeming abandon. They embraced alternative loan products, subprime loans and securities, and flexible product lines that provided 100% financing with as little as $500 down from borrowers. All three—Fannie Mae, Freddie Mac, and Ginnie Mae—pioneered the securitization of mortgage loans. Their securities were highly prized because they were deemed to be government guaranteed; strictly speaking, however, that was true only of Ginnie Mae securities.

To an important extent, the financial calamity of 2008 was greatly compounded by so-called "private-label" securitization of mortgages by Wall Street's credit derivative wizards. These securities were created using highly complex and opaque derivatives that magically made them seem—and be deemed—as creditworthy as the ones created by the GSEs, which of course they weren't.

All these factors combined to create one colossal mess that resulted in the financial crisis of 2008. However, before that major debacle, there was a warm-up act during the late 1980s and early 1990s involving the S&L industry. It provided a cautionary tale that was largely ignored. (Also see Appendix 8.1, Hollywood's S&L Cautionary Tale: *It's a Wonderful Life*.)

CAUTIONARY TALE

THE ESSENTIAL FEATURES of the modern American system regulating financial institutions and their lending practices were established during the early 1930s, when Congress enacted a number of banking bills in response to the financial panics of the Great Depression, as noted above. The FDIC was created in 1933 to insure bank deposits. And in 1934, insurance coverage was extended to S&Ls provided by the FSLIC.

Contrary to a widely held impression, however, Congress did not pledge the full faith and credit of the US government behind the guarantees of the FDIC and the FSLIC upon their inception. During his first press conference in office, President Franklin Roosevelt stated his opposition to deposit insurance: "As to guaranteeing bank deposits, the minute the government starts to do that . . . the government runs into a probable loss." And prophetically, he added, "We do not wish to make the United States government liable for the mistakes and errors of individual banks, and put a premium on unsound banking in the future." Nevertheless, Roosevelt ultimately succumbed to congressional pressure and agreed to the creation of the FDIC, but with insurance coverage backed by fees on the banks rather than a government guarantee. Come the 1980s, however—in 1982 and again in 1987—Congress passed nonbinding resolutions pledging to support the funds, although it didn't create any legal obligation to do so.

The federal government's regulatory system for the housing finance industry was clearly designed to promote homeownership, and it worked reasonably well for many years after the end of World War II. During the 1970s and 1980s, the postwar Baby Boom generation started boosting the demand for housing, and the S&Ls helped to finance the housing boom. By the mid-1970s, there were over 4,000 S&Ls, in just about every community in the United States. The S&Ls were mostly profitable because mortgage interest rates generally exceeded deposit rates. But by the late 1970s, the S&Ls had fallen into deep trouble.

Starting during October 1979, the Federal Reserve, under the leadership of Paul Volcker, pushed interest rates up to unprecedented heights to unwind a runaway inflation spiral, as I discuss in Chapter 1 and Chapter 9. The Federal Reserve was granted the power to set maximum deposit rates for commercial banks under the Glass–Steagall Act of 1933. The Interest Rate Control Act of 1966 extended deposit rate ceilings to the thrift institutions, which included S&Ls and mutual savings banks. When money-market interest rates soared above the ceilings imposed on deposits, depositors withdrew their funds and reinvested the proceeds in Treasury bills and other money-market instruments offering higher returns than available on fixed-rate deposits. The Fed's action immediately clobbered the market value of the mortgages and other fixed-income assets held by the S&Ls. The resulting credit crunch depressed housing activity.

The thrift industry's representatives turned to Congress for help, which they promptly received in the form of the Depository Institutions Deregulation and Monetary Control Act, signed by President Jimmy Carter on March 31, 1980. The Act phased out Regulation Q deposit rate ceilings so that S&Ls could pay much higher interest rates on deposits. Congress also permitted investors to open an unlimited number of accounts, each insured up to $100,000. Previously, $40,000 had been the limit on insured deposits.

These measures stopped the deposit outflows, but they battered profits because deposit rates soared well above the yields generated by the mortgage portfolios of the S&Ls. Once again, the industry turned to their friends in Washington for help. The Garn–St. Germain Depository Institutions Act of 1982 permitted thrifts to invest up to 55% of their assets in commercial real estate and other loans. Up to 30% of their portfolios could be in consumer loans.

State-chartered S&Ls in Texas and California were permitted by their regulators to plunge as much as 100% of their assets into practically anything. Now both their assets and their liabilities were deregulated. The federal regulators were also amazingly helpful. In 1981, the Federal Home Loan Bank Board issued a ruling permitting S&Ls to be owned by only one shareholder. Prior to this ruling, an S&L was required to have at least 400 shareholders to limit the influence of developers who might use the institution as a "cash cow."

Furthermore, the Bank Board lowered the minimum capital requirement from 5% to 3%. Some of this capital could be in the form of accounting "goodwill." Incredibly, the Bank Board issued "net worth certificates" (essentially temporary financial support) to institutions that could not meet even these liberalized capital requirements. But the greatest gimmick of all was the unique accounting system that the Bank Board used to determine the regulatory net worth of the thrifts. It was called "regulatory accounting principles," or "RAP."

As of October 1981, thrifts were allowed to amortize the losses on any assets sold over the remaining contractual life of the asset. The regulators thus encouraged the S&Ls to sell their "underwater" assets, which typically were packaged as MBSs, and to buy loans with higher yields, which would boost profits. This short-term fix was a huge gamble that interest rates would come down enough to reverse the capital losses created by the Fed's inflation fight. The 1981 rule change created an enormous divergence between net worth measured under RAP and GAAP (generally accepted accounting principles). In 1984, 877 S&Ls were bankrupt as defined under RAP, with a 3% capital requirement; under GAAP, with a 5% cut-off, 2,090 institutions were worthless! Rates had not fallen enough to save the day.

Why were Washington's politicians so helpful to the S&L industry? In a word: money. The S&Ls' troubles coincided with a dramatic increase in the funds needed to get elected to Congress. Ronald Reagan's landslide victory in the 1980 presidential race convinced the Democrats that they had to raise large sums to counter the Republican challenge, which was well financed by special interests. In 1986, the Democratic Congressional Campaign Committee, headed by Tony Coelho (D, CA), collected huge contributions from special-interest political action committees (PACs).

In *Honest Graft* (1988), Brooks Jackson, a former investigative reporter for *The Wall Street Journal*, wrote that the House of Representatives evolved "into a gigantic bureaucracy, a re-election machine designed principally to return incumbents to office." The S&L operators learned how to press all the right buttons to make this machine work for them. The chairman of the House Banking Committee, Henry B. Gonzalez (D, TX), observed that "everything the industry has wanted, Congress has rolled over and given to them." The S&L industry established over 150 PACs to funnel millions of dollars in campaign contributions to several congressmen, particularly key members of the House and Senate banking committees.

By far the most favored was former House Banking Committee Chairman Fernand St. Germain (D, RI), who was instrumental in raising the deposit insurance limit from $40,000 to $100,000. The contributions were mostly legal, but some gifts and favors were not. Representatives St. Germain and Coelho and Speaker of the House Jim Wright (D, TX) all lost their offices largely because of their unethical ties to the S&L industry. And other congressmen in both parties were under investigation.

Contributing to the political scandal that increasingly engulfed the S&L crisis were the "Keating Five." They were five US senators—Alan Cranston (D, CA), Dennis DeConcini (D, AZ), John Glenn (D, OH), John McCain (R, AZ), and Donald W. Riegle Jr. (D, MI)—who had received large political campaign contributions from Charles Keating Jr., chairman of the Lincoln Savings and Loan Association. When the bank ran into regulatory hot water in an investigation by the FHLBB, the Keating Five had the probe squelched. Lincoln subsequently collapsed, in 1989, and Keating was sent to prison for fraud.[9]

Why were Washington's regulators as helpful to the industry as the politicians? George Stigler, who won a Nobel Prize in economics for his pioneering work on the behavior of regulated firms, observed that such firms have an economic interest in "capturing" the regulator to achieve their own goals, thereby using "public resources and power to improve their economic status." Capture theory predicts that the most highly regulated industries will have the greatest influence over their regulators. That is exactly what happened in the thrift industry.

The United States League of Savings Institutions played a crucial role in establishing both the Federal Home Loan Bank System and the FSLIC. The League had a great deal of influence over the Bank Board, which provided liquidity to S&Ls and regulated and supervised their activities. The FSLIC was supposed to close insolvent institutions promptly. But under industry pressure, Congress refused to provide the FSLIC with enough money to do the job properly during the second half of the 1980s.

The results of Washington's assistance to the S&L industry were disastrous. For every three dollars in capital, the operators of an S&L could accept and raise $100 in government-insured deposits. Speculators and swindlers moved into the industry, offering very high rates to attract deposits. The fastest-growing thrifts paid the highest returns and invested in the most speculative projects. The depositors never worried about the riskiness of the S&Ls' assets because their deposits were widely believed to be insured by the government. As things turned out, many of the loans were extraordinarily risky.

The credit supplied by the S&Ls financed a building boom that created a glut of office buildings, condominiums, and shopping centers. As real estate prices started to sink, so did the net worth of more and more S&Ls. Congress responded to the crisis by restructuring and deregulating the industry and approving extra funds to pay depositors at failed institutions. The deposit insurance program was a major contributor to the S&L debacle.

The federal deposit guarantees were in fact a government subsidy rather than an insurance program. The thrifts paid the premiums to the FSLIC. Unlike most insurance programs, high flyers paid the same premiums as conservatively managed thrifts. And the FSLIC's reserves were never sufficient to cover the potential liabilities of the insurance fund.

The S&L crisis weighed on the economy during the second half of the 1980s. As the thrifts ran out of tricks to hide their losses on their dodgy loans, they were forced to reduce their lending for residential and commercial construction and mortgages. Housing completions fell from a cyclical peak during January 1987 of 1.86 million units, at a seasonally adjusted annual rate, to a cyclical low of 1.00 million units during December 1991.

Fixed investment on commercial and health-care structures in real GDP dropped 40% from the fourth quarter of 1985 to the fourth quarter of 1991 (Fig. 21). Commercial mortgages outstanding, which had risen by 240% from the first quarter of 1980 to peak at $829 billion during the second quarter of 1991, then fell 13% through the end of 1994 (Fig. 22).

The late 1980s and early 1990s were tumultuous. In addition to the S&L crisis, the stock market crashed during October 1987. The Cold War ended in 1989. Drexel Burnham Lambert, a major Wall Street investment banking firm, was forced into bankruptcy in February 1990. Under the direction of Michael Milken, the firm single-handedly created the junk-bond market. When Drexel shut down, that compounded the credit crunch resulting from the failures in the thrift industry. Then on August 2, 1990, Iraq invaded Kuwait, leading to the First Gulf War, which lasted from January 17 to February 28, 1991. Oil prices spiked.

Despite all the tumult, I predicted that the recession in residential and commercial construction wouldn't spread to the entire economy; this belief underpinned my continued bullishness on the stock market. However, all these events did push the economy into a recession during July 1990, according to the National Bureau of Economic Research. But the recession was a remarkably short one, lasting only eight months through March 1991. The Fed eased the credit crunch significantly by dropping the federal funds rate from 9.50% during June 1989 to 3.00% on September 4, 1992.

The S&L crisis of the 1980s resulted in billions of dollars of losses for the industry. It came to a head in 1989 when the FSLIC, which provided deposit insurance for thrift customers, became insolvent. In response, Congress moved to clean up the mess that Congress had created in the S&L industry. That year, the Financial Institutions Reform, Recovery, and Enforcement Act was enacted.

As a result of the Act, the following entities were added to the alphabet soup of regulatory bodies: The FHLB was abolished and replaced by the Federal Housing Finance Board to oversee the 11 Federal Home Loan Banks. The FSLIC was abolished and replaced by the Savings Association Insurance Fund (SAIF), which the FDIC administers.[10] The Office of Thrift Supervision (OTS), a bureau residing in the Treasury Department, was created to charter, regulate, examine, and supervise savings institutions. The Resolution Trust Corporation (RTC) was created as well, to dispose of failed thrift institutions that regulators had taken over. From its start on January 1, 1989 through mid-1995, the RTC shuttered 747 thrifts with assets totaling $394 billion. Also in 1989, Freddie Mac went public, becoming a for-profit corporation owned by private shareholders rather than by the FHLBs.

What did I learn from the S&L crisis? It was largely attributable to the S&Ls capturing the financial regulators who were supposed to regulate the thrift industry. Some observers blamed the crisis on deregulation of the industry, leading to an example of free-market capitalism gone wild. In fact, it is a perfect example of crony capitalism, where business interests bought influence in Congress to rig the system and markets in their favor. That's corruption, not capitalism.

The next big financial debacle was caused, to an important extent, by an even bigger and more widespread wave of corruption. However, so many perpetrators were involved that no one went to jail, unlike after the S&L crisis, when several perp walks occurred.

ROUNDING UP THE SUSPECTS

HOUSING CERTAINLY CONTRIBUTED to making the Great Recession the worst US economic downturn since the Great Depression. It lasted 18 months, from December 2007 through June 2009, which was longer than all the prior postwar recessions. Real GDP fell 4.2% from the end of 2007 through mid-2009. That was bad, but so were the recessions of the early 1970s and early 1980s. What made the Great Recession so great was that it was followed by a very weak recovery. The Great Recession was associated with a financial crisis deeply rooted in extraordinary excesses in the mortgage industry. The consequences lingered well past the official end of the recession and weighed heavily on the recovery. Arguably, Washington's policy responses to the Great Recession may also have dampened the recovery.

Ever since the magnitude of the crisis became apparent in 2007, people have been writing articles, books, and official reports on who caused it. In my home office library, I have three shelves of books rounding up numerous suspects. As in Agatha Christie's *Murder on the Orient Express*, all the suspects were guilty. There were 12 perpetrators in Christie's tale. *Time* put together a list titled "25 People to Blame for the Financial Crisis." The weekly news magazine accused the following:

Angelo Mozilo / Phil Gramm / Alan Greenspan / Chris Cox / American Consumers / Hank Paulson / Joe Cassano / Ian McCarthy / Frank Raines / Kathleen Corbet / Dick Fuld / Marion and Herb Sandler / Bill Clinton / George W. Bush / Stan O'Neal / Wen Jiabao / David Lereah / John Devaney / Bernie Madoff / Lew Ranieri / Burton Jablin / Fred Goodwin / Sandy Weill / David Oddsson / Jimmy Cayne

On the magazine's website are links to dossiers on each of the alleged perpetrators.[11] Plenty more "blameworthy" names and groups could be added to the list, including Henry Cisneros, Andrew Cuomo, Barney Frank (D, MA), Chris Dodd (D, CT), the Association of Community Organizations for Reform Now (ACORN), the credit rating agencies, and every person who made or took out a "liar's" mortgage loan based on false income information. Their common defense was that no one expected home prices nationwide could ever plummet "en masse," which is exactly what happened.

The stage was set for both the S&L crisis and the latest financial crisis way back in the early 1900s, when the housing industry teamed up with the financial industry to lobby the government for lots of support. Along the way, owning a home became part and parcel of the American Dream, and the government became increasingly committed to making the dream come true for as many Americans as possible, as described above. For the politicians who promoted this idea, there were lots of votes in this promise—and lots of campaign contributions.

The housing bust that started in 2007 was preceded by a housing boom that arguably started on April 6, 1998. That day, John Reed of Citicorp and Sandy Weill of Travelers Group announced their intention to merge the bank with the insurance company, forming Citigroup. One small roadblock: the law. The merger violated the Glass–Steagall Act of 1933 prohibiting any one financial institution from acting as any combination of an investment bank, commercial bank, and insurance company. Nevertheless, the Fed under Chairman Alan Greenspan gave Citigroup a temporary waiver in September 1998. (Weill and Greenspan were both on *Time*'s list of perps.)

Lo and behold, 14 months later, on November 12, 1999, Congress enacted the Gramm–Leach–Bliley Act, also known as the "Financial Services Modernization Act of 1999," which was strongly promoted by Senator Phil Gramm (R, TX) and signed into law by President Bill

Clinton. It swept away the Glass–Steagall barriers among financial institutions. They now could merge and acquire one another with abandon, becoming instant financial supermarkets. At the time, the popular rationale was that such modernization was necessary so that American banks could compete with Europe's "universal banks."[12] (Gramm is on the perps list.)

But the Clinton administration had threatened to veto the Act unless it included a provision—proposed by Senators Chris Dodd and Chuck Schumer (D, NY)—prohibiting from participating in a merger any financial holding company with a subsidiary that had received an unsatisfactory rating on its most recent Community Reinvestment Act (CRA) exam. CRA exams assessed banks' compliance with a 1977 law prohibiting banks from "redlining," or denying credit to qualified minority, low-income borrowers. The inclusion of this provision in Gramm–Leach–Bliley is important, in my opinion, because it gave the regulatory bodies that enforced the CRA say-so over which banks could and could not consider mergers, depending on their CRA performance.

Was the CRA—and particularly was hyper-empowering its enforcing agencies through the Gramm–Leach–Bliley Act—a major contributor to the subprime mortgage disaster? That question remains ensconced in controversy. The heightened importance to banks of earning satisfactory CRA ratings after passage of the Act no doubt encouraged subprime lending. And banks' necessity to score well on the CRA exam seemed to embolden community activist groups such as ACORN to virtually extort subprime lending—and contributions to their nonprofit organizations—from banks with low CRA scores. The activists' threat: lend below prime or deal with public shaming and be barred from any merger activity.

However, subsequent analyses of the subprime mortgage lending showed that mortgage brokers, who were not covered by the CRA, accounted for a significant portion of lending to people who should never have qualified for a loan. So the CRA was only partly to blame for the reckless proliferation of subprime lending.[13]

Fannie Mae and Freddie Mac also deserve some of the blame for accepting so many of the subprime loans made by the mortgage brokers as well as by the bankers. They were under political pressure to make the American Dream come true for more Americans during President Bill Clinton's administration. The push to expand homeownership continued under President George W. Bush, who, for example, introduced a "Zero Down Payment" initiative at the start of 2004 that under certain circumstances could remove the 3% down payment rule for first-time homebuyers with FHA-insured mortgages.[14] However, the Bush administration was troubled by the rapidly growing role of Fannie Mae and Freddie Mac in the mortgage market, especially since there was widespread belief that the GSEs were backed by the government, which they were not at that point.

The GSEs enjoyed great support from Senator Chris Dodd, chair of the Senate Banking Committee from 2007 to 2010. He was also the number one recipient of campaign funds from the GSEs from 1989 to 2008.[15] In the House, Representative Barney Frank—the powerful chairman of the House Financial Services Committee—defended Fannie Mae from the Republicans. He also had an alleged conflict of interest.[16]

The Fed deserves some of the blame too. Its easy monetary policy at the start of the decade and gradual rate hikes stimulated tremendous demand for yield. The Fed lowered the federal funds rate from 6.50% on January 3, 2001 to 1.00% on June 25, 2003, first in response to the recession and bear market in stocks that followed the bursting of the tech bubble. The residential and commercial construction markets were also under duress at the time. The 9/11 terrorist attacks only worsened the economic outlook. The Fed kept the federal funds rate at 1.00% until June 30, 2004. Then it proceeded to raise it at a "measured pace" of 25 basis points at each of the next 16 meetings of the Federal Open Market Committee (FOMC). That was a first: such a cautious and predictable normalization of monetary policy had never happened before.

The predictability of the Fed's measured rate hikes also increased the gains from carry trades in which bonds could be financed with short-term borrowing as long as the trader was reasonably confident that those borrowing costs would remain below the yield on the bonds. Of course, that trade wouldn't work if bond yields rose, causing bond prices to fall. However, yields didn't rise. Instead, the US Treasury 10-year bond yield fluctuated around 4.50% from 2001 to 2007. Mortgage rates also diverged from the upward march of the federal funds rate (Fig. 23). That was a big surprise given that short-term rates were almost certainly going to go up at every FOMC meeting, albeit at an incremental pace, once the Fed commenced its measured rate hikes.

That phenomenon became known as "Greenspan's conundrum." In his February 16, 2005 semiannual testimony to Congress on monetary policy, the former Fed chairman said globalization might be expanding productive capacity around the world and moderating inflation. It might also be increasing the size of the global savings pool. "But none of this is new and hence it is difficult to attribute the long-term interest rate declines of the last nine months to glacially increasing globalization. For the moment, the broadly unanticipated behavior of world bond markets remains a conundrum. Bond price movements may be a short-term aberration, but it will be some time before we are able to better judge the forces underlying recent experience," he concluded.[17]

Greenspan and other members of the FOMC were concerned about the fragility of the US economic recovery. They also feared deflation. In fact, Fed Governor Ben Bernanke addressed the issue in his November 21, 2002 speech "Deflation: Making Sure 'It' Doesn't Happen Here."[18] The PCED inflation rate on a year-over-year basis fell to a low of 0.7% at the start of 2002 (Fig. 24).

The demand for alternative investments such as those created by the GSEs was tremendous because other options to generate returns at a perceived low risk were scarce. The GSEs were the trailblazers in the MBS industry. Mortgages were originated and packaged together into these securities, which could be kept or sold to other financial institutions. Ginnie Mae securities were a big hit because they were, and still are, the only MBSs guaranteed by the US government, comparable to US Treasury securities in that respect. In effect, Ginnie Mae nationalized the mortgage market and untethered it from the banks and thrifts. Housing finance was no longer constrained by the resources of local depository institutions. The national, and increasingly the international, capital markets became a huge source of mortgage financing, supplementing and substituting for bank funding.

Wall Street recognized a great opportunity to monetize the growing demand for mortgages, no matter their credit rating, and to fund even more growth with credit derivatives. The Street mimicked the GSEs on a massive scale and ultimately deserves much of the blame for the financial crisis. Indeed, several of the names on *Time*'s list were among the titans of Wall Street back then—for example, Paulson, Fuld, O'Neal, and Cayne. It even included the chairman of the Securities and Exchange Commission (SEC) at the time, Chris Cox.

WEAPONS OF MASS FINANCIAL DESTRUCTION

CREDIT DERIVATIVES TURNED out to be weapons of mass financial destruction. They took off after the passage of the Commodity Futures Modernization Act of 2000. Once again, a key architect of the Act was Phil Gramm. His accomplices included Fed Chairman Alan Greenspan, Treasury Secretary Robert Rubin, Deputy Secretary Lawrence Summers, and SEC Chairman Arthur Levitt.[19] They all adamantly opposed what they viewed as a power grab by Brooksley Born, the head of the Commodity Futures Trading Commission (CFTC).

Born insisted that her agency should regulate the over-the-counter (OTC) credit derivatives market, which she wanted to see become an open exchange with strict rules, similar to the ones for commodities and financial futures. On May 7, 1998, the same day that the CFTC issued a concept release advocating her position, Rubin, Greenspan, and Levitt issued a joint statement denouncing her move: "We have grave concerns about this action and its possible consequences. . . . We are very concerned about reports that the CFTC's action may increase the legal uncertainty concerning certain types of OTC derivatives."[20] They proposed a moratorium on the CFTC's ability to regulate OTC derivatives.

A few months later, during September 1998, Long-Term Capital Management (LTCM) blew up. The huge hedge fund had accumulated on a notional basis more than $1 trillion in OTC derivatives and $125 billion in securities on $4.8 billion of capital. The Federal Reserve Bank of New York orchestrated a bailout of the firm by its 14 OTC dealers, who had been clueless about LTCM's enormous bets. This incident was a powerful indictment of the Rubin/Greenspan/Levitt position opposing tighter regulation of OTC derivatives and spoke volumes about the wisdom of Born's initiative. Incredibly, in October 1998, Congress passed the requested moratorium on her proposal.

LTCM's collapse should have been a victory for the CFTC's view. Born said on November 13, 1998 that the LTCM debacle raised important issues about hedge funds and their increasing use of OTC derivatives— including "lack of transparency, excessive leverage, insufficient prudential controls, and the need for coordination and cooperation among international regulators." She continued, "I welcome the heightened awareness of these issues that the LTCM matter has engendered and believe it is critically important for all financial regulators to work together closely and cooperatively on them."[21]

That turned out to be Born's swan song. Along with Greenspan, Rubin, and Levitt, Born sat on the President's Working Group on Financial Markets, which was charged with recommending reforms in response to the LTCM debacle. But she resigned as CFTC chair in January 1999, leaving the group before its report was released amid what *The New York Times* called infighting that had deteriorated into a "fray."[22] The group's report came out in April 1999, calling for new risk-reporting rules for hedge funds and others.[23]

But its message was not long remembered. The working group's next report, released in November 1999, did not recommend the regulation of derivatives that Born fought for—far from it. This later report suggested that Congress expressly exempt derivatives from oversight. Notably, it was produced after Larry Summers replaced Robert Rubin both as Treasury Secretary and on the working group, and after William J. Rainer had taken Born's former job and place in the group.[24] Without Born's advocacy, the notion of regulating derivatives died. The CFTC quietly withdrew its proposal.

The 2000 Act essentially prevented the regulation of credit derivatives. Derivatives products were deemed to be neither "futures," requiring regulation under the Commodity Exchange Act of 1936, nor "securities," subject to the federal securities laws. The Act's rationale in exempting them from any specific regulation beyond the general "safety and soundness" standards to which the vendors of these products—banks and securities firms—normally were held by their federal overseers was that OTC derivatives transactions occurred between "sophisticated parties," who presumably knew the risks they were undertaking. Therefore, the parties had no need for government protection; they watched out for themselves and kept each other honest.

The Gramm–Leach–Bliley Act of 1999 introduced the concept of functional regulation, a clever way of disempowering the regulators. This Act upended the system of regulatory checks and balances on the various special interest groups within the financial industry, replacing it with a divide-and-conquer system with respect to the regulators.[25] The 2000 Act simply barred financial industry regulators from any jurisdiction over credit derivatives. In effect, Phil Gramm's invisible hand gave Wall Street carte blanche. The 2000 legislation introduced the concept of self-regulation by Wall Street, which was presumed at the time to be the next logical extension of functional regulation.

No one back then seemed very troubled by the fact that shortly after these two deregulation acts were passed in 1999 and 2000, Enron Corporation—a Houston-based energy, commodities, and services company—blew up. Gramm–Leach–Bliley had exempted from government regulation trades on electronic energy commodity markets, in a provision that later came to be known as the "Enron Loophole." Exploiting this loophole, Enron had created the global market for energy-based derivatives. These customized risk-swapping contracts enabled parties to hedge their exposure to changing energy prices and supply fluctuations. Enron declared bankruptcy on December 2, 2001.

Wall Street's investment bankers proceeded to ramp up the assembly lines in their credit derivatives departments that transformed trash into gold. The alchemy was enabled with collateralized debt obligations and credit default swaps (CDOs and CDSs). Here are some of the basics of these credit derivatives:

- *Slice and dice.* "The CDO Machine" is the eighth chapter of *The Financial Crisis Inquiry Report*—released in January 2011 by the US government's Financial Crisis Inquiry Commission (FCIC) and updated in February of that year. It is devoted to understanding the huge role that CDOs played in the financial crisis of 2008.[26] This chapter explains that CDOs are "structured financial instruments that purchase and pool financial assets such as the riskier tranches of various mortgage-backed securities."

  The tranches into which many MBSs are structured divide pools of mortgage debt into higher and lower credit ratings. Whatever losses result from defaults on the underlying mortgages (or other credit events) are absorbed by lower-rated (typically termed "equity" or "mezzanine") tranches first, while the highest-rated (dubbed "senior") tranches are the most sheltered from credit risks.

  Wall Street piled the harder-to-sell lower-rated MBS tranches into CDOs, which were vouched to be sufficiently diversified that they were safer than their underlying MBS tranches. The credit rating agencies signed off on this sales pitch by giving AAA ratings to the vast majority of the CDO tranches even though they consisted mostly of lower-rated MBS tranches. After all, the thinking went, these instruments were secured by a diversified pool of underlying assets that were very unlikely to go belly up at the same time. The problems began when this is exactly what did happen: the underlying securities' performance started to correlate and, as the FCIC investigators wrote, "stopped performing at roughly the same time."

- *Full menu.* CDO products became more and more complicated. Some CDOs even had 80% to 100% of their assets in other CDOs, an instrument called "CDOs squared." Compounding the complexity, financial services companies, including American International Group (AIG)—an American multinational insurance corporation—offered CDSs to CDO investors. CDSs, the FCIC explained, "promis[ed] to reimburse [investors] for any losses on the tranches in exchange for a stream of premium-like payments. This credit default swap protection made the CDOs much more attractive to potential investors because they appeared to be virtually risk free, but it created huge exposures for the credit default swap issuers if significant losses did occur." There were also "synthetic" CDOs, which were "complex paper transactions involving credit default swaps." The inquiry report concluded that CDOs, especially synthetic ones, worked to magnify the risk built up in the structured finance markets, multiplying the effects of the crisis. (See Appendix 8.2, Credit Derivatives: Basic Definitions.)

With so much easy credit available in the mortgage market, lending standards deteriorated rapidly and significantly. The FCIC reported, "Lenders made loans that they knew borrowers could not afford and that could cause massive losses to investors in mortgage securities." Executives at Countrywide Financial Corporation, headed by Angelo Mozilo (on *Time*'s list of suspects) and the nation's biggest mortgage lender at the time, realized as early as September 2004 that the loans they were making could result in "catastrophic consequences." But they kept making more of them.[27]

Unregulated lenders jumped into the market. Many lenders no longer required down payments. Income verification was lax or nonexistent. Subprime mortgages jumped from 8% of mortgage originations in 2003 to 20% in 2005. The menu of mortgages expanded to include adjustable-rate mortgages (ARMs), interest-only mortgages, and payment-option ARMs. Lots of borrowers chose ARMs known as "2/28s" or "3/27s," with low "teaser rates" for the first two or three years of their 30-year mortgages. Most of them turned delinquent as soon as they were reset at the market rate after the teaser period. (See Appendix 8.2, Credit Derivatives: Basic Definitions.)

Orange County, California saw more than its share of unregulated lending companies sprouting up to meet Wall Street's heady demand for mortgages to securitize, according to CNBC's excellent special report on the financial crisis, *House of Cards* (first aired on February 12, 2009). People inexperienced and uneducated in banking were creating lending companies to get in on the action. Pizza boys were plucked from delivery trucks to become loan officers. Their only training was on the job—they learned to write mortgages by writing mortgages, according to the former head of such a company spotlighted in the documentary.

It was like the California Gold Rush all over again. For mortgage suppliers, the race was on to create more mortgages than the next guy. For their investment bank customers, the race was on to buy up more mortgage assets than the next guy and create more CDOs. Wall Street had discovered what seemed like a foolproof way to sell fool's gold as real gold.

After the fact, all the lenders claimed that the loans had made sense at the time because everyone expected home prices to keep rising, and almost nobody expected them to fall. For a short while, home prices didn't just rise, they soared—along with home sales, financed by an orgy of mortgage lending that was facilitated by the securitization of mortgages.

Sometimes, cover stories in major magazines can be contrary indicators. This is the front-cover curse I mention in Chapter 1 and Chapter 16. In 1997 and 1998, Rubin, Summers, and Greenspan worked with the International Monetary Fund and others to combat and contain financial crises in Russian, Asian, and Latin American financial markets; *Time*'s February 15, 1999 cover blared: "The Committee to Save the World: The inside story of how the Three Marketeers have prevented a global economic meltdown—so far."[28] Ironically, their opposition to any regulation of the credit derivatives market and their support for the 2000 Act certainly helped to set the stage for the 2008 meltdown.

By the way, Brooksley Born got to have the last word on the subject, as one of the members of the FCIC. Not surprisingly, the commission's report noted the irony of *Time*'s cover coming less than five months after LTCM hit the fan and three months after Congress buried the Glass–Steagall Act. The report took numerous direct swipes at Greenspan, Rubin, and Summers, not only for failing to stop the excesses that led to the financial crisis but also for helping to set the stage for it.

GREAT RECESSION

THE HOUSE OF cards came tumbling down. It all ended very badly indeed, as the following chronology recounts:

- *First half of 2007.* Everything started to come unglued during the fourth quarter of 2006 as delinquency rates on subprime mortgages rose, leading to a wave of bankruptcies among subprime lenders. On February 8, 2007, HSBC Holdings, the multinational bank headquartered in London, said it would have to add to loan loss reserves to cover bad debts in the subprime lending portfolio. On June 20, a couple of hedge funds at Bear Stearns announced major losses resulting from bad bets on securities backed by subprime loans.
- *Second half of 2007.* On July 30, German bank IKB announced losses linked to US subprime securities. On October 24, Merrill Lynch reported huge losses in its credit derivatives portfolio. The firm's CEO, Stanley O'Neal, left at the end of the month. MBIA announced a significant exposure to credit derivatives, which threatened its AAA rating as well as the value of its insurance on many municipal bonds.
- *First half of 2008.* On March 16, JP Morgan agreed to buy Bear Stearns, with the Fed agreeing to acquire up to $30 billion of Bear's distressed assets. On March 19, the government lowered capital requirements on Fannie Mae and Freddie Mac to provide liquidity to the mortgage market.
- *Second half of 2008.* On July 11, the FDIC assumed control of IndyMac, a California bank that had been one of the leading lenders making home loans to borrowers without proof of income. On July 13, the Fed authorized the GSEs to borrow from the discount window for emergency funding. On September 7, Fannie Mae and Freddie Mac were placed in conservatorship, with life support provided by the US Treasury.[29] On Monday, September 15, Bank of America agreed to acquire Merrill Lynch. The very same day, Lehman Brothers filed for bankruptcy due to losses resulting from holding onto large positions in subprime and other lower-rated tranches of securitized mortgages.

    On Thursday, September 16, AIG imploded following the failure of its Financial Products unit. This division was overseen by OTS, the thrift regulator, which *The New York Times* in a May 20, 2009 article called "arguably . . . the weakest of all the federal bank regulators."[30] Thanks to the Financial Services Modernization Act of 1999, AIG had been allowed to choose OTS as its noninsurance overseer in 1999, the article explained, after buying a small S&L. The FCIC concluded in January 2011 that "AIG failed and was rescued by the government primarily because its enormous sales of credit default swaps were made without putting up the initial collateral, setting aside capital reserves, or hedging its exposure."[31]

On Sunday, September 21, the Fed announced that Goldman Sachs and Morgan Stanley, the last two independent investment banks, would become bank holding companies, subjecting them to new regulation and supervision. The move also signaled that the Fed wouldn't let them fail, because it gave them access to the Fed's borrowing window. Why the same courtesy wasn't extended to Bear Stearns, Merrill Lynch, and Lehman Brothers remains a mystery. (See Appendix 8.3, Bernanke's Fed and the Lehman Bankruptcy.)

Here in brief is the credit history of the housing crisis:

- *Home prices, owners' equity, and mortgage debt.* On a 12-month average basis, the median existing single-family home price doubled from the fall of 1994 to peak at $224,283 during July 2006 (Fig. 25). Not surprisingly, this series is highly correlated with the value of real estate held by households—a data series, compiled quarterly in the Fed's *Financial Accounts of the United States*, that doubled from the second quarter of 2000 to peak at $22.7 trillion during the second quarter of 2006.

  The Fed also tabulates quarterly data on "owners' equity in household real estate." That doubled from the second quarter of 2000 to peak at $13.4 trillion during the first quarter of 2006 (Fig. 26). Over the same period, home mortgage debt also doubled.

  Home prices proceeded to drop 27% from July 2006 through February 2012. That doesn't seem like a big correction given the steep ascent of home prices since the early 1980s. However, mortgage leverage converted that into a 56% drop in owners' equity from the first quarter of 2006 through the first quarter of 2009. The aggregate value of owners' equity fell below the amount of mortgage debt outstanding, which was reflected in lots of "underwater" homeowners who owed more than their houses were worth.

- *Ratios of owners' equity to income.* The ratio of aggregate home values to disposable personal income soared from 1.4 at the start of 1998 to peak at a record high of 2.3 during the final quarter of 2005 (Fig. 27). The comparable ratio for owners' equity in their homes rose from 0.8 to 1.4 over this same period. That was a heady time to own a home. Almost no one seemed to recognize the bubble, inflated by the flood of mortgage credit, for what it was. The ratio of home mortgage debt to disposable income rose from 0.6 at the start of 1998 to a record high of 1.0 during the last half of 2007.

  Owners' equity as a percentage of the value of household real estate was 84% when the data started in 1945. It fell to a range of 60%–70% from the mid-1960s through the mid-2000s. It then fell from 60% during the last quarter of 2005 to a record low of 36% during the first quarter of 2009 (Fig. 28). The flip side of that story, of course, is that the amount of leverage—i.e., the percentage of mortgage debt on the underlying value of residential real estate—rose to a record high of 64% during the first quarter of 2009.

- *Borrowing binge.* During the 1990s, the annual pace of home mortgage borrowing was fairly steady around $200 billion (Fig. 29). It then went parabolic during the first six years of the 2000s, peaking at $1.3 trillion over the four quarters through the second quarter of 2006. Home equity loans also became a popular way to extract some of the real estate gains on home sweet home. The outstanding amount of such loans soared from $334 billion at the end of 1999 to peak at a record high of $1.1 trillion during the last quarter of 2007 (Fig. 30).

  Mortgage borrowing collapsed during the financial crisis, with loan repayments exceeding loan extensions from 2010 through 2013 before recovering from 2014 through 2016. Home equity loans dropped back down to $585 billion by mid-2017, the lowest since the third quarter of 2003.

- *ABS issuers.* In the private sector, the issuers of asset-backed securities (ABS) mimicked the GSEs and created credit derivatives with mortgages that didn't conform to the lending standards of the GSEs. From the first quarter of 2000, the debt of ABS issuers soared 391% from $815 billion to a record high of $4.0 trillion during the first quarter of 2008 (Fig. 31). It then plunged, returning to $1.2 trillion by the end of 2016, while the amount of home mortgages held by the ABS issuers fell from a peak of $2.4 trillion during the second quarter of 2007 to $521 billion by the end of 2016 (Fig. 32).

- *Commercial paper.* The commercial paper of ABS issuers turned toxic, peaking at a record $1.2 trillion during the week of August 8, 2007. It sank to $708 billion during the week of October 8, 2008, when the Fed set up an emergency facility to provide liquidity to the commercial paper market (Fig. 33).
- *Depository institutions.* Among FDIC-insured depository institutions, provisions for loan losses soared, along with delinquency rates. It didn't take long for spiraling delinquencies to turn into foreclosures, resulting in net charge-offs for bad loans (Fig. 34). Cumulative net charge-offs soared $693 billion from the fourth quarter of 2007 through the fourth quarter of 2012 (Fig. 35). The Fed's *Financial Accounts of the United States* shows that financial institutions were forced to shore up their badly depleted capital by issuing $720 billion in equities from the fourth quarter of 2007 through the fourth quarter of 2009 (Fig. 36).

The global economy sank into a severe synchronized recession as business activity fell off a cliff everywhere. Global industrial production dropped 12.8% from February 2008 through February 2009 (Fig. 37). The volume of world exports plunged 20.0% from January 2008 through January 2009. In the United States, real GDP declined by 4.2% from the last quarter of 2007 through mid-2009. It was the deepest recession since the Great Depression. However, it lasted only 18 months. So why has it been dubbed the "Great Recession," even by Fed officials who had touted the Great Moderation only a few years earlier? The answer is that the recovery was the weakest on record (Fig. 38).

Contributing to the weak recovery was housing starts, which plummeted from a high of 2.27 million units during January 2006, at a seasonally adjusted annual rate, to 478,000 units during April 2009, a record low since the start of the data in 1959. By the end of 2016, housing starts had recovered to 1.27 million units, a pace comparable to previous cyclical lows rather than cyclical highs.

This is in line with the history of bubbles: when a bubble in an asset or an industry bursts, it can take a painfully long time for the ensuing recovery in related prices and activity to unfold. That's because the flood of capital that poured into the asset or industry dries up while investors, lenders, and speculators lick their wounds.

PROPHETS OF DOOM

I FIRST SPOTTED trouble ahead in the spring of 2005, voicing my concern in a May 3, 2005 *Topical Study* titled "After Alan: HELs To Pay?"[32] I wrote that Greenspan, who was scheduled to retire at the start of 2006, had cleaned up the mess caused by the bursting of the tech bubble by creating another bubble with his "measured" approach to rate hikes. I warned, "This time it is in real estate finance."

I observed that there was plenty of anecdotal evidence showing that mortgage originators had lowered lending standards significantly in recent years. They were offering loans with all sorts of gimmicks, including no down payments, home equity loans equivalent to the down payment, below-market teaser rates for a year on variable-rate loans, balloon loans that were interest-only for several years before any principal was due, and heavily discounted closing costs. NINJA loans proliferated—i.e., mortgages extended to a borrower with "no income, no job, and no assets."

At the time, I concluded: "the housing bubble is more likely to get bigger than to pop." However, I didn't appreciate how big the bubble in the credit derivatives market was. Therefore, I didn't anticipate the calamity that resulted when it popped. On November 16, 2006, I appeared in a *PBS NewsHour* segment about the housing market. On the streets of Lower Manhattan, Paul Solman, the show's business and economics consultant, moderated a point–counterpoint debate between Nouriel Roubini and me on the outlook for the housing market. Roubini, a professor at New York University's Stern School of Business and chairman of Roubini Global Economics, had been vocally pessimistic since 2005, while I argued that even if housing was falling into a recession, the overall economy would continue to grow.

Roubini was right. The financial press dubbed him "Dr. Doom." David Rosenberg also correctly predicted the severity of the financial calamity. He was the chief North American economist at Bank of America Merrill Lynch in New York for seven years, prior to joining Gluskin Sheff in the spring of 2009. Ironically, while he was issuing his dire warnings, his firm was one of the leading manufacturers of CDOs.

Early in 2007, I concluded that the subprime problem was probably as big as the S&L crisis. While I expected that this might weigh on the economy, I also anticipated that the Fed would provide plenty of liquidity to ease the pain, just as it had during the early 1990s. One of my hedge fund accounts in London called and warned me that his sources in the credit markets were telling him the problem was much bigger and more widespread than generally recognized. Another account, an investment strategist at a major West Coast mutual fund company, also alerted me in mid-2007 that he had visited with several fixed-income professionals on Wall Street to get their read on the subprime problem. He said they were all very worried, mostly because they knew it was a big problem but had no clue how big it might be.

Lesson learned: I should have listened to those early prophets of doom and sought out more information from more knowledgeable people in the credit derivatives market. A handful of investors who did their homework and positioned for the calamity made fortunes, as chronicled by Michael Lewis in *The Big Short: Inside the Doomsday Machine* (2010). Instead, I concurred with Fed Chairman Ben Bernanke's relatively sanguine assessment, which he presented in a May 17, 2007 speech in Chicago titled "The Subprime Mortgage Market."[33] He certainly must regret coming to the following conclusion:

> The rise in subprime mortgage lending likely boosted home sales somewhat, and curbs on this lending are expected to be a source of some restraint on home purchases and residential investment in coming quarters. Moreover, we are likely to see further increases in delinquencies and foreclosures this year and next as many adjustable-rate loans face interest-rate resets. All that said, given the fundamental factors in place that should support the demand for housing, we believe the effect of the troubles in the subprime sector on the broader housing market will likely be limited, and we do not expect significant spillovers from the subprime market to the rest of the economy or to the financial system. The vast majority of mortgages, including even subprime mortgages, continue to perform well. Past gains in house prices have left most homeowners with significant amounts of home equity, and growth in jobs and incomes should help keep the financial obligations of most households manageable.

Following the financial crisis, the most prominent bears were joined by lots of other tardy doomsayers who warned that financial calamity might soon return. I fondly recall the yearly gatherings, always during the first weekend in June, of a few financial market economists together with the portfolio managers handling the Bahre family's investments—a tradition begun after the crisis. Gary Bahre and his parents, Bob and Sandy, were our gracious hosts at their magnificent estate overlooking Lake Winnipesaukee in New Hampshire. Over the years, these annual weekend retreats included Roubini and Rosenberg as well as Stephen Roach, Gary Shilling, and others. Gary Bahre told me that he invited me to counter the generally pessimistic outlook that many of the other participants shared.

FAULTY INSURANCE POLICIES

LLOYD BLANKFEIN, CEO of Goldman Sachs, wrote an article in the February 8, 2009 *Financial Times* titled "Do Not Destroy the Essential Catalyst of Risk."[34] He observed that it should have been obvious something wasn't right about CDOs: "In January 2008, there were 12 triple A-rated companies in the world. At the same time, there were 64,000 structured finance instruments, such as collateralised debt obligations, rated triple A." *Now* he tells us, I thought at the time. "It is easy and appropriate to blame the rating agencies for lapses in their credit judgments," Blankfein continued. "But the blame for the result is not theirs alone. Every financial institution that participated in the process has to accept its share of the responsibility." I guess mea culpas come more easily after all the profit opportunity has dried up.

In my June 9, 2009 commentary, I concluded that the "Credit Insurance Fraud Industry" (CIFI) caused the financial crisis that started in the US subprime mortgage market during 2007 and spread around the world. This industry emerged following the first of the three Basel Accords. In Basel I, the banking regulators of the major industrial nations agreed to impose uniform capital requirements on banks. Risky assets required more capital. The CIFI employed an army of financial engineers whose innovations magically transformed subprime mortgages, junk bonds, liars' loans, and other trashy debts into AAA-rated credits. Many of these products were defective. This financial engineering was a great business while it lasted. But it was mostly a huge fraud, at worst, or negligent malpractice, at best.

Among the major contributors to the debacle were the credit-rating agencies that had awarded AAA ratings to thousands of CDO tranches, as Goldman's Blankfein belatedly observed. The FCIC's January 2011 report was correct to call the rating agencies "essential cogs in the wheel of financial destruction" and "key enablers of the financial meltdown." There were only three big rating agencies—Moody's Investors Service, Standard & Poor's, and Fitch Ratings.

The FCIC concluded: "The three credit rating agencies were key enablers of the financial meltdown. The mortgage-related securities at the heart of the crisis could not have been marketed and sold without their seal of approval. Investors relied on them, often blindly. In some cases, they were obligated to use them, or regulatory capital standards were hinged on them. This crisis could not have happened without the rating agencies. Their ratings helped the market soar and their downgrades through 2007 and 2008 wreaked havoc across markets and firms."[35]

The securitization business brought the agencies huge fees. The raters were paid by the issuers to rate the CDOs that included bunches of tranched ABS. The more complex the security, the greater the fee generated. By the time Moody's became a public company, structured finance was its top source of revenue. Gretchen Morgenson of *The New York Times* reported on December 6, 2008 that Moody's fees for rating mortgage pools were four to five times more than fees for rating similarly sized municipal bonds.[36]

The rating agencies were operating as a government-sanctioned oligopoly without any government regulation—no federal agency was charged with oversight. Washington finally recognized that the rating agencies were running amok and needed to be reined in, so Congress passed the Credit Rating Agency Reform Act, and President George W. Bush signed it into law in late 2006.

Under the Act, the SEC filled the void and became the agencies' regulator. While the new law gave the Commission new powers to inspect and punish the agencies, it also prevented the SEC from regulating how ratings were determined. The SEC had no authority to make rules governing the agencies' business or to subject them to examinations as nationally recognized statistical rating organizations (NRSROs).

The Commission established its formal regulatory program for NRSROs in June 2007; seven firms applied to be registered, and all were approved. As SEC Chairman Christopher Cox testified on April 22, 2008, before the US Senate Committee on Banking, Housing and Urban Affairs, "as of the end of September 2007, seven credit rating agencies— including those that were most active in rating subprime RMBS [residential mortgage-backed securities] and CDOs—became subject to the

Commission's new oversight authority, and subject as well to our newly adopted rules."[37]

But September 2007 was too late. When the delinquency rates of mortgages started escalating in early 2007, calling into question the AAA ratings on many CDOs with subprime loan exposure, the rating agencies didn't fail to notice. The rating agencies lowered their credit ratings on $1.9 trillion in MBSs from the third quarter of 2007 through the second quarter of 2008, with dire implications for the credit quality of the CDOs composed of the downgraded MBSs. In other words, CDOs began to hit the fan.

Why hadn't Moody's noticed the rising delinquencies in early 2007? Moody's did have a US residential mortgage bond team in place to track troublesome developments, according to the October 17, 2008 issue of the *Financial Times*.[38] But the rising delinquencies seen in January 2007 didn't compel Moody's to take action. That's because rising delinquencies alone was only the first of three cautionary signals in Moody's alarm system—which was still flashing a "green light." True, the speed of delinquency escalation shocked analysts, but their system told them to sit tight. The *Financial Times* noted: "According to a report in March 2007, the risks of the defaults in subprime mortgage bond pools climbing further up the structured finance chain were 'mild to moderate.'" Soon after, the amber light flashed when the number of delinquencies exceeding 90 days shot through the roof. Still, "[o]utwardly, the agencies were sanguine," reported the *Financial Times*.

As US mortgages continued to sour at a breakneck pace, Moody's analysts, upon inputting the new data, were stunned by the severity of the mortgage crisis. In the final few months of 2007, the rating agency downgraded more bonds than it had over the previous 19 years combined, reported the *Financial Times*. Similar revelations must have occurred in the offices of Standard & Poor's and Fitch, which also began downgrading like mad.

Moody's abundant AAA ratings on pools tainted with subprime allowed for little possibility that the housing boom might go bust—even though Moody's very own in-house chief economist, Mark Zandi, had been warning of a US housing downturn since May 2006! According to the *Financial Times*, Zandi wrote in May 2006 that the housing market "feels increasingly ripe for some type of financial event."

We now know that the 800-pound gorilla in the credit insurance industry was AIG. In the Mayfair neighborhood of London dubbed "hedge fund alley" were the offices of AIG Financial Products—the business unit from which AIG issued its credit default swaps. It had been run for 21 years by American Joseph Cassano.[39] Most of those years were great ones financially, for both the high-performing subsidiary and its highly compensated leader. That all changed at the end of 2007. Cassano had built the credit default swap business so successfully that AIG Financial Products provided guarantees on more than $500 billion of assets by that point, including $61.4 billion in securities tied to subprime mortgages.[40]

An accounting shift that affected how the Financial Products unit valued collateral resulted in the markdown of these credit default swaps—and poof went $34 billion. In contrast to standard practice, AIG Financial Products did not hedge its exposure to a possible fall in the CDS market. When AIG's accountants asked the insurer to change the way it valued CDSs, the comparatively small base of capital on which AIG Financial Products had built a mountain of business became visible. This began the unravelling that led to AIG's central role in sparking the globalization of the US financial crisis, because many European banks had purchased AIG credit derivatives to insure their loan portfolios and bonds.[41]

On September 16, 2008, AIG suffered a liquidity crisis when its credit rating was downgraded. To avoid a financial meltdown, the US Treasury Department extended an $85 billion credit line in exchange for just under 80% of its equity. On March 2, 2009, AIG announced fourth-quarter 2008 results representing "the biggest quarterly corporate loss in US history," according to a March 4 *Washington Post* article: a loss of $61.7 billion.[42] The US government at about the same time re-restructured the terms of AIG's total bailout package, which by then had swelled to $152 billion—providing another $30 billion in taxpayer funds, eliminating dividend payments, and granting the government stakes in two of AIG's big insurance subsidiaries.

On Tuesday, March 3, 2009, testifying at a Senate hearing on the federal budget, Fed Chairman Ben Bernanke was really mad: "[I can't think of] a single episode in this entire 18 months that has made me more angry . . . than AIG." That was the first time the characteristically reserved central banker had publicly displayed any emotion about the financial crisis. What most got his goat reportedly was the way AIG had strayed from its core insurance business to take unmonitored and unnecessary risks; writing billions of dollars in exotic derivative contracts had nearly destroyed the company. "AIG exploited a huge gap in the regulatory system," Bernanke said. "There was no oversight of the Financial Products division. This was a hedge fund, basically, that was attached to a large and stable insurance company, made huge numbers of irresponsible bets—took huge losses. There was no regulatory oversight because there was a gap in the system."

On the same day that the Fed chairman was castigating AIG before the Senate, Treasury Secretary Timothy Geithner was over in the House trying to defend the government's ever-growing rescue of AIG to fuming lawmakers. The March 4, 2009 *Washington Post* quoted some of his testimony before the House Ways and Means Committee: "AIG is a huge, complex, global insurance company, attached to a very complicated investment bank hedge fund that built—that was allowed to build up without any adult supervision, with inadequate capital against the risks they were taking, putting your government in a terribly difficult position. . . . And your government made the judgment back in the fall that there was no way that you could allow default to happen without catastrophic damage to the American people."

In his mea culpa article on behalf of the financial industry, Blankfein admitted that it was all about making lots of money: "We rationalised and justified the downward pricing of risk on the grounds that it was different. We did so because our self-interest in preserving and expanding our market share, as competitors, sometimes blinds us—especially when exuberance is at its peak."

Blankfein didn't mention that his firm had been dangerously exposed to AIG. In 2007, Goldman began marking down the value of CDOs on its books that had been insured by AIG against the possibility of default. When Goldman requested that AIG put up more collateral to cover those losses, the insurance company sometimes posted half or less of the amount demanded, disputing Goldman's valuations. When the government took over AIG, its creditors, including Goldman, were made nearly whole. An April 15, 2009 editorial in *The Wall Street Journal* argued that the government's takeover of AIG amounted to a bailout of Goldman, though the firm claimed it had "no material economic exposure to AIG" when the insurer collapsed.[43]

FLAW IN THE MODEL

IN THE MOVIE *Casablanca* (1942), police Captain Louis Renault walks into the back room of Rick's Café and asserts, "I'm shocked, shocked to find that gambling is going on in here!" As he shuts the place down, the casino manager hands him his recent winnings. Likewise, Alan Greenspan repeatedly professed his shock at what had gone on in the credit casino under his watch, and he certainly lost some of his public admiration when he did so—though Greenspan's shock was a good deal more genuine than Renault's.

In the prepared remarks for his October 23, 2008 testimony before the House Committee on Oversight and Government Reform, at a hearing on the role of federal regulators in the financial crisis, the former Fed chairman noted that subprime mortgages were the root of the problem but indicated that the real crisis stemmed from the uncontrolled securitization of those mortgages: "The evidence strongly suggests that without the excess demand from securitizers, subprime mortgage originations (undeniably the original source of crisis) would have been far smaller and defaults accordingly far fewer." He went on: "[S]ubprime mortgages pooled and sold as securities became subject to explosive demand from investors around the world." Greenspan noted that there had been a surge in global demand for US subprime securities by banks, hedge funds, and pension funds that were supported by "unrealistically positive rating designations by credit agencies."[44]

Greenspan continued, "As I wrote last March: those of us who have looked to the self-interest of lending institutions to protect shareholders' equity (myself especially) are in a state of shocked disbelief. Such counterparty surveillance is a central pillar of our financial markets' state of balance. If it fails, as occurred this year, market stability is undermined." During his Q&A exchange, he said:

> I made a mistake in presuming that the self-interest of organizations, specifically banks and others, [was] such [that] they were best capable of protecting their own shareholders and their equity in the firms. . . . So the problem here is something which looked to be a very solid edifice and, indeed, a critical pillar to market competition and free markets did break down. And I think that, as I said, shocked me. I still do not fully understand why it happened and, obviously, to the extent that I figure out where it happened and why, I will change my views. And if the facts change, I will change.

Then he admitted, "I found a flaw in the model that I perceived is the critical functioning structure that defines how the world works, so to speak." He added, "That's precisely the reason I was shocked, because I had been going for 40 years or more with very considerable evidence that it was working exceptionally well."[45]

In his prepared remarks, Mr. Greenspan said that the models used by Wall Street's financial engineers were also flawed:

> In recent decades, a vast risk management and pricing system has evolved, combining the best insights of mathematicians and finance experts supported by major advances in computer and communications technology. A Nobel Prize was awarded for the discovery of the pricing model that underpins much of the advance in derivatives markets. This modern risk management paradigm held sway for decades. The whole intellectual edifice, however, collapsed in the summer of last year because the data inputted into the risk management models generally covered only the past two decades, a period of euphoria. Had instead the models been fitted more appropriately to historic periods of stress, capital requirements would have been much higher and the financial world would be in far better shape today, in my judgment.

Apparently, he was in so much shock that he offered the committee only one specific recommendation: "As much as I would prefer it otherwise, in this financial environment I see no choice but to require that all securitizers retain a meaningful part of the securities they issue. This will offset in part market deficiencies stemming from the failures of counterparty surveillance." Greenspan's reluctance to force securitizers to have skin in their own game is just plain odd.

Committee Chairman Henry Waxman (D, CA) blamed regulators and Congress alike. "Congress is not exempt from responsibility," he acknowledged. "We passed legislation in 2000 that exempted financial derivatives from regulation. And we took too long—until earlier this year—to pass legislation strengthening oversight of Fannie Mae and Freddie Mac. Over and over again, ideology trumped governance." Politics, greed, and outright corruption trumped governance as well.

Many lay blame for the subprime crisis on the GSEs' embrace of the low-end lending market—or, rather, their forced embrace. Former Senator Phil Gramm, the same fellow who had pushed for the law that outlawed regulating credit derivatives, drew such a linkage in a *Wall Street*

Journal editorial on February 20, 2009. He observed that when the housing market collapsed, Fannie Mae and Freddie Mac had to deal with three quotas: 56% of their mortgage holdings had to be loans to people with below-average incomes, 27% had to be loans to families with incomes at or below 60% of the area median income, and 35% had to target underserved geographic areas. Consequently, the subprime portion of the mortgage market shot up from 5% (with 31% of that securitized) in 1994 to 20% (81% securitized) in 2006.[46]

Needless to say, Gramm was doing his best to absolve himself and his two signature pieces of legislation in 1999 and 2000 from any responsibility for the financial disaster that seemed to ensue from them. Instead, he blamed it all on the "politicization of the mortgage market." He quoted from Greenspan's October 23, 2008 testimony that "the subprime market . . . essentially emerged out of CRA." In other words, the government made the lenders take on these riskier mortgages.

The GSEs initially resisted purchasing these risky mortgages. But they ended up going along for the ride. It was a win-win for everyone. Poor communities and their community organizers benefited from the surge in homeownership. Wall Street profited from increased sales of Fannie Mae, Freddie Mac, and guaranteed MBSs and derivatives. And the GSE heads were very richly rewarded, so they showered their political friends in Washington with campaign contributions.

In 2009, Henry Kaufman put the financial crisis into perspective in a book titled *The Road to Financial Reformation: Warnings, Consequences, Reforms*. A review of it in *The Economist* was titled "He Told Us So."[47] The reviewer wrote that he felt "shortchanged" because Kaufman didn't mention his role at Lehman and didn't "shed light on the failings of corporate governance that contributed to the humbling of high finance." Martin Feldstein, another paragon of financial conservatism, who had chaired the Council of Economic Advisers in the Reagan administration, was on AIG's board when it collapsed.

On April 18, 2010, former President Bill Clinton squarely blamed two of *Time*'s "Three Marketeers," Rubin and Summers, for their bad advice on the credit derivatives market, in an interview on ABC's *This Week* program: "On derivatives, yeah I think they were wrong and I think I was wrong to take [their advice] because the argument on derivatives was that these things are expensive and sophisticated and only a handful of investors will buy them and they don't need any extra protection, and any extra transparency. The money they're putting up guarantees them transparency," Clinton said. "And the flaw in that argument," he added, "was that first of all sometimes people with a lot of money make stupid decisions and make [them] without transparency."[48]

In response to the financial crisis of 2008, Congress passed the Dodd–Frank Wall Street Reform and Consumer Protection Act in 2010. Ironically, the sponsors were none other than US Senator Chris Dodd and US Representative Barney Frank, whom some believed should have been included in the list of people to blame for the crisis. The Act increases the amount of liquid assets and capital that banks must have to back up their activities. Large banks must pass an annual stress test administered by the Fed. The Act's so-called "Volcker Rule" bans the big banks' trading desks from proprietary trading, limiting them to making markets for their clients. The Trump administration is committed to easing some of the regulatory constraints imposed by the Act.

FEDDIE

WITH THE FINANCIAL crisis rapidly spreading during September 2008, US Treasury Secretary Henry Paulson proposed a plan under which the Treasury would acquire up to $700 billion worth of MBSs to relieve banks of these toxic assets. Only three pages long, the plan was called the Troubled Asset Relief Program (TARP). A longer version became the formal legislation enacted on October 3.

Just 10 days later, at a meeting with nine major US banks on October 13, TARP was changed. It became a program in which the Treasury would purchase individual banks' preferred shares to inject capital into the banking system. Some of the bankers initially balked, but Paulson made them an offer they weren't allowed to refuse.[49]

By the way, Paulson was the CEO of Goldman Sachs from 1999 until he became Treasury Secretary in 2006. He testified to the FCIC that by the time he became secretary, many bad loans already had been issued—"most of the toothpaste was out of the tube"—and that "there really wasn't the proper regulatory apparatus to deal with it." Paulson was on *Time*'s list and was blamed by the FCIC as follows: "Under Paulson's leadership, Goldman Sachs had played a central role in the creation and sale of mortgage securities. From 2004 through 2006, the company provided billions of dollars in loans to mortgage lenders; most went to the subprime lenders Ameriquest, Long Beach, Fremont, New Century, and Countrywide through warehouse lines of credit, often in the form of repos."[50]

More reassuring than TARP, which was poorly planned and executed, was the FDIC's Temporary Liquidity Guarantee Program, implemented on October 14. It fully guaranteed all noninterest-bearing transaction deposits at participating banks and thrifts through December 31, 2009. The deadline was extended twice and expired on December 31, 2010. In addition, the FDIC guaranteed certain newly issued senior unsecured debt of the banks.[51] At its peak, the guarantee covered $345.8 billion of outstanding debt through the end of 2012. Sheila Bair, FDIC chair at the time, deserves credit for her role in ending the crisis.

The Fed lowered the federal funds rate from 5.25% in mid-2006 to nearly zero near the end of 2008, the so-called "zero lower bound." Fed Chairman Ben Bernanke also responded to the crisis by flooding the financial system with liquidity. Under his leadership, the Fed was remarkably effective at creating numerous emergency credit facilities that helped to contain the crisis so that it wouldn't turn into a full-blown contagion and collapse of the financial system. As the crisis popped up in various parts of the financial system, Bernanke masterfully played "whack-a-mole" using three sets of tools:

- *Liquidity facilities for financial institutions.* The first set was closely tied to the central bank's traditional role as the lender of last resort for financial institutions. In addition to the Fed's discount window, the traditional facility for distressed banks, these facilities included the Term Auction Facility, Primary Dealer Credit Facility, and Term Securities Lending Facility. Credit swap agreements were approved on a bilateral basis with several foreign central banks to relieve liquidity problems arising in global bank funding markets (Fig. 39 and Fig. 40).

- *Liquidity facilities for borrowers and investors.* A second set of tools targeted distressed borrowers and investors in key credit markets, including the Commercial Paper Funding Facility, the Asset-Backed Commercial Paper Money Market Mutual Fund Liquidity Facility, the Money Market Investor Funding Facility, and the Term Asset-Backed Securities Loan Facility.[52] Collectively, the Fed's emergency loans rose from $391 billion during the first week of September 2008 to peak at $1.7 trillion during the week of December 10.

- *Quantitative easing programs.* In addition to these targeted facilities, the Fed expanded its traditional tools related to open-market operations. On November 25, 2008, the Fed announced the first round of a program of quantitative easing (QE). There were three rounds all told (Fig. 41 and Fig. 42):

QE1 from November 25, 2008 to March 31, 2010. The first round entailed the purchase of the direct obligations of housing-related GSEs—Fannie Mae, Freddie Mac, and the Federal Home Loan Banks—and MBSs backed by Fannie Mae, Freddie Mac, and Ginnie Mae. Over the next several quarters, the Fed would purchase up to $100 billion in GSE direct obligations and up to $500 billion in MBSs. The program was expanded on March 16, 2009 to include purchases of $300 billion in US Treasuries. Under QE1, the Fed purchased $1.5 trillion in bonds, including $1.2 trillion in US Agency debt and MBSs and $300 billion in US Treasuries.

QE2 from November 3, 2010 to June 30, 2011. The second round entailed the purchase of $600 billion of longer-term Treasury securities by the end of the second quarter of 2011, a pace of about $75 billion per month. Under the program, the Fed purchased $826 billion in US Treasuries, while its holdings of US Agency debt and MBSs declined $246 billion as securities matured.

QE3 from September 13, 2012 to October 29, 2014. The third round was open-ended, with the FOMC committing to purchase $40 billion per month in Agency MBSs. No total was announced, nor was a termination date. On December 12, 2012, the program was expanded to include $45 billion per month in "longer-term" Treasuries. On December 18, 2013, QE3 was tapered to $35 billion per month in MBSs and $40 billion per month in Treasuries. It was terminated on October 29, 2014 after the Fed had purchased $832 billion in MBSs and $808 billion in Treasuries.[53]

Ben Bernanke had transformed the Fed into "Feddie," supplementing and shoring up Fannie and Freddie. Because of the three rounds of QE from November 25, 2008 through October 29, 2014, the Fed's holdings of MBSs increased from zero to $1.8 trillion, and the Fed's holdings of Treasuries increased from $476 billion to $2.5 trillion.

Not widely recognized is that the Fed stepped in to buy Agency- and GSE-backed MBSs because overseas investors were bailing out of these securities (Fig. 43). Their holdings soared from $264 billion during the first quarter of 2000 to a record high of $1.6 trillion during the first half of 2008. By the end of the fourth quarter of 2014, when the QE program was terminated, they had dumped $734 billion of their holdings. Some of the foreign holders were central banks parking their international dollar reserves in these securities because they yielded more than US Treasury securities and were deemed to be just as safe.

There wasn't much the Fed could do for the ABS issuers. However, the Fed's purchases of Agency- and GSE-backed MBSs certainly propped up these financial institutions and the underlying mortgages they held (Fig. 44). Feddie had saved the day.

It was also a new day for central banks following the financial crisis. As I explore further in the next chapter, the Fed and the other major central banks evolved into central monetary planners, essentially grabbing more power to manage the economy via monetary policy—with tremendous consequences for the major capital markets around the world.

CHAPTER 9

Predicting the Fed

THE COMMITTEE

PREDICTING MONETARY POLICY is obviously very important for predicting financial markets. To do so, I learned early in my career the importance of trying to think like the Fed chairs. I've had to think like Paul Volcker, Alan Greenspan, Ben Bernanke, and Janet Yellen. As I will explain below, Volcker was the great price disinflator, Greenspan was the great asset inflator, and Bernanke was the great moderator. Yellen was the gradual normalizer.

To anticipate their policy moves, I've had to be their profiler. That requires very careful reading of their speeches and testimonies to assess their latest thinking. I also read the footnotes in their prepared remarks and the academic articles they cite in their footnotes to see who is influencing their thinking. This is an excellent way to stay current in the field of monetary macroeconomics. In addition, I often reread their previous pronouncements to monitor the evolution of their thinking. Some Fed chairs left a long paper trail revealing their thinking before they were chosen to run the Fed.

Volcker hadn't written much before he became the Fed chairman, and he didn't give many speeches after he assumed the top post. However, Volcker wasn't hard to figure out. He kept things simple, maybe because he isn't a PhD economist like the more loquacious Drs. Greenspan, Bernanke, and Yellen. Those three had many more speeches under their belts when they assumed the role, and as Fed chairs they testified in Congress more often than did Volcker. Moreover, these three PhDs already had lots in print before heading up the Fed. Getting up to speed on how each of them thought required a fair amount of ongoing effort.

The three PhDs also relished applying their favorite macroeconomic theories to managing the economy, a bit like mad scientists conducting experiments in a lab. In fact, Bernanke often expressed his admiration for President Franklin Roosevelt's willingness to experiment with new policies during the Great Depression. Occasional speeches before groups of fellow economists have allowed them to use more of their professional jargon and to theorize about some of the issues confronting them. Furthermore, by law, the chair reports to Congress twice a year, usually in February and July, on the Federal Reserve's monetary policy objectives. He or she also testifies before Congress on numerous other issues and meets regularly with the Treasury Secretary.

Looking back, I must say that I was very fortunate that my first 40 years on Wall Street coincided with the Fed chairmanships of these four extraordinary individuals, who contributed greatly to the remarkable bull markets in both stocks and bonds over this period (Fig. 1 and Fig. 2*). The three Fed chairmen prior to Volcker allowed inflation to rise rapidly, which led to a collapse in bond prices and weighed on stock prices, whereas Volcker decided to stop inflation no matter what happened to the financial markets and the economy. By doing so, he set the stage for the "long good buys," as I affectionately call the great bull markets in stocks and bonds during my career so far.

When Volcker started his chairmanship, on August 6, 1979, the S&P 500 was 104 and the US Treasury 10-year bond yield was 8.91%. By the end of 2016, the S&P 500 had soared 2,052% to close at 2239, while the bond yield was down to 2.45%. (Over this same period, the Dow Jones Industrial Average rose from 849 to 19763.) I stayed bullish for most of that time on stocks and bonds partly because the four Fed chairs adopted policies that were bullish for both asset classes, in my opinion.

In November 2017, President Donald Trump picked Fed Governor Jerome Powell as chair to replace Janet Yellen when her term expired on February 3, 2018. He has a law degree from Georgetown University and lots of experience on Wall Street. He became a Fed governor during December 2011. I expect that he will continue pursuing Yellen's gradual normalization of monetary policy.

---

* Figures, references, and appendices are linked on *yardenibook.com/resources*.

Of course, monetary policy is determined by the Federal Open Market Committee (FOMC), headed by the Fed chair. Let's begin with some background information:

- *Origin.* The Fed, which started to operate in 1914, was created by the Federal Reserve Act of 1913 "to furnish an elastic currency, to afford means of rediscounting commercial paper, to establish a more effective supervision of banking in the United States, and for other purposes."[1] The Act provided for the establishment of up to 12 Federal Reserve Banks (district banks) to coordinate policy, with the Federal Reserve Board of Governors in Washington consisting of seven members appointed by the President.[2]

    All nationally chartered banks are required to be members of the Federal Reserve System, while state-chartered banks can join if they meet certain requirements. Commercial banks that are members of the System are required by law to hold stock in the district Reserve Banks, which are not operated for profit.

- *Dual mandate.* The Employment Act of 1946 directed the federal government in general to promote maximum employment, production, and purchasing power. Back then, liberals wanted to call the act "The Full Employment Act," but conservatives resisted. In early 1975, Congress adopted Resolution 133, instructing the Federal Reserve to, among other things: "maintain long run growth of the monetary and credit aggregates commensurate with the economy's long run potential to increase production, so as to promote effectively the goals of maximum employment, stable prices, and moderate long term interest rates."[3]

    In 1977, Congress amended the Federal Reserve Act to incorporate the provisions of Resolution 133. The law requiring the semiannual testimony and monetary policy report by the chair is the Full Employment and Balanced Growth Act, known informally as the "Humphrey–Hawkins Full Employment Act." It was signed into law by President Jimmy Carter on October 27, 1978. This Act calls on the federal government to strive for full employment, production growth, price stability, and balanced trade and budget accounts. The Fed is specifically mandated to maintain long-run growth and minimize inflation. Fed officials have concluded that this legislation imposes a "dual mandate" on the Fed to keep the unemployment rate low and consistent with full employment, while achieving inflation so low that it amounts to "price stability."[4]

- *Governors.* After the President picks a candidate for an open position on the Board, he or she must then be confirmed by the full US Senate.[5] Governors serve 14-year terms and may not be reappointed. However, they can serve longer than 14 years if they are appointed to serve another member's uncompleted term, then subsequently appointed to a full term themselves. The nominees for chair and vice-chair may be chosen by the President from among the sitting governors for four-year terms; these appointments are also subject to Senate confirmation.

  Once appointed, governors may not be removed from office for their policy views. The appointments of governors are staggered so that one term expires on January 31 of each even-numbered year. The Fed's website notes: "The lengthy terms and staggered appointments are intended to contribute to the insulation of the Board—and the Federal Reserve System as a whole—from day-to-day political pressures to which it might otherwise be subject."[6] While those protections are good to have in place, Fed chairs in the past have tended to resist the formidable political pressure they've been under and managed to maintain the Fed's independence reasonably well, in my opinion, though it's not a spotless record.

- *FOMC.* All seven governors get to vote at every meeting of the FOMC, as does the president of the Federal Reserve Bank of New York. Four of the remaining 11 Reserve Bank presidents serve one-year terms on a rotating basis.[7] Nonvoting Reserve Bank presidents attend the meetings of the Committee, participate in the discussions, and contribute to the Committee's assessment of the economy and policy options.[8] In other words, when all positions are filled, there are up to 19 "participants" on this committee, who attend each of the eight regularly scheduled meetings per year, with up to 12 of them being voting "members."

I do my best to follow what they all are saying publicly. However, some are more important than others. The ones who seem to be most aligned with the views of the chair tend to provide more insights into the views of the majority, or the emerging majority, of the members. The Fed chair tends to spend a fair amount of time lobbying the other FOMC members to develop as much of a consensus as possible going into FOMC meetings. Volcker and Greenspan tended to lord over the FOMC as an assertive corporate board chairman might over a board of directors. Given their academic backgrounds, Bernanke and Yellen were more collegial in their approaches to managing the FOMC, seeking to build consensus as if they were the chairs of a college department of economics. Bernanke was especially committed to ending Greenspan's cult of personality.

The public comments of all Fed officials are picked up by the press and can sometimes move markets. That's especially so if they signal a change in policy that might not have been expected. In some cases, they may purposely be trying to change market expectations to reflect the likely course of policy at upcoming meetings of the FOMC. When more than one official does that, the markets tend to get the message, especially if the officials are the chair and one or more members deemed to be close in viewpoint to the chair. Sometimes, the Fed's message also will appear as a story in the financial press—especially *The Wall Street Journal*—that seems to be based on authoritative but unidentified sources inside the Fed.

Most annoying is when Fed officials simply float their own ideas as trial balloons. Increasingly over the years, participants on the FOMC, especially the regional presidents, have been happy to appear on televised financial news programs and to provide on-the-record interviews for the print media. This makes for lots of chatter that doesn't have much, if any, impact on policymaking. That's why I've occasionally expressed my frustration with the Fed's "talking heads" by dubbing them collectively the "Federal Open Mouth Committee."

Thankfully, we all get a regular break from the gabfest. Federal Reserve policy limits the extent to which FOMC participants and staff can speak publicly or grant interviews during Federal Reserve blackout periods, which begin the second Saturday preceding an FOMC meeting and end the Thursday following a meeting. But once that quiet time is over, they resume chattering. Sometimes, they feel compelled to do so if they perceive that the markets haven't properly understood the committee's latest message.

The FOMC's message is formally provided in a short statement released immediately after the latest meeting. It is only a few paragraphs long, starting with a brief description of how the economy has performed since the previous meeting and whether it is moving toward or away from the Fed's ideal scenario. There might be a sentence or two on how the committee expects the economy to continue to perform over the short term. The focus is always on the Fed's dual mandate, which is to keep the economy at "maximum sustainable employment" while maintaining "stable prices." Specific longer-run goals are developed by the Fed around these concepts. Then the statement announces whether the committee has decided to change its policy, aiming to achieve its goals. At the tail end is a list of how many members voted for the policy decision, which sometimes includes a line explaining dissenters' objections.

The statement is so important that *The Wall Street Journal* has a "Fed Statement Tracker" to help pundits and traders do what they have always done.[9] It parses the statement, comparing the latest one with the previous one to see how the wording has changed and what that might imply. If economic growth is upgraded from "moderate" to "solid," markets might adjust rapidly to reflect an increased chance of a Fed rate hike at the next meeting, if it didn't occur at the latest one. In the past, the appearance or disappearance of words like "uncertain," "measured," "gradual," "balanced," and "risks" could move markets. More often than not, Fed officials do their best not to surprise the markets, by preparing them with lots of guidance prior to the upcoming blackout period.

The first time the FOMC issued an explanatory statement immediately after a meeting was on February 4, 1994, to explain the first tightening decision since 1989.[10] Before then, no communication was provided on what was decided at the FOMC meetings. Market participants had to guess based on the actions of the System Open Market Account (SOMA), which is the trading desk at the Federal Reserve Bank of New York that implements the policies of the FOMC. After each policy meeting, the FOMC issues a directive to the SOMA manager, outlining the approach to monetary policy that the FOMC considers appropriate for the period between its meetings. The directive contains the rate at which the FOMC would like federal funds to trade over the coming intermeeting period. The FOMC's announcements of changes in monetary policy thus specify the changes in the Fed's target rate.

In February 1995, the committee decided to issue statements only to announce changes in the stance of monetary policy. Beginning in May 1999, statements were issued after every meeting, always including the federal funds rate target and "forward guidance" on the balance of risk.[11] If risk is deemed to be weighted to the upside for economic growth and inflation, that usually indicates the Fed is in tightening mode. If risk is perceived as weighted to the downside, then the Fed is usually in an easing or neutral mode.

The FOMC meets roughly every six to eight weeks, and the schedule is posted on the Fed's website.[12] On a quarterly basis, the Fed chair conducts a press conference after FOMC meetings. Fed Chairman Ben Bernanke held the first one on April 27, 2011. The chair starts with remarks that tend to be a longer version of the statement just issued by the FOMC. The conference ends with a usually informative Q&A session with the financial press.

The chair typically discusses the just-released quarterly "Summary of Economic Projections" (SEP) during both the prepared introductory comments and the Q&A. It includes the consensus economic projections of all the participants, whether they are voters or not. The projections reflect each participant's independent view of the outlook and policy. When there is disagreement within the Committee, the projections can vary widely. The SEP starts with a table showing the medians, central tendencies, and ranges of the forecasts for real GDP, the unemployment rate, the headline personal consumption expenditures deflator (PCED) inflation rate, and the core PCED inflation rate for the current year and the next three years. At the bottom of that table is a similar set of forecasts for the "projected appropriate policy path" for the federal funds rate. The fun continues with a "dot plot" chart that shows the unidentified forecast of each of the participants for the current year, the next three years, and the "longer run."

Like everyone else who closely watches the Fed, I carefully read the FOMC minutes, which are released three weeks after the Fed's policy-setting committee meetings.[13] They are a bit stale, with their key points often overshadowed by the latest comments of Fed officials. But importantly, the minutes often identify the general views attributed to unidentified members (who vote) and participants (unidentified nonvoters). That provides some insights into the breadth of the consensus view on key issues, as well as where the risks are deemed to be. The minutes are organized around a standard outline, with the second to last section covering the views of all participants and the last section reserved for the voting members only:

- *Developments in Financial Markets and Open Market Operations.* In this section, the deputy manager of the SOMA reports on developments in financial markets and open market operations during the period since the Committee's previous meeting.
- *Staff Review of the Economic Situation.* In this section, the staff reports on the latest developments in the major components of real GDP, focusing on monthly economic indicators that shed light on these developments. Of course, given the Fed's dual mandate, the staff also reports on employment, unemployment, and inflation.

- *Staff Review of the Financial Situation.* Financial conditions are reviewed by the staff in this section of the minutes. This overview covers credit availability, the quality of credit, interest rates, and the stock market. The dollar is rarely mentioned, though it is receiving more attention from Fed officials lately.
- *Staff Economic Outlook.* Instead of a quantitative presentation of the staff's economic projections, the minutes provide qualitative guidance on the likely direction of key economic variables. In addition, the staff provides an assessment of whether risks to the economic growth and inflation projections are likely to be on the downside or upside.
- *Participants' Views on Current Conditions and the Economic Outlook.* This section covers the views of the FOMC's official participants, i.e., all seven Board governors (assuming that all the positions are filled) and the 12 regional Fed bank presidents.
- *Committee Policy Action.* This section discusses only the views of the FOMC's 12 voting members (the seven governors, the Federal Reserve Bank of New York president, and the four currently voting regional presidents in the rotation of the 11 regional presidents), never mentioning the word "participant" (which also includes the nonvoting regional presidents). This last section ends with the same summary statement that is released to the press at 2:00 p.m. following the FOMC minutes.

On my firm's website, we post and update all the FOMC statements, with the record going back to 1997.[14] That allows me to search for key words and phrases when I'm writing about changes in Fed policy or trying to keep track of how long a key word appeared in the statements. We also provide links to all the FOMC minutes over that same period. Often when the minutes are released, I count certain key words to help assess whether increasing or decreasing frequency of mention suggests that something relevant to policymaking is becoming more important or less so.

Beyond their routine meetings, central bankers tend to socialize professionally on a regular basis. The Fed chair gets together with the heads of the other major central banks at the Bank for International Settlements, in Basel, Switzerland to meet and enjoy a fine dinner. They host conferences for one another in their respective countries. The Fed district banks regularly organize symposiums to discuss working papers by both Fed and academic economists on matters relevant to monetary policymaking.

One of the most important confabs is sponsored by the Federal Reserve Bank of Kansas City. The annual event started in 1978 and officially became known as the "Jackson Hole Economic Symposium" in 1982, when the location became a tradition. At Jackson Hole, Wyoming over a long weekend in late August, monetary policy experts gather to discuss a specific topic. In 2016, it was "Designing Resilient Monetary Policy Frameworks for the Future." In 2017, the topic was "Fostering a Dynamic Global Economy." Top officials from the Federal Reserve System and the major central banks around the world participate. The Fed chair usually does so as well and presents a speech that is widely followed. (See Appendix 9.1, Annual Jackson Hole Economic Symposium Themes: 1978–Present.)

Obviously, I'm not the only "Fed watcher" who has learned the importance of listening to the head of the Fed very carefully. In addition to paying close attention to the pronouncements of Fed chairs, I also learned early on that Martin Zweig was right when he said, "Don't fight the Fed." Zweig was a highly respected analyst and investor. He started his newsletter in 1971 and his hedge fund in 1984. On Friday, October 16, 1987, in a memorable appearance on *Wall Street Week with Louis Rukeyser*, he warned of an imminent stock market crash. It happened the following Monday, and Zweig became an investment rock star. His newsletter, *The Zweig Forecast*, had a stellar track record, according to Mark Hulbert, who tracks such things. I appeared several times on the widely watched show, which was the pacesetter for financial television programs. Louis was a class act, and so was Marty, who was one of the show's panelists.

In his 1986 book *Winning on Wall Street*, Zweig elaborated on his famous saying:

> Monetary conditions exert an enormous influence on stock prices. Indeed, the monetary climate—primarily the trend in interest rates and Federal Reserve policy—is the dominant factor in determining the stock market's major direction. . . . Generally, a rising trend in rates is bearish for stocks; a falling trend is bullish. Let's see why. First, falling interest rates reduce the competition on stocks from other investments, especially short-term instruments such as Treasury bills, certificates of deposit, or money market funds. . . . Second, when interest rates fall, it costs corporations less to borrow. . . . As expenses fall, profits rise. . . . So, as interest rates drop, investors tend to bid prices higher, partly on the expectation of better earnings. The opposite effect occurs when interest rates rise.[15]

Unlike Zweig's objective approach, most Fed watchers spend too much time critiquing the Fed. It's easy to do. Anyone can play the game. You don't need a PhD. Most Fed watchers are macroeconomists who would jump at the opportunity to be Fed chair or a Fed governor. Many would even settle for the presidency of one of the regional Fed banks. So naturally, they feel compelled to pontificate on what the Fed is doing wrong and what they would do differently. It's a fun and interesting exercise, but that's not what investors are paying Fed watchers to do. Investors want to know what the Fed is going to do next. That requires a good read on the Fed chair and other FOMC participants as well as a good read on the economy.

PUNCH BOWL

FROM MY UNDERGRADUATE days at Cornell onward, the courses I took in economics prepared me to be either a professor or a policymaker. My interest in managing the economy was only stoked by majoring in macroeconomics as a graduate student at Yale under Nobel Laureate James Tobin. This education trained me to meddle. Macroeconomists are professional meddlers who feel a calling to make the world a better place. Our ingrained conceit is that without our meddling, the economy would perform pitifully, stumbling into recessions on a regular basis. It might never even regain its footing without our help. Like the Hulk, we are superheroes with the power to lift economies out of ditches. We set economies back on the road to prosperity with just the right mix of fiscal and monetary policies to "fine-tune" the economy's performance to perfection.

I often must remind myself that my day job is to predict how the policy wonks will do their job, not to tell them how they should be doing it. I still struggle against the temptation to meddle. Admittedly, I did cross over to the dark side, petitioning lawmakers in Washington four times during my career: to promote the Real Interest Targeting Approach to monetary policy, raise awareness about Y2K, support the cessation of the double taxation of dividends, and call for the suspension of mark-to-market accounting—which I discuss in the first chapter. As I confess in Chapter 5, I'm a recovering macroeconomist.

Janet Yellen and I both received our PhDs from Yale and studied macroeconomics under Professor Tobin, as I mention in the first chapter. She graduated in 1971. I graduated in 1976. Despite our similar training, we do not share political views. She's a liberal. I'm a conservative. When she presided over the FOMC, she was powerful and could move markets. I wrote about her power to move the stock market higher, though that isn't technically a Fed mandate. Rich Miller posted a very interesting October 31, 2013 article about Yellen on Bloomberg.[16] He mentioned, "As a teaching assistant, Yellen was so meticulous in taking notes during Tobin's macroeconomics class that they ended up as the unofficial textbook for future graduate students." As I note in Chapter 1, I studied from those wonderfully useful Xeroxed notes. I must thank Yellen for helping me get through Yale's graduate program.

I still fondly recall the IS-LM Model from Yellen's notes. It's a Keynesian model that works great on paper but not so well in practice. Also known as the "Hicks–Hansen Model," it is usually shown in a chart where the vertical axis is the economy's interest rate and the horizontal axis is real GDP.[17] These two variables are determined by the intersection of the downward sloping "investment–saving" (IS) line and the upward sloping "liquidity preference–money supply" (LM) line. Stimulative fiscal policy—i.e., deficit-financed government spending or tax cuts—can be used to shift the IS curve to the right, thus boosting real GDP when it is depressed or not growing fast enough to lower the unemployment rate. Alternatively, stimulative monetary policy can shift the LM curve to the right to boost the economy.

The model is extremely simplistic, and macroeconomists have moved on to more complex ones. However, the simple one still seems to drive lots of policy thinking. It appeals to policymakers' need to meddle, since it posits that when the economy isn't performing well on its own, a dose of fiscal and/or monetary stimulus should do the trick. The model appeals to demand-side macroeconomists who believe, like John Maynard Keynes, that from time to time, demand needs to be lifted by more government spending, or easier monetary policy, or both.

In recent years, particularly since the Great Recession of 2008, monetary policy has been doing most of the heavy lifting around the world. That's because government deficits generally have been widening for many years to fund swelling social welfare programs. Most macroeconomists, at least the conservatively inclined bunch, deem that government debt is already too high relative to GDP. Besides, fiscal policy is messier than monetary policy. The former involves working with meddlesome politicians, who tend to see proposed legislation aimed at boosting economic growth as a wonderful opportunity to add provisions that benefit their own supporters. On November 18, 2008, Rahm Emanuel, the chief of staff for president-elect Barack Obama, famously stated, "You never want a serious crisis to go to waste. . . . This crisis provides the opportunity for us to do things that you could not before."[18] Lots of politicians and policymakers, not only the ones trained in macroeconomics, follow "Rahm's Rule for Politicians," as I call it.[19]

On the other hand, the Fed and the other major central banks are politically independent, at least in theory. They certainly have more centralized control of their policy than do fiscal policymakers, who must work with assorted politicians to get anything done. Not surprisingly, central bankers have been more than willing to take the leading policy role. That's because in recent years, they've been mostly overrun by macroeconomists, who were trained to play this role. In the past, there were more commercial bankers and business executives running monetary policy. They tended to be more conservative and less convinced that monetary policy could work as well as expected and promised by the macroeconomists.

The Fed's website includes a page titled "Meet the Economists." It notes that the Fed employs over 300 PhD economists, adding that they "represent an exceptionally diverse range of interests and specific areas of expertise. Board economists conduct cutting-edge research, produce numerous working papers, and are among the leading contributors at professional meetings and in major journals. Our economists also produce a wide variety of economic analyses and forecasts for the Board of Governors and the Federal Open Market Committee."[20] The website categorizes the Fed's economists under five fields of interest: Finance, International Economics, Macroeconomics, Mathematical and Quantitative Methods, and Microeconomics. Not surprisingly, macroeconomists form the clear majority, with only one-third of the Fed's economists interested mainly in microeconomics.

Justin Fox, a columnist for Bloomberg View, wrote an interesting article titled "How Economics PhDs Took Over the Federal Reserve" for the February 2014 *Harvard Business Review*.[21] He asked former Fed Vice Chairman Alan Blinder, a Princeton economics professor, whether an economics PhD basically had become a prerequisite for running the Fed. Blinder responded by email as follows: "I think the answer is 'probably yes' these days. Otherwise, the Fed's staff will run technical rings around you."

Fox also observed that "the Federal Reserve System is almost certainly the nation's largest employer of PhD economists." In addition to the ones working at the Board of Governors in Washington, there are plenty scattered around the research departments and the executive offices of the 12 regional Federal Reserve Banks. Among top Fed officials, there has been a noticeable shift in backgrounds from bankers, business professionals, and lawyers to economics PhDs, especially professors from top-ranked universities.

How was the Fed transformed from an organization run by business people to one run by economists? It was a transformation that started in 1933 when Congress reorganized the Fed after it was blamed for bungling monetary policy at the start of the Great Depression. The FOMC was created, giving the chairman in Washington more power. The Fed's power shift toward Washington continued with the Banking Act of 1935. It changed the name of the "Federal Reserve Board" to the "Board of Governors of the Federal Reserve System."

The first chairman under this new structure was Utah banker Marriner Eccles. His title was "Chairman of the Board of Governors of the Federal Reserve Board." The others prior to 1935 were "Chairman of the Board of Directors of the Federal Reserve System," with much more limited power. (See Appendix 9.2, Chairs of the Federal Reserve, a Chronology.)

Perversely, Eccles, who served from November 15, 1934 to February 3, 1948, believed that fiscal policy was much more effective than monetary policy. So the Fed didn't do much to stimulate the economy in the 1930s under his leadership. During World War II, the Treasury Department forced the Fed to buy US government securities to keep interest rates low. In effect, the Treasury was running a very easy monetary policy to finance the war and continued to do so after the war.

Once World War II was over, the Fed continued its wartime commitment of pegging interest rates. The Treasury-Fed Accord, announced March 4, 1951, freed the Fed from that obligation. A 2001 article in the Federal Reserve Bank of Richmond *Economic Quarterly* reviewed the story.[22] In April 1942, after the United States had entered the war, the Fed publicly committed itself to maintaining an interest rate of 3/8% on Treasury bills. In practice, it also established a ceiling for long-term government bonds at 2.50%. In the summer of 1947, the Fed raised the peg on the Treasury bill rate. However, the Treasury insisted that the bond yield stay put.

Postwar, policymakers in the Truman administration feared that the economy might fall back into a depression. Fed officials became increasingly concerned about inflation and wanted their independence back. Indeed, the primary problem turned out to be inflation rather than economic depression. There was a brief bout of inflation when wartime price controls ended during the summer of 1948. When inflation heated up again after the outbreak of the Korean War, five years of relative economic stability had greatly reduced the fear of falling into another depression.

According to the Richmond Fed article: "The prospect of a prolonged war created the likelihood of government deficits and the issuance of new government debt. Additional debt would force down the price of debt unless the Fed monetized it. That is, to prevent yields from rising above the 2½ percent rate peg, the Fed would have to buy debt and increase bank reserves. Banks would then fuel an inflationary expansion through increases in credit and the money supply." This led to a momentous change in the way Fed officials viewed their job. They came to believe that they had to control money creation to stabilize inflation.

In 1948, President Harry Truman appointed Scott Paper CEO Thomas McCabe to run the Fed. McCabe pushed to regain the Fed's power over monetary policy and did so with the Treasury-Fed Accord of 1951. He negotiated the deal with Assistant Treasury Secretary William McChesney Martin. McCabe returned to Scott Paper, and Martin took over as chairman of a re-empowered Federal Reserve on April 2, 1951, serving in that position until January 31, 1970 under five presidents.

In his article cited above, Fox observed that under Martin's leadership, "regulating the economy through monetary policy pushed aside bank regulation to become the central bank's No. 1 job. So hiring economists, and bringing people with serious economic backgrounds onto the FOMC, became a priority." The March 1951 Accord freed the Fed and marked the start of the modern Federal Reserve System.

Under Martin, the Fed's overriding goals became price and macro-economic stability, opening more jobs for economists. He believed that the Fed's job was to be a killjoy. His famous "punch bowl" metaphor seems to trace back to a speech given on October 19, 1955 in which he said: "In the field of monetary and credit policy, precautionary action to prevent inflationary excesses is bound to have some onerous effects—if it did not it would be ineffective and futile. Those who have the task of making such policy don't expect you to applaud. The Federal Reserve, as one writer put it, after the recent increase in the discount rate, is in the position of the chaperone who has ordered the punch bowl removed just when the party was really warming up."[23]

In this speech, Martin also observed that monetary policy needs to work with fiscal and budgetary policies: "But a note should be made here that, while money policy can do a great deal, it is by no means all powerful. In other words, we should not place too heavy a burden on monetary policy. It must be accompanied by appropriate fiscal and budgetary measures if we are to achieve our aim of stable progress. If we ask too much of monetary policy, we will not only fail but we will also discredit this useful, and indeed indispensable, tool for shaping our economic development."

If he were alive today, Martin would probably be shocked to see that the Fed has so many macroeconomists who are committed to moderating the business cycle. In his speech, he said, "The idea that the business cycle can be altogether abolished seems to me as fanciful as the notion that the law of supply and demand can be repealed." Yet he unwittingly unlocked the gate, allowing the barbarians to seize the Fed's fortress with the intention of using its power to slay the business-cycle beast, or at least tame it.

When President Richard Nixon entered the White House in 1969, he reportedly asked Martin to step aside. Nixon famously harbored grudges. He blamed Martin for his defeat in the 1960 presidential elections because the Fed chairman had refused to boost the economy by lowering interest rates, so nine years later, Nixon asked Martin to retire early. Martin refused. However, his term ended at the start of the following year, when Nixon appointed Arthur Burns, someone more to his liking.

ARTHUR BURNS: THE FIRST PROFESSOR

ARTHUR BURNS SERVED as Fed chairman from February 1, 1970 to January 31, 1978 under Presidents Nixon, Ford, and Carter. Burns was an academic, the first PhD macroeconomist to head the Fed. He taught economics at both Rutgers University (starting in 1927) and Columbia University (1945), having earned his PhD at the latter.

As a doctoral student at Columbia, Burns studied under Wesley Clair Mitchell, a founder of the National Bureau of Economic Research (NBER) and its chief researcher. Mitchell brought Burns into the NBER, where Burns began lifelong research into the business cycle. Together, in 1946, they published *Measuring Business Cycles*, which introduced the characteristic NBER methods of analyzing business cycles empirically.[24] It was Burns who started the NBER's academic tradition of determining recessions—a role that has been continued by the organization's Business Cycle Dating Committee. The NBER remains the preeminent authority on dating recessions, as I discuss in Chapter 5. (See Appendix 5.1, US Business Cycle Expansions and Contractions: 1854–Present.)

Burns served as president and chairman of the NBER at points throughout his teaching career. He also was chairman of the Council of Economic Advisers (CEA) from 1953 to 1956 under President Dwight Eisenhower. When Nixon was elected President in 1968, he persuaded Burns to become his White House counselor, with the understanding that Burns would be appointed chairman of the Fed when William McChesney Martin's term ended in early 1970.[25] (See Appendix 9.3, Chairs of the Council of Economic Advisers, a Chronology.)

Burns assumed leadership of the Federal Reserve in the middle of what would later become known as "the Great Inflation," which lasted from 1965 to 1982 (Fig. 3). During this period, the CPI inflation rate rose from 1.0% in January 1965 to peak at a record high of 14.8% during March 1980 before subsiding remarkably quickly to 2.5% in July 1983 owing to the unprecedented moves by Burns' successor, Paul Volcker.

Many Americans who lived through the Great Inflation remember the worst of it as a time of gasoline rationing and long lines at the gas pump. Paychecks didn't stretch nearly as far at the grocery store as they used to. It seemed to many that the inflation genie wreaking economic havoc would never get back into the bottle. Let's take a quick look at some of the reasons that US inflation spiraled out of control:

- *There were food, oil, and labor price shocks.* During this period, several price shocks exacerbated inflation. During 1972 and 1973, for the first time since the Korean War, farm and food prices began to contribute substantially to inflationary pressures in the economy. Also, there was a major oil price shock during 1973 and again in 1979 (Fig. 4). On January 16, 1979, the shah of Iran was forced to leave his country, replaced as leader soon after by Ayatollah Khomeini. The country's oil output plunged, and inflation soared along with oil prices. Finally, strong labor unions in the private sector succeeded in quickly boosting wages through cost-of-living clauses in their contracts. The result was an inflationary wage-price spiral to boot (Fig. 5).

- *The dissolution of the Bretton Woods system of international currency management caused an immediate inflationary shock to the US economy in 1971.* On August 15, 1971, Nixon suspended the convertibility of the dollar into gold, which ended the Bretton Woods system that had kept the dollar's value at a constant $35 per ounce of gold since the system was established in 1944. All other currencies were pegged to the dollar, so other countries could present their dollars to the United States and receive gold in exchange.

  The problem: By the summer of 1971, this system was no longer viable because other countries collectively had three times more dollars than the United States held in gold. Theoretically, if they had all chosen to redeem their dollars at once, the United States would not have been able to come up with enough gold. That's because the United States was running a mounting balance-of-payments deficit. Facing a crisis of confidence within the global financial system, the United States simply closed the gold window, refusing to exchange the foreign central banks' dollars for gold. The foreign currencies no longer were pegged to the dollar or to gold. It was a free market. The value of the dollar suddenly plummeted, causing spikes in import prices as well as the prices of most commodities priced in dollars (Fig. 6). Gold is such a commodity, and its price took off (Fig. 7).

- *Nixon's price-control measures were ineffective solutions.* With the 1972 election on the horizon, Nixon imposed wage and price controls. The 90-day freeze was followed by nearly 1,000 days of measures executed in four phases. Price controls were applied almost entirely to the biggest corporations and labor unions, which were seen as having price-setting power. However, when these companies and unions requested price increases, the vast majority of them were granted. The controls were lifted in 1973.

- *The Fed's monetary response under Burns was inadequate too.* Monetary policy during this period helped spur a surge in inflation and inflation expectations. The Fed did raise interest rates, but the rate hikes were too little, too late. The Fed was increasingly criticized for being "behind the curve."

At the end of his second term, late in 1977, Burns asked to be reappointed for another four years. But no such luck. I think President Carter didn't much like the pipe-smoking Fed chairman, maybe because he came across as an arrogant, pipe-smoking professor. Instead, Carter appointed G. William Miller, the chief executive of Textron Corporation.

G. WILLIAM MILLER: THE INFLATOR

BY SOME ACCOUNTS, Arthur Burns poured gasoline on inflation, while G. William Miller lit the match. Miller succeeded Burns as Fed chairman on March 8, 1978 but served only 17 months, until August 6, 1979. Inflation was accelerating. Miller remained eerily laid back, believing that the inflation spiral was a transient phenomenon, so he opposed raising interest rates. The trade-weighted dollar dropped 5.4% during Miller's brief tenure (Fig. 8). The Carter administration responded with a "dollar rescue package" that included emergency sales from the US gold stock, executed by borrowing from the International Monetary Fund, as well as auctions of Treasury securities denominated in foreign currencies.

Miller lacked the experience and the skills for his new job. Most observers were shocked that a few months after taking charge, Miller voted with the minority on the FOMC against raising interest rates. That quickly destroyed confidence in his leadership. The situation only got worse after he gave several interviews the day before the April 1979 FOMC meeting, expressing his view that there was no need to raise interest rates. Press leaks revealed that Miller's dovish stance against inflation was opposed by key administration officials who wanted the Fed to raise interest rates, including Treasury Secretary W. Michael Blumenthal and Charles Schultze, the chairman of the CEA. In any event, during Miller's brief tenure, the federal funds rate rose from 6.72% to 10.72%.

On July 15, 1979, President Carter responded to the decline in his popularity with his famous "malaise" speech, in which he lamented that the country had not come together to solve its problems. Carter never actually used the word "malaise," but he did use the phrase "crisis of confidence," which was the title of the speech. Carter bemoaned, "The erosion of our confidence in the future is threatening to destroy the social and the political fabric of America."[26] That had to have been among the most depressing speeches ever given to the nation by a sitting US president. Yet the speech was well received, and Carter's poll ratings rose significantly.[27]

Then he blew it just two days later when he fired five Cabinet members, including Blumenthal. Doing so suggested that Carter had lost control of his administration. He convinced G. William Miller to leave the Fed to replace Blumenthal at the Treasury. Carter picked Paul Volcker to replace Miller as the new Fed chairman. Volcker was not Carter's first choice, but the President was up for reelection in 1980 and was desperate to calm financial markets, which had responded badly to the White House meltdown. Volcker was highly respected in the investment community.

PAUL VOLCKER: THE GREAT DISINFLATOR

PAUL VOLCKER WAS Fed chairman from August 6, 1979 through August 11, 1987. He is widely credited with ending the inflationary spiral of the 1970s. Volcker didn't have a PhD, but he had a great résumé. After earning his MA in political economy from Harvard University in 1951, he joined the Federal Reserve Bank of New York as a staff economist in 1952. He then became a financial economist with the Chase Manhattan Bank.

In 1962, he was hired by the US Treasury undersecretary for monetary affairs, Robert Roosa, who had been his mentor in the research department of the New York Fed. Volcker started as the director of financial analysis and was promoted to deputy undersecretary for monetary affairs in 1963. He returned to Chase Manhattan Bank as vice president and director of planning in 1965. He was back at the Treasury from 1969 to 1974, serving as undersecretary for international monetary affairs.

Fed Chairman Arthur Burns developed a great respect for Volcker when Volcker was serving in the Treasury. In 1975, Burns picked Volcker to be the president of the Federal Reserve Bank of New York, where he stayed until 1979. That meant he sat next to Fed chairmen Burns and then Miller in FOMC meetings during the worst of the Great Inflation period.

In fact, Volcker was instrumental in convincing President Nixon to suspend gold convertibility by ending the Bretton Woods system, thereby contributing greatly to the inflationary spiral of the 1970s. That's the height of irony, because it was also Volcker who succeeded in breaking the back of inflation via bold and unprecedented monetary tightening once he took the Fed's helm.

Volcker assumed the Fed chairmanship at a time during the summer of 1979 when oil prices were soaring because of the second oil crisis. Seven months later, in March 1980, the CPI inflation rate crested at its record high of 14.8%. When Volcker left the Fed during August 1987, he had gotten it back down to 4.3%.

As I mention in Chapter 1, Paul Volcker was my first boss. He was the president of the Federal Reserve Bank of New York when I worked there for a year and a half at the start of my career. He was also the first Fed chairman of any meaningful duration in my career (given his predecessor G. William Miller's short stint). I learned a simple and important lesson from Volcker early on about how to predict Fed policymaking: don't second-guess the Fed chair. Volcker did what he said he would do, so betting that he would do so was a good bet and betting otherwise was a bad one.

Subsequent Fed chairs followed in Volcker's footsteps, i.e., doing what they said they would do as much as possible. So I didn't have to spend much time predicting their next moves. I just had to pay close attention to what they said they would do and make sure that my economic forecast and investment strategy were consistent with the likely course of monetary policy. The trick was to avoid letting my own views of what they should do derail my focus from what they were most likely to do. Of course, I also had to predict the economic outlook as best as I could, since that would influence Fed decision making.

Reading Paul Volcker wasn't very hard. He understood that part of his job was to communicate clearly and only as often as necessary to get his message across. He obviously dominated the FOMC and either discouraged public speaking by other FOMC participants overtly or kept them in line subliminally. In reviewing my commentaries from that time, I found relatively few quotes from Preston Martin, who was vice chairman of the Fed between 1982 and 1986. During his years at the Fed, Martin was known as a Reagan loyalist who challenged Volcker's tough anti-inflation policies. Martin was considered a possible successor to Volcker, but Alan Greenspan was appointed instead.

Volcker didn't waste any time attacking inflation. Eight days after starting his new job, he led the FOMC on August 14, 1979 to raise the federal funds rate (Fig. 9). On August 16, he called a meeting of the seven members of the Federal Reserve Board to increase the discount rate by half a percentage point (or 50 basis points) to 10.50% (Fig. 10). This confirmed that the federal funds rate had been raised by the same amount to 11.00%. Back then, FOMC decisions weren't announced. The markets had to guess.

On September 18, 1979, Volcker pushed for another discount-rate hike of 50 basis points to 11.00%. However, this time, the vote wasn't unanimous; the Board was split four to three.

Volcker, recognizing that the Fed's credibility along with his own were on the line, came up with a simple, though radical, solution that would take the economy's intractable inflation problem right out of the hands of the indecisive FOMC: the Fed's monetary policy committee would establish targets for the money supply and no longer target the federal funds rate. That would leave it up to the market to determine the federal funds rate; the FOMC no longer would vote to determine it!

This so-called "monetarist" approach to managing monetary policy had a longtime champion in Milton Friedman, who advocated that the Fed should target a fixed growth rate in the money supply and stick to it. Under the circumstances, Volcker was intent on slowing it down, knowing this would push interest rates up sharply. That's exactly what happened, and the economy fell into a deep recession. I called Volcker's approach "macho monetarism."

Holding an unusual Saturday night news conference on October 6, Volcker unleashed his own version of the "Saturday Night Massacre." He announced that the FOMC had adopted monetarist operating procedures effective immediately. Saying, "Business data has been good and better than expected. Inflation data has been bad and perhaps worse than expected," he also stated that the discount rate, which remained under the Fed's control, was being increased a full percentage point to a record 12.00%.[28]

The notion that the Fed would no longer target the federal funds rate but instead would target growth rates for the major money supply measures came as a shock to the financial community. It meant that interest rates could swing widely and wildly. And indeed they did. The federal funds rate, which was 10.70% when Volcker started his job as Fed chairman, soared to a peak of 22.36% in July 1981. At the end of 1980, the prime rate peaked at a record 21.50% (Fig. 11). The economy fell into a deep recession.

The Carter administration immediately endorsed Volcker's October 6 package. Press Secretary Jody Powell said that the Fed's moves should "help reduce inflationary expectations, contribute to a stronger US dollar abroad, and curb unhealthy speculation in commodity markets." He added, "The Administration believes that success in reducing inflationary pressures will lead in due course both to lower rates of price increases and to lower interest rates."[29] In a 1982 interview with *The New York Times*, Volcker recalled the events of late 1979:

> You had a sense in the summer of 1979 that psychologically and otherwise inflation was getting ahead of us. . . . [M]ore forceful action probably had to be taken, and it was only a couple of months after I was here that we adopted this new operating

technique—I'm not sure we understood all the implications. You never do. But we understood some of them certainly. . . . What we did was not basically a new idea. I'd thought about it some, but I can't say I'd been an advocate of it. It had some problems. What persuaded me was the need to somehow get a grip on the situation, and on psychology, and this seemed to me a way to do it.[30]

Those were not the words of an ideologue. Volcker was no born-again monetarist. He was a pragmatist. He understood the importance of credibility and psychology. He understood markets.

The Fed's experiment with monetarist operating procedures lasted only three years, ending at the October 1982 meeting of the FOMC. I anticipated this might happen at the start of that year, writing in my January 29 commentary: "Should the Fed abandon monetarism? It may be forced to do so shortly." I observed that high interest rates combined with a severe recession were increasing the demand for liquidity, which boosted the growth rate of the M1 money supply. I added, "Once the unemployment rate hits 10%, as we expect it soon will, the Fed will experience overwhelming political pressure to junk monetarism and lower interest rates."

The unemployment rate rose from 8.6% at the start of 1982 to peak at 10.8% during November and December, the highest since the Great Depression (Fig. 12). On Thursday, October 7, *The Wall Street Journal* reported that the FOMC had decided at its meeting on October 5 to temporarily suspend its monetarist operating procedures. Volcker confirmed the change in a speech to the Business Council on Saturday. "What is needed is market conviction that the fundamentals are consistent with lower interest rates, and I believe that is what we have been seeing for some months." He emphasized that lower interest rates are a "reward for success in dealing with inflation." He reiterated his pragmatic approach, saying, "you have also heard me repeatedly express caution about the validity of any single [money supply] measure, or even all the measures in the short run."

At the time, I wrote, "Mr. Volcker is a great practitioner of Pavlovian economics." He was also an astute politician. As I recount in the first chapter, during the summer of 1982, Democrat leaders in both the House and the Senate were writing bills that would have ordered the Fed to abandon the monetarist regime adopted during October 1979. According to an August 16, 1982 column in the *New York Post* by Rowland Evans and Robert Novak, I had a small hand in all this: "The lineal ancestor of the Democratic scheme is Dr. Edward Yardeni, chief economist of E.F. Hutton." They noted that in my January 29 newsletter, I predicted a 30% chance of a depression in 1982 unless the Fed abandoned monetarism. Just five years earlier, I had been a staff economist working near the bottom of the Fed's flow chart under Volcker.

My December 29, 1982 commentary was titled "Milton's Paradise Lost." I observed that in his December 27 *Newsweek* column, Milton Friedman, the father of monetarism, had sketched a hellish outlook for 1983 and 1984, clearly upset that the Fed had abandoned his approach. He warned that "the monetary explosion that started in July 1982 is almost certain to bring on a recovery starting within the next few months. As the recovery gathers steam, interest rates will erupt. The monetary explosion is then likely to end with a bang and be followed by negligible or negative monetary growth. As in 1982, that would abort the recovery and produce a renewed recession, probably starting in 1984."

I disagreed with what amounted to a "triple-dip scenario." I argued in my year-end commentary that the evidence strongly suggested individuals were responding to the world economic crisis at the time by building up precautionary balances of liquid assets: "So the increased demand for money actually reflects the effects of the recession; it does not foreshadow a super-hot recovery." I noted that my assessment was confirmed by the sharp decline in the ratio of nominal GDP to M1, the so-called "velocity of money." I sided with some members of the FOMC who, according to the November 16, 1982 minutes of the committee, believed that the falling velocity of money suggested "a distinct break from earlier postwar experience," resulting from "unusual economic and financial uncertainties." This was "inducing a greater desire to hold liquid assets than had been assumed in setting the annual [monetary] targets." Here's more from that commentary:

> In his November 24 testimony before the Joint Economic Committee, Volcker reiterated this view. In my year-end 1982 commentary, I concluded: Friedman's monetarism works best in Shangri-La, where the velocity of money is stable and predictable. In our economy, which is experiencing an infernal recession along with major structural and institutional changes, velocity is neither stable nor predictable. That's why the Fed abandoned "knee-jerk" monetarism in October and is now practicing

"judgmental" monetarism. We think the new, more eclectic approach can deliver lower inflation and a sustainable recovery. That would be paradise.

Monetarism never recovered following its short heyday. A 2017 Federal Reserve Bank of Richmond working paper by Robert Hetzel was titled "What Remains of Milton Friedman's Monetarism?"[31] Despite the author's best efforts to be constructive, I concluded that the answer to his question was "not much."

ALAN GREENSPAN: THE FLAWED MAESTRO

ALAN GREENSPAN SUCCEEDED Paul Volcker as Fed chairman, serving from August 11, 1987 until January 31, 2006. He was approved by a 91-to-2 vote in the Senate. Voting against the nomination were Senators Bill Bradley (D, NJ) and Kent Conrad (D, ND). Bradley presciently warned that Greenspan "will move too rapidly toward deregulation [of the banking industry], rather than showing the same caution as Chairman Volcker." Another senator for whom Greenspan's stance on banking deregulation didn't sit well was William Proxmire (D, WI), chairman of the Senate Banking Committee. Despite disagreeing with Greenspan that the banking industry needed more deregulation, however, Proxmire supported the nomination. He thought Greenspan would fight inflation as aggressively as Volcker did, according to *The New York Times*.[32]

Before he became chairman of the Federal Reserve Board, Greenspan had his own economic consulting firm. He also served from 1974 to 1977 as chairman of the CEA under President Gerald Ford. Greenspan had earned a PhD in economics from New York University decades after leaving graduate school at Columbia to start the consulting firm. At Columbia, Arthur Burns had been one of his professors. In his 2008 book, *Deception and Abuse at the Fed*, Robert Auerbach, a University of Texas professor, claimed that the PhD was actually only honorary, strongly implying that it was obtained in a few months just after Greenspan had completed a stint as chairman of the CEA for Presidents Nixon and Ford.[33]

Interestingly, Greenspan's dissertation was removed from the public shelves of New York University's (NYU) Bobst Library at the author's request in 1987, the year President Reagan appointed him chairman of the Federal Reserve Board. Upset that Auerbach was impugning NYU's reputation, Paul Wachtel, an NYU economics professor who was on Greenspan's thesis committee, provided a copy of the thesis to *Barron's* Jim McTague, who had reviewed the Auerbach book. The dissertation was unusual: a collection of previously published articles.[34]

Bob Woodward, the investigative reporter best known as the co-author of *All the President's Men* (1974), wrote a glowing book about Greenspan, published in 2000 and titled *Maestro*. Woodward revealed that at about the same time that the Fed chairman famously questioned whether stock investors had become irrationally exuberant, he was also trying to pop the marital question to television journalist Andrea Mitchell, his girlfriend of nearly 12 years: "He later confided to one person that he actually proposed to Mitchell twice before she accepted, but either she had not understood what he was saying or it had failed to register. His verbal obscurity and caution were so ingrained that Mitchell didn't even know that he had asked her to marry him. . . . On Christmas Day [1996], Greenspan finally asked, flat out, 'Do you want a big wedding or a small wedding?' It was a message no one could miss."

The Fed chairman's message has always been vitally important to investors and traders. This was true before Greenspan was appointed to replace Paul Volcker on August 11, 1987. It remains true today. Yet Greenspan was renowned for his "verbal obscurity and caution," as noted by Woodward. During his congressional testimonies, Greenspan was often asked to explain what he meant and left the questioner even more confused by his response.[35]

I didn't have much trouble deciphering the most important messages in Greenspan's often convoluted lexicon. Like a cryptographer, I simply looked for repetitive phrases and themes in his frequent public statements. He certainly enjoyed the limelight and spoke often. In addition to congressional testimonies, he gave lots of speeches, many more than his predecessors. I detected several themes along the way.

Greenspan was a big believer in free-market capitalism and deregulation, so he fit in very well with the Reagan team during the first two years of his tenure as Fed chairman. However, his policy moves on a few notable occasions showed that he wasn't averse to giving the stock market a lift occasionally when it seemed to need some help. He believed that it wasn't the Fed's job to stop asset bubbles because doing so might hurt the economy. In his view, it was better to let the bubbles pop and to clean up the mess afterward.

I knew that Greenspan was influenced by the free-market capitalistic views of Ayn Rand. In the early 1950s, Greenspan had become a member of Rand's inner circle, the Ayn Rand Collective, who read *Atlas Shrugged* while it was being written. He contributed several essays for Rand's *Capitalism: The Unknown Ideal* (1966), including one supporting the gold standard. Rand stood beside him at his 1974 swearing-in as chair of the CEA, and they remained friends until her death in 1982.

So I wasn't surprised that under Greenspan, the Fed focused even more on monetary policy and managing the economy and less on regulating banks. As a big champion of deregulation, he argued that it was necessary to allow US banks to compete with big foreign rivals. He also believed that deregulated capital markets would finance more startups and thus increase competition. Under Greenspan, the Fed essentially gutted the Glass–Steagall Act, which had barred commercial banks from the investment banking business. He did that even before Congress provided the final blow with the Gramm–Leach–Bliley Act of 1999, which I discuss in the previous chapter. Greenspan also strongly opposed any regulation of credit derivatives.

In 1996, the Fed allowed banks to derive 25% of their revenue from securities businesses, up from a previous cap of 10%, if they did so through a separate subsidiary. In April 1997, Bankers Trust bought the investment bank Alex. Brown & Co., becoming the first US bank to acquire a securities firm. Bankers Trust became a leader in the emerging derivatives business in the early 1990s. In early 1994, the bank suffered an embarrassment when some complex derivative transactions resulted in large losses for major corporate clients.

During August 1997, the Fed's Board of Governors stated that the risks of underwriting had proven to be "manageable" and granted banks the right to acquire securities firms outright. Deutsche Bank acquired Bankers Trust along with Alex. Brown in December 1998. The following year, in March, Bankers Trust pleaded guilty to institutional fraud for failure to turn over to the states funds from dormant customer accounts and uncashed dividend and interest checks, as required by law.

Greenspan's background as a director of several companies, including JP Morgan for 10 years, informed his view of the Fed's role—and its limitations. During the Q&A session following his February 17, 2009 speech on regulation before the Economic Club of New York, renowned Goldman Sachs investment strategist Abby Joseph Cohen asked Greenspan for his advice on setting up a new financial regulatory structure. Greenspan observed that as a member of the JP Morgan board, he had been very well informed about the bank's customers and counterparties, whereas at the Fed, "where we regulated these people, we knew very much less than did the Morgan people or indeed any of the other institutions." He suggested that the Fed's reliance on the banks to regulate themselves through "counterparty surveillance as the first line of defense" left no backup defense system. This approach worked just fine "for a goodly long period of time until it cracked in August of 2007." That is, it worked until it didn't. One of the important lessons from the latest financial crisis is that self-regulation is an oxymoron!

Yet during his long tenure at the Fed, Greenspan had great confidence in Wall Street, and Wall Street had great confidence in what came to be known as the "Greenspan Put," or actions Greenspan took to show investors he had their backs. That was quite different from Volcker's relationship with Wall Street. Volcker obviously was unperturbed by the bearish consequences of his policies on the stock market as he focused determinedly on breaking inflation. Nobody in the stock market thought he had their backs.

Two months after Greenspan's confirmation, the stock market crashed on Black Monday. The Fed immediately issued a statement affirming its readiness to serve as a source of liquidity to support the economic and financial system. The federal funds rate was lowered from 7.61% on October 19 to 5.69% on November 4. Gerald Corrigan, the president of the New York Fed, pressured the major New York banks to double their normal lending to securities firms, enabling brokers to meet cash calls. Greenspan later told the Senate Banking Committee that the Fed's strategy during Black Monday was "aimed at shrinking irrational reactions in the financial system to an irreducible minimum." That was the beginning of the Greenspan Put and affirmed my view that the financial crisis could mean buying opportunities in the stock market.

In response to the crisis, President Reagan signed an executive order that created the President's Working Group on Financial Markets, consisting of the Treasury Secretary and the chairpersons of the Fed, the Securities and Exchange Commission, and the Commodity Futures Trading Commission (CFTC). It came to be colloquially known as the "Plunge Protection Team." Conspiracy buffs have suspected that from time to time it has coordinated covert measures to support the stock market.

I recognized early on that Greenspan had turned into an enthusiastic cheerleader for the bull market of the 1990s. My own bullishness was buttressed by Greenspan's unabashed enthusiasm. He promoted the notion that the technology revolution might be boosting productivity growth. On several occasions, he speculated that "current developments are part of a once or twice in a century phenomenon that will carry productivity trends nationally and globally to a new higher track." Over the next few years, Greenspan made it very clear that he wasn't convinced stocks were in a bubble. As I note in Chapter 3 on technology, he believed even amid the near-vertical ascent in the prices of technology stocks during the late 1990s that the stock market might not be overvalued when viewed as a lottery.

Stock investors were taken by surprise when near the end of his speech on December 5, 1996, Greenspan asked, "But how do we know when irrational exuberance has unduly escalated asset values, which then become subject to unexpected and prolonged contractions, as they have in Japan over the past decade?"[36] That sounded like he was concerned about a bubble in the stock market. However, he was just asking the question, not answering it. He was thinking out loud, essentially. Indeed, right before posing the question, he suggested that stocks were *not* irrationally exuberant given that "sustained low inflation implies less uncertainty about the future, and lower risk premiums imply higher prices of stocks and other earning assets."

Greenspan liked to muse out loud as if he were chatting with an economist buddy over the phone and his words were not hung on by billions of people and acted upon in global financial markets. The key to interpreting what Greenspan meant was to stick with his underlying themes and not get sidetracked by his occasional Hamlet-like musings.

Greenspan's thinking about bubbles evolved over time. In that 1996 speech, he was the "two-handed economist," saying that on the one hand, the Fed shouldn't worry about bubbles that burst, as long as they didn't hurt the economy. He cited the example of the 1987 stock market crash. On the other hand, he said, the Fed shouldn't be complacent about them either, because they might be big enough to do real damage when they burst.

Greenspan was put to the test again when the Russian government defaulted on its debt on August 17, 1998, then, more importantly, during September 1998, when Long-Term Capital Management (LTCM) blew up. In retrospect, the LTCM incident foreshadowed the global economy-wide blow-up in 2008, holding advance warnings and cautionary lessons about leverage and risk that fell on deaf ears, as I note in the previous chapter. LTCM did business with nearly every major firm on Wall Street and was highly leveraged in various trading strategies that went awry. There was widespread fear on Wall Street that its failure could trigger a financial contagion, resulting in catastrophic losses throughout the financial system.

If the Fed hadn't yet existed, Wall Street would have had to clean up its own mess—as JP Morgan had done during the panic of 1907, prompting Congress to commission a 23-volume study on central banking that led to the formation of the Federal Reserve System. But in the LTCM panic, the Fed was there to coordinate the cleanup efforts that contained the damage, avoiding contagion…this time. The Federal Reserve Bank of New York organized a bailout of $3.625 billion by LTCM's major creditors. The FOMC also lowered the federal funds rate by 75 basis points from 5.50% on September 29, 1998 to 4.75% on November 17 of that year.

Once again, a financial crisis turned out to be a great buying opportunity thanks to the Greenspan Put. The S&P 500 jumped 59.6% from its post-Russian-default low on August 31, 1998 through the March 24, 2000 peak. Over this same period, the Nasdaq soared astonishingly by 231.0%. Investors got the reassuring message that the Fed would come to the rescue every time the financial markets got into trouble.

When the technology-led stock market bubble burst in 2000, the Fed once again responded quickly in an attempt to contain the adverse financial and economic impact. A severe bear market ensued nonetheless, and so did a recession. Most of the so-called "dot-com" companies, i.e., Internet startups, had burned through their cash. Investors were no longer willing to provide more, and many of these companies either slashed their spending or simply went out of business. Investors lost lots of money.

The stock market downturn was exacerbated by accounting scandals revolving around Enron (2001), Haliburton (2002), Tyco (2002), and Worldcom (2002). They all had criminally cooked their books to boost their earnings. With the benefit of hindsight, investors wondered whether technology companies had done the same by pushing the limits of legitimate accounting practices. Doubts about the quality of earnings accelerated the plunge in valuation multiples. The bear market in stocks, especially technology stocks, was severe.

The economic recession from March through November 2001 wasn't that bad, despite the horrible shock of the 9/11 terrorist attacks. Yet Fed officials seemed traumatized by the current events. They were particularly troubled by the sharp drop in the CPI inflation rate from 3.7% at the start of 2001 to 1.1% one year later. Deflation became a big worry. Fed Governor Ben Bernanke presented his famous speech "Deflation: Making Sure 'It' Doesn't Happen Here" on November 21, 2002.[37]

Although the economy started to recover at the end of 2001, the Fed delayed raising interest rates until the June 2004 meeting of the FOMC. The federal funds rate was increased by 25 basis points to 1.25%. That was followed by increases of 25 basis points at every one of the next 16 meetings, putting the rate at 5.25% during June 2006. Greenspan explained that the "measured pace" of tightening was necessary to sustain the recovery and avert deflation.

While Greenspan seemed ready, willing, and able to lend a very visible hand to the stock market as both a cheerleader and a savior, he was steadfastly hands-off when it came to the credit derivatives markets. The Fed submitted an extraordinary statement to Congress on June 10, 1998 defending Wall Street's right to be left alone when it came to credit derivatives:

> The Board is also dismayed by the prospect that legal uncertainties or unnecessary regulatory burdens could undermine the position of US institutions in what are intensely competitive global markets. We see no social benefits and clear social costs from pushing OTC derivatives activity offshore. . . . Institutional counterparties to privately negotiated contracts also have demonstrated their ability to protect themselves from losses from fraud and counterparty insolvencies. They have insisted that dealers have financial strength sufficient to warrant a credit rating of A or higher. Consequently, dealers are established institutions with substantial assets and significant investments in their reputations.[38]

The Fed warned Congress that any attempt to regulate derivatives would threaten the stability of the financial system. The Fed's position was that our team can't be expected to play by a rule book imposed by the CFTC or any other regulator when their competitors abroad are unregulated. In other words, if our competitors are unbound and we're bound, we don't stand a chance.

Let me interject my opinion here. The Fed's statement reflects just one of capitalism's many conundrums. How can a company compete fairly if its competitors are cheating, or at least are not burdened by the same regulatory rules if they happen to be overseas? Capitalism degenerates into corruption when one player or a few of them organized as a special interest group pay off politicians to rig the market in their favor with laws and regulations. The most regulated markets are often the most corrupted and least competitive ones. Banking and finance is particularly prone to "crony capitalism." The industry's standards often are set by the worst-run and most politically influential companies. A crisis follows, and then come mea culpas and professed stupidity by the perpetrators, who claim they are innocent of any wrongdoing. In other words, there is a case to be made for regulating and closely supervising financial institutions, especially since they mostly manage other people's money.

On July 24, 1998, Greenspan personally reiterated the Fed's position when he testified before a congressional committee on the regulation of over-the-counter (OTC) derivatives.[39] He stated that he opposed the CFTC's attempts to regulate this market. He stressed that derivatives are fundamentally different from commodities: it's almost impossible to corner the derivatives market, because most derivatives contracts are settled in cash rather than through the delivery of an underlying commodity, and derivatives prices will vary because contracts in these markets are usually privately negotiated and privately valued. He concluded by stating his confidence in the market professionals to manage their own affairs: "The primary source of regulatory effectiveness has always been private traders being knowledgeable of their counterparties. Government regulation can only act as a backup."

Remarkably, despite the collapse of LTCM, which resulted from its huge unregulated positions in derivatives, during September 1998, Greenspan continued to oppose any regulation of the OTC derivatives industry. On February 10, 2000, he once again testified before a congressional committee on this matter.[40] He started out by saying, "These instruments allow users to unbundle risks and allocate them to the investors most willing and able to assume them." He stated, "Imposing government regulation on a market can impair its efficiency." He also warned that Congress had to free the derivatives from the threat of regulation or else their markets would move "to foreign jurisdictions that maintain the confidence of global investors without imposing so many regulatory constraints." On June 21, also in congressional testimony, Treasury Secretary Lawrence Summers backed up Greenspan, saying, "In the absence of an updated legal and regulatory environment, needless systemic risk might jeopardize the broader vitality of the American capital markets."[41]

With lots of help from Greenspan, the Commodity Futures Modernization Act of 2000 was introduced in the House on December 14, 2000. The companion bill was introduced in the Senate on December 15, 2000, right before the Christmas holiday. It was never debated in the Senate. On December 21, 2000, Congress passed it, and President Clinton signed the legislation just before leaving office. The legislation expressly exempted the OTC derivatives market from CFTC oversight. That led directly to the excesses that fueled the housing bubble, as the previous chapter explains.

Greenspan sent a couple of mixed messages about the exuberance in the housing market. In a speech on February 23, 2004, he said, "Indeed, recent research within the Federal Reserve suggests that many homeowners might have saved tens of thousands of dollars had they held adjustable-rate mortgages rather than fixed-rate mortgages during the past decade, though this would not have been the case, of course, had interest rates trended sharply upward."[42] He was widely criticized for encouraging adjustable-rate lending, though his statement was clearly not an endorsement of such borrowing.

Finally, in a May 5, 2005 speech, he started to acknowledge the downside of the deregulation of derivatives. He correctly identified the potential dangers of the rapid growth of the derivatives market and the proliferation of new financial instruments in that market: "The rapid proliferation of derivatives products inevitably means that some will not have been adequately tested by market stress. Even with sound credit-risk management, a sudden widening of credit spreads could result in unanticipated losses to investors in some of the newer, more complex structured credit products, and those investors could include some leveraged hedge funds. Risk management involves judgment as well as science, and the science is based on the past behavior of markets, which is not an infallible guide to the future."[43] Nevertheless, he ended his speech on a lame note, saying "both market participants and policymakers must be aware of the risk-management challenges associated with the use of derivatives to transfer risk, both within the banking system and outside the banking system. And they must take steps to ensure that those challenges are addressed." He clearly continued to believe that market participants would properly manage their business and regulate themselves.

On Greenspan's watch, from August 1987 to January 2006, two asset bubbles inflated. The first was the bubble in the stock market. The price-to-earnings multiple of the S&P 500 based on trailing earnings rose to a record high of 29.0 during the first quarter of 2002 (Fig. 13). It was 20.1 when he assumed the chairmanship. The second was the bubble in residential real estate. The median price of a single-family home soared 161% from the start to the finish of his Fed tenure (Fig. 14).

After the housing bubble burst, Greenspan became convinced that it had been inflated by too much available credit because of what he called the "global saving glut." In other words, he solved his conundrum, but the consequences were still severe. Nevertheless, the Fed on Greenspan's watch failed to appreciate the magnitude of the financial excesses that were building in the housing finance industry. That was because Greenspan had a blind faith in the unregulated credit derivatives markets. His only concern seemed to be that many of the trades weren't being properly recorded. The Fed's staff continued to write lots of research studies, but virtually none of them focused on what was happening in the credit derivatives market since their boss showed no concern, let alone interest in the subject.

In his post mortem of the financial crisis provided in a February 17, 2009 speech, Greenspan concluded:

> The extraordinary risk management discipline that developed out of the writings of the University of Chicago's Harry Markowitz in the 1950s, produced insights that won several Nobel Prizes in Economics. It was widely embraced not only by academia but also by a large majority of financial professionals and global regulators. But in August 2007, the risk management structure cracked. All of the sophisticated mathematics and computer wizardry essentially rested on one central premise: that enlightened self-interest of owners and managers of financial institutions would lead them to maintain a sufficient buffer against insolvency by actively monitoring and managing their firms' capital and risk positions. When in the summer of 2007 that premise failed, I was deeply dismayed. I still believe that self-regulation is an essential tool for market effectiveness—a first line of defense. But, it is clear that the levels of complexity to which market practitioners, at the height of their euphoria, carried risk management techniques and risk-product design were too much for even the most sophisticated market

players to handle properly and prudently. Accordingly, I see no alternative to a set of heightened federal regulatory rules for banks and other financial institutions.[44]

It is ironic, in my opinion, that Sebastian Mallaby chose to title his very informative 2016 biography of Greenspan *The Man Who Knew*.

BEN BERNANKE: THE GREAT MODERATOR

BEN BERNANKE IS widely renowned as one of the world's leading macroeconomists. In other words, he is one of the world's greatest meddlers. Bernanke was Fed chairman from February 1, 2006 to January 31, 2014. On February 20, 2004, when he was a Fed governor, he delivered a remarkable speech titled "The Great Moderation," about the extraordinary decline in the variability of both output and inflation. In it, he marveled at what macroeconomists, particularly the ones at the Fed, had accomplished: "Reduced macroeconomic volatility has numerous benefits. Lower volatility of inflation improves market functioning, makes economic planning easier, and reduces the resources devoted to hedging inflation risks. Lower volatility of output tends to imply more stable employment and a reduction in the extent of economic uncertainty confronting households and firms. The reduction in the volatility of output is also closely associated with the fact that recessions have become less frequent and less severe."[45]

Lo and behold, macroeconomists—particularly those running the Fed—had finally found the Holy Grail! Their policies had succeeded in reducing the frequency and depth of recessions while subduing inflation (Fig. 15 and Fig. 16). It was truly a remarkable achievement, according to Bernanke. Macroeconomists had proven that they could deliver us to the Promised Land. Their theories weren't utopian; they weren't impossible dreams—they were pragmatic and successful!

Bernanke had been a great moderator since the start of his career as a macroeconomist. He was trained to be. He attended Harvard and graduated in 1975 with a BA in economics *summa cum laude*, followed by an MA, also from Harvard, and a PhD in economics from the Massachusetts Institute of Technology in 1979. His dissertation was titled *Long-Term Commitments, Dynamic Optimization, and the Business Cycle*, and his thesis adviser was Stanley Fischer, who became Fed vice chairman under Janet Yellen during 2014.

After stints at the Stanford Graduate School of Business and New York University, Bernanke became a tenured professor at Princeton. He was chair of the Economics Department for six years before going on public-service leave in 2002 to serve on the Fed's Board of Governors. He resigned from both Princeton and the Fed in the summer of 2005, when President George W. Bush appointed him to chair the CEA. If the CEA post was a test, he passed: within months, Bush appointed him to succeed Greenspan as chairman of the Federal Reserve, starting February 1, 2006.

Bernanke was reappointed by President Barack Obama for another four-year term in 2010 by a Senate vote of 70 to 30—the slimmest margin for a Fed chief ever. There was lots of dissatisfaction on Capitol Hill with the way the Fed had handled the financial crisis of 2008. However, there was widespread agreement that Bernanke had been the right man at the right time to avert a financial meltdown and a depression. I agree with that assessment. We were lucky he was running the show.

After all, Bernanke is one of the leading macroeconomic students of the Great Depression. He published numerous academic journal articles—with lots of econometric analyses of the subject—many of which were compiled into a 2004 book titled *Essays on the Great Depression*. Like Milton Friedman, he concluded that the Fed was mostly to blame for the Great Depression. The Fed "did it" as he said in his November 8, 2002 speech honoring Friedman's 90th birthday.

I am convinced that the Smoot–Hawley Tariff caused the Great Depression. It was enacted on June 17, 1930, triggering massive declines in world trade and commodity prices and an avalanche of bank bankruptcies and debt defaults, as I review in Chapter 2. Bernanke's narrative doesn't allow for the possibility that the tariff could have triggered the global collapse in business, trade, and prices. I concluded this after searching for "Smoot–Hawley Tariff" in the printed book's index. It's not listed. An electronic search of his book reveals that the term appears just twice. The first occurrence is not until page 266, and the second is in a footnoted reference. In the first spot, Bernanke discounts the "disruptive effect" of "trade restrictions" as a "theoretical possibility" based on weak direct evidence. In the footnote, he refers the reader to an August 1986 NBER working paper by Barry Eichengreen titled "The Political Economy of the Smoot–Hawley Tariff."[46]

In any event, Bernanke's findings convinced him that the Fed caused the Great Depression and that he must do whatever he could to ensure the Fed didn't make the same mistake again.

On March 20, 2012, in the first of four lectures on the history of the Fed that he delivered at George Washington University, Bernanke referred the students to the movie *It's a Wonderful Life*, starring Jimmy Stewart, for an example of a bank run.[47] Central banks were invented to stop such financial crises by acting as lenders of last resort, just as Walter Bagehot had explained in *Lombard Street: A Description of the Money Market*, Bernanke said. In an April 2012 *Atlantic* article about him, Bernanke cited Bagehot's *Lombard Street* as his guide book. "It's beautiful," Bernanke said. As I observe in Chapter 5, the 19th-century essayist had urged central bankers to take vigorous action to stop financial panics. Defending his own crisis measures, Bernanke said, "Some people don't understand— fulfilling the responsibility as lender of last resort is what the Fed was created to do. This is what central banks have been doing for 300 years."[48]

In his lecture, Bernanke accused the Fed of dereliction of duty at the start of the Great Depression. He didn't say what exactly triggered the downturn, though he implied that it might have been the stock market crash and US Treasury Secretary Andrew Mellon's puritanical response to the collapse of the debt-fueled speculative excesses of the Roaring '20s when Mellon heartlessly said, "Liquidate labor, liquidate stocks, liquidate the farmers, liquidate real estate." In Bernanke's opinion, the Fed failed its first major test, and it was left to President Roosevelt to abandon the gold standard on June 5, 1933, which "allowed monetary policy to be released and allowed the expansion of the money supply." The dollar was devalued by 40% relative to gold in 1933 and 1934. In 1934, the FDIC was created to provide deposit insurance, which also put an end to the bank runs.

It is quite ironic that roughly five years after Bernanke's Great Moderation speech, during 2008, the economy fell into what even he called the "Great Recession." He admitted that he hadn't seen it coming. But he was well prepared to come to the rescue. On November 21, 2002, in one of his first speeches as a Fed governor (the aforementioned "Deflation: Making Sure 'It' Doesn't Happen Here"), he outlined what has been referred to as "The Bernanke Doctrine."[49] He concluded, "Sustained deflation can be highly destructive to a modern economy and should be strongly resisted."

Bernanke discussed all the ways and means that the Fed could do so. He favored an inflation target of 1.0%–3.0% to provide enough of a buffer zone for inflation. He called on the Fed to use its "regulatory and supervisory powers to ensure that the financial system will remain resilient if financial conditions change rapidly." If the financial system and economy came unglued nonetheless, the Fed should use all its tools to stabilize them as quickly as possible. He believed in shock-and-awe tactics, with the Fed acting "more preemptively and more aggressively than usual in cutting rates."

In that speech, Bernanke also anticipated new unconventional monetary policy tools, particularly quantitative easing. He expressed confidence that even if the federal funds rate were cut to zero ("its practical minimum"), the Fed would have the tools to stop deflation; after all, in a worst-case scenario, the government could always print more money. He then backed off from this radical idea, saying the government wouldn't have to do that because the Fed could, in effect, do the same through various asset purchase programs, i.e., what came to be known as "quantitative easing."

Near the end of his speech, Bernanke rhetorically asked why Japan hadn't succeeded in ending deflation and gave an answer: political constraints had kept the Japanese from doing enough. It was the same conclusion he had offered in a widely read paper, "Japanese Monetary Policy: A Case of Self-Induced Paralysis?" delivered in January 2000 when he was a professor at Princeton.[50] Even back then, Bernanke was making a list of "nonstandard operations," including quantitative easing, that the Bank of Japan (BOJ) could implement to stop deflation. He extolled FDR: "But Roosevelt's specific policy actions were, I think, less important than his willingness to be aggressive and to experiment—in short, to do whatever was necessary to get the country moving again. Many of his policies did not work as intended, but in the end FDR deserves great credit for having the courage to abandon failed paradigms and to do what needed to be done."

Bernanke failed to appreciate the magnitude of the housing finance bubble, which started to show signs of stress in 2007. He first signaled his concern when he pushed for a 75-basis-point cut in the federal funds rate to 3.50% on January 22, 2008. That was quickly followed up with a 50-basis-point reduction on January 30 and another 75 basis points on March 18, down to 2.25%.

The Fed chairman probably first recognized that he was confronted by a financial and economic calamity potentially even worse than the Great Depression when Lehman Brothers and AIG collapsed during September 2008. It was time to implement the *Lombard Street* game plan. He teamed up with Treasury Secretary Hank Paulson to press Congress to enact the Troubled Asset Relief Program. He dusted off his 2002 speech and started methodically to implement his list of fail-safe measures. In late 2008, the Fed set up several emergency facilities to pump liquidity into the financial markets. The federal funds rate was lowered to the "zero bound" on December 16, 2008.

Unconventional monetary measures were first introduced on November 25, 2008 with the implementation of the first round of quantitative easing (QE1). I wasn't surprised, because Bernanke previously had revealed his game plan in response to such alarming circumstances. Furthermore, I noted in October and early November that mortgage interest rates hadn't dropped along with government bond yields. I predicted that the Fed would address this problem. The Fed did so with QE1, which was a commitment to purchase $600 billion in government-sponsored enterprise debt and mortgage-backed securities (Fig. 17 and Fig. 18).

The program was expanded on March 16, 2009 when the FOMC announced its intention to purchase "up to an additional $750 billion of agency mortgage-backed securities, bringing its total purchases of these securities to up to $1.25 trillion that year, and to increase its purchases of agency debt this year by up to $100 billion to a total of up to $200 billion. Moreover, to help improve conditions in private credit markets, the Committee decided to purchase up to $300 billion of longer-term Treasury securities over the next six months."[51]

I was all for QE1. I was not a fan of QE2. That second round of quantitative easing was introduced on November 3, 2010. The Fed said it would purchase "a further $600 billion of longer-term Treasury securities by the end of the second quarter of 2011, a pace of about $75 billion per month." Apparently, the Fed's staff ran the in-house econometric model and concluded around mid-2012 that QE1 wasn't enough to keep the economic recovery going. The model showed that a negative federal funds rate would be required to do so. But since no central bank had crossed the zero bound with negative interest rates back then, Bernanke must have asked the Fed staff to estimate how much in QE2 purchases would be required to have the same stimulative effect as a negative interest rate.

Bernanke first suggested the need for more quantitative easing in his Jackson Hole speech on August 27, 2010.[52] William Dudley, the president of the Federal Reserve Bank of New York, gave a speech on October 1, 2010, favoring another round of quantitative easing with specific numbers: "[S]ome simple calculations based on recent experience suggest that $500 billion of purchases would provide about as much stimulus as a reduction in the federal funds rate of between half a point and three quarters of a point." His basic argument was that despite the downside of additional quantitative easing, it was the only tool the Fed had left to meet its congressional mandate to lower the unemployment rate. Indeed, the speech was titled "The Outlook, Policy Choices and Our Mandate." The word "mandate" appeared 17 times in the speech, including the title.[53]

At the time, I argued that if the Fed's econometric model was calling for a negative official policy rate, then either there was something wrong with the model or the Fed was trying to fix economic problems that could not be fixed with monetary policy. In my opinion, when the federal funds rate was lowered to zero, Fed officials should have said that that was all they could do. While I expected and endorsed QE1, I am not convinced that QE2 and then QE3 were necessary. But there I go again, critiquing monetary policy.

Bernanke kept me focused on doing my job by explaining why he believed that his job was to implement QE2. He did so in a highly unusual op-ed article for the November 4, 2010 issue of *The Washington Post* appropriately titled "What the Fed Did and Why: Supporting the Recovery and Sustaining Price Stability."[54] In brief, the Fed wanted to drive up the prices of bonds and stocks: "Lower corporate bond rates will encourage investment. And higher stock prices will boost consumer wealth and help increase confidence, which can also spur spending. Increased spending will lead to higher incomes and profits that, in a virtuous circle, will further support economic expansion."

Bernanke made my job easier, which was to stay bullish on bonds and stocks. While QE2 and then QE3 didn't seem to be doing much to stimulate the economy and revive price inflation, they certainly fueled asset inflation, which was one of the reasons I remained bullish on stocks and bonds.

No one has been as committed to moderating the business cycle with monetary policy as former Fed Chairman Ben Bernanke. He reiterated this view in an October 4, 2015 *Wall Street Journal* op-ed titled "How the

Fed Saved the Economy," timed to coincide with the release of his new book, *The Courage to Act: A Memoir of a Crisis and Its Aftermath*:

> What the Fed can do is two things: First, by mitigating recessions, monetary policy can try to ensure that the economy makes full use of its resources, especially the workforce. High unemployment is a tragedy for the jobless, but it is also costly for taxpayers, investors and anyone interested in the health of the economy. Second, by keeping inflation low and stable, the Fed can help the market-based system function better and make it easier for people to plan for the future. Considering the economic risks posed by deflation, as well as the probability that interest rates will approach zero when inflation is very low, the Fed sets an inflation target of 2%, similar to that of most other central banks around the world.[55]

When Bernanke kindly gave me permission to quote from his op-ed, he informed me that he hadn't selected the title; the headline writers at *The Wall Street Journal* titled it.

In his memoir, Bernanke does acknowledge that the "experience of the Great Moderation had led both banks and regulators to underestimate the probabilities of a large economic or financial shock." In my opinion, attempts by the central banks to moderate the business cycle can have unintended consequences that make the economy *more vulnerable* to financial instability and deeper recessions.

JANET YELLEN: THE GRADUAL NORMALIZER

BEN BERNANKE'S TERM expired at the start of 2014. On February 3, 2014, Janet Yellen became the 15th chair of the Fed, having served as vice chair since October 4, 2010. Prior to joining the Federal Reserve Board in Washington, DC, she had served as the president of the Federal Reserve Bank of San Francisco since June 14, 2004. She had started her government service as the 18th chair of the CEA, from February 18, 1997 to August 3, 1999. In some ways, I found her easier to read than her three predecessors. Perhaps that was because we're both Yalies.

On April 16, 1999, CEA Chair Yellen gave a speech at a reunion of the Yale graduate economics department.[56] She declared that the liberal

Keynesian orthodoxy preached by James Tobin had conquered Washington. Tobin was one of the major disciples of John Maynard Keynes in the United States. According to Tobin's foremost disciple, everyone in the room shared the same goal—they all wanted to be do-gooders: "I suspect that many of us here tonight were attracted to economics and to policy positions in government because we believed in its potential for improving economic welfare."

She said Professor Tobin had suggested that the title of her speech be "Yale Economics in Washington." She readily obliged, saying, "I will try to make the case that the lessons that we learned here at Yale remain the right and relevant ones for improving economic performance, that Yale-trained economists in Washington are succeeding in making their voices heard, and, where Yale economics has been applied, it is working."

Then Yellen claimed that while most economists "appreciate the role of markets and incentives," only Yalies can see when they aren't working properly and know how to fix them: "I have noticed that Yalies often have a sharper eye for identifying market failures and greater concern for policies to remedy them than economists from institutions I will leave nameless." Her comments made me wonder whether at any time in her professional life Yellen considered the possibility that government policies can cause markets to fail, requiring more government policies to fix the failure that the government caused in the first place. At Yale, there were no courses in the unintended negative consequences of well-intentioned macroeconomic policies.

The original sin for macroeconomists, in my opinion, was the passage of the Employment Act of 1946 and its later amendments that established the CEA. As Yellen noted—favorably, of course—the Act mandated that the federal government should moderate the business cycle, thus "promoting balanced and noninflationary economic growth, and fostering low unemployment." The law has certainly been a full employment act for macroeconomists working for the Fed.

Yellen extolled the "Yale macroeconomic paradigm." She said that "as I have taught and hopefully practiced it," the model "combines a Keynesian understanding of economic fluctuations with a neoclassical perspective on long-run growth. . . . The IS-LM and aggregate demand/aggregate supply models, hopefully still staples in Yale's classes, provide the simplest description of the short run paradigm." She believes in this model more than ever, in my opinion.

Like a true-blue Yalie Keynesian, she claimed that a capitalist economy can't maintain full employment without the help of Yalie macroeconomists. "The Yale macroeconomic paradigm provides clear answers to key questions dividing macroeconomists along with policy prescriptions. Will capitalist economies operate at full employment in the absence of routine intervention? Certainly not. Are deviations from full employment a social problem? Obviously." Asking whether "policymakers have the knowledge and ability to improve macroeconomic outcomes rather than make matters worse," she replied to herself with an unequivocal, "Yes."

Near the end of her speech, Yellen raised one cautionary flag: "Decades ago, economists recognized an unfortunate implication of the IS-LM model: that the simultaneous attainment of financial market openness, monetary policy independence, and exchange rate stability—three desirable macroeconomic goals—was simply impossible! Countries would have to forego at least one or risk financial crisis." Less than a year after her pep talk, the US economy fell into a recession when the technology bubble in the stock market, inflated by Greenspan's Fed, popped.

Fed Chair Janet Yellen made her first rookie mistake during her first press conference on March 19, 2014, when she defined the "considerable time" mentioned in the latest FOMC statement to mean "something on the order of around six months or that type of thing."[57] That was widely interpreted as suggesting that the Fed might start raising the federal funds rate six months after QE was terminated. The termination was generally expected to happen by the end of 2014 and actually did occur that year in late October. However, the first rate hike after QE was terminated didn't occur until the end of the following year.

Yellen seemed to back away from that prediction in her extraordinarily impassioned and personal speech on Monday, March 31, 2014 in Chicago, when she said that the Fed remained committed "to do what is necessary to help our nation recover from the Great Recession."[58] In her speech, she briefly described the struggle of three workers in the Windy City—Dorine Poole, Jermaine Brownlee, and Vicki Lira—in the labor market, implying that she intended to maintain ultra-easy monetary policy until they and people like them had good jobs.

The next day, Jon Hilsenrath reported in *The Wall Street Journal*: "One person cited as an example of the hurdles faced by the long-term unemployed had a two-decade-old theft conviction. Another mentioned as an example of someone whose wages have dropped since the recession had a past drug conviction. Academic research suggests people with criminal backgrounds face unique obstacles to employment." Hilsenrath added that a "Fed spokeswoman said Tuesday that Ms. Yellen knew of the people's criminal backgrounds and that they were 'very forthright' about it in conversations with the chairwoman before the speech. In her remarks, she said they exemplified the trends she was discussing, such as downward pressure on wages or the challenge of finding a job for the long-term unemployed."[59]

Yellen's idea of humanizing the problem of the unemployed was a good one, but it should have been based on statistically valid samples rather than three people. The July 21, 2014 issue of *The New Yorker* included a lengthy article about Yellen.[60] It confirmed that she is an impassioned liberal: "Yellen is notable not only for being the first female Fed chair but also for being the most liberal since Marriner Eccles, who held the job during the Roosevelt and Truman Administrations. Ordinarily, the Fed's role is to engender a sense of calm in the eternally jittery financial markets, not to crusade against urban poverty."

Yellen intended "to help American families who are struggling in the aftermath of the Great Recession." She and her husband, George Akerlof, have published numerous papers on why labor markets don't automatically work to maintain full employment.[61] The government can do the job better: "I come from an intellectual tradition where public policy is important, it can make a positive contribution, it's our social obligation to do this. We can help to make the world a better place."

After she became Fed chair in early 2014, the FOMC finally terminated the QE program on October 29 of that year. There was lots of chatter among Fed watchers about rate hikes coming in 2015. Based on my assessment of Yellen, I concluded that she would be very slow and cautious in raising rates. Indeed, during September 2014, I predicted a "one-and-done" rate hike in the coming year. Yellen finally delivered that rate increase of 25 basis points at the very last meeting of 2015. At the end of that year, I predicted one-and-done again for 2016. Fed Vice Chairman Stanley Fischer rattled financial markets around the world at the very beginning of 2016, warning that they hadn't fully discounted the possibility of four rate hikes in 2016. I stuck with my forecast, and the next rate hike occurred at the last FOMC meeting of 2016. There were two more rate hikes during the first half of 2017.

Early on when Yellen became Fed chair (and even when she was vice chair, I noticed), the stock market often would rise after she gave a speech on the economy and monetary policy. She was among the most dovish members of the FOMC, and she now ruled the aviary, which also included a few hawks. So I remained bullish on the outlook for stocks, anticipating that under her leadership, the FOMC would normalize monetary policy at a very gradual pace.

On September 29, 2016, in a video conference with bankers in Kansas City, Yellen crossed the line, in my opinion, when she suggested that the Fed should be authorized by Congress to buy corporate bonds and stocks. After all, she noted, the BOJ had been buying corporate bonds and stocks for a while, and the European Central Bank (ECB) had been buying corporate bonds since June of that year. That's true, but there was no evidence that these purchases were boosting growth in either Japan or the Eurozone.

Yellen and I both learned from Professor Tobin about the "Portfolio-Balance Model." (My PhD dissertation was titled *A Portfolio-Balance Model of Corporate Finance*.) The idea is that assets are substitutable for each other. So if the Fed buys government bonds, reducing their supply, that will drive more demand into other bonds as well as equities. The resulting increase in wealth then should stimulate spending. In her video talk, Yellen said:

> Now because Treasury securities and, say, corporate securities and equities are substitutes in the portfolios of the public, when we push down yields—let's say on Treasuries—there's often and typically spillover to corporate bonds and to equities as well [such] that those rates fall or that equity prices rise, stimulating investment. But we are restricted from investing in that wider range of assets. And if we found—I think as other countries did—that [we] had reached the limits in terms of purchasing safe assets like longer-term government bonds, it could be useful to be able to intervene directly in assets where the prices have a more direct link to spending decisions.

Got that? If the Fed runs out of Treasuries, "it could be useful" to buy corporate bonds and stocks. Spoken like a true central monetary planner. She strongly suggested that she was all for adding that option to the Fed's toolkit just in case the other tools used to tinker with the economy didn't work. She was very blunt about her willingness to distort our capital markets because they clearly weren't working well enough on their own to achieve the Fed's goals. (See Appendix 9.4, Yellen's Comments on Fed Purchasing Corporate Bonds and Stocks.)

How can capitalism survive in the United States if the operation of its capital markets is completely distorted by the Fed? The economy certainly didn't seem to be getting any lift from all the distortions that occurred in the Treasury bond and money markets, caused by the Fed's policies since the financial crisis of 2008. Intervening so broadly in the capital markets is bound to disrupt the process of creative destruction that is integral to capitalism. It will keep zombie companies in business, which is deflationary and reduces profitability for well-run competitors. Investors won't get to determine the winners and losers if the Fed buys simply to prop up stock prices. Depending on the circumstances, the "Yellen Put" might have resulted in a speculative bubble.

In short, Fed intervention in the corporate bond and equity markets is a very bad idea, in my opinion.

The BOJ and ECB do it, so why shouldn't the Fed? Lots of reasons. For one, those policies certainly haven't been reviving capitalism's animal spirits in Japan and the Eurozone. Both have relatively inferior capital markets compared to the vibrant ones in the United States. They still depend too much on their banks for financial intermediation. Their banks have been broken for a long time, and the flat yield curve and negative interest-rate policies of the BOJ and ECB surely weren't helping their banks.

Yellen concluded her response by saying, "But while it's a good thing to think about, it's not something that is a pressing issue now, and I should emphasize that while there could be benefits to, say, the ability to buy either equities or corporate bonds, there would also be costs as well that would have to be carefully considered in deciding if it's a good idea."

On October 14, 2016, Yellen gave a speech at a conference sponsored by the Boston Fed and attended by Fed and academic economists—the topic of discussion: "The Elusive 'Great' Recovery: Causes and Implications for Future Business Cycle Dynamics." Her talk was titled "Macroeconomic Research After the Crisis." It was a remarkable speech that should have been titled "Macroeconomic Research in Crisis."[62] The unemployment rate had dropped from a peak of 10.0% during October 2009 to 4.9% in August 2016. The Fed had hiked once at the end of 2015 and was going to do it again at the end of 2016. Yet Yellen did her best to argue for a gradual normalization of monetary policy.

She talked about "hysteresis," the idea that persistent shortfalls in aggregate demand could adversely affect the supply side of the economy. Then she rhetorically asked: "If we assume that hysteresis is in fact present to some degree after deep recessions, the natural next question is to ask whether it might be possible to reverse these adverse supply-side effects by temporarily running a 'high-pressure economy,' with robust aggregate demand and a tight labor market." My commentary on her speech was titled "Some Like It Hot." I concluded that Yellen was in no hurry to rush the pace of rate hikes.

What I found unusual about her speech was that she admitted there might be "limits in economists' understanding of the economy." Then she proceeded to list several questions that she hoped "the profession will try to answer." Apparently, on-the-job experiences had moderated the confidence she had expressed at the Yalie reunion. She suggested that perhaps macroeconomists need to do more work using "disaggregated data and models." In other words, they should be microeconomists! I may, though, be putting words in her mouth. She got into some real meaning-of-life questions for macroeconomists. For example: "How does the financial sector interact with the broader economy?" Now get this one: "What determines inflation?" Remember, this is coming from the Fed chair who in a sense wrote the book on macroeconomics, or at least the Tobin notes!

Could this mean that Yellen is coming around to my strongly held view that economists need to go out and talk to real people instead of tweaking their models and having heated debates with one another over their theories that are divorced from reality? As a wise man once said: "In theory, there is no difference between theory and practice, but in practice, there is."[63]

During Yellen's term as Fed chair, she and other Fed officials were baffled that inflation remained below their 2.0% target, particularly when the unemployment rate suggested that the labor market was close to full employment during 2017. On numerous occasions, Yellen had expressed her faith in the Phillips Curve Model and used it to predict that wage inflation would move higher. I suggested that Fed officials needed to order from Amazon to understand one of the forces keeping inflation down. In a September 26, 2017 speech, Yellen for the first time conceded the point in public, saying, "The growing importance of online shopping, by increasing the competitiveness of the U.S. retail sector, may have reduced price margins and restrained the ability of firms to raise prices in response to rising demand."[64]

In a speech on October 15, 2017, Yellen candidly stated, "The biggest surprise in the U.S. economy this year has been inflation. . . . Inflation readings over the past several months have been surprisingly soft."[65]

Near the end of her term as Fed chair, Yellen faced a challenge launched by a few congressional Republicans to force the FOMC to follow a rules-based approach to setting monetary policy. The concept was originally pushed by Milton Friedman, who believed that the Fed should stick to a set growth rate in the money supply. The Fed's July 7, 2017 *Monetary Policy Report*, which accompanied Yellen's congressional testimony, included a section titled "Monetary Policy Rules and Their Role in the Federal Reserve's Policy Process."[66] The basic message was that the FOMC does pay attention to simple models such as the Taylor Rule, which prescribe the level of the federal funds rate based on two gaps: (1) the one between actual and targeted inflation and (2) the one between actual and potential real GDP. However, the Fed's policymakers believe that these models ignore too many "considerations" that require their judgment when setting the federal funds rate. In the "rules versus discretion" debate, they clearly favor the latter approach. For Fed watchers like myself, discretion means that we will continue to find gainful employment as profilers of Fed officials.

President Donald Trump did not reappoint Yellen for a second term to chair the Fed. He considered John Taylor, who devised the Taylor Rule, for the post. Instead, he chose Fed Governor Jerome Powell. I will miss Yellen. I think she did a very good job of managing the gradual normalization of monetary policy and solidifying Bernanke's achievement in reviving the economy. Under both of them, bond and stock investors enjoyed significant bull markets. I am looking forward to profiling the new Fed chairman.

CENTRAL MONETARY PLANNERS

DURING THE BULL market in stocks that began March 2009, I increasingly generalized Marty Zweig's famous dictum about not fighting the Fed to "Don't fight the central banks." I noted that the Fed, the ECB, the BOJ, and the People's Bank of China (PBOC) have an unlimited supply of dollars, euros, pounds, yen, and yuan that they can pour into the financial markets. They certainly demonstrated their willingness and ability to adopt unconventional, ultra-easy monetary policies during and after the financial crisis of 2008. The central bankers were like Walter Bagehot on steroids.

Most of the major central bankers also have stated explicitly that the transmission mechanism of their ultra-easy monetary policies works by boosting asset prices, with the resulting wealth effects stimulating their economies. Higher stock prices are expected to boost consumer spending. Lower bond yields are expected to stimulate business borrowing for capital spending. If some of the corporate borrowing is used to buy back shares, that's okay because it boosts stock prices.

This process has been great for stock and bond investors. However, the transmission mechanism hasn't worked as well as the central bankers expected. They struggled to avert deflation at times when economic growth remained subpar, with secular stagnation plaguing the Eurozone and Japan. So they persisted with their ultra-easy policies, which drove stock prices higher and bond yields to record lows.

During the latest bull market in stocks, there have been lots of vocal bearish prognosticators who warned that the stock market was on a "sugar high" from all the liquidity injected by the central banks into the financial markets. My response to their warnings: "So what's your point?" Their point was often simply that "this will all end badly." I retorted, "All the more reason to make lots of money before that happens." The pessimists countered that the central banks were just "kicking the can down the road." "That might be better than doing nothing" was my reply. The doomsayers said that it was all heading toward a widely dreaded "endgame" in a repeat of 2008 or worse. I countered with arguments suggesting there might be no end to this game.

I can understand why there was so much unease about the extreme measures that the major central banks took to avoid another financial crisis. They were indeed extreme, and without precedent. From time to time, I too was shocked by their latest maneuver and accused them of being "central monetary planners." I objected to their central conceit, namely that monetary policy could solve all our problems. The central bankers occasionally admitted that they didn't really believe that but had no choice except to do whatever it took to save the day, since fiscal policymakers seemed incapable of taking appropriate action.

"Whatever it takes" was uttered by none other than ECB President Mario Draghi in a pivotal unscripted speech at the Global Investment Conference in London on July 26, 2012.[67] Draghi succeeded Jean-Claude Trichet as the head of the central bank of the European Monetary Union (EMU) on November 1, 2011. He earned a PhD in economics from the

Massachusetts Institute of Technology in 1976. He worked at Goldman Sachs from 2002 until 2005 before becoming the governor of the Bank of Italy in December 2005, where he served until October 2011.

Draghi started his July 2012 speech by saying that the "euro is like a bumblebee. This is a mystery of nature because it shouldn't fly but instead it does." Near the end of his stream of consciousness, he suggested that the bee might need some help to keep flying, and he was ready to provide just that: "Within our mandate, the ECB is ready to do whatever it takes to preserve the euro. And believe me, it will be enough."

Two years earlier, in 2010, many people had started to question the stability and even the viability of the EMU, causing much angst in many quarters. The EMU had been adopted by the 19 countries that compose the Eurozone back on January 1, 1999, when they all agreed to scrap their own currencies and use only the euro from that day forward. Igniting the intense fears about the potential disintegration of the decade-old Eurozone were a chronic budget crisis and financial turmoil in Greece. Suddenly, investors around the world were alerted that not all bonds issued by Eurozone governments might be as sound as Germany's high-quality credits.

The yield spreads between the government bonds of the other Eurozone nations and Germany and France narrowed dramatically from 1995 through 1998 in anticipation of the formation of the Eurozone at the start of 1999 (Fig. 19). The spreads were close to zero across the region from 1999 through mid-2008. They started to widen as a result of the 2008 world financial crisis. The Greek crisis caused yields to soar on the government bonds issued by the so-called peripheral Eurozone countries—Portugal, Ireland, Italy, Greece, and Spain—from 2010 through 2012 (Fig. 20). Collectively, they were dubbed the "PIIGS." Their spreads widened dramatically relative to the yields of the "core" countries—France, Germany, and the Netherlands.

Draghi's speech worked wonders, even though he didn't follow up right away with any meaningful program. Nevertheless, the yield spreads of the PIIGS narrowed significantly relative to those of both France and Germany. The ECB had responded to the initial crisis by increasing its loans to Eurozone credit institutions from €0.4 trillion in early 2011 to €1.3 trillion by mid-2012, inflating its balance sheet by €1.2 trillion (Fig. 21 and Fig. 22). Draghi's July 2012 remarks not only narrowed the yield spreads in the Eurozone but also brought rates down across the board.

That allowed the ECB, near the end of 2014, to reduce its loans to credit institutions back down close to the early 2011 level.

However, subpar economic growth and mounting worries about deflation caused the ECB to break through the "zero bound." On June 5, 2014, the ECB announced that its official rate would be lowered to −0.10%. It was subsequently lowered three more times, to −0.40% on March 10, 2016. In addition, on January 22, 2015, the ECB adopted a QE program that on June 1, 2016 was expanded and extended to include corporate bond purchases. The ECB's holdings of the securities of Eurozone residents in euros soared by €1.7 trillion from the start of 2015 to €2.3 trillion by the end of 2016.[68]

Meanwhile, the BOJ also joined the "shock-and-awe" campaigns of the major central banks. In a political comeback, Shinzō Abe was elected Japan's prime minster on December 26, 2012, having resigned from that position in 2007 for health reasons. He pledged to revive the Japanese economy by focusing on stimulative fiscal and monetary policies as well as deregulation, his so-called "three arrows." During February 2013, he picked Asian Development Bank President Haruhiko Kuroda as head of the BOJ. Kuroda has a master's degree in economics from Oxford University. He had been an advocate of looser monetary policy in Japan.

Kuroda moved rapidly. The BOJ implemented its qualitative and quantitative easing (QQE) program on April 4, 2013. According to the bank's press release, the monetary base would be increased at an annual pace of ¥60–70 trillion, from ¥138 trillion at the end of 2012 to reach ¥200 trillion at the end of 2013 and ¥270 trillion at the end of 2014.[69]

The BOJ expanded and extended the program with its QQE program announced on October 31, 2014. According to the bank's press release, it aimed to triple the pace of its stock and property funds purchases, extend the average maturity of its bondholding by three years to 10, and raise the ceiling of its annual Japanese government bond purchases by ¥30 trillion to ¥80 trillion. In a separate announcement, Japan's huge public pension fund promised to invest more in stocks.[70] Japan's monetary base rose to ¥430 trillion by the end of 2016, up 210% since the start of QQE.

How did that all work out? The yen plunged 38% from late 2012 through mid-2015 (Fig. 23). That was great for the stock market, as the Nikkei rose 127% over the same period. However, exports didn't get the big boost that was widely expected. Inflation was still stuck near zero. Economic growth remained lackluster.

In his opening remarks at a conference in Tokyo on June 4, 2015, Kuroda said, "I trust that many of you are familiar with the story of Peter Pan, in which it says, 'The moment you doubt whether you can fly, you cease forever to be able to do it.'" *The Wall Street Journal* observed: "Japan's central bank chief invoked the boy who can fly to emphasize the need for global central bankers to believe in their ability to solve a range of vexing issues, whether stubbornly sluggish growth or entrenched expectations of price declines." Kuroda added, "Yes, what we need is a positive attitude and conviction."[71]

On January 21, 2016, Kuroda emphatically ruled out negative interest rates: "We are not considering a cut in interest on bank reserves," he told parliament. The BOJ feared that negative rates would make banks reluctant to sell their Japanese government bonds, thus undermining its asset purchase program. On January 29, the BOJ surprised everyone by lowering the official rate on new bank reserve deposits to –0.1%. Japan's Peter Pan was up to his old tricks.

So the Fed, the ECB, and the BOJ came up with lots of headline-grabbing shock-and-awe programs. Over time, they seemed to lose their effectiveness and ability to shock or awe. Nevertheless, the US economy had improved sufficiently by 2014 that the Fed terminated QE in October 2014 and started very gradually to raise interest rates. The ECB and BOJ weren't ready to move in that direction, but they seemed to have run out of new tricks.

Meanwhile, as Chapter 2 notes, the shockingly awesome program of central bank liquidity pumping was continuing in China without much fanfare. The PBOC has presided over one of the greatest expansions of credit in human history since the financial crisis of 2008. From December 2008 through September 2017, Chinese bank loans quadrupled from 30.3 trillion yuan to 117.8 trillion yuan. In dollars, they soared $13.5 trillion from $4.4 trillion to $17.9 trillion over this period (Fig. 24). China may very well be the epicenter of the world's next financial bubble. However, like Japan, the Chinese owe all that debt to themselves. That's confirmed by the rapid increase in the M2 money supply, which has kept pace with bank loans. The Chinese people have a very high saving rate, which is why bank deposit growth remains so strong.

The period from 2008 through 2016 was widely perceived to be the "Age of the Central Bankers." They undoubtedly view it as a Golden Age, in which they proved that they have the will and the means to stop a major financial contagion from turning into a financial meltdown, and a Great Recession from turning into another Great Depression. However, they must take some of the blame for having set the stage for the most recent world financial crisis by enabling too much credit expansion in the first place. Furthermore, there might still be some unintended consequences of their unprecedented experiments with central monetary planning.

As I've said before and will say again: I'm an investment strategist, not a preacher. I don't do right or wrong; I do bullish or bearish. While I have had many reasons to be critical of monetary policymaking in the United States and overseas, my job is to predict how long those policies will be bullish and when they might turn bearish.

CHAPTER 10

Predicting Bonds

HAT-SIZE BOND YIELDS

MY BAILIWICK WHEN I joined EF Hutton during the early 1980s was monitoring financial and monetary conditions. One of my main tasks was to work with the firm's chief economist to predict interest rates. Doing so has been a career-long preoccupation in my chosen occupation. Predicting short-term interest rates is really all about predicting the federal funds rate, which is all about correctly anticipating what the Fed will do, as the previous chapter examines. Forecasting short-term rates is one of the most important inputs for predicting bond yields, but there are plenty of other significant factors. There are also alternative models that can be used for predicting bond yields.

During the 1970s, Henry Kaufman, the chief economist of Salomon Brothers, was renowned for his interest-rate forecasts. He grew increasingly bearish on bonds over the course of that decade. It was a gutsy call, especially since his employer was a leading investment banking firm making markets in bonds and also raising lots of money for corporate clients in the capital markets. Kaufman was right for a long time because he was a conservative fellow and didn't like all the excesses he saw building in the credit markets and in the economy.[1]

Kaufman was especially concerned about the deregulation of the financial system. He believed that occasional credit crunches and recessions were important for maintaining some discipline in the financial markets. Deregulation meant that credit would be easier to obtain and that increased competition would lower lending standards, leading to higher inflation. Higher inflation is the second-biggest calamity bond holders can face—the biggest being defaults, which occur during credit crunches but affect fewer bond holders than rising inflation; that harms all bond holders.

The US Treasury 10-year bond yield rose from the decade's low of 5.38% on March 23, 1971 to peak at a record high of 15.84% on September 30, 1981 (Fig. 1*). The consumer price index (CPI) inflation rate rose from the decade's low of 2.7% on a year-over-year basis during June 1972 to peak at a record high of 14.8% during March 1980 (Fig. 2). The press started to refer to Kaufman as "Dr. Doom," though with admiration for having been rightly pessimistic.

Pessimism often sells well, and by the late 1970s, Kaufman was a virtual rock star on Wall Street, drawing thousands of investors to his annual presentation at the Waldorf Astoria Hotel in New York City. It certainly helped that his downbeat forecast had been consistently right on the money. Large crowds at financial conferences tend to be a contrary indicator, though. Sure enough, the 10-year yield plunged during 1982 to 10.36% at year-end. Kaufman did turn positive on bonds on August 17, 1982, but the yield had already dropped to 12.65% by that point. Kaufman's pronouncement set off an explosive stock market rally. After falling slightly lower to 10.12% on May 4, 1983, the bond yield proceeded to soar back to a peak of 13.99% on May 30, 1984 before resuming its decline.

Kaufman was also renowned for his detailed quarterly forecasts of the demand for credit by households, businesses, government, and foreigners and the supply of credit provided by individual savers, institutional investors, financial institutions, and foreigners. He based his analysis on the Fed's quarterly *Flow of Funds Accounts*. His interest-rate forecasts were very much influenced by his flow-of-funds analysis, as well as his assessment of other important influences on the credit markets, such as Fed policymaking and inflation.

Initially at EF Hutton, I followed in Kaufman's footsteps by analyzing the *Flow of Funds Accounts*, which was subsequently renamed the *Financial Accounts of the United States*.[2] This extraordinarily comprehensive database includes quarterly time series on the flow of funds in the capital markets and the levels of financial assets and liabilities, by sector and financial instrument, since 1952.[3] I had become quite familiar with the accounts

---

* Figures, references, and appendices are linked on *yardenibook.com/resources*.

in the course of writing my PhD dissertation, which was an econometric analysis of the corporate sector using data from this extensive source. (See Appendix 10.1, *Financial Accounts of the United States*: Instruments, and Appendix 10.2, *Financial Accounts of the United States*: Sectors.)

At first, Kaufman's flow-of-funds approach to forecasting the bond yield seemed plausible to me. The yield is simply the price of credit, so an accurate prediction of the balance between the demand for credit and the supply of credit should get the direction of the bond yield right. However, the more I analyzed the flow-of-funds data and tried to mimic Kaufman's approach to forecasting interest rates, the more convinced I became that it was a waste of time to use a framework that required such an enormous number of credit-market projections that were based on a bunch of educated guesses.

For Kaufman, it was a great marketing exercise and provided an aura of credibility based on the extraordinary amount of effort that had to go into this undertaking once a quarter. But there are too many moving parts to achieve an accurate forecast. While I agreed with Kaufman on the importance of credit flows in determining bond yields, I concluded that spending so much time and effort using this approach would distract me from seeing the big picture.

Not only was I starting to have my doubts about Kaufman's flow-of-funds analysis, but I also questioned the widespread view that inflation was an intractable structural problem. I didn't think so. I felt confident that the Reagan–Volcker tag team would break the back of inflation (as they proceeded to do), so I turned bullish on bonds during 1981 and increasingly so during 1982.

I started to talk about "hat-size" bond yields during the summer of 1981, when the yield still had a 15% "handle." As I note in Chapter 1, I first heard the expression from Van Hoisington, a fixed-income portfolio manager for Texas Commerce Bank I met that summer. We immediately bonded over our bullishness on bonds. Van and I disagreed with Dr. Doom and expected bond yields to fall sharply. "Ed," he said with a Texas drawl, "I think that the 10-year Treasury bond is heading toward hat-size yields." I loved Van's expression and marketed my forecast using it.

The late 1970s and early 1980s were extremely tumultuous in the credit markets. To review:

- Under Paul Volcker, the federal funds rate rose from around 11.00% on August 6, 1979—when he started his new job as Fed chairman—to peak three different times at around a record 22.00% during 1980 and

1981 (Fig. 3). The prime rate rose to a record 21.50% at the end of 1980, causing a severe credit crunch (Fig. 4).

- The economy fell into a long and deep recession as the unemployment rate rose from 5.6% during May 1979 to a postwar high of 10.8% during the last two months of 1982 (Fig. 5). Real GDP stopped growing for four years between the fourth quarter of 1978 and the final quarter of 1982 (Fig. 6).

- In addition, three financial crises developed during the spring and summer of 1982. Upstart Drysdale Government Securities failed to make an estimated $270 million of interest payments during May of that year. Penn Square Bank, a small commercial bank located in Oklahoma City, failed during July as a result of making a large amount of bad energy-related loans that also led to losses for other banks that had participated in these loans.[4] In August 1982, Mexican Secretary of Finance and Public Credit Jesús Silva Herzog Flores informed the Federal Reserve chairman, the US Treasury secretary, and the International Monetary Fund managing director that Mexico no longer would be able to service its debt, which at that point totaled $80 billion.

- The Fed reversed course and lowered the federal funds rate as the recession worsened. In addition, a "flight to quality" among investors during 1982 was triggered by the Mexican debt crisis.

But it was a wild ride all the way. From its record high of 15.84% on September 30, 1981, the US Treasury 10-year bond yield dropped sharply during the recession of 1982 and 1983. It rebounded in late 1983 and early 1984 before resuming its decline to a hat-size yield of 7.00% on August 20, 1986. To get there, I had to saddle up and ride along with my amigos, the Bond Vigilantes. As an alternative to Kaufman's flow-of-funds approach, I increasingly relied on what I call the "Bond Vigilantes Model." In the next section, I explain this model before exploring alternatives in the following sections, such as the Inflation Premium Model, the Yield Curve Model, and the global savings glut.

RIDING WITH THE BOND VIGILANTES

THE BOND VIGILANTES Model simply compares the bond yield to the growth rate in nominal GDP on a year-over-year basis (Fig. 7). Instead of spending lots of hours analyzing the ins and outs of the flow of funds, I do the best I can to forecast nominal GDP with the tools I discuss in Chapter 4 on predicting inflation and in Chapter 5 on predicting the business cycle.

This is a more straightforward approach but still requires plenty of work. My model shows that since 1953, the yield has fluctuated around the growth rate of nominal GDP. However, both the bond yield and nominal GDP growth tend to be volatile. While they usually are in the same ballpark, they rarely coincide. When their trajectories diverge, the model forces me to explain why this is happening. On occasions, doing so has sharpened my ability to see and understand important inflection points in the relationship.

Let's spend some time reviewing this relationship since the 1950s, and my ride with the Bond Vigilantes along the way:

- *1950s–1970s.* From the 1950s to the 1970s, the spread between the bond yield and nominal GDP growth was mostly negative (Fig. 8). Investors underestimated the growth rate of nominal GDP because they underestimated inflation. Bond yields rose during this period but remained consistently below nominal GDP growth.
- *1980s.* That changed during the 1980s, when investors belatedly turned much warier of inflation just as it was heading downward. As a result, the yield tended to trade above the growth in nominal GDP during that decade. Furthermore, there were two discernable episodes at the beginning of the decade when rising bond yields slowed the economy, which allowed them to fall again. A third episode preceded the 1987 stock market crash.

  I explained this phenomenon in the July 27, 1983 issue of my weekly commentary, which was titled "Bond Investors Are the Economy's Bond Vigilantes." I concluded: "So if the fiscal and monetary authorities won't regulate the economy, the bond investors will. The economy will be run by vigilantes in the credit markets." As the yield cycled in this vigilant fashion, the trend in nominal GDP growth moved downward along with inflation. Of course, bond investors don't have regulating the economy in mind but are simply acting in their perceived financial best interest—i.e., out of rising and falling concern that inflation might erode the effective purchasing power of their bond investment returns.

  In addition to the Bond Vigilantes, there were other players and forces at work bringing inflation and bond yields down during the

1980s. At the start of the decade, there was a severe recession triggered by the spike in oil prices in 1979 and by Paul Volcker's aggressive monetary policy measures to contain that inflationary shock. The
price of oil peaked during the summer and fell 71% through July 1986
(Fig. 9). That helped to moderate inflationary pressures. Economic
growth was weighed down during the mid-1980s by the recession in
the oil industry. During the second half of the 1980s, the mounting savings and loan (S&L) crisis depressed the housing market and
raised fears of a financial contagion (Fig. 10).

The end of the Cold War in 1989 was widely expected to boost
inflation because there would be more demand for goods and services
from the millions of people who had been liberated from the Soviet
system. Now they would want the same standard of living as West-
erners enjoyed, the thinking went. Bond yields were expected to rise,
as their credit needs would swell. None of that happened. Instead,
over the next couple of decades, the end of the Cold War contributed
to the forces of disinflation through more free trade that resulted in
more global competition, as Chapter 3 discusses.

That latter disinflationary scenario was the one I thought would
prevail, so I stayed bullish on bonds. In fact, in my June 20, 1988 *Topical
Study*, "The Coming Shortage of Bonds," not long after the stock market crashed during October 1987, I predicted that the bond yield would
fall to 5% by 1993 and that the Dow Jones Industrial Average (DJIA)
would soar to 5000 by then.[5] I revised that on January 6, 1994, when my
new mantra became "5, 5 by '95." I predicted that the DJIA would rise
to 5000 by 1995 and that the US Treasury 10-year bond yield would
fall to 5% by then. At the time, the DJIA was 3803 and the yield was
5.84%. The yield fell to 5.00% on September 9, 1998 for the first time
since June 13, 1967 (Fig. 11). That was well below most hat sizes. The
DJIA hit a record high of 5000 for the first time on November 21, 1995
(Fig. 12).

- *1990s.* The Bond Vigilantes' heyday was the Clinton years, from 1993
through 2001. Placating them was front and center on the administration's policy agenda. Indeed, Clinton political adviser James Carville
famously said at the time, "I used to think that if there was reincarna-
tion, I wanted to come back as the President or the Pope or as a .400
baseball hitter. But now I would like to come back as the bond market. You can intimidate everybody."

From October 15, 1993 to November 7, 1994, the 10-year yield climbed from 5.19% to 8.05%, fueled by concerns about federal government spending. With some guidance from Robert Rubin, who served in the White House as the President's assistant for economic policy from January 1993 to January 1995, the Clinton administration and Congress tried to reduce the federal budget deficit. The yield dropped to 4.16% on October 5, 1998.

After the mid-1990s, the Bond Vigilantes seemed less active, because they no longer had to be as vigilant. As inflation fell, the spread between the bond yield and nominal GDP growth narrowed and fluctuated around zero.

- *2000s.* While today the US government faces the problem of persistently big federal budget deficits, it's interesting to recall that at the start of 2001, a major topic of discussion was how big the coming *surplus* in the federal budget might get. It is truly remarkable to reread Fed Chairman Alan Greenspan's congressional testimony of January 25 that year.[6] He noted that the Office of Management and Budget projected that if current policies remained in place, the total unified surplus would reach $800 billion in fiscal year 2011, including an on-budget surplus of $500 billion. In his testimony, Greenspan added that the Congressional Budget Office was likely to report even larger surpluses. He concluded: "The most recent projections, granted their tentativeness, nonetheless make clear that the highly desirable goal of paying off the federal debt is in reach before the end of the decade." He spent most of the rest of his testimony discussing whether the government might have to buy private assets with the surpluses.

  During the 2000s, the Fed kept the federal funds rate too low for too long, mostly based on fears of deflation. According to both Alan Greenspan and Ben Bernanke, there was also a global savings glut back then. As a result, bond yields remained for the most part below nominal GDP growth. Mortgage rates and mortgage lending standards were too low. The result was a huge bubble in housing, which led to the Great Recession.

- *2010s.* From 2009 through late 2015, the Fed's response to the anemic recovery following the Great Recession was to peg the federal funds rate near zero. The Fed also purchased bonds under various quantitative easing (QE) programs from November 25, 2008 through October 29, 2014, as Chapter 9 discusses. These ultra-easy monetary policies effectively buried the Bond Vigilantes, because the Fed was now the 800-pound gorilla calling the shots in the credit markets. Betting against the Fed was likely to be a very bad bet since the "buyer of last resort" had opted to be the buyer of first resort in the bond market, scooping up large quantities of bonds on a predictable regular basis. The bond yield remained consistently below the growth in nominal GDP during this period.

My Bond Vigilantes concept was tested empirically by the Federal Reserve Bank of San Francisco, as detailed in its August 2015 working paper "Bond Vigilantes and Inflation." The authors developed "a simple model where bond issuance may lead to political pressure on the government to choose a lower inflation rate." Sure enough, they found that "inflation-targeting countries with bond markets experience inflation approximately three to four percentage points lower than those without." The authors of this study explained: "Our model suggests that when a domestic bond market is created, the rich find themselves holding assets exposed to inflation, and respond by lobbying to lower inflation. Our model is stylized and not meant to be taken literally. Still, it formalizes our contention that domestic financial market developments can influence macroeconomic outcomes. By issuing debt that is not protected from inflation, the government creates a powerful political group opposed to inflation, and ends up choosing less inflation than it would otherwise."[7]

SURFING THE AGE WAVE

MY LONG-TERM BULLISH posture on bonds obviously was directly related to my view that inflation had peaked in the early 1980s and was likely to move lower for many years. Initially, I perceived that Paul Volcker would probably break the back of inflation with monetary policy. Ronald Reagan seemed to have done the same in the labor markets by firing striking air traffic controllers. More importantly, even before the end of the Cold War there were mounting pressures on US companies to move abroad because labor costs were too high in the United States. Unions were losing members as a result of what was widely called "deindustrialization." Furthermore, manufacturers were starting to use more automation to replace workers. Union members no longer received automatic cost-of-living adjustments, as their leaders had lost bargaining clout.

In addition, in the early 1980s I concluded that demographic factors might contribute to lowering inflation and bond yields. I argued that the influx of young adult Baby Boomer workers during the 1980s would reduce wage inflation. The downside was that these new entrants into the labor force were inexperienced, so their productivity might be low, but it likely would improve as they aged. I also anticipated that they would become more financially conservative over time. As they approached retirement, they might load up on bonds since older people tend to depend more on income from fixed-income assets.

This "Age Wave" scenario, as I dubbed it, panned out and had the expected effects on inflation and the bond market as the workforce aged. To monitor it, I devised a simple chart showing the Age Wave as the percentage of the labor force that is 16 to 34 years old versus the trends in both the CPI inflation rate and the 10-year Treasury yield using the five-year moving averages of monthly data (Fig. 13). The Age Wave rose from a low of 37% during April 1962 to a high of 51% during January 1981. It then dropped to a low of 35% during August 2012. Sure enough, the downward trend in the Age Wave since the start of the 1980s was matched by similar downward trends in inflation and in bond yields. My motto: "Have chart, will travel."[8]

As the Baby Boomers aged, inflows into bond mutual funds soared. From 1990 through 2016, net new inflows into bond mutual funds totaled $3.0 trillion (Fig. 14). However, with Baby Boomers living—and working—longer than previous generations, the Age Wave remains very low even as the labor force absorbs the influx of young Millennials.

AN r-STAR IS BORN

THE INFLATION PREMIUM Model posits that the nominal interest rate is equal to the real interest rate plus a premium reflecting inflation expectations. That sounds plausible in theory, but it's not particularly useful for predicting interest rates. It certainly doesn't make very much sense for short-term interest rates—particularly not for the overnight federal funds rate, since inflationary expectations over such a short period are irrelevant unless the economy is plagued by hyperinflation.

The model seems to be more useful for decomposing the nominal bond yield than predicting it. I can come up with some alternative measures of expected inflation to subtract from the nominal yield to derive the real rate. What do I do next with this information? I haven't found any practical way to use the Inflation Premium Model to forecast the bond yield. But I have to monitor it as best I can, especially on the rare occasions when Fed officials mention it in their policy deliberations.

Very often, economists approximate the real interest rate simply by subtracting the actual inflation rate from the nominal interest rate. The problem with this simple approach is that the actual inflation rate is history as far as fixed-income investors are concerned. What they are concerned about is future inflation over their investment horizon. It is the *expected* inflation rate that determines the inflation insurance premium in nominal interest rates. There are a couple of ways to measure these expectations:

- *TIPS.* The US Treasury first started issuing Treasury Inflation-Protected Securities (TIPS) on January 29, 1997 in an auction of 10-year TIPS.[9] These bonds provide protection against inflation. The principal of a TIPS increases with inflation and decreases with deflation, as measured by the CPI. When a TIPS matures, the owner is paid the adjusted principal or original principal, whichever is greater. The security pays interest twice a year at a fixed rate. The rate is applied to the adjusted principal; so, like the principal, interest payments rise with inflation and fall with deflation.

  When investors expect inflation to move higher, it stands to reason that demand for TIPS should increase, all else remaining equal, and increased demand would reduce their yields. On the other hand, higher inflationary expectations would tend to push nominal bond yields higher. So the yield spread between the nominal Treasury bond yield and the same maturity TIPS yield should reflect inflationary expectations—i.e., a widening (or conversely narrowing) spread suggests rising (falling) inflation expectations. That's the theory. In practice, all else doesn't remain equal. There are often other influences on the spread, which make theory a less useful measure of the market's inflationary expectations. Nevertheless, recognizing its limitations, I regularly monitor the yield spread between the 10-year bond and the comparable TIPS (Fig. 15 and Fig. 16).

- *Surveys.* There are also survey-based measures of inflationary expectations. The Fed's staff and policy officials often mention the Philadelphia Fed's survey of economists' inflationary expectations, which is the median forecast of the year-over-year CPI inflation rate over the next 10 years. I derive a monthly series interpolated from quarterly data starting as two quarters per year during the fourth quarter of 1979 until the fourth quarter of 1991, when the data continue with four quarters a year. The economists' expectations change slowly from quarter to quarter according to the survey data available since 1979 (Fig. 17). Since the mid-1980s, the survey data haven't diverged very much or very often from the actual "core" inflation, i.e., the CPI excluding the volatile food and energy components. Since 2003, this consensus has often been above inflationary expectations in the TIPS market (Fig. 18).

The widespread assumption seems to be that the real interest rate is relatively stable, implying that inflationary expectations account for most of the volatility in the nominal interest rate. The data for the US Treasury 10-year bond yield suggest otherwise:

- *Real monthly.* Since 1960, the bond yield clearly has been highly correlated with the CPI inflation rate on a year-over-year basis (Fig. 19). The spread between the two is one way to measure the real interest rate, but that's assuming expected inflation is usually the same as actual inflation, which may not always be a safe assumption. In any event, this measure has shown numerous significant swings along the way, with some stability for relatively short periods of time (Fig. 20).
- *Real daily.* Daily data are available for the yield on the 10-year US TIPS since 2003. Presumably, it should be a market-based measure of the real interest rate, and the yield spread between the nominal 10-year Treasury bond and its comparable TIPS should be a measure of inflationary expectations over the next 10 years at an annual rate, as noted above. In the short period of available data, the nominal 10-year Treasury bond yield has been more highly correlated with the TIPS yield than with the yield spread between the two. This suggests that the TIPS and Treasury yields share a common driver, and that it's not inflation but the other component of their yields—i.e., the real interest rate, which is hardly a stable fixture.

Presumably, the real interest rate may also be indirectly affected by inflation. Changes in public-sector economic policies and private-sector behavior caused by inflation can impact the real rate. Had enough? Sorry, but there's more.

The Inflation Premium Model assumed even greater importance in the fall of 2015. The minutes of the October Federal Open Market Committee (FOMC) meeting began with a very dense section titled "Equilibrium Real Interest Rates."[10] It focused on the concept of r-star (r*), which is the "neutral" or "natural" real interest rate. This was defined in the minutes as "the level of the real short-term interest rate that, if obtained currently, would result in the economy operating at full employment or, in some simple models of the economy, at full employment and price stability." The minutes reported that a number of FOMC participants believed that "the longer-run downward trend in real interest rates suggested that short-run r* would likely remain below levels that were normal during previous business cycle expansions, and that the longer-run normal level to which the nominal federal funds rate might be . . . consistent . . . with maximum employment and 2 percent inflation . . . would likely be lower than was the case in previous decades."

In theory, the nominal interest rate is r* plus inflation expectations. Fed officials were arguing that the "normal" nominal federal funds rate should be lower than in the past, because they believed that various cyclical and secular forces were depressing r*. So, for example, in a situation where r* is zero, if expected inflation is 2%, then the nominal federal funds rate should be 2% as well, rather than 3% if r* were 1%.

Increasingly, Fed officials used the concept as an excuse for why their policies hadn't worked as well as they'd expected. For example, in a December 2, 2015 speech, Federal Reserve Chair Janet Yellen explained: "Had the neutral rate been running closer to the levels that are thought to have prevailed prior to the financial crisis, current monetary policy settings would have been expected to foster a very rapid economic expansion, with inflation likely rising significantly above our 2 percent objective." She dedicated her closing remarks to r*, stating: "The marked decline in the neutral federal funds rate after the crisis may be partially attributable to a range of persistent economic headwinds that have weighed on aggregate demand. . . . As the restraint from these headwinds further abates, I anticipate that the neutral federal funds rate will gradually move higher over time."[11]

Yellen did assign a high degree of uncertainty to that expectation. But her speech was the lead-in to signal December's first rate hike of the economic expansion that followed the Great Recession, so she obviously wasn't too concerned about it.

The turning point for many Fed officials seemed to be the release of an August 15, 2016 *Economic Letter* by President John Williams of the Federal Reserve Bank of San Francisco. It was titled "Monetary Policy in a Low R-star World." Williams warned: "Economics rarely has the benefit of a crystal ball. But in this case, we are seeing the future now and have the opportunity to prepare for the challenges related to persistently low natural real rates of interest. Thoroughly reviewing the key aspects of inflation targeting is certainly necessary, and could go a long way towards mitigating the obstructions posed by low r-star. But that is where monetary policy meets the boundaries of its influence."[12]

The fact that "the neutral rate is likely to remain low for some time" was one of five key reasons that the Fed should hold off on raising rates, according to Fed Governor Lael Brainard in a September 12, 2016 speech, which seems to have heavily influenced the decision to do so at the September and November FOMC meetings. She stated: "Several econometric models and estimates from market participants suggest the current real neutral rate is at or close to zero, and any increase is likely to be shallow and slow. These estimates imply that it may require a relatively more modest adjustment in the policy rate to return to neutral over time than previously anticipated."[13]

Federal Reserve Board Vice Chairman Stanley Fischer dedicated his October 5, 2016 speech, "Low Interest Rates," to r* and shared his anxieties on the subject.[14] First on his worry list was that with low r*, "the economy is more likely to fall into the liquidity trap" and "becomes more vulnerable to adverse shocks that might render conventional monetary policy ineffective." Second, "it may hurt financial stability by causing investors to reach for yield, and some financial institutions will find it harder to be profitable." Third, "a decline in longer-run equilibrium real rates . . . could be yet another indication that the economy's growth potential may have dimmed considerably." In his speech, Fischer gave a brief history of the origin of r*:

> Knut Wicksell, the great Swedish economist, emphasized the concept of an equilibrium level of interest rates in his influential work. In his 1898 book, *Interest and Prices*, he wrote that "there is a certain level of the average rate of interest which is such that the general level of prices has no tendency to move either upwards or downwards." In modern language, this level of the interest rate is usually referred to as the natural rate of interest. Applying Wicksell's insights to the

circumstances we face today, the fact that both inflation and interest rates have remained very low over the past several years suggests
that our current interest rate environment may well reflect, at least in
part, a very low level of the natural rate of interest.

(I can't help but be reminded here of the following quote from John
Maynard Keynes: "Practical men who believe themselves to be quite
exempt from any intellectual influence, are usually the slaves of some
defunct economist. Madmen in authority, who hear voices in the air, are
distilling their frenzy from some academic scribbler of a few years back."
In this case, Fischer named the long defunct economist who still influenced his thinking in 2017. Of course, Keynes is now part of that club of
defunct economists, and remains very influential too.)

Does r* have any practical significance? In the past, there was a presumption that it is reasonably stable, yet as I note above, I can't find a way
to measure it that results in a reasonably stable metric. More importantly,
Fed officials have acknowledged that it might have been lower than they
expected following the Great Recession.

Furthermore, the October 2015 FOMC minutes cited earlier refer to
r* as a real "short-term" interest rate. How would it be calculated? It makes
no sense to me to subtract longer-run inflation expectations from the nominal federal funds rate, which is an overnight rate (Fig. 21). It makes more
sense to subtract the 10-year inflation expectations derived from the survey
of economists from the 10-year bond yield (Fig. 22). If this is a measure of
r*, then it certainly isn't stable: it has been trending downward in a volatile
fashion since the early 1980s, from 8% to about zero by 2015.

While Fed officials have yet to provide a consistent way to measure r*,
there's consensus on a theoretical level that r* has fallen to zero during the
period of low interest rates. Theories about why abound. Many Fed officials
blamed the drop in r* down to zero on the weak performance of productivity. They also blamed it on demographic factors, including the aging of the
Baby Boomers. Another theory relates to the Bernanke/Greenspan global
savings glut supposition that there aren't enough investment opportunities
to sop up the surplus of savings around the world. This is a very Keynesian
notion, and the solution to the problem is more fiscal spending, since monetary policy has already been ultra-easy. Both Larry Summers' secular stagnation thesis and the New Normal view share this idea, i.e., that monetary
stimulus has done its part, so it's time for more fiscal stimulus.

None of the official and academic macroeconomists have seriously considered what might be the real problem: too much government and policy intervention are constraining the economy's potential! Could it be that taxes have been too high? Could it be that there have been too many regulations on business? Could it be that too many unconventional monetary policy tools have become all too conventional? I think so. Government doesn't need to do more in the way of fiscal stimulus; it just needs to step out of the way.

Fed officials concluded that unless r* moved higher (and who would know when it did, since it's just an abstract, not a concretely measurable, concept?), they might not have to increase the nominal federal funds rate much to normalize monetary policy. I looked at the same relationship between the real rate and the nominal federal funds rate and saw not a justification for continuing the Fed's ultra-easy monetary policies but an indictment of them, wondering whether these unusual policies had contributed to an unusually low r* in the first place. Looking to r* for guidance on the course of monetary policy, therefore, is like a dog chasing its tail.

YIELD CURVE'S SLIPPERY SLOPE

THE YIELD CURVE Model is more fun and potentially more useful (and profitable) than the Inflation Premium Model. It posits that bond yields are determined by expectations for short-term interest rates over the maturity of the bond. These expectations are imbedded in the "term structure of interest rates," as reflected in the shape of the yield curve.

The yield curve is simply a table showing the yield on various-maturity US Treasuries at any point in time. When shown as a chart at a point in time, it usually connects the market yields of the three-month, six-month, and 12-month Treasury bills, the two-year and five-year notes, and the 10-year and 30-year bonds at that time. The so-called "short end" of the yield curve tends to be very sensitive to actual and expected short-term changes in the federal funds rate. The "long end" of the curve can be more or less sensitive to such changes, depending on longer-term expectations for the federal funds rate.

The slope of the yield curve reflects the "term structure" of interest rates. Think of the 10-year yield as reflecting the current one-year bill rate and expectations for that rate over the next nine years. The one-year bill rate reflects the current six-month bill rate and expectations for the six-month bill rate six months from now. Of course, there are plenty of other combinations of shorter-term rates and expectations about them that are reflected in longer-term rates.

Over time, the overall slope of the yield curve is typically measured as the difference between the 10-year yield and the federal funds rate (Fig. 23 and Fig. 24). As I observe in Chapter 5, this spread is one of the components of the Index of Leading Economic Indicators (LEI). Let's look at this business cycle indicator in the context of forecasting the interest-rate cycle:

- *An ascending yield curve* indicates that investors expect short-term interest rates to rise over time; they demand higher rates for tying their money up longer with long-maturing bonds. So a positive yield curve spread implies market expectations of rising interest rates.

- *A flat yield curve* suggests that investors expect short-term rates to remain stable for the future. For example, today's six-month Treasury bill rate should be the same as today's three-month Treasury bill rate if the latter is expected to be unchanged three months from now, and so on all along the maturity spectrum of the yield curve. At times, the Fed has raised the federal funds rate sharply, yet bond yields didn't rise as much as rates on bills and notes. Such flattening of the yield curve tended to happen when investors expected that the tightening of monetary policy was likely to cause a recession and bring down inflation.

- *An "inverted" yield curve* has a downward slope, suggesting that investors are scrambling to lock in long-term yields before they fall. The yield curve spread is negative. This typically happens when short-term rates soar above bond yields as the Fed tightens monetary policy to fight inflation. An inverted yield curve suggests that investors believe this will cause a recession, with short-term interest rates heading back down below bond yields. They expect locked-in yields to exceed the short-term interest rates during most of the investment horizon. The yield curve might then invert, with short-term rates rising above long-term rates as investors become more convinced that rising short-term rates will cause an economic downturn, prompting the Fed to yank the federal funds rate back down. Then, short-term rates will drop back below long-term rates, and the yield curve once again will signal better economic times ahead.

In the years prior to my career, the yield curve was a very useful tool for those forecasting the business cycle. During the 1960s and 1970s, the financial markets were highly regulated. For example, the Fed's Regulation Q allowed the central bank to set ceilings on interest rates paid on deposits by commercial banks and by S&Ls. When the Fed raised the federal funds rate to slow the economy and bring down inflation, it all happened rapidly once money-market interest rates rose above the Regulation Q ceilings. That's because money poured out of deposits and into money-market instruments.

The process is called "disintermediation," as I note in previous chapters. Its consequence is a credit crunch, which Kaufman well understood. Financial intermediaries facing deposit outflows would stop extending credit to consumers, homebuyers, and businesses. Kaufman believed that these credit crunches and the busts they caused were necessary from time to time to eliminate the financial excesses that always occur during booms.

From that perspective, Regulation Q was a very useful and effective way for the Fed to put an end to booms. However, banks hated disintermediation and the public hated credit crunches, so political pressure led to a wave of financial market deregulation. Regulation Q deposit ceilings were phased out from 1981 to 1986 by the Depository Institutions Deregulation and Monetary Control Act of 1980, as Chapters 1 and 8 discuss.

Nevertheless, the yield curve continued to work as a business-cycle indicator. The spread between the 10-year Treasury bond yield and the federal funds rate has been one of the components of the LEI since 1996.[15] For many years, the index reflected the month-to-month changes in the spread. So if the spread widened, that would contribute positively to the LEI, pulling the index higher, and if it narrowed, the spread's contribution would be negative, pulling the index lower. During 2005, the spread's contribution was changed to put more weight on whether it was positive or negative. That way, the spread contributes positively (negatively) to LEI only when it is itself positive (negative), not when it rises (falls).[16] The Conference Board, which compiles the LEI every month, cumulates the spread month by month.

Since the Great Recession of 2008, the Fed and other central banks have played a much bigger role in influencing bond yields. They've always had a big impact on the long end of the yield curve since they have a big influence on expectations about the course of short-term rates. What changed is that they started buying bonds often and in size through their various QE programs.

The credit markets clearly are very efficient and competitive. They are free markets and remain less regulated now than they were in the 1960s and 1970s. However, the central banks (a.k.a. "central monetary planners") have become the biggest buyers in the bond market in recent years. In other words, the free markets for credit are hardly free of the influence of the central banks. This means that the central banks may be distorting the viability of the yield curve as a business-cycle indicator.

Nevertheless, if and when the yield curve inverts again, it will still get my attention as a warning signal that something isn't right with the economy. Pessimistically inclined prognosticators undoubtedly will warn that a recession is imminent.

In this Yield Curve Model, inflation matters a great deal to markets because it matters to the central bank. Investors have learned to anticipate how the Fed's inflationary expectations might drive short-term interest rates, and to determine yields on bonds accordingly. So the measure of inflationary expectations deduced from the yield spread between the Treasury bond and the TIPS might very well reflect not only the expectations of borrowers and lenders but also their assessment of the expectations and the likely response of Fed officials! The data are very supportive of these relationships among inflation, the Fed policy cycle, and the bond yield.

The Fed policy cycle is easy to depict. Tightening occurs from a cyclical trough to a cyclical peak in the federal funds rate. Easing occurs between the peaks and the troughs. Not surprisingly, since 1960, tightening has occurred during periods of rising inflation, while easing has occurred during periods of falling inflation or relatively low and stable inflation (Fig. 25). Sure enough, the yield curve spread tends to widen from its negative trough to its positive peak during the early stage of monetary easing (Fig. 26). The yield curve spread tends to peak during the late stage of monetary easing. When monetary tightening begins, the spread falls, turning less positive and then going negative during the late stage of tightening.

The interest-rate forecasting models discussed above aren't mutually exclusive. All three are based on the premise that inflation is the main driver of interest rates; the flow of funds is a sideshow. Here's how they differ:

- *The Bond Vigilantes Model* relates the bond yield to the growth rate in nominal GDP, which reflects inflation as well as the real growth of the economy. The divergence between the nominal growth rate and the bond yield may very well be influenced by the inflationary expectations of investors as well as by their expectations for monetary policy.

• *The Inflation Premium Model* is based on the inflationary expectations of investors. In my opinion, it's not as useful to view the bond yield as some vague hypothetical real rate plus investors' inflation expectations, unless that mumbo jumbo is influencing Fed policymaking.

• *The Yield Curve Model* is based on investors' expectations of how the Fed will respond to inflation. It is more practical for predicting interest rates than is the Inflation Premium Model. It makes sense that the federal funds rate depends mostly on the Fed's inflation outlook, and that all the other yields to the right of this rate on the yield curve are determined by investors' expectations for the Fed policy cycle.

GLUT RIDDEN

KAUFMAN'S FLOW-OF-FUNDS APPROACH to predicting, or at least to explaining, the bond yield made a comeback of sorts in early 2005. The comeback started on February 16 of that year when Fed Chairman Alan Greenspan presented his famous "conundrum" testimony during his semiannual report on monetary policy to Congress. Greenspan said he was puzzled that bond yields were falling while the Fed was raising the federal funds rate:

> This development contrasts with most experience, which suggests that, other things being equal, increasing short-term interest rates are normally accompanied by a rise in longer-term yields. The simple mathematics of the yield curve governs the relationship between short- and long-term interest rates. Ten-year yields, for example, can be thought of as an average of ten consecutive one-year forward rates. A rise in the first-year forward rate, which correlates closely with the federal funds rate, would increase the yield on ten-year U.S. Treasury notes even if the more-distant forward rates remain unchanged. Historically, though, even these distant forward rates have tended to rise in association with monetary policy tightening.[17]

On March 10, 2005, Fed Governor Ben Bernanke sought to solve the puzzle that Greenspan had presented just three weeks earlier. Bernanke did so in a speech titled "The Global Savings Glut and the U.S. Current Account Deficit."[18] Bernanke argued that the US bond market during the 2000s was increasingly driven by countries outside of the United States. In his narrative, there was a "global savings glut." The United States was running large trade deficits with the rest of the world, and increasingly with emerging market economies such as China. Chinese and other foreign investors reciprocated by buying our bonds rather than our companies' exported goods, which increasingly were manufactured overseas.

In an April 1, 2015 blog post, Bernanke continued to promote this thesis:

> Some years ago I discussed the macroeconomic implications of global flows of saving and investment under the rubric of the "global savings glut". My conclusion was that a global excess of desired saving over desired investment, emanating in large part from China and other Asian emerging market economies and oil producers like Saudi Arabia, was a major reason for low global interest rates. I argued that the flow of global saving into the United States helped to explain the "conundrum" (to use Alan Greenspan's term) of persistently low longer-term interest rates in the mid-2000's while the Fed was raising short-term rates. Strong capital inflows also pushed up the value of the dollar and helped create the very large U.S. trade deficit of the time, nearly 6 percent of U.S. gross domestic product in 2006.[19]

The global savings glut thesis explained Greenspan's conundrum and allowed both Greenspan and Bernanke to blame foreign investors for the US housing bubble. Foreigners purchased lots of mortgage-backed bonds, which kept credit conditions too loose in the housing market, despite the Fed's attempts to tighten credit conditions.

There are plenty of critics of the global savings glut hypothesis. They blame the Fed for keeping interest rates too low for too long, then raising them too slowly and predictably. The federal funds rate was lowered from 6.50% on May 16, 2000 to 1.00% on June 25, 2003, where it stayed for the next year. A June 30, 2004 rate hike of 25 basis points was followed by the same at each of the next 16 FOMC meetings.

Keep in mind that the Fed was concerned about deflation at the time (as evidenced by Bernanke's famous November 21, 2002 speech on the subject, "Deflation: Making Sure 'It' Doesn't Happen Here"[20]). In addition, the unsettling bursting of the tech bubble at the beginning of the decade and the terrorist attacks of September 11, 2001 likely contributed to the Fed's cautious policy stance. This stance, the critics contend, resulted in excessive credit demands in the United States that were readily met as investors reached for yield.

I tend to agree with the critics, though I also think that there may be some validity to the glut view. After all, in an increasingly globalized world, external forces affect the US credit market too. The Fed isn't totally to blame for creating the credit conditions that led to the housing boom and subsequent bust.

UNCONVENTIONAL GLOBAL NORM

I AM OFTEN asked what happened to the Bond Vigilantes. Governments around the world continue to run large budget deficits. Why aren't the Bond Vigilantes protesting the ongoing fiscal excesses around the world? They did their job during the 1980s and early 1990s, but when inflation continued to moderate after that, they perceived inflation as less of a threat to their future investment returns. So understandably, the Vigilantes became less vigilant.

They reappeared briefly when the bond yield rose from a low of 2.08% on December 18, 2008 to a high of 4.01% on April 5, 2010. According to a May 29, 2009 *Wall Street Journal* article titled "The Bond Vigilantes":

> They're back. We refer to the global investors once known as the bond vigilantes, who demanded higher Treasury bond yields from the late 1970s through the 1990s whenever inflation fears popped up, and as a result disciplined U.S. policy makers. The vigilantes vanished earlier this decade amid the credit mania, but they appear to be returning with a vengeance now that Congress and the Federal Reserve have flooded the world with dollars to beat the recession.

The *Journal* further opined:

> The Obama Administration's epic spending spree means the Treasury will have to float trillions of dollars in new debt in the next two or three years alone. Meanwhile, the Fed has gone beyond cutting rates to directly purchasing such financial assets as mortgage-backed securities, as well as directly monetizing federal debt by buying Treasurys for the first time in half a century. No wonder the Chinese and other dollar asset holders are nervous. They wonder—as do we—whether the unspoken Beltway strategy is to pay off this debt by inflating away its value.[21]

That was the Bond Vigilantes' last hurrah for a while.[22] Following the Great Recession of 2008, they were essentially buried by the central bankers, who lowered their countries' official interest rates to zero and then purchased lots of bonds through their various QE programs.

The Fed and the other major central banks announced that their goal was to bring bond yields down to encourage more risk-taking and borrowing by consumers and businesses. As the previous chapter mentions, in a November 4, 2010 *Washington Post* article, Fed Chairman Ben Bernanke wrote that the Fed had responded to the financial crisis of 2008 by lowering the federal funds rate to zero and purchasing "more than a trillion dollars' worth of Treasury securities and US-backed mortgage-related securities, which helped reduce longer-term interest rates, such as those for mortgages and corporate bonds." The purchase program was the first round of the Fed's quantitative easing, or QE1. In this article, Bernanke stated that a second round (QE2), which had been announced the day before his article was published, would entail purchasing an additional $600 billion of long-term Treasury securities by mid-2011.[23]

Bernanke claimed that "lower mortgage rates will make housing more affordable and allow more homeowners to refinance. Lower corporate bond rates will encourage investment. And higher stock prices will boost consumer wealth and help increase confidence, which can also spur spending. Increased spending will lead to higher incomes and profits that, in a virtuous circle, will further support economic expansion."

What was billed as "unconventional" monetary policies became more conventional as the Fed unveiled yet a third round of purchases

(QE3).[24] On September 13, 2012, the Fed announced a program to purchase $40 billion per month in mortgage securities. Unlike the previous two programs, QE3 was open-ended with no set termination date. The program was expanded on December 12 to include $45 billion in Treasuries (Fig. 27 and Fig. 28).

The bond yield fell from 3.11% at the start of QE1 to 2.27% by the end of QE3. However, along the way, it perversely tended to rise more during the QE programs, while falling in between them (Fig. 29). Interestingly, the bullish performance of the S&P 500 tended to be highly correlated with the Fed's rising holdings of securities during the QE period (Fig. 30).

The Bond Vigilantes weren't completely dead and buried by the Fed's actions. They showed up during the Greek crisis of 2010. To understand what happened then, we first need to step back about 20 years.

During the 1990s, the European economies were suffering from what was widely described as "Eurosclerosis." Economic growth was anemic in most of the major European economies. The cure was expected to be the creation of the Eurozone, the monetary unification of the region's economies. (There are currently 19 member states.) The euro was introduced on January 1, 1999. The immediate impact of the euro was to narrow the spreads between government yields in the region. They all converged down toward the German yield (Fig. 31). Investors seemed to believe that monetary unification had reduced the riskiness of government debt issued by the monetary union's so-called peripheral countries, i.e., Portugal, Ireland, Italy, Greece, and Spain (the "PIIGS").

That assumption was discredited (literally) when Greece first threatened to default in 2010. At the time, I explained to our accounts, "With the benefit of hindsight, it is now easy to see that the Eurozone had allowed Greek taxi drivers to buy spacious Mercedes Benz sedans with money borrowed from Deutsche Bank at German rates." The 10-year government bond yield of Greece soared to peak at 39.85% on March 8, 2012 (Fig. 32). The crisis quickly turned into a contagion affecting all five of the PIIGS. The bond yields of Italy and Spain peaked at 6.61% and 7.61%, respectively, during July 24, 2012 (Fig. 33).

In response to the crisis, the European Central Bank (ECB) lowered its official deposit rate for bank reserves from 0.75% on November 8, 2011 to zero on July 11, 2012 in three steps, following the lead of the Fed, which had dropped the federal funds rate to zero on December 16, 2008. As I note in the previous chapter, ECB President Mario Draghi on July 26, 2012 uttered the following magic words: "Within our mandate, the ECB is ready to do whatever it takes to preserve the euro. And believe me, it will be enough."[25] Remarkably, that's all it took to bring the PIIGS yields down dramatically from their peaks during the summer of 2012. The ECB took no announced follow-up actions until mid-2014.

My guess is that Draghi was just as amazed by the power of his speech as I (and anyone else who was paying attention). I was puzzled by the power of Draghi's words and made some inquiries. One of my accounts in London told me he had heard rumors that the ECB followed up by asking some of the big banks in the Eurozone to step up their bond buying. I contacted a few knowledgeable friends in the European bond market. They had heard the rumor but could not confirm that the ECB had verbally intervened in the bond market.

Nevertheless, the region's economy remained moribund, and bank loans stayed dead in the water. The ECB's Governing Council proceeded to implement a number of extraordinarily unconventional measures to revive lending and growth. On June 5, 2014, the official interest rate on bank deposits at the ECB was lowered to –0.10%. It was lowered again to –0.20% on September 4, 2014 and to –0.30% on December 3, 2015 (Fig. 34). A QE program was implemented on January 22, 2015 and expanded to include corporate bond purchases starting June 1, 2016 (Fig. 35).[26] The German 10-year government bond yield dropped below zero for the first time ever on June 15, 2016.

As dramatic as the ECB's moves were, another central bank was really the pioneer in the realm of unconventional ultra-easy monetary policy: the Bank of Japan (BOJ). Japan's central bank responded to the bursting of the country's stock market and real estate bubbles of the late 1980s by lowering interest rates dramatically during the 1990s. The official rate was lowered from 8.56% on March 29, 1991 to 0.43% on October 6, 1995. It was pegged around that rate until it was lowered during 1998 and then set to zero on March 5, 1999 (Fig. 36). From 2001 to 2005 and again from 2011 to 2012, the BOJ implemented a couple of relatively small QE programs that boosted reserve balances held at the central bank by 69% and 28%, respectively (Fig. 37).

The BOJ's real shock-and-awe show started after "Abenomics" was implemented. This package of economic policies—proposed by Shinzō Abe, who was running for prime minister of Japan in late 2012—included more monetary easing as one of the program's "three arrows."

Abe succeeded in replacing the governor of the BOJ on March 20, 2013 with Haruhiko Kuroda, who was gung-ho to provide unconventional ultra-easy monetary policies. In short order, Kuroda launched a quantitative and qualitative easing (QQE) program on April 4, 2013. It was followed by an expanded and extended version (QQEE). On January 29, 2016, the BOJ went negative, cutting the official central bank rate to −0.10%.

It all led to a 38% plunge in the yen from late 2012 through mid-2015 (Fig. 38). In theory, that should have boosted exports and real GDP growth. It should also have lifted inflation above zero and closer to the BOJ's target of 2.0%. The results were disappointing.

Meanwhile, the Fed terminated QE3 on October 31, 2014. Bond investors started to fret that the long-term bull market was over for them. I argued that the Fed was likely to move very slowly in normalizing monetary policy. I also observed that US bonds had become increasingly globalized as foreign investors facing negative interest rates in the Eurozone and in Japan reached for yield in the United States.

After terminating the QE program, the FOMC rolled over maturing securities on its balance sheet so that the total of these assets remained around $4.3 trillion. The committee moved to gradually normalize monetary policy by raising the federal funds rate target range from 0.00%–0.25% to 0.25%–0.50% at the end of 2015 and again at the end of 2016 to 0.50%–0.75%. There were two more rate hikes in early 2017 that brought the range up to 1.00%–1.25%. On September 9, 2017, the FOMC announced that the Fed would gradually pare down its balance sheet as securities matured. The following month, the Fed started to do so.

The ECB and the BOJ were widely expected to start normalizing their monetary policies in 2018, also in a very gradual fashion. Nevertheless, the line had been crossed between the conventional and the unconventional approach to running monetary policy. The central monetary planners had devised new tools, including QE, ZIRP (zero-interest-rate policies), and NIRP (negative-interest-rate policies).

The US Treasury 10-year bond yield fell to a record low of 1.37% on July 8, 2016. That same day, the comparable Japanese and German bond yields were −0.27% and −0.19% (Fig. 39). That might have marked the end of the great bull market in bonds, which had started on September 30, 1981, near the beginning of my career on Wall Street. It was a great ride, for sure. Too bad I didn't have the money to load up on bonds back then.

The great bond bull market may be over, though I wouldn't rule out even lower yields in coming years. A bear market is conceivable if inflation makes a comeback, though that's not the most likely outlook, in my opinion. More likely is that bond yields will meander for a prolonged period.

HIGH YIELD, HIGH RISK

DURING MY CAREER, I haven't spent much time predicting corporate bond yields. However, I do follow the yield spreads between corporate bonds and the US Treasury bond closely, because they tend to be very good indicators of financial and economic distress. More specifically, I track the yield spread using the Bank of America Merrill Lynch A-BBB corporate bond yield composite (Fig. 40 and Fig. 41). That's still investment grade, but it has a higher yield than the top-rated AAA corporate bond composite. I also monitor the yield spread using noninvestment-grade bonds, which are rated accordingly and called "high-yield bonds" or "junk bonds."

The corporate yield spread is extremely cyclical. It widens dramatically during recessions as higher-yielding bonds earn their "junk" nickname. During economic downturns, credit quality deteriorates, especially for noninvestment-grade bonds. During economic recoveries, the spread tends to narrow rapidly and to continue doing so during economic expansions. In other words, credit quality is extremely procyclical.

The corporate spread isn't included in the LEI, as is the yield-curve spread. Perhaps it should be. When investors in the bond market sense that trouble is coming, they tend to sell their lower-quality bonds and move into investment-grade bonds. When they get really scared, they pile into US Treasuries. The spread can suddenly spike higher if junk bond yields soar at the same time as the rush for safety pushes Treasury yields lower.

The spread widens dramatically during recessions because the most popular junk bonds during the preceding good times tend to have lots of sellers with few buyers. During good times, there's often at least one relatively risky industry that attracts bond investors. Lots of demand for the industry's bonds creates a big supply of them, suddenly flooding into the market with a big "for sale" sign.

During the late 1990s, plenty of junk bonds were issued by telecommunications hardware companies. They were for sale when the tech bubble burst. During the housing boom of the 2000s, lots of junky asset-backed securities were issued and snapped up by investors. Some of them were layered into credit derivative products that turned totally illiquid when the housing boom turned into a bust. During 2008, there were lots of sellers and few buyers for these products, and the rush out of corporate bonds was widespread as well. When oil prices plunged during the second half of 2014 through early 2015, there were more sellers than buyers of bonds issued by energy companies, requiring bond prices to drop in order to clear the market; high-yield bonds suddenly had high yields.

Not surprisingly, the high-yield spread is highly correlated with other procyclical measures such as the S&P 500's VIX, which is a measure of stock market volatility (Fig. 42). It is also highly inversely correlated with the Weekly Leading Index compiled by the Economic Cycle Research Institute (ECRI), suggesting that it is one of the major components of this proprietary index, i.e., an ingredient of the ECRI's secret sauce (Fig. 43).

DEFICITS AND HELICOPTER MONEY

I STARTED THIS chapter by discussing my early career doubts about using a Kaufmanesque flow-of-funds approach to forecasting bond yields. There are simply too many moving parts in the demand and supply of credit. While I am a big fan of microeconomics, a macroeconomic approach to forecasting bond yields has worked better for me.

Over time, I became more convinced of this as I saw so many bearish forecasts for bonds that were based on a pessimistic view of the federal budget deficit turn out to be so wrong. During the 1970s through the 1990s, the widening federal deficit was a big concern. More supply of government bonds implied higher bond yields. In addition, most economists agreed that the widening federal deficit was inflationary so it had to be bearish for bonds. I wasn't as concerned. On the contrary, I observed that some of the best bond rallies occurred when the federal deficit was widening (Fig. 44 and Fig. 45). Of course, that happened most often when the economy was falling into a recession, as tax revenues fell while so-called countercyclical government spending tended to rise.

During recessions, private credit demands weaken. The stock market falls. Investors seek the safety of US Treasury bonds. More importantly, the Fed responds to recessions by lowering short-term rates, which makes bonds even more attractive. When the federal funds rate fell to zero in 2008, the

Fed implemented a series of QE programs, buying lots of bonds. From March 2009 through October 2014, the Fed purchased $3.64 trillion in US Treasuries, financing 62.5% of the federal deficit over that period.

While Fed officials have insisted that their QE programs weren't the same as monetizing the debt, what else can you call a bond-buying program other than an exchange of debt for money? Fortunately, all the liquidity they pumped into the financial markets didn't revive price inflation. As it turns out, powerful secular forces have kept a lid on inflation, as I discuss in Chapter 4.

If inflation ever makes a comeback, imagine the impact on the federal deficit. In this scenario, the Fed presumably would have to raise interest rates. Bond yields could soar, especially since so many investors have piled into bonds as they reached for yield when money-market rates were pegged close to zero by the Fed. Net interest paid by the federal government could swell and bloat the deficit, which would put more upward pressure on interest rates.

A second scenario would be a continuation of secular stagnation with subpar economic growth and subdued inflation. That would be more of the same for the foreseeable future. However, the economy would be vulnerable to stalling into a recession. In this third recessionary scenario, the Fed might work with Congress to stimulate the economy with so-called "helicopter money."

The term comes from economist Milton Friedman. In *The Optimum Quantity of Money* (1969), Friedman wrote, "Let us suppose now that one day a helicopter flies over this community and drops an additional $1,000 in bills from the sky, which is, of course, hastily collected by members of the community. Let us suppose further that everyone is convinced that this is a unique event which will never be repeated."

Friedman focused on the effects of monetary policy on inflation and the costs of holding money, rather than making an actual policy proposal. However, the idea has caught on with a few economists as a serious monetary policy instrument of last resort. In their view, helicopter money would best boost aggregate demand in a "liquidity trap" situation when central banks have reached the so-called "zero lower bound" and no other stimulus has worked.

In an April 11, 2016 blog post, Ben Bernanke acknowledged that "the benefits of low rates may erode over time, while the costs are likely to increase. Consequently, at some point monetary policy faces diminishing returns."[27] When that happens, he implied, the central banks should get the choppers ready. Bernanke noted that Friedman defined "helicopter money" as money-financed (as opposed to debt-financed) tax cuts.

To me, that sounds like QE earmarked to fund a specific variety of fiscal stimulus, namely tax cuts. There's no reason why the targeted QE program couldn't be used to finance infrastructure spending instead of, or in addition to, the tax cuts. If the financial statements of the US Treasury and the Fed are consolidated, it simply means that the government is self-financing either or both varieties of fiscal stimulus by printing so-called "high-powered money"—which shows up on the Fed's balance sheet as bank reserves on the liabilities side and as the Treasury's IOUs on the assets side.

In his blog post, Bernanke confirmed this point: "[A] 'helicopter drop' of money is an expansionary fiscal policy—an increase in public spending or a tax cut—financed by a permanent increase in the money stock. To get away from the fanciful imagery, for the rest of this post I will call such a policy a Money-Financed Fiscal Program, or MFFP." (He has always loved acronyms!) Bernanke concluded his blog post as follows:

> Money-financed fiscal programs (MFFPs), known colloquially as helicopter drops, are very unlikely to be needed in the United States in the foreseeable future. They also present a number of practical challenges of implementation, including integrating them into operational monetary frameworks and assuring appropriate governance and coordination between the legislature and the central bank. However, under certain extreme circumstances—sharply deficient aggregate demand, exhausted monetary policy, and unwillingness of the legislature to use debt-financed fiscal policies—such programs may be the best available alternative. It would be premature to rule them out.

GO WITH THE FLOWS

HENRY KAUFMAN WAS renowned for his detailed quarterly flow-of-funds analyses and forecasts, which he used to forecast interest rates, as I noted at the beginning of this chapter. That process seemed to work brilliantly during the 1970s. However, I think his success back then had more to do with his prescient insight that the deregulation of financial markets and mounting federal deficits would drive inflation higher—which is what happened. I don't recall that he predicted the two OPEC oil price shocks, but they certainly supported his view that the financial and economic systems were biased toward rising inflation. The important point is that he was correctly bearish on bonds.

Even though I rejected Kaufman's flow-of-funds approach to forecasting interest rates early in my career because it didn't seem worth all the effort it took, I do believe that anyone seriously interested in predicting financial markets and the economy should take a deep dive into the Fed's *Financial Accounts of the United States*. The quarterly database is a treasure trove of very valuable information on the capital markets, showing supply and demand by sectors for all financial instruments, including money-market securities, loans, bonds, mortgages, and equities.[28]

While tracking the flows in the credit markets may not be the best way to predict interest rates, it can be very helpful for seeing supply and demand trends in the financial markets, and thus for recognizing where credit market excesses might be occurring, as I demonstrate in Chapter 8, which focuses on the financial crisis of 2008. Likewise, tracking the flow of funds in the corporate equity market helps immensely in understanding which groups of buyers and sellers are driving trends in stock prices, as I show in Chapter 15.

Several series in the *Financial Accounts of the United States* provided early warnings about the speculative extravaganza in the housing market before the housing bubble burst in 2007. They included the rapidly increasing quarterly series tracking home mortgages and home equity loans, as well as corporate bonds and commercial paper issued by asset-backed security issuers. The problem is that no one at the Fed paid much, if any, attention to them, even though the data are compiled by the Fed! I know it may be hard to believe, but the reality is that the Fed's economists don't spend much time analyzing credit trends in the economy. I've skimmed through the titles of all the working papers posted by the Fed's staff since 2005 on the Fed's website and found that very few of them seem to be about credit issues, and even fewer about credit derivatives.

Interestingly, the Fed's data lend some support to the global savings glut argument made by both Alan Greenspan and Ben Bernanke after the fact to explain—and to blame foreign investors for financing—the housing bubble that preceded the bust. From 2004 through 2007, foreign investors purchased $751 billion of US agency and GSE-backed securities (Fig. 46). Over this same period, they purchased $928 billion in US Treasury bonds (Fig. 47). They thus helped to keep bond yields and mortgage rates down even as the Fed raised the federal funds rate at a "measured pace."

Throughout my career, there have been occasional flow-of-funds data scares, prompting alarmists to predict dire consequences that haven't materialized, at least so far. Rising debt-to-income ratios should alert us to possible debt-financed excesses in the economy. Sometimes they do, and sometimes they don't. The economy's total debt at the end of 2016 was a record $65.9 trillion, or 354% of GDP, just below the record high of 379% during the third quarter of 2009 (Fig. 48 and Fig. 49). Total non-financial debt of households, business, and government reached a record $47.2 trillion, or a record 254% of GDP, at the same time (Fig. 50 and Fig. 51). There was lots of chatter about "deleveraging" following the financial crisis of 2008. It's hard to see it in these numbers, though the ratio of financial-sector debt to GDP fell from a record high of 123% during the third quarter of 2008 to 84% at the end of 2016.

The financial crisis of 2008 should have stimulated deleveraging by not just financial services companies but also nonfinancial ones. However, historically low interest rates allowed households and businesses to refinance their debts and to carry more debt. So, for example, while household debt rose to a record $12.6 trillion during the fourth quarter of 2016, the household debt-servicing burden remained at an historical low (Fig. 52 and Fig. 53).

So what do all the available data we have today tell us about bond markets in the predictable future? We can safely predict that bond yields will either rise, fall, or stay the same. That covers all the possibilities. As for the probabilities of these three scenarios, I'm inclined to predict that the bond yield will remain relatively flat for quite some time. The secular forces that have brought bond yields down since the early 1980s remain intact and in some ways are more powerful than ever. These same forces are keeping a lid on inflation. They are global competition, technological innovation, and aging populations.

As I note above, I can even see some merit in the global savings glut thesis to explain why bond yields might remain low for quite some time. Anecdotally, global savers seem to be hard pressed to find enough good investment opportunities for all their savings and continue to reach for higher bond yields and better equity returns by taking on more risk. They might continue to do so if inflation remains low, causing central banks to keep short-term interest rates low.

Ironically, taking the other side of the trade is none other than Alan Greenspan. In an August 4, 2017 CNBC interview, he said, "The current level of interest rates is abnormally low, and there's only one direction in which they can go, and when they start they will be rather rapid." He added, "I have no time frame on the forecast. I have a chart which goes back to the 1800s and I can tell you that this particular period sticks out. But you have no way of knowing in advance when it will actually trigger."[29] I suppose this means that Greenspan no longer gives much weight to the savings glut notion.

I do admire Greenspan's intellectual agility. It's important to stay open-minded in the forecasting business, willing to change one's views. It was economist Paul Samuelson (not John Maynard Keynes) who famously said, "Well, when events change, I change my mind. What do you do?" On the other hand, consistency is also important when forecasting. President Harry Truman famously complained, "Give me a one-handed economist! All my economists say, 'On the one hand...on the other.'"

CHAPTER 11

Predicting Commodities

OLD ADAGE FROM THE PITS

MY JOB ON Wall Street requires me to concentrate my attention on the financial markets. At the same time, the markets can be a big distraction from doing my job. That's because there is always the temptation to trade. I discovered early on that I was most productive and did my best work when I wasn't staring at the quote screen on my desk because I had placed short-term bets on a bunch of securities whose prices were flashing green on upticks and red on downticks. I recognized before long that fast gains, especially if they were achieved with leveraged positions, were followed by fast losses. That led me to adopt a very conservative personal investment approach. In most businesses, having skin in the game shows commitment. For my job as an economist and investment strategist, I felt that short-term investing reduced the objectivity I needed.

I learned these lessons mostly by trading commodity futures. I didn't know it at the time, but Hillary Rodham Clinton and I both started trading futures in 1978. Reportedly, she traded cattle futures but closed her account the following year with a gain. I wish I'd had that discipline. I managed a few times to make money, only to stay in the game and give it back. Then I called it quits.

In the late 1970s and early 1980s, EF Hutton had a very big and well-regarded commodity operation, with traders in the pits of the major futures exchanges in New York and Chicago. The firm also was one of the first to set up a small trading desk in Treasury bill futures contracts, which were introduced on the Chicago Mercantile Exchange in 1976. The trading operation was extremely profitable at first because the fellows who started it recognized that there were huge discrepancies between the cash market and the new futures market, resulting in lots of arbitrage opportunities and big gains for the desk.

The head of Hutton's commodities department was one of the firm's stars because his operation was very lucrative. He had lunch with some of his top lieutenants almost every day at an Italian restaurant across the street from the firm's headquarters in downtown Manhattan. The maître d' provided a telephone just for him at his table so he could keep in touch with his staff, who mostly ate lunch at their desks. His department showed some interest in my work on the economy, but not much.

The commodities department had a news desk tasked with disseminating pertinent information via the "hoot-and-holler" system to Hutton's traders and sales force. Occasionally, the two ladies who ran the desk would broadcast my spin on some of the economic indicators. However, there was much more interest in the latest weather forecast that might impact grain prices, provided by Hutton's meteorologist.

Commodity traders tend to focus on the fundamentals unique to their market rather than on the impact of macroeconomic developments. Actually, many of them tend to use technical analysis more than fundamental analysis. They look at the charts of the past price action for patterns that might provide some clues to the next move or trend in prices. I studied technical analysis after work in the evenings for a short while, hoping that I too could find the clues and get rich. It didn't happen for me. The action was too volatile and risky. Besides, I already had a full-time day job.

Nevertheless, I did develop some understanding and respect for technical analysis. It's definitely not science. Proponents of the efficient-market theory argue that gazing at charts is as useful as gazing at one's navel. In their opinion, all available information is discounted in current prices, so using past prices to forecast future prices is a waste of time. That makes sense. Technicians counter that the very fact that all fundamental information is already reflected in prices makes their pattern-watching approach useful—it can provide valuable information on how the markets' participants are responding to, and anticipating, relevant news events. That makes sense too. It's a bit like solving a puzzle by looking over the shoulder of someone who is a few steps ahead of you in solving the same puzzle.

Technicians are particularly fond of drawing horizontal lines at the lows and highs in previous price action and extrapolating them to determine key "support" and "resistance" levels in their charts. If the price drops below an important support level, they believe that's a bearish signal. It suggests that the market expects the fundamentals might continue to be bearish. If support holds and prices move higher, that suggests a bullish move that presumably will be confirmed by the next batch of fundamental news. Breaking out above a resistance level is deemed to be bullish. Failing to do so is bearish. If these signals don't pan out, there's always new price action that can be extrapolated.

A truism I learned over the years is one that all traders in the commodity pits agree on: "The best cure for high commodity prices is high commodity prices." In other words, high commodity prices tend to boost supply and trim demand. So high prices are usually followed by falling prices. Low prices tend to reduce supply and lift demand. So they are usually followed by rising prices.

Commodity futures are traded in so-called "auction" markets in the major exchanges. The markets are highly competitive and transparent, driven mostly by publicly available information. The exchanges keep a fairly level playing field for all the participants, enforcing rules to reduce corrupt practices such as cornering a market. The prices are constantly changing to reflect the latest balance between supply and demand. They differ significantly from "administered" markets, where prices tend to be set by companies. Administered prices change, but not as frequently as auction prices.

At Hutton, I lost my interest in trading commodities along with a bit of money, which was a lot of money for me at the time. Professionally, as a macroeconomist working on Wall Street, I became more interested in understanding how commodity prices are affected by and reflect the performance of the US and global economies.

INDUSTRIAL SPOT PRICES ARE SPOT ON

MY FAVORITE OF all the economic indicators that I track is the raw industrials spot price index compiled daily by the Commodity Research Bureau (CRB). It is composed of the spot prices of the following 13 commodities: copper scrap, lead scrap, steel scrap, tin, zinc, burlap, cotton, print cloth, wool tops, hides, rosin, rubber, and tallow (Fig. 1*). I've been relying on it for years as a very sensitive indicator of both global and US economic activity. I like it because it does not include any petroleum or lumber products; these tend to have their own unique supply and demand dynamics, which I also monitor. Furthermore, several of the 13 commodities are traded only in spot markets, not in futures markets, so they are likely to be driven less by speculators and more by underlying supply/demand factors. (See Appendix 11.1, CRB Raw Industrials Spot Price Index Basic Facts.)

Over the years, I've found that the CRB raw industrials spot price index is highly correlated not only with almost all the major US business-cycle indicators but also with global ones. However, most of them are available only monthly, and often with a lag of at least one month. This CRB index goes back to 1951 on a weekly basis and May 27, 1981 on a daily basis. The boom-and-bust cycle of the US and global economies is very well reflected in the CRB index. It tends to drop sharply during US economic recessions and to rise when the US economy is growing. However, it doesn't always work that way. When it doesn't, figuring out why can provide some useful insights. Let's review the performance of the CRB raw industrials index since the start of the data:

- *Not much action during the 1950s and 1960s.* This commodity price measure—which is indexed to equal 100 in 1967—didn't do much during the 1950s and 1960s. It mostly fluctuated around 100, within a range of 89 to 126. Global demand for commodities was lackluster. While the US economy recovered smartly from World War II, the rest of the world took much longer to do so.

- *Soaring during the 1970s, then meandering through mid-1990.* The index soared during the 1970s, tripling to a peak of 327 near the start of 1980. The two oil price shocks of the 1970s triggered a worldwide inflationary spiral that drove up industrial commodity prices; the growing economic strength of the European and Japanese economies was a catalyst. Along the way, the CRB index fell sharply during the recessions of 1973–1974 and the early 1980s. Then during the rest of the 1980s and the first half of the 1990s, it once again meandered, this time at around 300, with somewhat more volatility than during the 1950s and 1960s.

- *Bear market during tech boom of late 1990s.* During the second half of the 1990s, the index mostly fell despite an economic boom in the

* Figures, references, and appendices are linked on *yardenibook.com/resources*.

United States. Leading the boom was the high-tech industry, which was much bigger in the United States than anywhere else. This industry doesn't use industrial commodities as intensively as other manufacturing industries. Silicon, abundant in sand, is the key ingredient for producing semiconductors.

In Europe, policymakers were scrambling to form a monetary union scheduled to start at the beginning of 1999. They hoped that such a union would help to revive their economies, which had been suffering from Eurosclerosis. Emerging markets were just starting to emerge, but those in Southeast Asia were hit by a financial crisis in 1997. In 1998, the Russian ruble crisis was another setback for emerging markets.

The CRB index fell to 214 on November 5, 2001, the lowest reading since September 1, 1986. That year's recession in the United States and the 9/11 attacks depressed the global economy and industrial commodity prices. That low also marked the beginning of what came to be called a commodity "supercycle."

• *China joins the WTO in 2001, triggering a supercycle.* The rebound from the low in late 2001 coincided with China's admission to the World Trade Organization (WTO) on December 11, 2001 (Fig. 2). As commodity prices continued to rise for the next few years, more investors came around to the view that they might do so for a couple of decades, given China's extraordinary demand for raw materials. Commodities—which tend to have short price cycles, lasting no more than a couple of years—now were deemed to be potentially great long-term investments.

That was my opinion too. On November 7, 2003, I wrote a *Topical Study* titled "China for Investors: The Growth Imperative," in which I concluded that greater urbanization and car ownership would dramatically boost Chinese demand for industrial commodities, including crude oil, over the next few years. I also observed that the Chinese were rushing to buy the steel and copper they needed to construct the urban infrastructure for all those migrants from the rural sector.[1] Steel imports were skyrocketing, even though China's domestic steel output was bigger than that of the United States and Japan combined. Surging auto production and the construction boom drove up steel demand exponentially.

Chinese industrial production soared by 168% from December 2001 through December 2008 (Fig. 3). Real GDP growth on a year-over-year basis, which had been running between 7% and 11% from 1998 to 2005, heated up to peak at 15.0% in mid-2007 (Fig. 4). The CRB raw industrials spot price index and the price of copper—which is a component of the index and a very sensitive economic indicator—both have been highly correlated with the growth rate of Chinese industrial production (Fig. 5 and Fig. 6).

- *The Great Recession hits hard in 2008.* During 2008, the commodity supercycle went from boom to bust along with the global economy. The CRB index had peaked at a record 526 on May 13, 2008, a 145% increase from its 2001 low. It then plunged by 40% to 316 through December 5, 2008. The global financial crisis triggered a global recession, which greatly depressed the demand for commodities.

- *An impressive snapback after the recession.* However, the CRB's supercycle wasn't over just yet: the index bungeed 102% over the next two years to its all-time record high of 638 on April 11, 2011. The snapback reflected massive economic stimulus provided by the Chinese government. On November 9, 2008, 26 days before the index troughed, the State Council of the People's Republic of China announced a four trillion yuan ($586 billion) stimulus program, the largest in the country's history at the time. "Over the past two months, the global financial crisis has been intensifying daily," the State Council said in a statement. "In expanding investment, we must be fast and heavy-handed." The required reserve ratio for large depository institutions was cut three times, from 17.5% in early October 2008 to 15.5% at the end of 2008 (Fig. 7). It was slashed from 16.5% to 13.5% for smaller lenders at the same time. The result was an explosive rise in bank loans, which increased at a record pace of 34% over the 12 months through October 2009 (Fig. 8).

- *Beyond the supercycle.* After the Chinese stimulus-triggered spike in commodity prices peaked at a record high during the spring of 2011, the CRB index fell sharply over the remainder of 2011, eventually stabilizing at just north of 500 during 2012 through mid-2014. It remained north of the previous record high before the Great Recession. Then it proceeded to fall sharply again during the second half of 2014 through 2015, when the plunge in oil prices depressed the global energy industry, which weighed on world economic growth. Once again, rebounding demand out of China boosted prices during 2016 through 2017.

The supercycle's apparent demise was just another confirmation of the old traders' maxim, "The best cure for high commodity prices is high commodity prices." Commodity producers around the world responded to the prospect of a multidecade boom in demand from China by expanding their operations. Capital spending on mining equipment soared. Roads were built and train tracks laid to transport the commodities to the ports, which were also enlarged.

Once again, however, rebounding demand out of China boosted prices during 2016 through 2017. It's still possible that the record high of 2011 marked the end of the supercycle, which therefore lasted only 10 years. That wasn't so super. I'm inclined to think that supercycles should last 20 years or longer. On the other hand, perhaps the super-cycle concept isn't very useful, given the inherent volatility of commodity prices.

A discussion of the commodities supercycle during the previous decade just wouldn't be complete without mentioning one of the period's more popular indicators of the boom times for industrial commodities: the Baltic Dry Index (BDI) (Fig. 9). The BDI is a shipping and trade index compiled by the London-based Baltic Exchange, which contacts shipping brokers to collect prices for various routes, cargo, and delivery times. So it measures changes in the cost to transport various raw materials. The BDI is a composite of three subindexes that measure different sizes of dry bulk carriers, or merchant ships: Capesize, Panamax, and Supramax.

The BDI soared by 1,300% from its 2001 low to its 2008 record high. Most of that jump occurred during 2006 and 2007. This surge coincided with lots of news stories about a shortage of freighters, attributed to China's booming demand for commodities. Even if more ships were available, they might be stuck waiting for weeks to pick up their cargoes in jammed ports from Australia to Brazil that couldn't handle all the traffic.

During the global recession of 2008, the BDI collapsed by 94%. It didn't recover much during the subsequent economic upturn. That's because shipyards around the world produced more freighters to accommodate the commodity supercycle. So the best cure for high freight rates was high freight rates.

While the concept of a multidecade supercycle turned out to be a flawed one, the old adage from the pits remains spot on. The CRB raw industrials spot price index bottomed at 398 on November 23, 2015 and rose 24% through the end of 2016. The drop in prices from mid-2014 through the end of 2015 caused producers to cut their output and boosted demand. Commodity prices will continue to cycle.

COMMODITY CORRELATIONS

THE CRB INDEX is highly correlated with lots of important economic and financial indicators. The spot price of copper scrap is one of the components of the CRB index and is highly correlated with it (Fig. 10). Use of the copper price as a gauge of the US economy was popularized years ago by my friend James Grant, the widely followed credit market strategist. He wrote, "Professor Copper is the metal with a PhD in economics." Since 2001, though, it's probably been a better indicator of China's economy than of the US economy.

Another commodity-related economic indicator that has stood the test of time for me so far is my weekly Boom-Bust Barometer (BBB). It is simply the weekly average of the CRB index divided by weekly initial unemployment claims. The data are available from the start of 1967, and since then through 2017, the BBB has been highly correlated with the US business cycle (Fig. 11). The BBB has tended to peak before or at the same time as the business cycle, because that's when commodity prices tend to make their cyclical highs while jobless claims tend to be at their cyclical lows. The BBB has tended to bottom at the trough of recessions, when commodity prices start to rebound and initial unemployment claims start to fall.

From the start of its data, the BBB has also shown a good correlation with the stock market's bull-and-bear cycle, which makes sense since the stock market is a reflection of economic conditions, as perceived by investors (Fig. 12). The bust phase of the BBB is associated with bear markets, while the boom phase coincides with bull markets. The BBB was highly correlated with the S&P 500 stock price index from 2000 through 2016—though not so much before that period, and we'll have to see whether that relationship continues (Fig. 13). Over the same period, the BBB was highly correlated with S&P 500 forward earnings, which is a weekly proxy for actual earnings, as I explain in Chapter 13 (Fig. 14).

My three favorite economic indicators are: first, the CRB raw industrials spot price index; second, the BBB; and third, the S&P 500 forward earnings. All three are high-frequency indicators, available essentially on a real-time basis, and almost never revised.

The BBB has helped me to stay on the right side of the bull market that spanned from 2003 to 2007 and the one since 2009. It didn't help much to predict the stock market debacle of 2008 other than to confirm the freefall in stock prices with a 67% plunge of its own from August 2007 to the bitter end of the bear market on March 9, 2009. The BBB bottomed on March 28, 2009, then proceeded to trace out a V-shaped recovery through the end of 2010.

During the equity bull market from March 11, 2003 through October 9, 2007, I recommended overweighting what I called the "MEI" sectors of the S&P 500—i.e., Materials, Energy, and Industrials—as they would be the most likely to benefit from a global economic boom led by Chinese demand for commodities. They were among the best performing of the 10 sectors in the S&P 500 during that bull market: Energy soared 223%, Materials climbed 154%, and Industrials rose 125%, outpacing the 95% gain in the S&P 500 (Fig. 15). Over this period, three other sectors outpaced the S&P 500: Utilities (139%), Telecommunication Services (112%), and Information Technology (102%).

The best-performing asset classes during that bull market were actually overseas. The Emerging Markets MSCI stock price index (in US dollars) rose 367% (Fig. 16). Trailing behind were the MSCI stock prices indexes for the European Monetary Union (215%), the United Kingdom (142%), Japan (123%), and the United States (97%). Many emerging markets were very dependent on commodity exports, especially to China. In turn, the strength in commodity prices confirmed the rapid pace of growth in China.

Therefore, there was a strong correlation between the Emerging Markets MSCI stock price index (in local currencies) and the CRB raw industrials spot price index (Fig. 17). The surprise was that they remained highly correlated following the Great Recession, during the years from 2009 through 2016, suggesting that the emerging economies haven't emerged from their dependence on commodity exports. The same story underlies the strong relationship between the Emerging Markets MSCI currency index and the CRB index (Fig. 18). The correlation suggests that many emerging economies continue to have so-called "commodity currencies," i.e., currencies that tend to appreciate and depreciate relative to the US dollar as commodity prices move higher or lower.

During most of 2017, the Emerging Markets MSCI stock price index was much stronger than the CRB index. This divergence suggests that perhaps emerging markets are finally starting to emerge with more spending on services, a sure sign of rising standards of living.

While I'm on the subject of intermarket correlations, there is a close correlation between the CRB raw industrials spot price index and the ratio of the S&P 500 Materials stock price index to the S&P 500 index (Fig. 19). That's logical since Materials stocks represent the producers of industrial commodities. For the same reason, we see a high correlation between the price of a barrel of oil and the ratio of the S&P 500 Energy stock price index—representing energy producers—to the S&P 500 (Fig. 20).

FROM PEAK OIL TO CHEAP OIL

THE WORLD HAS had plenty of cyclical episodes during which high oil prices led to low oil prices followed by high prices, and so on. Global oil demand can be approximated using data on global supply compiled by the Energy Information Administration of the US Department of Energy (Fig. 21). The yearly percent change in this series is certainly procyclical. It can be used as an indicator of global economic growth, though it does a mediocre job and isn't very timely because the latest monthly data are stale by several months (Fig. 22).

Since the first oil crisis back in 1973, soaring oil prices have tended to be followed by recessions and falling oil prices (Fig. 23). They seem to have become integral to the booms and busts of the business cycle. In the past, rapidly rising gasoline prices were covered daily by television evening news programs. Congress would respond by holding hearings with oil company managements to berate them about their "windfall profits." Soaring pump prices would depress the spending of consumers, who had less money to spend on other goods and services, including gasoline (Fig. 24). The resulting recession would bring oil prices back down.

On a secular basis, the high oil prices of the past and fears that they might continue to rise have stimulated conservation on the demand side and technological innovations to produce more oil more cheaply on the supply side. Let's review some of the highs and lows of the oil market in recent years:

- *The cartel.* OPEC, which stands for "Organization of the Petroleum Exporting Countries," is a cartel of oil-producing and oil-exporting countries founded at the Baghdad Conference on September 10–14,

1960 by Iran, Iraq, Kuwait, Saudi Arabia, and Venezuela. Other countries joined these five founding members later; the cartel had 14 members at year-end 2017.[2] The oil cartel's objective is to increase member countries' oil profits by acting jointly to limit global oil supplies and thereby artificially inflate, or "fix," prices. To this end, OPEC's power was consolidated in the 1960s and 1970s when various countries expropriated their oil reserves from the "Seven Sisters" multinational oil companies (Anglo-Iranian, Esso, Gulf, Royal Dutch Shell, Socal, Socony, and Texaco) and created their own nationalized oil companies.

Cartels are inherently unstable because members have an incentive to cheat by exceeding their cartel-set production quotas, thus undercutting the cartel's price target. OPEC has been relatively successful, mostly because Saudi Arabia, which has dominated the cartel with its huge oil reserves, has been willing to be the "swing" producer most times, taking a big share of any cutbacks aimed at shoring up or boosting prices.

- *First shock.* By the early 1970s, OPEC accounted for more than half of worldwide oil production. During October 1973, the Organization of Arab Petroleum Exporting Countries (consisting of the Arab majority of OPEC plus Egypt and Syria) declared an oil embargo against the United States and other industrialized nations that supported Israel in the Yom Kippur War, which lasted from October 6–25, 1973. The embargo ended in March 1974.

  The price of a barrel of West Texas crude oil jumped 213% from $3.56 during July 1973 to $11.16 during October 1974. It triggered a severe recession, but the price only stalled briefly before it continued rising to $15.85 during February 1979. OPEC was on a roll, as higher prices didn't lead to lower prices.

- *Second shock.* The second oil shock was also associated with events in the Middle East. The Iranian Revolution began in early 1978 and ended a year later, when the royal reign of Shah Mohammad Reza Pahlavi collapsed and Sheikh Khomeini took control as grand ayatollah of the Islamic republic. Iranian oil output dropped sharply, prompting fears of additional supply disruptions and spurring widespread speculative hoarding. Oil prices more than doubled, from $15.85 during April 1979 to a peak of $39.50 during April 1980.

  The two oil shocks stimulated more oil production among non-OPEC producers and prompted oil conservation efforts around the world. Energy efficiency increased for cars and appliances. The second shock also caused another recession, which did depress oil prices. They remained weak through 1984, drifting down to $25.43 by the end of that year despite the economic recovery.

- *Swinging Saudis.* In a *Topical Study* titled "The Case for Lower Oil Prices," dated December 12, 1984, I concluded that OPEC had two unpleasant alternatives: lose market share to non-OPEC producers or cut prices to revive worldwide oil consumption.[3] Saudi Arabia initially responded to the weakness in oil prices by slashing its production (Fig. 25). When that didn't work, the Saudis reversed course and flooded the market, causing the price to plunge to a low of $10.40 a barrel on March 31, 1986. As the world's major low-cost producer, the Saudis hoped to shut down high-cost production elsewhere and force other OPEC members to agree to limit production to bolster prices, while reviving demand for its crude oil. Other OPEC producers such as Iran and Iraq were dominated by Saudi Arabia (Fig. 26).

- *Saddam's gambit.* The cartel's overproduction problem evaporated during the second half of the 1980s and early 1990s as non-OPEC production trended downward (Fig. 27). OPEC's market share rose from a low of 28% in 1985 to roughly 44% by the second half of the 1990s (Fig. 28).

Iraqi President Saddam Hussein desperately needed higher prices to rebuild his country following the Iran–Iraq War that lasted from 1980 through 1988. He tried to solve his problem by invading Kuwait during August 1990. The oil price jumped briefly until military forces led by the United States repelled his invasion. As chart watchers would say, it "retested" the previous record high set after the second oil shock. The price of oil declined again as a result of recessionary pressures and the resumption of Kuwaiti exports. The price then remained volatile but range-bound between the high set by the second oil shock and 1985's low.

Following the recession at the start of the current millennium, the price moved higher again after bottoming on November 15, 2001, coinciding with China entering the WTO at the end of 2001. Initially, the upturn was attributed to America's response to the 9/11 terrorist attacks in September 2001. The Bush administration claimed that Iraq had supported al-Qaeda's attacks on the United States and also possessed nuclear and chemical weapons of mass destruction. At first, the United States worked through the United Nations to disarm

Iraq. However, on March 20, 2003, the United States invaded Iraq and overthrew Saddam Hussein. The oil price was back at the top of its range since 1979.

- *Emerging demand.* On July 14, 2006, the price of oil broke out to a new record high. It was another golden period for OPEC as global oil demand was boosted by rapidly growing emerging market economies. The cartel produced more to meet demand. Oil demand in the "Old World" countries of the United States, Western Europe, and Japan peaked during 2005 thanks to conservation and aging demographic trends. That same year, demand everywhere else, i.e., in the "New World," rose above Old World demand for the first time in history and never looked back or down. I wasn't surprised by the surge in oil prices.

- *Hubbert's peak.* On July 3, 2008, the price of a barrel of Brent crude oil rose to a record high of $146.08. The press was full of articles about market experts who promoted the "peak oil" thesis. The world was running out of oil, the theory went. New reserves were getting harder to find, and as oil became more difficult to access, the cost of producing it would head higher. So oil prices would continue to rise.

    Peak oil was popularized by M. King Hubbert, a geologist who worked for years at Shell Oil. In a 1956 paper, he predicted that US oil production would peak, probably in the early 1970s, and then decline in a bell curve fashion.[4] Hubbert's peak oil theory gained enormous credibility when US oil output did in fact peak in the early 1970s and the OPEC oil crises caused oil prices to soar during the decade.

- *Great Recession.* Yet once again, recessionary pressures sent the Brent price tumbling 75% from that record high, on July 3, 2008, to $36.61 by December 24 of that year. While the doubling in the price of oil from August 28, 2007 to that record high undoubtedly contributed to the recession, there were plenty of other reasons why global economic activity nosedived during the Great Recession, taking oil prices along for the ride.

- *Sanctioning Iran.* As the global economy recovered, there was a dramatic rebound back over $100 a barrel by early 2011. While the pace of economic growth was relatively subpar after the initial recovery from the Great Recession, the price bounced around $100 through mid-2014. Mounting tension and turmoil in the Middle East threatened supplies.

    On June 9, 2010, the United Nations Security Council passed a resolution that further tightened sanctions first imposed in 2006 over Iran's nuclear weapons program. A US law that took effect in 2012 threatened sanctions on foreign banks, including the central banks of US allies, if they failed to significantly reduce their imports of Iranian oil. The result was a drastic drop of about 1.0 million barrels per day in Iran's oil output. It remained severely curtailed through 2014 as the country's oil industry was hard-pressed to get parts and services to maintain its facilities. In addition, following the so-called Arab Spring, Libya's Muammar Gaddafi was overthrown during October 2011, which virtually shut down the country's production from around 1.3 million barrels a day during 2010.

Offsetting the cuts in Iran and Libya was Iraqi output, which increased by about 2.0 million barrels per day to a new record high of 4.7 million barrels per day during 2016. In addition, Russian oil production—which had stalled around 6.0 million barrels per day during the 1990s, following the end of the Cold War—doubled from 2000 through the end of 2016. That period coincided with the leadership in Russia of Vladimir Putin, who clearly wanted more oil revenues to fund his various ambitions, as well as his personal bank accounts. Russia has been outproducing Saudi Arabia since 2003.

- *Freefall.* On November 23, 2014, with the groundwork laid by secret US–Iran talks, Iran and six major powers—the United States, Britain, China, France, Germany, and Russia—reached an interim pact called the "Joint Plan of Action," under which Iran agreed to curb its nuclear work in return for limited sanctions relief. The deal was finalized in 2015. Iran's output quickly rebounded to its pre-2012 level. Coincidentally, Saudi Arabia the month before had lowered the price charged to its Asian customers. The Saudis refused to support the price above $100 a barrel if other OPEC members wouldn't abide by their quotas. Needless to say, the Saudis' attempts to get the Iranians to agree were futile. The Russians, however, who are not members of OPEC, agreed to join the Saudis in a production freeze.

  The Saudis' price cut triggered a freefall similar to the one in 2008. However, this time there was no recession depressing demand. There was simply too much supply. The price of a barrel of Brent crude oil, which had peaked on June 19, 2014 at $115.06, dropped below $100 on September 9 and finally bottomed out at $27.88 on January 20, 2016. The problem for OPEC, particularly the Saudis, was that US cowboys were now running wild in their own sizable oil fields.

- *Fracking USA.* As mentioned earlier, US oil production did peak in the 1970s and declined for decades after, exactly as the peak oil theory had predicted (Fig. 29). But then it started rising again in 2009 thanks to major advances in oil-field technology. Energy companies combined hydraulic fracturing and horizontal drilling to extract oil out of rock formations in North America. They did so by pumping mixtures of chemicals, water, and sand into shale, creating thousands of fractures in the rock and forcing oil into a well. Technological innovations also allowed the frackers to pick their drilling spots with better accuracy. Oil company geologists are exploring more ways to extract more oil from known reserves using nanochemistry.

  The fracking revolution in the oil industry led to a dramatic increase in US oil production, which rose from about five million barrels per day during 2007 to more than nine million barrels per day by late 2014 and early 2015 (Fig. 30). As a result, non-OPEC oil production rose faster than OPEC output. That set the stage for the dramatic 76% plunge in the price of oil from mid-2014 through early 2016.

  That price freefall forced the US frackers to cut their production. However, their output dropped only 12% by mid-2016. They proved to be remarkably resilient. They quickly lowered their costs, allowing them to produce at their former high levels of early 2015. It helped that the price of a barrel of West Texas crude oil nearly doubled from a low close to $26 on February 11, 2016 to about $50 during the first half of 2017.

- *Lesson learned.* The frackers offer a great example of how unexpected technological innovations tend to solve problems when market forces can work relatively freely. Their story is also a reminder of the ability of entrepreneurs to see inherent opportunities in solving problems. In the midst of widespread pessimism about an economic problem, entrepreneurs find a solution that benefits all consumers. In other words, one of the reasons that high prices lead to low prices is that entrepreneurs figure out how to increase supplies with new technological innovations.

During October 2016, the World Energy Council (WEC), which advises governments and other organizations on energy policy, published a report titled *World Energy Scenario 2016: The Grand Transition.*[5] It amounted to a prediction of peak demand for oil, outlining three scenarios for oil demand:

- *In the first scenario*, rapid adoption of new technologies and business models would seriously disrupt demand, which would peak in 2030 at 103 million barrels a day, compared with about 86 million in 2014, and decline by 0.9% a year to 80 million in 2060.
- *In the second scenario*, the adoption of more aggressive low-carbon policies could bring the 2030 peak down to 94 million barrels a day.
- *In the status quo scenario*, demand would reach a plateau of about 104 million barrels per day between 2040 and 2050.

To monitor the likelihood of these long-term projections, I watch a couple of key related short-term variables in the US. Although total vehicle miles traveled by Americans once again rose into record territory from 2015 through 2017, their gasoline usage remained below its record high during 2007 (Fig. 31). Both series are compiled by the US Department of Energy. I approximate fuel efficiency as the ratio of vehicle miles traveled to gasoline usage. This derived series increased from about 19.5 miles per gallon in January 1991, when the series starts, to 22.5 by mid-2017 (Fig. 32).

Eventually, there will be peak oil, most likely as a result of peaking demand rather than peaking supplies. Demand peaked for coal, and it certainly could for oil. The most obvious reason for peak demand would be the widespread adoption of electric cars—but that won't happen until the vehicles become more affordable and can travel farther before needing a recharge, charging stations become readily available, and recharge times shorten. These are significant technological challenges that most of the major auto manufacturers are taking on. If they succeed, there will be plenty of natural gas with which to produce more electricity, and there will be more electricity coming from solar power.

Meanwhile, oil supplies remain abundant. Of course, the peak oil supply theory is based on the widely held notion that oil is a finite "fossil" fuel. There is a minority view—some would say a "fringe" view—that oil is "abiotic," i.e., a natural renewable product of the earth. Proponents of this theory note that the core temperature of the earth is over 6,000 degrees centigrade. The temperature of erupting lava is 700–1,200 degrees centigrade. All that heat combined with carbon, one of the most abundant elements in the earth's crust, must generate all sorts of gasses and pressures that could produce oil on an ongoing basis.

I've found that the price of crude oil is highly correlated with the CRB raw industrials spot price index (Fig. 33). That's logical since oil products are industrial commodities, after all. The price of oil is also highly correlated with the price of copper (Fig. 34). In other words, while oil has its own unique supply and demand dynamics (which is why I'm glad the CRB excludes it), oil's price fluctuations are heavily influenced by the business cycle, just as the CRB index and the copper price are.

Accordingly, July 3, 2008 marked the peak in the price of oil—not long after the CRB had peaked in May of that year. The oil price plunged to a low of $36.61 on December 24, 2008—the same month that the CRB found its bottom, on December 5. Then the oil price recovered smartly along with other commodity prices during 2009 and 2010, back to around $100, and fluctuated there until mid-2014, when the price plunged by 76% through early 2016.

The shocking plummet in oil prices from mid-2014 through the end of 2015 depressed capital spending by the oil industry. While the recession in the oil industry didn't cause a worldwide recession, it did cause a worldwide slowdown. That was the main event that broke the back of the supercycle in other industrial commodity prices. However, the initial negative impact on the oil industry was mitigated by the positive impact on world demand for oil. The price recovered to around $55 by early 2017.

I calculated that global consumers of oil had a windfall of roughly $2.2 trillion as their collective oil bill dropped from an annual rate of $3.2 trillion in mid-2014 to about $1.0 trillion at the start of 2016 (Fig. 35). That helped to revive global economic growth from the initial negative shock effect of the oil price plunge. In the United States, the windfall over this period was about $230 billion, by my estimate (Fig. 36).

MALTHUSIANS AND THEIR DISMAL SCIENCE

THERE IS NO better example of the role of high prices and technological innovation in bringing down commodity prices than the history of wheat and other grain prices. During my career on Wall Street, there were several major spikes in grain prices. Inevitably, doomsayers would pop out of the ground, declaring that an era of chronic food shortages was at hand. Farmers would respond to the jump in grain prices by planting from fence post to fence post, and new technologies allowed them to increase their yields per acre.

The first economist in recorded history was renowned for his great forecast in the grain market. He was Joseph, the 11th of Jacob's 12 sons in

Genesis and Rachel's firstborn. Joseph was sold into slavery by his jealous brothers. He then was thrown into prison in Egypt when his master's frisky wife falsely accused him of sexual misconduct after he spurned her advances. Joseph won his freedom and a promotion to chief economist by interpreting the Pharaoh's dreams as foretelling seven years of abundance followed by seven years of famine. On Joseph's advice, surplus grain was stored during the abundant years. When the famine arrived, it was so severe that people "from all over the earth" came to Egypt to buy bread, as it was the only kingdom prepared for the seven-year drought. It was a brilliant forecast.

The most famous grain economist was Thomas Robert Malthus. He was among the first classical economists. Between 1798 and 1826, he published six editions of his widely read treatise *An Essay on the Principle of Population*. He rejected the notions about the future improvement in mankind that were popular at the time, believing instead that poverty cannot be eradicated but is a permanent fixture in the economic firmament. He explained this supposed principle by arguing that population growth generally expanded too fast in times and regions of plenty, until the size of the population relative to the primary resources, particularly food, caused distress. Famines and diseases were nature's way of keeping population growth from outpacing the food supply: "That the increase of population is necessarily limited by the means of subsistence, that population does invariably increase when the means of subsistence increase, and, that the superior power of population is repressed, and the actual population kept equal to the means of subsistence, by misery and vice."

Malthus was the original "dismal scientist." His pessimistic outlook was probably the most spectacularly wrong economic forecast of all times, and a classic for contrarian thinkers. Grain production soared during the 1800s thanks to new technologies, more acreage, and rising yields. During the first half of the century, chemical fertilizers revived the fertility of European soil, and the milling process was automated using steam engines. During the second half of the century, vast new farmlands were opened in the United States under the Homestead Act of 1862, and agriculture's productivity soared with the proliferation of mechanical sowers, reapers, and threshers.

Malthusians just don't learn from their mistakes, though. In 1968, Stanford University Professor Paul R. Ehrlich published *The Population Bomb*, a best-selling book that warned of mass starvation in the 1970s and

1980s as a result of overpopulation. The alarmist tone was set in the book's preface: "The battle to feed all of humanity is over. In the 1970s hundreds of millions of people will starve to death in spite of any crash programs embarked upon now. At this late date nothing can prevent a substantial increase in the world death rate."

Ironically, in 1968, the same year that Ehrlich rang the alarm bell, the term "Green Revolution" was born. William Gaud, the former director of the US Agency for International Development, coined the phrase to describe the spread of new agricultural technologies: "These and other developments in the field of agriculture contain the makings of a new revolution. It is not a violent Red Revolution like that of the Soviets, nor is it a White Revolution like that of the shah of Iran. I call it the Green Revolution."

In 1970, Norman Borlaug—often called "the father of the Green Revolution"—won the Nobel Peace Prize. A January 1997 article about him written by Gregg Easterbrook in *The Atlantic* was titled "Forgotten Benefactor of Humanity."[6] Easterbrook wrote that the agronomist's techniques for high-yield agriculture were "responsible for the fact that throughout the postwar era, except in sub-Saharan Africa, global food production has expanded faster than the human population, averting the mass starvations that were widely predicted." Borlaug may have prevented a billion deaths.

In 1968, a small international group of people from the fields of academia, civil society, diplomacy, and industry met in a villa in Rome to fret about the world's problems. They raised a global fright with a report published in 1972 titled *The Limits of Growth*. The book's authors—Donella H. Meadows, Dennis L. Meadows, Jørgen Randers, and William W. Behrens III—based their analysis on a computer simulation model. Like all good Malthusians, they simulated a world where population grows exponentially but technology increases resource availability only linearly. The book sold 30 million copies in 30 languages, making it the best-selling environmental book ever. The 1973 oil crisis certainly gave the book credibility, as it had for Hubbert's peak and Ehrlich's bomb.

During my lifetime, the first major spike in grain prices occurred when I was an undergraduate at Cornell. The price of a bushel of soybeans soared 283% from mid-1972 through mid-1973 (Fig. 37). Farm prices rose at a record pace as a result during 1973, adding to the inflationary pressures caused by the first OPEC oil crisis. During 1972, harvests were poor in Russia, Asia, and Africa. Demand for corn and soybeans was boosted by a temporary shortage of Peruvian anchovies, a source of protein for farm animals. In the United States, the food component of the consumer price index (CPI) rose 92% from 1973 through 1979 (Fig. 38). But it didn't take long for the anchovies to return to the waters off Peru or for the high grain prices to lead to more grain production and lower grain prices.

Many more food price spikes came and went quickly. One in the late 1980s coincided with the end of the Cold War. While all those people liberated from Soviet communism undoubtedly wanted to eat better, they did so with food prices remaining, on balance, relatively low during the 1990s.

The next significant food price spike occurred during 2008. The April 17, 2008 issue of *The Economist* included an article, "The New Face of Hunger," that warned: "But the food scare of 2008, severe as it is, is only a symptom of a broader problem. The surge in food prices has ended 30 years in which food was cheap, farming was subsidised in rich countries and international food markets were wildly distorted."[7]

The following year, the July 2 issue of the magazine ran a story, "Whatever Happened to the Food Crisis? It Crept Back" that explained: "On the face of things, markets last year were adjusting exactly as economic theory predicts they should: prices rose, drawing investment into farms; supplies then rose sharply, pushing prices down."[8]

Although soybean prices were at their lows near the end of 2008, they remained well above their previous cyclical lows despite the global recession. Then they proceeded to move higher, spiking to a record high during September 4, 2012. Once again, the alarmists rang the alarm bells. This time, they also could argue that food shortages and soaring prices were causing social and political unrest, particularly in the Arab world.

The 2007–2008 food crisis triggered riots in countries from Haiti to Bangladesh to Mozambique. The Arab Spring during 2012 started with riots in response to high food prices in Algeria and Tunisia. The revolutions that swept the Middle East that year primarily reflected the population's frustration with decades of dictatorship and corruption, but the food crisis arguably touched off the fury. It wasn't until 2013 and 2014 that grain prices came tumbling down after supplies had been increased yet again in response to high prices.

The conclusion is that the good earth has been very good to all the people who have to be fed, even as the world's population has increased from about a billion in 1800 to over seven billion in 2016. Nearly all the major famines along the way were man-made calamities attributable to totalitarian regimes. Like most commodity markets, the markets for food are very competitive on a global basis and respond rapidly to imbalances between supply and demand without requiring the dire Malthusian solution to the problem of too many mouths to feed.

Looking ahead, the world's population growth is expected to slow. It doubled from 3.7 billion people in 1970 to 7.4 billion in 2015 (Fig. 39). According to the United Nations, global population growth will slow due to lower fertility rates; the UN's medium variant forecast anticipates the world population reaching around 11.2 billion by 2099. The annual growth rate is projected to fall from 1.1% during 2015 to nearly zero by the end of the century (Fig. 40). That's because the global fertility rate is projected to fall below the population replacement rate of 2.1 children per woman almost everywhere over the next few years (Fig. 41). I believe that's mostly because technological innovations in agriculture have forced migration from rural to urban areas, where childrearing has fewer benefits and more costs (Fig. 42). Malthusians never saw any of this coming.

Another Malthusian mini-crisis erupted in the market for rare-earth minerals during 2011. Most of the supplies of these minerals are based in China, which limited exports of them in 2009 and 2010. They are used to make wind turbines, certain light bulbs, computers, and many other high-tech products. A 2010 US Department of Energy report titled *Critical Materials Strategy* identified a possible "critical shortage" of five rare-earth elements.[9] At the time, China accounted for 95% of their global production.

As this problem was making headlines, the prices of these rare commodities spiked, peaking around mid-2011 before tumbling. Shortages never happened, because manufacturers found ways to reduce their need for the materials; one such innovation was light-emitting diode (LED) bulbs, which contain less rare-earth minerals than fluorescent bulbs. Also, mines outside of China were opened when prices rose in 2010 and 2011, increasing supply.

GOLD RUSH

GOLD IS PROBABLY the most controversial commodity. That's because there has been an age-old debate on whether it should be used as the sole monetary standard. Proponents of the gold standard believe that only gold should be the basis of a country's monetary system. The purists among them rail at "fiat" monetary systems that allow the government to print money. Gold is unique among commodities in having its own fan club, with its members called "gold bugs."

Their basic concern is that fiat systems tend to generate inflation. Governments are likely to print more and more money as long as the resulting inflation doesn't trigger social unrest, threatening their survival. By printing more money, governments are said to be "debasing" their currencies. Ironically, that term originally was coined to describe what governments sometimes did to the gold and silver coins they minted; the sovereign would reduce the size and content of gold and silver in the coins. Nevertheless, gold's fans view it as the ultimate inflation hedge. If the government prints too much money, some of that money is bound to boost the price of gold, which has a relatively fixed supply.

In the United States, gold has long been a politically charged commodity. The dollar became the official currency of the United States when Alexander Hamilton recommended and Congress passed the Coinage Act of 1792. Through the following century, the United States was on a bimetal standard, with the dollar backed by a ratio of gold to silver. It was a fixed ratio but was changed by law from time to time. On March 14, 1900, the Gold Standard Act guaranteed the dollar's convertibility into 1.5 grams of gold.

The gold standard didn't last long in the United States. On March 6, 1933, just 36 hours after taking the oath of office, President Franklin Roosevelt declared a nationwide bank moratorium to stop the run on the banks. They were forbidden to pay out gold or to export it. On April 5, Roosevelt issued an executive order outlawing gold hoarding and requiring all persons to exchange their gold at the Federal Reserve Banks by May 1. The exchange price was set at $20.67 per ounce. In 1934, this was increased to $35.00.

The 1944 Bretton Woods agreement fixed the exchange rate of currencies to the US dollar as a reserve currency convertible to gold. The United States pledged to redeem any and all US dollars held by foreigners, at $35.00 per ounce; later, this promise was limited to foreign central banks. The monetary system was called a "gold exchange standard."

As Chapter 9 reviews, on August 15, 1971, President Nixon closed the gold window. Foreign central banks no longer could get gold for their dollars, which had been fixed relative to gold for almost 30 years. The US government thus abrogated the financial commitment it had made to the rest of the world at the Bretton Woods Conference, which had set up the post-war monetary system.

In 1974, President Gerald Ford signed legislation that permitted Americans again to hold gold bullion. The price of gold soared to a 1974 peak of $194 per ounce (Fig. 43). After a brief decline through mid-1976, the price ascended to a 1980 peak of $850. It then trended back down to a low of $252 on July 20, 1999. A great bull market followed for bullion, with its price soaring 650% to a record high of $1,895 per ounce on September 6, 2011. It fell by 45% through December 17, 2015, possibly bottoming as gold bugs rooted for a renewed bull market in the precious metal.

I'm not a gold bug. To me, gold is just another commodity. The difference is that speculators and inflation hedgers tend to be more important sources of demand than commercial users. A bar of gold doesn't generate any earnings or dividends. It doesn't pay interest. On the contrary, interest payments have to be made if it is bought on margin, and storage costs are another consideration. In other words, it's hard to value gold unless the value to the gold bugs can somehow be determined.

Gold is widely regarded as a hedge against inflation as well as against financial and social instability. A look at the dollar price of gold divided by the US CPI shows that gold was a good inflation hedge during the second half of the 1970s (Fig. 44). It was a terrible hedge during the early 1980s and kept up with the CPI over the remainder of the decade. It wasn't a good hedge during the 1990s. However, inflation was trending downward, so there wasn't much demand for gold to hedge against inflation. Besides, stocks significantly outperformed gold during the 1990s, with the S&P 500 rising 316%, while gold fell 28% from the start of the decade through the end. Gold started to outpace the CPI again, especially after the 9/11 terrorist attacks. The real price of gold continued to soar during the financial crisis of 2008 and didn't peak until September 6, 2011.

Gold also is often viewed as an alternative currency to the dollar, rising in value when the dollar is weak and falling in value when it's strong (Fig. 45). Gold's sensitivity to interest rates is another salient characteristic; bullish speculators can increase their leverage by buying the bullion with borrowed funds.

Of gold's many attributes, though, the most important one for understanding its price behavior, I've found, is that gold acts like a commodity. The price of gold seems to track the underlying trend in the CRB raw industrials spot price index (Fig. 46).

From time to time, I've had an opinion on the outlook for the price of gold, For example:

- In my November 7, 2003 *Topical Study* on China, I wrote that the country's rapid growth would be bullish for commodities in general, including gold.[10] I observed that the May 8, 2003 issue of *The Economist* included an interesting article titled "Bullion for a Billion." It suggested that Chinese demand, which had been unleashed by government deregulation, might have contributed to the jump in gold prices since the prior summer. Until 2002, China's central bank had fixed the domestic price of gold, as it played the role of intermediary, purchasing all the gold produced by China's mines and allocating it to jewelers.

  This intermediary role of the central bank ended in October 2002 when a gold exchange opened in Shanghai, offering producers and wholesalers a place to trade directly with each another. In March 2003, the central bank went further and gave up its power to license producers and retailers, so anyone could enter the gold business in China. During June 2002, laws changed to allow individuals to invest in gold.

- During the summer and fall of 2012, I observed that while gold rallied strongly after European Central Bank (ECB) President Mario Draghi pledged on July 26, 2012 to do "whatever it takes" to defend the euro, it did not beat the 2011 record high (Fig. 47). An even more bearish sign for gold was that its price dropped sharply on April 4, 2013 when the Bank of Japan formally implemented the ultra-easy monetary policy component of "Abenomics."

While I typically don't have much to say about the gold price outlook, I continue to monitor the close inverse relationship between the price of gold and the yield of 10-year Treasury Inflation-Protected Securities (TIPS) (Fig. 48). It tends to confirm that gold behaves as an inflation hedge. Since 2006, the price of gold has tended to rise when a declining TIPS yield suggested increasing demand for inflation protection. Conversely, the gold price tends to fall when the TIPS yield is rising, suggesting less demand from investors seeking to hedge against inflation.

GOLDMAN'S INDEX

GOLDMAN SACHS DESERVES a mention in a chapter on commodities, as the firm has been at the forefront of convincing institutional investors that commodities should be another asset class in their portfolios, promoting the idea that including this asset class would achieve better portfolio diversification. The firm has touted its Goldman Sachs Commodity Index (GSCI) as the best way to do so (Fig. 49).[11] The firm was bullish on emerging economies during the early 2000s, particularly the so-called BRICs (Brazil, Russia, India, and China) and believed in the commodity supercycle.

Betting on the supercycle was a good idea during the early 2000s. It was a bad idea during 2014 and 2015, when the price of oil crashed. The price of oil tends to dominate the moves in the GSCI because energy commodities account for a large portion of the index (Fig. 50).

Moreover, the CRB raw industrials spot price index long has been highly correlated with the Emerging Markets stock price index in both local currencies and even more so in dollars, as I noted above. So owning commodities in a diversified portfolio actually may blunt the benefits of diversification if the portfolio already includes energy stocks and emerging market stocks. I think investors are best served by understanding the forces that move commodity prices and the composition of commodity indexes sold to them rather than simply accepting the diversification argument without question.

CHAPTER 12

Predicting Currencies

CURRENCIES HAVE CONSEQUENCES

I'VE BEEN A prognosticator for a number of Wall Street firms over the past 40 years. Occasionally, I run into former colleagues who greet me with, "Hello, Dr. Ed. We worked together many years ago." I'm often slightly embarrassed that they know me but I don't remember them. These are usually people who had worked at EF Hutton or Prudential-Bache Securities in the 1980s and who forgive my lapse given that both firms had big retail branch systems with hundreds of brokers. Nevertheless, I do enjoy hearing some of them tell me that I helped them make a lot of money in the bond and stock markets back then. Once in a while, I'm complimented for forecasts that weren't even mine (so the lapses of memory go both ways). One fellow thanked me for his windfall based on my forecast for the Turkish lira, a currency that I've never had an opinion on in my life! I'm sure about that.

Back in the early 1980s, I was rarely asked about the outlook for the foreign-exchange value of the dollar or any other currency when I met with our accounts in the United States. On the other hand, when I visited our accounts overseas, that was one of the first questions they would ask. Historically, US institutional investors have tended to invest domestically, for the most part, and foreign investors have tended to invest globally—so foreign investors have been much more exposed to currency risk. That's been less true in recent years, though, as American investors have allocated more of their portfolios to overseas assets.

The US stock market still has a bigger market capitalization than other stock markets around the world and has tended to be more liquid as a result. Buying and selling large blocks of stocks is easier to do in the United States than in most overseas financial markets. However, that has also changed as they've become bigger and more liquid too. Consider the following developments:

- Data compiled by the Investment Company Institute show that Americans started to warm up to global investing right after China joined the World Trade Organization (WTO) in December 2001. Since the beginning of 2000, cumulative net inflows into US equity mutual funds investing internationally increasingly have outpaced those for funds investing just in the United States (Fig. 1 and Fig. 2*). Indeed, from December 2001 through December 2016, the percentage of cumulative net inflows going into equity mutual funds attributable to international funds rose from 11% to 91%. Starting in late 2009, domestic funds have been plagued by persistent net outflows through 2016.

- The Fed's *Financial Accounts of the United States* includes a quarterly series on the market value of all equities held by US residents since 1952 and a similar series that excludes their holdings of foreign corporate equities and investment fund shares, as well as American Depositary Receipts, a.k.a. "ADRs" (Fig. 3). The percentage of foreign equities in the total holdings of equities by US residents was below 2% from 1952 through the end of 1985 (Fig. 4). Then this percentage remained on an uptrend until it peaked at a record high of 22% during the third quarter of 2010. It meandered on a slight downtrend to 18% by the end of 2016, when Americans held $39.0 trillion in equities in total, with $7.1 trillion in foreign issues.

Of course, many US companies do lots of business overseas. By investing in these companies, US investors indirectly accrue plenty of exposure to the global economy. Many of these corporations not only export goods and services made in America but also generate profits from their overseas subsidiaries. Accordingly, the foreign-exchange value of the dollar greatly affects the profits of many US companies. Currency impacts are often discussed during quarterly earnings calls held by corporate managements

---

* Figures, references, and appendices are linked on *yardenibook.com/resources*.

with investors and industry analysts. Available data can provide some perspective:

- *Revenues from abroad.* On average, the S&P 500 companies derive roughly half of their revenues and profits from abroad. In 2016, the actual percentage of S&P 500 companies' sales from foreign countries was 43% of their total sales, down from 44% in 2015 and 48% in 2014. Importantly, however, S&P 500 foreign sales represent only goods and services produced and sold outside of the United States; they don't include US-made products that are exported and sold abroad.[1]

- *Earnings from abroad.* Standard & Poor's provides no comparable figures for the percentage of profits earned overseas by the S&P 500 companies. However, it's likely to be close to the percentage of revenues from abroad. The National Income and Product Accounts of the United States does have a data series on pretax corporate profits receipts from the rest of the world. It has risen from $3 billion at the start of 1959, accounting for 5.7% of total pretax profits, to $699 billion at the end of 2016, accounting for 32.4% of profits (Fig. 5 and Fig. 6).

If all else were equal, one could expect a straightforward, consistent impact of currency-exchange effects on corporate profits: 10% appreciation (or depreciation) of the dollar should decrease (or increase) S&P 500 profits by 5%, assuming roughly half of the index companies' earnings come from abroad. But the fact that Standard & Poor's excludes export revenues in its calculation of revenues from abroad—lumping export sales together with domestic sales—means that all else isn't equal; there's more to the story, because export revenues are affected by currency impacts as well.

In other words, there is no simple rule of thumb for estimating the impact of a currency's move on either overall profits or an individual company's earnings. Here are some of the "microeconomic" complications for US companies and industries:

- *Lags.* The currency impact on US earnings from abroad is immediate since a stronger (or weaker) dollar automatically reduces (or boosts) the dollar value of foreign currency earnings. On the other hand, the impact on US exports might lag, depending on how demand changes overseas and on how the exporters adjust their prices.

- *Winners and losers.* It's not always simple to extrapolate the winners and losers among industries or types of companies because any given company could be both beneficiary and victim of a currency move. For example, US exporters that suffer when the dollar appreciates relative to a currency of a country where they do business may also benefit from reductions in the prices of imported materials and parts used to produce their products if they are tied to currencies that are depreciating relative to the dollar.

- *Overall profits.* In the relationship of the dollar to overall corporate profits, when the greenback goes down, the net impact tends to be positive for corporate-sector profits generally; when it goes up, the net impact should depress profits on balance.

More specifically, a weak dollar tends to be good for US corporations that export and have operations overseas. Conversely, a strong dollar tends to benefit companies that do most of their business in the United States but rely on imported goods and services to do what they do. Retailers, for example, may enjoy a profits windfall when the dollar is strong since they will spend fewer dollars on imports, which they may be able to sell at the same price as before the dollar strengthened. But they are likely to face stiff competition from other retailers who see an opportunity to attract more customers by passing on their foreign-exchange windfall in the form of lower prices.

So directionally, the effects of currency changes on profits are relatively easy to predict; more difficult is getting the degree of impact correct.

The macroeconomic consequences of currency moves are much more complicated than their direct microeconomic relationship with corporate profits. There are lots of feedback loops between a country's currency and forces in its economy, and between the country and all the foreign countries that have trading and financial relationships with that country. These complications result from the fact that a currency has three broad prices, or exchange rates, since it can be exchanged for goods and services, for financial assets, and for other currencies:

- *Exchange for goods and services.* The exchange rate of a currency for goods and services can be approximated by a country's GDP price deflator. Presumably, the rate of inflation in goods and services determines the buying power of a country's currency over time at home. However, the purchasing power of domestic consumers can increase as long as their wages are rising faster than prices.

- *Exchange for financial assets.* It's not as simple to find a single price for financial assets. However, one of the most important is the price of bonds, which determines their yields. More generally, interest rates reflect the exchange rate between current and future spending. Savers are postponing their current spending so that they can earn a return on their fixed-income securities and deposits. Borrowers are willing to pay the going interest rates to borrow currency to spend today on goods and services rather than waiting until tomorrow.

- *Exchange for other currencies.* Finally, currencies can be exchanged for other currencies in the foreign-exchange markets. This market is a huge one, operating 24/7 around the world. It is an extremely liquid market for most of the major foreign currencies. It is also frequently "managed" by central banks that are "intervening" in this market to peg their currencies' exchange rate to the dollar. Occasionally, they step away to allow market forces to either appreciate or depreciate their currencies, sometimes because the alternative would bring unacceptable consequences.

The Purchasing Power Parity (PPP) Theory holds that currency-exchange rates should tend to equal the ratio of a basket of goods priced in one currency to the same basket priced in another. The UN, International Monetary Fund (IMF), and World Bank monitor PPPs. I've never had occasion to apply this model in my work, though.

Since 1986, *The Economist* has been calculating PPPs for the prices of McDonald's Big Mac™ burgers in many countries. A 2003 article by two economists at the Federal Reserve Bank of St. Louis, titled "Burgernomics: A Big Mac™ Guide to Purchasing Power Parity," rates PPP as a "useful benchmark" but a poor "predictive tool." They conclude: "It is interesting to find that the simple collection of items comprising the Big Mac sandwich does just as well (or just as poorly) at demonstrating the principles and pitfalls of PPP as do more sophisticated measures."[2] Would you like fries with that?

The macro impacts of currency moves are measured economy-wide. They are felt in a country's merchandise trade balance of exports and imports and its foreign capital flows in and out, so they affect its balance of payments. Macro currency impacts also affect prices in the country's domestic markets and thus its rates of inflation, with ramifications for consumer spending and monetary policy. Naturally, all these effects can impact the pace of GDP growth and the strength of the country's economy. And since shifts in the value of one country's currency are mirrored in other countries' currencies, the intricate web of impacts reaches around the globe. For a sense of how complicated this all gets, consider the following:

- *The three prices of a currency are interdependent.* Rising inflation tends to push up interest rates. If inflation rises faster than interest rates, the foreign-exchange value of the currency is likely to depreciate. A depreciating currency is likely to put upward pressure on inflation and interest rates. If interest rates rise faster than inflation—as a result of central bank tightening, for example—the currency is likely to strengthen, and inflation is likely to moderate. There are many more possibilities, depending not only on domestic developments but also on international ones. The latter include monetary policies pursued by foreign central banks.

- *In addition to the "price effects" of currency moves on trade are "income effects," which often dominate.* Imports tend to rise along with domestic demand in so-called "open economies," i.e., those where some of the demand is satisfied with imported goods and services. Rapid domestic growth sometimes boosts imports even as the home currency depreciates in value, because it empowers consumers to make purchase decisions not based solely on price. A government that depreciates its currency to stimulate growth might be frustrated by domestic consumers continuing to spend on imports, even though they've gotten more expensive, while exporters run into weak demand growth overseas. Instead of more export-led growth, the unintended consequence might be higher inflation driven by higher-priced imports.

- *The common notion that a widening trade deficit is bearish for a currency isn't always true.*[3] A country's currency may strengthen despite a widening trade deficit if the economy is booming and attracting lots of foreign capital that easily offsets the trade deficit. In other words, currency moves are driven not just by the current account balances, which consist mostly of the trade balance between exports and imports of goods and services. They also reflect the financial account of investment inflows and outflows for both portfolio and direct investments.

- *Since the end of the Cold War, globalization has affected the advanced economies in ways similar to the effects of their currencies appreciating.* That's because globalization opened up these economies to cheaper imports of products manufactured in emerging economies, which had much lower labor costs. So consumers in advanced economies enjoyed lower prices for imported products. However, many workers in those countries either lost their jobs to foreigners or were forced to take pay cuts.

If your head is spinning by now, all I can say is: "Welcome to my world." I've learned over the years that there are a lot of moving parts when analyzing and predicting currency moves and their impacts on economic growth, inflation rates, interest rates, and profits. I've also found some reliable relationships between currencies and other macroeconomic variables. Before exploring them, a very brief review of events related to the trade-weighted dollar is worthwhile.

BRIEF HISTORY OF THE DOLLAR

I MONITOR A few measures of the trade-weighted dollar, which are indexes reflecting the foreign-exchange value of the dollar compared to the selected foreign currencies of countries that have significant trading relationships with the United States. The currencies in the index are weighted to reflect their countries' share of trade with the United States. The one with the most history is the Fed's index based on the major currencies (Fig. 7). It is available on a weekly basis and goes back to 1973. The Fed also compiles a broader index containing daily figures from 1995 to the present, which is also updated on a weekly basis. Neither is updated fast enough for my needs, so I've come to depend more on the JP Morgan Nominal Broad Effective Exchange Rate, which has been available daily since 1995 (Fig. 8).[4]

I also track the exchange-rate indexes that MSCI uses to calculate the dollar values of the many foreign stock market price indexes it compiles.[5] That means there are currency indexes for all of the various MSCI stock market composites, such as for emerging market economies and developed economies excluding the United States (Fig. 9 and Fig. 10).

As I discuss in Chapter 9, on August 15, 1971, when I was still in college, President Richard Nixon announced that the United States would no longer redeem currency for gold. Nixon's move made no impression on me at the time, though it unleashed the inflationary forces that crested just as my career on Wall Street began in the late 1970s. Nixon's decision to close the so-called "gold window" ended the gold standard and the Bretton Woods system, which had been in effect since 1946.

In 1944, 730 delegates from all 44 nations that made up the Allies in World War II gathered at the Mount Washington Hotel in Bretton Woods, New Hampshire for the United Nations Monetary and Financial Conference, also known as the "Bretton Woods Conference." From July 1 to July 22, the delegates deliberated, signing the Bretton Woods agreement on the final day. The goal was to create rules and institutions that would stabilize the postwar international financial system. The World Bank and IMF were established. Furthermore, the US government promised to redeem other central banks' holdings of dollars for gold at a fixed rate of $35.00 per ounce, as I mention in Chapter 11. Under this system, the participating countries agreed to settle their international balances in US dollars. The signing of the formal documents took place in the Gold Room, located off the hotel lobby and now preserved as a historic site.

During the late 1960s, persistent US balance-of-payments deficits steadily reduced US gold reserves as some central banks exchanged their dollars for gold, as permitted by the Bretton Woods system. Foreign governments did make sure to keep their currencies from appreciating relative to the dollar (as appreciation would harm the competitiveness of their exporters in the United States), so their coffers stayed stocked with plenty of dollars. By the summer of 1971, the rest of the world held three times more dollars than the United States had in gold.[6] Confidence in the ability of the United States to redeem its currency in gold fell sharply, forcing the Nixon administration to abandon the gold standard. Paul Volcker, who was undersecretary of the US Treasury at the time, was the architect of the bold move. The consequences were immediate and significant:

- *CRB index.* The price of gold soared 352% from $41.00 per ounce in July 1971 to peak at $185.25 on February 24, 1975 (Fig. 11). The CRB raw industrials spot price index, which does not include any petroleum products, had been fluctuating in a flat range since 1952 but broke out to a record high during the week of November 14, 1972 and continued to rise sharply by 88% through early 1974, when a severe recession temporarily depressed commodity prices (Fig. 12).
- *Oil price.* The price of a barrel of West Texas crude oil remained stable at $3.56 from the start of 1971 through July 1973, but over the next six months it jumped 184% to $10.11 (Fig. 13). That was the first oil crisis triggered by OPEC's decision to drive prices higher. Contributing to that move was the cartel's concern that the dollar might depreciate now that it was no longer fixed to gold.

- *Trade-weighted dollar.* However, the foreign-exchange value of the dollar didn't fall, as many had expected seeing the gold price's extraordinary rise. That's because closing the gold window meant central banks no longer could redeem their dollars at a fixed price. If they dumped their dollars in the foreign-exchange market, their countries' currencies would appreciate, which would hurt their exports to the United States. So more central banks held dollars than before, supporting the dollar's value.

The dollar did weaken a bit late in the 1970s, but then it soared by 55% from the start of the 1980s to peak at a record high on February 25, 1985. Volcker—who by then was Federal Reserve chairman—raised interest rates dramatically during that time. The global economy, which was also hit by the second OPEC price shock, in 1979, fell into a severe recession, with mounting fears of a global financial contagion. There was a "flight to safety" into the US dollar. Adding to the demand for dollars was the need by global oil users to get more US currency to pay for the commodity, which is priced in dollars.

Interest rates fell during the mid-1980s, and so did the price of oil. The dollar plunged along with both, by the end of the decade losing 38% of its value measured from its record high. The dollar remained relatively weak until the mid-1990s despite another spike in the price of oil during the first Iraq War. During the second half of the 1990s through the beginning of the following decade, the dollar experienced another bull market, ascending 43% from April 19, 1995 through January 28, 2002.

Following the end of the Cold War in the late 1980s, the United States emerged as the world's sole superpower. That became obvious in the early 1990s as the Soviet Union disintegrated. On October 3, 1990, East and West Germany were reunited after 45 years. The Soviet Union was dissolved on December 26, 1991 in a formal declaration that acknowledged the independence of the former Soviet republics. The previous day, Soviet President Mikhail Gorbachev, the eighth and last leader of the Soviet Union, had resigned, handing over the executive powers of his office to Russian President Boris Yeltsin. That same evening, the Soviet flag was lowered from the Kremlin for the last time, replaced with the pre-revolution Russian flag.

Less obvious at that time was that America's economy, which had been struggling with deindustrialization during the 1970s and 1980s, was emerging as the world's technology leader. As that became increasingly apparent during the 1990s, investors from around the world poured money into US technology stocks. They soared, and so did the dollar, as dollars were needed by foreign investors to buy US stocks. The booming US economy and a strong dollar widened the US trade deficit, meaning that America was importing more value than it was exporting (Fig. 14). The United States became increasingly dependent on imported crude oil, which also widened the trade deficit.

So why didn't the dollar weaken as the trade deficit widened, as textbooks suggest happens when a country's imports exceed its exports? Because the capital inflows—as foreign investors bought dollars to participate in US financial markets and as foreign central banks bought dollars to weaken their currencies and thereby strengthen their exports—were more than sufficient to keep the dollar strong. In addition, the US economic boom converted the US federal government's budget deficit into a surplus during the late 1990s (Fig. 15). The publicly held marketable US Treasury debt outstanding declined 22%, by $779 billion, from March 1997 through July 2001 (Fig. 16). Fewer Treasury bonds on the market meant that the US fiscal outlook was improving rapidly, which also bolstered the dollar.

The party for the dollar bulls ended after the 9/11 terror attacks. The United States was still perceived to be the world's preeminent military and economic superpower. However, the peace dividend, which helped to boost the US economy during the 1990s, was about to disappear as America started to wage the "War on Terror." The Cold War was replaced with hot wars in the Middle East against Islamic jihadists. The US federal budget surplus turned into a deficit very quickly.

The value of the dollar proceeded to fall 27% from February 27, 2002 through July 15, 2008. Contributing to the reversal of the dollar's fortune at the start of the decade was the bursting of the tech bubble in the stock market. The Fed responded to the resulting recession by lowering interest rates and keeping them very low following the 9/11 attacks. Fed officials feared a prolonged recession and fretted about deflation. They didn't start raising the federal funds rate until June 30, 2004. Then they raised it by 25 basis points at each of the next 16 Federal Open Market Committee (FOMC) meetings, at what was billed as a "measured pace."

It all added up to a bearish environment for the dollar. Contributing to the dollar's weakness was the emergence of emerging markets and their bullish impact on commodity prices.

The JP Morgan trade-weighted dollar peaked at the start of 2002. Since then, it has developed a very tight inverse correlation with the CRB raw industrials spot price index, the price of a barrel of Brent crude oil, and the Emerging Markets MSCI stock price index (in local currencies):

- The JP Morgan trade-weighted dollar fell 27% from its February 27, 2002 peak to its July 15, 2008 low.
- The CRB raw industrials spot price index rose 145% from November 5, 2001 to May 13, 2008 (Fig. 17). The price of oil soared 777% from November 15, 2001 to July 3, 2008 (Fig. 18).
- The Emerging Markets MSCI, in dollars, soared 425% from October 10, 2002 to October 29, 2007 (Fig. 19). As noted at the start of this chapter, US international equity mutual funds saw significant inflows after China joined the WTO, as investment demand for stocks exposed to emerging economies took off globally. Many of these economies were significant producers of commodities, which were in great demand (particularly in China); most major commodities are priced in dollars.

So why didn't the dollar soar along with commodity prices? How come an inverse correlation developed instead? The producers in the emerging markets chose to diversify their dollar windfalls into other major currencies. The international capital that had poured into the United States during the tech boom of the late 1990s poured out of emerging economies and made them vulnerable to a financial crisis, specifically in Southeast Asia during 1997 and Russia during 1998. From 2002 to 2008, international capital flows reversed, rushing into emerging economies, especially the commodity producers.

The Emerging Markets MSCI, which had plunged 43% in US dollars from the start of 1995 through to October 10, 2002, then rose 425% to October 29, 2007. It would have increased much more but for all the foreign-exchange intervention of the central banks in the emerging world. These policymakers didn't want their countries' currencies to get too strong, fearing that their exports then would be less competitive in world markets. In addition, this was a great opportunity for them to build up their dollar reserves as a cushion against a financial crisis like the ones of the late 1990s. So they accumulated lots of dollars while satisfying the high demand for their currencies. Consequently, the dollar value of non-gold international reserves—which includes currencies other than the dollar held by the central banks of emerging economies—soared by $1.4 trillion to $2.6 trillion from the start of 2000 through mid-2008 (Fig. 20).

The trade-weighted dollar soared during the financial crisis of 2008. Ironically, the US was the epicenter of that crisis thanks to the contagion that spread through most of the US fixed-income markets and overseas once the US housing bubble burst. Yet investors around the world still viewed the United States as the safest place to park their funds, so the dollar spiked by 21% from its low in mid-2008 through early 2009.

As the crisis eased, the dollar fell again, this time by 18% through mid-2011. It moved erratically higher through mid-2014 on mounting evidence that the US economy was recovering from the financial crisis and recession of 2008 much better than were Europe and Japan. It became increasingly likely that the Fed would move toward normalizing monetary policy ahead of the other major central banks. This was confirmed during May 2013, when Fed Chairman Ben Bernanke triggered a "taper tantrum" in financial markets—i.e., fears that the Fed might soon taper down and end its quantitative easing (QE) program. The dollar jumped.

Sure enough, the Fed terminated QE at the end of October 2014. During December 2015, the Fed raised the federal funds rate by 25 basis points. Meanwhile, the other major central banks expanded and extended their ultra-easy monetary policies. Consequently, the dollar soared by 23% from July 1, 2014 through January 20, 2016. It weakened a bit over the rest of the year, but then it rebounded dramatically following Donald Trump's victory on November 8, 2016. It peaked again on January 11, 2017, 26% above its mid-2014 level.

The dollar's subsequent weakness in 2017 may seem counterintuitive, since the Fed continued to raise the federal funds rate and started to reduce its balance sheet that year. Meanwhile, the European Central Bank (ECB) and the Bank of Japan maintained their ultra-easy monetary policies. However, the foreign-exchange market had already discounted the divergence in monetary policies. Now it was starting to anticipate that improving economic activity in the Eurozone and Japan might cause their central banks to reverse course and join the Fed in gradually normalizing their monetary policies. Furthermore, economic growth overseas was showing more signs of picking up, which tends to strengthen foreign currencies relative to the dollar. The rebound in global growth was reflected in rising commodity prices, particularly oil prices, which continued their inverse correlation with the dollar.

THE OIL STANDARD

I WASN'T SURPRISED by the strength in the dollar from mid-2014 through early 2016. In 2014, I concluded that the commodity supercycle might be over, and I had also been monitoring the close inverse correlation between the dollar and commodity prices, especially the price of oil. The increasingly obvious divergence between the monetary policy paths of the Fed versus those of the other major central banks also supported a stronger dollar forecast. The inverse correlation between the dollar and the price of oil seemed to be tighter than ever from mid-2014 through 2016.

The simplest explanation for this relationship may also be the best one. When the price of oil is relatively high, oil-exporting nations are earning lots of dollars. Some of them may prefer to diversify their currency holdings, which depresses the value of the dollar relative to the currencies purchased in exchange for their dollars. That's especially likely if their governments have a hostile relationship with the United States. Iran, Russia, and Venezuela come to mind, but even friendlier regimes are unlikely to put all their international currency reserves in one currency basket, especially since their oil reserves are priced in dollars. When the price of oil is relatively low, oil exporters simply don't accumulate as many dollars to convert to other currencies. With less selling of the dollar by oil exporters, its value tends to rise relative to other currencies.

This explanation probably also works for most of the other commodities priced in dollars. Of course, there is a feedback loop in this story too: a strong dollar increases the local currency prices of commodities priced in dollars, thus reducing demand, which depresses their dollar prices; a weak dollar boosts demand for such commodities because their local currency prices are lower.

Every now and then, just when I find a strong correlation such as the one between commodity prices and the inverse of the dollar, and come up with a good theory to explain it, the relationship breaks down. Rather than view this as a setback, I see it as an opportunity to assess what has changed in the relationship that might have important investment implications.

I believe that the relationship between commodity prices and commodity currencies is likely to remain very close, almost by definition. Both will remain hard to predict, of course, but they are likely to stay bound to one another. Among the most liquid and heavily traded commodity currencies are the Canadian dollar and the Australian dollar. Both are highly correlated with one another and with the CRB raw industrials spot price index (Fig. 21 and Fig. 22).

THE BALANCE OF PAYMENTS ALWAYS BALANCES

FORECASTING CURRENCIES BASED on fundamentals can be very challenging, as I noted before, because there are so many variables that influence the value of a currency relative to other currencies. The best way to understand the complexity of this exercise is to examine the balance-of-payments accounts. There are three broad components of these accounts:

- *The current account.* The current account includes the trade balance, i.e., the difference between exports and imports of goods and services. Also included is the difference between income receipts and payments resulting from overseas transactions.

   This account saw a widening deficit in the United States during the 1980s as a result of costlier oil imports and rising auto and semiconductor imports from Japan, plus a growing dependence on foreign oil (Fig. 23). It was briefly back in balance during the four quarters of 1991. Then it widened significantly during the 1990s and 2000s, reaching a record $207 billion over the four quarters ending with the third quarter of 2006. Soaring imports from China accounted for a significant portion of this swelling current account deficit. It narrowed following the Great Recession but remained relatively large despite the drop in the price of oil imports from mid-2014 through the end of 2016.

- *The financial account.* The financial account shows the difference between capital inflows and outflows, both of which include direct investments and portfolio investments.

   The widening US current account deficit was offset in a mirror-like fashion by the widening surplus in the financial account. Countries running large trade surpluses with the US purchased US securities with their trade windfalls. Much of that buying was by America's Asian trading partners, especially by the central banks that aimed to keep their currencies from appreciating.

- *Statistical discrepancy.* The balance of payments must always balance. For the United States, this is done by showing a statistical discrepancy item for the difference between the current account and the financial account (Fig. 24). (See Appendix 12.1, US International Transactions.)

- *International reserves.* Other countries also report a statistical discrepancy. But that's after they buy or sell the foreign currency reserves held by their central banks to manage the foreign-exchange values of their currencies relative to the US dollar as well as relative to other currencies.

When Nixon closed the gold window, he effectively forced the world to accept a "dollar standard." The dollar, which already was the pre-eminent reserve currency held by central banks, now could no longer be exchanged for gold. Other central banks could balance their current and capital accounts by intervening in the foreign-exchange market to purchase or sell dollars. Since the United States was running a widening trade deficit with the world, most central banks purchased dollars to balance their balance of payments as their current accounts expanded faster than their capital accounts.

Alternatively, they could have done nothing, which would have caused their currencies to appreciate relative to the dollar. That exchange rate-adjustment mechanism would have balanced their balance of payments by depressing their exports and boosting their imports. That wasn't a desirable outcome for many of America's trading partners, so they accumulated dollar reserves. In other words, they chose to manage their exchange rate, pegging it to the dollar rather than letting it float freely to whatever level was necessary to balance their balance of payments.

Foreign economies benefited greatly from the forces that were widening the US trade deficit, making America's exports less competitive in marketplaces abroad and the foreign-made goods that America imported very competitive in the US marketplace. So their central banks were more than willing to fund the widening of the US trade deficit by converting the dollars pouring into their countries' export industries into their local currencies. That kept the dollar strong and their currencies weak as their international dollar reserves piled up.

The dollar standard has been very advantageous for the United States. Since the dollar is the key international reserve currency, any differences between the US current account and the portion of the US financial account related to net purchases of US securities by private foreign investors were completely financed by foreign central banks' purchases of US government securities. Because the overall balance of payments always balances, the role of the dollar in international finance virtually guarantees that foreign central banks provide some, and maybe much, of the financing of both the US trade deficit and the US federal deficit.

The dollar standard encouraged chronic US trade and budget deficits. It also made other countries dependent on the US economy as a "locomotive" pulling their economies along via their trade surpluses with the United States. This means that US economic policies can have a powerful impact on other countries. Here is a stylized rundown of what often happens during the business cycle:

- *US monetary easing and economic recovery expand US trade deficit.* During recessions, the United States tends to adopt stimulative monetary and fiscal policies to revive US economic growth. The resulting rebound in demand typically widens the US merchandise trade deficit because imports rise faster than exports. The growth of imports is boosted by recovering domestic demand. The growth of exports usually lags because overseas economic growth tends to trail recoveries in the United States. So the US trade deficit as a percentage of nominal GDP is likely to narrow during recessions and widen during recoveries and expansions.

- *Expanding trade deficit depresses value of US dollar.* As the trade deficit widens during recoveries, the trade-weighted foreign-exchange value of the dollar tends to fall. This happens because the widening trade deficit increases the supply of dollars in the foreign-exchange market as US importers seek the foreign currencies they need to buy foreign-made goods. Foreign exporters who are paid in dollars by US customers seek to convert their dollar receipts into their local currencies.[7]

- *Foreign central banks buy dollars, propping up the dollar's value.* At this early stage of a global recovery, foreign central bankers often choose to prop up the dollar relative to their currency. To do so, they purchase dollars and sell their own currency in the foreign-exchange market. Why? To keep their currencies from appreciating, because when a nation's currency does so relative to the dollar, the nation's exports to the United States become more expensive and therefore less competitive in the world's biggest and most rapidly recovering consumer and business market. To fully benefit from the recovery in the United States, central bankers naturally tend to intervene in the currency markets by buying dollars. Rapidly growing exports to the United States spread the US boom to the rest of the world.

- *Such foreign intervention spreads US monetary ease globally.* The central banks also tend to spread and to amplify the Fed's easy monetary policy worldwide. If they don't "sterilize" their US dollar purchases (and domestic currency sales) through open-market sales of domestic bonds—thus buying back their local currency—then the rapid growth of their international reserves, i.e., dollars, will increase their domestic monetary base and money supply.

- *When the Fed tightens, the dollar strengthens and foreign central banks' intervention slows.* When the Federal Reserve tightens monetary policy, dollar reserves growth tends to slow. The dollar typically strengthens when monetary policy turns more restrictive. Foreign central banks no longer must intervene as aggressively in the currency markets to support the dollar. Also, as noted above, when the global economic expansion matures, policy-driven liquidity tends to be replaced by prosperity-driven liquidity, i.e., more jobs, more incomes, more consumption, and more private savings.

CAPITAL FLOWS IN AND OUT

THE PROBLEM WITH the balance-of-payments accounts for those of us who need to predict currencies is that while there are plenty of monthly data series for merchandise trade balances around the world, financial accounts are mostly reported quarterly with a lag. Trade surpluses and deficits tend to be fairly persistent and somewhat predictable. Capital flows, on the other hand, can be quite volatile because they include lots of short-term "hot money" that can come and go from a country overnight. A country that has become very dependent on short-term loans from foreigners is a prime target of speculators who will depreciate its currency if they believe that those inflows might reverse quickly for one reason or another. Of course, such speculative attacks can be self-fulling prophecies, especially if the central bank is running out of reserves to defend its currency against the speculators.

The best I can do to quantify all these relationships as simply as possible and with relatively current data is to reverse-engineer the financial account. I derive a proxy for the international capital flows of a country by subtracting the country's trade balance, which is available monthly for almost all countries, from the change in the non-gold international reserves held by the country's central bank. This approach requires smoothing out the data by using the 12-month sum of the trade surplus (or deficit) and the year-over-year change in reserves.

From an accounting perspective, if a country is accumulating reserves, it may have a current account and financial account surplus, a current account surplus that exceeds the financial account deficit, or a financial account surplus that exceeds the current account deficit. Of course, if the country's central bank chooses not to accumulate reserves under any of these three scenarios, its currency will appreciate.

This residual approach to calculating capital flows was very useful for detecting a sudden and massive net outflow of capital from China starting in 2014. Since January 2002, just after China joined the WTO, through August 2014, capital inflows totaled $1.6 trillion according to this approach. From September 2014 through December 2016, net capital outflows were $2.2 trillion (Fig. 25 and Fig. 26).

Now keep in mind that these calculations are in dollars. The outflows were so large that the People's Bank of China had to intervene in the foreign-exchange market by purchasing its currency with its dollar reserves. It did so to slow the depreciation of its currency. China's reserves peaked at a record high of $4.0 trillion during June 2014 and fell to $3.0 trillion by the end of 2016. Not surprisingly, there has been a strong correlation between China's reserves and the foreign-exchange value of the yuan (Fig. 27).

Every month, I review the available monthly data for the 12-month trade balances and the 12-month changes in reserves of several major countries. I look for any early warning that something important is changing in one or more of those countries. In China's case, the capital outflows suggest that the government's anti-corruption drive, which started during 2013, may have triggered an exodus of capital by wealthy Chinese, who were trying to protect their wealth by moving more of it overseas.

Over the years, I've learned that one insight can lead to another. My analysis of country data was like looking at the trees without seeing the forest. It dawned on me that maybe I could create a monthly capital flows series for the world excluding the United States, and that it might help to explain, if not forecast, the moves in the trade-weighted dollar.

On a 12-month basis, the United States has been running widening trade deficits for many years (Fig. 28). The trade deficit of the United States must equal the trade surplus of the rest of the world. So the 12-month change of non-gold international reserves held by all central banks (with the notable exception of the Fed, thanks to the dollar standard) minus the trade surplus of the rest of the world should be a proxy for capital inflows (outflows) to the rest of the world from (to) the United States (Fig. 29). The global capital flows proxy series starts in 1995. Here is what it shows:

- *High-tech boom years.* Capital flowed out of the rest of the world and into the United States during the second half of the 1990s, presumably reflecting foreign investors' pouring of money into the US tech-stock boom. Those inflows stopped during the early 2000s following the tech-stock bust.

- *Housing bubble years.* Capital rushed out of the United States during 2007 and early 2008, presumably as global investors decided to overweight emerging market economies. By the way, this seems to raise some doubts about the Bernanke/Greenspan "global savings glut" that purportedly flooded the US mortgage market at the time, thereby causing the housing bubble. Or, more likely, there was enough global liquidity to inflate assets all around the world.

- *Great Recession years.* The United States was a safe haven during the financial crisis of late 2008 through 2009 as the international capital flows proxy turned negative, suggesting net inflows to the United States.

- *Reaching for yield.* From 2010 through early 2012, the rest of the world experienced large capital inflows—again, mostly to emerging economies as global investors "reached for yields" in reaction to developed economies' zero-interest-rate policies and QE programs. Such extreme monetary ease suppressed yields on interest-earning investments in developed nations to such a degree that investors flocked into emerging economies' credit markets in their quest for acceptable yields.

- *Oil price plunges.* For a brief period during 2013 and early 2014, world capital flows were roughly in balance. But the extraordinary plunge in the price of oil that started during the summer of 2014 and lasted through early 2016 seemed once again to cause global investors to seek shelter in safe-haven assets in the United States. At about the same time, China's international capital flows proxy also showed huge outflows to the rest of the world, with much of that probably going to the United States.

The credibility of my proxy for international capital flows between the United States and the rest of the world is confirmed by its high inverse correlation with the yearly percent change in the trade-weighted dollar (Fig. 30). This makes a great deal of sense. It suggests that the dollar is much more sensitive to capital flows than to trade. When the rest of the world is experiencing capital inflows, the dollar tends to be weak. When capital is pouring out of the rest of the world and into the United States, the dollar tends to be strong.

The non-gold international reserves component of my proxy tends to be much more volatile than the trade component, reflecting the greater volatility of capital flows than of merchandise trade. Therefore, it isn't surprising to see that the inverse of the yearly percent change in the trade-weighted dollar is also highly correlated with both the 12-month absolute change and the 12-month percent change in non-gold international reserves (Fig. 31 and Fig. 32).

This is certainly consistent with the tendency of the financial press to explain sharp short-term increases in the foreign-exchange value of the dollar as "flights to safety." When the world is experiencing financial or geopolitical turmoil, global investors tend to seek safe-haven investments. Gold may seem to be the obvious choice, but US government securities are also deemed safe havens. To buy them, foreigners first need to buy dollars with their currencies.

There is one important caveat when analyzing any global economic data, especially when comparing different countries. In this case, my proxy for international capital flows is based on the dollar values of both the 12-month sum of trade balances and the 12-month change in international reserves. In a world of pegged exchange rates, the proxy should be a good one for capital flows. However, it might be distorted by currency swings.

In China's case, the dollar was strong from 2014 to 2016; this depressed the dollar value of reserves held by China's central bank, which include not only dollars but also euros and yen. Those foreign currencies were worth less in dollars. At the same time, China's trade surplus was expanding in yuan but flat in dollars. It's difficult to sort out the net effect other than to assume that it probably doesn't distort the conclusion about capital flows much since both reserves and the trade surplus in dollars are depressed by a weak yuan.

Finally, I should note that in addition to monthly data on the non-gold international reserves of the world's central banks, the IMF compiles quarterly data on their total foreign-exchange holdings. There isn't much difference between the quarterly series and the monthly one for all the central banks (Fig. 33). The IMF posts the quarterly data in a publication titled *Currency Composition of Official Foreign Exchange Reserves*. Not all of the central banks disclose these figures, so the IMF shows the composition of so-called "allocated" reserves, for which data are available. These indicate that the dollar accounted for roughly 72% of allocated reserves in 1999, falling to about 61% in 2011 (Fig. 34), then rising to about 64% during 2016.

THE FED AND THE DOLLAR

THE FOREIGN-EXCHANGE VALUE of the dollar is rarely mentioned in the minutes of the FOMC, strongly suggesting that it is rarely discussed during the committee's monetary policy deliberations. A scan of the Federal Reserve System's various websites shows very few research papers focused on currency markets. On the other hand, the FOMC meeting minutes always are full of discussions about inflation and interest rates, and even asset prices. Why? Traditionally, the US Treasury has been deemed the government agency in charge of foreign-exchange policy. In the past, whenever the United States was involved in international negotiations on global exchange-rate issues, US Treasury officials represented the United States.

During my entire career, the only time the dollar was discussed much at FOMC meetings was during 2015 and early 2016. The 26% appreciation of the trade-weighted dollar from mid-2014 through early 2017 certainly raised some concerns about its negative impact on exports at a time when the Fed was worrying about the slow pace of economic activity. In addition, the strong dollar weighed on import prices and inflation at a time when the Fed was hoping that its policies would boost inflation toward its 2.0% target.

The Fed began to normalize monetary policy in late 2014 when it terminated QE at the end of October and hiked the federal funds rate by 25 basis points during December 2015; meanwhile, the other major central banks continued to pursue their ultra-easy monetary policies. As a result, the dollar soared just as the Fed was achieving its dual mandate, with the unemployment rate down to around 5.0% and core inflation approaching 2.0%. Fed officials mentioned their concerns about the adverse impact of a strong dollar on their dual-mandate mission but expected that it would have a transient impact once the dollar had peaked.

On September 12, 2016, Fed Governor Lael Brainard presented a speech titled "The 'New Normal' and What It Means for Monetary Policy," calling for "prudence in the removal of policy accommodation."[8] She listed several reasons for this, including a very specific estimate of the impact of the strong dollar on the economy. She said, "In particular, estimates from the FRB/US model suggest that the nearly 20 percent appreciation of the dollar from June 2014 to January of this year could be having an effect on US economic activity roughly equivalent to a 200-basis-point increase in the federal funds rate." I had been making the same point since late 2015. It was good to see a top Fed official acknowledge that the foreign-exchange value of the dollar matters.

There was much angst when the dollar continued to move higher through early 2017. Following the election of Donald Trump on November 8, 2016, it jumped 5.4% to peak on January 11, 2017 at 126.2, putting the dollar 26% above its mid-2014 low. I wasn't convinced that it was likely to head higher, given how much it had appreciated already. As noted above, it seemed to me that the foreign-exchange markets had already discounted the fact that the Fed had been normalizing monetary policy since October 2014. While the ECB's QE program pushed the bank's assets above the Fed's assets during April 2017, economic growth in the Eurozone was showing signs of improving (Fig. 35). This suggested that the ECB would move toward normalizing monetary policy for the Eurozone sooner rather than later. We'll see. At the end of October 2017, the ECB halved its monthly bond purchases to €30 billion starting January 2018 but extended the bond-purchase program until at least September 2018.

From late 2015 through June 2017, the Fed raised the federal funds rate four times. The last two rate hikes occurred after the dollar peaked (Fig. 36). This was an important signal suggesting the foreign-exchange markets were starting to anticipate that the Fed's monetary normalization was well advanced. In addition, the so-called "Trump bump" seemed to have run its course as the markets concluded that his fiscal stimulus agenda was running into lots of speed bumps in Washington, DC.

In a July 11, 2017 speech titled "Cross-Border Spillovers of Balance Sheet Normalization," Fed Governor Brainard said that there would not be "much more additional work to do on moving to a neutral stance" from the current moderately accommodative stance.[9] She added that the FOMC "decided to delay balance sheet normalization until the federal funds rate had reached a high enough level to enable it to be cut materially if economic conditions deteriorate." She mentioned "exchange rate" 47 times in her comments and footnotes, obviously acknowledging that the foreign-exchange value of the dollar is now an important consideration in the setting of monetary policy. Brainard seemed to conclude that it is best to lean toward reducing the balance sheet, as in her opinion, that should put less upward pressure on the dollar than raising interest rates. In other words, rate hikes might end soon once balance-sheet reductions start.

There are lots of lessons to be learned from my adventures in forecasting bonds, commodities, and currencies. Three that I can't emphasize strongly enough are:

- Paying close attention to what central banks are doing and are likely to be doing is extremely important. Markets discount the future, not the past or the present. However, the past and the present always remain relevant to predicting the future.
- When markets don't behave as expected in response to current events and indicators, that may be a tipoff suggesting an important inflection point in what matters to the markets.
- Reversion to the mean is always relevant when forecasting markets, especially currency and commodity markets. They tend to be much more cyclical than stock markets, which generally trend higher along with earnings. So anytime I see a commodity price or a currency move either straight up or straight down, my contrary instincts go on full alert.

All these lessons are relevant to forecasting the stock market as well. Without any further ado, that's what we'll explore in the next three chapters.

CHAPTER 13

Predicting Corporate Earnings

INDUSTRY OF INDUSTRIOUS ANALYSTS

MY CAREER BEGAN with a stint at the Federal Reserve Bank of New York as a staff economist, then took me to the research departments of several Wall Street firms as their chief economist. I learned much at each of these positions. In particular, I have fond memories of working closely with two remarkable chief investment strategists—Greg Smith at both EF Hutton and Prudential-Bache Securities, and Jim Moltz at CJ Lawrence and Deutsche Bank's US equities division. These mentors taught me a great deal about forecasting corporate earnings, valuation, and the stock market. When it came to learning about investment strategy, they were my Jedi masters.

In April 1999, I jumped at the opportunity that opened for me at Deutsche Bank to take on a dual role as the chief investment strategist *and* chief economist of the bank's US equities division. This was a new role among the major Wall Street firms, and it's one I've played ever since.

I occasionally quipped in meetings with accounts that I took on the extra chores of an investment strategist because they're easy: I only needed to forecast two numbers, earnings and the price-to-earnings ratio, in the stock market equation:

$$P = P/E \cdot E$$

P = *Stock price index*

P/E = *Price-to-earnings ratio*

E = *Earnings*

Forecasting these is easy; getting them right is the hard part. Providing an informed prediction of the stock market requires good forecasts of all the key economic indicators that I have to monitor as an economist, along with lots of other variables that drive stock prices. At the end of the day, all forecasts are opinions, but they should be well-informed opinions based on all the relevant available data. My goal was to achieve fact-based, rather than faith-based, predictions of the stock market.

Greg and Jim were great mentors. They were very solid, traditional investment strategists who focused on the fundamentals and the valuation of earnings. That was my focus as well. Nevertheless, everyone has their own approach and style. As an economist, I wanted to get closer to the underlying data driving the stock market. I needed to develop a database with analytics that would guide my forecasts. In the process of doing so, I developed my own tools for predicting the stock market.

Greg and Jim focused their work on their own "top-down" earnings forecasts for the current year and coming year. I started to modify this approach during 2001 with my "Earnings Squiggles" analytical framework, which focuses on the "bottom-up" earnings expectations of industry analysts.

Why use analysts' expectations? Think about it: the stock market discounts future expected earnings. Past and current earnings are relevant, but only to the extent that they influence the outlook for earnings. Whose earnings expectations does the market discount, and how far into the future? The market doesn't discount the earnings expectations of individual investment strategists or even the consensus expectations of top-down strategists. It discounts the bottom-up consensus earnings expectations of industry analysts. It's those expectations that I want to quantify and use in the stock market equation as a benchmark for my own forecasts.

Therefore, the bottom-up earnings expectations data that I use are an aggregation of the estimates for all the stocks in the index covered by analysts. As the saying goes, the stock market is a market of stocks. So using bottom-up earnings estimates makes more sense than using top-down forecasts.

On Wall Street, I was a member of the equity research departments in the firms where I worked, so I was surrounded by industry analysts. I listened to them at our morning meetings with the sales force. I had lunch with them. Many were good friends. Industry analysts are particularly well informed about the companies they follow. Wall Street research firms hire them, and they are very well compensated.

Investors closely follow the analysts' earnings forecasts and the revisions to their forecasts. Publicly traded corporations report their earnings on a quarterly basis and provide guidance about their prospects. They do so in quarterly conference calls attended by industry analysts as well as investors. Investors react to what they hear on the calls and rely on the analysts for additional analysis and insights.

Every business morning, Wall Street firms have their research meetings, which typically last about 30–45 minutes. They are usually run by a senior person in research who is charged with supervising the analysts. He or she schedules the analysts who have something important to say about their companies and industries. The audience is the equity sales force. Some are there in person, while others listen in using various telecommunication devices. After the morning meetings, which always occur before the market opens, the salespeople call their institutional accounts. They relay the information and opinions provided by the analysts about the earnings outlooks of the companies they follow in their specific industries and related issues.

The analysts maintain detailed financial spreadsheets of key metrics for the companies they follow and update them regularly as new information becomes available. They run "channel checks" to assess the business environment for their companies. They formulate quarterly earnings estimates for the current year and the next one. Most also provide their estimates of earnings growth over the next three to five years. The more influential ones can move the stock prices of the companies they follow when they change their earnings estimates and their buy/sell/hold stock ratings.

Of course, company managements are the most important source of information about earnings. Federal securities laws require publicly traded companies to disclose certain information, both periodically and as specific events occur.

During the quarterly "earnings seasons," companies report their financial results for the recently concluded quarter. The news comes out in press releases summarizing the details shown in Form 10-Q, a comprehensive financial performance report that all public companies submit quarterly to the Securities and Exchange Commission (SEC). In the 10-Q, firms are required to disclose relevant information regarding their financial situation, including unaudited financial statements. The exact filing deadlines depend on the firm's fiscal year, but three 10-Q reports must be filed each year. After fiscal fourth quarters conclude, companies file with the SEC an annual 10-K report, which is audited. Both the 10-Qs and the 10-Ks are publicly released.

The quarterly earnings seasons during which publicly traded corporations report their results start the week after the end of each calendar quarter and last about six weeks. Investors are very sensitive to earnings surprises. If a company's management reports even a penny per share better or worse than expected, the company's valuation and stock price may change in response, causing total gains or losses measured in the millions, and sometimes even billions, of dollars.

The chief executive officer and chief financial officer usually schedule a conference call to discuss their company's results and the outlook for the future. The calls are open to the public and attended by analysts who cover the company. The conference call may prompt a stock's price to react to the quarterly results for a second time as management elaborates on the reasons for the results and the reasoning behind their forward guidance, as well as answers questions from analysts and investors.

At times, managements provide guidance to analysts several weeks before the quarterly results are released. Such a "preannouncement" is usually aimed at either lowering or raising the analysts' earnings expectations to avoid a big surprise and an excessive plunge or jump in the company's stock price. Guidance most often occurs during earnings seasons conference calls. For example, management might warn during a call reviewing the quarter's results that future quarters may be more challenging and explain why. This is why analysts' forecasts usually show little dispersion. If the guidance triggers a significant change in analysts' assessment of the prospects for the company, the stock price can undergo a seismic move that day. Moreover, big price moves can occur even without any new guidance if a single well-regarded analyst changes his or her outlook for the company for any reason at all.

During August 2000, the SEC introduced Regulation Fair Disclosure, more commonly known as "Reg. FD." This measure was aimed at limiting the widespread practice by top officials at publicly traded companies of selectively disclosing important information to their favorite securities analysts and biggest institutional investors. Individual investors had been at a disadvantage because they often obtained the information days or even weeks later from the financial press. Indeed, prior to Reg. FD, most companies did not allow small investors to attend their conference calls.

To level the playing field, the SEC mandated publicly traded companies to disclose any information deemed material to all market participants at the same time. That ruling resulted in the current protocol—which entails releasing corporate information in press releases that are disseminated to everyone simultaneously via newswires and social media, broadcasting conference calls live online, providing access to archived recordings of the conference call webcasts, and making available online the transcripts of the calls.[1]

All this public disclosure hasn't changed the way analysts forecast earnings, but it has restricted their ability to talk to managements. So it is harder for analysts to glean important insights that might help them to estimate the latest earnings more accurately than their competitors. In other words, they must work harder and smarter to shine than they did in the old days.

How do analysts analyze companies? Most develop earnings models, which essentially are income statement spreadsheets that change based on assumptions for key revenue and cost drivers. The top line is revenues; the bottom line is earnings per share. From the top line to the bottom line, analysts must project numerous variables, including prices, unit sales, the cost of goods sold, depreciation, taxes, interest expense, and shares outstanding. They must assess the competitive environment in their industry and the overall business climate and outlook. For companies with overseas businesses, global economic activity and foreign-exchange rates can have a significant impact on financial statements. (See Appendix 13.1, S&P 500 Summary Income Statement.)

Some companies' profitability can be impacted dramatically by new legislation or changes in government regulations. Wall Street research firms therefore usually have analysts who cover legislative and regulatory developments in Washington, DC. Analysts generally forecast "operating" earnings rather than "reported" earnings, which are hard to predict because they include discontinued operations and extraordinary one-time losses and gains.

Some businesses are highly leveraged to the economy; others are less so. Clearly, analysts who cover companies in industries with relatively stable earnings growth don't need to spend much time worrying about the business cycle. They are more likely to focus on company-specific developments, such as new products, processes, management, and competition. Analysts covering industries that are sensitive to the business cycle must also place greater weight on the outlook for the economy in their earnings estimates.

As an economist in a large Wall Street firm, I had some of my closest professional relationships with the analysts who covered "cyclicals," such as automobile manufacturing and semiconductors, since those industries' profits often determined the direction of S&P 500 earnings. These analysts needed to keep abreast of my thoughts on the economic outlook, and I gleaned insights on the economy from their feedback on the companies they covered.

DISCOUNTING FORWARD EARNINGS

THE STOCK MARKET is forward-looking, and stock prices discount future earnings prospects, so I rarely use so-called "trailing earnings" in the stock market equation. More specifically, I believe that stock investors are basing their decisions on the outlook for earnings over the year ahead, i.e., the next 12 months (or 52 weeks). Experienced investors recognize that anything beyond that is too far off to forecast with any degree of accuracy. Investors obviously rely on industry analysts for their insights about earnings. Consequently, I view analysts' consensus forecasts as a treasure trove of valuable information on earnings for the stock market equation.

Unfortunately, analysts don't provide rolling earnings forecasts for the coming 12 months; like company managements, they focus on quarterly estimates for the remainder of the current year and the following one. Fortunately, Thomson Reuters' I/B/E/S fills this void. In addition to compiling analysts' consensus revenues and earnings expectations for individual corporations and calculating aggregate revenues and earnings series for industries, sectors, and broad stock market indexes, Thomson Reuters provides a useful proxy called "12-month forward consensus expected earnings" for the S&P 500, which starts during September 1978. This series supplies the forward-looking earnings (E) and the forward-looking valuation (P/E) I need to assess the stock market.

In 2000, I hired Joe Abbott to help me develop an in-house database and analytical tools to monitor and analyze the consensus data from I/B/E/S, which stands for "Institutional Brokers' Estimate System," so that we could track forward earnings for the S&P 500, its 11 sectors, and the more than 100 industries that compose them.[2] Joe had been a senior equity strategist at I/B/E/S for 14 years, before it was acquired by Thomson Financial during 2000, so he was exceptionally well qualified for the job. Together, we developed a simple graphical framework for visualizing the I/B/E/S consensus data.

We dubbed the framework "Earnings Squiggles" because the time series for each calendar-year forecast, which we update monthly and weekly, tend to look like squiggly lines (Fig. 1 and Fig. 2*). Forward earnings is simply a time-weighted average over the next 12 months of the analysts' latest consensus estimates of earnings for the current year and for the coming year. At the start of a year (i.e., in January), forward earnings is identical to the current year's consensus forecast. One month later (i.e., in February), forward earnings is the weighted average of 11/12 of the current year's estimate and 1/12 of the coming year's estimate. So as any given year progresses, forward earnings gradually converges with the estimate for the coming year, and by January it is once again fully reflective of that next year's outlook. Of course, next year's earnings estimate is a moving target because it changes as analysts revise their earnings estimates, as does the current year's estimate. (See Appendix 13.2, Deriving 12-Month Forward Earnings.)

In the monthly charts, we show every year's squiggle spanning 25 months from February to February, i.e., 11 months before the year begins and two months after it ends. That's because for calculating forward earnings, the next year only enters the calculation once the current year is one month old, as just noted above. Then the squiggles run through the 12 months of the actual year and another two months after it ends. That's because the fourth quarter's results for each year are reported in the earnings season during January, with some stragglers during February. Each annual squiggle starts one year early since it needs to be time-weighted with the current year. Each annual squiggle ends after earnings are released for the final quarter of the year it covers, though it only matters through the end of its year.

This may be a bit confusing, so a more specific example should help to make sense of it all. During January 2016, forward earnings was identical to the consensus estimate for all of 2016. No weight was given to 2017's estimate. During February 2016, we started to track the 2017 squiggle

---

* Figures, references, and appendices are linked on *yardenibook.com/resources*.

because forward earnings represented 11/12 of the latest 2016 estimate and 1/12 of the latest 2017 consensus estimate. By January 2017, the 2016 squiggle was no longer relevant, but we plotted the squiggle through February 2017 (when data for the final quarter of 2016 were available) to show that it had converged to closely match the actual result for 2016.

One of the biggest advantages of Thomson Reuters' I/B/E/S forward earnings is that the data are available much more frequently than the measures of actual profits that are provided quarterly, with a lag of a few weeks, for the S&P 500 by Standard & Poor's and for the corporate sector broadly in the National Income and Product Accounts (NIPA), compiled by the Bureau of Economic Analysis (BEA). The Earnings Squiggles and forward earnings for the S&P 500 are available not only monthly from September 1978 but also weekly from March 1994 (Fig. 3 and Fig. 4).

We have 37 years of complete annual squiggles from 1980 through 2016, i.e., with 25 months of data for each one of them. From the beginning to the end of each annual squiggle, estimates fell for 29 of those years and rose for eight of them. The squiggles tend to decline over time because analysts tend to be overly optimistic about the outlook for their companies' earnings the further out in the future they are. The up-year exceptions were 1980, 1988, 1995, 2004, 2005, 2006, 2010, and 2011 (Fig. 5). Of course, the steepest downward slopes occur during recessions, when analysts are scrambling to cut their estimates. The few years when they raised their estimates in the past tended to be during economic recoveries, especially following bad recessions during which analysts had become too pessimistic. The overall average decline for the 25 months of the 37 years was −12.9%, with the 29 down years averaging −18.3% and the eight up years averaging 6.7%.

Joe and I track Net Earnings Revisions Indexes (NERIs) for the S&P 500 as well as its 11 sectors and 100-plus industries. We do the same for numerous other composites, including MSCI Inc.'s stock market indexes for the major countries of the world. NERIs show the percentage of analysts' forward earnings estimates that have been revised higher minus the percentage that has been revised lower, divided by the total number of forward earnings estimates. The resulting indexes are extremely volatile on a weekly and monthly basis and tend to be most volatile around earnings seasons, when analysts are more likely to adjust their forecasts. We've found that the three-month average of NERIs provides the most useful information, since it encompasses the entire quarterly earnings cycle. Our data start during March 1985.

The S&P 500's NERI turns negative during recessions and positive during recoveries (Fig. 6). During expansions, it has shown mixed performances. Given that most Earnings Squiggles have downward slopes, NERIs tend to have a negative bias. So during expansions, we are not overly concerned to see negative NERIs and give more weight to the positive ones.

It's human nature for industry analysts to be biased toward optimism about the prospects of the companies they follow. Most have a strong professional interest in their designated industries and companies. Most prefer to give buy ratings rather than sell ratings, which is why they have more of the former than the latter. Analysts don't want to follow companies that are likely to go out of business. If they are following a dying industry, they can score points by being bearish ahead of the curve; however, eventually they'll have to start all over again covering a different industry. Also, analysts are loath to get too negative on companies that have investment banking relationships with their firm. Given analysts' inherent optimism, savvy investors know that when the analysts downgrade their recommendation on a stock from "buy" to "hold," they probably mean "sell."

Forward earnings can rise even as overly optimistic analysts lower their estimates for the current year and/or the coming one. That happens if the coming year's estimate remains higher than forward earnings. Arithmetically, forward earnings converges to next year's consensus estimate. While it is possible for forward earnings to rise if the current-year consensus plunges, it's hard to imagine that next year's estimate won't take a dive too.

Imagine the following stylized conversation between a "sell-side" industry analyst and a "buy-side" portfolio manager:

Jane: Jim, thanks for visiting us today and sharing your earnings outlook for your industry, especially for ABC Corp., which we own. We always value your insights and analysis. However, you're always too optimistic on earnings and invariably lower them. When might you be cutting your estimates yet again for this year?

Jim: Jane, thanks for taking the meeting. Look, this year is half over. Let's not dwell on it too much. Let's talk about next year. It's going to be a great one for the company.

That in a nutshell is how earnings are discounted by the stock market, in my opinion, and why I'm a fan of forward earnings as the "right" earnings measure to use in the stock market equation to forecast the market. The average portfolio manager is relying on the earnings expectations of the average analyst over the next 12 months. The earnings valuation multiple, however, is determined by investors, not analysts. It's up to them to decide how much they are willing to pay for the time-weighted average of analysts' consensus earnings expectations for this year and next year.

Let me stress a very important point about the Earnings Squiggles and forward earnings: the stock market can go up when analysts are reducing their earnings estimates for the current year and the coming year. I'm often asked how this can be. The answer is that if next year's estimate exceeds the time-weighted average, forward earnings will rise as next year gets more weight while this year gets less. Let's continue the above conversation:

> Jane: Okay, we can talk about next year now that it's fast approaching. However, I see in your spreadsheet that you've already started lowering your estimate for next year!
>
> Jim: That's true, but my forecast for this year is still better than last year's result, and next year still exceeds my number for this year. Things are continuing to get better for the company, though not quite as great as I had been predicting.

Institutional investors (on the buy side) clearly value the opinions of industry analysts (on the sell side). Why else would Wall Street hire them and pay them so well? Few investors have the time or the in-house resources to do their own industry-specific research and channel checks. Those who do have their own analysts sometimes hire them from Wall Street. In-house analysts are deluged by research provided by Street analysts and often develop a close professional relationship with the ones they respect most. Indeed, many buy-side money management firms have a voting system whereby their internal analysts collectively allocate commission dollars to the sell-side firms whose analysts have helped them the most.

To assess its accuracy, forward earnings can be pushed ahead by a year and compared to actual quarterly S&P 500 operating earnings on a four-quarter-trailing basis, i.e., the moving sum over the past four quarters (Fig. 7 and Fig. 8). The former turns out to be a very good leading indicator of the latter, with one rather important exception: collectively, industry analysts generally don't do a very good job of anticipating recessions, which causes them to slash their earnings estimates for both the current and the coming years. Conversely, during economic expansions (which fortunately tend to last much longer than recessions), they do a very good job of forecasting earnings over the year ahead using the forward earnings proxy.

This raises an interesting question: why should we pay any attention to the forecasts of industry analysts if they have a long track record of being too optimistic? That's the reason for using forward earnings rather than the squiggles themselves. What about failing to forecast recessions? Analysts aren't economists. It isn't their job to see a recession coming. Besides, investors would probably ignore such warnings coming from an analyst unless he or she had insights from a company that was especially well positioned to see a recession coming. That may happen occasionally, but there is certainly no evidence that analysts collectively provide any early warnings of a coming recession.

Predicting recessions is what economists are supposed to do, and we don't do a very good job of it. Indeed, it seems that every recession produces a superstar economist who was alone in anticipating the latest downturn. Of course, at the end of the day, it is up to investors to anticipate recessions. Some rely on their favorite economists to assess this risk. Most simply react to the news headlines. If the economic news is bad, many will sell stocks and raise their cash position even if industry analysts remain upbeat on earnings. If the news turns good, then stocks will rebound and the analysts' forecasts will have more credibility.

Since Joe and I also track analysts' consensus earnings expectations for each of the quarters of the current and coming years on a weekly basis, we have a window into a strange tendency of the "too-high" analysts to lower their estimates as earnings seasons approach and the "low or just-right" analysts to hold their forecasts steady. The widespread view is that company managements guide selected analysts down so that their company's results will be better than expected. I'm not sure why analysts are so cooperative. Why don't they confront managements? "Look, I've lowered my estimates every quarter for the past six years as you suggested. I'm not playing that game anymore. Give me more accurate guidance, please!"

Analysts' quarterly consensus earnings expectations for the S&P 500 are available on a weekly basis from 1994. Joe and I track them in our chart publication titled *Stock Market Briefing: S&P 500 Earnings Squiggles Annually & Quarterly*.[3] From the first quarter of 1994 through the third quarter of 2017, there were 95 quarterly squiggles. Of these, 76 were shaped in what we call "earnings hooks," where the actual results were better than analysts predicted at the start of the earnings season by at least 0.1%. Squiggles reflecting estimates that were "beat" by 3.0% or more totaled 43, while only 13 squiggles reflected big positive surprises exceeding 5.0%. The longest streak of positive surprises occurred during every quarter from the first quarter of 2009 through the third quarter of 2017. Such upward surprises don't happen during recessions, when actual results often turn out to be worse than the rapidly falling estimates, so the earnings hook is much smaller.

Of course, most of the information provided by companies during an earnings season is old news, having happened last quarter. However, the information does provide insights into the likely future course of a company's earnings. From the perspective of our forward earnings analytical approach, the fourth quarter of each year is the least important. That's because by the time the results are reported during January and February of the next year, the previous year (including the fourth quarter, of course) is irrelevant to forward earnings, which no longer gives any weight to it. However, each quarter's results can significantly impact earnings revisions for coming quarters.

FLYING WITH THE BLUE ANGELS

INDUSTRY ANALYSTS PROVIDE the earnings estimates that are discounted in stock prices. Investors determine the valuation of those earnings. While forward earnings isn't an infallible measure of earnings for forecasting purposes, I'm convinced that the market is discounting the time-weighted average of analysts' consensus earnings expectations for the current and coming years. In my analysis of the stock market equation, I can specify that "E" is S&P 500 forward earnings. "P" is the S&P 500 stock price index. "P/E" is the ratio of the S&P 500 stock price index to the S&P 500 forward earnings. Industry analysts' consensus expectations are used to derive the forward E, and investors determine the forward P/E.

I devised "Blue Angels" charts to monitor these three variables in a visually useful way. In the monthly version, I multiply the S&P 500's forward earnings by forward P/Es of 5.0 to 25.0 in increments of 5.0 (Fig. 9).

The result is five different time series of an implied S&P 500 index price at various P/E levels that move in parallel formation. So they never collide, just like the parallel vapor trails left behind the Navy's famous Blue Angels jets.[4] Superimposing the actual S&P 500 index price shows when the index is breaking into new valuation territory, i.e., changing P/E "altitude" by moving toward a new higher or lower P/E series "jet trail." In my presentations to clients, I often refer to the S&P 500 series as "the stunt plane flying through the vapor trails of the Blue Angels." The same framework can be constructed using weekly data to keep a more frequent watch on the Blue Angels relationships among P, E, and P/E (Fig. 10).

As the S&P 500 ascends or descends through the Blue Angels, we can see how much of the move is attributable to forward earnings and the forward P/E. As a general rule, the forward earnings isn't as volatile as the forward P/E. So big short-term moves in the stock index most often reflect changes in the forward P/E that cause the index to climb or fall toward the next Blue Angel P/E-level data line. Conversely, moves in the actual index price that do not bring it closer to a nearby Blue Angel P/E line confirm that changes in the earnings outlook are driving the S&P 500's price action.

Forward earnings tends to rise fastest during economic recoveries and fall fastest during recessions. My simple Blue Angels framework clearly shows that bull markets typically occur when forward earnings and forward valuation are rising. Bear markets typically occur when both are falling. Short-term bull-market selloffs, a.k.a. "corrections," occur when valuation declines while forward earnings continues to rise. There was a rare bear market in 1987 when the forward P/E fell sharply while forward earnings continued to rise.

The bottom line is that I use Earnings Squiggles and Blue Angels as tools to benchmark my own forecasts to the earnings expectations and the valuation levels that the market is discounting. I monitor the trends of earnings expectations for the current year and next year as well as for forward earnings. I watch to see how much altitude the S&P 500 "stunt plane" is gaining or losing as a result of changes in forward earnings and valuation. In the bull market since 2009, as in the previous one from 2003 through 2007, I have stayed bullish during stock price swoons when I saw that forward earnings was still rising. I remained bullish during the stock market crash of 1987 for the same reason. These tools are like my air traffic control system, providing me with guidance through market turbulence.

So what I actually do for a living is this: I forecast the forecast. I predict where forward earnings will be at the end of the current year and the coming year. That amounts to forecasting next year's and the following year's earnings since those will be the forward earnings at the end of the current year and the coming year, assuming that industry analysts eventually concur with my earnings outlook. My outlook reflects a synthesis of everything else I forecast and cover in all the foregoing chapters of this book. Of course, it doesn't end there: to convert my forecasts for forward earnings to S&P 500 targets at the end of the current year and the coming year, I also need to forecast where the forward P/E will be at both points in time. The next chapter focuses on predicting valuation.

For now, let's resume the analysis of my methods by comparing the alternative measures of profits to forward earnings. I use those alternative measures to study the secular and cyclical trends of profits since they have longer histories than forward earnings does.

LOTS OF S&P 500 EARNINGS MEASURES

ABOVE, I EXAMINED the relationship between forward earnings and the actual operating earnings of the S&P 500, both calculated by Thomson Reuters. The former tends to be a good leading indicator of the latter when the economy is growing but not when it is falling into a recession. Other measures of profits are worth analyzing to provide useful insights for predicting future profits. They aren't forward-looking or available weekly; only forward earnings has those advantages. The rest represent actual quarterly results compiled by either private-sector data vendors or the government's accountants. What many of these series offer are more historical data than are available for forward earnings, which starts in September 1978. So they can provide a longer-term perspective on the trends and cyclical performance of profits.

Let's start our survey of these other measures with the quarterly data available for the S&P 500:

- *Reported (GAAP) earnings (since 1935).* Standard & Poor's has compiled S&P 500 quarterly earnings on a reported basis since the first quarter of 1935 (Fig. 11). As noted earlier in this chapter, the SEC requires that publicly traded companies include financial statements in their (unaudited) 10-Q and (audited) 10-K forms, showing figures based on generally accepted accounting principles (GAAP).

- *Operating earnings (Standard & Poor's data since 1988).* Since the first quarter of 1988, Standard & Poor's has provided an operating version of the quarterly earnings of the S&P 500 companies (Fig. 12). It excludes one-time items that are included in the fully loaded reported series. Both are available on a per-share as well as an aggregate basis. The operating measure almost always exceeds the reported one because one-time write-offs and charges tend to occur more frequently than one-time income windfalls. Standard & Poor's determines the one-time items that are included and excluded from the firm's reported data series for the S&P 500 "operating" earnings series.

- *Operating earnings (Thomson Reuters data since 1993).* To complicate matters, other widely respected data vendors calculate S&P 500 operating earnings differently than does Standard & Poor's. The most widely used numbers are compiled by Bloomberg, FactSet, Thomson Reuters, and Zacks. I prefer the longer data history of the Thomson Reuters version, which tends to be the same as the Standard & Poor's series but has diverged at times (Fig. 13). Both the Thomson Reuters and Standard & Poor's series' data are on a pro forma basis, which means that they reflect the composition of the S&P 500's portfolio as it was in each period. So the value of today's index is being compared to the values of past versions of the index, when its composition of companies was different, before some companies were dropped from the index and others added to it. Mergers and acquisitions also can change the composition of the index.

The big difference between the Standard & Poor's and Thomson Reuters measures of operating earnings per share is that the former determines which one-time items to exclude and include in reported earnings, while the latter is based on "majority rule." In other words, it is based on the industry analysts' consensus on operating earnings, which tends to be the same as the operating numbers reported by the companies in their quarterly filings.

Obviously, company managements prefer to determine their own operating earnings and are more favorably disposed toward industry analysts who follow their guidance. The SEC has warned some companies about hyping up their operating results by excluding bad stuff that shouldn't be excluded. Importantly, industry analysts and investors who are after the unvarnished truth can always analyze the GAAP results, which must be reported in the quarterly filings and reconciled back to any non-GAAP measures presented. Not surprisingly, the net write-offs for bad stuff tend to be greater for the Thomson Reuters' than for the Standard & Poor's measure of operating earnings (Fig. 14).

Some strategists disparage the concept of operating earnings as "earnings before bad stuff," which is sometimes shortened to "EBBS." They insist that reported earnings is the only correct measure. I prefer following both measures, since reported earnings tend to diverge most from operating earnings during downturns and bounce back when operations are back to normal. Nevertheless, even during normal times, the Standard & Poor's measure of operating earnings tends to exceed reported earnings. One major reason is that Standard & Poor's doesn't concur with the relatively widespread practice, especially among technology companies, of excluding stock option compensation as an expense when calculating operating earnings.

I believe that the stock market reflects the Thomson Reuters measure of operating earnings since most industry analysts follow the guidance provided by company managements for what is considered to be one-time bad stuff. That's why all of our work on the S&P 500's Earnings Squiggles, forward earnings, and the Blue Angels is based on Thomson Reuters data.

SLICING AND DICING NIPA'S PROFITS

THE US GOVERNMENT also compiles, in the NIPA (which, as a reminder, stands for "National Income and Products Accounts"), various measures of corporate profits that are used to derive GDP.[5] Corporate profits is one of the major components of national income. Again, before I proceed to examine the trends and cycles in profits, it's worth understanding the government's profits data and how they compare to the series available for the S&P 500. Useful information and insights can be gleaned from all these measures of profits.

The NIPA profits data are included in the GDP report released by the BEA on a quarterly basis. When they are released, I start with the top line, which is profits before tax (PBT)—sometimes referred to as "book profits." The NIPA's series is primarily based on tax-return information provided by the Internal Revenue Service (IRS) in its SOI (Statistics of Income) Tax Stats – Corporation Tax Statistics, which is adjusted to conform to BEA coverage and definitions.[6]

The NIPA measures are aggregate measures rather than per-share ones and are not adjusted for bad stuff. However, two adjustments are added to PBT to derive a measure often called "profits from current production," which is consistent with GDP accounting (Fig. 15):

- *Inventory valuation adjustment (IVA).* The IVA eliminates gains and losses that result from holding goods in inventory, which are not considered income from current production and thus are removed from business income.
- *Capital consumption adjustment (CCAdj).* The CCAdj adjusts tax-reported depreciation to the NIPA concept of economic depreciation (or "consumption of fixed capital"), which values fixed assets at current cost and uses consistent depreciation profiles based on used asset prices. This eliminates any gains or losses attributable to accounting for depreciation.

I prefer to call profits from current production "cash-flow profits." That's because after taxes are subtracted, corporations use some of the proceeds to pay dividends. The remainder is known as "undistributed profits with IVA and CCAdj." The sum of the retained profits and economic depreciation is equal to corporate cash flow, which is available for capital spending as well as corporate finance activities, including stock buybacks, mergers, and acquisitions. (See Appendix 13.3, Corporate Profits.)

The BEA also shows a breakdown of pretax profits from current production attributable to domestic financial and nonfinancial industries and the "rest of the world," which is equal to receipts from the rest of the world less payments to the rest of the world.[7]

In March 2011, Andrew W. Hodge published a *BEA Briefing*, "Comparing NIPA Profits with S&P 500 Profits."[8] He observed:

> NIPA profits measures are designed to reflect the national economic accounting concept of "income from current production" and to provide consistent coverage over time of all U.S. corporations, including private corporations and S corporations. Primarily reflecting this broader coverage, total after-tax NIPA profits are typically about twice as high as S&P 500 operating earnings during expansions. In contrast, the purpose of the S&P 500 earnings measures is to serve as benchmarks for comparing the performance of individual companies, which are reported on a financial accounting basis that reflects "generally accepted accounting principles," or GAAP, accounting.

In his article, Hodge broadly compared the NIPA's current production measure of profits and S&P 500 operating earnings. Here are a few of the differences:

- *Coverage.* NIPA profits include all US-based corporations. The Standard & Poor's measure is limited to the largest 500 of them, excluding not only small ones but also all private C corporations and all S corporations.
- *Industry representation.* The S&P 500 isn't as broadly based as the NIPA measure. The former may not represent the industry composition of the US economy. There have been times when a few sectors have been disproportionately represented in S&P 500 profits.
- *Accounting.* The NIPA profits series are based on tax accounting because the source data are from corporate tax returns filed with the IRS. The S&P 500 ones are based on financial accounting as reflected in reports filed with the SEC.
- *Gains and losses.* The NIPA receipts exclude income in the form of dividends as well as capital gains and losses, which are included in S&P 500 earnings. Capital gains and losses in corporate pension plans are reflected in the S&P 500 profits but not in the NIPA. NIPA expenses exclude bad debts. S&P 500 operating earnings tend to include write-offs of bad debts.
- *Stock options.* Hodge reports that "NIPA accounting and tax accounting have always treated employee stock options as an expense only when (and if) options are exercised. It is an operating expense and therefore always a cost deduction in the NIPA profits calculation." Prior to 2006, "GAAP option expense reporting was completely at a company's discretion and reported as a nonoperating expense or, often, not reported at all. Since 2006, options grant expense was mandated by GAAP. It was included in the Standard & Poor's reporting starting in 2006 as an operating profits deduction."[9]
- *Foreign profits.* Both NIPA and S&P 500 profits include the global profits of corporations headquartered in the United States. The NIPA's "profits component includes income earned abroad by US corporations and excludes income earned in the United States by foreign corporations or their subsidiaries." There is limited specific information about overseas results for the S&P 500 companies. However, Standard & Poor's uses the available data in an annual study of the percentage of S&P 500 revenues earned abroad, which excludes exports to the US.[10]

The book and cash-flow NIPA profits series are available before and after taxes. I focus my work on the after-tax measures, which I can compare to the S&P 500's reported and operating aggregate net income data compiled by Standard & Poor's, which is used to calculate the per-share measures (Fig. 16). They are hard to compare on an apples-to-apples basis. That's because the NIPA book profits series is based on tax accounting as shown in tax returns filed with the IRS and is adjusted using the IVA and CCAdj to derive cash-flow profits. S&P 500 aggregate net income is based on financial accounting as shown in reports filed with the SEC and is adjusted for one-time items to derive aggregate operating income. S&P 500 aggregate operating net income seems more in sync with the NIPA current production measure of profits (Fig. 17).

Furthermore, S&P 500 aggregate reported net income seems to better track the BEA's measure of after-tax profits reported on tax returns (Fig. 18). That makes sense since the S&P 500 reported earnings and the NIPA book profits exclude any adjustments and mainly differ because of coverage and accounting methodologies. Taking the ratio of these two unadjusted measures shows that S&P 500 corporations have accounted for roughly 50% of total corporate profits most of the time since 1964, when the data start (Fig. 19). This ratio also confirms Hodge's observation that the "S&P 500 earnings measures fall by larger percentages during recessions than the NIPA measures and then rise faster to converge back toward NIPA profits trends."

THE TREND IN EARNINGS

NOW THAT I have chosen the most important measures of profits, let's see what they tell us about the trend in profits. Then let's study the profits cycle. The goal is to develop a historical understanding of profits so that we can predict them. There's another important accounting identity we need to guide us:

$$E = R \cdot E/R$$

E = *Earnings*

R = *Revenues*

E/R = *Profit margin*

Translated, that means earnings is equal to revenues times the profit margin. Over time, the earnings trend must be the same as the trend of revenues. The profit margin is a trendless cyclical variable. The economic system wouldn't work if profits' share of revenues grew either too large or too small. Think of the two extreme cases: if profits were 100% of gross national product (GNP), there wouldn't be any consumers. If it were zero percent, there would be no producers.

To analyze the trend and the cycle in profits, we need to pick measures of revenues that are comparable to the measures of earnings discussed above. Consider the following:

- *S&P 500 revenues (S&P data since 1992)*. Since most of my work focuses on the S&P 500, the quarterly aggregate revenues of this index is the obvious choice (Fig. 20). The problem is that the S&P 500 data series is available only quarterly, beginning with the first quarter of 1992. I need a measure that's available more frequently to keep close tabs on the stock market. And because industry analysts forecast revenues for their companies along with earnings, I have one: S&P 500 forward revenues. This, you may have guessed, is the time-weighted average of analysts' consensus estimate for this year's and next year's revenues. S&P 500 forward revenues tends to coincide with the actual quarterly data. It is available monthly from January 2004 and weekly from January 2006, which makes it a very useful weekly window into the direction of revenues.

- *NIPA revenues (BEA data since 1947)*. For NIPA profits, I use nominal GNP as the most comparable measure of revenues. It is the same as GDP but includes net income receipts from the rest of the world. Nominal GNP data are available on a seasonally adjusted quarterly basis from the first quarter of 1947. The two revenues series do have very similar trends, with the ratio of S&P 500 aggregate revenues to GNP hovering between 50% and 65% most of the time since 1992 (Fig. 21 and Fig. 22).

  GNP reflects the final value of all goods and services produced by US residents at home and overseas. It is the sum of all the value added by intermediaries in their production. On the other hand, S&P 500 revenues reflects all the sales of the 500 companies in the index, whether those sales are intermediate or not. For example, it includes the sales of cars as well as all the materials and parts that go into cars. It makes more sense to compare it to total manufacturing shipments and distributors' sales, though this monthly series—often referred to as "business sales"—is only available for goods, not services. Sales of S&P 500 companies obviously include both goods and services. Nevertheless, there is a closer fit between S&P 500 revenues and the business sales of goods series, with the ratio of the two fluctuating around 65% since 2002.

Let's proceed with an analysis of the trends in revenues and earnings, followed by their cycles. Given that the S&P 500 revenues series starts in 1992, my trend work is based on the relationship of nominal GNP and NIPA profits as reported to the IRS and on a current-production basis. Since the start of 1949, all three have been trending along a 7% annual growth path (Fig. 23).

The S&P 500's forward earnings has also been trending around 7%. Actual operating and reported earnings, using the four-quarter average, have been more volatile, bouncing within a growth range of 5% and 7% since 1960 (Fig. 24). S&P 500 reported earnings, available since 1935, has also been bouncing along a mostly 6% growth path within a 5%–7% range (Fig. 25).

No wonder an age-old adage among stock investors is: "Let the trend be your friend." Since its 1935 inception, the S&P 500 stock price index likewise has tracked the 7% trend line along with earnings (Fig. 26). This is the most convincing argument for the thesis that stocks are among the best investments in the long run. That's assuming stock investors will continue to enjoy a compounded annual appreciation rate of roughly 7%, which is determined by the trend growth in revenues and earnings.

Be warned that picking different starting points can produce different growth rates. If the time period being measured begins at the peak of a bull market or the trough of a bear market, the trend-lines growth rate is going to be lower or higher than 7%. Obviously, that will make a difference for individual investors, depending on when they started investing and when they'll retire.

In recent years, it seems that the growth rate of nominal GNP has slowed along with the growth of real GNP and the lower trend in the inflation rate. Does this mean that 7% will no longer be the yellow brick road for the S&P 500? Not necessarily. Many companies have been deriving more of their revenues and earnings from abroad in recent years, especially from fast-growing emerging economies. So revenue and earnings growth—and the share price performance they drive—are less linked to GNP growth than in decades past.

ON THE MARGIN

NOW LET'S DISCUSS the profits cycle, which is determined by the cycle in revenues and in the profit margin.

Not surprisingly, there is a good correlation between the year-over-year growth rate in S&P 500 revenues and nominal GNP (Fig. 27). So S&P 500 revenues are procyclical, i.e., driven concurrently by the business cycle. In other words, revenues tend to grow during economic recoveries and expansions, while they tend to fall during recessions. Indeed, S&P 500 revenues is highly correlated with lots of other procyclical domestic economic indicators, especially manufacturing and trade sales, even though they don't include services, as noted above (Fig. 28). It is also highly correlated with durable goods orders, US exports, the value of world exports, and the Commodity Research Bureau raw industrials spot price index. It may or may not be a small world, but it certainly has been a cyclical one over the years.

The amplitude of the profits cycle relative to the revenue cycle is amplified by the cycle in the profit margin. Here is the relevant accounting identity for the profit margin:

$$E/R = (R - C)/R = 1 - C/R$$

$$
\begin{aligned}
R\ &=\ Revenues \\
C\ &=\ Costs \\
E\ &=\ Earnings\ (R - C) \\
E/R\ &=\ Profit\ margin
\end{aligned}
$$

The profit margin is the ratio of after-tax profits to revenues. Earnings are revenues less costs. During recessions, revenues tend to fall faster than costs, squeezing margins. During recoveries, revenues rebound faster than costs, thus boosting margins significantly. During the boom phase of expansions, businesses tend to ramp up costs rapidly by expanding their payrolls and production capacity. So margins tend to peak before recessions.

Since the revenues series available for the S&P 500 starts during the first quarter of 1992, the profit margin doesn't have much history (Fig. 29). However, the S&P 500 profit margin has been highly correlated with the NIPA profit margin, which is after-tax profits as reported to the IRS (i.e., without the IVA and CCAdj) divided by nominal GNP, which is nominal GDP plus net overseas receipts (Fig. 30). This measure of the profit margin is available back to the start of 1947 (Fig. 31). It confirms that the profit margin cycle has been procyclical and trendless. It tends to peak before recessions because labor costs and capital spending tend to rise faster than GNP during late expansions, when economic growth has tended to boom (Fig. 32). When costs rise faster than revenues, the profit margin tends to fall.

Booms typically set the stage for busts. In the past, booms have been associated with rising inflation, tighter monetary policies, and tougher credit conditions. The resulting recessions usually cause the profit margin to plunge. When the economy recovers, revenues rise faster than labor costs and capital spending. In addition, there is typically a cyclical rebound in productivity, which also lowers labor costs and boosts margins.

So profits follow the trend of revenues. The profits cycle and business cycle coincide because each impacts the other. Causality runs both ways. The business cycle drives the profits cycle because all the economic factors at play in the economy at large influence how much revenue comes in companies' doors and what managements choose to do with it, resulting in their profits. Conversely, the profits cycle drives the business cycle because when their profits are rising, companies tend to expand their payrolls and their capacity; when their profits are falling, they tend to retrench. Those decisions in aggregate feed into GNP growth; notably, however, the profits cycle is much more volatile than GNP because it is amplified by the cycle in the profits margin. I discuss more ways that the business cycle is driven by the profits cycle in Chapter 5.

Since 1947, there have been 10 cyclical peaks in the NIPA profits margin. They ranged between a low of 6.5% during the third quarter of 1997 and a high of 10.6% during the first quarter of 2012. They averaged 8.3%. Over the same period, there were 10 troughs in the margin, ranging between 3.3% during the third quarter of 1986 and 8.1% at the end of 2015, and averaging 5.2%.

The fact that profit margins are cyclical has led to the widespread view that profit margins tend to revert to their means. This reversion-to-the-mean model is often deemed to apply to any trendless cyclical economic series, especially those tied to the business cycle. In fact, business cycle-related series *only briefly* revert to their means. What they do is fall toward and through their means on their way to their cyclical troughs during recessions. Then they rebound, reverting once again to their means and rising above them to their cyclical peaks. Previous cyclical peaks and troughs are useful benchmarks for assessing the current position of the profits cycle.

With forward earnings and forward revenues for the S&P 500 in hand, we can calculate the implied forward profit margin for the index (Fig. 33, Fig. 34, and Fig. 35). The resulting series is available monthly from January 2004 and weekly from January 2006. Since forward earnings and revenues are time-weighted measures of analysts' expectations for the current and coming years, the forward profit margin—for which they are the sole inputs—is too. In other words, tracking the forward margin calculation tells us when analysts collectively are becoming more or less optimistic about businesses' margin potential over the coming 12 months. That's valuable to know for forecasting the stock market and the economy. The forward profit margin measure that I calculate can be compared to the Standard & Poor's four-quarter-trailing actual profit margin but has the advantages of more frequent availability and being forward looking versus backward looking, like the stock market itself.

FINANCIAL ENGINEERING

IN THE NEXT chapter, I examine stock market valuation models that use actual earnings as well as the market's earnings expectations. In my opinion, the market discounts the consensus expectations of industry analysts, as I explain above. The analysts tend to have earnings models that are based on the accounting framework used by the companies to show their operating results as presented in their quarterly filings with the SEC. Results on a GAAP basis must also be shown, with explanations of why adjustments are made to the reported results to generate operating earnings. The quality of expected operating earnings will be flawed if the analysts are basing their expectations on misleading adjustments and information.

This problem can occur during bull markets. Typically, the bull market initially is driven by better-than-expected earnings. But along the way, many company managers find that delivering better-than-expected earnings becomes harder and harder. So some of them start spending more time managing their earnings rather than their companies.

Japanese corporate managers played this game with their earnings during the late 1980s stock market bubble in Japan, just before it crashed. They called it "*zaitech*," i.e., financial engineering. Many Japanese companies attempted to boost their depressed profitability by speculating in the stock market. During the late 1990s, managing earnings became a widespread practice in the United States. I warned about this problem in my August 16, 1999 *Topical Study*, "Earnings: The Phantom Menace, Episode I." I wrote, "A related problem is that many companies are overstating their earnings by using questionable accounting and financial practices. Some are significantly overstating their profits, and they tend to have the highest valuation multiples in the stock market. This suggests that investors are not aware that the quality of earnings may be relatively low among some of the companies reporting the fastest earnings growth."[11]

I certainly was not the first to warn about this issue. In a September 28, 1998 speech, SEC Chairman Arthur Levitt blasted many of the most egregious accounting practices, in a speech titled "The Numbers Game."[12] He warned that companies were crossing the line from managing their earnings to manipulating them:

> Increasingly, I have become concerned that the motivation to meet Wall Street earnings expectations may be overriding common sense business practices. Too many corporate managers, auditors, and analysts are participants in a game of nods and winks. In the zeal to satisfy consensus earnings estimates and project a smooth earnings path, wishful thinking may be winning the day over faithful representation. As a result, I fear that we are witnessing an erosion in the quality of earnings, and therefore, the quality of financial reporting. Managing may be giving way to manipulation; integrity may be losing out to illusion.

"Manipulation" is a strong word. In his speech, Levitt also called some of the accounting practices "hocus pocus," "trickery," and "gimmicks." He went on to list several of the worst tricks in the accounting-for-earnings book.

The 1998 annual report of Berkshire Hathaway included a letter to the shareholders from Chairman and CEO Warren Buffett, dated March 1, 1999.[13] He railed against what he perceived as widespread accounting abuses: "Clearly the attitude of disrespect that many executives have today for accurate reporting is a business disgrace." He was particularly incensed by corporate managements that didn't expense compensation paid in the form of stock options. The Oracle of Omaha famously asked three simple rhetorical questions: "If options aren't a form of compensation, what are they? If compensation isn't an expense, what is it? And, if expenses shouldn't go into the calculation of earnings, where in the world should they go?"

When the stock market bubble burst in 2000, all the accounting excesses that had been so widely ignored by investors suddenly came to the fore. The S&P 500 plunged 49% from March 24, 2000 through October 9, 2002. Investors were shocked by the rigged earnings games played by so many companies. They wanted the usual suspects rounded up. They found that many technology companies, particularly those that sold telecommunications equipment, boosted their sales by offering their customers very generous credit terms. Such seller financing was a quick road to ruin for many of them. Some companies had been recognizing revenues before a sale was completed, before the product was delivered to a customer, or at a point in time when the customer still had the option to terminate, void, or delay the sale. Some companies treated acquisitions as a "one-time" charge—removing any future earnings drag.

A series of accounting scandals ensued, including at Computer Associates (2000), Lernout & Hauspie (2000), Xerox (2000), Enron (2001), AOL (2002), Global Crossing (2002), Haliburton (2002), Sunbeam (2002), Tyco (2002), and WorldCom (2002). The charges included falsifying financial statements, inflating revenues, and cooking up fictitious transactions. A few high-profile executives faced criminal charges and went to jail.

Congress responded by enacting the Public Company Accounting Reform and Investor Protection Act, also known as the "Sarbanes–Oxley Act," on July 30, 2002.[14] It contains 11 sections covering the responsibilities of a public corporation's board of directors, adds criminal penalties for certain misconduct, and requires the SEC to create regulations to define how public corporations are to comply with the law. In my opinion, one of the most important provisions requires top corporate executives to take personal individual responsibility for the accuracy and completeness of corporate financial reports.

The Financial Accounting Standards Board (FASB) responded belatedly by ruling at the end of 2004 that stock options would have to be expensed in GAAP earnings effective as of fiscal year 2006. During 1973, the SEC designated the FASB as the organization responsible for setting accounting standards for public companies in the United States.[15] The FASB's primary purpose was to establish and improve GAAP to serve the public's interest.

Also, after the fact, Fed Chairman Alan Greenspan, in a March 26, 2002 speech, reported: "The Federal Reserve staff estimates that the substitution of unexpensed option grants for cash compensation added about 2½ percentage points to reported annual growth in earnings of our larger corporations between 1995 and 2000. Many argue that this distortion to reported earnings growth contributed to a misallocation of capital investment, especially in high-tech firms."[16] He added that the FASB "proposed to require expensing in the early to middle 1990s but abandoned the proposal in the face of significant political pressure."

US public companies are required to report their earnings per share in their financial statements based on GAAP. In short, GAAP earnings are fully loaded with all income-statement line items pertinent to the reporting period. Even when facing a judgment call, GAAP accountants lean toward the outcome that reveals the least amount of profit. That's because GAAP accountants are trained to follow the principle of conservatism in accordance with GAAP.

Public companies report on several variations of earnings per share. Those include basic and diluted earnings per share based on total net income, or loss, with further subdivision by continuing and discontinued operations. They also report on other variations.

"Unusual" exclusions are usually not GAAP. Public companies typically want to demonstrate the best view of their results to investors and so may wish to exclude (or include) items considered unusual in nature from their earnings calculations. Any such related financial measures would be considered non-GAAP. It's no surprise that non-GAAP measures of earnings tend to be more favorable than GAAP ones, given the bias toward conservativism in GAAP.

As previously noted, Standard & Poor's releases two series for earnings per share, namely "as reported per share" and "operating per share." The former is derived from income from continuing operations as defined by GAAP. Their "operating per share" series further adjusts for unusual items based on their own interpretation of such items. Importantly, Standard & Poor's does not always exclude (or include) the same unusual items as companies and analysts do. That's because their goal is to ensure comparability across industry groups.

As mentioned earlier, the rule for Thomson Reuters' operating earnings per share is "majority rule," i.e., the firm takes no position on which one-time items ought to be included or excluded in calculating its earnings estimates but simply aims to align its estimates with those of analysts to give an accurate snapshot of analyst projections. Since analysts often work closely with companies to ensure that forecasts are consistent with how "adjusted" earnings will be reported, analysts tend to exclude (or include) the same line items that companies do. So through the majority-rule approach, Thomson Reuters' earnings estimates achieve a close approximation of the earnings calculation methods that companies actually use, different though they may be from company to company. Notably, the firm also collects data on a variety of different measures of earnings per share, including a GAAP and an adjusted one.

Thomson Reuters' July 2015 proprietary "Methodology for Estimates" notes:

> When a company reports their earnings, the data is evaluated by a Market Specialist to determine if any Extraordinary or Non-Extraordinary Items (charges or gains) have been recorded by the company during the period. . . . If one or more items have been recorded during the period, actuals will be entered based upon the estimates' majority basis at the time of reporting. Any submission of an estimate by a contributing analyst using a non majority [sic] actual or on a non majority basis results in a call from a Thomson Reuters Market Specialist requiring the contributing analyst to adjust to the majority basis or have their estimates footnoted for an accounting difference and excluded from the mean calculation for the fiscal years in question.[17]

Where do I stand? I go with the flow and follow the Thomson Reuters data, which reflect analysts' consensus estimates; that's because I believe it's the consensus estimates that stock prices typically reflect.

In his February 27, 2016 letter to Berkshire Hathaway shareholders, Buffett was back at it, lambasting "phony" earnings based on accounting measures that don't follow GAAP:[18]

> [I]t has become common for managers to tell their owners to ignore certain expense items that are all too real. . . . And, if real and recurring expenses don't belong in the calculation of earnings, where in the world do they belong? Wall Street analysts often play their part in this charade, too, parroting the phony, compensation-ignoring

"earnings" figures fed them by managements. Maybe the offending analysts don't know any better. Or maybe they fear losing "access" to management. Or maybe they are cynical, telling themselves that since everyone else is playing the game, why shouldn't they go along with it. Whatever their reasoning, these analysts are guilty of propagating misleading numbers that can deceive investors.

Buffett also noted in this letter that depreciation is a "real" cost and shouldn't be excluded from results for most companies: "When CEOs or investment bankers tout pre-depreciation figures such as EBITDA [earnings before interest, taxes, depreciation and amortization] as a valuation guide, watch their noses lengthen while they speak."

The FASB in its Concepts Statement No. 8 states that the objective of general purpose financial reporting "is to provide financial information about the reporting entity that is useful to existing and potential investors, lenders, and other creditors in making decisions about providing resources to the entity. . . . However, general purpose financial reports do not and cannot provide all of the information that existing and potential investors, lenders, and other creditors need. Those users need to consider pertinent information from other sources."

In other words, non-GAAP information may in some cases be useful to investors. That's especially true when one-time nonrecurring events might make "real" results less meaningful for assessing underlying profitability. Non-GAAP earnings often do exclude both bad and good stuff for sensible reasons.

In any case, the SEC's rules protect against the overuse of such information in a way that might mislead investors. When filers with the SEC disclose non-GAAP financial measures, they are required (with a few exceptions) also to present the comparable GAAP measures and show a reconciliation of them. In addition, "for financial information to be understandable, users should have a reasonable degree of financial knowledge and a willingness to study the information with reasonable diligence," according to the FASB. That means it's up to the users of financial statements to diligently study all the publicly available information provided by companies.

The job of most sell-side analysts is to sell investment ideas to generate trades as well as to attract investment banking business. Buy-side analysts are more likely than sell-siders to be paid based on the performance of their stock recommendations, according to a 2016 study by Lawrence Brown (et al.), *Skin in the Game: The Activities of Buy-Side Analysts and the Determinants of Their Stock Recommendations*.[19] Importantly, the study also found that buy-side analysts say recent 10-K or 10-Q reports tend to be more useful for decision making than quarterly conference calls, management earnings guidance, or recent earnings performance.

The study highlighted that most buy-siders say "they never exclude depreciation expense, and more analysts say they never exclude stock option expense and amortization expense than say they always exclude these items." More generally speaking, an analyst was quoted as saying, "We're more concerned with the core operations of the company and what's going to happen over the next couple of years or so." That's as opposed to a quarterly beat or miss based on "adjusted" consensus-based earnings. Another analyst added, "We're going to make [our own] adjustments that adhere to what we think the true earnings power of the business is."

CORPORATE FINANCE 101

FINANCIAL ENGINEERING BY corporations gets lots of press, particularly when the faulty financial structures collapse. However, the clear majority of businesses are run soundly and for the benefit of their customers, their workers, and their shareholders. America's free-market capitalism continues to boost the prosperity of most Americans, in my opinion. There is certainly room for improvement in corporate governance, which continues to be afflicted by excessive cronyism on boards of directors. Nevertheless, most corporate managers are driven to make their companies as successful as possible.

Some corporate executives are paid too much and spend too much time boosting their stock prices. They claim that their job is to enhance "shareholder value." Most of them are shareholders and claim this gives them a tremendous incentive to work hard to manage their companies very well. Ironically, many became even bigger shareholders after President Bill Clinton changed the tax code in 1993, when he signed into law his first budget, creating Section 162(m) of the Internal Revenue Code. This provision placed a $1 million limit on the amount that corporations could treat as a tax-deductible expense for compensation paid to the top five executives (this was later changed by the SEC under Bush to the top four execs). It was hoped that would put an end to skyrocketing executive pay.

The law of unintended consequences trumped the new tax provision, which had a huge flaw—it exempted "performance-based" pay, such as stock options, from the $1 million cap. Businesses started paying executives more in stock options, and top executive pay continued to soar. Liberal critics, notably Senator Elizabeth Warren (D, MA), concluded that the 1993 tax code change had backfired badly and that soaring executive pay has exacerbated income inequality.

Furthermore, say the critics, executive officers aren't spending enough on capital and labor to promote the long-term health of their companies. Instead, they're spending too much on buying back their shares to boost their stock prices. Exhibit A for the prosecution is that during 2015 and 2016, share buybacks and dividend payouts equaled roughly 100% of S&P 500 operating profits, as compiled by Standard & Poor's (Fig. 36).

This situation provides a useful case study to illustrate how the data I track can be applied to analyze trends in corporate finance:

- *Dividends and retained earnings.* The available data show that 84% of S&P 500 companies paid dividends in 2016 (Fig. 37). That's down from the high of 94% at the start of the data in 1980. But it's up from the low of 70% during both 2001 and 2002. During the late 1990s, the fad, especially among hot technology companies, was to pay no dividends at all, reinvest all the retained profits, and buy other tech companies. That strategy blew up along with the tech bubble. That's one reason why more companies have been paying dividends since then. In addition, the valuation of dividend-paying stocks was boosted by the sustained plunge in interest rates after the financial crisis of 2008.

  Collectively, since the mid-1960s, the corporate dividend payout ratio (dividends divided by after-tax S&P 500 reported earnings or NIPA book profits) has fluctuated around 50% (Fig. 38). For the S&P 500, there has been a steady uptrend in dividends since the start of the data in the mid-1940s (Fig. 39). There have been downturns along the way during recessions, but the big declines occurred in retained earnings (after-tax reported earnings less dividends), which have been fluctuating in a procyclical fashion along with the business cycle but have been doing so along the trend set by dividends. By the way, the trend growth rate in NIPA corporate dividends has been just over 6% since the fourth quarter of 1946 (Fig. 40).

- *Cash flow.* Retained earnings represent a small portion of corporate cash flow, which is equal to retained earnings including the IVA (to eliminate inventory profits) plus tax-reported depreciation. Tax-reported depreciation is the consumption of fixed capital plus the CCAdj. So the CCAdj is tax-reported depreciation minus economic depreciation. In the NIPA, tax-reported depreciation is called the capital consumption allowance (Fig. 41 and Fig. 42).

  I prefer to focus on the cash flow of nonfinancial corporations (NFCs), which accounts for most of corporate cash flow (Fig. 43). The income statement data for NFCs are updated quarterly in Table F.103 of the Fed's *Financial Accounts of the United States*. During 2016, the cash flow of all corporations was a record $2.2 trillion, with NFCs accounting for 87% of this total.

- *Capital spending.* What do NFCs do with all this cash? They mostly spend it on capital outlays for intellectual property (e.g., software and R&D), equipment, and structures (Fig. 44). Remember that wages and salaries are a cost paid out of revenues, and dividends come out of after-tax profits. That leaves retained earnings plus the capital consumption allowance (i.e., tax-reported depreciation), which is basically a big pile of profits that is exempt from taxation.

  The difference between gross fixed investment and the capital consumption allowance (i.e., tax-reported depreciation) is net fixed investment (Fig. 45 and Fig. 46). The Fed's data for NFCs show that net capital spending (above and beyond what is spent to replace depreciating assets) during the latest economic expansion has been comparable to that of the previous two cycles. The notion that companies haven't spent enough to ensure their long-term viability isn't supported by the data for the overall NFC sector. As I review in Chapter 3, companies are spending an increasing portion of their capital budgets on high-tech equipment, software, and R&D. The first two categories have gotten cheaper over the years, which means that companies are getting more bang for their bucks spent on these.

- *Bond issuance and buybacks.* In addition to cash flow, another source of cash is the capital markets. Companies can issue stocks and bonds to raise funds. The Fed's data show that since the mid-1990s, NFCs have been actively selling bonds while buying back their shares (Fig. 47).

Data compiled by Standard & Poor's show that gross stock buybacks for the S&P 500 totaled $3.4 trillion from 2009 through 2016, while dividends totaled $2.4 trillion—both clearly driving stock prices higher (Fig. 48).

My conclusion: the notion that corporate financial behavior on balance has been skewed toward driving up stock prices in the short run at the expense of sound management for the long-term success of corporate America is not supported by the data. There is certainly plenty of room for improving corporate governance in ways that might reduce cronyism and excessive compensation paid to top executives. Still, the data show that corporate profits and cash flow continue to move higher in record territory, suggesting that corporate managements are spending most of their internal funds and funds raised in the capital markets wisely.

Now that I have sliced and diced corporate profits every which way, let's turn in the next chapter to how investors value those earnings.

CHAPTER 14

Predicting Valuation

JUDGING A BEAUTY CONTEST

STOCK MARKET FORECASTING is easy on one level, as I observe in the previous chapter. All you've got to do is predict two variables: earnings (E) and the price-to-earnings (P/E) ratio—i.e., what investors will pay per dollar of those prospective earnings, or "valuation." On another level, few things in life can be more difficult than getting these predictions right. If that weren't the case, we'd all be a lot richer!

As an economist, I've always felt relatively comfortable with predicting earnings, since they are mostly determined by the performance of the economy. Assessing the outlook for the P/E is the tougher of the two variables, in my opinion.

Judging valuation in the stock market is akin to judging a beauty contest. Episode 42 of the television series *The Twilight Zone* is titled "Eye of the Beholder." It's about a woman who undergoes her 11th and last legally allowed facelift to correct her looks, as required by the totalitarian regime. When the bandage is removed, the doctors are disappointed and can barely hide their disgust: she is still beautiful. Then the camera reveals the faces of the doctors and nurses. They look horrifying to us viewers, with their pig-like snouts, though clearly pleasing to one another. The beautiful misfit escapes with a handsome man to a village of their "own kind," where the rest of society won't be subjected to their repellent good looks. "Beauty is in the eye of the beholder," the man tells the woman.

Not only is beauty subjective, Hollywood tells us—it can be dangerous. At the end of the original version of the movie *King Kong* (1933), the big ape's death is blamed by his handler on Ann Darrow, Kong's blonde love interest, played by Fay Wray: "It was beauty that killed the beast."

Valuation is in the eye of the beholder too. And buying stocks when they are most loved and very highly valued can also be deadly. For example, during the late 1990s, investors scrambled to purchase high-tech stocks in the United States. The forward P/E of the S&P 500 peaked at a record 24.5 during July 1999, led by a surge in the forward P/E of the S&P 500 Information Technology sector to a record high of 48.3 during March 2000 (Fig. 1*). When that bubble burst, many investors suffered crushing losses in their portfolios. They weren't killed by their losses, but they certainly were hurt badly.

As I discuss in the previous chapter, stocks tend to rise along a long-term trend line that is determined by the long-term growth rate of earnings. In the past, 7% has been the growth rate trend. Nevertheless, a long-term investor who hopes to earn this projected return may get less if stocks are bought when they are overvalued and more if bought when undervalued. A short-term trader doesn't care about long-term returns, but buy-and-hold investors should care about buying stocks when they are relatively cheap, rather than too expensive.

How can we judge whether stock prices are too high, too low, or just right? Investment strategists are fond of using stock valuation models to do so. Some of these are simple. Some are complex. The levels and changes in numerous variables—such as earnings, dividends, inflation, interest rates, and various risk metrics—all are thrown into the pot to cook up a "fair value" for the stock market. If the stock market's price index exceeds the number indicated by the model, then the market is overvalued. If it is below fair value, then stocks are undervalued. As a rule, investors should buy when stocks are undervalued and sell when they are overvalued.

A model can help us to assess value. But any model is just an attempt to simplify reality, which is always a great deal more complex and unpredictable. Valuation is ultimately a judgment call. It tends to be controversial, since everyone has their own opinion on what's a pig of a stock and what's a knockout at various levels of valuation.

---

* Figures, references, and appendices are linked on *yardenibook.com/resources*.

Valuation is not only subjective; it's also relative. Stocks are cheap or dear relative to other assets, such as bonds, for example. There are no absolutes. Even this statement is controversial since some observers swear by a reversion-to-the-mean approach, which compares stock valuation to its historical average rather than to other asset classes. When the P/E is above the historical mean, they warn that stocks are overvalued and vulnerable to reverting to the mean.

These diehards ignore all other factors that may be boosting valuations, and occasionally die waiting to be proven that they were right after all. It's been said that history doesn't repeat itself, but it rhymes. Similarly, history shows that valuation multiples do revert to their means, though only briefly as they transition from overvalued to undervalued and back. Insights into how much time they might spend above and below their means and the magnitude of the deviations are not provided by simple reversion-to-the-mean models.

A model can always be constructed to explain nearly 100% of what happened in the past. "Dummy variables" can be added to account for one-time unpredictable events or shocks that have already occurred. But how useful is a model explaining the past when the future is always full of surprises that create "outliers," i.e., valuations that can't be explained by the models? For investors, these anomalies present both the greatest potential risks and the greatest potential rewards.

IRRATIONAL EXUBERANCE AND THE FED'S MODEL

THE VALUATION QUESTION isn't as existential as Hamlet's "To be or not to be" soliloquy. The question is: "How can we judge whether stocks are overvalued or undervalued?" I've been working on answering this question for many years. I started thinking more about it after Alan Greenspan, former chairman of the Federal Reserve Board, famously asked the valuation question near the end of a speech he gave on December 5, 1996, "The Challenge of Central Banking in a Democratic Society."[1]

In that speech, the Fed chairman mostly talked about the importance of maintaining the independence of the Fed from political influences. Nevertheless, he acknowledged, "Our monetary policy independence is conditional on pursuing policies that are broadly acceptable to the American people and their representatives in the Congress." He also observed that the

Fed would face challenges in managing an economy that is constantly changing. "But one factor that will continue to complicate that task is the increasing difficulty of pinning down the notion of what constitutes a stable general price level. . . . [W]hat about futures prices or more importantly prices of claims on future goods and services, like equities, real estate, or other earning assets? [Is the] stability of these prices essential to the stability of the economy?"

Then Greenspan discussed how low price inflation could boost valuation multiples to levels that might indicate "irrational exuberance." He asked the valuation question as follows: "Clearly, sustained low inflation implies less uncertainty about the future, and lower risk premiums imply higher prices of stocks and other earning assets. We can see that in the inverse relationship exhibited by price/earnings ratios and the rate of inflation in the past. But how do we know when irrational exuberance has unduly escalated asset values, which then become subject to unexpected and prolonged contractions as they have in Japan over the past decade?" (See Appendix 14.1, Greenspan's Fed on Stock Market Valuation.)

This was the first time any Fed chairman had mused publicly about the impact of monetary policy on the interaction between the inflation rate for goods and services and the valuation of equities. If the Fed were to succeed in stabilizing inflation at a low rate, he suggested, that could drive up P/Es in the stock market, possibly causing a speculative bubble. When that bubble burst, it could trigger a severe recession, as happened in Japan during the 1990s after the country's stock market and real estate bubbles burst at the end of the 1980s. But then he let the Fed off the hook, asking "how do we know" when bubbles are inflating?

After Greenspan famously worried out loud for the first time about irrational exuberance, his staff apparently examined various stock market valuation models to help him evaluate the extent of the market's exuberance. One such model was made public, albeit buried in the Fed's *Monetary Policy Report* to Congress that accompanied Greenspan's testimony on July 22, 1997.[2]

While the semiannual congressional testimonies on monetary policy presented by Fed chairs are widely followed and analyzed, virtually no one reads the actual policy reports that accompany the testimonies. I do this regularly, because I find that there is much useful information available about "Fed Think" in the supporting documents and research reports cited by Fed officials. In July 1997, I noticed that for the first time, the report discussed stock market valuation. It did so in a single paragraph:

> The run-up in stock prices in the spring was bolstered by unexpectedly strong corporate profits for the first quarter. Still, the ratio of prices in the S&P 500 to consensus estimates of earnings over the coming twelve months has risen further from levels that were already unusually high. Changes in this ratio have often been inversely related to changes in long-term Treasury yields, but this year's stock price gains were not matched by a significant net decline in interest rates. As a result, the yield on ten-year Treasury notes now exceeds the ratio of twelve-month-ahead earnings to prices by the largest amount since 1991, when earnings were depressed by the economic slowdown. One important factor behind the increase in stock prices this year appears to be a further rise in analysts' reported expectations of earnings growth over the next three to five years. The average of these expectations has risen fairly steadily since early 1995 and currently stands at a level not seen since the steep recession of the early 1980s, when earnings were expected to bounce back from levels that were quite low.

This brief discussion of valuation was followed by a chart showing a strong correlation between the US Treasury 10-year bond yield and the S&P 500 forward earnings yield—i.e., the ratio of the year-ahead forward consensus expected operating earnings to the price index for the S&P 500 companies (Fig. 2). The monthly chart compared the two series starting in 1982 and extending through July 1997. This model was first developed in the mid-1980s by Dirk van Dijk at I/B/E/S, which had started compiling the forward earnings series on a monthly basis during September 1978.[3] (Founded in 1976, I/B/E/S changed hands numerous times before becoming part of Thomson Reuters in 2008.)

The S&P 500 is fairly valued when the index's forward earnings yield is equal to the 10-year Treasury bond yield, the model suggests. It is overvalued (undervalued) when the earnings yield is below (above) the bond yield. It is easier to visualize this model by calculating the implied fair value price (FVP) of the S&P 500, which is simply the year-ahead forward earnings (E) series divided by the US Treasury 10-year bond yield (TBY) (Fig. 3):

$$FVP = E / TBY$$

FVP = *S&P 500's fair value price*
E = *Year-ahead forward earnings*
TBY = *US Treasury 10-year bond yield*

As I note in the previous chapter, in most of my analyses I use forward earnings rather than either reported or operating earnings because market prices reflect earnings *expectations*. The past is relevant, but only to the extent that it is influencing the formation of current expectations about the outlook for earnings, which are largely determined by industry analysts. Apparently, the folks at the Fed likewise considered forward earnings to be the right variable to use in a valuation model.

I first wrote about my discovery of the "Fed's Model" in my July 28, 1997 commentary, a week after noticing it in the July 22 report to Congress. In his accompanying congressional testimony, as so often in the past, Greenspan played the role of a "two-handed economist." I pointed out, though, that he was clearly inclined to be bullish. He said: "Without question, the exceptional economic situation reflects some temporary factors that have been restraining inflation rates. In addition, however, important pieces of information, while suggestive at this point, could be read as indicating basic improvements in the longer-term efficiencies of the economy." He added that the economy's great performance could be "a once or twice in a century phenomenon."[4]

My *Topical Study* dated August 25, 1997 was titled "Fed's Stock Market Model Finds Overvaluation."[5] I noted that in September 1987, just prior to the October crash, stocks were 34% above fair value, according to the model (Fig. 4). Immediately after the crash, stocks were about 10% undervalued. They were slightly overvalued at the start of the 1990s, then generally undervalued from 1993 through 1995. Stocks were fairly valued at the end of 1996, not irrationally exuberant as Greenspan had wondered about out loud. The S&P 500 was overvalued, according to the model, by 18% at the time I was writing in August 1997. Nevertheless, in my study, I remained bullish.

Later on, the model showed that after a brief period of undervaluation by 10% during the October 1998 financial crisis (precipitated by the collapse of Long Term Capital Management), the S&P 500 became overvalued by a record 63% during January 2000. I started to turn more bearish during 1999. When Greenspan began to justify the high valuations of technology companies with his "lottery principle," I became more concerned about the overvaluation shown by the Fed's Model, especially since I expected that Y2K might cause a recession at the beginning of the new millennium. (See Chapter 3 for more on this.) It did, though not because computers failed but rather because spending on making systems Y2K compliant contributed to the pre-millennium boom and its subsequent bust when the spending abruptly stopped.

The Fed's Stock Valuation Model worked relatively well until 2000. Since then, it has shown that stocks have been consistently undervalued relative to bonds, so it has been useless to investors for asset allocation purposes. It certainly did not give a sell signal during 2007, when it showed that stocks remained roughly 25% undervalued relative to bonds. Nevertheless, I continue to tinker with similar versions of it as well as alternative valuation models.

AN EXPANDED VALUATION MODEL FOR CFAs

GREENSPAN NEVER SAID specifically that he was tracking a data series collected by I/B/E/S on consensus annual long-term earnings growth (LTEG) for the S&P 500. But I know that he was, because it is the only series available for such expectations (Fig. 5).

The July 22, 1997 *Monetary Policy Report* mentioned LTEG as follows: "One important factor behind the increase in stock prices this year appears to be a further rise in analysts' reported expectations of earnings growth over the next three to five years." Greenspan also mentioned LTEG in a September 5, 1997 speech at Stanford University, saying: "the equity market itself has been the subject of analysis as we attempt to assess the implications for financial and economic stability of the extraordinary rise in equity prices—a rise based apparently on continuing upward revisions in estimates of our corporations' already robust long-term earning prospects."[6]

The monthly data for LTEG start in January 1985 and are based on industry analysts' annualized growth projections for the next three to five years.[7] In July 1997, the consensus LTEG forecast was 13.5%, the highest recorded since the start of the data at that time. The LTEG series rose even higher during the next few years, peaking at a record 18.7% during August 2000 (Fig. 6). That was mostly because technology analysts in the late 1990s were under the influence of extreme irrational exuberance. Their LTEG expectations for the S&P 500 Information Technology sector soared to a record 28.7% during October 2000.

Over the next decade, the analysts lowered their annual long-term growth expectations for the overall S&P 500 so sharply that LTEG was halved to 9.3% by January 2010. From 2010 through 2015, the consensus hovered mostly around 10.0%. It started moving higher in 2016, returning to 12.9% by December 2017.

The simple version of the Fed's Stock Valuation Model seemed to be missing a variable for LTEG. After all, investors make decisions based heavily on expected earnings growth. It may have been missing some other important variables too. It was just too simplistic to explain valuation. That's why it worked only until it didn't, i.e., after 2000.

I started tinkering with the model in 1999. I reckoned that it needed to include variables that differentiate stocks from bonds. If stock earnings were fixed for the next 10 years (and beyond), then the price of the S&P 500 would be at a level that equates the current earnings yield to the US Treasury 10-year bond yield, according to the simple model. But there is no such guarantee for stocks. Earnings can go down. Companies can lose money or go out of business. On the other hand, earnings can also go up. The model needed a variable to capture earnings expectations beyond just the next 12 months and a second variable to reflect business risk to those expected earnings.

Before proceeding any further, let me address a question that might be on your mind. In the previous chapter, I explain why I believe that the stock market discounts earnings over the year ahead, i.e., the next 12 months, or 52 weeks. So did I just contradict myself by saying that the Fed's Model needed to capture longer-term earnings expectations? I don't think so, because I also believe that the often relatively optimistic earnings growth expectations beyond the next 12 months that are provided by industry analysts aren't embraced with much conviction by investors. Risk increases with the length of the time horizon. So my hunch is that more often than not, the long-term earnings growth variable is offset by the business risk variable.

I could test this hypothesis with my expanded version of the Fed's Model, which I first wrote about in a July 26, 1999 *Topical Study*, "New, Improved Stock Valuation Model."[8] The variable I chose to reflect business risk to earnings was the spread between the A-rated seasoned corporate bond yield composite compiled by Moody's and the US Treasury

10-year bond yield. For the corporate bond yield, I now prefer to use the average of the AA-AAA and BBB-A bond yield composites compiled by Bank of America Merrill Lynch (Fig. 7). This spread tends to widen during recessions and narrow during expansions, reflecting the procyclical nature of credit quality (Fig. 8).

The data series I chose for the second variable was the one Greenspan was tracking on long-term earnings growth. To keep it simple, I opted for a straightforward linear relationship:

$$FEY = a + b \cdot TBY + c \cdot DRP - d \cdot LTEG$$

FEY = *S&P 500's year-ahead forward earnings divided by S&P 500 price index*

TBY = *US Treasury 10-year bond yield*

DRP = *Default risk premium. Yield spread between corporate and Treasury 10-year bond*

LTEG = *Analysts' consensus long-term expected earnings growth*

Notice that if the last two terms offset each other—i.e., net out to zero—then the equation turns into the simple version of the Fed's Stock Valuation Model, assuming that a = 0 and b = 1 when stocks are fairly valued relative to bonds. When FEY (the forward earnings yield) is less than (greater than) TBY, stocks are deemed to be overvalued (undervalued) relative to bonds.

Of course, given that bond yields have fallen to historical lows since 2009, it's important to stress that the Fed's Stock Valuation Model is in fact a *stocks–versus–bonds* valuation model. In other words, when FEY is less than (greater than) TBY, it may be that bonds are undervalued (overvalued) relative to stocks.

Chartered financial analysts (CFAs) studying for their Level III credentials are required to spend some time reading about the Fed's Model. The CFA Institute's study guide warns that the model ignores the equity risk premium, which is the extra compensation required by investors for the greater risk of investing in equities compared to investing in default-risk-free debt. On the other hand, the guide observes that the model ignores earnings growth opportunities that benefit equity, but not bond, investors. There is a huge advantage in owning the equities rather than the bonds of blue-chip companies that have a history of increasing their dividends, because their earnings are growing while their bond coupon payments remain fixed.

The CFA Institute's Level III study guide then proceeds to discuss the "Yardeni Model." It's the expanded model that I discuss above and developed in my 1999 study. The CFA guide notes that while using the corporate bond yield does incorporate default risk into the expanded model, it does not fully capture the risk of equities.

To provide some empirical guidance on valuation with the expanded model, I simplified it to:

$$FEY = CBY - d \cdot LTEG$$

CBY = Corporate bond yield after assuming that
a = 0, b = 1, and c = 1 in the expanded model

This stripped-down version of the expanded model simply assumes that the forward earnings yield should fully reflect the corporate bond yield less some fraction of long-term earnings growth expectations. Recognizing all the pitfalls, I can try different weights that investors might be willing to give to the long-term earnings growth forecast of industry analysts, to judge which one fits the model best. I can use my Blue Angels technique, which I explain in the previous chapter, to create a series of fair-value forward earnings with d = 0.0, d = 0.1, d = 0.2, etc. When d is set to zero, the expanded model is the same as the original Fed's Model, with the corporate bond yield replacing the Treasury yield (Fig. 9).

My tinkering with the weight for LTEG shows that historically investors haven't given much weight to this variable—somewhere between zero and 0.2 (Fig. 10). The growth variable improved the "fit" of the model during the late 1990s, when investors and their analysts were especially exuberant about the outlook.

In any event, after all that effort, I found that the expanded model produces more or less the same results as the simple one, suggesting that the risk and the growth terms do tend to offset one another (Fig. 11 and Fig. 12). That makes sense to me. Stocks may be riskier than bonds, but if a company does well, it can increase its dividend, while its coupon remains fixed. If a company does poorly, both its coupon and its dividend will be at risk, though dividends will be cut before there is a default on the company's bonds.

With the benefit of hindsight, the simplest version of the Fed's Model was right about stocks during the late 1990s: they were wildly overvalued. The problem is that the model stopped working after that great call. It did signal that stocks were very cheap again by September 2002, but they remained cheap during the bull market from 2003 through 2007. That market was driven higher by earnings even as valuation multiples continued to decline from their heights at the end of the previous bull market. In other words, it was an earnings-led, rather than a valuation-led, bull market. The model lost any remaining credibility when it signaled that stocks were cheap even as they crashed from October 2007 through early February 2009.

FED'S MODEL DRIVES BUYBACKS

THE FED'S MODEL started rising from the ashes around 2004. While it still wasn't useful as a stocks-versus-bonds asset allocation model, it found new life as a model for corporate finance, specifically for stock buybacks and for mergers and acquisitions (M&A).

Thanks to falling inflation and relatively easy monetary policies since 2004, the corporate bond yield has consistently traded below the forward earnings yield of the S&P 500 (Fig. 13). That has created a big arbitrage incentive for corporations to borrow money in the bond market with which to buy back their shares; doing so is advantageous for companies as long as the after-tax cost incurred is below their forward earnings yield. That incentive also applies to M&A deals: if the companies' cost of borrowing money is below the forward earnings yield of the combined enterprise, there's incentive to merge and acquire with borrowed funds.

It may surprise you to learn that for many years after the Great Crash of 1929, the Securities and Exchange Commission (SEC) viewed buybacks as bordering on criminal activity. That was the case up until the Reagan years, when the SEC began to ease the rules on buybacks, under John Shad, chairman from 1981 to 1987. Our paths crossed very briefly when I joined EF Hutton, shortly before he left his position as the firm's vice chairman. He believed that the deregulation of securities markets would be good for the economy.

William Lazonick, a professor of economics at the University of Massachusetts Lowell and the co-director of its Center for Industrial Competitiveness, believes that buybacks are effectively a form of stock price manipulation. He explained in a September 2014 *Harvard Business Review* article, "Profits Without Prosperity":

Companies have been allowed to repurchase their shares on the open market with virtually no regulatory limits since 1982, when the SEC instituted Rule 10b-18 of the Securities Exchange Act. Under the rule, a corporation's board of directors can authorize senior executives to repurchase up to a certain dollar amount of stock over a specified or open-ended period of time, and the company must publicly announce the buyback program. After that, management can buy a large number of the company's shares on any given business day without fear that the SEC will charge it with stock-price manipulation—provided, among other things, that the amount does not exceed a "safe harbor" of 25% of the previous four weeks' average daily trading volume. The SEC requires companies to report total quarterly repurchases but not daily ones, meaning that it cannot determine whether a company has breached the 25% limit without a special investigation.[9]

In Lazonick's opinion, trillions of dollars have been spent to artificially boost earnings per share by lowering the share count. The money should have been used to invest in the capital and labor of corporations to make them more productive. At the end of the previous chapter, I question the assertion that managements haven't done enough of this.

In any case, my job as an investment strategist isn't to judge whether buybacks are good or bad for companies, for capital formation, for capitalism, or for society. I've said it before, and I'll say it again: I'm not a preacher. Instead of good or bad, I do bullish or bearish.

I didn't pay that much attention to buybacks during the bull market of 2003 to 2007, when corporations in the S&P 500 repurchased $1.7 trillion worth of their shares. But my bullishness on stocks during the bull market that started in 2009 was increasingly based on the significant rise in buyback activity. From the start of that bull market during the first quarter of 2009 through the third quarter of 2017, S&P 500 companies repurchased $3.8 trillion worth of their shares, well exceeding purchases by individual, institutional, and foreign equity buyers (Fig. 14).

The valuation consequences of this development are significant, in my opinion. As mentioned above, corporate finance managers have a big incentive to buy back their companies' shares when the forward earnings of their corporations exceeds the *after-tax* cost of borrowing funds in the bond market. Using the pretax corporate bond yield composite overstates the after-tax cost of money borrowed in the bond market. The spread between the forward earnings yield and the pretax cost of funds did widen after 2004 and remained wide well into the next decade. Obviously, it did the same on an after-tax basis.

So, for example, if the forward earnings yield exceeds the after-tax cost of borrowing of, say, 4%, then corporations have an incentive to buy shares until the forward earnings yield is down to 4%. That would imply a forward P/E of 25, which is the reciprocal of 4%. If the after-tax borrowing cost is 3%, that would be consistent with a forward P/E of 33. Notice this is the same math that applies to the Fed's Stock Valuation Model. However, while it hasn't been relevant to the asset allocation decisions of investors since maybe 2000, it has been increasingly relevant to the stock repurchase decisions of corporate managements since 2004.

The bottom line is that as corporate managers have increased their buyback activities, their version of the Fed's Model has probably had more weight in the valuation of stocks. In theory, this means that valuation should be determined by the corporate version of the model. In practice, if that pushes valuation multiples to historically high or record-high levels, nervous investors who are uncomfortable with such high valuations probably will be selling their stocks.

Always remember: Valuation is in the eye of the beholder. Also: Like the two sides to every story, there are two sides to the Fed's Model—the one driving investors' asset allocation decisions and the one driving corporate finance decisions.

GETTING REALLY REAL

AFTER I STARTED writing about the "Fed's Model," as I called it, the name caught on, and the model became an overnight sensation, receiving lots of press and buzz. Not widely recognized was that the Fed seemed to rush to disown it. Indeed, seven months after the July 1997 report, the Fed signaled that it was agnostic about how to value stocks—and certainly wasn't endorsing the I/B/E/S model just because it had been briefly mentioned in that report—by changing the subject: the February 1998 *Monetary Policy Report* to Congress included a short paragraph comparing the earnings yield to the inflation-adjusted 10-year Treasury bond yield, which was defined as the difference between the nominal yield and the average consumer price index (CPI) inflation expected over the next 10 years (Fig. 15).[10] (See Appendix 14.1, Greenspan's Fed on Stock Market Valuation.)

The source of the inflationary expectations data was a quarterly survey of economists conducted by the Federal Reserve Bank of Philadelphia. There are two series available from this survey, one showing the median and the other the mean of the expectations data. The median data are available twice a year from 1979 through 1991 and quarterly thereafter, while the mean data start in the fourth quarter of 1991 on a quarterly basis. The inflation-adjusted Fed's Model interpolated the data to generate a monthly series, which I continued to monitor.

So this was the *real* version of the Fed's Stock Valuation Model (double entendre intended). The Fed continued to track this relationship in subsequent semiannual reports to Congress, never mentioning the nominal version again. Here is how the new model was discussed back in the February 1998 *Monetary Policy Report*:

> Despite the strong performance of earnings and the slower rise of stock prices since last summer, valuations seem to reflect a combination of expectations of quite rapid future earnings growth and a historically small risk premium on equities. The gap between the market's forward-looking earnings-price ratio and the real interest rate, measured by the ten-year Treasury rate less a survey measure of inflation expectations, was at the smallest sustained level last year in the eighteen-year period for which these data are available. Declines in this gap generally imply either that expected real earnings growth has increased or that the risk premium over the real rate investors use when valuing those earnings has fallen, or both. Survey estimates of stock analysts' expectations of long-term nominal earnings growth are, in fact, the highest observed in the fifteen years for which these data are available. Because inflation has trended down over the past fifteen years, the implicit forecast of the growth in real earnings departs even further from past forecasts. However, even with this forecast of real earnings growth, the current level of equity valuation suggests that investors are also requiring a lower risk premium on equities than has generally been the case in the past, a hypothesis supported by the low risk premiums evident in corporate bond yields last year.

The difference between the S&P 500 forward earnings yield and the real bond yield is deemed to be the "risk premium on equities" (Fig. 16). In other words, in the real version of the Fed's valuation model, the forward earnings yield is equal to the real 10-year riskless yield plus an equity risk premium:

$$FEY = (TBY / CPI) + ERP$$

FEY = *Forward earnings yield*
TBY = *US Treasury 10-year bond yield*
CPI = *Expected inflation over the next 10 years*
ERP = *Equity risk premium*

The last variable may have some value in explaining valuation *ex post facto*, i.e., after it is derived from the three known variables. However, I don't think that ERP is forecastable. It must be a hodgepodge variable reflecting stocks' advantage of earnings and dividends growth versus bonds' fixed coupons and the higher risk inherent in stocks versus bonds. Furthermore, I am not convinced that investors compare the earnings yield to the real, rather than the nominal, bond yield. Maybe they should, but they probably don't, in my opinion.

Hedge fund manager and co-founder of AQR Capital Management Clifford Asness, in his December 2002 article "Fight the Fed Model," argued that the original Fed's Stock Valuation Model is seriously flawed because it compares a real variable, i.e., the earnings yield, to a nominal bond yield. He believed that the earnings yield should be compared to the real bond yield.[11] Then again, investors may suffer from "money illusion," as Asness acknowledged.

There is a widespread notion that stocks are riskier than Treasury bonds; so, the thinking goes, the forward earnings yield must include a premium to offset this risk. That's only true if the bonds are held to maturity. Trading bonds can be quite risky: you can lose plenty of money in bonds if rates are rising and you cash out before the maturity of the bond. On the other hand, an equity portfolio indexed to the S&P 500 should earn 7% per year on average before dividends are reinvested over a long enough period, assuming the historical trend continues. Of course, short-term investors can suffer losses if they buy high and sell low.

The equity risk premium data start in 1979, when it was around 1,000 basis points. It dropped to about 400 basis points by the mid-1980s and stayed there through the mid-1990s. It plunged to zero by the end of the decade. Then it jumped back to around 400 basis points from 2003 through 2006. It's been mostly above 600 basis points since then. The average value from 1979 to 2016 was 500 basis points.

Should we conclude from this limited data set that investors usually require about 500 basis points above the real bond yield to invest in stocks? In that case, if the real bond yield is 3%, then the market's forward earnings yield should be 8%, implying a fair-value P/E of 12.5. Let's say, instead, that the P/E is 18.0. You then could conclude that stocks are overvalued because the risk premium is too low. If the real bond yield is 2%, then the forward yield should be 7%, implying a fair-value P/E of 14.2. There are a lot of assumptions in this analysis, bringing us back to judging a beauty contest.

Even getting a measure of what ERP *was* can be as imprecise as predicting what it should be. There are alternative measures of inflationary expectations. The Fed chose to use the Philadelphia Fed's survey of economists. What do economists know? Their expectations change slowly from quarter to quarter, according to the survey data available since 1979 (Fig. 17). Since 1997, real-time market data for inflationary expectations can be derived from the yield on Treasury Inflation-Protected Securities (TIPS). The spread between the nominal 10-year Treasury bond and the comparable inflation-protected security is a measure of the bond market's expected inflation rate over the next 10 years. Since 1997, this rate has often been below the consensus of professional forecasters (Fig. 18).

MEAN REVERSION

THE FED'S JULY 1997 *Monetary Policy Report*, as noted above, featured the model comparing the S&P 500 forward earnings yield to the nominal US Treasury 10-year bond yield just once. Subsequent reports switched gears, comparing the S&P 500 forward earnings yield to the real bond yield. Then in February 2001, the report focused on the forward P/Es (the reciprocal of the forward earnings yield) of the S&P 500 composite index, the S&P 500 Information Technology sector, and the overall index excluding Information Technology. At that point, it was obvious that the stock market bubble had clearly burst by the end of 2000. The market finally had provided a clear affirmative answer to the question Greenspan had asked about irrational exuberance at the end of 1996.

Over the next three years, investors did become overly exuberant about tech stocks, especially the dot.com stocks. Most of these companies were burning through their cash at an unsustainable pace. When investors refused to provide more financing, the dot.com stocks plunged, and so did their spending on technology hardware and software. That coincided with the abrupt plunge in Y2K-related spending on technology at the start of the new millennium.

I believe that a March 20, 2000 *Barron's* cover story provided the pin that pricked the tech bubble. Written by Jack Willoughby, the article "Burning Up" was subtitled "Warning: Internet Companies Are Running Out of Cash—Fast."[12] The remarkably prescient and timely article warned: "When will the Internet Bubble burst? For scores of 'Net upstarts, that unpleasant popping sound is likely to be heard before the end of this year. Starved for cash, many of these companies will try to raise fresh funds by issuing more stock or bonds. But a lot of them won't succeed. As a result, they will be forced to sell out to stronger rivals or go out of business altogether. Already, many cash-strapped Internet firms are scrambling to find financing."

The Fed's February 2001 *Monetary Policy Report* noted that "the most dramatic" plunges in share prices in 2000 took place among technology, telecommunications, and Internet shares. "While these declines partly stemmed from downward revisions to near-term earnings estimates, which were particularly severe in some cases, they were also driven by a reassessment of the elevated valuations of many companies in these sectors." This time, the Fed staff picked a chart showing the aforementioned P/E ratios.[13] The ratios were based on forward earnings. That clearly highlighted the extreme overvaluation of technology stocks, with the benefit of hindsight.[14]

Like the Fed's staff, I give more weight to forward P/Es than to the Fed's Model when I assess valuation. But the exercise is still a beauty contest. Common sense strongly suggests that the best time to buy stocks is when forward P/Es are low, while the best time to sell is when P/Es are high. However, doing so is not that simple. Stocks seemed relatively expensive in late 1996, which is why Greenspan asked the valuation question, but they proceeded to soar for another three years. Lots of money can be made during bubbles, if you know enough to get out at the top or take timely advice such as Willoughby's in *Barron's*.

Another issue regarding forward P/E data for the S&P 500 is that it's available only from September 1978 onward. That was a limiting feature of the Fed's Model, which is based on the inverse of this series. More years of data are necessary to determine whether the valuation multiple is high or low within an historical context. Besides, more data might suggest other testable models of valuation. Fortunately, as the previous chapter discusses, there are other earnings series going back much further that can be used to construct lots of different valuation models. They are often referred to as "trailing earnings."

The advocates of trailing earnings models do have the choice of using either reported earnings or operating earnings, i.e., excluding one-time extraordinary gains and losses. Of course, the more pessimistically inclined analysts focus on reported earnings, the lower of the two measures. In either case, the data are available only on a quarterly basis with a lag of three to six weeks, and in any event, stock prices should be based on *expected* earnings, not trailing earnings, in my opinion. Forward earnings data reflect expectations and are available on a more timely basis, though with less history than trailing earnings.

Models with P/Es based on trailing earnings often produce valuation conclusions quite different from those of models with P/Es based on forward expected earnings. Comparing the S&P 500 P/E based on actual reported and operating quarterly earnings to the S&P 500 forward P/E shows that the latter has always been lower than the former two (Fig. 19 and Fig. 20). Not surprisingly, given that they are using past earnings, trailing P/Es tend to show overvaluation well ahead of forward P/Es, so they tend to get bearish too early in bull markets. On the other hand, when recessions hit, forward earnings expectations turn out to be too high and are slashed, confirming with the benefit of hindsight that forward P/Es had seriously understated the overvaluation of the market.

I do track all the measures of the P/E both in absolute terms and relative to their means, along with similar valuation ratios deemed to be mean-reverting. However, I don't buy the idea that the mean is determined by the laws of nature and exerts some sort of inherent gravitational pull on valuation, surrounding it with a force field that deflects all other influences. The simple "reversion-to-the-mean" models are worth tracking, in my view, although they ignore how changes in interest rates, inflation, and technologies might impact valuation on a short-term and a long-term basis. Let's have a look at the most popular reversion-to-the-mean models, then turn to a couple of models that account for inflation:

- *Trailing P/Es.* Standard & Poor's has a quarterly series for the reported earnings of the S&P 500 since 1935. That's as far back as I can calculate the quarterly P/E using quarterly averages of daily data on the S&P 500 closing price and the four-quarter trailing average of reported earnings, to smooth out seasonal earnings volatility (Fig. 21). What does this sweep of valuation history tell us, for perspective? The average of this measure of valuation was 16.1 from the end of 1935 through the third quarter of 2017. It has had a spotty record as a market-timing tool if stocks were bought whenever it was below that average and sold when it was above it.

  Robert J. Shiller earned much fame and fortune with his book *Irrational Exuberance* (published March 2000), in which he argued that the market's P/E was too high by historical standards. Along with his colleague John Campbell, Shiller devised a valuation measure called the "cyclically adjusted price-earnings ratio," widely known as "CAPE." Using inflation-adjusted figures, they divide stock prices by corporate earnings averaged over the preceding 10 years. Their ratio differs from a conventional price-to-earnings ratio in that it uses 10 years, rather than one year, in the denominator. In an August 16, 2014 *New York Times* article, Shiller wrote, "In the last century, the CAPE has fluctuated greatly, yet it has consistently reverted to its historical mean—sometimes taking a while to do so. Periods of high valuation have tended to be followed eventually by stock-price declines."[15] CAPE has a bias of being too pessimistic long before bear markets begin. Eventually, it turns out to be right because eventually bear markets will occur.

- *PEG ratios.* The PEG ratio is equal to the forward P/E divided by LTEG, i.e., long-term consensus expected earnings growth (Fig. 22). Conceptually, it makes lots of sense. When long-term investors buy stocks, they aren't focusing on earnings just over the coming year but rather over the next several years. The higher the expected growth in earnings, the more dearly an investor is likely to value a stock.

  However, what makes sense for an individual stock may not be as sensible for the overall market. Overall earnings growth is limited by the nominal growth rate of overall revenues, which depends on the growth of nominal global economic activity, as discussed in the previous chapter. So the model suggests that if earnings growth expectations for the overall market were to exceed the growth potential of the global economy, that would be a sign of overvaluation.

The PEG measure is more likely to run into trouble at the sector level, where irrational exuberance may distort earnings growth expectations—as happened during the second half of the 1990s, when industry analysts raised their earnings growth expectations for technology. It seems to me that they were doing so mostly to justify the rapid ascent in prices. Hey, even Fed Chairman Alan Greenspan justified high stock prices during the tech bull market by noting that industry analysts were raising their growth expectations.

What he forgot to mention is that this is exactly why irrational exuberance always ends badly. It attracts too much buzz, too much press, too many speculators, and most importantly too much capital that funds new competitors in the hot industry. While valuations are soaring, competition from new entrants starts to squeeze margins and saturates the market. Once investors recognize analysts' earnings growth expectations as too optimistic, they scramble to get out as P/Es drop even faster than growth expectations.

- *Buffett ratio.* Another set of ratios I follow includes various price-to-sales (P/S) measures. The S&P 500 stock price index can be divided by forward revenues instead of forward earnings (Fig. 23). However, the forward P/S ratio is very highly correlated with the forward P/E ratio, so it doesn't really add any value to the valuation assessment.

A measure that's correlated with the P/S ratio and one that Warren Buffett has said he favors is the ratio of the value of all stocks traded in the US to nominal GNP, which is nominal GDP plus net income receipts from the rest of the world (Fig. 24). The data for the numerator are included in the Fed's quarterly *Financial Accounts of the United States* and lags the GNP report, which is available on a preliminary basis a couple of weeks after the end of a quarter. Needless to say, they aren't exactly timely data.

However, the forward P/S ratio, which is available weekly, has been tracking Buffett's ratio very closely (Fig. 25). In an essay for *Fortune* in December 2001, Buffett said: "For me, the message of that chart is this: If the percentage relationship falls to the 70% or 80% area, buying stocks is likely to work very well for you. If the ratio approaches 200%—as it did in 1999 and a part of 2000—you are playing with fire."[16]

During the latest bull market, Buffett remained bullish when his ratio rose back to 200% in 2017, observing that historically low inflation and interest rates were major considerations. On September 19, 2017, speaking at an event in New York City marking the 100th anniversary of *Forbes* magazine, he predicted that the Dow Jones Industrial Average will be over one million in 100 years. Buffett noted that 1,500 different individuals have been featured on *Forbes'* list of 400 wealthiest Americans since the start of that tally in 1982. "You don't see any short sellers" among them he said, referring to those who expect equity prices will fall. "Being short America has been a loser's game," he added. "I predict to you it will continue to be a loser's game."[17]

- *Tobin's q.* Another interesting valuation model is Tobin's *q*. I learned about the model directly from the late Professor James Tobin, the chairman of my PhD committee at Yale. In his model, *q* is the ratio of the market capitalization of a corporation to its replacement cost. When *q* is greater than one, it makes more sense to rebuild the company at cost than to buy it in the market. When *q* is less than one, it is cheaper to buy the corporation in the market than to build it from scratch.

  It is possible to derive a *q* ratio for all US nonfinancial corporations using data in the Federal Reserve's *Financial Accounts of the United States* on the "market value of all equities" and the "net worth at market value."[18] Obviously, the cost of replacing most operating enterprises must exceed the replacement cost of just the firm's infrastructure. The data are quarterly and available with a lag of two to three months, which also limits their usefulness for assessing and forecasting valuation. Furthermore, the *q* ratio is highly correlated with the Buffett ratio (Fig. 26). So although it may be theoretically sound, it doesn't provide any useful insights into the valuation question.

  The credibility of Tobin's *q* model received a big boost after the publication in March 2000 of *Valuing Wall Street* by Andrew Smithers and Stephen Wright. According to the book's website, "The US stock market is massively overvalued. As a result, the Dow could easily plummet to 4,000—or lower—losing more than 50% of its value[,] wiping out nest eggs for millions of investors. . . . Using the *q* ratio developed by Nobel Laureate James Tobin of Yale University, Smithers & Wright present a convincing argument that shows the Dow plummeting from recent peaks to lows not seen in a decade."[19] The Dow plummeted to a low of 7286 during October 2002, then bounced back to around 10000.

A Fed staff economist, Michael Kiley, wrote a research paper in January 2000 titled "Stock Prices and Fundamentals in a Production Economy."[20] Based on a model like Tobin's, he concluded that "the skyrocketing market value of firms in the second half of the 1990s may reflect a degree of irrational exuberance." That was the same conclusion suggested by the Fed's Model, which showed that the S&P 500 was overvalued by nearly 70% at the time.

Kiley's goal was to demonstrate that some of the more bullish prognosticators in the late 1990s based their conclusions on exuberant assumptions. He specifically mentioned *Dow 36,000* by James K. Glassman and Kevin A. Hassett (1999), who argued that stocks were much less risky than widely believed, so a lower equity risk premium justified higher P/Es. Kiley also mentioned Jeremy J. Siegel's widely read book *Stocks for the Long Run*. In the second edition (1998), the dust jacket claimed that "when long-term purchasing power is considered, stocks are actually safer than bank deposits!" Siegel's book was in its fifth edition during 2017 when the new record highs in stock prices gave his thesis much more credibility.

INFLATION'S IMPACT ON VALUATION

MISSING IN ALL the mean-reverting ratios is any consideration of extenuating circumstances that might cause them to remain higher above their means—or vice versa—for longer than usual. During the 1960s and 1970s, rapidly rising inflation and interest rates seemed to depress all the valuation measures mentioned above. It follows that historically low inflation and interest rates might boost these measures for a while.

The trailing P/E does seem to have been influenced by the underlying trends in both inflation and the 10-year bond yield (Fig. 27 and Fig. 28). It tended to fall below its mean and remain in single digits as inflation and yields rose during the 1960s and 1970s. The periods of low inflation during the 1950s and since 1983 generally have been associated with double-digit valuation multiples at or above the historical mean. While the Fed's Model, relating the S&P 500 forward earnings yield and the bond yield, hasn't been very useful for asset allocation purposes for a while, there remains a strong secular correlation between the trailing earnings yield and the bond yield (Fig. 29).

Now consider the following valuation measures that reflect the possible impact of inflation on valuation:

- *Real earnings yield.* The earnings yield of the S&P 500, which is simply the reciprocal of the P/E based on reported earnings, is highly correlated with the CPI inflation rate on a year-over-year basis (Fig. 30). The real earnings yield (REY) of the S&P 500 is the difference between the nominal yield and the inflation rate (Fig. 31). The result is a mean-reversion valuation model that logically includes inflation. The average of the real yield since 1952 is 3.3%. The model tends to anticipate bear markets when the yield falls close to zero. John Apruzzese, the Chief Investment Officer of Evercore Wealth Management, examined this model in a November 2017 paper titled "A Reality Check for Stock Valuations." Based on the REY model, he found that "stocks appear more reasonably priced than the conventional P/E ratio suggests during periods of low inflation and rising markets, and more expensive during periods of high inflation and falling markets when they otherwise might seem cheap."[21]

- *Rule of 20.* The "Rule of 20" was devised by Jim Moltz, my mentor at CJ Lawrence. It simply compares the S&P 500 forward P/E to the difference between 20 and the inflation rate, using the year-over-year percent change in the CPI (Fig. 32). When the sum of the forward P/E and the inflation rate is above (below) 20, stocks are deemed to be overvalued (undervalued) (Fig. 33). This rule of thumb has had a few hits and misses, as have more sophisticated models.

- *Misery-adjusted P/E.* Sticking with the forward P/E, I've found that it is reasonably well inversely correlated with the so-called Misery Index, which is the sum of the unemployment rate and the inflation rate (Fig. 34). The Misery Index tends to fall during bull markets and to bottom before bear markets (Fig. 35). That makes sense to me. When we are already miserable, we aren't in the mood to drive up the valuation multiple; we have to be happy to do so. For what it's worth, my homebrewed "Misery-adjusted forward P/E" (MAPE), which is the sum of the Misery Index and the S&P 500 forward P/E, averaged 23.9 from 1979 through 2017 (Fig. 36). It correctly warned that stocks were overvalued prior to the bear markets of the early 1980s and 2000s. It did not anticipate the last bear market, but that's because the problem back then was the overvaluation of real estate, not stocks.

During today's divisive times, it might be better to compare valuation to a talent show rather than a beauty contest. Like any objective judge at a talent show, I want to see all the contestants compete before I pick the winner. That's what I do on a regular basis when I assess the various valuation models. In recent years, I've given more of my votes to the contestants that incorporate inflation and interest rates into their acts. That's led me to a more sanguine opinion about stock valuation than suggested by the more traditional reversion-to-the-mean models, especially the ones based on trailing earnings.

DISCIPLINE OF DIVIDENDS

THE FOCUS ON valuing earnings is a relatively new phenomenon that started with the bull market of the 1990s. Before then, most valuation models focused on dividends, not earnings. The dividend yield, not the current earnings yield, was compared to the bond yield. Corporations were valued on their ability to pay and grow dividends, which represented a tangible return to investors. Retained earnings—profits after taxes and dividends—were reinvested in the business, presumably to increase the capacity of the corporation to pay more dividends in the future.

Investors could analyze the dividend payout history of a company. Then they could project a reasonable future payment stream to shareholders and calculate the present discounted value of the firm using a dividend-discount model. If the present discounted value were less than the share price in the market, then an investor could expect to get a better than average return by investing in the company's stock. Of course, if the present discounted value of the projected future stream of dividends were greater than the share price in the market, then a prudent investor might sell the stock, or at least underweight it in the portfolio.

This dividend-centric valuation discipline provided a powerful and conservative system of checks and balances for corporate managers. Dividends are cash payments. There is no way to print the money; it must be available from a company's cash position. Managers were under pressure to deliver dividend growth, but they also had to retain enough of their earnings to reinvest in their companies so that dividends would continue to grow.

This conservative but disciplined system was replaced during the bull market of the 1990s by a more entrepreneurial system that was more easily abused to boost stock prices to levels that could never be justified by dividends. Indeed, many companies reduced their dividend payouts or just eliminated them entirely. More earnings were retained, and fewer dividends were paid out to investors. The rationale in most cases was sensible: growth companies experiencing rapid increases in their earnings could reinvest their profits and get a better long-term return for their investors through share price appreciation as the companies expanded and became more valuable. Besides, investors couldn't reinvest the dividends on their own and do as well as a growth company because they would have to pay taxes on the dividend income after it had already been taxed at the corporate level.

The new system of valuation based on earnings rather than dividends was both a blessing and a curse. Under the dividend regime, most managers adopted a slow but steady and conservative approach. As long as dividends were growing, investors should be content with managements' performance. Growing dividends was a long-term process occasionally disrupted by economic downturns. Reinvesting retained earnings required a great deal of planning, and the projected returns had to be just high enough to boost dividends without subjecting the company to a great deal of risk.

Under the earnings-centric valuation regime, companies no longer faced the quarterly grind of delivering cash dividends. The cash could be plowed back into the business. Greater risk was acceptable because there was less pressure to deliver the cash to investors every quarter. This meant that managers could be more entrepreneurial. It also meant that some could abuse the system by artificially boosting their earnings. Managing earnings rather than managing the business became an increasing problem during the bull market of the 1990s.

During 2002, many of the most abusive practices in managing earnings came to light as a consequence of numerous corporate scandals. Undoubtedly, the system needed to be reformed, and it was through the Sarbanes–Oxley Act of 2002, which I discuss in the previous chapter.

Dividends did matter a great deal prior to 1982 but subsequently seemed to matter less and less. That year, a simple regulatory move, combined with the different tax rates on dividend income and capital gains, set the stage for the accounting excesses of the 1990s.

As I mention earlier in this chapter, in 1982 the SEC gave companies a safe harbor to conduct share repurchases without risk of investigation. Repurchases raise per-share earnings through share reduction. Before that point in time, companies that repurchased their shares risked an SEC investigation for price manipulation.

This rule change provided a big incentive for companies to buy back their shares rather than pay dividends. Shareholders enjoyed a tax benefit if the buybacks generated long-term capital gains, which were taxed at a lower rate than dividends.[22] The dividend payout ratios of the S&P 500, which averaged 51% from 1946 to 1982, then averaged 45% through the third quarter of 2017 (Fig. 37). Contributing to the decline in this ratio was the sharp drop in the percentage of S&P 500 companies paying dividends—from 87% during 1982 to 73% in 2001 and 2002 (Fig. 38). However, that was the low, and it was back up to 84% in 2016.

As the saying goes, hindsight is 20/20. The bespectacled Fed Chairman Alan Greenspan put the stock market bubble of the 1990s into perspective on March 26, 2002 in a speech on "Corporate Governance" that he presented at New York University.[23] Greenspan observed that shareholders' obsession with earnings was a relatively new phenomenon: "Prior to the past several decades, earnings forecasts were not nearly so important a factor in assessing the value of corporations. In fact, I do not recall price-to-earnings ratios as a prominent statistic in the 1950s. Instead, investors tended to value stocks on the basis of their dividend yields."

Greenspan also pointed out that earnings accounting is much more subjective than that for cash dividends, "whose value is unambiguous." More specifically, "Although most pretax profits reflect cash receipts less out-of-pocket cash costs, a significant part results from changes in balance-sheet valuations. The values of almost all assets are based on the assets' ability to produce future income. But an appropriate judgment of that asset value depends critically on a forecast of forthcoming events, which by their nature are uncertain."

So, for example, depreciation expenses are based on book values but are approximations of the actual reduction in the economic value of physical plant and equipment and the asset's life. "The actual deterioration will not be known until the asset is retired or sold." Greenspan also took a swipe at corporate pension plan accounting: "projections of future investment returns on defined-benefit pension plans markedly affect corporate pension contributions and, hence, pretax profits."

Because earnings are "ambiguous," they are prone to manipulation and hype. During a period of rapid technological change, innovative companies are likely to be especially profitable over the short run. But this tends to increase the incentive for competitors to enter the market and reduce profitability in the long run. Greenspan noted:

> Not surprisingly then, with the longer-term outlook increasingly amorphous, the level and recent growth of short-term earnings have taken on special significance in stock price evaluation, with quarterly earnings reports subject to anticipation, rumor, and "spin." Such tactics, presumably, attempt to induce investors to extrapolate short-term trends into a favorable long-term view that would raise the current stock price.

> This led to the sorry state of corporate affairs during the 1990s, which became all too obvious at the start of the subsequent decade. CEOs, under increasing pressure from the investment community to meet short-term elevated expectations, in too many instances were drawn to accounting devices whose sole purpose was arguably to obscure potential adverse results. Outside auditors, on several well-publicized occasions, sanctioned such devices, allegedly for fear of losing valued corporate clients. Thus, it was not surprising that earnings restatements proliferated in the late 1990s. This situation is a far cry from earlier decades when, if my recollection serves me correctly, firms competed on the basis of which one had the most conservative set of books. Short-term stock price values then seemed less of a focus than maintaining unquestioned credit worthiness.

Greenspan concluded his speech on an optimistic note, seeing signs that the market was already fixing the problem as the sharp decline in stock and bond prices following Enron's collapse punished many of the companies that used questionable accounting practices. "Markets are evidently beginning to put a price-earnings premium on reported earnings that appear free of spin." In other words, market discipline was already raising corporate accounting and governance standards.

The Fed chairman was all for legislative and regulatory initiatives that provided incentives for corporate officers to act in the best interests of their shareholders. He warned against excessive regulation, which "has, over the years, proven only partially successful in dissuading individuals from playing with the rules of accounting."

Personally, I am all for eliminating the taxation of dividend income. I believe that this should be a very effective way to fix most of the problems with the system that Greenspan identified so well in his speech. Shareholders should be encouraged to act as owners of the corporations in which they invest. Managers should be encouraged to treat them as owners, too. It is the owners of the corporation who pay taxes on profits. Why should they be taxed again on that same money when it is distributed as their dividend income?

Double taxation of dividends created a tremendous incentive for management to retain rather than distribute earnings. It gave management a convincing story to tell shareholders: "Instead of paying you dividends, we will invest retained earnings on your behalf to grow our business even faster, and we will also buy back our stock to boost earnings per share." This system gave too much power to management and tended effectively to disenfranchise the shareholder, in my opinion. In other words, this system was prone to abuse and corruption. Without the discipline of dividend payments, management has great incentive to use every trick in the rule book and every conceivable accounting gimmick to boost earnings. Investors are forced to value stocks on easily manipulated and inflated earnings, rather than on the cold, hard cash of dividends.

If, instead, dividends were exempt from personal income tax, then investors would tend to favor companies that paid dividends and had established a record of steadily raising their payouts to shareholders. Shareholders then could decide for themselves whether to reinvest their dividend income in the corporation, based on management's ability to grow dividend payments rather than earnings. Obviously, dividends would grow at the same rate as earnings, assuming a fixed payout ratio. But paying dividends would impose discipline on how managements account for earnings, since they can't pay cash to shareholders unless the cash is available to do so.

The good news is that dividends have been making a comeback since the financial crisis of 2008. As bond yields have plunged since then, dividend-yielding stocks have come back into favor, especially those of companies with a long record of raising their dividends. I often show the power of dividends by calculating the current dividend yield of an S&P 500 portfolio purchased in 1970, 1980, 1990, and 2000. At the end of 2017, those hypothetical portfolios were yielding 57%, 36%, 15%, and 4%, respectively (Fig. 39).

Unlike the forward earnings yield, or even the trailing earnings yield, the dividend yield of the S&P 500 doesn't correlate enough with either the Treasury or the corporate bond yield to inspire the construction of a valuation model (Fig. 40). As inflation soared from the 1950s through the 1970s, the bond yield rose much faster than the dividend yield. During the disinflationary 1980s and 1990s, the bond yield fell faster than the dividend yield. Since 2000, the dividend yield has been on a slight uptrend, while the bond yield has continued to fall. Since the financial crisis of 2008, the bond yield and the dividend yield have been about the same for the first time since the late 1950s.

I've extended my Blue Angels framework to track the relationship of the S&P 500 dividend and dividend yield to the S&P 500 stock price index (Fig. 41). The arithmetic relationship is simple:

$$P = D / Y$$

P = *S&P 500 stock price index*
D = *Aggregate dividends paid by the S&P 500 corporations*
Y = *Dividend yield, or D/P*

The Blue Angels show the hypothetical value of the S&P 500 using the actual dividends paid out divided by dividend yields from 1.0% to 6.0%. The Blue Angels analysis reveals what's propelling the S&P 500's price performance. If the "plane" (index) is flying along a particular "vapor trail," then the dividend yield is propelling the plane (i.e., the index's performance). Diversions above or below a vapor trail indicate rising or falling valuation. The conclusion of this Blue Angels analysis is similar to the one derived from analyzing the Blue Angels based on earnings: the long-term uptrend in the S&P 500 has been driven by the long-term uptrend in S&P 500 dividends, which has been roughly 6% since the end of 1946 (Fig. 42).

GREENSPAN ON BUBBLES

BEFORE MOVING ON, I would like to spend some more time examining Greenspan's views on stock market valuation, especially the role of the Fed in dealing with speculative bubbles. Following his December 5, 1996 speech, Greenspan and his staff searched for a way to value stocks. At first, his staff compared the 12-month forward earnings yield of the S&P 500 to the 10-year Treasury bond yield. This led Greenspan to conclude that investors must have very high expectations for earnings growth and very low risk assessments to justify the market's lofty valuation levels. He implied that these assumptions might be irrational. Along the way, Greenspan frequently wavered and suggested that there might be some method to the madness of stock price performance. For example, in January 1999, he suggested that the stock market had become a lottery and that valuations could be justified based on a "lottery principle," as I discuss in Chapter 3.

There is one school of market thought that has no place for valuation conundrums, however: the efficient market theory. The stock market is very efficient, and efficient markets are always "correctly" valued. All buyers and all sellers have access to exactly the same information. They are completely free to act upon this information by buying or selling stocks as they choose, so the market price is always the "correct" price, reflecting all available information.

In his June 17, 1999 congressional testimony, Greenspan soliloquized yet again about valuation, this time sounding almost as though he were trying to convince himself that "hundreds of thousands of informed investors can't be wrong":

> The 1990s have witnessed one of the great bull stock markets in American history. Whether that means an unstable bubble has developed in its wake is difficult to assess. A large number of analysts have judged the level of equity prices to be excessive, even taking into account the rise in "fair value" resulting from the acceleration of productivity and the associated long-term corporate earnings outlook. But bubbles generally are perceptible only after the fact. To spot a bubble in advance requires a judgment that hundreds of thousands of informed investors have it all wrong. Betting against markets is usually precarious at best.[24]

This was another of the chairman's ambiguous insights that may have contributed to inflating the very bubble he was fretting over. He seemed to be saying that the stock market might be a bubble, but since the market efficiently reflects the expectations of "thousands of informed investors," maybe the market is right, because all those people can't be wrong. So what looked like a bubble might be no such thing.

They *were* wrong, though; it was a bubble. And the Fed chairman was wrong about the judgment of all those folks.

The information available at the time obviously convinced the crowd that stocks were worth buying. But information that's available now, in retrospect, would not have been bullish. Hence, the crowd didn't realize it was a bubble until it burst. In other words, efficient markets can experience bubbles when investors irrationally buy into unrealistically bullish assumptions about the future prospects of stocks. The trick to seeing bubbles for what they are before they burst is keeping an eye out and ears pricked for pertinent information that might not be widely known or appreciated—and keeping an open mind about what that information may portend.

In a speech on August 30, 2002, Greenspan based much of his discussion of valuation on a model very similar to the expanded version of the Fed's Stock Valuation Model. In footnote 3 of his speech, Greenspan wrote: "For continuous discounting over an infinite horizon, $k(E/P) = r + b - g$, where k equals the current, and assumed future, dividend payout ratio, E current earnings, P the current stock price, r the riskless interest rate, b the equity premium, and g the growth rate of earnings."[25] In my expanded version of the Fed's Model, k = 1 because I believe that the market discounts earnings, not dividends. Furthermore, r = the 10-year Treasury bond yield, b = the default risk premium in corporate bonds, and g = long-term expected earnings growth. In his speech, Greenspan concluded that the Fed has no unambiguous tools to gauge whether stocks are overvalued or undervalued. Therefore, he claimed, the Fed could do nothing about stock market bubbles other than to wait to see whether they burst.

Laurence H. Meyer, who was a governor of the Federal Reserve Board from June 1996 to January 2002, wrote in his 2006 book *A Term at the Fed: An Insider's View* that the stock market bubble was a result of the "Greenspan Put." This was the general feeling in the markets—i.e., that the Fed chairman wouldn't raise the federal funds rate to restrain stock prices, but he would intervene quickly to cushion a sharp decline.

Back then, the Federal Open Market Committee (FOMC) basically had one tool (the federal funds rate) to achieve two objectives, i.e., full employment and price stability. Stopping bubbles—which are hard to recognize until they've burst—was one objective too many for the Fed, according to Greenspan. Nevertheless, Meyer regretted that there had been no formal discussion of raising margin requirements, which Greenspan was against doing. Meyer believed the FOMC was too accommodating during much of the second half of the 1990s.

In my opinion, Greenspan was wrong that it was beyond the Fed's purview to deflate bubbles. Asset inflation, like consumer price inflation, distorts economic behavior and poses just as much of a threat to achieving the Fed's goal of full employment with price stability. Asset inflation, like consumer price inflation, leads to a misallocation of resources. Too much capital pours into the asset that has attracted the speculative frenzy. If the Fed doesn't prick the bubble, it gets bigger, creating enormous excess capacity and oversupply. This overhang takes a long time to work down, putting deflationary pressures on the economy. When bubbles burst, deflation can become a serious problem for the economy, and the immediate consequence is often high unemployment. Case in point: the financial crisis of 2008 and its aftermath in economies around the world.

Greenspan's unwillingness to have his staff research this issue and offer policy alternatives was simply bizarre, in my opinion. It was a cop-out.

In a January 3, 2004 speech, "Risk and Uncertainty in Monetary Policy," Greenspan spelled out his side of the story:

> It is far from obvious that bubbles, even if identified early, can be preempted at lower cost than a substantial economic contraction and possible financial destabilization—the very outcomes we would be seeking to avoid. In fact, our experience over the past two decades suggests that a moderate monetary tightening that deflates stock prices without substantial effect on economic activity has often been associated with subsequent *increases* in the level of stock prices. Arguably, markets that pass that type of stress test are presumed particularly resilient. The notion that a well-timed incremental tightening could have been calibrated to prevent the late 1990s bubble while preserving economic stability is almost surely an illusion. Instead of trying to contain a putative bubble by drastic actions with largely unpredictable consequences, we chose, as we noted in our mid-1999 congressional testimony, to focus on policies "to mitigate the fallout when it occurs and, hopefully, ease the transition to the next expansion."[26]

In other words, Greenspan once again claimed that it's not the Fed's job to stop bubbles, only to clean up the mess once market forces have pricked the bubble.

CHAPTER 15

Predicting Stocks

PATH OF LEAST RESISTANCE

I SAVED MY discussion of what I have learned about predicting the stock market for the tail end of my book because the stock market tends to be influenced by all the other economic variables and financial markets that I've analyzed in the previous chapters. All financial markets are affected by the business cycle and inflation. All are affected by interest rates and Fed policy. The financial markets affect each other too, but the bond market isn't as sensitive to the stock market as the stock market is to the bond market. The same can be said about the relationship of the commodity and currency markets to the stock market.

My career up until now has spanned an extraordinary secular bull market in stocks, with plenty of nasty corrections and a few wicked bear markets along the way. Before my Wall Street career began in January 1978 at EF Hutton, the Dow Jones Industrial Average (DJIA) had been trading around 1000 since 1971 (Fig. 1*). It continued to do so until October 11, 1982, when it finally rose above that level, and it hasn't gone that low since. It increased five-fold to 5000 by November 21, 1995 and 10-fold to 10000 by March 29, 1999. The DJIA then revisited 10000 a few times before finally kissing this level goodbye, hopefully for good, on August 27, 2010. On January 25, 2017, it rose to 20000, a 20-fold increase since I started on the Street. It closed above 24000 on November 30, 2017.

---

* Figures, references, and appendices are linked on *yardenibook.com/resources*.

I was bullish most of the time those 40 years. I remained bullish during all the corrections. I was bearish when the tech and housing bubbles burst, but not bearish enough. However, I correctly saw both selloffs as buying opportunities, as selloffs within a secular bull market always are.

Where is the stock market headed next? While there are only two variables to predict—earnings (E) and the price-to-earnings (P/E) ratio—they are not so easy to get right given that a myriad of factors collectively determine them.

Valuation is the tougher of the two to predict because it's more subjective, as I show in the previous chapter. The earnings variable is determined by such as factors as economic growth, inflation, and interest rates. Valuation is influenced by the same factors but is also subject to hard-to-assess psychological influences that affect investor behavior, such as confidence, fear, and greed. And of course, valuation is not independent of earnings. The level of conviction investors have about their earnings expectations also affects how much they are willing to pay for a dollar of prospective earnings.

The earnings series tends to be more predictable than valuation, because it has the same upward trend as the economy does over the long run, which we can predict, and it fluctuates with the business cycle over the short run, which we also can predict—all of which I discuss in Chapter 13.

An error in forecasting the market can be compounded by missing a key variable that drives both earnings and valuation. This risk is most common during recessions, when both earnings and P/E ratios tend to fall together. During expansions, earnings will rise and so should valuations, though that's not as certain as the positive outlook for earnings.

That's why I firmly believe and often say that recessions are the major risk for stock investors. The stock market tends to rise along with earnings as long as the economy is expanding, not contracting. No recession on the horizon? Don't worry, be happy, but be vigilant too. As Chapter 5 reviews, since World War II, recessionary periods have been infrequent and relatively short. From 1948 through 2016, real GDP rose during 236 quarters and fell during just 39 of them, with one showing no change.

Furthermore, from 1928 through 2017, the S&P 500 rose during 60 of those years, was flat during just one year (1947), and declined during 29 years (Fig. 2). After the Great Depression and World War II, from 1946 through 2016, the S&P 500 increased during 50 of the years, was flat one year, and decreased during 20 years. Since 1946, there have been several periods of consecutive annual gains in the stock market. Importantly, declines lasted just one year, with only two exceptions, i.e., 1973 to 1974 and 2000 to 2002. Incredibly, during the Great Recession, the S&P 500 declined only during 2008, though it was a significant plunge of 38.5%. Of course, the actual bear market back then lasted from October 9, 2007 to March 9, 2009 and slashed the S&P 500 by 56.8% over that period.

By common convention, bear markets are defined as declines in the S&P 500 of 20% or more. Bull markets are the advances of 20% or more in between bear markets. Corrections are declines of 10% to 20% that occur during bull markets. More precise definitions would probably account for the length of time that each occurs. But that would make the whole exercise more scientific than it is. In my opinion, bona fide bear markets are caused by recessions that depress both earnings and the valuation of earnings.

My Blue Angels analysis, which I introduce in Chapter 13, is a useful way to depict this relationship (Fig. 3). The monthly version is available from September 1978. Most of the bear markets since then have been associated with declines in forward earnings and in forward P/Es. The 1987 crash stands out as an exception because forward earnings continued to rise. The crash happened so fast that most investors had no chance to sell. However, it was a great buying opportunity, which is how I saw it at the time based on my assessment that it was primarily caused by a proposal in the House Ways and Means Committee to end the tax deductibility of interest expense incurred in leveraged buyouts, as I review in Chapter 1.

My Blue Angels analysis of the market can also be constructed with weekly data for the S&P 500 since March 1994 (Fig. 4). It shows that the 49.1% decline in the S&P 500 from March 24, 2000 through October 9, 2002 was caused by an 8.2% drop in forward earnings and a 44.6% fall in the forward P/E. It also shows that the 56.8% drop in the stock index from October 9, 2007 through March 9, 2009 was attributable to a 36.3% plunge in forward earnings and a 32.2% drop in the forward P/E.

The bull market after that through late 2017 had plenty of P/E-led corrections that were not confirmed by declines in forward earnings. Of course, in this business there are always exceptions to the rule, such as when earnings were weak in 2015 and again in 2016 because the S&P 500 Energy sector's earnings plunged along with oil prices. That resulted in a couple of wicked but relatively short-lived selloffs; the bull market resumed in 2016 after earnings recovered along with oil prices.

The S&P 500's valuation multiple is greatly affected by the monetary policy cycle. Splicing together quarterly data for the reported four-quarter-trailing P/E from 1960 to 1978 and the monthly forward P/E since January 1979 shows that the valuation multiple typically decreases during periods of monetary tightening and increases during periods of monetary easing (Fig. 5). Recessions tend to exacerbate declines in the S&P 500's valuation multiple that were already under way, usually because the Fed had been raising interest rates to recession-triggering levels. While it is much more cyclical and volatile than earnings, the P/E ratio has had a few significant long-term moves, such as the decline from about 22 in the early 1960s to around six in the early 1980s. From there, it rose in a volatile fashion to a record high of 24.5 during 1999. It was back down to 10.4 during the financial crisis of 2008. By the end of 2017, it had climbed back to 18.5.

Splicing together quarterly data for the reported four-quarter-trailing earnings of the S&P 500 from 1960 to 1978 and the composite's monthly forward earnings since January 1979 shows that this series is procyclical, rising and falling with the business cycle. But it also has a well-defined uptrend that tracks the secular ascent in economic activity (Fig. 6). Let's review the secular uptrends in earnings and stock prices:

- *Trends in earnings.* For S&P 500 monthly forward earnings, the trend growth rate since January 1979 has been around 7% during cyclical peaks in the series and around 5% to 6% during cyclical troughs (Fig. 7). S&P 500 quarterly reported earnings has been growing mostly between 5% and 7% since the start of the data during the first quarter of 1935 (Fig. 8).
- *Trends in stock prices.* A similar trend analysis of the S&P 500 stock price index starting December 1920 shows that since the beginning of the 1960s, the index's appreciation rate ranged between 4% and 7% (Fig. 9). At the end of 2017, it was around 6%, roughly the same as the trend in forward earnings. Assuming no change in the forward P/E, which was very high at the end of 2016, the 6% trajectory would put the S&P 500 stock price index around 3300 by 2025. These levels may or may not answer where the stock market is going—depending on, well, just about everything discussed in this book.

Just for fun: Starting from the last trading day of 2016, when the DJIA was at 19763, I calculate the following DJIA targets for 100 years from then, in round numbers: 54000 (using a 1% compounded annual growth rate), 146000 (2%), 391000 (3%), 1038000 (4%), and 2729000 (5%). Buffett's target of 1000000 in 100 years should easily be hit if the DJIA grows at a subpar annual rate of 4%.

- *Trends in stock price returns.* The trend growth rate of the S&P 500 including reinvested dividends has tended to follow a compounded annual growth rate of roughly 10% since the mid-1950s (Fig. 10). It has provided a solid inflation-adjusted annual return ranging between 6% and 8% over this same period.

TIMELINE

BACK IN 1966, Professor Paul Samuelson, the first American to win the Nobel Prize in economics, famously quipped, "The stock market has forecast nine of the last five recessions." That doesn't quite jibe with my analysis. However, the underlying premise makes sense. The stock market tends to get very jumpy when recessions seem to be coming. Bull markets occasionally are interrupted by corrections, which tend to occur when investors suddenly fear that a recession might be imminent because of some unanticipated event. If they are wrong and earnings continue to grow, stocks will recover. With the benefit of hindsight, everyone breathes a sigh of relief, agreeing that the scare was a great buying opportunity.

The popular view is that occasional selloffs are "healthy" pauses in a bull market. On a regular basis, market watchers will warn that the stock market is "overdue for a correction" simply because stocks have risen too far and/or too fast without one, in their opinion. Sometimes they are right, but more often they are wrong. In any event, corrections are very hard to time. In addition, to profit from them requires two remarkably prescient decisions, namely when to get out and when to get back in.

Since 1945, there have been just four bear markets that weren't associated with recessions, during: 1946 (–27%, lasting 133 days), 1962 (–28%, lasting 196 days), 1966 (–22%, lasting 240 days), and 1987 (–34%, lasting 101 days). They were relatively short and attributable to swoons in the P/E that weren't validated by earnings, which continued to rise. Also since 1945, there have been seven bear markets associated with recessions. They were deeper and longer because tightening monetary policy often triggered not only recessions but also financial crises that exacerbated the recessions and the bear markets (Fig. 11 and Fig. 12). (See Appendix 15.4, S&P 500 Bear Markets and Corrections Since 1928.)

Going back further to 1920, there have been 23 bull markets since 1920. About half, or 11, happened after World War II ended in 1945. All

11 have had at least one correction; contrary to popular belief, corrections are not frequent events during bull markets. (See Appendix 15.3, S&P 500 Bull Markets Since 1928.)

The S&P 500 didn't recover its losses following the Great Crash of 1929 until September 22, 1954, or 25 very long years after the September 7, 1929 high. Along the way, there were 13 bull markets by my definition, which arguably were just rallies in a secular bear market since they all peaked at levels below the 1929 high.

Every bull market since the one that started on June 13, 1949 has peaked at a new record high, suggesting that we've been in a very long secular bull market since then. A few market pundits did make the argument that the stock market was back in a secular bear market once the S&P 500 had peaked on March 24, 2000 at 1527.46.[1] The index surpassed that peak in the following bull market, although not by much, rising to 1565.15 on October 9, 2007. But the subsequent trough at 676.53 on March 9, 2009 was below the previous bear-market trough of 776.76 on October 9, 2002. Notwithstanding the semantics, the latest bull market has gone where no bull market has gone before, suggesting that the secular bull is alive and well.

To get a better understanding of bull and bear markets, let's put on our diving suits once again and have a closer look at the ones in the S&P 500 since World War I:

- *Roaring '20s bull market.* Following the end of the Great War on November 11, 1918, the economy fell into a recession from January 1920 through July 1921. The S&P 500 bottomed at an average monthly price of 6.45 during August 1921.[2] There were two more relatively short recessions during the Roaring '20s preceding the Great Depression, which started at the end of the decade. They didn't stop the S&P 500 from roaring ahead during the decade, as it rose 394.9% to the record high of 31.92 on September 7, 1929. The postwar economy was booming, led by new technologies such as the automobile and electric lights and appliances.

- *The 1929 plunge and 1930 rebound.* The Great Crash started on September 7, 1929. The S&P 500 initially plunged by 44.7% through November 13, 1929 to 17.66. It then soared 46.8% through April 10, 1930 and closed at 25.92, the best level since Saturday, October 26, 1929, the last trading day before the big selloffs during Black Monday and Tuesday. It was still down 18.8% from 1929's record high, but hardly a great crash.

In Chapter 2, I explain why I am convinced that the Great Depression was not caused, or even triggered, by the stock market's decline from early September through mid-November 1929. In my opinion, the Great Depression and the resumption of the bear market were caused by the Smoot–Hawley Tariff, enacted June 17, 1930.

- *The crashes and rebounds of the 1930s.* Anticipating the tariff, the S&P 500 peaked on April 10, 1930. It proceeded to crash 83.0% through June 1, 1932 to bottom at 4.40, down 86.2% from the 1929 peak. It mostly rallied from there by 324.5% to 18.68 by March 6, 1937, despite three bear markets along the way. Then it dropped again by 60.0% because of four more bear markets, to bottom finally at 7.47 on April 28, 1942. The US entered World War II on December 7, 1941 after Japan attacked Pearl Harbor.

- *Postwar ups and downs.* Stocks rallied during most of World War II, gaining 157.7% from the 1942 low to peak at 19.25 on May 29, 1946. Germany unconditionally surrendered on May 7, 1945. The US dropped an atomic bomb on Hiroshima on August 6, 1945 and a second one on Nagasaki three days later. World War II ended on September 2, 1945.

  A brief bear market occurred from May 29, 1946 to October 9, 1946 (lasting 133 days, down 26.6%). There was widespread concern that the end of the war might result in what was called "secular stagnation" at the time or even a renewed depression. Instead, the returning soldiers went to college, found jobs, got married, and fathered the Baby Boom generation. The subsequent bull market lasted until June 15, 1948 (615 days, up 20.8% to peak at 17.06). There were two significant corrections along the way, with declines of 14.7% and 14.1%.

- *Seven-year bull market of the 1950s.* The bear market from June 15, 1948 to June 13, 1949 (down for 363 days, by 20.6%) occurred when the postwar surge in demand tapered off and Americans poured their money into savings, pushing the economy into a sharp "inventory recession" in 1948. It was followed by a seven-year bull market (up for 2,607 days, by 267.1% to 49.74) through August 2, 1956. There were four corrections during the bull market, with declines of 14.0%, 14.8%, 10.6%, and 14.8%. All of that happened despite the Korean War, which lasted from June 25, 1950 to July 27, 1953.

- *The bull market of the early 1960s.* There was a very short bear market from July 15, 1957 through October 22, 1957 (down for 99 days, by

20.7%). The subsequent bull market through December 12, 1961 (up for 1,512 days, by 86.4% to 72.64) had one correction, with a decline of 13.6%.

- *Before and after the Cuban Missile Crisis.* The next bear market lasted from December 12, 1961 to June 26, 1962 (down for 196 days, by 28.0%). The economy grew and stocks rallied despite the Cuban Missile Crisis of October 1962, which sparked Cold War jitters. The bull market through February 9, 1966 (up for 1,324 days, by 79.8% to 94.06) had one correction (–10.5%).

- *The mid-1960s bull run.* There was another short bear market from February 9, 1966 to October 7, 1966 (down for 240 days, by 22.2%). It was followed by a bull market through November 29, 1968 (up for 784 days, by 48.0% to 108.37) that had one 10.1% correction.

- *Turbulence during the late 1960s and early 1970s.* The US became increasingly mired in the war in Vietnam during the bear market from November 29, 1968 to May 26, 1970 (down for 543 days, by 36.1%), the longest and deepest since the 1930s. Nixon was elected president after a year of assassinations and riots. Inflation soared, and there was a short recession from December 1969 to November 1970. The bull market through January 11, 1973 (up for 961 days, by 73.5% to 120.24) had only one correction (–13.9%).

- *The first oil shock and Watergate.* The next bear market was even more severe, lasting from January 11, 1973 through October 3, 1974 (down for 630 days, by 48.2%). The Yom Kippur War between Israel and a coalition of Arab states led by Egypt and Syria triggered the first Arab oil embargo, which sent energy prices soaring, sparking a severe recession. The annual consumer inflation rate peaked at 12.3% during December 1974. The Watergate scandal forced President Nixon to resign on August 9, 1974. Saigon fell on April 30, 1975. The bull market through November 28, 1980 (up for 2,248 days, by 125.6% to 140.52) was interrupted by six significant corrections along the way (ranging from –10.2% to –19.4%).

- *Volcker's round trip.* The bear market from November 28, 1980 to August 12, 1982 (down for 622 days, by 27.1%) was caused by the recession that resulted when the Fed allowed interest rates to soar freely to combat inflation, which had been exacerbated by a second oil shock caused by the Iranian Revolution during the late 1970s. Ronald Reagan defeated Jimmy Carter in the 1980 presidential campaign, promising to cut taxes and regulations. Volcker lowered interest rates in 1982. The subsequent bull market through August 25, 1987 (up for 1,839 days, by 228.8% to 336.87) had one correction (–14.4%).

- *Black Monday 1987.* The bear market from August 25, 1987 through December 4, 1987 was short but steep and deep (down for 101 days, by 33.5%). It started with concerns about rising bond yields in the United States and a debate between the United States and Germany over the value of the dollar. The actual trigger for the debacle was a House Ways and Means Committee bill to eliminate the deductibility of interest expense in corporate takeovers, announced on Wednesday, October 14. This led to an avalanche of selling on Monday of the following week. That day, the S&P 500 plunged 22.6% as computerized "portfolio insurance" programs caused massive selling.

- *The bull market of the 1990s.* The following 12-year bull market through March 24, 2000 (up for 4,494 days, by 582.1% to 1527.15) had five corrections, of which two were borderline bear markets (–19.9% and –19.3%). Most of the gains occurred during the late 1990s as technology stock prices soared.

- *The Y2K bear market.* The bear market from March 24, 2000 to October 9, 2002 was the longest and one of the deepest on record (down for 929 days, by 49.1%). It was caused by the bursting of the dot.com bubble that had caused tech stocks to soar to extraordinary valuations. It was followed by a bull market through October 9, 2007 (up for 1,826 days, by 101.5% to 1565.15) and had just one relatively brief correction (–14.7%).

- *The Great Recession's bear market.* The bear market from October 7, 2007 through March 9, 2009 was long and the deepest since the Great Depression (down for 517 days, by 56.8%). The housing bubble burst, causing a financial crisis in the credit derivatives market that turned into a worldwide financial contagion.

- *The bull's latest charge.* The latest bull market through the end of 2017 record high (up for 3,219 days, by 295.2% to 2673.61) has four corrections so far (ranging from –12.4% to –19.4%).

Brief as this chronology has been, it does provide a couple of important lessons. As Robert Louis Stevenson observed, "To travel hopefully is a better thing than to arrive." Geopolitical troubles aren't necessarily bad for stocks if investors can hope that better times are coming. Notice that the stock market rallied less than five months after Pearl Harbor. After World

War II, it stalled for a short while. Stocks rallied through the Korean War, the Cuban Missile Crisis, and much of the war in Vietnam. The only geopolitical crises that arguably caused bear markets were the two oil shocks of the 1970s because both triggered recessions. Geopolitical crises that don't cause recessions don't usually trigger bear markets.

DANCING WITH BULLS AND BEARS

UNTIL APRIL 1999, my role on Wall Street was chief economist, for the firms of EF Hutton, Prudential-Bache, and CJ Lawrence. My job was to forecast the economy, not the stock market. However, I did work closely with two outstanding investment strategists during the 1980s and 1990s, Greg Smith and Jim Moltz. Neither objected when I crossed the line in my role as an economist and presented my views about the outlook for stocks, which coincided with their views since we worked so well together.

Greg and I turned bullish on the stock market on August 16, 1982, as I note in Chapter 1. Together, we developed what Greg dubbed "the greatest financial story ever told." We believed that the combination of deregulation, disinflation, and demographics would be very bullish for stocks. My work on globalization and the Baby Boomers contributed to this thesis. We stayed bullish over the rest of the 1980s.

When I moved to CJ Lawrence in 1991, Jim was just as bullish as I on the outlook for stocks. Jim devised the Rule of 20, which I discuss in the previous chapter. It states that the stock market is fairly valued when the sum of the average P/E ratio and the rate of inflation is equal to 20.0. Above that level, stocks are overvalued; below it, they are undervalued. The rule has yielded some excellent calls—it was wildly bullish for stocks in the early 1980s, very bearish in the late 1990s, and bullish again a couple of years later in mid-2002. However, like every other valuation model, it didn't signal the bear market that lasted from October 9, 2007 through March 9, 2009. At the end of 2008, the Rule of 20 was as bullish as it was in the early 1980s, another spot-on call. During 2017, it was signaling that stocks were fairly valued for the first time since the early 2000s.

CJ Lawrence, which was merged into Deutsche Bank while I was there, was a great place to develop my thesis about the High-Tech Revolution, which I review in Chapter 3. The firm was investing in developing its technology investment banking division and in 1996 hired Frank Quattrone to head it up. He brought several star technology analysts with him. The team took Amazon.com public during 1997 at just $18 per share. (Don't ask: I never bought a single share.) Once, in 1997, Frank invited me to be the dinner speaker at a ski outing in Beaver Creek, Colorado for his high-powered, high-tech clients. They chatted loudly with one another during my presentation but heartily enjoyed the karaoke performances by Frank and others that came afterward. The next year, Frank moved on to Credit Suisse First Boston.

Jim Moltz also moved on to join his former colleague, Ed Hyman, who had left CJ Lawrence to found his own very successful investment research company, ISI Group, as I note in the first chapter. I became the chief investment strategist at Deutsche Bank's US equities division in New York City during April 1999. By then, I had turned more cautious on the market in general and on technology stocks in particular because of my concerns about Y2K. In addition, my work on the Fed's Stock Valuation Model also led me to ring the alarm bell as the market rose to record-high valuation multiples during 1999.

In a September 6, 1999 article I wrote for *Barron's*, "Next: Dow 8000?" I warned that "I've recently done some tinkering with a widely-followed valuation model, and the results are disturbing. My new, improved model shows that the market's assumptions about risk, and especially about long-term earnings growth, are unrealistically optimistic, leaving stocks ripe for a big fall." I noted that at the end of August, the consensus forecast for earnings growth was around 15% per year for the foreseeable future, the highest long-term growth rate forecast recorded since the data had been compiled. I observed, "The stock market is clearly priced for perfection," and concluded: "Of course, there is one other variable that would bring the model back into line all by itself, and that would be a sharp pullback in the Dow to just under the 8000 mark."[3] At the time, the DJIA was just over 11000. After the tech bubble burst early the following year, the resulting bear market took the DJIA down to a low of 7286.27 on October 9, 2002.

Ultimately, Y2K was a nonevent, but the S&P 500 tumbled 49.1% from March 24, 2000 through October 9, 2002, led by an 82.3% plunge in the S&P 500 Information Technology sector (Fig. 13). I was wrong about Y2K but on the money about valuation, thanks to the Fed's Stock Valuation Model.

I turned increasingly bullish again during the following bull market. Initially, I emphasized the themes I had developed during the previous two decades relating to demographics (i.e., the aging of the Baby Boomers) and geopolitics (i.e., the end of the Cold War). During 2003 and 2004, I focused more of my research on the importance of China to the global economy, devoting three of my *Topical Studies* to the subject, as I review in Chapter 2. Consequently, I was bullish on commodities. In the stock market, I recommended overweighting the sectors that would most benefit from this development. I dubbed them the "MEIs," namely Materials, Energy, and Industrials. During the previous bull market, I was a fan of the "TMT" sectors—Technology, Media, and Telecommunications.

I expanded my bullish case for the stock market in an April 19, 2004 *Barron's* article, "Global Synchronized Earnings Boom." I wrote: "The global synchronized boom should continue to be good for profits both in the United States and around the world. So should operating leverage and productivity. Pricing power is also improving, especially for materials, energy, and industrials. Forward earnings are rebounding strongly among all the major industrial economies, with new record highs in the United States, Canada, and Japan."[4]

While I was focusing on China and the global economic boom, the subprime mortgage problem was emerging on the home front in late 2006 and early 2007. I turned bearish on the S&P 500 Financials sector on June 25, 2007, writing:

> I have to conclude that it might be a good idea to implement defensive portfolio strategies for the next few weeks. It is just too hard to assess how the repricing of illiquid assets held by hedge funds will play out. Reading the *WSJ* stories on the Bear Stearns funds reminded me of the technology companies that boosted their sales during the late 1990s by lending their customers the money they needed to buy their products. In the current case, Wall Street firms and money center banks financed the leveraging up of hedge funds that purchased the exotic and illiquid fixed-income securities produced by the very same Wall Street firms and money center banks. I've previously suggested that [z]aitech (financial engineering) might be the biggest risk for us stock market bulls. This risk may be about to play out sooner than I expected as some of the structured securities designed by the financial engineers crumble. As a result, I am downgrading the S&P 500 Financials today from overweight to underweight.

The sector's stock price index had dropped only 3.9% from its record-high peak on February 20, 2007 when I turned bearish on it (Fig. 14).

It then plunged another 83.3% from June 25, 2007 (when I began to advise underweighting the sector) through March 6, 2009, for a total loss of 84.0% from the February peak. While I got that right, I didn't anticipate the severity and breadth of the unfolding bear market. I expected that the Federal Open Market Committee (FOMC) would ease aggressively, which is what the committee had always done in the past when confronted with financial crises. Sure enough, the Fed slashed the federal funds rate by 75 basis points, from 5.25% to 4.50%, from September 18 to October 31. By April 30, 2008, the rate had been cut five more times to 2.00%. But it turned out to be too little, too late.

Keep in mind that the S&P 500 had dropped by 20.0% from its October 9, 2007 peak through Friday, September 12, 2008. That was well into the financial crisis, yet the stock market was just crossing the border from correction territory into bear-market country.

When Treasury Secretary Henry Paulson and Fed Chairman Ben Bernanke opted to let Lehman fail on Monday, September 15, the stock market went into a freefall. That was a shocker, for sure. At the time and ever since, both claimed that they had no legal authority to support Lehman. I'm not convinced, especially given what happened next. On Sunday, September 21, less than a week after Lehman failed, the Fed announced that both Goldman Sachs and Morgan Stanley would become bank holding companies.[5] They would have full access to the Fed's emergency liquidity facilities, i.e., the full support of the bank of last resort! (See Appendix 8.3, Bernanke's Fed and the Lehman Bankruptcy.)

The situation went from really bad to horrendous for the Financials and the overall market when Larry Summers weighed in as the director-elect of the National Economic Council of the incoming Obama administration at the start of 2009. In a Monday, January 12 letter to the congressional leadership, he assured them that everything would be done to avoid an economic catastrophe. The letter was very populist in tone: financial executives had benefited, while working stiffs and small business owners had not, according to Summers.

So Summers pledged: "We will ensure that resources are directed to increasing lending and preventing new financial crises and not to enriching shareholders and executives. Those receiving exceptional assistance will be subject to tough but sensible conditions that limit compensation until taxpayer money is paid back, ban dividend payments beyond *de minimis* amounts, and put limits on stock buybacks and the acquisition of already financially strong companies."

On January 14, 2009, I wrote, "Shoot me now. Let's kill the capital market for bank common and preferred shares by banning dividends!" On January 22, *The New York Times* hosted a discussion by experts on nationalizing US banks.[6] The S&P 500 Financials stock price index dropped another 47.5% from Friday, January 9, the trading day before the Summers letter, through the March 6 record-low bottom for the Financials sector.

As I note in Chapter 1, I turned bullish in March a few days after the S&P 500 hit an intraday low of 666 on March 6, 2009. The closing low occurred on March 9, but the intraday low of 666 was the very lowest point in the market's post-crisis downward spiral.

By the next week, I suspected as much. As I recount in Chapter 11, I wrote on March 16, 2009: "We've been to Hades and back. The S&P 500 bottomed last week on March 6 at an intraday low of 666. This is a number commonly associated with the Devil. . . . The latest relief rally was sparked by lots of good news for a refreshing change, which I believe may have some staying power. . . . I'm rooting for more good news, and hoping that 666 was THE low." The same day, the Fed's first round of quantitative easing was expanded to $1.25 trillion in mortgage-related securities and $300 billion in Treasury bonds.

During the bear market, I had written on several occasions that mark-to-market accounting rules had created a death spiral in the credit markets. Ben Bernanke, Fed chairman at the time, was asked about this at a congressional hearing and responded that changing the rule during a crisis didn't make sense to him. I argued that doing so made lots of sense if the rule was exacerbating the crisis. Here is what I wrote about this on March 5, 2008:

Last Thursday, Senator Chuck Schumer asked the Fed Chairman about the role of fair-value accounting in exacerbating the turmoil in the credit markets. Mr. Bernanke responded, "I think . . . it's one of the major problems that we have in the current environment. I don't know how to fix it. I don't know what to do about it." When the Senator suggested modifying the mark-to-market rule, Mr. Bernanke lamented, "I agree there's a severe problem. It's difficult to change the rules in the middle of a crisis." Well, how about cutting the federal funds rate by another 100bps in the middle of the crisis? And can't the Fed's huge staff of economists come up with any suggestions for the accountants on how to tweak the mark-to-market rules to stop the downward spiral in bank asset values? Why not just price all loans and related derivatives at par as long as they are current, while marking down only those that are experiencing delinquencies?

Mark-to-market accounting adjusts balance-sheet values to reflect current market asset prices. In contrast, historical cost accounting is based on the original purchase price of assets. The former generally makes sense, except when asset markets seize up, providing very faulty pricing information. During September 2006, the FASB issued its Statement of Financial Accounting Standards No. 157, titled "Fair Value Measurements." "FAS 157," as it is commonly known, took effect on November 15, 2007, just in time to worsen the financial crisis by forcing companies to write down billions in hard-to-value assets!

As I note in Chapter 1, following a contentious hearing before the US House Financial Services Committee on March 12, the FASB eased the mark-to-market rules through the release of three FASB Staff Positions (which are a type of ruling). Legislators at the hearing urged the FASB to act quickly, indicating that any failure to do so could result in congressional intervention. The Committee held the hearing after the American Bankers Association, the US Chamber of Commerce, the Federal Home Loan Banks, and numerous industry groups requested that federal regulators urge the FASB to issue guidance expeditiously. On March 17, 2009, the FASB issued FAS 157-e, "Determining Whether a Market is Not Active and a Transaction is Not Distressed," which provided revised guidance on mark-to-market accounting. In effect, the FASB eased up on the mark-to-market rule, which increased my bullish outlook on the stock market.

I realized early on that the bull market since March 2009 was likely to be plagued by frequent anxiety attacks, because the trauma of 2008 had left investors feeling overly jittery. Their PTSD was understandable, certainly, given the S&P 500's 56.8% plunge in less than a year and a half, from October 9, 2007 through March 9, 2009. But investors' fears that a similar calamity might strike their world again at any moment clearly were overblown. So I predicted that panic attacks would be followed by relief rallies once proven to be false alarms, i.e., when nothing bad happened. Indeed, the pattern I had foreseen unfolded as if scripted: recurring panic attacks were followed by relief rallies, carrying the market to new cycle highs and then on to new record highs after March 28, 2013, when the S&P 500 exceeded its previous record high of October 9, 2007.

As I had told our accounts back in the early days of the bull market, the financial crisis of 2008 and the resulting bear market were so traumatic that it wouldn't take much to convince investors that another calamity was imminent. Quite a few vocal bears repeatedly sounded the alarm, warning about a coming "endgame." I argued that they were fighting the major central banks that had committed to doing whatever it took to avoid another financial debacle. The bears insisted that the central bankers were simply "kicking the can down the road." I countered that it was too soon to see the end to the game or a cliff at the end of the road.

From 2009 through 2017, there were four major corrections and several significant scares. I kept track of them and the main events that seemed to cause them (Fig. 15). By my count, there were 59 panic attacks from 2009 through 2017, with 2012 being especially anxiety-prone, seeing 12 attacks.[7] From 2010 through 2012, there were recurring fears that the Eurozone might disintegrate. There were Greek debt crises and concerns about bad loans in the Italian banking sector. Investors were greatly relieved when European Central Bank President Mario Draghi pledged during the summer of 2012 to do whatever it took to defend the Eurozone. China also popped up from time to time as concerns mounted about real estate bubbles, slowing growth, and capital outflows over there. At the end of 2012, fear of a "fiscal cliff" in the United States evaporated when a budget deal was struck at the start of 2013 between Democrats and Republicans. I expected a deal would be struck, though I certainly had no idea that it would be worked out between Vice President Joe Biden and Senate Minority Leader Mitch McConnell (R, KY) on New Year's Eve.

On January 29, 2013, I wrote that following the fiscal cliff nonevent, there was "nothing to fear but nothing to fear." Investors will always find something to worry about, and now I noticed that some were concerned that there might be too many bulls! In a November 9, 2013 *Barron's* interview, I observed that investors seemed to have "anxiety fatigue":

> I have met a lot of institutional investors I call "fully invested bears" who all agree this is going to end badly. Now, they are

a bit more relaxed, thinking it won't end badly anytime soon. Investors have anxiety fatigue. I think it's because we didn't go over the fiscal cliff. We haven't had a significant correction since June of last year. We had the fiscal cliff; they raised taxes; then there was the sequester, and then the latest fiscal impasse. And yet the market is at a record high. Investors have learned that any time you get a selloff, you want to be a buyer. The trick to this bull market has been to avoid getting thrown off.[8]

In that interview, I said I was more concerned about a meltup than a meltdown in the stock market: "Since the beginning of the year, I've been forecasting 60% probability of a rational exuberance scenario, 30% meltup, and 10% meltdown. I'm still there, but I'm wavering and leaning toward the meltup." During 2017, as the stock market continued to soar to new highs with valuation multiples nearing previous record highs, I raised the odds of a meltup to 55%. I also raised the odds of a meltdown to 25%, since such events naturally tend to follow meltups. That left me with 20% odds for rational exuberance but still 75% in the bullish camp.

The phrase "meltup" is unambiguously associated with soaring stock prices. The *Financial Times* defines it as "the informal term used to describe markets that experience a rapid rise in valuations due to a stampede of investors anxious not to miss out on a rising trend. Gains caused by meltups are usually followed quite quickly by meltdowns." One meaning of the word "meltdown" is "an accident in a nuclear reactor in which the fuel overheats and melts the reactor core or shielding." Since the 1987 stock market crash, the word has also been defined as "a disastrous event, especially a rapid fall in share prices." Of course, stressed humans can sometimes exhibit signs of a meltdown, a phenomenon that can coincide with a meltdown in one's stock portfolio.

There was another nasty selloff at the start of 2016 as two Fed officials warned that the FOMC was likely to follow 2015's one rate hike at the end of that year with four hikes in 2016. I had predicted "one-and-done" for 2015 and again for 2016.

A strange coincidence occurred on January 19, 2016, when I registered for a room at the Radisson Blu Hotel in Zurich, Switzerland, where I was scheduled to be a keynote speaker at an investment conference the next day. I was taken aback when the front-desk clerk handed me a key for room 666—the S&P 500's post-crisis intraday low, hit on March 6, 2009.

The number represents a career highlight for me since I called that point the probable bottom just days after it was hit; but its association with the Devil didn't escape me, either in 2009 or in early 2016. "My initial reaction was to ask for a different room," I wrote at the time, "since that number is associated with the Devil in folklore. I'm not superstitious, but then again, why tempt the Fates? However, I spent the night in 666, because I actually have fond memories about this number."

Contributing to the selloff in early 2016 was the plunge in the price of oil, which had started on June 20, 2014. That triggered a significant widening in the yield spread between high-yield corporate bonds and the US Treasury 10-year bond yield from 2014's low of 253 basis points on June 23 to a high of 844 basis points on February 11, 2016. The widening was led by soaring yields of junk bonds issued by oil companies. There were widespread fears that all this could lead to a recession. In addition, the Chinese currency was depreciating amid signs of accelerating capital outflows from China.

I remained bullish. I argued on Monday, January 25, 2016 that "it may be too late to panic" and that the previous "Wednesday's action might have made capitulation lows in both the stock and oil markets." Sure enough, the price of a barrel of Brent crude oil did bottom on Wednesday, January 20. The S&P 500 bottomed on February 11, the same day that the high-yield spread peaked. The S&P 500 Energy sector dropped 47.3% from its high on June 23, 2014 to bottom on January 20, 2016 (Fig. 16).

In a February 6, 2016 *Barron's* interview, "Yardeni: No U.S. Recession in Sight," I reiterated my forecast that the Fed was unlikely to hike the federal funds rate more than once that year, and that the secular bull market remained intact.[9] During the summer of 2016, I perceived the end of the energy-led earnings recession and was quoted as saying so in an August *Barron's* story.[10]

The bull market rose to a new record high at the end of 2016. Following the surprising Brexit vote that summer, the stock market declined for just two days, despite lots of gloomy predictions, which I didn't share, about the turmoil that it would unleash. Just prior to the US presidential election, I argued that the rebound in earnings—following the recession in the energy industry—would likely push stock prices higher no matter who won. A few weeks after Donald Trump was elected—the Republican party having won majorities in both the Senate and the House of Representatives—I raised my 2017 outlook for the S&P 500, expecting that a combination of deregulation and tax cuts would boost earnings. In another *Barron's* interview, on February 4, 2017, I said:

> It would be a mistake to bet against what President Trump might accomplish on the policy side. I'm giving him the benefit of the doubt, hoping good policies get implemented and bad ones forgotten. We could get substantial tax cuts. All his proposals don't need to be implemented for the Trump rally to be validated. If you got $1 trillion to $2 trillion coming back from overseas because of a lower tax on repatriated corporate earnings, that would be very powerful in terms of keeping the market up.[11]

I anticipated that Trump would move quickly to push Congress to enact his tax reform plan. Instead, he pressed for the repeal of Obamacare, which ran into fierce opposition even from a few congressional Republicans. I argued that it didn't much matter whether the tax-cutting plan was implemented in 2017 or 2018. At the start of 2018, after Trump had signed the Tax Cut and Jobs Act at the end of 2017, the stock market continued to climb to new highs. I remained bullish and lifted my odds of a meltup from 55% to 70%. However, I also observed in my January 16 commentary: "We may be experiencing an extremely unusual earnings-led meltup. If so, it is more likely to be sustainable than the run-of-the-mill P/E-led meltup, as long as it doesn't morph into one. For now, sit back and enjoy the show."

ACTIVE VERSUS PASSIVE

IN THIS BOOK, I focus primarily on the S&P 500 stock price index. There are numerous alternative price indexes, of course. (See Appendix 15.1, Major US Stock Market Indexes.) The most comprehensive measures of the value of the stock market are compiled by the Fed in the *Financial Accounts of the United States*, which shows the value of all equities traded in the US as well as the total excluding foreign issues (Fig. 17). Both series are available only quarterly, though.

Among the broadest daily indexes is the Wilshire 5000 Total Market Index, which measures the market capitalization of its constituents. Named for the nearly 5,000 stocks it contained at launch, it then expanded to a high count of 7,562 on July 31, 1998. After that, the count fell steadily to 3,776 on December 31, 2013; from there, it bounced back to 3,818 on September 30, 2014. The last time the Wilshire 5000 contained 5,000 or more companies was December 29, 2005.[12]

Another comprehensive measure is the S&P 1500, which includes the constituents of the S&P 500, S&P 400, and S&P 600. Since March 10, 2017, when Standard & Poor's updated its market-cap guidelines, the S&P 500 has consisted of "LargeCap" companies with market capitalizations of $6.1 billion or more.[13] The S&P 400 MidCaps comprise companies with market capitalizations of $1.6 billion to $6.8 billion, while the S&P 600 SmallCaps range between $450 million and $2.1 billion. The market capitalization of the S&P 1500 has tended to be nearly the same as that of the Wilshire 5000.

So why choose to focus on an index that covers just 500 stocks? Good historical earnings measures are not readily available for the other major price indexes, but they are for the S&P 500 composite. The S&P 500 is one of the stock price indexes most closely tracked by institutional portfolio managers. It is also one of the most widely used benchmarks of US equity performance. Indeed, in 2015, over $2 trillion in assets were benchmarked to the S&P 500.[14] Among assets that were not exchange-traded funds (ETFs), the year-end total was $1.79 trillion, while ETFs that directly tracked the index totaled $354 billion.

The companies represented in the index tend to be among the largest ones headquartered in the United States. The S&P 500 is a market-value-weighted index (i.e., stock price times the number of shares outstanding), with each stock's weight in the index proportionate to its market value. The S&P 500 accounts for nearly all the market value of both the Wilshire 5000 and the S&P 1500.

The Standard & Poor's Index Committee examines several criteria when searching for suitable Index candidates from a universe of over 10,000 stocks.[15] The shares must have sufficient liquidity, with a turnover ratio—i.e., the dollar value of shares traded annually relative to their market cap—of at least 1.00. The constituents of the S&P 500 are US companies that file 10-K annual reports and are traded on US exchanges. The public float must equal at least 50% of the company's stock. The sum of the most recent four consecutive quarters' GAAP earnings should be positive, as should the GAAP earnings of the most recent quarter.

The S&P 500 Index is clearly "dressed for success." Only successful candidates are likely to make the team. Losers are booted out if their market capitalization or share prices drop too low. Companies experiencing financial distress are also likely to be excommunicated. The Committee does strive to minimize turnover by not making too many changes. However, some turnover is a natural consequence of mergers and acquisitions.

Along with the S&P 500, I keep track of the S&P 400 MidCaps and the S&P 600 SmallCaps (Fig. 18). Like the S&P 500, there are data series available for their forward revenues and forward earnings, which provide additional insights into the stock market. Besides, while most of my accounts manage portfolios benchmarked to the S&P 500, quite a few manage MidCap and SmallCap portfolios. Some institutional investors prefer to use the Russell 1000 and Russell 2000 as their LargeCap and SmallCap benchmarks. For almost all institutional investors, the name of the game is to beat their benchmark as well as their "peers," i.e., their competitors who use the same benchmark.

Increasingly in recent years, the benchmarks themselves have become major competitors for institutional investors who actively manage funds, as ETFs have been created to mimic just about every imaginable index and investment style. These "passive funds" continue to attract lots of inflows that in the past might have gone into traditional mutual funds. Their proponents claim that active managers don't beat their benchmarks, on average, yet charge more in management fees than investors pay for passive funds.

This rationale would be hard to refute if the entire universe of stocks consisted only of the S&P 500 and everyone investing in this limited market was attempting to overweight and underweight different stocks, industries, and sectors to beat the market. On average, that's impossible to do, since all the money collectively invested in the market must necessarily have the exact same market cap as the market and its constituents!

However, my experience has been that actively managing around a portfolio's benchmark by overweighting (and/or underweighting) just one, two, or maybe three sectors can result in the portfolio outperforming the benchmark if the choices are based on strongly held views that turn out to be right.

For example, overweighting the Information Technology sector of the S&P 500 was a winning strategy for me during the bull market of the 1990s (Fig. 19). It soared 1,697% back then, significantly outpacing all the other sectors. Admittedly, I started cooling to the sector by 1999, when it managed to double before it peaked in early 2000. Underweighting Utilities, Energy, and Materials helped performance at that time. I wasn't much interested in the latter two sectors given the weakness in commodity prices and my view that the only commodity necessary for the High-Tech Revolution is sand to make silicon chips.

During the following bull market, the MEI sectors were among the outperforming sectors (Fig. 20). Energy led the way with a gain of 242%. I was all in on the China-led commodity boom and its positive implications for the MEI sectors. Consumer Staples and Health Care were notable laggards. During the bull market from 2009 through 2016, the Consumer Discretionary sector beat the other sectors. Energy significantly underperformed (Fig. 21).

Of course, the equity market isn't limited to the S&P 500 or even the S&P 1500. Even the Wilshire 5000 doesn't cover all the choices available for equity investors. There's the FTSE, the Nikkei, the Dax, and lots of other stock market indexes around the world. Indeed, there's literally an entire world of stock market indexes constructed by MSCI (formerly known as "Morgan Stanley Capital International"): "MSCI's All Country World Index (ACWI) is composed of 2,400 constituents, 11 sectors, and is the industry's accepted gauge of global stock market activity. It provides a seamless, modern and fully integrated view across all sources of equity returns in 46 developed and emerging markets."[16]

Among the major MSCI indexes are those for the United States, the European Monetary Union, Japan, the United Kingdom, and the Emerging Markets. During the bull market from 2002 through 2007, the United States was the laggard, rising 102%. In dollar terms, the Emerging Markets MSCI was the big winner, with a gain of 386% (Fig. 22). During the bull market from 2009 through the end of 2017, there was a remarkable reversal, with the United States up 294% while the other indexes were up around 125% each, in dollars (Fig. 23). My advice to global active managers during most of the latest bull market was to "stay home" in the United States rather than to "go global." That worked out very well and was premised on my view that the US economy had adjusted best to the traumatic shock of the financial crisis of 2008. Daily, I track the ratio of the US MSCI stock price index to the All Country World excluding the US indexes, in both dollars and local currencies (Fig. 24).

By the way, I also monitor the market-capitalization shares of the S&P 500's sectors. The composite is divided into 11 economic sectors:

Consumer Discretionary, Consumer Staples, Energy, Financials, Health Care, Industrials, Information Technology, Materials, Real Estate, Telecommunication Services, and Utilities. The Standard & Poor's Index Committee tries to maintain some balance among the sectors to reflect their relative importance in the economy. I do that by comparing the earnings share of the sectors using forward earnings to their market-capitalization shares.

I've found that when a sector's market-capitalization share and/or earnings share rises close to 30%, that's a sign of possible trouble ahead for the sector as well as the market. That was the case for Information Technology during the late 1990s and for Financials during the years prior to the financial crisis of 2007 and 2008 (Fig. 25 and Fig. 26).

In any event, the main point to remember in the active-versus-passive debate is that asset allocation is always an active choice.

GO WITH THE FLOWS

USEFUL INSIGHTS INTO the performance of the stock market also can be gleaned by a careful analysis of the available data on the demand and supply sides of the equity market. The major source of this information is the Fed's *Financial Accounts of the United States*. The good news is that it is all-inclusive, covering the issuance of equities by nonfinancial and financial corporations. It also tracks the net purchases (or sales) by households, mutual funds, ETFs, institutional investors, and foreign investors.[17] The bad news is that the data are all quarterly and compiled with a lag of about two and a half months. Nevertheless, trends in the flows can persist and provide a better understanding of what is driving the stock market. To smooth out the volatility in data, I prefer to track the four-quarter averages of the various time series.

The Fed also provides monthly data on the new issuance of corporate equities and corporate bonds for both nonfinancial and financial corporations. These include both initial public offerings (IPOs) and secondary issues. The Investment Company Institute compiles monthly data on bond and equity mutual funds and ETFs. I prefer to accentuate their trends by tracking the 12-month sums of these often volatile data series. All together, they provide useful clues to how the underlying fundamentals that drive stock prices are showing up in the stock market's flow of funds.

Here's a quick tour of some of the series that I follow closely to track the equity market from a flow-of-funds perspective:

- *Mergers and acquisitions.* Let's start by examining the flows attributable to corporations. Data available since 1995 from Dealogic show a distinct cyclical pattern in merger and acquisition (M&A) activity (Fig. 27). Over that period, during the past three bull markets, M&A activity measured in billions of dollars rose along with stock prices. One reason this happens is that when share prices are on the rise, company managements get more optimistic about the future and see more opportunities to profit by either combining with or acquiring another company. In addition, their rising stock prices can provide currency with which to finance such deals when transactions include company stock. So M&A activity may or may not reduce the supply of stock, but it certainly tends to feed bullish sentiment—until it doesn't. During bear markets, M&A activity drops along with stock prices.

- *Gross issuance.* The Fed compiles monthly data on new issuance of stocks. They are volatile, so again I prefer to track the 12-month sum (Fig. 28). However, there are clearer patterns in the disaggregated data for stock issuance by nonfinancial and financial corporations. The former tend to raise money in the equity market during bull markets (Fig. 29). That makes sense, especially for IPOs, which proliferate when investors are particularly bullish and keen on owning companies that may provide lots of upside in new businesses. Financial corporations tend to issue stocks when they need to raise capital, which sometimes happens during bear markets resulting from financial crises, as was most evident in 2008 and 2009 (Fig. 30).

- *Buybacks.* In addition to issuing new stock, corporations can also buy back their shares. The Fed's quarterly data show the *net* issuance of stocks by all corporations. It includes share issuance by ETFs. I subtract the latter from the former to get a better sense of corporate finance trends (Fig. 31 and Fig. 32). My preference is to focus on the Fed's data on net equity issuance by nonfinancial corporations, which closely track Standard & Poor's data on share buybacks for the S&P 500 since the first quarter of 1998 (Fig. 33 and Fig. 34). That's because share buybacks have greatly exceeded new issuance in recent years.

  Both series show that buybacks were a major driver of the previous and most recent bull markets. From the fourth quarter of 2002 through the third quarter of 2007, S&P 500 buybacks totaled $1.6 trillion, while the Fed's data showed net issuance of equities of *minus* $1.4 trillion for all nonfinancial corporations. From the first quarter of 2009 through the third quarter of 2017, S&P 500 buybacks added up to $3.8 trillion, while the Fed's data, which include the impact of M&A activity, summed to *minus* $3.4 trillion. The Fed's data show a spike in issuance by domestic financial corporations, excluding ETFs, during 2008 and 2009, when they scrambled to raise capital (Fig. 35).

- *ADRs.* In the equity issuance data, the Fed includes net purchases of foreign corporate equities and investment fund shares by US residents (Fig. 36). This series includes American depositary receipts, commonly known as "ADRs." Americans tend to be consistent buyers of foreign equities, with slowdowns in such activities occurring during recessions.

- *Households.* Flow-of-funds geeks should take note that the Fed's data on total net issuance of equity by financial corporations includes shares issued by ETFs. Furthermore, net purchases of equities by the various sectors include these ETF shares. That clouds the picture provided by the data. For example, net purchases by households include their acquisition of ETFs while excluding their buying of mutual fund shares. Furthermore, the household sector is a residual that includes not only households but also nonprofit organizations as well as domestic hedge funds, private equity funds, and personal trusts. Therefore, I don't give much weight to the household sector's data in the Fed's flow-of-funds database.

- *Institutional investors.* More useful, I find, are the Fed's data on the activity of institutional investors. I track these data by summing the net purchases of equities of property-casualty insurance companies, life insurance companies, private pension funds, state and local retirement funds, and federal government retirement funds. This statistic shows institutional investors have been significant net sellers of equities for most of the time since the mid-1990s (Fig. 37).

- *Foreign investors.* Foreign investors tended to do most of their buying of US equities near the tops of the previous two bull markets, suggesting that their buying and selling might be useful as contrary signals, i.e., signaling points in time when investors would be better off doing the opposite (Fig. 38). Sure enough, foreign investors were significant sellers during 2015 and 2016, just before the S&P 500 vaulted into record territory in early 2017.

- *Mutual funds and ETFs.* The Fed's data on equity mutual funds once reliably reflected the sentiment of individual investors. That was before

ETFs surged in popularity over the past few years. Mutual fund data suggest that individual investors were big buyers of equities during the bull market of the 1990s (Fig. 39). They weren't fazed as much as widely believed by the bursting of the tech bubble. They came roaring back into the equity mutual funds from roughly 2003 through early 2007. They've been less reliable buyers of equity mutual fund shares during the latest bull market that started in 2009. That might be because equity ETFs have been attracting more and more net inflows; that's been true since the start of the data in the late 1990s but particularly so in recent years (Fig. 40).

The Fed also compiles data on the net inflows into equity mutual funds and ETFs—both US-based—by investment objective, focusing on those that invest in domestic stocks only and those that invest around the world. They show that at the beginnings of the previous two bull markets, domestic funds collectively had significant net inflows that dissipated rather quickly (Fig. 41). World funds saw more significant and consistent increases in net inflows during the previous two bull markets, though they lost their momentum during the second half of 2016 (Fig. 42).

To get a better handle on net inflows into mutual funds and ETFs, I like to track the data compiled monthly by the Investment Company Institute. They show that during the latest bull market, from March 2009 through November 2017, equity mutual funds had net inflows of just $142 billion, while equity ETFs attracted $1.4 trillion over this same period (Fig. 43 and Fig. 44).

LEADING THE WAY

PREDICTING THE STOCK market shouldn't be all that difficult since only two variables drive it, as I've noted repeatedly in these pages—earnings and the valuation of those earnings. But it's tougher than it sounds, because both of those variables are driven by so many others. That doesn't stop stock gurus and their followers from searching for leading indicators of the stock market. Some believe that the Holy Grail is hiding in plain sight, in the chart patterns that the stock market traces all the time.

Technical analysts focus solely on stock performance-related charts and data, paying little attention to the fundamentals that determine companies' earnings. These readers of tea leaves, as I sometimes call them, believe that the market is always dropping clues about where it is going next. Sometimes, they're right for a while and develop a cult following. Sadly for them and their disciples, one great call that leads to instant fame is often followed by a really bad one just when everyone is paying attention. The list of has-beens, now forgotten, is a long one.

Then again, I've met plenty of market-savvy investment advisers, institutional investors, and individual investors who do very well without much fanfare. Few of them claim that the charts provide useful guidance about the long-term outlook for the stock market. But they do see levels that might provide "support" that could end a selloff and "resistance" to a further upside advance. The chart watchers may also compare the current level of the market to various moving averages (typically of the 50-day and 200-day varieties) to assess whether price momentum is picking up or tapering off. Some are awfully good at seeing developing relationships among sectors within the stock market. Others are good at "macro" trades that often involve perceiving how developments in bond, currency, and commodity markets provide early signals for important moves in the stock market.

The challenging truth for us fortune-seeking fortune-tellers is that we are all amateurs compared to the most seasoned fortune-teller, the stock market itself. The S&P 500 is one of the 10 components of the Index of Leading Economic Indicators (LEI) because it is forward looking by its very nature. It reflects investor expectations for the future. That might be why no one seems to have found a leading index for the stock market itself.

Could the LEI's other nine components be tapped for confirmation of the signal that the stock market is sending? The problem is that only the S&P 500 and the interest-rate spread between the US Treasury 10-year bond yield and the federal funds rate are available daily. Initial unemployment claims are available weekly. The other seven components of the LEI are monthly and are old news by the time they are released. The overall index is released two to three weeks after the end of each month. I examine all of this in Chapter 5.

Notwithstanding the above cautionary advice, I do look at the charts. I do follow moving averages. I've even dabbled in constructing leading indicators for the stock market. That effort did yield some coincident, though not leading, indicators of the S&P 500, which can either confirm or challenge the direction of this stock index. Here are a couple:

- *Boom-Bust Barometer.* In Chapter 11, I introduce my Boom-Bust Barometer (BBB). This ratio of the CRB raw industrials spot price index and initial unemployment claims was a good coincident indicator of S&P 500 forward earnings from 2000 through 2017 (Fig. 45). However, the former tends to be more volatile than the latter. Not surprisingly, the BBB also has tracked the S&P 500 over the same period (Fig. 46).
- *Weekly Leading Indicator.* Averaging the BBB with Bloomberg's Weekly Consumer Comfort Index (WCCI) reduces some of its volatility and provides a closer fit with the S&P 500 (Fig. 47). I call this expanded version of the BBB the "YRI Weekly Leading Index" (YRI-WLI) and compare it to a similar index constructed by the folks at the Economic Cycle Research Institute (ECRI-WLI) (Fig. 48).

My index is an open-source indicator, i.e., you can have the recipe: it is simply the average of the BBB and WCCI. The ECRI index is proprietary, with a secret sauce. My hunch is that it includes the same variables I am using and several financial ones, such as the S&P 500, the yield-curve spread, and the credit-quality yield spread. In any event, the ECRI didn't track the S&P 500 performance as closely as my index, measured since 2000 (Fig. 49). Of course, past performance is no guarantee of future success, as we say in the stock market forecasting trade. Besides, both indexes tend to be coincident rather than leading indicators of the stock market, so their usefulness as prediction tools is limited.

My BBB and YRI-WLI are fundamental in nature, i.e., they combine economic indicators rather than financial ones. There are also plenty of internal technical indicators generated by the market's own action. Consider the following:

- *Margin debt.* The monthly series on debt balances in margin accounts at brokers and dealers is highly correlated with the S&P 500 (Fig. 50). Bearish strategists tend to warn that record highs in margin debt can signal a market top. They see it as a clear sign of speculative excess, making the market vulnerable to a selloff exacerbated by margin calls. It's hard to argue with the logic of this view, but margin debt doesn't provide a useful sell signal or any insights into when the next bear market is likely to occur, since it is a coincident indicator of the stock market. It has rarely, if ever, triggered a significant market decline. However, margin calls can certainly worsen a selloff. Keep in mind that margin debt tends to be a very tiny fraction of the stock market's capitalization.

- *Moving averages.* The most widely followed are various moving averages. Bearishly inclined stock market technicians tend to warn that the market's price momentum has accelerated unsustainably when the S&P 500 well exceeds its widely followed 200-day moving average. But if the index falls well below this average, some will warn this *too* might be bearish, signaling diminished price momentum that might continue. The big problem with this technical tool is that in a bull market, falling below the moving average can signal a buying opportunity.

- *Breadth.* Another related set of internal technical indicators measures the breadth of market advances and declines. The broader the participation of stocks in a rally, the more likely the rally is to be sustainable. If a rally is led by fewer and fewer stocks, it might be more vulnerable to ending badly. In any event, in this scenario, many investors are losing money and aren't taking much comfort in the narrowly led rise in a broad stock index such as the S&P 500. Of course, a sudden broad selloff could signal the end of a bull market and the beginning of a bear market.

  Among measures of breadth is the percentage of S&P 500 stocks that are above their 200-day moving averages (Fig. 51). A variation of this measure is the percentage of S&P 500 stocks that are up on a year-over-year basis (Fig. 52). I keep track of them, but I've found that they are not consistently helpful in assessing the direction of the market. I must say the same about other commonly followed breadth measures, such as the ratio of the S&P 500 on an equal-weighted basis to the market-cap-weighted basis (Fig. 53). The New York Stock Exchange advance/decline line is another indicator that I glance at from time to time, just out of curiosity (Fig. 54).

- *VIX.* The VIX measure of volatility is also a popular technical series. However, it is a coincident indicator for the overall market. It is based on options prices on the S&P 500 index and tends to move in the opposite direction of the index. It is also known as the "fear gauge" and closely tracks other fear gauges, such as the high-yield corporate bond spread and the percentage of bears, as tracked by Investors Intelligence in a widely followed survey of investment newsletters (Fig. 55 and Fig. 56).

- *Bull-to-bear ratio.* The stock market is essentially a tug-of-war between bullish and bearish investors. The bulls are optimistic about the prospects for the economy and profits. The bears have a pessimistic view of the future. The market reflects the balance of these dueling viewpoints. Obviously, the market tends to rise during good times and fall during bad ones. There are times, usually around turning points, when the balance is either overly optimistic or overly pessimistic.

  Often, stock market tops follow a long bull market, with mounting optimism right before the top. Investors talk about "new eras" and see no end to prosperity, or at least no cloud on the foreseeable horizon. They are exuberant about the immediate outlook and have great confidence in the long-term prospects for the economy, earnings, and stock prices. It is hard for them to imagine what could go wrong. But like a bipolar person during a manic episode, their judgment is impaired. At such times, the market's valuation multiple is well above its mean, which has been around 15 since the fourth quarter of 1935.

  At major bottoms, conversely, investors have lost almost all hope in a better tomorrow. They see only downside risk and no meaningful upside potential. It is hard for them to imagine what could go right. The market's multiple is well below 15 at such times.

  Sentiment indicators, including various "fear and greed" indexes, are widely followed by contrarian investors. I have a few personal favorites. I am particularly fond of the sentiment readings produced by Investors Intelligence, which reports on a weekly basis the percentages of bullish and bearish market letter writers that the organization tracks. There is also a percentage for those who are in the correction camp, anticipating a selloff but not an outright bear market.

  This survey's bull-to-bear ratio is widely followed as a contrary indicator (Fig. 57). I've found that when it falls below a reading of 1.00, it works quite well as a signal to buy stocks (Fig. 58). On the other hand, when it exceeds 3.00, it doesn't work as well as a sell signal (Fig. 59). So the message is: don't sell just because it's over 3.00, but do load up on stocks the next time the ratio is at 1.00 or less. This advice does not come with a money-back guarantee, of course.

Mark Twain famously said, "October: This is one of the peculiarly dangerous months to speculate in stocks. The others are July, January, September, April, November, May, March, June, December, August, and

February." Indeed, there seems to be some relationship between every month and the stock market:

- *January.* The January Effect is a seasonal increase in stock prices during the month of January. The explanation for it is that investors tend to sell their losers during December for tax purposes, depressing share prices and thus creating good buying opportunities at the start of the new year.
- *May to October.* Then there's this old adage: "Sell in May and go away, and come on back on St. Leger Day." This English saying refers to the custom of aristocrats, merchants, and bankers to leave the city of London and go to the country to escape the heat during the summer months. St. Leger Day is the day in mid-September of the St. Leger Stakes—a thoroughbred horse race and the last leg of the British Triple Crown. In the US, Wall Street's traders have tended to take long vacations between Memorial Day and Labor Day. However, they now can execute trades very efficiently from anywhere over their laptops and smartphones.

  So the American version of the adage "Sell in May and go away" may no longer have vacation schedules working in its favor. It certainly doesn't jibe with the widely held notion that summer rallies happen often, which they often do. Another problem with heeding the adage is that even when May turned out to be a good month to be out of the market, coming back directly after summer vacations didn't always work. During the latest bull market, selling on the first day of May was usually a bad idea. Halloween found the S&P 500 higher in six of the eight years from 2009 through 2017, with double-digit gains in both 2009 and 2013 over the intervening months.
- *October.* Twain was wrong about October. It hasn't been the worst month for stock investors. September wins first place in this losers' derby (Fig. 60). However, October has had a couple of harrowing sell-offs during 1929 and 1987, though Twain didn't know that, having passed away in April 1910. It doesn't follow that there is something fundamentally wrong with the month of October or that it is somehow cursed.
- *December.* One of the problems with the January Effect is that it is at odds with so-called "Santa Claus rallies," which tend to happen between Christmas and New Year's Day.

Finally, I should note that some investors look for clues to stock market behavior in the political cycle, particularly the S&P 500's performance during each of the four years that a US president is in the White House. Ignoring the possibility that the second terms of presidencies might affect stocks differently than first terms, the resulting pattern since 1928 through 2016 is that stocks do best, on average, during third years as follows: first year 5.9%, second year 4.8%, third year 12.8%, and fourth year 7.1%. There is quite a bit of variability around those averages.

FRONT-COVER CURSE

AS OLD-TIMERS SAY: "Don't fight the tape." Truisms aren't always true, but they are true often enough to be called "truisms." The market is constantly forecasting the outlooks for the economy, inflation, interest rates, profits, policies, politics, etc. The market isn't about reality; it's about the perception of reality by all the investors, traders, and speculators who are in the market.

What any individual investor or forecaster believes is moot unless it jibes with how the market actually moves. Only then do investors make money and forecasters get credit. Lamely protesting, "But the market is wrong, and I'm right," is useless. Investors can also lose a fortune, and forecasters can lose their followers, by betting that the market will see the error of its ways. That's why the old-timers warn against fighting the tape. When the market is moving against you, move out of the way.

Despite this age-old wisdom, it is also true that some of the greatest fortunes have been made by betting against the market's perceptions. The historical reality is that some, and perhaps many, of the great fortunes were made with the benefit of inside information, i.e., information not readily available to the trading public. This was an accepted road to riches in the past. The gains from inside information became ill-gotten and illegal after Congress investigated the excesses of the 1920s that contributed to the Great Crash of 1929. In 1933, Congress enacted legislation that outlawed the use of inside information in investing.

Assuming, therefore, that all publicly available information is reflected in the stock market, how can an investor make money? Investment advisers recommend that investors diversify their stock portfolios and hold their stocks for a long period. They also advise: "Buy low, sell high." In other words, buy stocks when they are relatively cheap and hold them for a long time, until they get very expensive, then sell. This long-term approach is simply a bet that stocks will offer a good rate of return if held long enough. In other words, without inside information, you can't get rich quick. So get rich slowly by betting that stock prices will rise over time, as they have in the past. This is good advice and consistent with my analysis showing that the uptrend in earnings drives the uptrend in stock prices.

However, human nature is such that many of us want to get rich quick. Many of us tend to buy high and to sell low when we can't stand the pain of losing any more money. Why do we buy high? It's no fun to see our friends and relatives getting rich in the stock market when we're not. To get a piece of the action, we jump in with them, often just before stock prices tumble. When the masses are moved to act, it's usually too late.

Similarly, front-cover stories about the economy or the stock market often are great contrary indicators. That's because once the media folk get excited enough about a story to put it on their cover, it's often too late to invest in the idea. Front-cover stories usually mark a major turning point for the economy and the stock market.

Over the years, I've collected and laminated some of the best contrary front covers from the leading financial magazines. Here is a sample of the classic cover stories in my file:

- "The Death of Equities," *Businessweek*, August 13, 1979.[18] It was subtitled "How Inflation Is Destroying the Stock Market." The CPI inflation rate peaked at a record high during March 1980. Equities continued to rise until November 28, 1980. Then they fell into a bear market. However, they didn't die. A great bull market started almost exactly three years later, on August 12, 1982.
- "The Pacific Century: Is America in Decline?" *Newsweek*, February 22, 1988. With the benefit of hindsight, the answer was "no." In fact, Japan was about two years away from a prolonged depression during the 1990s.
- "Taking Stock: Is America In Decline?" *The New York Times Magazine*, April 7, 1988. On the cover was a caricature of an old, overweight, stooping bald eagle, dressed in red, white, and blue. The old bird held a cane for support and stared anxiously into a small mirror. Ironically, the United States was less than two years away from winning the Cold War and embarking on one of the most prosperous periods in history.

- "The Recession: How Bad Is It?" *Time*, January 13, 1992. Pictured on the cover was a man selling apples, suggesting a comparison to the Great Depression. The recession officially started in July 1990 and ended in March 1991. It was one of the shorter ones, having lasted only eight months. However, it didn't seem so back then, as evidenced by the fact that the Dating Committee of the National Bureau of Economic Research didn't officially announce the end of the recession until December 22, 1992!
- "Downward Mobility: Even a Recovery Will Not Bring Back the Thousands of Jobs Lost by Managers and Professionals. Here's How Some People Cope," *Businessweek*, March 23, 1992. Of course, the fastest-growing employment categories during the 1990s boom were managers and professionals.
- "Corporate Killers: Wall Street Loves Layoffs but the Public Is Scared as Hell. Is There a Better Way?" *Newsweek*, February 26, 1996. The photos of four top CEOs, each of whom had cut more than 10,000 jobs, were framed between the bold red letters of the headline. One week later, the Labor Department reported a huge jump in employment during February, marking one of the best economic booms in American history during the second half of the 1990s.
- "Our Love Affair with Stocks: Never Before Have So Many People Had So Much Riding on the Market. Should We Worry?" *Businessweek*, June 3, 1996. There was nothing to worry about at that time, since the stock market continued to soar to new highs over the next three and a half years.
- "Like It or Not, You're Married to the Market. More Americans Than Ever Are Betting on Stocks. A Hard Look at Today's Rewards—and Tomorrow's Risks," *Newsweek*, April 27, 1998. Gracing the cover was a cartoon of a female bull in a white wedding dress holding a bouquet of roses (um, aren't bulls necessarily male?). Many Americans filed for divorce after the tech bubble burst in 2000.
- "The Whine of '99: Everyone's Getting Rich but Me," *Newsweek*, July 5, 1999. A cartoon of the face of a square-jawed man with a very anxious expression is featured on the cover. Very few of the nouveau riche cashed in their stock market gains before they disappeared in a blink during the bear market of 2000 to 2002.
- "GetRich.com: Secrets of the New Silicon Valley," *Time*, September 27, 1999. Many people in the Valley and their investors became very

poor during 2000, 2001, and 2002. Most tech professionals watched in disbelief as their stock options expired worthless. Many lost their jobs.

- "Person of the Year: Amazon.com's Jeff Bezos. E-Commerce Is Changing the Way the World Shops," *Time*, December 27, 1999. The dot.com bubble burst in 2000. Amazon survived the crash; most dot.coms did not.

Like *Businessweek* and *Time*, *The Economist* has racked up some impressive contrary cover stories since the financial crisis, including: "Bubble Warning" (January 9, 2010), "New Dangers for the World Economy" (February 13, 2010), "Fear Returns" (May 29, 2010), "Nowhere to Hide" (October 15, 2011), "Over the Cliff?" (December 15, 2012), "That Sinking Feeling (Again)" (August 30, 2014), "Living in a Low-Rate World" (September 24, 2016), and "The Mighty Dollar" (December 3, 2016).

In 2016, Gregory Marks and Brent Donnelly, analysts at Citibank, looked at every cover story from *The Economist* going back to 1998, selecting those stories that covered "an emotional or hyperbolic portrayal of an asset class or market-related theme." They selected 44 cover stories that had either an optimistic or a pessimistic point. They found that impactful covers with a strong visual bias proved after one year to be contrarian 68% of the time.[19] That's high enough for market watchers to suggest that market watchers should keep the front-cover curse on their radar.

CHAPTER 16

Predicting the Future

FUTURE OF FORECASTING

VITTORIO DE SICA'S classic 1963 comedy film *Yesterday, Today, and Tomorrow*, starring Sophia Loren and Marcello Mastroianni, is an anthology of three short stories about couples in different parts of Italy. What does it have to do with this book? Nothing, other than the title. I've learned a great deal from the past. Economic forecasters who fail to study history are doomed to be consistently wrong because they aren't attuned to the consistencies and inconsistencies of human nature. When all is said and done, economic forecasting is about understanding and predicting human behavior. The same goes for predicting markets, which are uniquely human inventions.

So yesterday matters a great deal because it provides important context for understanding today and tomorrow. A sound analysis of what is happening today can confirm that the lessons of the past are still relevant or alternatively can alert a forecaster to important shifts in the environment that render extrapolations from the past less useful for predicting the future. Of course, accurately predicting what will happen tomorrow is the ultimate test of whether the lessons of yesterday and today have been properly learned.

In any event, as economist Edgar Fiedler quipped, "If you have to forecast, forecast often." There's not much choice about that, since the future is turning into both the present and the past every day. The trick is to learn from the hits and misses of the never-ending forecasting process. That's what makes this occupation so interesting. You never stop learning because there are always new topics to study, and plenty of opportunities to reassess previous notions of how the world works.

In the first chapter, I wrote that I hope my book will provide a very solid education in "current analysis." I noted that former Fed Chairman Ben Bernanke, despite his stellar academic credentials, regretted that he hadn't been taught about it in graduate school. He speculated that was probably because current analysis "seems more amenable to on-the-job training" and added: "It's an intellectually challenging activity." As a practitioner of current analysis for 40 years, I completely agree.

First and foremost, current analysis requires a thorough grounding in the economic and financial data. Since the first chapter, I've taken you on lots of deep dives into quite a bit of the data. I certainly recommend frequent plunges into the National Income and Product Accounts compiled quarterly by the Bureau of Economic Analysis, and the Fed's quarterly *Financial Accounts of the United States*.[1] That's just for starters, to get a good sense of the accounting framework for the US economy and financial markets. Then, of course, there are numerous daily, weekly, and monthly data series reflected in these accounts. And that's just in the United States. There are plenty of places around the world to take interesting deep dives into data that provide great insights into yesterday, today, and tomorrow.

While my strong preference is to see as much data as I can with the help of a few thousand charts in hundreds of publications that thematically organize them, I'm no fan of stuffing the data into black-box econometric models or pasteurizing the stats with other "quant" methods. I like my data raw, with a touch of seasonal adjustment. Before I give you my predictions for the future, I'd like to reiterate how they're derived—and, importantly, how they aren't.

The macroeconomic profession continues to rely on quantitative models for predicting the economy. Their proponents claim that the models have become more realistic and more sophisticated. Maybe so, but that doesn't mean they are more accurate or provide more insights into how the economy works. The major problem is that models are deemed to work just because they've been back-tested with historical data to see whether they accurately predict recent developments. The key assumption is that yesterday's relationships to today and tomorrow haven't changed significantly. However, change in the course of human affairs is a constant.

When the models fail to work (as most do sooner or later), they are sent back to the garage for a tune-up, if not a major overhaul. A good example of this is the "comprehensive revision" of the Index of Leading Economic Indicators (LEI) during January 2012. The redesign replaced a few old components with new ones to keep the index working as advertised, i.e., as a leading indicator of economic activity.[2]

The LEI is a rather elementary example of a quant model. Far more complex are "dynamic stochastic general equilibrium" (DSGE) econometric models of the economy. Everyone seems to agree that a model of the economy should be dynamic (rather than static) and stochastic (to reflect uncertainty). In my opinion, the biggest positive development is that DSGE models incorporate a microeconomic foundation to be consistent with the economy's general equilibrium. That's some progress toward a long overdue reconciliation of the unnatural division of the economics profession into macro and micro camps.

The move toward bridging the two camps was catalyzed by the "Lucas Critique." In a seminal 1976 paper, University of Chicago Professor Robert Lucas Jr.—who won the 1995 Nobel Prize in economics—pointed out that rational consumers and business managers regularly update their expectations and change their behavior in response to macroeconomic policy changes.[3] As a result, macroeconomists started to incorporate changes in rational expectations and other microfoundations into their models. Nevertheless, not a single major econometric model predicted the 2008 financial crisis that triggered the Great Recession. In fact, five years before, in 2003, Lucas began an address before the American Economic Association by proclaiming that macroeconomics "has succeeded: Its central problem of depression prevention has been solved."[4]

Such overconfidence runs rampant in the field of economics. Economists have a habit of coming up with their theories and models first, then torturing the data until it supports their narrative. I'm not the only one to point this out:

- *Mathiness.* In a 2015 paper, Professor Paul M. Romer of New York University critiqued the obsession of economists with quantitative methods as follows: "The style that I am calling mathiness lets academic politics masquerade as science. Like mathematical theory, mathiness uses a mixture of words and symbols, but instead of making tight links, it leaves ample room for slippage between statements in natural versus formal language and between statements with theoretical as opposed to empirical content."[5]

In a 2016 paper titled, "The Trouble With Macroeconomics," Romer bemoaned that economic models "attribute fluctuations in aggregate variables to imaginary causal forces that are not influenced by the action that any person takes." He added, "The trouble is not so much that macroeconomists say things that are inconsistent with the facts. The real trouble is that other economists do not care that the macroeconomists do not care about the facts."[6]

- *Algorithms.* Gary Smith, a professor of economics at Pomona College, wrote an August 31, 2017 opinion piece for MarketWatch titled "This Experiment Shows the Danger in Black-Box Investment Algorithms."[7] Gary was an assistant professor at Yale when I attended the graduate program in economics, and I learned much from him. We remain good professional friends and like-minded about the cluelessness and irrelevance of most macroeconomic research.

In the article, Gary reported running big-data, black-box investment algorithms to explain the S&P 500 daily for 2015. He let data-mining software loose on 100 variables that might be correlated with the S&P 500 stock price index. His experiment considered all possible combinations of one to five variables, including all 75,287,520 possible combinations of five variables. Several of them worked great but then failed miserably in 2016. He wisely concluded: "We should not be intimidated into thinking that computers are infallible, that data-mining is knowledge discovery, that black boxes should be trusted. Let's trust ourselves to judge whether statistical patterns make sense and are therefore potentially useful, or are merely coincidental and therefore fleeting and useless."

Contributing to the cockiness of economists is that their social science is the only one to have a Nobel Prize, thanks to a grant from the Bank of Sweden to the Nobel Foundation. Economists are among the best-paid professors, earning more not only than other social scientists but also than physicists and mathematicians. Only computer scientists and engineers get paid more, on average.[8]

In his *Essays in Persuasion* (1931), John Maynard Keynes bemoaned, "If economists could manage to get themselves thought of as humble, competent people, on a level with dentists, that would be splendid!"[9] I find that remarkably ironic since the title of his most celebrated work was *The General Theory of Employment, Interest, and Money* (1936), obviously suggesting that Keynes had discovered a universal theory in economics as important as the general theory of relativity in physics published by Albert Einstein in 1915!

My complaint with treating economics and the other "social sciences" as sciences—governed by the immutable laws of physics and nature—is that they aren't. The social sciences are concerned with human behavior, and human behavior is quite mutable, constantly changing in response to the ever-changing course of human events. The laws of physics have been discovered over time, gradually advancing our understanding of our universe. Similar progress has eluded social scientists trying to understand, predict, and even change human nature. It's hard enough to get humans to obey their own laws let alone any universal laws of human behavior. The natural universe is much more stable and predictable than human society.

Social scientists often aspire to be like natural scientists, though. They envy the precision of the scientific method and mimic it with mathiness. Oxford Dictionaries defines the scientific method as "a method or procedure that has characterized natural science since the 17th century, consisting in systematic observation, measurement, and experiment, and the formulation, testing, and modification of hypotheses." Experiments need to be designed to test hypotheses. The most important part of the scientific method is the experiment. Applying this paradigm to social sciences in general and economics in particular is a lost cause. Economists can observe human behavior and collect data to quantify it. They can develop theories and models to explain and predict human behavior. But they can't run controlled experiments on humans the way psychologists do with lab rats.

Economists might develop better insights by getting to know the data first. I'm all for theories and for models too if they reliably work. But theories and models should be inspired by quantitative analysis—not the black-box variety, which keeps the actual source data in the dark, but analysis involving deep dives with a big floodlight into the original, raw, unfiltered data.

In this concluding chapter, I would like to shine a light into the future as best I can, informed by what current analysis has taught me about the past and the present.

GLOBALIZATION AND GEOPOLITICS

AS I'VE DISCUSSED throughout the book, the end of the Cold War in the late 1980s marked the beginning of a period of globalization, with far-reaching consequences for the global economy and financial markets. The same can be said about China joining the World Trade Organization in late 2001. The formation of the Eurozone in 1999 was a big deal for that region and the world. Meanwhile, the emergence of emerging economies continues apace. Globalization has been good for them.

However, not everyone has benefited from globalization, particularly not factory workers in advanced economies who feel robbed of their high-paying jobs by foreign workers in places such as China and Mexico. The result has been a political backlash in the form of populist movements that oppose the global integration of national economies through the free trade of goods and services, with open labor and capital markets. These movements gained some momentum with Britain's Brexit vote on June 23, 2016 and America's election of Donald Trump as President on November 8, 2016. They lost some momentum when populist and nationalist politicians were defeated in elections in the Netherlands and France during the first half of 2017.

President Trump's anti-trade campaign rhetoric became much more nuanced once he took office. He backed away from his pledge that on the day he entered the White House, he would declare China a "currency manipulator." Rather than repeal the North American Free Trade Agreement with Mexico and Canada, as promised during the campaign, he moved toward renegotiating the deal on a more bilateral basis. Such an approach to trade deals, as opposed to the post-World War II multilateral approach, might save globalization from a populist onslaught, as I suggest in Chapter 2.

National labor markets also have become much more globalized since the end of the Cold War. That has led to some deindustrialization in the United States, which has been the main complaint of American populists bemoaning the loss of high-wage manufacturing jobs to foreign countries where labor costs less. However, technological innovation likewise has eliminated lots of jobs. As in the past, it also has created plenty of jobs of a different sort. However, today there seems to be more of a skills mismatch between the new jobs and the available workers.

Capital markets long have been globalized, since the merchants of Florence and Venice financed world trade during the 14th and 15th centuries. Dutch merchant banks played a similar role during the 16th and 17th centuries. London emerged as the next major center for global finance during the 19th century.

After World War II, the United States ran widening trade deficits, which provided lots of financial capital to the rest of the world. Some of it, such as the so-called "petrodollars" accumulated by OPEC's oil exporters, was recycled into deposits in London and New York money center banks, which then lent the funds to emerging economies in Latin America and Asia. Unfortunately, those flows stopped abruptly with the debt crises in Latin America during the early 1990s and in Asia during the late 1990s. The global savings glut that preceded the 2008 financial debacle set the stage for it as Asians poured large sums into the US mortgage market.

I will continue to monitor the course of globalization with the available indicators (i.e., puzzle pieces) that have proven quite useful in the past in seeing the unfolding picture of the future:

- *Commodity prices.* On a very short-term basis, the CRB raw industrials spot price index remains my favorite gauge (Fig. 1*). Even though it's a very low-tech indicator that includes some funky legacy components (such as the spot prices of hide, rosin, and tallow), it remains an extremely reliable economic barometer, in my opinion.

- *MSCI metrics.* While one of my jobs is to predict the outlook for broad stock market indexes, they can be useful for economic forecasting too. Like the CRB index, the All Country World MSCI stock market index is a sensitive gauge of the prospects for the global economy (Fig. 2). I continue to rely on the consensus expected forward revenues of the All Country World MSCI, which is the time-weighted average of analysts' consensus expectations for the current and coming years, reflecting the insights of *thousands* of industry analysts around the world on a weekly basis (Fig. 3). It serves as an excellent leading indicator of the 12-month sum of the value of world exports, a series compiled by the International Monetary Fund (IMF).

Just as useful as forward revenues is the forward earnings of the All Country World MSCI, which is among the key drivers of world stock prices (Fig. 4). I also track these weekly MSCI metrics for all the major subindexes around the world. However, since most of the companies they include are doing business on a worldwide basis, they are unlikely to tell a different story unless their domestic or regional business activities are diverging significantly from the global trend.

---

* Figures, references, and appendices are linked on *yardenibook.com/resources*.

- *Export volumes.* There aren't many inflation-adjusted measures of global economic activity. The CPB Netherlands Bureau for Economic Policy does compile a world industrial production index and another for the volume of world exports (Fig. 5). The year-over-year growth rate in the latter is particularly useful for gauging real global economic activity, though the latest available data make it stale by two to three months (Fig. 6). I previously showed that the growth rate of the volume of world exports is highly correlated with the growth rate in the sum of inflation-adjusted US exports plus imports, which I also monitor.

Among the most predictable developments on a worldwide basis is that emerging economies will continue to emerge. They have come a long way over the past two decades. The IMF's data on the value of world trade show that the G7 industrial economies accounted for 50% of the total during 1996 (Fig. 7). By the end of 2016, their share had fallen to 33%, while the rest of the world's share had risen to 67%. This helps to quantify the impact of globalization through trade. In terms of the value of export shares, the winners clearly have been emerging economies at the expense of industrial economies. That's why populist political movements have found fertile soil in the United States and Europe. In any case, it's unlikely that emerging markets will gain much more export share given how high their shares are now and the resulting political backlash in industrial economies.

Economic emergence entails the formation and expansion of a middle class with a rising standard of living. Middle classes develop and grow when consumers spend more of their budgets on services than on goods, especially food and fuel. One way to get a glimpse of this trend globally is to track the monthly data on the purchasing managers' indexes in emerging economies for manufacturing versus non-manufacturing industries (Fig. 8). The latter have tended to exceed the former in recent years.

By the way, the weekly consensus expected forward revenues of the Emerging Markets MSCI is a leading indicator of the value of exports of emerging economies in a similar fashion as the comparable world data (Fig. 9). For stock investors, what matters is how forward earnings are determined by forward revenues and forward profit margins for the Emerging Markets MSCI (Fig. 10). The bottom line is performance, both the absolute performance of the actual Emerging Markets MSCI stock price index and its relative performance to the All Country World MSCI stock price index.

Here are a few of the pictures I have in mind when putting together the puzzle pieces related to the future of globalization:

* *Asia.* The Asian economies clearly have benefited from the rapid pace of growth of the largest economy in the region, namely China. Asia's emerging market economies have been running trade surpluses with countries in the rest of the world. Most have had net capital inflows over the past few years, with the notable exception of China, as I discuss in Chapter 12.

  To an important extent, the future of Asia depends on the future of China, which faces increasingly challenging demographic trends. The country's future growth may also be weighed down by the rapid pace of debt accumulation that continues unabated. However, I'm not ready to bet against a country with over a billion aspirational, entrepreneurial, hard-working, and materialistic people. Their economy remains centrally planned, but the government has proven that it can boost growth by rapidly implementing and executing massive infrastructure spending programs.

  The Chinese government's latest plan is its grand vision for China called "One Belt, One Road." It is the foreign policy proposed by the Chinese President Xi Jinping to build roads, ports, and railways to connect Eurasia, much as the historic Silk Road trade route did centuries ago. The initiative spans over land and across the oceans, involving 60 countries along the two routes; those 60 countries represent 4.4 billion people and account for over 40% of the world's GDP.

  China has no plans to link India into the Silk Road. That's not surprising since the two nations have had an adversarial relationship for decades. They are also very unlike each other. For one thing, China and India are governed very differently. China has succeeded up until now with a central planning system flexible enough to permit more entrepreneurship. Central planners continue to run a significant portion of the Chinese economy and have been very effective at getting mammoth projects completed and operational. Conversely, India's government has burdened its economy with too many stifling regulations, and corrupt bureaucratic practices are commonplace. However, India is currently striving to reform its political and economic systems. The two nations' demographic circumstances also are very different and point, in my view, to much better economic prospects for India than for China.

- *Middle East.* The economic prospects of the Middle East remain unsettled. The centuries-old schism between Sunni and Shiite Moslems remains deeper than ever, and potentially more lethal.

    Compounding the region's troubles is the likelihood that crude oil may lose its value over time, for multiple reasons. For one, US entrepreneur Elon Musk intends to harvest solar energy on the roofs of American homes, storing the electricity generated in large batteries while also charging up Americans' electric cars. As long as the sun will come out tomorrow, solar energy is likely to get increasingly cheaper and fuel a growing fleet of electric passenger cars. Meanwhile, America's frackers are using every trick in their books to reduce the cost of pumping more crude oil and of extracting more natural gas. Rather than trying to prop up the price of oil, Middle Eastern producers with large reserves would be better off selling as much of their oil as they can at lower prices to slow down the pace of technological innovation that may eventually put them out of business.

- *Eurozone.* The future of the Eurozone remains debatable. The Greek debt crisis, which started in 2010, heightened fears that the monetary union would disintegrate. Pessimistically inclined economists and bearish investment strategists put high odds on this happening. They noted that other members of the Eurozone also had too much debt and vulnerable banking systems. Sentiment seemed to turn less dire after European Central Bank (ECB) President Mario Draghi pledged at the end of July 2012 to do whatever it took to defend the monetary union. Britain's vote in the summer of 2016 to leave the European Union (EU) raised questions about the viability of that organization, which is the political and economic union of 28 member states that are located primarily in Europe. Brexit from the EU is slated to occur on March 29, 2019.

    Disintegration may be a smaller threat to the future of both the EU and the Eurozone than declining and aging populations throughout Europe prove to be. Mass immigration from the Middle East and Africa might provide younger blood. However, this influx is bound to exacerbate the culture clashes. The fact that many of the immigrants are living in insular communities and are adding to the already bloated European welfare rolls can't be helping to assimilate them into their economies and societies.

On the other hand, history shows that mass migration has usually boosted economic growth. Germany's economic growth increased during 2017 after the country took in more than a million migrants, many fleeing war and poverty in the Middle East and Africa in 2015 and 2016. The number of immigrants in Germany rose 8.5% during 2016 to a record 18.6 million, largely due to an increase in refugees.[10]

- *United States.* What about the United States? The population is aging and is growing at a slower pace. Real GDP growth hovered around 2.0% on a year-over-year basis from the second half of 2010 through mid-2017. Trump's election boosted consumer and business confidence. High hopes that his administration would implement Trump's economic agenda, including a major reform of the tax code with lower tax rates, shortly after gaining office were mugged by the reality of Washington's bitter bipartisan divide and by the divide within the Republican party. However, Congress enacted a major tax reform plan at the end of 2017. Forecasting legislative outcomes in Washington, DC remains one of the most challenging tasks for prognosticators.

  When I visit some of our bearishly inclined accounts, who bemoan the mess that is our gridlocked political system, I accentuate the positive: "Look how well our economy has done despite Washington!" The US economy remains very competitive and entrepreneurial, more so than almost all other economies. It is highly diversified among numerous very dynamic and profitable industries. It remains the global epicenter of technological innovation.

By its very nature, globalization is a wide-ranging phenomenon demanding an interdisciplinary course of study. Its implications for business and financial markets can't be fully grasped simply by following a bunch of economic and financial indicators, although these are a good place to start. First and foremost, it requires peace and relatively free trade. Political events that might lead to protectionism bear close watching, as do demographic trends and technological innovations. Central bankers' monetary policies certainly matter a great deal to the global capital markets as well and will continue to matter in the ongoing evolution of those markets.

DEMOGRAPHY AND GROWTH

DEMOGRAPHIC TRENDS MATTER for every economy, and they have had a great impact on the US economy. Yet demography isn't usually taught in economics courses, tending instead to be covered in college sociology departments. Many corporations have strategic planners who carefully study the demographic trends that influence the demand for their products and services. Yet Wall Street spends very little time on the subject.

In the 1980s, I made my mark partly by focusing on the impact of the Baby Boomers on the economy and financial markets. Along the way, I had one significant competitor on Wall Street. From 1995 to 2000, Richard Hokenson was the chief economist at Donaldson, Lufkin & Jenrette, where he focused on the application of demographics to economic and financial market forecasting. He went on to head global demographic research at Credit Suisse First Boston and then at ISI Group Inc. He is widely respected for his insights in this field.

While Hokenson went global, I continued to focus on US demographic developments. However, I also sharpened my other economic tools to be more useful in my second day job as an investment strategist. Over the past few years, I've been spending more time again on US demography, focusing on the Millennials in addition to the Baby Boomers. I've also been getting up to speed on global demographic developments of late, though I've always kept abreast of them in China and Japan.

Globally, the most significant demographic development has been the collapse in recent years of fertility rates around the world. The Voluntary Human Extinction Movement (VHEMT), founded in 1991, believes that human extinction is the best solution to the problems facing the Earth's biosphere and humanity. Their motto is "May we live long and die out," and they sell t-shirts stating "When You Breed, the Planet Bleeds" and "Thank You for Not Breeding."[11] Sure enough, the pace of human breeding has slowed, but for reasons that have nothing to do with the VHEMT.

All around the world, humans are not having enough babies to replace themselves. There are a few significant exceptions, such as India and Africa. Working-age populations are projected to decline along with general populations in coming years in Asia (excluding India), Europe, and Latin America. The United States has a brighter future, though the pace of its population growth is projected to slow significantly in coming years.

The world fertility rate was around 5.0 children per woman in the mid-1950s through the 1960s (Fig. 11).[12] It dropped to 2.5 by 2015. The United Nations projects that it will fall to 2.0 by the end of this century. The world population is expected to grow by 3.8 billion from 2015 through 2099, reaching 11.2 billion (Fig. 12). However, the annual growth rate is projected to decline from 1.2% during 2015 to half that by mid-century and nearly zero by the end of the century (Fig. 13).

There are many explanations for the decline in fertility rates around the world to below the replacement rate—estimated to be 2.1 children born per woman in developed countries and higher in developing countries, where mortality rates are higher. I believe that the most logical explanation is urbanization.

The UN estimates that the percentage of the world population living in urban communities rose from 30% in 1950 to 53% during 2013 (Fig. 14).[13] This percentage is projected to rise to 66% by 2050.

Why would urbanization lower fertility rates? Families are likely to have more children in rural communities than urban ones. Housing is cheaper in the former than in the latter. In addition, rural populations are much more dependent on agricultural employment; their children are likely to be viewed as economic contributors once old enough to work in the field or tend the livestock. Adult children are expected to support and care for their extended families by housing and feeding their aging parents in their own huts and yurts. In urban environments, children tend to be expensive to house, feed, and educate. When they become urban-dwelling adults, they are less likely to welcome an extended family living arrangement together with their aging parents in a cramped city apartment.[14]

In my opinion, the urbanization trend since the end of World War II was attributable in large part to the "Green Revolution," as I discuss in Chapter 11. The resulting productivity boom in agriculture eliminated lots of jobs and forced small farmers to sell their plots to large agricultural enterprises that could use the latest technologies to feed many more people in the cities with fewer workers in the fields. Ironically, then, the Green Revolution provided enough food to feed a population explosion, but the population instead moved from the farms to the cities and had fewer kids!

Thomas Malthus, the dismal scientist of economics and demographics, never anticipated technological progress in agriculture and urbanization. Back in the early 1800s, he also couldn't foresee the birth control pill, which was invented in the 1950s and proliferated as a means of family planning during the 1960s. Fertility rates plunged during the 1960s and 1970s, mostly in developed economies, then in developing countries during the 1980s and 1990s. Now consider the following related demographic developments and projections from the UN:

- *Japan.* Among modern industrial economies, Japan is the poster child for the economic impact of aging demographics. Japan's overall population is now declining at the fastest pace on the globe (Fig. 15). Its dearth of workers to support an aging population is depressing economic growth. Japan's fertility rate fell below the replacement rate of 2.1 children per woman during 1977 and is projected to remain below this rate through the end of the century (Fig. 16). Over the 12 months through June 2017, marriages totaled just 51,301, the lowest on record (Fig. 17). The number of deaths has exceeded the number of births since July 2007 (Fig. 18). The primary working-age population, spanning 15 to 64 years old, peaked at a record 87.8 million during 1995 (Fig. 19). It fell to 78.1 million during 2015 and is projected to be down to 55.6 million by 2050. In 1955, the elderly dependency ratio, which I define as the primary working-age population divided by the number of seniors who are 65 and older, was nearly 12.0 (Fig. 20). Now the ratio is just barely above 2.0 workers per senior.

  During October 2017, Prime Minister Shinzō Abe announced a goal to raise the birth rate to 1.8 per woman from 1.4. He proposed to loosen regulations on childcare providers, making it easier for women to return to work after a child is born. The government was also considering easing the tax burden for some part-time employees and making interest-free loans available for higher education.

- *China.* The fertility rate in China plunged from 6.1 in the mid-1950s to below 2.0 during 1996 (Fig. 21). Still below 2.0, it's projected to remain so through the end of the century. Initially, the drop was exacerbated by the government's response to the country's population explosion, which was to introduce the one-child policy in 1979. While that slowed China's population growth—to a 10-year growth rate of 0.5% at an annual rate in 2016 from a 3.0% pace in 1972—it also led to a shortage of young adult workers and a rapidly aging population.

  So the government reversed course, with a two-child policy effective January 1, 2016. Births soared by 7.9% that year with the deliveries of about 18 million newborns. But that was still short of the government estimates and might not be sustainable. At least 45% of the babies born during 2016 were to families that already had one child.[15]

Meanwhile, urbanization has proceeded apace, with the urban population rising from about 12% in 1950 to 49% during 2010; it was an estimated 57% in 2016 (Fig. 22). The urban population has been increasing consistently by around 20 million in most years since 1996 (Fig. 23). To urbanize that many people requires the equivalent of building one Houston, Texas per month, as I discuss in Chapter 2. I first made that point in a 2004 study.

The move to a two-child policy is coming too late, in my opinion. China's primary working-age population peaked at a record high of just over 1.0 billion during 2014 and is projected to fall to 815 million by 2050 (Fig. 24). By then, the primary working-age population in China will represent 60% of the total population, below the peak of 74% during 2010 (Fig. 25). The elderly dependency ratio will drop from 7.5 workers per senior in 2015 to 2.3 by 2050 (Fig. 26).

In any event, despite the initial mini baby boom, the fertility rate is unlikely to rise much in response to the government's new policy. Many young married couples living in China's cities are hard-pressed to afford having just one child. An October 30, 2015 blog post on the *Washington Post* website, titled "Why Many Families in China Won't Want More than One Kid Even if They Can Have Them," made that point, observing that education is particularly expensive, as parents feel compelled to prepare their child to compete for the best colleges and jobs. Another problem is that most couples are the only offspring of their aging parents, who require caregiving resources that rule out having a second child.[16] As it says in the Bible, "As you sow, so shall you reap."

- *Europe.* The fertility rate in Europe fell from 2.7 during 1955 to below 2.0 during 1980 and has remained below that level ever since; it's projected to remain below the replacement rate through the end of the century (Fig. 27). Europe's primary working-age population peaked at a record 503 million during 2010 and is expected to decline to 361 million by the end of the century (Fig. 28). The immigration during 2015 and 2016 was significant but probably not big enough to change the UN's projections much.

- *United States.* The fertility rate in the United States was over 3.0 during the second half of the 1950s, when the postwar Baby Boom was at its height (Fig. 29). It fell to just below 2.0 during 2013 and has been hovering around this level since then. The percentage of Americans living in rural areas fell from 30% during 1960 to 18% during 2015. The UN projects that the primary working-age population will continue to grow through 2050, though the growth rate will be very low, never exceeding 0.5% per year. Data compiled by the Bureau of Labor Statistics show that the 120-month (i.e., 10-year) average annual growth rate of the US civilian labor force peaked at a record 3.1% during January 1979 (Fig. 30). It has been declining ever since, having fallen to just 0.5% at the end of 2016.

- *Latin America.* The fertility rate in Latin America was down to 2.2 during 2015 from almost 6.0 during the late 1950s and is expected to fall to 1.8 by 2050. The region's working-age population was 422 million during 2015 and is projected to peak during the early 2040s at 500 million before heading downward to 390 million by the end of the century (Fig. 31).

- *Russia.* The fertility rate in the Russian Federation has dropped from 2.9 during 1955 to 1.7 during 2015 and is projected to remain below 2.0 through the end of the century. The country's working-age population peaked during 2009 at 103.1 million. It is projected to fall below 80.0 million during the second half of the century (Fig. 32).

- *India and Africa.* During 2015, among the highest fertility rates were those of India, at 2.5, and Africa, at 4.7. They are projected to decline to 1.9 and 3.1, respectively, by 2050. India's primary working-age population is projected to rise from 860 million during 2015 to peak at 1.1 billion during 2050 before heading back below 1.0 billion over the remainder of the century (Fig. 33). Africa's primary working-age population stands out, as it is projected to rise from 663 million during 2015 to 1.6 billion during 2050 and 2.8 billion by the end of the century. India and Africa remain predominantly rural (Fig. 34).

The world population is getting older as people live longer yet have fewer babies. The percentage of children aged five years or younger has already declined globally from 15% during 1956 to 9% during 2015. It is projected to fall to 7% by 2050 (Fig. 35). The percentage of seniors, which rose from 5% during the 1950s and early 1960s to 8% in 2015, is projected to rise to 16% by 2050.[17] The elderly dependency ratio is projected to fall from 7.9 workers per senior in 2015 to just 2.8 by the end of the century (Fig. 36).[18]

There is increasing buzz about the need for a universal basic income to support people who can't compete with robots, as I discuss in Chapter 3. Maybe what we need instead is a fertility income subsidy to encourage married couples to have children. In early 2017, a Chinese vice-minister of the National Health and Family Planning Commission said the government was considering "birth rewards and subsidies."[19] Such incentives for couples to make babies for fun and profit might be increasingly necessary to boost fertility rates. Otherwise, the members of VHEMT will have their wish come true, as homo sapiens are on the long, slow road to self-extinction.

Before it ends, that road takes us to slower economic growth around the world, based on the UN projection of the world population growth rate. From a supply-side perspective, the potential growth of real GDP is determined by the growth of the civilian working-age population and productivity. It is much harder to predict productivity than to predict population dynamics. Perhaps productivity growth will improve and offset the demographic drag on growth. However, there is also a demand side to productivity. The most efficient widgets factory in the world will have zero productivity if there is no demand for widgets. The slowdown in population growth with an aging profile suggests that consumer-spending growth may weaken, which could weigh on productivity growth from the demand side. This all adds up to slower economic growth. While the global economy showed signs of faster growth during 2017, the jury is still out on secular stagnation.

TECHNOLOGY, INFLATION, AND PRODUCTIVITY

THE GOOD NEWS is that robots may not eliminate lots of jobs done by humans, as is widely feared. Instead, they may be filling the gap as shortages of working human stiffs become more prevalent. Japan is the most automated economy in the world, with a proliferation of robots doing all sorts of jobs, yet the jobless rate in Japan is below 3.0%. The country is suffering from a chronic labor shortage.

The demand for technological innovations is largely driven by demographic imperatives, i.e., the needs of human societies as they evolve. Hunter-gatherer tribes lived in mobile homes such as teepees and yurts because they had to follow the food. They settled down in one location once they mastered agricultural techniques such as soil tilling and basic irrigation. Their small villages grew into towns with markets where produce could be exchanged for goods manufactured by cottage industries. A few tradesmen became industrial capitalists when they built factories. Merchants became bankers and financiers. Soldiers were hired to protect the farms, villages, and cities. Roads were built between the cities, later becoming exits on superhighways and connected by airports. Indoor plumbing, electric lights and appliances, air conditioning, vaccines and antibiotics, radio and television, mainframe computers and PCs, the Internet and email, GPS navigation, and smartphones all have improved the quality and length of life. This outline of human progress in one paragraph was enabled by technological innovations that met the individual and collective needs of people.

The supply side of technological innovations is mostly driven by entrepreneurs, who see a need for a product or service that is either brand new or significantly improved over what is currently available. If they are right, and the market is big enough without much, if any, competition initially, then they stand to get very rich very fast. This is what drives entrepreneurial capitalism. As long as governments don't meddle too much in this beneficial relationship between entrepreneurs and their customers, more innovations benefit more people.

The High-Tech Revolution that I started to analyze during the early 1990s continues apace. In my opinion, it has a long way to go. Given that so many of the new technologies supplement or replace the brain, they lend themselves to many more applications than did the technologies of the Industrial Revolution, which were mostly about replacing brawn. (See Appendix 16.1, Technological Innovations: Yesterday, Today, and Tomorrow.)

One of the main themes of my book is that economists, especially of the pessimistic persuasion, rarely pay much attention to technological developments. Yet these developments regularly transform the course of human history. Human nature may not change much over time, but technology often does so in ways that profoundly impact human societies and their economies and financial markets.

The demographic projections discussed above show that the world is heading down the same road as Japan, with labor shortages likely to be widespread. Even the United States, which stands out with a relatively upbeat demographic profile, is already showing signs of labor shortages. The reasons may be partly cyclical rather than structural. But whatever their cause, tightening labor markets will revive inflation, won't they?

This may be the most important question for investors to accurately answer in coming months and years. My working hypothesis is that inflation is likely to remain extremely low for all the reasons I discuss repeatedly in this book. On a worldwide basis, I will continue to monitor the CPI inflation rates data compiled by the IMF for advanced economies as well as emerging ones (Fig. 37 and Fig. 38).

The US economy is less prone to transmit inflationary shocks today and in the future than in the past. The oil price shocks of 1973 and 1979 were rapidly passed through to wages by cost-of-living adjustments in the labor contracts of unionized workers. Today and tomorrow, similar price shocks are much less likely to trigger a broad and sustained upturn in inflation. That's as long as globalization persists and perhaps even proliferates despite populist resistance.

Despite the weak pace of productivity growth in the United States, inflation is very low. There's a lot of anecdotal evidence that productivity-enhancing technological innovations are proliferating in many industries. The cloud allows for much more efficient use of high-tech hardware and software across the economy. Automation and robotics have been integrated over the Internet to communicate and to interact seamlessly. The Great Disruptors among companies—including Alphabet, Amazon, Tesla, and Uber—are forcing competitors to boost their efficiency or risk going out of business. Perhaps no industry has made more progress in increasing its productivity than the oil and gas producers, thanks to fracking technologies.

Yet none of these productivity-boosting developments is showing up in the official productivity numbers. Why not? Lots of explanations have been proffered by economists and technologists. Economists are notorious for basing explanations on assumptions:

- *Common explanation #1:* The optimists assume that the data are wrong and will eventually be revised higher. That once happened, in the late 1990s. The optimists say that the government's bean counters may be underestimating the economy's output.
- *Common explanation #2:* The pessimists assume that we are in a period of secular stagnation. Some of them claim that all the latest and future technological innovations are unlikely to boost productivity to the extent that the truly revolutionary technologies of the past did—such as the steam engine, electricity, indoor plumbing, automobiles, air conditioning, and computers. They even question whether computers have

done much to increase productivity beyond boosting the production of computers.

Instead, I wonder: could it be that technological innovation aimed at complementing (or unemploying) the brain has a different impact on productivity than innovations that replace brawn? The proliferation of the cloud explains why spending on IT hardware and software has slowed, since we can all just rent what we need from the cloud vendors, who are using their resources much more efficiently than we did when we owned our own software and servers, housed them at server farms, and woefully underutilized them. Uber undoubtedly is increasing the efficiency of the auto fleet, while it must be weighing on car sales. But how would we even measure the impact of self-driving cars on productivity?

While I have my own explanations, I don't have the definitive answers for the many questions raised by the weak productivity statistics. However, I'm impressed that corporate profit margins rose to record highs in recent years despite the dismal productivity numbers. Also encouraging is that real wages have not stagnated for the past 15–20 years, as is widely and wrongly believed (see Chapter 7). Over the past 20 years, real compensation in the nonfarm business (NFB) sector is up roughly 25% (Fig. 39). The laggard has been manufacturing, yet in this sector real compensation has risen about 20% over the past 20 years.

Over this period, real average hourly earnings (using the NFB price deflator) for production and nonsupervisory workers, who currently account for 82% of total private payroll employment, rose 30%, continuing to track productivity (Fig. 40). Nominal wages are growing remarkably slowly given the tight labor market. However, adjusted for inflation, they are keeping pace with productivity, which still is trending upward. Wages are rising faster than prices, but prices are rising very slowly for reasons that may not have much to do with productivity. Global competition, disruptive technology, and aging demographics may be playing a much greater role in keeping a lid on prices, which are also keeping a lid on wages.

In other words, the Phillips curve has flattened. Low inflation can coexist with tight labor markets today (Fig. 41 and Fig. 42). If it does so tomorrow, then macroeconomists once again will have to reconsider the relevance of their models for both explaining current developments and predicting future outcomes. They may have to spend more time on current analysis—which is, by its nature, always relevant.

CENTRAL BANKS AND CRYPTOCURRENCIES

HOW MUCH LONGER must inflation remain subdued for central bankers to consider the possibility that inflation may not be a monetary phenomenon, or at least not solely a monetary phenomenon? Their central conceit is that they can control the economy thanks to the quantity theory of money MV = PY, as Chapter 4 reviews. This assumes that they can determine the money supply (M) and that the velocity of money (V) is constant or at least predictable. If so, then they can drive nominal GDP (PY) and raise the price level (P) once real GDP (Y) is equal to or exceeds its noninflationary potential. By the way, they also need to have a constant or predictable money multiplier (m), i.e., the ratio of the broad money supply (M) to high-powered money (H), which is mostly bank reserves under their control. Neither the money multiplier nor the velocity have been constant, or even predictable, for a very long time, and even less so since the financial crisis of 2008.

Since late 2008, high-powered money has soared thanks to the central banks' various quantitative easing (QE) programs, yet the growth rates in broad measures of the money supply have remained subdued as the money multiplier has plunged. While the central bankers can take some credit for reviving economic growth, I think that's what economies naturally do. In the US, Fed officials have been mystified that the tightening of the labor market hasn't boosted wages, which would then bring inflation closer to their target. When might they consider the possibility that the forces subduing price inflation are keeping a lid on wage inflation?

When might the central bankers realize that concepts such as the non-accelerating inflation rate of unemployment (NAIRU) and the natural real rate of interest (r*), while interesting as intellectual exercises, cannot actually be measured? Attempts to estimate them have strongly suggested that they aren't constants. For central bankers, utopia would be a world where m, V, NAIRU, and r* are all constant or at least measurable *and* predictable. By the way, the word "utopia" comes from the fictional society in Sir Thomas More's 1516 book *Utopia*. He created the name from the ancient Greek words for "no" and "place."

I find contrarian perspectives intellectually refreshing, especially if they come from important central bankers. That gives me a hint that the consensus views they tend to share may be changing. I particularly enjoyed an October 4, 2017 speech by Daniel Tarullo, who served as a

Fed governor from January 2009 through April 2017. It was titled "Monetary Policy Without a Working Theory of Inflation."[20] Tarullo provides an insider's view on what has and hasn't been "useful for policymaking." He has become increasingly skeptical about the Fed's focus on unobservable variables such as the ones I just described. He then discusses why the Phillips Curve Model also is useless. One of his main conclusions is that "monetary policy will need to confront the likelihood that we may be in for an indefinite period in which no Phillips Curve or other model will be a workable guide to policy."

Another interesting speech by a central banker was delivered on September 22, 2017 by Claudio Borio, the head of the Monetary and Economic Department of the Bank for International Settlements.[21] It was titled "Through the Looking Glass." I appreciated it because we are like-minded about the groupthink of central bankers. Regarding inflation, he says, "Yet the behaviour of inflation is becoming increasingly difficult to understand. If one is completely honest, it is hard to avoid the question: how much do we really know about the inflation process?" He follows up with two seemingly rhetorical questions: "Could it be that we know less than we think? Might we have overestimated our ability to control inflation, or at least what it would take to do so?" The rest of the speech essentially answers "yes" to both questions.

Borio, a master of rhetorical questions, then asks: "Is it reasonable to believe that the inflation process should have remained immune to the entry into the global economy of the former Soviet bloc and China and to the opening-up of other emerging market economies? This added something like 1.6 billion people to the effective labour force, drastically shrinking the share of advanced economies, and cut that share by about half by 2015."

Borio deduces that measures of domestic slack are insufficient gauges of inflationary or disinflationary pressures. Furthermore, there must be more global slack given "the entry of lower-cost producers and of cheaper labour into the global economy." That must "have put persistent downward pressure on inflation, especially in advanced economies and at least until costs converge."

Borio explains that technological innovation might also have rendered the Phillips curve comatose or dead, by reducing "incumbent firms' pricing power—through cheaper products, as they cut costs; through newer products, as they make older ones obsolete; and through more transparent prices, as they make shopping around easier." He concludes: "No doubt, globalisation has been the big shock since the 1990s. But technology threatens to take over in future. Indeed, its imprint in the past may well have been underestimated and may sometimes be hard to distinguish from that of globalisation."

He adds a final zinger, arguing that the impact of real factors on inflation has been underestimated and that the impact of monetary policy on the real interest rate has been underestimated too.

These are all points I've been puzzling out over the past 40 years.

End the Fed is a 2009 book by Ron Paul, a former Republican congressman from Texas and a vocal libertarian. The book advocates abolishing the Federal Reserve System. It debuted at number six on *The New York Times*' Best Sellers list. The congressman blamed the Fed for the financial crisis of 2008. The Fed has had lots of critics over the years, especially among progressives, who believe it was founded by a cabal of bankers and remains that way. There are lots of Germans who feel the same way about the ECB. In her 2017 book, *Fed Up*, Danielle DiMartino Booth argues that the Fed has morphed into a cabal of PhD macroeconomists who are clueless about how the economy works. She wants to mend the Fed, not end it. I'm sympathetic to that view, as I discuss throughout this book.

However, my focus from the beginning of my career has been on objective, rather than subjective, analysis. I'm not advocating either ending the Fed or changing it. My job is to understand the Fed and the other central bankers as they are, not as I think they should be, and to predict their actions accordingly. Nevertheless, I do try occasionally to puzzle out whether technological innovation might put the central bankers out of business or radically change their modus operandi.

I'm particularly intrigued by the impact of bitcoin and other cryptocurrencies on our monetary system. Blockchain, the software that runs these digital currencies, is allowing banks to eliminate clearinghouse intermediaries in their transactions and to clear them much more rapidly. Smartphone apps allow consumers to use these digital devices to deposit checks and make payments. These innovations could reduce employment and bank branches in the financial sector, much as Amazon is doing in the retail space.

Central bankers are scrambling to understand the implications of bitcoin and blockchain. In time, central banks likely will incorporate these technologies into their operations, perhaps spawning bitdollars, biteuros, bityen, etc. So far, the cybercurrencies have been too volatile and prone to speculative moves to function as elastic currencies. Bitcoin soared during 2017, leaving gold in the dust (Fig. 43 and Fig. 44). Libertarians might long for a day when central banks are replaced by a monetary system based on a digitized currency that is unregulated by governments. I doubt that the central monetary planners will allow that to happen. But who knows? Technology has disrupted major industries. Maybe it will disrupt central banking!

BONDS, STOCKS, AND SWANS

IF INFLATION REMAINS subdued and the economic expansion continues, bond investors should earn yields on their bonds surpassing inflation. If this scenario persists for five to 10 years, they should earn a modest real return if their bonds mature over the same period. They are unlikely to have significant capital losses or gains along the way. Stock prices should continue to rise along with earnings and dividends.

Of course, it's never quite so easy to predict the outlook for bonds and stocks. There are those pesky Black Swans that could show up when least expected.[22] Black Swan events were discussed by Nassim Nicholas Taleb in his 2001 book *Fooled by Randomness*, which focused on financial events. His 2007 book *The Black Swan: The Impact of the Highly Improbable* generalized the metaphor as follows:

> What we call here a Black Swan (and capitalize it) is an event with the following three attributes. First, it is an outlier, as it lies outside the realm of regular expectations, because nothing in the past can convincingly point to its possibility. Second, it carries an extreme "impact". Third, in spite of its outlier status, human nature makes us concoct explanations for its occurrence after the fact, making it explainable and predictable. I stop and summarize the triplet: rarity, extreme "impact", and retrospective (though not prospective) predictability. A small number of Black Swans explains almost everything in our world, from the success of ideas and religions, to the dynamics of historical events, to elements of our own personal lives.

Since the financial crisis of 2008, pessimistic prognosticators have done an admirable job of anticipating all sorts of Black Swan scenarios. For example, in late 2012, a widely feared and anticipated Black Swan event was that the US economy would fall off a "fiscal cliff" in early 2013 because Democrats and Republicans couldn't agree on a federal budget. I expected that they would come to terms.

When they did so at the start of the new year, I wrote that investors might have "anxiety fatigue" as a result of all the false alarms issued by the bears since the start of the latest bull market. I've been raising the odds of a meltup in stock prices since then, as I note in the previous chapter. A meltup would constitute a Black Swan event, according to Taleb, since it doesn't matter whether such an event is bearish or bullish; it just has to be a big surprise.

Meanwhile, stock market bears warned that once the Fed terminated its QE program, stock prices would fall. The program was terminated at the end of October 2014, yet the S&P 500 rose 32.5% through the end of 2017 to yet another record high. Now the bears are saying that stocks will fall once the ECB and the Bank of Japan terminate their QE programs and start to normalize their monetary policies (Fig. 45 and Fig. 46).

Despite the symmetry of Taleb's argument, Black Swans are widely associated with bad outcomes for the economy and financial markets. Here are a few that come to mind:

- *Inflation comeback.* If inflation were to rear its ugly head again, that would force central banks to raise their official interest rates. Bond prices would fall, and stock markets might do so once rates got high enough to cause a recession, which might be signaled by an inverted yield curve. Then again, inflation might remain a no-show.
- *Financial crises.* Financial crises always seem to happen unpredictably, with adverse consequences for most investments other than government securities. Since the Great Recession, pessimistic prognosticators have predicted several financial calamities, including the disintegration of the Eurozone, a debt crisis in China, currency wars, and many more. None of these scenarios has played out so far.
- *Flash crash.* During 2017, money poured into exchange-traded funds (ETFs). That influx was driving a broad-based surge in stock prices, since the most popular ETFs tend to track the broad market indexes. It increasingly looked like the meltup that I had begun to anticipate in early 2013. The problem with the popularity of this investment

vehicle is that while it works great on the way up, it has the potential to worsen future corrections and bear markets. A "flash crash" can occur as indiscriminate selling of ETFs causes indiscriminate selling of all the stocks they include, however strong might be the companies' underlying fundamentals. Unlike mutual funds, ETFs don't hold liquid assets to meet redemption orders; they have to sell stocks when investors decide to redeem.

- *Geopolitical crises.* The Trump administration may take a tougher stance against the nuclear ambitions of North Korea and Iran, raising the chances of a military confrontation between the US and one or both of these rogue regimes. Another oil crisis is always possible if political instability worsens in Saudi Arabia or if a military conflict breaks out between the oil kingdom and Iran, its archrival in the Middle East. Tensions between China and its neighbors, especially the ones allied with the US, could flare as China continues to build small islands in the South China Sea to claim sovereignty over this important trade route. Already testy relations between Russia and the West could flare up, with the potential for dangerous skirmishes with NATO forces. In recent years, however, and certainly during the current bull market, stock investors have learned that selloffs triggered by geopolitical crises tend to be short-lived buying opportunities.

Contrarians were put on high alert in June 2017, when Fed Chair Janet Yellen said at a London conference: "Would I say there will never, ever be another financial crisis? You know probably that would be going too far, but I do think we're much safer, and I hope it will not be in our lifetimes, and I don't believe it will be." Yet she also described asset valuations as "somewhat rich if you use some traditional metrics like price earnings ratios." Yellen turned 71 on August 13, 2017, so her lifetime may not be yours (for someone who tends to be very precise, her use of "our lifetimes" sure leaves room for interpretation!). In any event, her comment is reminiscent of other ill-fated predictions by Fed chairs— like Greenspan's "once-in-a-century" technology and productivity revolution and Bernanke's no "significant spillovers" stance on the subprime mortgage debacle.[23]

I'll go out on a limb and predict that there will be another financial crisis in our lifetimes. However, like previous ones, it probably will offer a great opportunity for buying stocks.

THE SCIENCE OF PROSPERITY

FINALLY, I WOULD like to editorialize briefly on the economics profession. Economics gets a bad rap. It's often called "the dismal science," but I think of it as the science of prosperity—and what could be less dismal than prosperity? Yet given the way it's taught in most universities, it certainly can be dismal to study. Too much time is devoted to unrealistic theories and abstract mathematical models, and too little time is spent on studying current analysis, which by its very nature is more realistic and objective. The excitement and drama of economic life are lost in lifeless econometric regressions and algebraic matrixes. The gap between interesting, dynamic, albeit messy economic reality and the boring, static, antiseptic, orderly theories taught in academia is so wide, in my opinion, that the two barely resemble each other.

Economic history—presumably the inspiration for the theoretical models—is mostly ignored or taught in elective courses. And there are few, if any, courses on the manic-depressive market cycles of greed and fear that are amplified by debt and recur along with business cycles. I would like to see at least 101-level courses on Entrepreneurial Capitalism, the History of Globalization and Trade, Creative Destruction and Technological Disruption, the History of Financial Crises, the Political Economy of Corruption, and Demography for Economists. Ideally, an introductory course in Current Analysis would be required, with my book as assigned reading!

The predictions of economists are often dismally wrong because they're based on theory instead of reality. Economists like to predict but can't do so very well, led in wrong directions by their faulty theoretical tools. That's why economists are the Rodney Dangerfields of the sciences: they get no respect, or not much anyway.

But irrelevant lectures and erroneous forecasts are not the reason that economics is known as the dismal science. The reason, in a nutshell, is that economists all too often are pessimists. They tend to predict dismal outcomes for us. The bad reputation originated with the work of Thomas Malthus. Ever since, economics professors have taught their students that economics is about "the optimal allocation of scarce resources." This focus on scarcity is anxiety provoking.

Actually, economics isn't inherently dismal at all. There is no reason economists can't be optimists. Indeed, many have been in the past, and many are today. Perhaps the press is to blame: the pessimists get all the attention because bad news sells better than good news.

Nevertheless, some of the blame must rest with the economics profession. Is economics really about the optimal allocation of scarce resources? "Do the best you can with what you have, because there ain't no more." I believe that the focus on limits is misguided. Limits are broken by human ingenuity all the time. More often than not, limits are mental blocks that vanish thanks to outside-the-box thinking.

Perhaps it is all a big misunderstanding. When economists talk about scarce resources, they mean resources that aren't free like air and sand. You have to pay a price to get them. The more the demand relative to the supply, the higher the price, i.e., the "scarcer" the resource. However, the supply of most resources isn't as limited as "scarce" suggests. Higher prices in most cases stimulate the production of more of the desired resource. Also, higher prices often stimulate substitution with alternative resources that then become more affordable. And higher prices stimulate technological innovations that create a new abundant resource, destroying the need for the resource that was previously deemed to be scarce, or at least too expensive.

In other words, economics isn't about limits at all. The price mechanism linking demand with supply has the potential to increase the supply of resources as demand expands or else to satisfy demand with other relatively more abundant substitutes. There are no limits. Economics is about our *unlimited* potential to prosper, both collectively and individually. There are no natural resource limits, only man-made obstacles. Ideally, economists can help us eliminate the obstacles that we place in the way of our own well-being, rather than doing the opposite.

Economics is really all about power—purchasing power, that is. Most of us want as much of this power as possible. More is better than less.

This is an admittedly materialistic view of humankind. Some people seem content to earn just enough to afford a simple lifestyle. Maybe we would all be happier living frugally and ascetically on the shores of Walden Pond, in the footsteps of Henry David Thoreau. Thoreau maligned materially focused folks as living "lives of quiet desperation." I think his thinking was wrong. Most of us know that "money doesn't buy happiness," as the old saying goes. However, we also know that if the choice is between being miserably poor or miserably rich, the latter is the far better alternative if possible. At least having enough money reduces one source of stress, namely not having enough of it. Most of us do desire to earn more so we can spend more and have more for ourselves and our families.

As I discuss in Chapter 7, purchasing power is best measured as real disposable income per household. Economic well-being can be measured in terms of what purchasing power actually buys—namely, real consumption per household, i.e., the standard of living. More than 240 years ago, Adam Smith concluded that "consumption is the sole end and purpose of all production; and the interest of the producer ought to be attended to only so far as it may be necessary for promoting that of the consumer." As Smith put it, "The maxim is so perfectly self-evident that it would be absurd to attempt to prove it." I concur.

Now that you are well acquainted with why I think what I think and how I arrive at my conclusions, here are my major predictions. I predict that prosperity will prevail in our interconnected global economy long into the future. If so, then so should the bull market in stocks, as it has over the past 40 years.

EPILOGUE

I'VE REALLY ENJOYED writing my professional autobiography. I was warned by those who have done so that writing a book can be a tiresome and lonesome experience. It requires late nights to make the time to write after coming home from work. Fortunately for me, writing my professional autobiography complemented my day job. I was warned that it can take a long time from start to finish. That wasn't the case either; I wrote most of the book from the summer of 2016 to the summer of 2017.

I've essentially been writing this book for 40 years, because it reflects what I have learned on Wall Street since I started my career there in 1978. When it came to getting it down on paper, I didn't have to spend much time on research—I use everything I write about too often not to know it like the back of my hand.

However, writing the book taught me much more about what I thought I had already learned. I examined more closely many of the data resources that I have used for many years. I also refreshed my memory about the exact definitions and derivations of numerous indicators that have been my stock in trade. I spent lots of time picking from my company's vast virtual library the more than 700 charts that most clearly support my approach to predicting the markets. I hope you've had the time to look at them on the book's website to improve your understanding of current analysis.

While I have spent much of the past four decades doing my own research—with the support of my longtime colleagues at Yardeni Research and the other Wall Street firms we worked at—I've also learned a great deal from lots of very smart people who are in the business of managing money and companies. One of the advantages of my day job is that I am very privileged to have access to so many of them. My frequent discussions with them provide me with valuable insights, many arising through emails and phone calls. Quite a bit of that interaction has also been through frequent marketing trips to meet with our accounts in their offices or in a restaurant for a small-group breakfast, lunch, or dinner. I always enjoy the in-person discussions with our accounts and learn much from them. I also get ideas for new research topics based on their questions. I figure if even one account is puzzling over an issue, there are probably many more who would value some insight about it.

Some of my most popular commentaries are the ones reviewing my discussions with institutional investors with whom I've met during a recent marketing trip. I frequently travel in the United States and overseas for such excursions, which can last from one to four days, packed with one-hour, back-to-back meetings. It can be a hectic schedule, but I always learn a great deal and have lots to write about when I get home. It's professional gossip, but there is always plenty of interest in what everyone else is doing in their portfolios and thinking about.

Another source of very useful information for me is everyday conversations. I start conversations with almost everyone I meet. Relatives, friends, handymen, and perfect strangers are a fount of surprisingly interesting, and occasionally useful, insights into our economy from a bottom-up perspective. When I go on business trips, I've found that limo drivers know a great deal about the current state of their local economy. I ask them whether they are busy and which businesses seem to be getting better or worse, based on the demand for their service. Those who wouldn't rather gripe about how Uber is cutting into their business occasionally share insights that I sometimes incorporate into my *Morning Briefing* commentaries and my blog posts. We should all talk to our children and their friends more often. Ask Millennials when they are planning to get married, have children, and buy a house. Ask your Gen Z kids which social media platform is hot right now and why.

Peter Lynch, the legendary manager of the Fidelity Magellan mutual fund from 1977 to 1990, generated extraordinary returns in the stock market for many of those years. His most famous investment principle was: "Invest in what you know." Lynch observed that many of his best stock ideas came to him while walking through the grocery store or chatting casually with friends and family. As a top-down investment strategist, I've always focused on the broad market indexes along with their sectors and industries, not on recommending individual stocks. In my own personal stock account, I wish I had taken Lynch's advice to heart and invested in the companies that produced the goods and services I purchased. After all, I am a Baby Boomer, and there have been lots of us buying the same products at the same time.

I've often accused the members of the Federal Open Market Committee of engaging in groupthink. I think they need to spend more time with people other than macroeconomists. To be fair, the Fed's *Beige Book* is an attempt to get a grassroots perspective on the economy, as described on the Fed's website: "Each Federal Reserve Bank gathers anecdotal information on current economic conditions in its District through reports from Bank and Branch directors and interviews with key business contacts, economists, market experts, and other sources. The Beige Book summarizes this information by District and sector. An overall summary of the twelve district reports is prepared by a designated Federal Reserve Bank on a rotating basis."[1]

Several of the Fed district banks conduct monthly surveys of business conditions in their regions. I've found that the average of the general business indexes for five of the districts (Dallas, Kansas City, New York, Philadelphia, and Richmond) is highly correlated with the national manufacturing purchasing managers' index.[2] The Fed also surveys senior loan officers of up to 80 large domestic banks and 24 US branches and agencies of foreign banks on a quarterly basis.[3] That doesn't sound very folksy, but at least the Fed is trying to get some feedback on regional economies from the local folks.

Every profession has its opportunities and challenges. The downside of doing what I do is that I don't get enough physical exercise, though I do manage to play tennis for an hour a couple of days a week. I sit at the computer for too many hours during the day, when I'm not on the road. On the other hand, I get lots of mental exercise. Working all day with markets and other people who do the same sharpens the mind, in my opinion. It forces one to process an enormous amount of information and make efficient decisions about what is important, and not so, for the markets. This may not yield great insights into the meaning of life, but it does provide lots of insights into how the world works.

Here, in summary, are a few of the lessons I have learned over the years from doing what I do:

- *Be an investor, not a preacher.* Investing isn't a moral pursuit. It's not about right or wrong, good or evil. It's about bullish or bearish. In other words, don't let your political views bias your investment decisions.[4] Buy low, sell high, but invest for the long run, if you are young enough.

- *Be an empiricist, not a dogmatist.* Get to know the data before you come up with your theory. This helps to avoid the curse of faith-based, rather than fact-based, analysis. Recognize that there are lots of intellectual hucksters promoting their theories without ever letting the facts get in the way. When the facts suggest a scenario that you didn't expect, be open-minded enough to recognize its import. Don't let cognitive bias blind you to what's really going on. Be willing to change what you believe if the facts warrant it. Staying wedded to constructs or ideas that have outlived their usefulness is a sure way to lose money.

- *Be a policy wonk, not a critic.* Don't second-guess policymakers and expect them to change course just because you are convinced they are on the wrong one. However, as I learned along the way, pay close attention to new legislation that changes taxes or regulations. I wish I had paid more attention to the unintended consequences of some of the major laws that deregulated the financial industry.

- *Be a lender, not a borrower.* While we all know that Polonius said, "Neither a borrower nor a lender be," there's no evidence that Einstein said, "Compound interest is the eighth wonder of the world. He who understands it, earns it. He who doesn't, pays it." But it sounds like something he might have said. You can make a bundle of dough by borrowing money and buying stocks on margin. But you can also lose lots of money that way. If day trading isn't your day job, succeed at what you do best and let dividend-yielding companies work their magic of compounding your return.

- *Be revolutionary, not evolutionary.* I'm not advocating that you conspire to overthrow the government. However, change happens, and sometimes it happens much faster than was widely anticipated or even perceived as it was happening. The end of the Cold War and China entering the World Trade Organization were revolutionary changes with major consequences for the global economy and financial markets. While such dramatic events might be infrequent, the revolutionary impact of technological innovation on our lives seems to be moving at a faster and faster pace.

- *Be an optimist, not a pessimist.* History shows that optimistic investment strategies tend to work better over time than pessimistic ones. Doomsdays occur from time to time, but they don't last as long as the good times. If you are going to be bearish, try to be so when everyone is too bullish. Then when everything falls apart, you can say, "I told you so." However, don't forget to turn optimistic once everyone else is pessimistic. Remember: don't worry, be happy, but stay informed!

To sum up, in the realm of forecasting, keeping an open mind is critically important. While I am not a big fan of the theories of John Maynard Keynes, I agree with a quote that is widely attributed to him: "When the facts change, I change my mind. What do you do, sir?" There's no clear evidence that he actually said that, by the way. However, Daniel Patrick Moynihan, a former senator from New York, undeniably once said, "Everyone is entitled to his own opinion, but not to his own facts."

A combination of these two sayings essentially sums up my approach to forecasting. Start with the facts to produce well-thought-out opinions and theories that have plenty of empirical support, but keep an open mind should you need to change your views along the way as you learn more about how the world works and as the world changes the way it works.

Perhaps the best way to end this book is to put it in perspective. It covers only 40 years of history as I have experienced them during my career so far. That's not even a speck in the cosmic timeline. What is likely to happen over the next 40 years? History has a tendency to repeat itself because human nature hasn't changed much, if at all, since the beginning of recorded time. Nevertheless, there is no doubt in my mind that the next 40 years will be significantly different from the past 40. The powerful technological and demographic trends I discuss in the book strongly suggest that robots with artificial intelligence and populations with fewer babies and more seniors will radically transform human societies and our economies—creating exciting challenges, considerable risks, and glorious opportunities along the way.

I hope my insights into predicting the economy and financial markets will prove useful to you in your professional life as well as your financial life. We've examined the past 40 years to learn how current analysis can help us to understand yesterday and today so that we can do a better job of anticipating tomorrow. We've traveled down a long road together. Now, let's get back to the future. "Where we're going, we don't need roads."[5]

ACKNOWLEDGMENTS

A BOOK PROJECT that spans the first 40 years of my career on Wall Street reflects the influence and support of many people.

First and foremost, my colleagues at Yardeni Research deserve a great deal of credit for helping to put it all together. Debbie Johnson and Mali Quintana spent countless hours checking the data that are shown in the book's text and in the more than 700 charts on the book's website. Melissa Tagg provided insightful research and fact-checking assistance. Joe Abbott and I have worked together for many years to develop some of the investment strategy tools highlighted in the book. Jackie Doherty provided numerous good editorial suggestions. Mary Fanslau helped to administer the project. Geoff Moore and Steve Rybka delivered great tech support. Our in-house editor, Sandra Cohan, cheerfully and masterfully pulled double duty by editing the book and our daily commentary. Her dedication to making the book happen was impressive.

Special thanks go to several professional friends who closely read the manuscript and came back with very helpful suggestions for making the book more accurate and readable. They are Andrew Bell, James Codrington, Max King, and Jim Solloway. I am also grateful for useful advice from Mike Avery, Hank Herrmann, Van Hoisington, Simon Owen-Williams, Francis Scotland, and Steve Smith. Of course, any remaining errors or omissions are solely my own.

My award-winning consulting editor, Dania Sheldon, was supremely thorough in covering all the necessary bases for this project. Alex Hennig's design work contributed greatly to the book's visual appeal. Additional editorial and design assistance was ably provided by Ruth McGuire, Tom Clemmons, and Jim Dissette.

Last but not least, I must thank my wife, Valerie, for encouraging me to write this book. She is my biggest fan, and I am hers.

NOTES

Find links for references, figures, and appendices at *yardenibook.com/resources*.

INTRODUCTION

1 "The Transition from Academic to Policymaker," Bernanke's remarks on a panel discussion, January 7, 2005.

2 I also email my daily "What I Am Reading" to our accounts, most of whom find this to be very helpful.

CHAPTER 1: PREDICTING THE PAST

1 R-squared is a statistical measure of how close the data are to the fitted regression line. It is also known as the "coefficient of determination," or the "coefficient of multiple determination" for multiple regression.

2 For more information, visit the Federal Reserve Bank of New York's webpage "About the Building."

3 The Federal Reserve Bank of New York's website states: "Gold custody is one of several financial services the Federal Reserve Bank of New York provides to central banks, governments and official international organizations on behalf of the Federal Reserve System. The New York Fed's gold vault is on the basement floor of its main office building in Manhattan. Built during the construction of the building in the early 1920s, the vault provides account holders with a secure location to store their monetary gold reserves. None of the gold stored in the vault belongs to the New York Fed or the Federal Reserve System. The New York Fed acts as the guardian and custodian of the gold on behalf of account holders, which include the US government, foreign governments, other central banks, and official international organizations. No individuals or private sector entities are permitted to store gold in the vault."

4 GDP is the most commonly used measure of the market value of all goods and services produced in an economy. It is limited to production in the United States, while GNP measures the production of American or American-owned entities anywhere in the world.

5 "About as Low as They'll Go," *Barron's*, November 26, 2001.

6 The parenthetical abbreviations after the names of US senators and members of the House of Representatives mentioned in this book indicate their political party affiliation if not already mentioned (D for Democrat, R for Republican) and home state.

7 "Wall St. Securities Firm Files for Bankruptcy," *The New York Times*, August 13, 1982.

8 For more information, refer to James M. Boughton's *Silent Revolution: The International Monetary Fund 1979–1989*, Chapter 7, "The Mexican Crisis: No Mountain Too High?"

9 Market index values have been rounded to the nearest whole number at most mentions throughout the book. Notable exceptions are Chapter 15 and elsewhere that percentage performance numbers calculated using unrounded numbers are provided.

10 The bottom was made on Black Monday for the DJIA, which was the 55th day of the bear market, with the DJIA down 36.1% from the peak. However, that bottom was retested on December 4, 1987, which I view as the end of the bear market. That's confirmed by the broader S&P 500 stock price index, which bottomed on December 4 with a drop of 33.5%. For the year, the DJIA rose 2.3% and the S&P 500 increased 2.0%.

11 For more details, see Mark Carlson's "A Brief History of the 1987 Stock Market Crash," Board of Governors of the Federal Reserve, November 2006.

12 "A Computer Lesson Still Unlearned," *The New York Times*, October 18, 2012.

13 Refer to the article "Triggering the 1987 Stock Market Crash," in the September 1989 *Journal of Financial Economics*, by Mark L. Mitchell and Jeffrey M. Netter.

14 In my *Topical Study* "Dow 5000," dated May 9, 1990, I predicted that the DJIA could nearly double, from 2700 to 5000 by 1993, if earnings and the valuation multiple each rose by 50%, as I expected. It took a little longer than I expected. The Dow rose to 5000 on November 21, 1995. I then wrote another *Topical Study*, "10,000 in 2000," dated November 6, 1995. This time, it happened a bit ahead of schedule: the Dow rose to 10,000 on March 29, 1999.

15 See YRI's *Topical Studies* archive.

16 See my *Topical Study* (co-authored with David Moss) "The New Wave Manifesto," October 5, 1988.

17 See my *Topical Study* "The Triumph of Capitalism," August 1, 1989.

18 See my *Topical Study* "The Collapse of Communism Is Bullish," September 4, 1991.

19 See my *Topical Study* "The End of the Cold War Is Bullish," September 10, 1993.

20 The SEC form 10-Q is a comprehensive report of a company's performance that must be submitted to the SEC quarterly by all public companies. In the 10-Q, firms are required to disclose relevant information regarding their financial position. There is no filing after the fourth quarter, because that is when the 10-K is filed.

21 "Why Ed Yardeni Is an MVP in the Victory over Y2K Bugs," *Businessweek*, January 5, 2000.

22 The original Cyrus J. Lawrence & Sons was founded in 1864 and thrived as an independent investment and research firm until it was acquired 1986 by the London-based Morgan Grenfell Group, which was, in turn, acquired by the Frankfurt-based Deutsche Bank A.G. in 1989.

23 "Congress Helped Banks Defang Key Rule," *The Wall Street Journal*, June 3, 2009.

24 See my movie review webpage at *yardeni.com/movies*.

CHAPTER 2: PREDICTING THE WORLD

1 "Getting It Straight," *Cornell Alumni Magazine*, March 3, 2009.

2 Jones has been a director of Altria Group, trustee of The Economic Club of New York, and trustee emeritus of Cornell University. Past board positions included Vice Chairman of the Federal Reserve Bank of New York, Freddie Mac, Travelers Group, Pepsi Bottling Group, Eastern Enterprises, Thomas & Betts Corporation, and Investment Company Institute.

3 "Sykes–Picot: The Map that Spawned a Century of Resentment," BBC News, May 16, 2016.

4 The full August 4, 1997 *Barron's* article "Wall Street Seer" is reproduced in Appendix 1.3.

5 *The Reagan Record on Trade: Rhetoric vs. Reality*, Cato Institute Policy Analysis No. 107, May 30, 1988.

6 See my *Topical Study* "The Protectionist Road to Depression," September 9, 1985.

7 See John Maynard Keynes' *The Economic Consequences of the Peace* (1919).

8 "Smoot–Hawley Tariff: A Bad Law, Badly Timed," Gordon's article in *Barron's*, April 21, 2017.

9 "The Gold Standard, Deflation, and Financial Crisis in the Great Depression," Bernanke's *NBER Working Paper* No. 3488, October 1990 (co-authored with Harold James).

10 Again, as a reminder: GDP is the most commonly used measure of the market value of all goods and services produced in an economy. It is limited to production in the United States, while GNP measures the production of American or American-owned entities anywhere in the world.

11 "The Recession of 1937–38," *federalreservehistory.org*.

12 "The Lessons of 1937," *The Economist*, June 18, 2009.

13 "Gold Sterilization and the Recession of 1937–38," Douglas Irwin's September 9, 2011 paper.

14 "Reconsidering Expectations of Economic Growth After World War II from the Perspective of 2004," Robert W. Fogel, *NBER Working Paper* No. 11125, February 2005.

15 See my *Topical Study* "The Economic Consequences of the Peace," May 7, 1997.

16 See my *Topical Study* "A Bullish Post-War Scenario," February 4, 2003.

17 See my *Topical Study* "China for Investors I: The Growth Imperative," November 7, 2003.

18 See my *Topical Study* "China for Investors II: The Games," January 21, 2004.

19 *An Aging World: 2015*, the United States Census Bureau, March 2016.

20 Composite, manufacturing, and services PMIs are available for numerous countries on IHS Markit's website.

21 See the European Commission's webpage "Business and Consumer Surveys."

22 See Eurostat's webpage "Retail Trade Volume Index Overview."

23 Refer to the CESifo Group's webpage "IFO Business Climate Index."

24 Refer to the International Monetary Fund's *World Economic Outlook*.

25 *An Aging World: 2015*, the United States Census Bureau, March 2016.

26 "How Are Populations Shifting within Developed Countries?" Federal Reserve Bank of St. Louis, August 11, 2016 blog post.

27 *An Aging World: 2015*, the United States Census Bureau, March 2016.

28 "Why Stagnation Might Prove to Be the New Normal," Larry Summers' op-ed in the *Financial Times*, December 15, 2013.

29 "Debt Supercycle, Not Secular Stagnation," Kenneth Rogoff's April 22, 2015 commentary.

30 "Short-Run Effects of Lower Productivity Growth: A Twist on the Secular Stagnation Hypothesis," Peterson Institute for International Economics *Policy Brief*, February 2017.

CHAPTER 3: PREDICTING TECHNOLOGY AND PRODUCTIVITY

1 Access the Federal Reserve Bank of St Louis' "FRED Economic Data" website.

2 See my *Topical Study* "The High-Tech Revolution in the US of @," March 20, 1995.

3 Chapter 13 explains forward earnings.

4 "Cramming More Components onto Integrated Circuits," Moore's article in *Proceedings of the IEEE*, January 1998, reprinted from his original April 19, 1965 study.

5 Professor Nordhaus explained in an August 30, 2001 paper titled "The Progress of Computing" that "the simplest version of MIPS is defective in several respects. First, it does not specify the size of the word or the nature of the instruction. Long words have more computational value than short words. Some instructions (such as division) require much more computer power than simple instructions (such as addition). The definition does not consider the mix or the number of instructions. In short, it violates the central rule of index numbers by failing to consider an invariant bundle of characteristics." He noted that complex sets of performance benchmark tests can better assess the speed of real-world applications that depend upon memory, input-output speed, and the instruction mix. MIPS is limited to the speed of the central processing unit.

6 "The World's Technological Capacity to Store, Communicate, and Compute Information," *Science*, April 1, 2011.

7 Again, see "The World's Technological Capacity to Store, Communicate, and Compute Information," *Science*, April 1, 2011.

8 *Two Centuries of Productivity Growth in Computing*, Nordhaus' January 2007 study.

9 "The Rise of the Intangible Economy: U.S. GDP Counts R&D, Artistic Creation," Bloomberg, July 18, 2013.

10 For an explanation of how the Bureau of Economic Analysis calculates deflators for software, refer to "Private Fixed Investment," pp. 30–31.

11 "The Challenge of Central Banking in a Democratic Society," Greenspan's December 5, 1996 speech.

12 See my *Topical Study* "The Technology Lottery," November 22, 1999.

13 See my *Topical Study* "The Baby Boom Chart Book 1991," October 9, 1991.

14 "In Search of Productivity," Roach's article in the *Harvard Business Review*, September–October 1998.

15 "Alternative Hours Data and Their Impact on Productivity Change," Bureau of Labor Statistics, July 2003, p. 9.

16 See Laurence H. Meyer's book *A Term at the Fed: An Insider's View* (2006), pages 6 and 16.

17 Refer to Meyer, page 18.

18 Refer to Meyer, page 38.

19 Refer to Meyer, page 135.

20 Refer to Meyer, page 132.

21 Refer to Meyer, page 126.

22 "The Productivity Mirage," Cassidy's article in *The New Yorker*, November 27, 2000.

23 "Bundesbank Mocks US IT Book-Cooking," Grant's article in the *Financial Times*, September 4, 2000.

24 "A Note on the Impact of Hedonics and Computers on Real GDP," in the Bureau of Economic Analysis (BEA) *Survey of Current Business*, December 2000.

25 "Who's Afraid of Stephen Roach?" *Barron's*, December 6, 2004.

26 "Silicon Valley Doesn't Believe U.S. Productivity Is Down," *The Wall Street Journal*, July 16, 2015.

27 "Does the United States Have a Productivity Slowdown or a Measurement Problem?" *Brookings Papers on Economic Activity*, Spring 2016.

28 "The Coming Productivity Boom: Transforming the Physical Economy with Information," Technology CEO Council, March 2017.

29 Robert J. Gordon, *The Rise and Fall of American Growth: The U.S. Standard of Living Since the Civil War* (2016).

30 "Why Innovation Won't Save Us," Gordon's article in *The Wall Street Journal*, December 21, 2012.

31 See my November 27, 2012 *Morning Briefing*, "Woe Is Us!"

32 Philippe Harelle was quoted in the November 23, 2016 Bloomberg article "Solar-Panel Roads to Be Built on Four Continents Next Year."

33 "Rethinking Transportation 2020–2030," May 2017 report by James Arbib and Tony Seba.

34 "Daddy, What Was a Truck Driver?" *The Wall Street Journal*, June 23, 2013.

35 "Terry Gou: Managing '1m Animals' [updated with Foxconn statement]," *Financial Times*, January 20, 2012.

36 Watch the robot "Baxter" at work on YouTube.

37 "A Revolution in the Making," *The Wall Street Journal*, June 10, 2013.

38 "A San Francisco Startup 3D Printed a Whole House in 24 Hours," March 7, 2017 article on *engadget.com*. Don't miss the embedded video.

39 "How 3-D Printers Could Erase a Quarter of Global Trade by 2060," Bloomberg, October 3, 2017.

40 George Gilbert, "Wikibon Trip Report from IBM's Watson Developer Conference: Keep It Simple, Geniuses," blog post, SiliconANGLE, November 15, 2016.

41 "Quantum Computers Ready to Leap Out of the Lab in 2017," *Scientific American*, January 4, 2017.

42 "Moore's Law at 50: The Performance and Prospects of the Exponential Economy," American Enterprise Institute, November 10, 2015.

43 I am including employment in: publishing; motion picture and sound recording; broadcasting; telecommunications; data processing, hosting, and related services; computer and electronic products manufacturing; and other information services.

44 "A Warning from Bill Gates, Elon Musk, and Stephen Hawking," freeCodeCamp, February 18, 2017.

45 "The Robot that Takes Your Job Should Pay Taxes, says Bill Gates," Quartz Media, February 17, 2017.

46 "Why Taxing Robots Is Not a Good Idea," *The Economist*, February 25, 2017.

47 "Draft Report with Recommendations to the Commission on Civil Law Rules on Robotics," European Parliament Committee on Legal Affairs, May 31, 2016.

48 "Robots Are Wealth Creators and Taxing Them Is Illogical," Summers' article in the *Financial Times*, March 5, 2017.

CHAPTER 4: PREDICTING INFLATION

1 *Cost-of-Living Adjustment Clauses in Union Contracts: A Summary of Results*, July 1983 study by Ronald G. Ehrenberg of Cornell University, Leif Danziger of Tel Aviv University, and Gee San of Cornell University.

2 Stuart E. Weiner, "Union COLA's on the Decline," Federal Reserve Bank of Kansas City, June 1986.

3 See my *Topical Study* "Economic Consequences of the Internet," October 22, 1996.

4 "Deflation: Making Sure 'It' Doesn't Happen Here," Bernanke's November 21, 2002 speech.

5 See my *Topical Study* "The Economic Consequences of the Peace," May 7, 1997.

6 The quote appears on p. 150 of Ron Chernow's *Titan: The Life of John D. Rockefeller, Sr.* (1998).

7 The Bank for International Settlements compiled in October 1998 a list of sound banking practices. See Basle Committee on Banking Supervision, "Sound Practices for Loan Accounting, Credit Risk Disclosure and Related Matters."

8 Countries that have the best legal protection for investors tend to have the biggest capital markets and the least concentration of share ownership. See Rafael La Porta, Florencio Lopez-de-Silanes, Andrei Shleifer, and Robert W. Vishny, "Law and Finance," *NBER Working Paper* No. 5661, July 1996. See also their *NBER Working Paper* No. 5879, "Legal Determinants of External Finance," January 1997.

9 Sheryl WuDunn wrote an interesting article, "In Asia, Firms 'Fail' but Stay Open," in the *International Herald Tribune* dated September 9, 1998 (the link no longer is available). She discussed the systems that allowed "failed" Asian corporations to remain in business nonetheless. "[G]overnments and legal systems routinely protect tycoons from their own incompetence, setting the stage not for a Darwinian struggle but for the survival of the flimsiest." In many countries in Asia, the legal framework for bankruptcy is vague and loosely formed.

10 Yellen's March 19, 2014 press conference.

11 "The 'New Normal' and What It Means for Monetary Policy," Brainard's September 12, 2016 speech.

12 Refer to the Bureau of Labor Statistics' latest JOLTS press release.

13 In 1977, country singer Johnny Paycheck popularized a song titled "Take This Job and Shove It." It's about the bitterness of a man who worked long and hard with no apparent reward. However, he quit not for a better job but because his "woman done left and took all the reasons" for working.

14 See the latest monthly Employment Situation release from the Bureau of Labor Statistics.

15 "Opening Pandora's Box: The Measurement of Average Wages," Ritter's article in the Federal Reserve Bank of St. Louis' *Review*, March/April 1996.

16 See the latest Employment Cost Index report from the Bureau of Labor Statistics.

17 Again, see "Opening Pandora's Box: The Measurement of Average Wages."

18 See the latest Productivity and Costs report from the Bureau of Labor Statistics.

19 "Reconciling the Divergence in Aggregate U.S. Wage Series," *BLS Working Paper* No. 486, January 2016.

20 See the Federal Reserve Bank of Atlanta's "Wage Growth Tracker" website.

21 See the first footnote in the Federal Reserve Board's *Monetary Policy Report* submitted to Congress on February 17, 2000.

22 "Transparency in Monetary Policy," Greenspan's October 11, 2001 speech.

23 "Federal Reserve issues FOMC statement of longer-run goals and policy strategy," January 25, 2012 press release.

24 "Final Report of the Advisory Commission to Study the Consumer Price Index," the December 1996 report of the US Senate Committee on Finance.

25 "Price Measurement in the United States: A Decade After the Boskin Report," *Monthly Labor Review*, May 2006.

26 See the first footnote in the Federal Reserve Board's *Monetary Policy Report* submitted to Congress on February 17, 2000.

27 "How the CPI measures price change of owners' equivalent rent of primary residence (OER) and Rent of primary residence (Rent)," factsheet prepared by the Bureau of Labor Statistics.

28 According to the Bureau of Labor Statistics, "These include fees (not recouped through health insurance) that consumers paid directly to retail outlets for medical goods and to doctors and other medical providers for medical services, as well as health insurance premiums that consumers paid (including Medicare Part B). To arrive at the consumer out-of-pocket medical expense, the [Consumer Expenditure Survey] nets out direct insurance reimbursements to the consumer from the total amounts paid by the consumer. Since medical care only includes consumers' out-of-pocket expenditures (and excludes employer provided health care), its share in the CPI is smaller than its share of gross domestic product (GDP) and other national accounts measures." See "Measuring Price Change for Medical Care in the CPI."

29 "Comparing the Consumer Price Index and the Personal Consumption Expenditures Price Index," the Bureau of Economic Analysis' *Survey of Current Business*, November 2007.

30 The Bureau of Labor Statistics discusses this perception discrepancy in "The Consumer Price Index—Why the Published Averages Don't Always Match An Individual's Inflation Experience."

CHAPTER 5: PREDICTING BUSINESS CYCLES

1 The BEA switched in 1991 to emphasizing GDP rather than GNP. GDP is the most commonly used measure of the market value of all goods and services produced in an economy. It is limited to production in the United States, while GNP measures the production of American or American-owned entities anywhere in the world.

2 Real GDP is the broadest measure of the goods and services produced in an economy, while real GDI measures the total income generated by that production. In theory, the two should be equal, though in practice, there is a small statistical discrepancy.

3 For more information, see the NBER's webpage "Business Cycle Dating Procedure: Frequently Asked Questions."

4 See the Federal Reserve Bank of Atlanta's "GDPNow" webpage and the Federal Reserve Bank of New York's "Nowcasting Report" webpage.

5 The six financial indicators of the Leading Credit Index are: 2-year swap spread (real time), 3-month LIBOR less 3-month Treasury-Bill yield spread (real time), debit balances at margin account at broker dealer (monthly), AAII Investors Sentiment Bullish (%) less Bearish (%) (weekly), Senior Loan Officers C&I loan survey's bank tightening credit to large and medium firms (quarterly), and securities repurchases (quarterly) from the Total Finance-Liabilities section of the Federal Reserve's flow of funds report. See the Conference Board's December 2011 *Working Paper* No. 11-05, "Using the Leading Credit Index™ to Predict Turning Points in the U.S. Business Cycle."

6 Irving Fisher was prominent among the 1,028 economists who in vain petitioned Herbert Hoover to veto the Smoot–Hawley tariff of 1930. He was adamant that ending deflation required abandoning the gold standard.

7 "The Debt-Deflation Theory of the Great Depression," Fisher's 1933 article.

8 "The Financial Accelerator and the Flight to Quality," *NBER Working Paper* No. 4789, July 1994.

9 "The Financial Accelerator and the Credit Channel," Bernanke's June 15, 2007 speech.

10 For more background on this, see *federalreservehistory.org*'s webpage on the "Full Employment and Balanced Growth Act of 1978," commonly called the "Humphrey–Hawkins Act."

11 "The Great Moderation," Bernanke's February 20, 2004 speech.

12 See the May 9, 1939 meeting transcript from the Franklin D. Roosevelt Library's online "Henry Morgenthau Diary."

13 *The Job Impact of the American Recovery and Reinvestment Plan*, the January 9, 2009 report by Christina Romer and Jared Bernstein.

14 See the BEA's website for links to *Measuring the Economy: A Primer on GDP and the National Income and Product Accounts* and *Concepts and Methods of the U.S. National Income and Product Accounts*.

CHAPTER 6: PREDICTING CONSUMERS

1 The US Census Bureau reckons that the Millennials were born between 1982 and 2000. See the Bureau's webpage "Millennials Outnumber Baby Boomers and Are Far More Diverse, Census Bureau Reports."

2 The Pew Research Center divides the generations in the same way as I do; see "Comparing Millennials to Other Generations" on Pew's website.

3 See the latest JOLTS release from the Bureau of Labor Statistics (BLS).

4 Total separations includes quits, layoffs and discharges, and other separations. Total separations is referred to as "turnover." Quits are generally voluntary separations initiated by the employee. Therefore, the quits rate can serve as a measure of workers' willingness or ability to leave jobs. Layoffs and discharges are involuntary separations initiated by the employer. Other separations include ones due to retirement, death, disability, and transfers to other locations of the same firm.

5 See the "Employment Situation Technical Note" on the BLS website.

6 According to the BLS: "People are classified as employed if they did any work at all as paid employees during the reference week; worked in their own business, profession, or on their own farm; or worked without pay at least 15 hours in a family business or farm. People are also counted as employed if they were temporarily absent from their jobs because of illness, bad weather, vacation, labor-management disputes, or personal reasons. People are classified as unemployed if they meet all of the following criteria: they had no employment during the reference week; they were available for work at that time; and they made specific efforts to find employment sometime during the 4-week period ending with the reference week. Persons laid off from a job and expecting recall need not be looking for work to be counted as unemployed. The unemployment data derived from the household survey in no way depend upon the eligibility for or receipt of unemployment insurance benefits." Again, refer to the BLS's latest "Employment Situation Technical Note."

7 Again, see the "Employment Situation Technical Note" on the BLS website.

8 See the BLS's "CES Net Birth/Death Model."

9 The authors of a fall 2016 Brookings Institution paper attributed more than half of the increase in labor force participation over the past decade to retirees; see Stephanie Aaronson et al., *Labor Force Participation: Recent Developments and Future Prospects.*

10 For more information, refer to the BEA's detailed explanation of "Compensation of Employees."

11 Refer to the BEA's detailed explanation of "Nonfarm Proprietors' Income."

12 See the BEA's explanation of "Housing Services in the National Economic Accounts."

13 "Alternative Measures of Personal Saving," BEA, *Survey of Current Business*, March 2012.

14 "This Is Your Brain at the Mall: Why Shopping Makes You Feel So Good," *The Wall Street Journal*, December 6, 2005.

15 "Shopping, Dopamine, and Anticipation," *Psychology Today*, October 22, 2015.

CHAPTER 7: PREDICTING DEMOGRAPHY

1 See, for example, "People Around You Control Your Mind: The Latest Evidence," *The Washington Post*, December 4, 2014.

2 "Mother's Little Helper" was released in 1966 on the album *Aftermath.*

3 "*State-Specific Healthy Life Expectancy at Age 65 Years—United States, 2007–2009*," Centers for Disease Control and Prevention, July 19, 2013.

4 "Technical Notes: International Comparisons of Annual Labor Force Statistics, 1970–2012," BLS.

5 "Boomers Spend Their Kids' Inheritance—on Supporting Them," *Barron's*, June 26, 2015.

6 See the Fed's October 3, 2016 study, *Understanding the New Normal: The Role of Demographics.*

7 "The Effect of Population Aging on Economic Growth, the Labor Force and Productivity," *NBER Working Paper* No. 22452, July 2016.

8 See the December 28, 2015 report by Arlene Wong, "Population Aging and the Transmission of Monetary Policy to Consumption."

9 "Why Are Interest Rates So Low? Causes and Implications," Fischer's October 17, 2016 speech.

10 As I note in the previous chapter, the US Census Bureau defines the Millennials as people born between 1982 and 2000. See the Bureau's June 25, 2015 press release titled "Millennials Outnumber Baby Boomers and Are Far More Diverse, Census Bureau Reports." On the other hand, the Pew Research Center divides the generations in the same way as I do; see "Comparing Millennials to Other Generations."

11 "Mean Age of Mothers Is on the Rise: United States, 2000–2014," *NCHS Data Brief*, No. 232, January 2016.

12 "The Changing Economics and Demographics of Young Adulthood: 1975–2016," Census Bureau, April 2017.

13 "Student Debt and the Class of 2015," The Institute for College Access & Success, October 2016.

14 "Quick Facts about Student Debt," The Institute for College Access & Success, March 2014.

15 "Are Student Loans as Big of a Problem as People Think?" *USA Today*, July 7, 2017.

16 "Singles, Mingles and Wedding Jingles: Partnerships and Living Arrangements from 1967 to 2014," Census Bureau blog, July 13, 2015.

17 "Definitions and Explanations," Census Bureau.

18 "About Income," Census Bureau.

19 The Census Bureau uses the research series of the Consumer Price Index (CPI-U-RS), provided by the BLS, to adjust for changes in the cost of living. See Appendix A in *Income and Poverty in the United States: 2016*. Also see the BLS statement on "Updated CPI-U-RS, All items and All items less food and energy, 1978–2016."

20 See the Census Bureau Current Population Survey's "Income Definitions."

21 See the IRS's "2017 EITC Income Limits, Maximum Credit Amounts and Tax Law Updates."

22 "Alternative Measures of Household Income: BEA Personal Income, CPS Money Income, and Beyond," BEA and Census Bureau study, November 2004.

23 More information can be found in the Census Bureau report *Income and Poverty in the United States: 2016*.

24 See Table 3 on p. 30 of "A Consistent Data Series to Evaluate Growth and Inequality in the National Accounts," the National Poverty Center's *Working Paper* 16-04, July 2016.

25 Productivity and Costs, BLS report.

26 A June 2017 BLS study titled "Understanding the Labor Productivity and Compensation Gap" concluded: "A full 83 percent of industries studied here had productivity–compensation gaps when the same deflator was used for output and compensation. These gaps came from a declining labor share of income. Sectors with the strongest declines in labor share included manufacturing, information, retail trade, and transportation and warehousing. Although the causes of the decline in labor share are still unclear, focusing on industries may help to isolate and understand the causes unique to each industry."

CHAPTER 8: PREDICTING REAL ESTATE

1 The Monthly New Residential Construction releases are issued jointly by the US Census Bureau and the US Department of Housing and Urban Development.

2 The Monthly New Residential Sales releases are issued jointly by the US Census Bureau and the US Department of Housing and Urban Development.

3 "Center for Microeconomic Data," New York Federal Reserve Bank webpage.

4 See the Federal Reserve's latest *Financial Accounts of the United States*.

5 A good source of information on US housing policy and mortgage lending from the early 20th century through the late 1980s is a paper by Marc A. Weiss titled "Marketing and Financing Home Ownership: Mortgage Lending and Public Policy in the United States, 1918–1989."

6 For more information, refer to the report of the Federal Housing Finance Agency (Office of Inspector General) titled *A Brief History of the Housing Government-Sponsored Enterprises*.

7 "Tax Break May Have Helped Cause Housing Bubble," *The New York Times*, December 18, 2008.

8 Wayne Barrett, "Andrew Cuomo and Fannie and Freddie," *Village Voice*, August 5, 2008.

9 Following a lengthy investigation, the Senate Ethics Committee concluded in 1991 that Cranston, DeConcini, and Riegle had improperly interfered with the FHLBB's investigation

of Lincoln Savings. Senators Glenn and McCain were cleared but were chastised for their "poor judgment." Keating's convictions were overturned in 1996.

10 The SAIF and its sister fund for banks, the Bank Insurance Fund, were administered by the FDIC until 2006, when they were merged by the Federal Deposit Insurance Reform Act of 2005 to create the Depositor Insurance Fund.

11 "25 People to Blame for the Financial Crisis," *Time* magazine's website.

12 "Citi's Creator: Alone With His Regrets," *The New York Times*, January 2, 2010. The article reported that Citigroup CEO Sandy Weill hung in his office "a hunk of wood—at least 4 feet wide—etched with his portrait and the words 'The Shatterer of Glass-Steagall.'"

13 On this subject, *The Financial Crisis Inquiry Report* (2011) stated, "The Commission concludes the CRA was not a significant factor in subprime lending or the crisis. Many subprime lenders were not subject to the CRA. Research indicates only 6% of high-cost loans—a proxy for subprime loans—had any connection to the law. Loans made by CRA-regulated lenders in the neighborhoods in which they were required to lend were half as likely to default as similar loans made in the same neighborhoods by independent mortgage originators not subject to the law." See p. xxvii.

14 "Zero Down Payment," HUD's January 19, 2004 press release.

15 See "Fannie Mae and Freddie Mac Invest in Democrats" on *opensecrets.org.*

16 "Lawmaker Accused of Fannie Mae Conflict of Interest," Fox News, October 3, 2008.

17 "Federal Reserve Board's Semiannual Monetary Policy Report to the Congress," Greenspan's February 16, 2005 congressional testimony.

18 "Deflation: Making Sure 'It' Doesn't Happen Here," Bernanke's November 21, 2002 speech.

19 See the *US Commodity Futures Trading Commission Handbook.*

20 "Joint Statement" by Rubin, Greenspan, and Levitt, US Treasury, May 7, 1998.

21 "Regulatory Responses to Risks in the OTC Derivatives Market," Born's November 13, 1998 speech.

22 "Who's in Charge? Agency Infighting and Regulatory Uncertainty," *The New York Times*, December 15, 1998.

23 *Hedge Funds, Leverage, and the Lessons of Long-Term Capital Management*, President's Working Group on Financial Markets report, April 28, 1999.

24 *Over-the-Counter Derivatives Markets and the Commodity Exchange Act*, President's Working Group on Financial Markets report, November 9, 1999.

25 "Securities Regulation After Glass–Steagall Reform," SEC Commissioner Norman S. Johnson's March 3, 2000 speech.

26 *The Financial Crisis Inquiry Report*, specifically Figure 7.2 on p. 116, Figure 8.1 on p. 128, and Figure 8.2 on p. 144.

27 *The Financial Crisis Inquiry Report*, p. xxii.

28 Check out the cover of the February 15, 1999 issue of *Time*, featuring Robert Rubin, Alan Greenspan, and Larry Summers, and the corresponding article, "The Three Marketeers."

29 For more on the housing GSEs' conservatorship, see the Federal Housing Finance Agency's "FHFA as Conservator of Fannie Mae and Freddie Mac."

30 "Regulator Shopping," editorial in *The New York Times*, May 20, 2009.

31 "What the Financial Crisis Commission Concluded About AIG's Failure," *Insurance Journal*, January 27, 2011.

32 See my *Topical Study* "After Alan: HELs To Pay?" May 3, 2005.

33 "The Subprime Mortgage Market," Bernanke's May 17, 2007 speech.

34 "Do Not Destroy the Essential Catalyst of Risk," Blankfein's *Financial Times* op-ed of February 8, 2009.

35 *The Financial Crisis Inquiry Report*, p. xxv.

36 "Debt Watchdogs: Tamed or Caught Napping?" Morgenson's article in *The New York Times*, December 6, 2008.

37 "Testimony Concerning Oversight of Nationally Recognized Statistical Rating Organizations," Cox's April 22, 2008 congressional testimony.

38 "How Moody's Faltered," *Financial Times*, October 17, 2008.

39 "AIG Trail Leads to London 'Casino'," *The Telegraph*, October 18, 2008.

40 "AIG Said to Pay $450 Million to Retain Swaps Staff (Update1)," Bloomberg News, January 27, 2009.

41 Again, see "AIG Trail Leads to London 'Casino'."

42 "Bernanke Blasts AIG for 'Irresponsible Bets' that Led to Bailouts," *The Washington Post*, March 4, 2009.

43 "The Goldman Two-Step," *The Wall Street Journal*, April 15, 2009.

44 See "Testimony of Dr. Alan Greenspan," October 23, 2008, before the US House of Representatives' Committee of Government Oversight and Reform. The Q&A portion is available in an October 24, 2008 *Washington Times* article titled "He Found the Flaw?"

45 Again, see Greenspan's October 23, 2008 testimony and the October 24, 2008 *Washington Times* article for the Q&A portion.

46 "Deregulation and the Financial Panic," Gramm's op-ed in *The Wall Street Journal*, February 20, 2009.

47 "Henry Kaufman on Financial Reform: He Told Us So," *The Economist*, August 27, 2009. Kaufman did have more to say about Lehman in *Tectonic Shifts in Financial Markets* (2016). However, rather than recounting his experiences at Lehman as board director, he blamed US Treasury Secretary Henry Paulson and Fed Chairman Ben Bernanke for letting the firm fail. See Appendix 8.3, Bernanke's Fed and the Lehman Bankruptcy.

48 "Clinton: I Was Wrong to Listen to Wrong Advice Against Regulating Derivatives," ABCNews.com, April 18, 2010.

49 "How the Bailout Bashed the Banks," *Fortune*, June 22, 2009.

50 *The Financial Crisis Inquiry Report*, p. 142.

51 "Temporary Liquidity Guarantee Program," FDIC factsheet.

52 "Credit and Liquidity Programs and the Balance Sheet," Federal Reserve Board webpage.

53 "Chronology of Fed's Quantitative Easing," YRI webpage.

CHAPTER 9: PREDICTING THE FED

1 "Federal Reserve Act," Federal Reserve Board webpage.

2 The 12 district banks are headquartered in Atlanta, Boston, Chicago, Cleveland, Dallas, Kansas City, Minneapolis, New York, Philadelphia, Richmond, San Francisco, and St. Louis.

3 For more information on the Employment Act of 1946, see *federalreservehistory.org*.

4 "The Federal Reserve's 'Dual Mandate': The Evolution of an Idea," Federal Reserve Bank of Richmond, *Economic Brief*, December 2011.

5 By law, Federal Reserve Board appointments must yield a "fair representation of the financial, agricultural, industrial, and commercial interests and geographical divisions of the country," and no two governors may come from the same Federal Reserve District.

6 "Who are the Members of the Federal Reserve Board, and How Are They Selected?" Federal Reserve Board webpage.

7 The rotating seats are filled from the following four groups of Federal Reserve Banks, with one bank president from each group: Boston, Philadelphia, and Richmond; Cleveland and Chicago; Atlanta, St. Louis, and Dallas; and Minneapolis, Kansas City, and San Francisco.

8 The Fed district presidents are chosen by a search committee composed of the regional banks' directors. Once a candidate is formally appointed, he or she must be approved by the Board of Governors.

9 See the *The Wall Street Journal*'s "Fed Statement Tracker."

10 "A Short History of FOMC Communication," Dallas Federal Reserve Bank article, September 2013.

11 For more information, refer to the "FOMC Meeting Calendars, Statements, and Minutes."

12 Again, see the "FOMC Meeting Calendars, Statements, and Minutes."

13 In 1993, Representative Henry B. Gonzalez (a Democrat from Texas and Chairman of the House Banking Committee) attacked the FOMC's disclosure policy on the grounds that the public deserved more detailed coverage of FOMC meetings. In response, the Federal Reserve instituted its current minutes policy and subsequently released historical transcripts, after light editing, with a five-year lag.

14 "FOMC Statements since 1997," YRI webpage.

15 Martin Zweig, *Winning on Wall Street* (New York: Warner Books, 1986), pp. 42–43.

16 "Yalies Yellen-Hamada Put Tobin Twist Theory to Work in QE," Bloomberg, October 31, 2013.

17 The model was developed by John Hicks in 1937 and later extended by Alvin Hansen. It remains the leading framework shown in macroeconomic textbooks, as it has been since the 1940s.

18 "Rahm Emanuel on the Opportunities of Crisis," *The Wall Street Journal*, November 18, 2008.

19 If Rahm's advice seems Machiavellian, well, it is. Sixteenth-century Italian political theorist Niccolò Machiavelli advised in his famous treatise *The Prince*: "Never waste the opportunity offered by a good crisis." However, it was Winston Churchill who reputedly popularized the sentiment.

20 "Meet the Economists," Federal Reserve Board webpage.

21 "How Economics PhDs Took Over the Federal Reserve," *Harvard Business Review*, February 3, 2014.

22 "The Treasury-Fed Accord: A New Narrative Account," by Hetzel and Leach, in the Federal Reserve Bank of Richmond *Economic Quarterly*, Winter 2001.

23 See the transcript of Martin's "Address before the New York Group of the Investment Bankers Association of America," October 19, 1955.

24 Refer to the 1946 book *Measuring Business Cycles*, written by Burns and Mitchell and published by the NBER.

25 See former Fed Chairman Arthur Burns' obituary, *The New York Times*, June 27, 1987.

26 Watch Carter's televised speech "Crisis of Confidence," delivered on July 15, 1979.

27 "Jimmy Carter's 'Malaise' Speech Was Popular!" *The Washington Post*, August 9, 2013.

28 For more on Volcker's impactful October 6, 1979 monetary policy announcement, see the Federal Reserve Bank of San Francisco's December 3, 2004 *Economic Letter* titled simply "October 6, 1979." Also, see the collection of articles on this subject in the *Federal Reserve Bank of St Louis' Review*, March/April 2005.

29 "Fed Squeezes Credit, Raises Lending Rate," *The Washington Post*, October 7, 1979.

30 "A Talk With Paul Volcker," *The New York Times*, September 19, 1982.

31 "What Remains of Milton Friedman's Monetarism?" Hetzel's Federal Reserve Bank of Richmond working paper, July 13, 2017.

32 "Senate, by 91 to 2, Backs Greenspan as Fed Chief," *The New York Times*, August 4, 1987.

33 "Dr. Greenspan's Amazing Invisible Thesis," *Barron's*, March 31, 2008.

34 "Looking at Greenspan's Long-Lost Thesis," *Barron's*, April 28, 2008.

35 According to Wikiquote.com, there's no hard evidence that Greenspan said the following, although it is often attributed to him: "I know you think you understand what you thought I said, but I'm not sure you realize that what you heard is not what I meant." Nevertheless, it did apply to many of his public pronouncements, especially when he testified in Congress.

36 "The Challenge of Central Banking in a Democratic Society," Greenspan's December 5, 1996 speech.

37 "Deflation: Making Sure 'It' Doesn't Happen Here," Bernanke's November 21, 2002 speech.

38 See the Federal Reserve Board of Governors' statement "Application of the Commodity Exchange Act to Transactions in Over-the-Counter Derivatives," submitted before the House of Representatives Agricultural Committee's Subcommittee on Risk Management and Specialty Crops on June 10, 1998.

39 "The Regulation of OTC Derivatives," Greenspan's July 24, 1998 congressional testimony.

40 "Over-the-Counter Derivatives," Greenspan's February 10, 2000 congressional testimony.

41 See the transcript of the congressional "Testimony of Lawrence H. Summers," June 21, 2000.

42 "Understanding Household Debt Obligations," Greenspan's February 23, 2004 speech.

43 "Risk Transfer and Financial Stability," Greenspan's May 5, 2005 speech.

44 See Greenspan's February 17, 2009 speech before the Economic Club of New York.

45 "The Great Moderation," Bernanke's February 20, 2004 speech.

46 "The Political Economy of the Smoot-Hawley Tariff," Eichengreen's *NBER Working Paper* No. 2001, August 1986.

47 "The Federal Reserve and the Financial Crisis Origins and Mission of the Federal Reserve," Bernanke's March 20, 2012 lecture. Also see Appendix 8.1, Hollywood's S&L Cautionary Tale: *It's a Wonderful Life.*

48 See Roger Lowenstein's article on Bernanke, "The Villain," *The Atlantic*, April 2012.

49 "Deflation: Making Sure 'It' Doesn't Happen Here," Bernanke's November 21, 2002 speech.

50 "Japanese Monetary Policy: A Case of Self-Induced Paralysis?" Bernanke's January 9, 2000 speech.

51 "Chronology of Fed's Quantitative Easing," YRI webpage.

52 "The Economic Outlook and Monetary Policy," Bernanke's remarks at the August 27, 2010 Jackson Hole symposium.

53 "The Outlook, Policy Choices and Our Mandate," Dudley's October 1, 2010 speech.

54 "What the Fed Did and Why: Supporting the Recovery and Sustaining Price Stability," Bernanke's op-ed in *The Washington Post*, November 4, 2010.

55 "How the Fed Saved the Economy," Bernanke's op-ed in *The Wall Street Journal*, October 4, 2015.

56 "Yale Economics in Washington," Yellen's April 16, 1999 speech.

57 See the transcript of Yellen's March 19, 2014 press conference.

58 "What the Federal Reserve Is Doing to Promote a Stronger Job Market," Yellen's March 31, 2014 speech.

59 "Janet Yellen's Human Message Gets Clouded," *The Wall Street Journal*, April 1, 2014.

60 See the July 21, 2014 *New Yorker* profile of Janet Yellen, "The Hand on the Lever," by Nicholas Lemann.

61 George Akerlof won the 2001 Nobel Prize in economics mostly for his work on asymmetrical information in an article titled "The Market for Lemons: Quality Uncertainty and the Market Mechanism," published in the *Quarterly Journal of Economics* in 1970. He shared the prize with Michael Spence and Joseph Stiglitz for their research related to asymmetric information.

62 "Macroeconomic Research After the Crisis," Yellen's October 14, 2016 speech.

63 The speaker is unknown, but Snopes.com asserts that it definitely wasn't Yogi Berra, to whom it's commonly attributed.

64 "Inflation, Uncertainty, and Monetary Policy," Yellen's September 26, 2017 speech.

65 "The U.S. Economy and Monetary Policy," Yellen's October 15, 2017 speech.

66 See "Monetary Policy Rules and Their Role in the Federal Reserve's Policy Process," pp. 36–39 in the *Monetary Policy Report*, July 2017.

67 "Whatever It Takes," Draghi's July 26, 2012 speech.

68 "Chronology of ECB Monetary Policy Actions: 2014–Present," YRI webpage.

69 See the BOJ's April 4, 2013 press release on its QQE program: "Introduction of the 'Quantitative and Qualitative Monetary Easing.'"

70 See the BOJ's October 31, 2014 press release on the expansion of its QQE program: "Expansion of the Quantitative and Qualitative Monetary Easing."

71 "Bank of Japan's Kuroda Channels Peter Pan's Happy Thoughts," *The Wall Street Journal*, June 4, 2015.

CHAPTER 10: PREDICTING BONDS

1 In 1948, Kaufman received a BA in economics from New York University, followed by an MS in finance from Columbia University in 1949 and a PhD in banking and finance from New York University Graduate School of Business Administration in 1958. Kaufman worked in commercial banking and served as an economist at the Federal Reserve Bank of New York. After the Federal Reserve, he spent 26 years with Salomon Brothers, where he was the managing director, a member of the executive committee, and in charge of the firm's four research departments.

2 You can find the latest version of the Federal Reserve Board's comprehensive quarterly data release online in the *Financial Accounts of the United States*. The report provides full balance sheets, including net worth, for households and nonprofit organizations, nonfinancial corporate businesses, and nonfinancial noncorporate businesses—with supplemental details as well.

3 Annual data for outstanding levels start in 1945, and flows start in 1946.

4 For example, in May 1984, Continental Illinois National Bank and Trust Company experienced a bank run after troubles that originated with nonperforming loans purchased from the failed Penn Square.

5 See my *Topical Study* "The Coming Shortage of Bonds," June 20, 1988.

6 "Outlook for the Federal Budget and Implications for Fiscal Policy," Greenspan's January 25, 2001 congressional testimony.

7 "Bond Vigilantes and Inflation," Federal Reserve Bank of San Francisco's August 2015 *Working Paper*, p. 25.

8 *Have Gun—Will Travel* was an American Western television series from 1957 through 1963. It starred Richard Boone in the lead role as Paladin, a mercenary gunfighter who would provide his services for a fee, or for free to those who had a good cause but not enough money.

9 See the US Treasury's "Timeline of Treasury Inflation-Protected Securities (TIPS)."

10 See the FOMC October 27–28, 2015 meeting minutes.

11 "The Economic Outlook and Monetary Policy," Yellen's December 2, 2015 speech.

12 "Monetary Policy in a Low R-star World," Williams' August 15, 2016 commentary.

13 "The 'New Normal' and What It Means for Monetary Policy," Brainard's September 12, 2016 speech.

14 "Low Interest Rates," Fischer's October 5, 2016 speech.

15 The Conference Board added the difference between the 10-year Treasury note yield and the federal funds rate to the LEI in 1996 in a revision that also deleted two components of the LEI, the change in the index of sensitive materials prices, and the change in manufacturers' unfilled orders for durable goods.

16 *The New Treatment of the Yield Spread in the TCB Composite Index of Leading Indicators*, Conference Board 2005 report.

17 "Federal Reserve Board's Semiannual Monetary Policy Report to the Congress," Greenspan's February 16, 2005 congressional testimony.

18 "The Global Saving Glut and the U.S. Current Account Deficit," Bernanke's March 10, 2005 speech.

19 "Why Are Interest Rates So Low, Part 3: The Global Savings Glut," Bernanke's April 1, 2015 blog post.

20 "Deflation: Making Sure 'It' Doesn't Happen Here," Bernanke's November 21, 2002 speech.

21 "The Bond Vigilantes," *The Wall Street Journal*, May 29, 2009.

22 A Google search for the phrase "bond vigilantes" on January 18, 2018 yielded approximately 64,500 links.

23 "What the Fed Did and Why: Supporting the Recovery and Sustaining Price Stability," Bernanke's op-ed in *The Washington Post*, November 4, 2010.

24 "Chronology of Fed's Quantitative Easing," YRI webpage.

25 "Whatever It Takes," Draghi's July 26, 2012 speech.

26 "Chronology of ECB Monetary Policy Actions," YRI webpage.

27 "What Tools Does the Fed Have Left? Part 3: Helicopter Money," Bernanke's April 11, 2016 blog post.

28 See the Fed's *Financial Accounts of the United States*. Also see outlines of the financial instruments and sectors included in this database in Appendix 10.1 and Appendix 10.2.

29 The video of Greenspan's interview is embedded in the article "Greenspan: Bond Bubble About to Break Because of 'Abnormally Low' Interest Rates," CNBC, August 4, 2017.

CHAPTER 11: PREDICTING COMMODITIES

1   See my *Topical Study* "China for Investors: The Growth Imperative," November 7, 2003.

2   At the end of 2017, the following countries were members of OPEC: Algeria, Angola, Ecuador, Equatorial Guinea, Gabon, Iran, Iraq, Kuwait, Libya, Nigeria, Qatar, Saudi Arabia, United Arab Emirates, and Venezuela.

3   See my *Topical Study* "The Case for Lower Oil Prices," December 12, 1984.

4   See the report *Nuclear Energy and the Fossil Fuels* by M. King Hubbert, dated June 1956.

5   *World Energy Scenario 2016: The Grand Transition*, World Energy Council.

6   See "The Forgotten Benefactor of Humanity," *The Atlantic*, January 1997.

7   "The New Face of Hunger," *The Economist*, April 17, 2008.

8   "Whatever Happened to the Food Crisis? It Crept Back," *The Economist*, July 2, 2009.

9   *Critical Materials Strategy*, US Department of Energy's report, December 2010.

10 See my *Topical Study* "China for Investors: The Growth Imperative," November 7, 2003.

11 *S&P GSCI Methodology*, S&P Global, April 2017.

CHAPTER 12: PREDICTING CURRENCIES

1   *S&P 500 2016 Global Sales*, S&P Global report, July 2016.

2   "Burgernomics: A Big Mac™ Guide to Purchasing Power Parity," *Federal Reserve Bank of St. Louis Review*, November/December 2003.

3   A "trade deficit" is the gap between the values of imports and exports when imports are greater; when the value of exports exceeds that of imports, a country is said to have a "trade surplus."

4   The JP Morgan Nominal Broad Effective Exchange Rate reflects the currencies of Hungary, India, Indonesia, Israel, Italy, Japan, Korea, Kuwait, Malaysia, Mexico, Morocco, New Zealand, Nigeria, Norway, Pakistan, Panama, Peru, Philippines, Poland, Romania, Russia, Saudi Arabia, Singapore, South Africa, Spain, Sweden, Switzerland, Taiwan, Thailand, Turkey, Ukraine, the United Kingdom, Uruguay, Venezuela, and Vietnam.

5   For more about MSCI (formerly known as "Morgan Stanley Capital International") and its global stock market indexes, see "Our Story" on MSCI's website.

6   Joseph B. Treaster, *Paul Volcker: The Making of a Financial Legend* (2004), p. 39.

7   The dollar doesn't have to weaken if foreign capital inflows from private sources are large enough to offset the US trade deficit. This might happen if foreign investors were attracted by rising returns in a rebounding US economy. Indeed, it is conceivable that the dollar might even strengthen in value if enough foreign capital were attracted by investment opportunities in the United States. However, the actual experience over the past three and a half decades has been that the dollar has weakened as the US economy has recovered from recessions.

8   "The 'New Normal' and What It Means for Monetary Policy," Brainard's September 12, 2016 speech.

9   "Cross-Border Spillovers of Balance Sheet Normalization," Brainard's July 11, 2017 speech.

CHAPTER 13: PREDICTING CORPORATE EARNINGS

1 The SEC still allows company managements to meet privately with investors, and that special access has raised questions about whether some continue to have an advantage in obtaining material information.

2 The 11 S&P sectors are Consumer Discretionary, Consumer Staples, Energy, Financials, Health Care, Industrials, Information Technology, Materials, Real Estate, Telecommunication Services, and Utilities. Prior to September 1, 2016, when Real Estate was split from the Financials sector to become a sector in its own right, there were 10 sectors.

3 See YRI's *Stock Market Briefing: S&P 500 Earnings Squiggles Annually & Quarterly.*

4 The different time series lines in our Blue Angels charts would collide if forward earnings turned negative, but this rarely happens for the broad market averages we track.

5 The NIPA profits measures are based on data from sources that provide information on a financial accounting basis and on a tax-accounting basis. Several adjustments are made in the source data to meet the criteria for measuring profits on a NIPA basis. The IRS provides accounting measures, but this information, based on federal corporate income tax returns, is only published annually and with a two-year lag. Other more current sources are the Census Bureau's Quarterly Financial Report and the Federal Deposit Insurance Corporation's report on insured institutions, in the *Quarterly Banking Profile*. Any gaps in coverage are filled with estimates based on surveys of financial accounts from publicly available sources.

6 See the Internal Revenue Service's "SOI Tax Stats — Corporation Tax Statistics" webpage.

7 Receipts by all US residents (including both corporations and persons) includes dividends from foreign corporations and US corporations' share of the reinvested earnings of their incorporated foreign affiliates, and the earnings of unincorporated foreign affiliates, net of corresponding payments. The profits component of domestic income excludes the income earned abroad by US corporations and includes the income earned in the United States by foreign residents. See the BEA's explanation of Corporate Profits, available on their website.

8 "Comparing NIPA Profits with S&P 500 Profits," BEA, *Survey of Current Business*, March 2011.

9 "Employee Stock Options and the National Economic Accounts," BEA, *Survey of Current Business*, February 2008.

10 *S&P 500® 2016: Global Sales*, S&P Global's July 2017 report.

11 See my *Topical Study* "Earnings: The Phantom Menace, Episode I," August 16, 1999.

12 "The Numbers Game," Levitt's September 28, 1998 speech.

13 See Buffett's March 1, 1999 letter to shareholders.

14 Sarbanes–Oxley Act of 2002.

15 The private, non-profit FASB replaced the American Institute of Certified Public Accountants' Accounting Principles Board in this role on July 1, 1973.

16 "Corporate Governance," Greenspan's March 26, 2002 speech.

17 Quoted from p. 6 of Thomson Reuters' proprietary *Methodology for Estimates, A Guide to Understanding Thomson Reuters Methodologies, Terms and Policies for I/B/E/S Estimates Databases*, dated July 2015.

18 See Buffett's February 27, 2016 letter to shareholders.

19 For more information, read the March 2016 report *Skin in the Game: The Activities of Buy-Side Analysts and the Determinants of Their Stock Recommendations*, by Lawrence D. Brown, Andrew C. Call, Michael B. Clement, and Nathan Y. Sharp.

CHAPTER 14: PREDICTING VALUATION

1 "The Challenge of Central Banking in a Democratic Society," Greenspan's December 5, 1996 speech.

2 "Economic and Financial Developments in 1997," the Fed's *Monetary Policy Report*, Section 2, July 22, 1997.

3 The model can be updated weekly from March 1994, when I/B/E/S started to compile weekly forward earnings data for the S&P 500.

4 *Testimony of Chairman Alan Greenspan*, the Federal Reserve's semiannual monetary policy report to Congress, July 22, 1997.

5 See my *Topical Study* "Fed's Stock Market Model Finds Overvaluation," August 25, 1997.

6 "Rules vs. Discretionary Monetary Policy," Greenspan's September 5, 1997 speech.

7 Weekly data are available from January 19, 2006.

8 See my *Topical Study* "New, Improved Stock Valuation Model," July 26, 1999.

9 "Profits Without Prosperity," *Harvard Business Review*, September 2014.

10 "Economic and Financial Developments in 1997 and Early 1998," Fed's *Monetary Policy*, Section 2, February 24, 1998.

11 "Fight the Fed Model: The Relationship between Stock Market Yields, Bond Market Yields, and Future Returns," Asness' December 2002 study.

12 "Burning Up. Warning: Internet Companies Are Running Out of Cash—Fast," *Barron's*, March 20, 2000.

13 "Economic and Financial Developments in 2000 and Early 2001," Fed's *Monetary Policy Report*, Section 2, February 13, 2001.

14 As I noted at the beginning of this chapter, the forward P/E of the S&P 500 peaked at a record 24.5 during July 1999, up from 15.6 at the end of 1996, when Greenspan raised the valuation question. It fell to 21.9 by the end of 2000 and to 9.5 by November 2008. The forward P/E of the Technology sector peaked at a record 48.3 during March 2000, up from 13.9 at the end of 1995. It plunged to 31.2 by the end of 2000 and recovered to 47.8 in December 2001 before declining steadily over the next seven years to a record low of 10.4 in November 2008. The Technology sector's share of the market capitalization of the S&P 500 soared from 8.9% during March 1995 to a record high of 32.9% during March 2000. Industry analysts who collectively had increased their long-term earnings growth expectations from 17.0% during March 1995 to 28.7% in March 2000 subsequently proceeded to curb their enthusiasm.

15 "The Mystery of Lofty Stock Elevations," *The New York Times*, August 16, 2014. By the way, Robert Shiller and John Campbell on December 3, 1996 presented to the Fed's Board of Governors their research showing that stocks were running well ahead of earnings. One week later, Greenspan gave his "irrational exuberance" speech.

16 "Warren Buffett on the Stock Market," *Fortune*, December 10, 2001.

17 "Buffett Calls Pessimists about United States 'Out of Their Mind'," Reuters, September 19, 2017.

18 Refer to Table B.102 Balance Sheet of Nonfarm Nonfinancial Corporate Business. Net worth at market value includes real estate (i.e., land and structures) at market value and equipment, software, and inventories at replacement cost.

19 Visit the website for *Valuing Wall Street: Protecting Wealth in Turbulent Markets*.

20 "Stock Prices and Fundamentals in a Production Economy," Kiley's January 2000 paper.

21 "A Reality Check for Stock Valuations," Apruzzese's study, November 2017.

22 With rare exceptions, the marginal individual tax rate on dividends had always exceeded the marginal tax rate on capital gains until July 2003, when the dividend and long-term capital gains tax rates were lowered to 15%. Short-term capital gains are still taxed the same way as personal income.

23 "Corporate Governance," Greenspan's March 26, 2002 speech.

24 "Monetary Policy and the Economic Outlook," Greenspan's June 17, 1999 congressional testimony.

25 "Economic Volatility," Greenspan's August 30, 2002 speech.

26 "Risk and Uncertainty in Monetary Policy," Greenspan's January 3, 2004 speech.

CHAPTER 15: PREDICTING STOCKS

1 While I have rounded stock market index numbers to the nearest whole number throughout most of this book, for this chapter alone I am providing the unrounded index numbers on which all of the performance percentages are calculated.

2 Daily S&P 500 price data start during January 1928.

3 See my "Next: Dow 8000?" article, *Barron's*, September 6, 1999.

4 See my "Global Synchronized Earnings Boom" article, *Barron's*, April 19, 2004.

5 Lloyd C. Blankfein, Goldman Sachs' chairman and chief executive, stated: "While accelerated by market sentiment, our decision to be regulated by the Federal Reserve is based on the recognition that such regulation provides its members with full prudential supervision and access to permanent liquidity and funding." See the September 21, 2008 Goldman Sachs press release "Goldman Sachs to Become the Fourth Largest Bank Holding Company."

6 "Should the Government Nationalize U.S. Banks?" *The New York Times*, January 22, 2009.

7 See YRI's chart book *S&P 500 Panic Attacks: 2009–2017*.

8 "Lifting the Odds for a Market Melt-Up," my *Barron's* interview, November 9, 2013.

9 "Yardeni: No U.S. Recession in Sight," my *Barron's* interview, February 6, 2016.

10 "Yardeni: It's Official. The Earnings Recession Is Over," *Barron's*, August 22, 2016.

11 "Ed Yardeni Sees Upside of 10% for U.S. Stocks," my *Barron's* interview, February 4, 2017.

12 "Wilshire 5000 Family: Wilshire 5000 Total Market Index."

13 "S&P Dow Jones Indices Announces Changes to U.S. Indices and Updates to U.S. Indices Methodology and Market Cap Guidelines," S&P Global, March 10, 2017 press release.

14 *"Annual Survey of S&P Indexed Assets: As of December 31, 2015,"* S&P Global.

15 *S&P US Indices Methodology*, S&P Global report, April 2017.

16 For more information, visit MSCI's website.

17 Institutional investors consist of property-casualty insurance companies, life insurance companies, private pension funds, state and local retirement funds, and federal government retirement funds. Foreign investors are classified as the "rest of the world" in the Fed's *Financial Accounts of the United States*.

18 "The Death of Equities: How Inflation Is Destroying the Stock Market," *Businessweek*, August 13, 1979.

19 "The Fascinating Theory that 'The Economist' Magazine Covers Are Like Cabbies Offering Share Tips," *Business Insider*, October 31, 2016.

CHAPTER 16: PREDICTING THE FUTURE

1   See the BEA's NIPA and the Fed's *Financial Accounts of the United States*.

2   See "2012 Comprehensive Revisions to The Conference Board Leading Economic Index (LEI) for the United States."

3   "Econometric Policy Evaluation: A Critique," Lucas' paper in Brunner and Meltzer (eds.), *The Phillips Curve and Labor Markets* (1976).

4   "Macroeconomic Priorities," Lucas' January 4, 2003 speech.

5   "Mathiness in the Theory of Economic Growth," Romer's 2015 article in *American Economic Review*.

6   "The Trouble With Macroeconomics," Romer's working paper, September 14, 2016.

7   "This Experiment Shows the Danger in Black-Box Investment Algorithms," Smith's article at MarketWatch, August 31, 2017.

8   See "The Superiority of Economists," by Marion Fourcade et al., in *Journal of Economic Perspectives*, Winter 2015.

9   John Maynard Keynes, *Essays in Persuasion* (1931).

10 "Immigrant Population Hits New High in Germany," Reuters, August 1, 2017.

11 See the Voluntary Human Extinction Movement's website.

12 See YRI's Global Demography chart book *Fertility Rates*.

13 See YRI's Global Demography chart book *Urbanization*.

14 For more on this subject, see the UN's 2014 report *World Urbanization Prospects*, and iied's December 2013 working paper *Urbanization and Fertility Decline: Cashing in on Structural Change*.

15 "China's Population Boom: Nation sees 18 Million Babies Born after Dropping One-child Policy," *Express*, January 23, 2017.

16 "Why Many Families in China Won't Want More than One Kid Even if They Can Have Them," *The Washington Post*, October 30, 2015 blog post by Ana Swanson.

17 See the YRI Global Demography chart book *Children vs. Seniors, Percent of Population*.

18 See YRI's Global Demography chart book *Elderly Dependency Ratios*.

19 "China Considers Financial 'Rewards' for Second Child after Baby Boom Fails to Materialise," *The Telegraph*, February 28, 2017.

20 "Monetary Policy Without a Working Theory of Inflation," Tarullo's October 4, 2017 speech.

21 "Through the Looking Glass," Borio's September 22, 2017 speech.

22 According to *blackswanevents.org*, "The term Black Swan originates from the (Western) belief that all swans are white because these were the only ones accounted for. However, in 1697 the Dutch explorer Willem de Vlamingh discovered black swans in Australia. This was an unexpected event in (scientific) history and profoundly changed zoology. After the black swans were discovered, it seemed obvious that black swans had to exist just as other animals with varying colors were known to exist as well."

23 See Bernanke's May 17, 2007 speech, "The Subprime Mortgage Market," and Greenspan's January 13, 2000 speech, "Technology and the Economy," which began as follows: "We are within weeks of establishing a record for the longest economic expansion in this nation's history. The 106-month expansion of the 1960s, which was elongated by the Vietnam War, will be surpassed in February. Nonetheless, there remain few evident signs of geriatric strain that typically presage an imminent economic downturn. Four or five years into this expansion, in the middle of the 1990s, it was unclear whether, going forward, this cycle would differ significantly from the many others that have characterized post-World War II America. More recently, however, it has become increasingly difficult to deny that something profoundly different from the typical postwar business cycle has emerged. Not only is the expansion reaching record length, but it is doing so with far stronger-than-expected economic growth. Most remarkably, inflation has remained subdued in the face of labor markets tighter than any we have experienced in a generation. Analysts are struggling to create a credible conceptual framework to fit a pattern of interrelationships that has defied conventional wisdom based on our economy's history of the past half century. When we look back at the 1990s, from the perspective of say 2010, the nature of the forces currently in train will have presumably become clearer. We may conceivably conclude from that vantage point that, at the turn of the millennium, the American economy was experiencing a once-in-a-century acceleration of innovation, which propelled forward productivity, output, corporate profits, and stock prices at a pace not seen in generations, if ever."

EPILOGUE

1 See the Federal Reserve Board's "Beige Book" webpage.

2 See YRI's chart book *Regional Business Surveys*.

3 The Fed's website explains: "The Federal Reserve generally conducts the survey quarterly, timing it so that results are available for the January/February, April/May, August, and October/November meetings of the Federal Open Market Committee. The Federal Reserve occasionally conducts one or two additional surveys during the year. Questions cover changes in the standards and terms of the banks' lending and the state of business and household demand for loans. The survey often includes questions on one or two other topics of current interest." See the Fed's "Senior Loan Officer Opinion Survey on Bank Lending Practices."

4 Of course, I'm referring to decisions based on your beliefs about the direction of the overall market; if you are a socially conscious investor, limiting your investing to companies that meet ethical or moral standards, that's your choice.

5 The quote is the last line of a 1985 classic movie, *Back to the Future*.

ACRONYMS AND ABBREVIATIONS

ABS	asset-backed securities
ACORN	Association of Community Organizations for Reform Now
AHE	average hourly earnings
AI	artificial intelligence
ARMs	adjustable-rate mortgages
BBB	Boom-Bust Barometer
BDI	Baltic Dry Index
BDM	Birth/Death Model
BLS	Bureau of Labor Statistics
BOJ	Bank of Japan
CAPE	cyclically adjusted price-earnings ratio
CBO	Congressional Budget Office
CCAdj	capital consumption adjustment
CCI	Consumer Confidence Index
CDO	collateralized debt obligation
CDS	credit default swap
CEA	Council of Economic Advisers
CEI	Index of Coincident Economic Indicators
CFA	chartered financial analyst
CFTC	Commodity Futures Trading Commission
COLA	cost-of-living adjustment
CPB	CPB Netherlands Bureau for Economic Policy Analysis
CPI	consumer price index
CPS	Current Population Survey
CRB	Commodity Research Bureau
CSI	Consumer Sentiment Index

D	Democrat
DJIA	Dow Jones Industrial Average
DSGE	dynamic stochastic general equilibrium
ECB	European Central Bank
ECI	Employment Cost Index
ECRI	Economic Cycle Research Institute
EEC	European Economic Community
EIP	Earned Income Proxy
EITC	Earned Income Tax Credit
EMU	European Monetary Union
ESI	Economic Sentiment Indicator
ETF	exchange-traded fund
EU	European Union
FASB	Financial Accounting Standards Board
FBI	Federal Bureau of Investigation
FCIC	Financial Crisis Inquiry Commission
FDIC	Federal Deposit Insurance Corporation
FDR	Franklin Delano Roosevelt
FHA	Federal Housing Administration
FHLB	Federal Home Loan Bank
FHLBB	Federal Home Loan Bank Board
FOMC	Federal Open Market Committee
FRB	Federal Reserve Board
FRB-NY	Federal Reserve Bank of New York
FSLIC	Federal Savings and Loan Insurance Corporation
FVP	fair value price
G7	Group of Seven
GAAP	generally accepted accounting principles
GATT	General Agreement on Tariff and Trade
GDI	gross domestic income
GDP	gross domestic product
GNP	gross national product
GSE	government-sponsored enterprise
HOLC	Home Owners' Loan Corporation
HUD	Department of Housing and Urban Development
IMF	International Monetary Fund
IPO	initial public offering

IRS	Internal Revenue Service
ISM	Institute for Supply Management
IVA	inventory valuation adjustment
JOLTS	Job Openings and Labor Turnover Survey
LDC	less-developed country
LEI	Index of Leading Economic Indicators
LTCM	Long-Term Capital Management
LTEG	long-term earnings growth
M&A	merger(s) and acquisition(s)
MBS	mortgage-backed security
MFN	most-favored-nation
MIPS	millions of instructions per second
MIT	Massachusetts Institute of Technology
MSCI	Morgan Stanley Capital International
NAFTA	North American Free Trade Agreement
NAIRU	non-accelerating inflation rate of unemployment
NATO	North Atlantic Treaty Organization
NBER	National Bureau of Economic Research
NERI	Net Earnings Revisions Index
NFC	nonfinancial corporation
NFIB	National Federation of Independent Business
NILF	not in the labor force
NIPA	National Income and Product Accounts
NIRP	negative-interest-rate policies
NRSRO	nationally recognized statistical rating organization
OECD	Organisation for Economic Co-operation and Development
OPEC	Organization of the Petroleum Exporting Countries
OTS	Office of Thrift Supervision
PAC	political action committee
PATCO	Professional Air Traffic Controllers Organization
PBT	profits before tax
PCED	personal consumption expenditures deflator
P/E	price-to-earnings ratio
PIIGS	Portugal, Ireland, Italy, Greece, Spain
PMI	purchasing managers' index
PPI	producer price index
PPP	purchasing power parity
P/S	price-to-sales

QE	quantitative easing
QQE	qualitative and quantitative easing
R	Republican
RAP	regulatory accounting principles
RPI	Retail Prices Index
RTAA	Reciprocal Trade Agreements Act
RTC	Resolution Trust Corporation
RUR	Resource Utilization Rate
S&L	savings and loan association
S&P	Standard & Poor's
SAIF	Savings Association Insurance Fund
SEC	Securities and Exchange Commission
SEP	Summary of Economic Projections
SEZ	Special Economic Zone
SOMA	System Open Market Account
TARP	Troubled Asset Relief Program
TBY	10-year bond yield
TIPS	Treasury Inflation-Protected Securities
UN	United Nations
UBI	universal basic income
VA	Veterans Administration (now Veterans Affairs)
WCCI	Weekly Consumer Comfort Index
WEO	*World Economic Outlook*
WLI	Weekly Leading Index
WTO	World Trade Organization
YRI	Yardeni Research, Inc.
ZIRP	zero-interest-rate policies

CREDITS AND PERMISSIONS

Every reasonable effort has been made to trace and contact copyright holders. The publisher would be pleased to hear from any copyright holders not acknowledged here, so that these credit pages may be amended at the earliest opportunity.

INTRODUCTION

CHAPTER 1

CHAPTER 2

Pages 51-52: Excerpts from Jonathan Laing, "Wall Street Seer," *Barron's*, August 4, 1997. Reprinted with permission of *Barron's*, Copyright © 1997 Dow Jones & Company, Inc. All Rights Reserved Worldwide. License number 4212010603762.

CHAPTER 3

Page 103: Excerpt from Michael Mandel and Bret Swanson, "The Coming Productivity Boom: Transforming the Physical Economy with Information," published by the Technology CEO Council, March 2017. Reprinted with permission of the authors.

Page 104: Excerpt from Robert Gordon, "Why Innovation Won't Save Us," *The Wall Street Journal*, December 21, 2012. Reprinted with permission of *The Wall Street Journal*. Copyright © 2012 Dow Jones & Company, Inc. All Rights Reserved Worldwide. License number 4194341423558.

Page 110: Excerpt from George Gilbert, Analyst, Wikibon: "Wikibon Trip Report from IBM's Watson Developer Conference: Keep It Simple, Geniuses." Blog post, SiliconANGLE, November 15, 2016. Reprinted with permission of Wikibon.

Pages 111–112: Excerpt from Davide Castelvecchi, "Quantum Computers Ready to Leap Out of the Lab in 2017," *Nature*, January 4, 2017. Reprinted with permission from Macmillan Publishers Ltd: *Nature* (Volume 541, Number 7), copyright 2017. License number 4194350395516.

Page 112: Excerpt from Bret Swanson, "Moore's Law at 50: The Performance and Prospects of the Exponential Economy," published by the American Enterprise Institute, November 2015. Reprinted with permission of the author.

CHAPTER 4

Page 120: Excerpt from Ronald G. Ehrenberg, Leif Danziger, Gee San. (1983). "Cost-of-Living Adjustments Clauses in Union Contracts: A Summary of Results." *Journal of Labor Economics*, *1*(3), 215–245. © 1983 The University of Chicago. Reprinted with permission of The University of Chicago and with permission of the authors.

CHAPTER 8

Pages 269 and 273: Excerpts from Lloyd Blankfein, "Do Not Destroy the Essential Catalyst of Risk," *Financial Times*, February 8, 2009. © Lloyd Blankfein. Reprinted with permission of the author.

CHAPTER 9

Pages 301–302: Excerpt from Andrew Tobias, "A Talk with Paul Volcker," *The New York Times*, September 19, 1982. Copyright © 1982 Andrew Tobias. Reprinted with permission of the author.

Pages 319–320: Excerpt from Ben S. Bernanke, "How the Fed Saved the Economy," *The Wall Street Journal*, October 4, 2015. © 2015 Ben S. Bernanke. Reprinted with permission of the author.

Pages 320–322: Excerpt from Janet Yellen, "Yale Economics in Washington," a speech delivered at the Yale Economics Reunion, New Haven, CT, April 16, 1999. © 1999 Janet Yellen. Reprinted with permission of the author.

Pages 322–323: Excerpts from Jon Hilsenrath, "Janet Yellen's Human Message Gets Clouded," *The Wall Street Journal*, April 1, 2014. Reprinted with permission of *The Wall Street Journal*, Copyright © 2014 Dow Jones & Company, Inc. All Rights Reserved Worldwide. License number 4194350610297.

CHAPTER 10

Page 352: Excerpt from Ben S. Bernanke, "Why Are Interest Rates So Low, Part 3: The Global Savings Glut," blog post, Brookings Institution, April 1, 2015. © 2015 Ben S. Bernanke. Reprinted with permission of the author.

Pages 353–354: Excerpts from "The Bond Vigilantes," *The Wall Street Journal*, May 29, 2009. Reprinted with permission of *The Wall Street Journal*, Copyright © 2009 Dow Jones & Company, Inc. All Rights Reserved Worldwide. License number 4194350733611.

Pages 360–361: Excerpts from Ben S. Bernanke, "What Tools Does the Fed Have Left? Part 3: Helicopter Money," blog post, Brookings Institution, April 11, 2016. © Ben S. Bernanke. Reprinted with permission of the author.

CHAPTER 13

Pages 437–438: Excerpts from Warren Buffett's "Letter to Shareholders," March 1, 1999. Copyright © 1999 Warren Buffett. Reproduced with permission of the author.

Page 440: Excerpt from Thomson Reuters, *Methodology for Estimates: A Guide to Understanding Thomson Reuters Methodologies, Terms and Policies for I/B/E/S Estimates Databases*, July 2015. Reproduced with permission of Thomson Reuters.

Pages 440–441: Excerpts from Warren Buffett's "Letter to Shareholders," February 27, 2016. Copyright © 2016 Warren Buffett. Reproduced with permission of the author.

CHAPTER 14

Page 462: Excerpt from Jack Willoughby, "Burning Up. Warning: Internet Companies Are Running Out of Cash—Fast," *Barron's*, March 20, 2000. Reprinted with permission of *Barron's*, Copyright © 2000 Dow Jones & Company, Inc. All Rights Reserved Worldwide. License number 4211690401731.

Page 465: Excerpt from Warren Buffett, "Warren Buffett on the Stock Market," *Fortune*, December 10, 2001. Copyright © 2001 Warren Buffett. Reprinted with permission of the author.

Page 466: Excerpt from Andrew Smithers and Stephen Wright, *Valuing Wall Street: Protecting Wealth in Turbulent Markets*, McGraw-Hill, 2000. Copyright © 2000 Andrew Smithers and Stephen Wright. Reprinted with permission of the authors.

CHAPTER 15

Figures 56, 57, 58, and 59 (online): With data from Investors Intelligence. Copyright © Investors Intelligence. Used with permission.

CHAPTER 16

Pages 515–516: Excerpt from Paul Romer, "Mathiness in the Theory of Economic Growth," *American Economic Review*, vol. 105, no. 5, May 2015 (pp. 89–93). © 2015 American Economic Review. Reprinted with permission.

Page 516: Excerpt from Gary Smith, "This Experiment Shows the Danger in Black-Box Investment Algorithms," MarketWatch, August 31, 2017. Copyright © 2017 Gary Smith. Reprinted with permission of the author.

Pages 533–534: Excerpt from Daniel Tarullo, "Monetary Policy Without a Working Theory of Inflation," Hutchins Center Working Paper No. 33, October 2017. Copyright © Daniel Tarullo. Reprinted with permission of the author.

Pages 534–535: Excerpts from Claudio Borio, "Through the Looking Glass," OMFIF City Lecture, September 22, 2017, London. Copyright © Claudio Borio and Bank for International Settlements. Reprinted with permission of the author. The speech is available in full on the Bank for International Settlements' website free of charge.

Page 536: Excerpt from Nassim Nicholas Taleb, *The Black Swan: The Impact of the Highly Improbable*, Random House, 2007. Copyright © 2007 Nassim Nicholas Taleb. Reprinted with permission of the author.

Page 569, note 22: Excerpt from "What are Black Swan Events?" © The Black Swan team, Hasso Plattner Institute. Reprinted with permission of Felix Naumann.

Appendix 16.1 (online): Graph of "Estimated Productivity Impact of Innovation Platforms. Historical and Future." © ARK Investment Management LLC. Used with permission.

INDEX